MATHEMATICS FOR BUSINESS, ECONOMICS, AND MANAGEMENT

Marvin L. Bittinger
J. Conrad Crown

INDIANA UNIVERSITY-
PURDUE UNIVERSITY AT
INDIANAPOLIS

▲▼ **ADDISON-WESLEY
PUBLISHING COMPANY**

Reading, Massachusetts ■ Menlo Park, California
London ■ Amsterdam ■ Don Mills, Ontario ■ Sydney

Library of Congress Cataloging in Publication Data

Bittinger, Marvin L.
  Mathematics for business, economics, and management.

  Based on: Finite mathematics, a modeling approach /
J. Conrad Crown, Marvin L. Bittinger. 2nd ed. c1981 and
Calculus, a modeling approach / Marvin L. Bittinger.
2nd ed. 1980.
  Includes index.
  1. Mathematics—1961-   . I. Crown, J. Conrad.
II. Title.
QA37.2.B583   510   81-14910
ISBN 0-201-10104-1   AACR2

ISBN 0-201-10104-1
ABCDEFGHIJ-DO-898765432

PREFACE

The material in this book continues on from basic algebra and introduces the student to areas of finite mathematics and calculus which have applications in business, economics, and management. The basic material can be covered in two semester courses.

While most of the material in this book has been taken from *Finite Mathematics: A Modeling Approach*, second edition, by Crown-Bittinger, and *Calculus: A Modeling Approach*, second edition, by Bittinger, many sections have been rewritten after extensive class testing.
There are several features of the book as follows.

1. Intuitive Approach. While this word has many meanings and interpretations, its use here, for the most part, means "experience based." That is, when a concept is being taught, the learning is based on the student's prior experience or new experience given before the concept is formalized. For example, in a maximum-minimum problem a function is usually derived which is to be maximized or minimized. Instead of forging ahead with the standard calculus solution, the student is asked to stop and compute some function values. This experience provides the student with more insight into the problem. Not only does the student discover that different dimensions yield different volumes, if volume is to be maximized, but the dimensions which yield the maximum volume might even be conjectured as a result of the calculations. Provision for use of the hand calculator also provides for an intuitive approach.

2. The Hand Calculator.   Exercises in this text can be done with or without a hand calculator. Most students, we find, not only have calculators but assume that calculators are *always* helpful to them. While there are many types of problems for which the calculator can reduce the work of computation, there are also many problems where there are naturally occurring fractions, and automatic conversion of all fractions to decimals may bring more distress than relief. For example, in the solution of systems of linear equations, fractions such as one-third have no exact decimal conversion and consequently conversion to decimals introduces the problem of "round-off" error. In general, we feel that calculators should *not* be used automatically but rather reserved for cases where they are necessary (or tables would be required), or where they reduce the tedium of computation.

3. Applications.   Relevant and factual applications are included throughout the text to maintain interest and motivation. Problems in linear programming are of particular interest to students in business and management curricula. Problems in natural growth and decay (involving exponential and logarithmic functions) have applications in almost all areas ranging from population growth to continuously compounded interest to present value. The notions of total revenue, cost, and profit, together with their related derivatives (marginal functions) are threads which run through the text, providing continued reinforcement and unification.

4. Tests.   Each chapter ends with a review. All the answers to these reviews are in the back of the book. A test on each chapter appears, classroom-ready, in the *Instructor's Manual*.

5. Exercises.   Great care has been given to constructing the exercises. Many of the linear programming exercises have been designed to simplify the calculations and minimize the occurrence of fractions. The first exercises in each set are quite easy, while later ones become progressively more difficult. Most of the exercises are similar to examples worked out in that section of the text, and are arranged in matching pairs. That is, each odd-numbered exercise is very much like the one immediately following. The odd-numbered exercises have answers in the book, while the even-numbered exercises have answers in the *Instructor's Manual*.

The authors wish to acknowledge the assistance of Charles N. Kellog of Texas Tech University, Jeff Mock of Diablo Valley College, and Peter Rice of the University of Georgia, whose professional reviews were extremely valuable to the preparation of this book.

Indianapolis, Indiana   M.L.B.
January 1982   J.C.C.

CONTENTS

CHAPTER **3**   **THE ECHELON METHOD AND MATRICES**

CHAPTER **4**   **LINEAR PROGRAMMING—GRAPHICAL TECHNIQUES**

CHAPTER **5**   **LINEAR PROGRAMMING—ALGEBRAIC TECHNIQUES**

CHAPTER 10   INTEGRATION

CHAPTER 11   APPLICATIONS OF INTEGRATION

CHAPTER 12   SETS AND COUNTING TECHNIQUES

CHAPTER 13   PROBABILITY: BASIC CONCEPTS

BASIC CONCEPTS OF ALGEBRA

1.1 THE REAL NUMBERS*

Real Numbers

In this table of stock market quotations are many kinds of numbers.

Rohr	5¼s86	7.0	75	−2	StOlin	9.20s04	14.	64	+ ¾
Ryder	11½ 90	13.	90½	......	StOInd	7⅞s07	14.	56	+1
Ryder	8⅛s92	13.	63¼	−4⅛	St OilInd	6s91	10.	59	......
StRegs	10⅝10	16.	66⅛	+3⅛	St OilInd	.6s98	12.	49½	......
SanDgo	10s06	16.	61	+ ⅞	Std Oh	8⅜s07	16.	54	−2
SFelnd	6¼ 98	3.2	195	+7	StdOh	7.60s99	14.	54¼	+2
Savin	14s00	21.	67½	− ¼	Std Oh	7½s86	11.	71½	− ½
Savin	11⅜s98	21.	55½	− ⅜	St Pak	5¼s90	12.	43½	+ ¼
SCM	5½s88	8.6	64⅛	−- ⅞	Stauffr	8⅛s96	14.	58	−1
Seafist	9¼s01	15.	64	+5	Storage	9s01	8.6	105	+2
SearsR	8⅝ 95	14.	62¼	− ¾	Storag	10¼00	7.6	135	+4
Sears Ro	8s06	15.	55¼	+ ¾	Storer	8½s05	9.7	87¼	− ¾
SearsR	7⅞07	14.	55⅛	+ ⅛	SunCo	10¾ 06	12.	89	......
SearsR	6⅜ 93	12.	55	− ½	Sun M	8½95D	10.	83	+2
SearsR	4¾ 83	5.6	84⅞	+ ¾	SunMn	8½s95	10.	83¾	− ¾
SecPc	8.80s85	11.	77½	+1⅜	Tandy	10s91	15.	67	−1¾
SecPc	7.70s82				Teldyne	10s04	15.	64⅞	+1½
		8.0	96 5-16	+ ½	Teldy	10 04C	16.	64	+ ¼
SheLR	15¼90	17.	91⅞	......	Teledyn	7s99	14.	48½	......
SheLR	10¾03	17.	64	−1	Telex	11¾s96	18.	67⅛	+1⅝
ShellO	14¼11	15.	92⅝	+ ¼	Telex Cp	9s96	16.	55⅝	......

**To the Instructor*: Chapters 1 and 2 of this book can be considered review and omitted by students with adequate preparation.

The numbers we use most in algebra are the *real numbers*. The real numbers are often pictured in one-to-one correspondence with the points of a line, as follows.

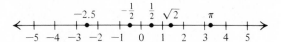

The positive numbers are pictured to the right of 0 and the negative numbers to the left. Zero itself is neither positive nor negative.

There are several subsets of the real numbers. They are as follows.

Natural Numbers. **The counting numbers 1, 2, 3, ...**
Whole Numbers. **The natural numbers and 0; that is, 0, 1, 2, 3, ...**
Integers. **The whole numbers and their additive inverses,**

$$0, 1, -1, 2, -2, 3, -3, \ldots .$$

Rational Numbers. **The integers and all quotients of integers (excluding division by 0). For example,**

$$\frac{3}{5}, \frac{-5}{6}, \frac{8}{1}, 7, -19, 0, \frac{59}{-8}, -\frac{8}{3} \left(\text{can also be named } \frac{-8}{3}, \text{ or } \frac{8}{-3} \right).$$

Any real number that is not rational is called *irrational*. The rational numbers and the irrational numbers can be described in several ways.

The *Rational Numbers* are

1. **Those numbers that can be named with fractional notation a/b, where a and b are integers and $b \neq 0$ (definition).**
2. **Those numbers for which decimal notation either ends or repeats.**

All of the following numbers are rational.

Example 1 $\dfrac{7}{16} = 0.4375$ (This is an ending or terminating decimal.)

Example 2 $-\dfrac{9}{7} = -1.285714285714 \ldots = -1.\overline{285714}$ (The bar indicates the repeating part.)

Example 3 $\dfrac{4}{11} = 0.363636\ldots = 0.\overline{36}$ (Repeating decimal)

Irrational Numbers **are**

1. **Those real numbers that are not rational (definition).**
2. **Those real numbers that cannot be named with fractional notation** *a/b,* **where** *a* **and** *b* **are integers and** *b* ≠ **0.**
3. **Those real numbers for which decimal notation does not end and does not repeat.**

There are many irrational numbers. For example, $\sqrt{2}$ is irrational. We can find rational numbers *a b* for which $(a/b) \cdot (a/b)$ is close to 2, but we cannot find such a number for which $(a/b) \cdot (a/b)$ is *exactly* 2.

Unless a whole number is a perfect square its square root is irrational. For example, $\sqrt{4}$ and $\sqrt{49}$ are rational, but all of the following are irrational:

$$\sqrt{5}, \; -\sqrt{12}, \; \sqrt{37}.$$

There are also many irrational numbers that cannot be obtained by taking square roots. The number π is an example. Decimal notation for π does not end and does not repeat.

All of the following are irrational.

Example 4 $\pi = 3.1415926535\ldots$ (Numeral does not repeat. $\frac{22}{7}$ and 3.14 are only rational approximations to the irrational number π.)

Example 5 $-7.202002000200002000002\ldots$ (Numeral does not repeat.)

Example 6 $\sqrt[3]{2} = 1.25992105\ldots$ (Numeral does not repeat.)

In Example 5, there is a pattern, but it is not a repeating pattern.

Algebra and Properties of Real Numbers

In arithmetic we use numbers, performing calculations to obtain certain answers. In algebra, we use arithmetic symbolism, but in addition we use symbols such as *a, b, c, x, y,* and *z* to represent unknown numbers. We do calculations and manipulations of symbols, based upon properties of numbers, which we review now. Algebra is thus an extension of arithmetic and a more powerful tool for solving problems. We will study even more powerful mathematical tools later in the book.

Addition

Assuming that addition of nonnegative real numbers is familiar, let us review how the definition of addition is extended to include the negative numbers. Recall first that the absolute value of a nonnegative number is that number itself. To get the absolute value of a negative, change its sign (make it positive). The absolute value of a number x is denoted $|x|$. Thus, $|5| = 5$, $|0| = 0$, and $|-2.7| = 2.7$.

To add

1. **Two negative numbers, add their absolute values (the sum is negative).**
2. **A negative and a positive number, find the difference of their absolute values. The result will have to have the sign of the number with the larger absolute value. If the absolute values are the same, the sum is 0.**

For example,

$$-7 + (-8) = -15, \quad -\frac{5}{6} + \left(-\frac{7}{12}\right) = -\frac{17}{12}, \quad 9 + (-6) = 3,$$

$$-7 + 3 = -4, \quad 9.7 + (-5.2) = 4.5, \quad -\pi + \pi = 0,$$

$$-\frac{7}{6} + \frac{3}{6} = -\frac{2}{3}, \quad -\sqrt{2} + (-8\sqrt{2}) = -9\sqrt{2}.$$

Properties of Real Numbers under Addition

The following are the fundamental properties of real numbers under addition. These are properties upon which algebraic manipulations are based, especially when symbols are used.

Commutative. **For any real numbers a and b, $a + b = b + a$. (The *order* in which numbers are added does not affect the sum.)**

Associative. **For any real numbers a, b, and c, $a + (b + c) = (a + b) + c$. (When only additions are involved, parentheses for *grouping* purposes may be placed as we please without affecting the sum.)**

Identity. **There exists a unique real number 0, such that for any real number a, $a + 0 = 0 + a = a$. (Adding 0 to any number gives that same number as the sum.)**

Inverses. **For every real number a, there exists a unique number, denoted $-a$, for which $-a + a = a + (-a) = 0$.**

CAUTION! It is common to read an expression such as $-x$ as "negative x." This can be confusing, indeed incorrect, because $-x$ may be positive, negative, or zero, depending on the value of x. The symbol $-$, used in this way, indicates an *additive inverse*; somewhat unfortunately the same symbol may also indicate a negative number, as in -5, or it may indicate subtraction, as in $8 - x$.

CAUTION! An initial $-$ sign, as in $-x$, or $-(x^2 - 3x + 2)$ should always be interpreted as meaning "the additive inverse of." The entire expression may be positive, negative, or zero, depending upon the value of the part of the expression that follows the $-$ sign. Taking the additive inverse is sometimes called "changing the sign."

Find the additive inverse for each of the following expressions.

Example 7 $-x$, when $x = 3$ $-(3) = -3$ (Negative 3)

Example 8 $-x$, when $x = -8$ $-(-8) = 8$

Example 9 $-x$, when $x = 0$ $-(0) = 0$

Example 10 $-(x^2 + 8x + 2)$, when $x = 4$ $-(4^2 + 8 \cdot 4 + 2) = -50$

when $x = -4$ $-((-4)^2 + 8(-4) + 2) = 14$

It can be easily shown that $-1 \cdot x = -x$ for any number x. That is, multiplying a number x by negative 1 results in the additive inverse of x. This can be proved as a theorem but we will not do that here.

THEOREM   **For any real number x, $-1 \cdot x = -x$. (Negative one times any number is its additive inverse.)**

Multiplication

Assuming that multiplication of nonnegative real numbers is familiar, let us review how the definition of multiplication is extended to include the negative numbers.

To multiply

1. **Two negative numbers, multiply their absolute values (the product is positive).**

2. **A positive number and a negative number, multiply their absolute values and take the additive inverse of the result (the product is negative).**

For example,

$$5 \cdot (-4) = -20, \quad 1.6 \cdot (-3.8) = -6.08, \quad -8 \cdot (-6) = 48,$$
$$-\tfrac{2}{3} \cdot (-\tfrac{4}{5}) = \tfrac{8}{15}, \quad -3 \cdot (-2) \cdot (-7) = -42.$$

We now list the properties of real numbers under multiplication. Recall that ab is an abbreviation for $a \cdot b$.

Commutative. **For any real numbers a and b, $ab = ba$. (The *order* in which numbers are multiplied does not affect the product.)**

Associative. **For any real numbers a, b, and c, $a(bc) = (ab)c$. (When only multiplications are involved, parentheses for grouping purposes may be placed as we please without affecting the product.)**

Identity. **There exists a unique number 1, such that for any real number a, $a \cdot 1 = 1 \cdot a = a$. (Multiplying any number by 1 gives that same number as the product.)**

Inverses. **For each nonzero real number a, there exists a unique number $\dfrac{1}{a}$ or a^{-1}, for which $a\left(\dfrac{1}{a}\right) = \left(\dfrac{1}{a}\right)a = 1$.**

Multiplicative inverses are also called *reciprocals.*

Example 11   The multiplicative inverse, or reciprocal, of 8 is $\tfrac{1}{8}$.

Example 12   The multiplicative inverse of $-\tfrac{4}{5}$ is $-\tfrac{5}{4}$.

Example 13   The reciprocal of 0.32 is 3.125.

There is a very important property, or law, that connects addition and multiplication, as follows.

Distributive. **For any real numbers a, b, and c,**

$$a(b + c) = ab + ac.*$$

(This is called the distributive law of multiplication over addition.)

---

* The expression $ab + ac$ means $(a \cdot b) + (a \cdot c)$. By agreement, we can omit parentheses around multiplications. According to this agreement, multiplications are to be done before additions or subtractions.

Subtraction

Many other properties, important in algebraic manipulations, can be proved from those already considered. We will now consider some of these. We first consider the definition of subtraction.

DEFINITION
SUBTRACTION

For any real numbers a and b, $a - b = c$ if and only if $b + c = a$. ($a - b$ is that number which when added to b gives a.)

We can subtract by adding an inverse.

THEOREM

For any real numbers a and b, $a - b = a + (-b)$.

This can be proved immediately from the definitions of subtraction and additive inverse. It says that to subtract a number we can add its additive inverse. For example,

$$9 - 6 = 9 + (-6) = 3, \quad 4 - 9 = 4 + (-9) = -5,$$
$$11 - (-2) = 11 + 2 = 13, \quad 9.7 - (-4.8) = 9.7 + 4.8 = 14.5,$$
$$-17 - (-9) = -17 + 9 = -8, \quad \tfrac{3}{8} - \tfrac{7}{8} = \tfrac{3}{8} + (-\tfrac{7}{8}) = -\tfrac{4}{8} = -\tfrac{1}{2}.$$

Multiplication is also distributive over subtraction.

Distributive. **For any real numbers a, b, and c,**

$$a(b - c) = ab - ac.$$

(This is called the distributive law of multiplication over subtraction.)

Division

Division is the operation opposite to multiplication, as given in the following definition.

DEFINITION
DIVISION

For any number a and any nonzero number b, $a \div b = c$ if and only if $bc = a$. ($a \div b$ is that number which when multiplied by b gives a.)

We can divide by multiplying by a reciprocal.

THEOREM

For any real number a and nonzero number b,

$$a \div b = a\left(\frac{1}{b}\right).$$

Divide by multiplying by a reciprocal.

Example 14 $\frac{3}{4} \div (-\frac{3}{2}) = \frac{3}{4}(-\frac{2}{3}) = -\frac{1}{2}$

Example 15 $-\frac{5}{8} \div (-\frac{7}{12}) = -\frac{5}{8}(-\frac{12}{7}) = \frac{15}{14}$

It can be proved that the quotient of two negative numbers is negative and the quotient of a positive number and a negative number is negative.

Order

On a number line if a number a is located to the left of b, then a is less than b, $a < b$. In such a case, if we subtract a from b, the result will be a positive number. This motivates the following definition.

DEFINITION   **For any real numbers a and b,**

$$a < b \quad \text{if and only if} \quad b - a \text{ is positive.}$$

Verify each inequality using the definition of $<$.

Example 16 $3 < 8$ $8 - 3 = 5$ and 5 is positive.

Example 17 $-4 < 11$ $11 - (-4) = 15$ and 15 is positive.

Example 18 $-6 < -2$ $-2 - (-6) = 4$ and 4 is positive.

The symbol for "greater than" ($>$) is defined in terms of $<$. We say that $a > b$ if and only if $b < a$. Thus, to show that $a > b$, we show that $a - b$ is positive.

The Use of Calculators

In the exercise set that follows you will find problems designed for the use of a calculator. These and other discussions will be denoted with the symbol ▦. Although a calculator is not essential for working the problems in this text, you will find a calculator extremely useful. An eight- or ten-digit calculator with an x^y key and the exponential and natural logarithm function keys would be the most useful. Calculators with all of the aforementioned keys are available for under $20. If you do not already have a calculator, it might be wise to consult with your instructor in this course before such a purchase.

EXERCISE SET 1.1

Given the numbers

$$-6,\ 0,\ 3,\ -\tfrac{1}{2},\ \sqrt{3},\ -2,\ -\sqrt{7},\ \sqrt[3]{2},\ \tfrac{5}{8},\ 14,\ -\tfrac{9}{4},\ 8.53,\ 9\tfrac{1}{2}.$$

Which are

1. natural numbers? 2. whole numbers? 3. irrational numbers?
4. rational numbers? 5. integers? 6. real numbers?

Which of the following are rational? irrational?

7. $-\tfrac{6}{5}$ 8. $-\tfrac{3}{7}$ 9. -9.032 10. 3.14

11. $4.51\overline{6516}$ (Numeral repeats) 12. $-7.32\overline{3232}$ (Numeral repeats)

13. $4.303003000300003 \ldots$ (Numeral does not repeat) 14. $6.414114111411114 \ldots$ (Numeral does not repeat)

15. $\sqrt{6}$ 16. $\sqrt{7}$ 17. $-\sqrt{14}$ 18. $-\sqrt{12}$

19. $\sqrt{49}$ 20. $-\sqrt{16}$ 21. $\sqrt[3]{5}$ 22. $\sqrt[4]{10}$

Simplify.

23. $|12|$ 24. $|-2.56|$ 25. $|-47|$ 26. $|0|$

Find $-x$ and $-1 \cdot x$, when

27. $x = -7$ 28. $x = -\tfrac{10}{3}$ 29. 57 30. $\tfrac{13}{14}$

For Exercises 31 and 32, find $-(x^2 - 5x + 3)$, when For exercises 33 and 34, find $-(7 - y)$, when

31. $x = 12$ 32. $x = -8$ 33. $y = -9$ 34. $y = 19$

Compute.

35. $-3.1 + (-7.2)$ 36. $-735 + 319$ 37. $\tfrac{9}{2} + (-\tfrac{3}{5})$ 38. $-6 + (-4) + (-10)$

39. $-7(-4)$ 40. $-\tfrac{8}{3}(-\tfrac{9}{2})$ 41. $(-8.2) \times 6$ 42. $-6(-2)(-4)$

43. $-7(-2)(-3)(-5)$ 44. $(-7.1)(-2.3)$ 45. $-\tfrac{14}{3}(-\tfrac{17}{5})(-\tfrac{21}{2})$ 46. $-\tfrac{13}{4}(-\tfrac{16}{5})(\tfrac{23}{2})$

47. $\dfrac{-20}{-4}$ 48. $\dfrac{49}{-7}$ 49. $\dfrac{-10}{70}$ 50. $\dfrac{-40}{8}$

51. $\tfrac{2}{7} \div (-\tfrac{14}{3})$ 52. $-\tfrac{3}{5} \div (-\tfrac{6}{7})$ 53. $-\tfrac{10}{3} \div (-\tfrac{2}{15})$ 54. $-\tfrac{12}{5} \div (-0.3)$

55. $11 - 15$ 56. $-12 - 17$ 57. $12 - (-6)$ 58. $-13 - (-4)$

59. $15.8 - 27.4$ 60. $-19.04 - 15.76$ 61. $-\tfrac{21}{4} - (-\tfrac{7}{4})$ 62. $\tfrac{10}{3} - (-\tfrac{17}{3})$

The symbol ▦ indicates an exercise meant to be done with a calculator.

Calculate. Round to six decimal places.

63. a) ▦ $(1.4)^2$
$(1.41)^2$
$(1.414)^2$
$(1.4142)^2$
$(1.41421)^2$

b) What number does the sequence of numbers 1.4, 1.41, 1.414, and so on, seem to approach as a limit?

64. a) ▦ $(2.1)^3$
$(2.15)^3$
$(2.154)^3$
$(2.1544)^3$
$(2.15443)^3$

b) What number does the sequence of numbers 2.1, 2.15, 2.154, and so on, seem to approach as a limit?

What property is illustrated by each of the following sentences?

65. $k + 0 = k$

66. $ax = xa$

67. $-1(x + y) = (-1x) + (-1y)$

68. $4 + (t + 8) = (4 + t) + 8$

69. $c + d = d + c$

70. $-67 \cdot 1 = -67$

71. $4(xy) = (4x)y$

72. $5(a + t) = 5a + 5t$

73. $y(\frac{1}{y}) = 1, y \neq 0$

74. $-x + x = 0$

1.2   EXPONENTIAL NOTATION

Integers As Exponents

Let us review the meaning of an expression

$$a^n,$$

where n is an integer. The number a above is called the *base* and n is called the *exponent*. When n is larger than 1, then

$$a^n = \underbrace{a \cdot a \cdot a \cdots a}_{n \text{ factors}}$$

In other words, a^n is the product of n factors, each of which is a.
Rename without exponents.

Example 1 $4^3 = 4 \cdot 4 \cdot 4$, or 64

Example 2 $(-2)^5 = (-2)(-2)(-2)(-2)(-2)$, or -32

Example 3 $(1.08)^2 = 1.08 \times 1.08$, or 1.1664

Example 4 $\left(\frac{1}{2}\right)^3 = \frac{1}{2} \cdot \frac{1}{2} \cdot \frac{1}{2}$, or $\frac{1}{8}$

Example 5 $-8^2 = -(8)(8) = -64$

When a minus sign occurs with certain kinds of exponential notation, a certain caution is in order. For example, $(-8)^2$ means that -8 is raised to the second power. Hence $(-8)^2 = (-8)(-8) = 64$. On the other hand, -8^2 represents the additive inverse of 8^2. Thus $-8^2 = -64$. It may help to think of $-x^2$ as $-1 \cdot x^2$, according to a property in Section 1.1.

We define an exponent of 1 as follows:

$$a^1 = a, \text{ for any number } a.$$

That is, any number to the first power is that number itself. We define an exponent of 0 as follows:

$$a^0 = 1, \text{ for any nonzero number } a.$$

That is, any nonzero number a to the 0 power is 1.

Rename without exponents.

Example 6 $(-2x)^0 = 1$

Example 7 $(-2x)^1 = -2x$

Example 8 $\left(\frac{1}{2}\right)^0 = 1$

Example 9 $e^0 = 1$

Example 10 $e^1 = e$

Example 11 $\left(\frac{1}{2}\right)^1 = \frac{1}{2}$

The meaning of a negative integer as an exponent is as follows:

$$a^{-n} = \frac{1}{a^n}, \text{ for any nonzero number } a.$$

That is, any nonzero number a to the $-n$ power is the reciprocal of a^n.

Rename without negative exponents.

Example 12 $2^{-5} = \dfrac{1}{2 \cdot 2 \cdot 2 \cdot 2 \cdot 2} = \dfrac{1}{32}$

Example 13 $10^{-3} = \dfrac{1}{10 \cdot 10 \cdot 10} = \dfrac{1}{1000}$, or 0.001

Example 14 $\left(\frac{1}{4}\right)^{-2} = \dfrac{1}{\left(\frac{1}{4}\right)^2} = \dfrac{1}{\frac{1}{4} \cdot \frac{1}{4}} = \dfrac{1}{\frac{1}{16}} = 1 \cdot \dfrac{16}{1} = 16$

Example 15 $x^{-5} = \dfrac{1}{x^5}$

Example 16 $e^{-k} = \dfrac{1}{e^k}$

Example 17 $t^{-1} = \dfrac{1}{t^1} = \dfrac{1}{t}$

Properties of Exponents

Note the following:

$$b^5 \cdot b^{-3} = (b \cdot b \cdot b \cdot b \cdot b)\, \dfrac{1}{b \cdot b \cdot b}$$
$$= \dfrac{b \cdot b \cdot b \cdot b \cdot b}{b \cdot b \cdot b}$$
$$= \dfrac{b \cdot b \cdot b}{b \cdot b \cdot b} \cdot b \cdot b$$
$$= 1 \cdot b \cdot b$$
$$= b^2.$$

The result could have been obtained by adding the exponents. This is true in general.

For any number a, and any integers n and m,

$$a^n \cdot a^m = a^{n+m}.$$

(To multiply when the bases are the same, add the exponents.)

Multiply.

Example 18 $x^5 \cdot x^6 = x^{5+6} = x^{11}$

Example 19 $x^{-5} \cdot x^6 = x^{-5+6} = x$

Example 20 $2x^{-3} \cdot 5x^{-4} = 10x^{-3+(-4)} = 10x^{-7}$

Example 21 $r^2 \cdot r = r^{2+1} = r^3$

Note the following:

$$b^5 \div b^2 = \frac{b^5}{b^2} = \frac{b \cdot b \cdot b \cdot b \cdot b}{b \cdot b} = \frac{b \cdot b}{b \cdot b} \cdot b \cdot b \cdot b = 1 \cdot b \cdot b \cdot b = b^3.$$

The result could have been obtained by subtracting the exponents. This is true in general.

> **For any nonzero number a and any integers n and m,**
> $$\frac{a^n}{a^m} = a^{n-m}.$$
> **(To divide when the bases are the same, subtract the exponents.)**

Divide.

Example 22 $\dfrac{a^3}{a^2} = a^{3-2} = a^1 = a$

Example 23 $\dfrac{x^7}{x^7} = x^{7-7} = x^0 = 1$

Example 24 $\dfrac{e^3}{e^{-4}} = e^{3-(-4)} = e^{3+4} = e^7$

Example 25 $\dfrac{e^{-4}}{e^{-1}} = e^{-4-(-1)} = e^{-4+1} = e^{-3}$, or $\dfrac{1}{e^3}$

Note the following:

$$(b^2)^3 = b^2 \cdot b^2 \cdot b^2 = b^{2+2+2} = b^6.$$

The result could have been obtained by multiplying the exponents. This is true in general.

> **For any number a, and any integers n and m,**
> $$(a^n)^m = a^{nm}.$$
> **(To raise a power to a power, multiply the exponents.)**

Simplify.

Example 26 $(x^{-2})^3 = x^{-2 \cdot 3} = x^{-6}$, or $\dfrac{1}{x^6}$

Example 27 $(e^x)^2 = e^{2x}$

Example 28 $(3x^3y^4)^2 = 3^2(x^3)^2(y^4)^2 = 9x^6y^8$

Example 29 $(2x^4y^{-5}z^3)^{-3} = 2^{-3}(x^4)^{-3}(y^{-5})^{-3}(z^3)^{-3}$

$$= \frac{1}{2^3}x^{-12}y^{15}z^{-9}, \quad \text{or} \quad = \frac{y^{15}}{8x^{12}z^9}$$

EXERCISE SET 1.2

Rename without exponents.

1. 5^3 **2.** 7^2 **3.** $(-7)^2$ **4.** $(-5)^3$

5. $(1.01)^2$ **6.** $(1.01)^3$ **7.** $(\frac{1}{2})^4$ **8.** $(\frac{1}{4})^3$

9. $(6x)^0$ **10.** $(6x)^1$ **11.** t^1 **12.** t^0

13. $(\frac{1}{3})^0$ **14.** $(\frac{1}{3})^1$

Rename without negative exponents.

15. 3^{-2} **16.** 4^{-2} **17.** $(\frac{1}{2})^{-3}$ **18.** $(\frac{1}{2})^{-2}$

19. 10^{-1} **20.** 10^{-4} **21.** e^{-b} **22.** t^{-k}

23. b^{-1} **24.** h^{-1}

Multiply.

25. $x^2 \cdot x^3$ **26.** $t^3 \cdot t^4$ **27.** $x^{-7} \cdot x$ **28.** $x^5 \cdot x$

29. $5x^2 \cdot 7x^3$ **30.** $4t^3 \cdot 2t^4$ **31.** $x^{-4} \cdot x^7 \cdot x$ **32.** $x^{-3} \cdot x \cdot x^3$

33. $e^{-t} \cdot e^t$ **34.** $e^k \cdot e^{-k}$

Divide.

35. $\dfrac{x^5}{x^2}$ **36.** $\dfrac{x^7}{x^3}$ **37.** $\dfrac{x^2}{x^5}$ **38.** $\dfrac{x^3}{x^7}$

39. $\dfrac{e^k}{e^k}$ **40.** $\dfrac{t^k}{t^k}$ **41.** $\dfrac{e^t}{e^4}$ **42.** $\dfrac{e^k}{e^3}$

43. $\dfrac{t^6}{t^{-8}}$ **44.** $\dfrac{t^5}{t^{-7}}$ **45.** $\dfrac{t^{-9}}{t^{-11}}$ **46.** $\dfrac{t^{-11}}{t^{-7}}$

Simplify.

47. $(t^{-2})^3$ **48.** $(t^{-3})^4$ **49.** $(e^x)^4$ **50.** $(e^x)^5$

51. $(2x^2y^4)^3$ **52.** $(2x^2y^4)^5$ **53.** $(3x^{-2}y^{-5}z^4)^{-4}$ **54.** $(5x^3y^{-7}z^{-5})^{-3}$

55. $(-3x^{-8}y^7z^2)^2$ **56.** $(-5x^4y^{-5}z^{-3})^4$

1.3   ADDITION AND SUBTRACTION OF ALGEBRAIC EXPRESSIONS

Polynomials

Expressions like these are called *polynomials in one variable:*

$$-7x + 5,$$

$$3y^3 - 5y^2 + 7y - 4,$$

$$0,$$

$$-5t^4,$$

$$x^5 - 9.$$

DEFINITION

A *polynomial in one variable* is any expression of the type

$$a_n x^n + a_{n-1} x^{n-1} + \cdots + a_2 x^2 + a_1 x + a_0,$$

where *n* is a non-negative integer and $a_n, \ldots, a_0$ are real numbers, called *coefficients*. Some or all of the coefficients may be 0. Each $a_i x^i$ is called a *term*.

Expressions like the following are called *polynomials in several variables:*

$$5x^2 y^3 + 17x^2 y - 2, \quad 14a^2 b, \quad \pi r^2 + 2\pi rh.$$

Example 1   The polynomial $5x^3 y - 7xy^2 + 2$ has three terms. They are

$$5x^3 y, \ -7xy^2, \text{ and } 2.$$

The coefficients of the terms are 5, -7, and 2.

The *degree of a term* is the sum of the exponents of the variables. The *degree* of a nonzero polynomial is the degree of the term of highest degree. The polynomial consisting only of the number 0 has no degree.

Example 2   In the polynomial $5x^3 y - 7xy^2 + 2$, the degrees of the terms are 4, 3, and 0. The polynomial is of degree 4.

A polynomial with just one term is called a *monomial*. If there are just two terms, a polynomial is called a *binomial*. If there are just three terms, it is called a *trinomial*.

Much of the algebraic manipulation we do with polynomials can also be done with expressions that are not polynomials. Following are some expressions that are not polynomials:

$$3\sqrt{x} + 4y, \quad \frac{3x^2 + 2}{x - 1}, \quad 4x^{1/2} - 5y^{3/2}.$$

If two terms of an expression have the same letters raised to the same powers, the terms are called *similar*. This is true even if the expression is not a polynomial. Similar terms can be "combined" using the distributive laws.

Example 3 $3x^2 - 4y + 2x^2 = 3x^2 + 2x^2 - 4y$ (Rearranging)
$= (3 + 2)x^2 - 4y$ (Using the distributive laws)
$= 5x^2 - 4y$

Example 4 $4x^{1/2}y + 7x^{1/2}y = 11x^{1/2}y$

Example 5 $-2x^2\sqrt{y^3} + 5x^2\sqrt{y^3} = 3x^2\sqrt{y^3}$

Addition

The sum of two polynomials can be found by writing a plus sign between them and then combining similar terms.

Example 6   Add $-3x^3 + 2x - 4$ and $4x^3 + 3x^2 + 2$.

$$(-3x^3 + 2x - 4) + (4x^3 + 3x^2 + 2) = x^3 + 3x^2 + 2x - 2.$$

Additive Inverses

The additive inverse of a polynomial can be found by changing the sign of every term.

THEOREM   **The additive inverse of a polynomial can be found by replacing every term by its additive inverse.**

Example 7   The additive inverse of $-3xy^2 + 4x^2y - 5x - 3$ is

$$3xy^2 - 4x^2y + 5x + 3.$$

Example 8   The additive inverse of $7xy^2 - 6xy - 4y + 3$ can be symbolized as

$$-(7xy^2 - 6xy - 4y + 3).$$

Thus,

$$-(7xy^2 - 6xy - 4y + 3) = -7xy^2 + 6xy + 4y - 3.$$

The preceding example may recall the following rule: To remove parentheses preceded by an additive inverse sign, change the sign of every term inside the parentheses.

Subtraction

We know we can subtract by adding an inverse. Thus to subtract one polynomial from another, we add its additive inverse. We change the sign of each term of the subtrahend and then add.

Example 9 Subtract.

$$
\begin{aligned}
(-9x^5 - x^3 &+ 2x^2 + 4) - (2x^5 - x^4 + 4x^3 - 3x^2) \\
&= (-9x^5 - x^3 + 2x^2 + 4) + [-(2x^5 - x^4 + 4x^3 - 3x^2)] \\
&= (-9x^5 - x^3 + 2x^2 + 4) + (-2x^5 + x^4 - 4x^3 + 3x^2) \\
&= -11x^5 + x^4 - 5x^3 + 5x^2 + 4
\end{aligned}
$$

On occasion, it may be helpful to write polynomials to be subtracted with similar terms in columns.

Example 10 Subtract the second polynomial from the first.

$$
\begin{array}{l}
4x^2y - 6x^3y^2 \qquad\quad + x^2y^2 - 5y \\
\underline{4x^2y + x^3y^2 + 3x^2y^3 \qquad\quad + 6y} \\
 - 7x^3y^2 - 3x^2y^3 + x^2y^2 - 11y
\end{array}
$$
(Mentally change signs and add.)

EXERCISE SET 1.3

Determine the degree of each term and the degree of the polynomial.

1. $-11x^4 - x^3 + x^2 + 3x - 9$

2. $t^3 - 3t^2 + t + 1$

3. $y^3 + 2y^6 + x^2y^4 - 8$

4. $u^2 + 3v^5 - u^3v^4 - 7$

5. $a^5 + 4a^2b^4 + 6ab + 4a - 3$

6. $8p^6 + 2p^4t^4 - 7p^3t + 5p^2 - 14$

Add.

7. $5x^2y - 2xy^2 + 3xy - 5$ and
$-2x^2y - 3xy^2 + 4xy + 7$

8. $6x^2y - 3xy^2 + 5xy - 3$ and
$-4x^2y - 4xy^2 + 3xy + 8$

9. $- 3pq^2 - 5p^2q + 4pq + 3$ and
$- 7pq^2 + 3pq - 4p + 2q$

10. $- 5pq^2 - 3p^2q + 6pq + 5$ and
$- 4pq^2 + 5pq - 6p + 4q$

11. $2x + 3y + z - 7$ and
$4x - 2y - z + 8$ and
$- 3x + y - 2z - 4$

12. $2x^2 + 12xy - 11$ and
$6x^2 - 2x + 4$ and
$- x^2 - y - 2$

13. $7x\sqrt{y} - 3y\sqrt{x} + \frac{1}{5}$ and
$- 2x\sqrt{y} - y\sqrt{x} - \frac{3}{5}$

14. $10x\sqrt{y} - 4y\sqrt{x} + \frac{4}{3}$ and
$- 3x\sqrt{y} - y\sqrt{x} - \frac{1}{3}$

Rename each additive inverse without parentheses.

15. $- (5x^3 - 7x^2 + 3x - 6)$

16. $- (-4y^4 + 7y^2 - 2y - 1)$

Subtract.

17. $(3x^2 - 2x - x^3 + 2)$
$- (5x^2 - 8x - x^3 + 4)$

18. $(5x^2 + 4xy - 3y^2 + 2)$
$- (9x^2 - 4xy + 2y^2 - 1)$

19. $(4a - 2b - c + 3d)$
$- (-2a + 3b + c - d)$

20. $(5a - 3b - c + 4d)$
$- (-3a + 5b + c - 2d)$

21. $(x^4 - 3x^2 + 4x)$
$- (3x^3 + x^2 - 5x + 3)$

22. $(2x^4 - 5x^2 + 7x)$
$- (5x^3 + 2x^2 - 3x + 5)$

23. $(7x\sqrt{y} - 4y\sqrt{x} + 7.5)$
$- (-2x\sqrt{y} - y\sqrt{x} - 1.6)$

24. $(10x\sqrt{y} - 4y\sqrt{x} + \frac{4}{3})$
$- (-3x\sqrt{y} + y\sqrt{x} - \frac{1}{3})$

1.4 MULTIPLICATION OF POLYNOMIALS

Multiplication of polynomials is based on the distributive laws. To multiply two polynomials, we multiply each term of one by every term of the other and then add the results.

Example 1   Multiply $4x^4y - 7x^2y + 3y$ by $2y - 3x^2y$.

$$4x^4y - 7x^2y + 3y$$
$$2y - 3x^2y$$
$$\overline{\hphantom{-12x^6y^2+}8x^4y^2 - 14x^2y^2 + 6y^2} \quad \text{(Multiplying by } 2y\text{)}$$
$$-12x^6y^2 + 21x^4y^2 - \hphantom{1}9x^2y^2 \quad \text{(Multiplying by } -3x^2y\text{)}$$
$$\overline{-12x^6y^2 + 29x^4y^2 - 23x^2y^2 + 6y^2} \quad \text{(Adding)}$$

Products of Two Binomials

We can find a product of two binomials mentally. We multiply the first terms, then the outside terms, then the inside terms, then the last terms (this procedure is sometimes abbreviated FOIL), and then add the results. This also works for expressions that are not polynomials.

Multiply.

Example 2 $(3xy + 2x)(x^2 + 2xy^2) = 3x^3y + 6x^2y^3 + 2x^3 + 4x^2y^2$

$$\overset{\text{F}}{\quad} \overset{\text{O}}{\quad} \overset{\text{I}}{\quad} \overset{\text{L}}{\quad}$$

Example 3 $(x + \sqrt{2})(y - \sqrt{2}) = xy - \sqrt{2}y + \sqrt{2}x - 2$

Example 4 $(2x - \sqrt{3})(y + 2) = 2xy + 4x - \sqrt{3}y - 2\sqrt{3}$

Example 5 $(2x + 3y)(x - 4y) = 2x^2 - 5xy - 12y^2$

Squares of Binomials

Multiplying a binomial by itself, we obtain the following:

$$(a + b)^2 = a^2 + 2ab + b^2$$

and

$$(a - b)^2 = a^2 - 2ab + b^2.$$

Thus, to square a binomial we square the first term, add twice the product of the terms, and then add the square of the second term.

Multiply.

Example 6 $(2x + 9y^2)^2 = (2x)^2 + 2(2x)(9y^2) + (9y^2)^2$
$$= 4x^2 + 36xy^2 + 81y^4$$

Example 7 $(3x^2 - 5xy^2)^2 = (3x^2)^2 - 2(3x^2)(5xy^2) + (5xy^2)^2$
$$= 9x^4 - 30x^3y^2 + 25x^2y^4$$

Products of Sums and Differences

The following multiplication gives a result to be remembered:

$$(a + b)(a - b) = (a + b) \cdot a - (a + b) \cdot b$$
$$= a^2 + ab - ab - b^2$$
$$= a^2 - b^2.$$

The result to be remembered is as follows:

$$\mathbf{(a + b)(a - b) = a^2 - b^2.}$$

The product of a sum and a difference of the same two terms is the difference of their squares. Thus to find such a product, we square the first term, square the second term, and write a minus sign between the results. Multiply.

Example 8 $(y + 5)(y - 5) = y^2 - 25$

Example 9 $(3x + 2)(3x - 2) = (3x)^2 - 2^2$
$$= 9x^2 - 4$$

Example 10 $(2xy^2 + 3x)(2xy^2 - 3x) = (2xy^2)^2 - (3x)^2$
$$= 4x^2y^4 - 9x^2$$

Example 11 $(5x + \sqrt{2})(5x - \sqrt{2}) = (5x)^2 - (\sqrt{2})^2$
$$= 25x^2 - 2$$

Example 12 $(5y + 4 + 3x)(5y + 4 - 3x) = (5y + 4)^2 - (3x)^2$
$$= 25y^2 + 40y + 16 - 9x^2$$

Example 13 $(3xy^2 + 4y)(-3xy^2 + 4y) = -(3xy^2)^2 + (4y)^2$
$$= 16y^2 - 9x^2y^4$$

In the following exercises you should do as much of the calculating mentally as you can. If possible, write only the answer. Work for speed with accuracy.

EXERCISE SET 1.4

Multiply.

1. $2x^2 + 4x + 16$ and $3x - 4$
2. $3y^2 - 3y + 9$ and $2y + 3$
3. $4a^2b - 2ab + 3b^2$ and $ab - 2b + 1$
4. $2x^2 + y^2 - 2xy$ and $x^2 - 2y^2 - xy$
5. $(a - b)(a^2 + ab + b^2)$
6. $(t + 1)(t^2 - t + 1)$
7. $(2x + 3y)(2x + y)$
8. $(2a - 3b)(2a - b)$
9. $(4x^2 - \frac{1}{2}y)(3x + \frac{1}{4}y)$
10. $(2y^3 + \frac{1}{5}x)(3y - \frac{1}{4}x)$
11. $(\sqrt{2}x^2 - y^2)(\sqrt{2}x - 2y)$
12. $(\sqrt{3}y^2 - 2)(\sqrt{3}y - x)$
13. $(2x + 3y)^2$
14. $(5x + 2y)^2$
15. $(2x^2 - 3y)^2$
16. $(4x^2 - 5y)^2$
17. $(2x^3 + 3y^2)^2$
18. $(5x^3 + 2y^2)^2$
19. $(\frac{1}{2}x^2 - \frac{3}{5}y)^2$
20. $(\frac{1}{4}x^2 - \frac{2}{3}y)^2$

21. $(0.5x + 0.7y^2)^2$
22. $(0.3x + 0.8y^2)^2$
23. $(3x - 2y)(3x + 2y)$
24. $(3x + 5y)(3x - 5y)$
25. $(x^2 + yz)(x^2 - yz)$
26. $(2x^2 + 5xy)(2x^2 - 5xy)$
27. $(3x^2 - \sqrt{2})(3x^2 + \sqrt{2})$
28. $(5x^2 - \sqrt{3})(5x^2 + \sqrt{3})$
29. $(2x + 3y + 4)(2x + 3y - 4)$
30. $(5x + 2y + 3)(5x + 2y - 3)$
31. $(x^2 + 3y + y^2)(x^2 + 3y - y^2)$
32. $(2x^2 + y + y^2)(2x^2 + y - y^2)$
33. $(x + 1)(x - 1)(x^2 + 1)$
34. $(y - 2)(y + 2)(y^2 + 4)$
35. $(2x + y)(2x - y)(4x^2 + y^2)$
36. $(5x + y)(5x - y)(25x^2 + y^2)$
37. Find a formula for $(a + b)^3$.
38. Find a formula for $(a - b)^3$.

Use the formulas of Exercises 37 and 38 to multiply each of the following.

39. $(x + h)^3$
40. $(x - h)^3$
41. $(x - 5)^3$
42. $P(1 + i)^3$
43. $(2x + 3)^3$
44. $(3t^2 - 4)^3$

1.5 FACTORING

To factor a polynomial we do the reverse of multiplying; that is, we find an expression that is a product. Facility in factoring is an important algebraic skill.

Terms with Common Factors

When an expression is to be factored, we should always look first for a possible factor that is common to all terms. We then "factor it out" using the distributive laws.

Factor.

Example 1 $4x^2 + 8 = 4(x^2 + 2)$

Example 2 $12x^2y - 20x^3y = 4x^2y(3 - 5x)$

Example 3 $7x\sqrt{y} + 14x^2\sqrt{y} - 21\sqrt{y} = 7\sqrt{y}(x + 2x^2 - 3)$

Example 4 $(a - b)(x + 5) + (a - b)(x - y^2) = (a - b)[(x + 5) + (x - y^2)]$
$$= (a - b)(2x + 5 - y^2)$$

In some polynomials pairs of terms have a common factor that can be removed, as in the following examples. This process is called *factoring by grouping*, and uses the distributive laws repeatedly.

Factor.

Example 5 $y^2 + 3y + 4y + 12 = y(y + 3) + 4(y + 3)$
$$= (y + 4)(y + 3)$$

Example 6 $ax^2 + ay + bx^2 + by = a(x^2 + y) + b(x^2 + y)$
$$= (a + b)(x^2 + y)$$

Differences of Squares

Recall that $(a + b)(a - b) = a^2 - b^2$. We can use this equation in reverse to factor an expression that is the difference of two squares.
    Factor.

Example 7 $x^2 - 9 = (x + 3)(x - 3)$

Example 8 $y^2 - 2 = (y + \sqrt{2})(y - \sqrt{2})$

Example 9 $9a^2 - 16x^4 = (3a + 4x^2)(3a - 4x^2)$

Example 10 $9y^4 - 9x^4 = 9(y^4 - x^4)$
$$= 9(y^2 + x^2)(y^2 - x^2)$$
$$= 9(y^2 + x^2)(y + x)(y - x)$$

Trinomial Squares

You should recall that $a^2 + 2ab + b^2 = (a + b)^2$ and $a^2 - 2ab + b^2 = (a - b)^2$. We can use these equations to factor trinomials that are squares. To factor a trinomial, you should check to see if it is a square. For this to be the case, two of the terms must be squares and the other term must be twice the product of the square roots.
    Factor.

Example 11 $x^2 - 10x + 25 = (x - 5)^2$

Example 12 $16y^2 + 56y + 49 = (4y + 7)^2$

Example 13 $-4y^2 - 144y^8 + 48y^5 = -4y^2(1 + 36y^6 - 12y^3)$ (We first removed
$$= -4y^2(1 - 12y^3 + 36y^6)$$ the common
$$= -4y^2(1 - 6y^3)^2$$ factor.)

Trinomials That Are Not Squares

Certain trinomials that are not squares can be factored into two binomials. To do this, we can use the equation

$$acx^2 + (ad + bc)x + bd = (ax + b) \times (cx + d).$$

Example 14 Factor $x^2 - 5x - 14$.

$$x^2 - 5x - 14 = (x - 7)(x + 2) \qquad \text{(Here we looked for factors of } -14 \text{ whose sum is } -5.)$$

Example 15 Factor $2x^2 + 11x + 12$.

We look for binomials $(ax + b)$ and $(cx + d)$. The product of the first terms must be $2x^2$. The product of the last terms must be 12. When we multiply the inside terms, then the outside terms, and add, we must get $11x$. By trial, we thus determine the factors to be as follows: $(x + 4)$ $(2x + 3)$.

In later work we will consider expressions like

$$(x + h)^2 - x^2.$$

To simplify this, first note that

$$(x + h)^2 = x^2 + 2xh + h^2.$$

Subtracting x^2 on both sides of this equation, we get

$$(x + h)^2 - x^2 = 2xh + h^2.$$

Factoring out an h on the right side we get

$$(x + h)^2 - x^2 = h(2x + h).$$

Let us now use this result to compare two squares.

Example 16 How close is $(3.1)^2$ to 3^2?

Solution Substituting $x = 3$ and $h = 0$ in equation (1) we get

$$(3.1)^2 - 3^2 = 0.1(2 \cdot 3 + 0.1) = 0.1(6.1) = 0.61.$$

So $(3.1)^2$ differs from 3^2 by 0.61.

Compound Interest

Suppose we invest P dollars at interest rate i, compounded annually. The amount A_1 in the account at the end of 1 year is given by

$$A_1 = P + Pi = P(1 + i) = Pr,$$

where, for convenience,

$$r = 1 + i.$$

Going into the second year we have Pr dollars, so by the end of the second year we would have the amount A_2 given by

$$A_2 = A_1 \cdot r = (Pr)r = Pr^2.$$

Going into the third year we have Pr^2 dollars, so by the end of the third year we would have the amount A_3 given by

$$A_3 = A_2 \cdot r = (Pr^2)r = Pr^3.$$

In general,

If an amount P is invested at interest rate i, compounded annually, in t years it will grow to the amount A given by

$$A = P(1 + i)^t.$$

Example 17 Suppose \$1000 is invested at 18% compounded annually. How much is in the account at the end of 2 years?

Solution We substitute into the equation $A = P(1 + i)^t$ and get

$$A = 1000(1 + 0.18)^2 = 1000(1.18)^2 = 1000(1.3924) = \$1392.40.$$

If interest is compounded quarterly, we can find a formula like the one above as follows:

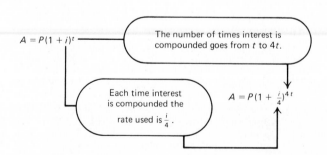

In general,

THEOREM   **If a principal P is invested at interest rate i, compounded n times a year, in t years it will grow to the amount A given by**

$$A = P\left(1 + \frac{i}{n}\right)^{nt}.$$

Example 18   Suppose $1000 is invested at 18% compounded quarterly. How much is in the account at the end of 2 years?

Solution   We substitute into the equation $A = P\left(1 + \dfrac{i}{n}\right)^{nt}$ and get

$$A = 1000\left(1 + \frac{0.18}{4}\right)^{4\times 2} = 1000(1 + 0.045)^8 = 1000(1.045)^8,$$
$$\approx 1000(1.422100613)$$
$$= 1422.10$$
$$\approx \$1422.10.^*$$

EXERCISE SET 1.5

Factor.

1. $18a^2b - 15ab^2$
2. $4x^2y + 12xy^2$
3. $a(b - 2) + c(b - 2)$
4. $a(x^2 - 3) - 2(x^2 - 3)$
5. $x^2 + 3x + 6x + 18$
6. $3x^3 + x^2 - 18x - 6$
7. $9x^2 - 25$
8. $16x^2 - 9$
9. $4xy^4 - 4xz^2$
10. $5xy^4 - 5xz^4$
11. $y^2 - 6y + 9$
12. $x^2 + 8x + 16$

---

* A CALCULATOR NOTE: A calculator with a y^x key and a ten-digit readout was used to find $(1.045)^8$ in Example 17. This power could also be found on a calculator without a y^x key by multiplying 1.045 by itself eight times. In this case, the answer is approximated by the calculator to fit its readout, ten digits. The number of places on the calculator may affect the accuracy of the answer. Thus, you may occasionally find your answers do not agree with those in the key, which were found on a calculator with a ten-digit readout. In general, if you are using a calculator, do all your computations, and round only at the end, as in Example 17. Usually, your answer should agree to at least four digits. It might be wise to consult with your instructor on the accuracy required.

13. $1 - 8x + 16x^2$

14. $1 + 10x + 25x^2$

15. $4x^2 - 5$

16. $16x^2 - 7$

17. $x^2y^2 - 14xy + 49$

18. $x^2y^2 - 16xy + 64$

19. $4ax^2 + 20ax - 56a$

20. $21x^2y + 2xy - 8y$

21. $a^2 + 2ab + b^2 - c^2$

22. $x^2 - 2xy + y^2 - z^2$

23. $x^2 + 2xy + y^2 - a^2 - 2ab - b^2$

24. $r^2 + 2rs + s^2 - t^2 + 2tv - v^2$

25. $5y^4 - 80x^4$

26. $6y^4 - 96x^4$

27. $(x + h)^3 - x^3$
[*Hint:* Use Exercise Set 1.4, Exercise 39.]

28. $(x + 0.01)^2 - x^2$

Use the following for Exercises 29 and 30: $(x + h)^2 - x^2 = h(2x + h)$

29. a) How close is $(4.1)^2$ to 4^2?

    b) How close is $(4.01)^2$ to 4^2?

    c) How close is $(4.001)^2$ to 4^2?

30. a) How close is $(2.1)^2$ to 2^2?

    b) How close is $(2.01)^2$ to 2^2?

    c) How close is $(2.001)^2$ to 2^2?

From Exercise 27 it follows that $(x + h)^3 - x^3 = h(3x^2 + 3xh + h^2)$. Use this for Exercises 31 and 32.

31. a) How close is $(2.1)^3$ to 2^3?

    b) How close is $(2.01)^3$ to 2^3?

    c) How close is $(2.001)^3$ to 2^3?

32. a) How close is $(4.1)^3$ to 4^3?

    b) How close is $(4.01)^3$ to 4^3?

    c) How close is $(4.001)^3$ to 4^3?

The symbol ▓ indicates an exercise designed to be done using a calculator.

33. Suppose $1000 is invested at 8%. How much is in the account at the end of 1 year, if interest is compounded

    a) annually?

    b) semiannually?

    c) quarterly?

    d) daily? (▓ with y^x key.)

    e) hourly?

34. Suppose $1000 is invested at 10%. How much is in the account at the end of 1 year, if interest is compounded

    a) annually?

    b) semiannually?

    c) quarterly?

    d) daily? (▓ with y^x key.)

    e) hourly?

1.6   FRACTIONAL EXPRESSIONS

Expressions like the following are called *fractional expressions*:

$$\frac{8}{5}, \quad \frac{5}{x - 2}, \quad \frac{3x^2 + 5\sqrt{x} - 2}{x^2 - y^2}.$$

Fractional expressions represent division. Certain substitutions are not sensible in such expressions. Since division by 0 is not defined, any number that makes a denominator zero is not a sensible replacement.

Multiplication and Division

To *multiply* two fractional expressions, we multiply the two numerators (to obtain the numerator of the product) and multiply the two denominators (to obtain the denominator of the product).

To *divide* a given fractional expression by a fractional expression divisor, we multiply the given fractional expression by the reciprocal of the divisor. This involves two steps. First, we obtain the reciprocal of the divisor, as in Section 1.1, by *inverting*; that is, the reciprocal is a fraction with a numerator equal to the denominator of the divisor and with a denominator equal to the numerator of the divisor. Next, we *multiply* the given expression by the reciprocal of the divisor just found.

Example 1 Multiply.

$$\frac{x + 3}{y - 4} \cdot \frac{x^3}{y + 5} = \frac{(x + 3)x^3}{(y - 4)(y + 5)}$$

$$= \frac{x^4 + 3x^3}{y^2 + y - 20}$$

Example 2 Divide.

$$\frac{x - 2}{x + 1} \div \frac{x + 5}{x - 3} = \frac{x - 2}{x + 1} \cdot \frac{x - 3}{x + 5} \qquad \text{(Inverting)}$$

$$= \frac{(x - 2)(x - 3)}{(x + 1)(x + 5)} \qquad \text{(Multiplying)}$$

$$= \frac{x^2 - 5x + 6}{x^2 + 6x + 5}$$

Simplifying

The basis of simplifying fractional expressions rests on the fact that certain expressions are equal to 1 for all sensible replacements. Such expressions have the same numerator and denominator.* Here are some examples:

$$\frac{x - 2}{x - 2}, \quad \frac{3x^2 - 4x + 2}{3x^2 - 4x + 2}, \quad \frac{4x - 5}{4x - 5}.$$

---

* From Section 1.1, $a \div a = \frac{a}{a} = a\left(\frac{1}{a}\right)$, and since a and $\frac{1}{a}$ are reciprocals, their product is 1.

When we multiply by such an expression we obtain an equivalent expression. This means that the new expression will name the same number as the first for all sensible replacements. The set of sensible replacements may not be the same for the two expressions.

Example 3   Multiply.

$$\frac{y + 4}{y - 3} \cdot \frac{y - 2}{y - 2} = \frac{(y + 4)(y - 2)}{(y - 3)(y - 2)}$$

$$= \frac{y^2 + 2y - 8}{y^2 - 5y + 6}$$

The expressions $(y + 4)/(y - 3)$ and $(y^2 + 2y - 8)/(y^2 - 5y + 6)$ are equivalent. That is, they will name the same number for all sensible replacements. The only nonsensible replacement in the first expression is 3. For the second expression the nonsensible replacements are 2 and 3.

Simplification can be accomplished by reversing the procedure in the above example; that is to say, we try to factor the fractional expression in such a way that one of the factors is equal to 1, and then we "remove" that factor.

Example 4   Simplify.

$$\frac{15x^3y^2}{20x^2y} = \frac{(5x^2y)3xy}{(5x^2y)4} \qquad \text{(Factoring numerator and denominator)}$$

$$= \frac{5x^2y}{5x^2y} \cdot \frac{3xy}{4} \qquad \text{(Factoring the expression)}$$

$$= \frac{3xy}{4} \qquad \text{("Removing" a factor of 1)}$$

Note that in the original expression neither x nor y can be 0. In the simplified expression, however, all replacements are sensible.

Example 5   Simplify.

$$\frac{x^2 - 1}{2x^2 - x - 1} = \frac{(x - 1)(x + 1)}{(2x + 1)(x - 1)} = \frac{x - 1}{x - 1} \cdot \frac{x + 1}{2x + 1}$$

$$= \frac{x + 1}{2x + 1}$$

In the original expression the sensible replacements are all real numbers except 1 and $-\frac{1}{2}$. In the simplified expression the sensible replacements are all real numbers except $-\frac{1}{2}$.

Canceling

Canceling is a shortcut for part of the procedure in the preceding examples. Canceling gives rise to a great many errors, particularly when it is not well understood. It should therefore be used with caution.

Example 6 Simplify.

$$\frac{x^3 - 27}{x^2 + x - 12} = \frac{(x - 3)(x^2 + 3x + 9)}{(x + 4)(x - 3)}$$

$$= \frac{x^2 + 3x + 9}{x + 4}$$

Note that the canceling is a shortcut for "removing" a factor of 1. When fractional expressions are multiplied or divided, they should be simplified when possible.

Example 7 Multiply and simplify.

$$\frac{x + 2}{x - 2} \cdot \frac{x^2 - 4}{x^2 + x - 2} = \frac{(x + 2)(x^2 - 4)}{(x - 2)(x^2 + x - 2)} \qquad \text{(Multiplying)}$$

$$= \frac{(x + 2)(x + 2)(x - 2)}{(x - 2)(x + 2)(x - 1)} \qquad \text{(Factoring)}$$

$$= \frac{x + 2}{x - 1} \qquad \text{("Removing" a factor of 1)}$$

Example 8 Divide and simplify.

$$\frac{a^2 - 1}{a + 1} \div \frac{a^2 - 2a + 1}{a + 1} = \frac{a^2 - 1}{a + 1} \cdot \frac{a + 1}{a^2 - 2a + 1}$$

$$= \frac{(a + 1)(a - 1)(a + 1)}{(a + 1)(a - 1)(a - 1)}$$

$$= \frac{a + 1}{a - 1}$$

Addition and Subtraction

When fractional expressions have the same denominator, we can add or subtract them by adding or subtracting the numerators and retaining the common denominator. If denominators are not the same, we then find equivalent expressions with the same denominator and add. If one denominator is the additive inverse of another, we can find a common denominator by multiplying by $\dfrac{-1}{-1}$.

Example 9 Add.

$$\frac{3x^2 + 4x - 8}{x^2 + y^2} + \frac{-5x^2 + 5x + 7}{x^2 + y^2} = \frac{-2x^2 + 9x - 1}{x^2 + y^2}$$

In the following example, one denominator is the additive inverse of the other.

Example 10 Add.

$$\frac{3x^2 + 4}{x - y} + \frac{5x^2 - 11}{y - x} = \frac{3x^2 + 4}{x - y} + \frac{-1}{-1} \cdot \frac{5x^2 - 11}{y - x}$$

$$= \frac{3x^2 + 4}{x - y} + \frac{-1(5x^2 - 11)}{-1(y - x)}$$

$$= \frac{3x^2 + 4}{x - y} + \frac{11 - 5x^2}{x - y} \quad (-1(y - x) = -y + x = x - y)$$

$$= \frac{-2x^2 + 15}{x - y}$$

When denominators are different, but not additive inverses of each other, we find a common denominator by factoring the denominators. Then we multiply by 1 to get the common denominator in each expression.

Example 11 Add $\dfrac{1}{2x} + \dfrac{5x}{x^2 - 1} + \dfrac{3}{x + 1}$.

We first find the *Least Common Multiple* (LCM) of the denominators. The denominators, when factored, are

$$2x, \quad (x + 1)(x - 1), \quad x + 1.$$

The LCM is $2x(x + 1)(x - 1)$.

Now we multiply each fractional expression by 1 appropriately.

$$\frac{1}{2x} \cdot \frac{(x + 1)(x - 1)}{(x + 1)(x - 1)} + \frac{5x}{(x + 1)(x - 1)} \cdot \frac{2x}{2x} + \frac{3}{(x + 1)} \cdot \frac{2x(x - 1)}{2x(x - 1)}$$

$$= \frac{(x + 1)(x - 1) + 10x^2 + 6x(x - 1)}{2x(x + 1)(x - 1)}$$

$$= \frac{17x^2 - 6x - 1}{2x(x + 1)(x - 1)} \quad \text{or} \quad \frac{17x^2 - 6x - 1}{2x^3 - 2x}$$

Example 12   Subtract.

$$\frac{x}{x^2 + 5x + 6} - \frac{2}{x^2 + 3x + 2}$$

$$= \frac{x}{(x + 2)(x + 3)} - \frac{2}{(x + 1)(x + 2)} \quad \text{(The LCM is } (x + 1)(x + 2)(x + 3)\text{)}$$

$$= \frac{x}{(x + 2)(x + 3)} \cdot \frac{x + 1}{x + 1}$$

$$\quad - \frac{2}{(x + 1)(x + 2)} \cdot \frac{x + 3}{x + 3}$$

$$= \frac{x(x + 1) - 2(x + 3)}{(x + 1)(x + 2)(x + 3)} \quad \text{(It is important to subtract the } \textit{entire} \text{ numerator, not just part of it.)}$$

$$= \frac{x^2 + x - 2x + 6}{(x + 1)(x + 2)(x + 3)}$$

$$= \frac{x^2 + x - 2x - 6}{(x + 1)(x + 2)(x + 3)}$$

$$= \frac{x^2 - x - 6}{(x + 1)(x + 2)(x + 3)}$$

$$= \frac{(x - 3)(x + 2)}{(x + 1)(x + 2)(x + 3)}$$

$$= \frac{x - 3}{(x + 1)(x + 3)} \quad \text{(Always simplify at the end if possible.)}$$

Complex Fractional Expressions

A complex fractional expression is one that has a fractional expression in its numerator or denominator or both. To simplify such an expression, we can combine as necessary in numerator and denominator in order to obtain a single fractional expression for each. Then we divide the numerator by the denominator.

Example 13 Simplify.

$$\frac{x + \dfrac{1}{5}}{x - \dfrac{1}{3}} = \frac{x \cdot \dfrac{5}{5} + \dfrac{1}{5}}{x \cdot \dfrac{3}{3} - \dfrac{1}{3}}$$

$$= \frac{\dfrac{5x + 1}{5}}{\dfrac{3x - 1}{3}}$$ (Now we have a single fractional expression for both numerator and denominator.)

$$= \frac{5x + 1}{5} \cdot \frac{3}{3x - 1}$$ (Here we divided by multiplying by the reciprocal of the denominator.)

$$= \frac{15x + 3}{15x - 5}$$

Example 14 Simplify.

$$\frac{a^{-2} - b^{-2}}{a^{-1} + b^{-1}} = \frac{\dfrac{1}{a^2} - \dfrac{1}{b^2}}{\dfrac{1}{a} + \dfrac{1}{b}} = \frac{\dfrac{b^2}{b^2} \cdot \dfrac{1}{a^2} - \dfrac{a^2}{a^2} \cdot \dfrac{1}{b^2}}{\dfrac{b}{b} \cdot \dfrac{1}{a} + \dfrac{a}{a} \cdot \dfrac{1}{b}} = \frac{\dfrac{b^2 - a^2}{a^2b^2}}{\dfrac{b + a}{ab}}$$

$$= \frac{b^2 - a^2}{a^2b^2} \cdot \frac{ab}{b + a}$$

$$= \frac{(b - a)(b + a)ab}{(b + a)a^2b^2}$$

$$= \frac{ab(b + a)}{ab(b + a)} \cdot \frac{b - a}{ab} = \frac{b - a}{ab}$$

EXERCISE SET 1.6

In Exercises 1 through 3, determine the sensible replacements.

1. $\dfrac{3x - 2}{x(x - 1)}$

2. $\dfrac{(x^2 - 4)(x + 1)}{(x + 2)(x^2 - 1)}$

3. $\dfrac{7y^2 - 2y + 4}{x(x^2 - x - 6)}$

In Exercises 4 through 6, simplify. Then determine the replacements that are sensible in the simplified expression.

4. $\dfrac{25x^2y^2}{10xy^2}$

5. $\dfrac{x^2 - 4}{x^2 + 5x + 6}$

6. $\dfrac{x^2 - 3x + 2}{x^2 + x - 2}$

Multiply or divide, and simplify.

7. $\dfrac{x^2 - y^2}{(x - y)^2} \cdot \dfrac{1}{x + y}$

8. $\dfrac{r - s}{r + s} \cdot \dfrac{r^2 - s^2}{(r - s)^2}$

9. $\dfrac{x^2 - 2x - 35}{2x^3 - 3x^2} \cdot \dfrac{4x^3 - 9x}{7x - 49}$

10. $\dfrac{x^2 + 2x - 35}{3x^3 - 2x^2} \cdot \dfrac{9x^3 - 4x}{7x + 49}$

11. $\dfrac{a^2 - a - 6}{a^2 - 7a + 12} \cdot \dfrac{a^2 - 2a - 8}{a^2 - 3a - 10}$

12. $\dfrac{a^2 - a - 12}{a^2 - 6a + 8} \cdot \dfrac{a^2 + a - 6}{a^2 - 2a - 24}$

13. $\dfrac{m^2 - n^2}{r + s} \div \dfrac{m - n}{r + s}$

14. $\dfrac{a^2 - b^2}{x - y} \div \dfrac{a + b}{x - y}$

15. $\dfrac{3x + 12}{2x - 8} \div \dfrac{(x + 4)^2}{(x - 4)^2}$

16. $\dfrac{a^2 - a - 2}{a^2 - a - 6} \div \dfrac{a^2 - 2a}{2a + a^2}$

17. $\dfrac{x^2 - y^2}{x^2 + y^2} \cdot \dfrac{x^4 - y^4}{x^2 + 2xy + y^2}$

18. $\dfrac{c^2 + 4}{c^2 - 4} \div \dfrac{c^4 - 16}{c^2 - 4c + 4}$

19. $\dfrac{(x - y)^2 - z^2}{(x + y)^2 - z^2} \div \dfrac{x - y + z}{x + y - z}$

20. $\dfrac{(a + b)^2 - 9}{(a - b)^2 - 9} \cdot \dfrac{a - b - 3}{a + b + 3}$

Add or subtract, and simplify.

21. $\dfrac{3}{2a + 3} + \dfrac{2a}{2a + 3}$

22. $\dfrac{a - 3b}{a + b} + \dfrac{a + 5b}{a + b}$

23. $\dfrac{y}{y - 1} + \dfrac{2}{1 - y}$

24. $\dfrac{a}{a - b} + \dfrac{b}{b - a}$

25. $\dfrac{x}{2x - 3y} - \dfrac{y}{3y - 2x}$

26. $\dfrac{3a}{3a - 2b} - \dfrac{2a}{2b - 3a}$

27. $\dfrac{3}{x + 2} + \dfrac{2}{x^2 - 4}$

28. $\dfrac{5}{a - 3} - \dfrac{2}{a^2 - 9}$

29. $\dfrac{y}{y^2 - y - 20} + \dfrac{2}{y + 4}$

30. $\dfrac{6}{y^2 + 6y + 9} - \dfrac{5}{y + 3}$

31. $\dfrac{3}{x + y} + \dfrac{x - 5y}{x^2 - y^2}$

32. $\dfrac{a^2 + 1}{a^2 - 1} - \dfrac{a - 1}{a + 1}$

33. $\dfrac{9x + 2}{3x^2 - 2x - 8} + \dfrac{7}{3x^2 + x - 4}$

34. $\dfrac{3y}{y^2 - 7y + 10} - \dfrac{2y}{y^2 - 8y + 15}$

35. $\dfrac{5a}{a - b} + \dfrac{ab}{a^2 - b^2} + \dfrac{4b}{a + b}$

36. $\dfrac{6a}{a - b} - \dfrac{3b}{b - a} + \dfrac{5}{a^2 - b^2}$

37. $\dfrac{7}{x+2} - \dfrac{x+8}{4-x^2} + \dfrac{3x-2}{4-4x+x^2}$

38. $\dfrac{6}{x+3} - \dfrac{x+4}{9-x^2} + \dfrac{2x-3}{9-6x+x^2}$

39. $\dfrac{1}{x+1} - \dfrac{x}{x-2} + \dfrac{x^2+2}{x^2-x-2}$

40. $\dfrac{x-1}{x-2} - \dfrac{x+1}{x+2} + \dfrac{x-6}{x^2-4}$

Simplify.

41. $\dfrac{\dfrac{x^2-y^2}{xy}}{\dfrac{x-y}{y}}$

42. $\dfrac{\dfrac{a-b}{b}}{\dfrac{a^2-b^2}{ab}}$

43. $\dfrac{a-a^{-1}}{a+a^{-1}}$

44. $\dfrac{a-\dfrac{a}{b}}{b-\dfrac{b}{a}}$

45. $\dfrac{c^2-16c^{-2}}{1-2c^{-1}}$

46. $\dfrac{x^{-1}-y^{-1}}{x^{-2}-y^{-2}}$

47. $\dfrac{x^2+xy+y^2}{\dfrac{x^2}{y}-\dfrac{y^2}{x}}$

48. $\dfrac{\dfrac{a^2}{b}+\dfrac{b^2}{a}}{a^2-ab+b^2}$

49. $\dfrac{\dfrac{x}{y}-\dfrac{y}{x}}{\dfrac{1}{y}+\dfrac{1}{x}}$

50. $\dfrac{\dfrac{a}{b}-\dfrac{b}{a}}{\dfrac{1}{a}-\dfrac{1}{b}}$

51. $\dfrac{x^2y^{-2}-y^2x^{-2}}{xy^{-1}+yx^{-1}}$

52. $\dfrac{a^2b^{-2}-b^2a^{-2}}{ab^{-1}-ba^{-1}}$

53. $\dfrac{\dfrac{a}{1-a}+\dfrac{1+a}{a}}{\dfrac{1-a}{a}+\dfrac{a}{1+a}}$

54. $\dfrac{\dfrac{1-x}{x}+\dfrac{x}{1+x}}{\dfrac{1+x}{x}+\dfrac{x}{1-x}}$

55. $\dfrac{\dfrac{1}{a^2}+\dfrac{2}{ab}+\dfrac{1}{b^2}}{\dfrac{1}{a^2}-\dfrac{1}{b^2}}$

56. $\dfrac{\dfrac{1}{x^2}-\dfrac{1}{y^2}}{\dfrac{1}{x^2}-\dfrac{2}{xy}+\dfrac{1}{y^2}}$

■ ───

Simplify.

57. $\dfrac{(x+h)^2-x^2}{h}$

58. $\dfrac{\dfrac{1}{x+h}-\dfrac{1}{x}}{h}$

59. $\dfrac{(x+h)^3-x^3}{h}$

60. $\dfrac{\dfrac{1}{(x+h)^2}-\dfrac{1}{x^2}}{h}$

61. $\left[\dfrac{\dfrac{x+1}{x-1}+1}{\dfrac{x+1}{x-1}-1}\right]^8$

62. $1+\dfrac{1}{1+\dfrac{1}{1+\dfrac{1}{1+\dfrac{1}{x}}}}$

1.7 SOLVING EQUATIONS

Solutions and Solution Sets

DEFINITION **SOLUTION**	A *solution* of an equation is any number that makes an equation true when that number is substituted for the variable.

Thus, 3 is a solution of $5x = 15$ because $5(3) = 15$ is true. But, -4 is not a solution of $5x = 15$ because $5(-4) = 15$ is false.

DEFINITION **SOLUTION SET**	The set of *all* real numbers which are solutions of an equation form the *solution set.*

For example, 3 is the only solution of $5x = 15$, so the solution set consists of the number 3 and is denoted $\{3\}$.

When we find all the solutions of an equation (find its solution set), we say we have *solved* it.

Example 1   Solve $y^2 - y = 0$.

We can see that 0 will make the equation true when substituted for y; so 0 is a solution. But, 1 also makes the equation true. There are no other solutions. The solution set is $\{0, 1\}$.

Equation-solving Principles

Basic to the solution of many equations are these two simple principles.

> *The Addition Principle.* If an equation $a = b$ is true, then the equation $a + c = b + c$ is true for any number c.
>
> *The Multiplication Principle.* If an equation $a = b$ is true, then the equation $ac = bc$ is true for any number c.

Example 2   Solve $-\frac{5}{6}x + 10 = \frac{1}{2}x + 2$.

Solution   We first multiply on both sides by 6 to clear of fractions.

$$6\left(-\tfrac{5}{6}x + 10\right) = 6\left(\tfrac{1}{2}x + 2\right) \qquad \text{(Multiplication Principle)}$$

$$6\left(-\tfrac{5}{6}x\right) + 6 \cdot 10 = 6\left(\tfrac{1}{2}x\right) + 6 \cdot 2 \qquad \text{(Distributive Law)}$$

$$-5x + 60 = 3x + 12 \qquad \text{(Simplifying)}$$

$$60 = 8x + 12 \qquad \text{(Addition Principle: We add } 5x \text{ to get}$$

the variable by itself on one side of the

equation.)

$$48 = 8x \qquad \text{(We add } -12.\text{)}$$

$$\tfrac{1}{8} \cdot 48 = \tfrac{1}{8} \cdot 8x \qquad \text{(We multiply by } \tfrac{1}{8}.\text{)}$$

$$6 = x$$

The number 6 checks when it is substituted into the original equation; thus it is the solution. The solution set is {6}.

Example 3   Solve $3(7 - 2x) = 14 - 8(x - 1)$.

Solution

$$21 - 6x = 14 - 8x + 8 \qquad \text{(Multiplying to remove parentheses)}$$

$$21 - 6x = 22 - 8x \qquad \text{(Simplifying)}$$

$$8x - 6x = 22 - 21 \qquad \text{(Adding } 8x \text{ and also } -21)$$

$$2x = 1 \qquad \text{(Combining like terms and}$$

simplifying)

$$x = \tfrac{1}{2} \qquad \text{(Multiplying by } \tfrac{1}{2})$$

The solution is $\frac{1}{2}$. The solution set is $\{\frac{1}{2}\}$.

Example 4   Solve $x + 4 = x$.

Solution

$$-x + x + 4 = -x + x \qquad \text{(Adding } -x)$$

$$4 = 0$$

In Example 4 we get a false equation. No replacement for x will make the equation true. Thus, there are no solutions. The solution set is the *empty set*, denoted $\emptyset$.

The third principle for solving equations is

> **The Principle of Zero Products.** For any numbers a and b, if $ab = 0$, then $a = 0$ or $b = 0$; and if $a = 0$ or $b = 0$, then $ab = 0$.

To solve an equation using this principle, there *must* be a 0 on one side of the equation and a product on the other. The solutions are then obtained by setting each of the factors equal to 0 and solving the resulting equations.

Example 5   Solve $3x(x - 2)(5x + 4) = 0$.

Solution $3x(x - 2)(5x + 4) = 0$

$\qquad 3x = 0 \quad$ or $x - 2 = 0$ or $5x + 4 = 0 \qquad$ (Principle of Zero Products)

$\qquad \frac{1}{3} \cdot 3x = \frac{1}{3} \cdot 0$ or $\qquad x = 2$ or $\qquad 5x = -4 \qquad$ (Solve each separately.)

$\qquad x = 0 \quad$ or $\qquad x = 2$ or $\qquad x = -\frac{4}{5}$

The solutions are 0, 2, and $-\frac{4}{5}$. The solution set is $\{0, 2, -\frac{4}{5}\}$.

Example 6   Solve $x^2 - x = 20$.

Solution $\qquad\qquad\qquad x^2 - x = 20$

$\qquad\qquad\qquad x^2 - x - 20 = 0 \qquad$ (Adding -20)

$\qquad\qquad (x - 5)(x + 4) = 0 \qquad$ (Factoring)

$\qquad x - 5 = 0 \quad$ or $\quad x + 4 = 0 \qquad$ (Principle of Zero Products)

$\qquad\quad x = 5 \quad$ or $\qquad x = -4$

The solution set is $\{5, -4\}$.

Example 7   Solve $4x^3 = x$.

Solution

$$4x^3 = x$$

$$4x^3 - x = 0 \quad \text{(Adding } -x\text{)}$$

$$x(4x^2 - 1) = 0$$

$$x(2x - 1)(2x + 1) = 0 \quad \text{(Factoring)}$$

$$x = 0 \quad \text{or} \quad 2x - 1 = 0 \quad \text{or} \quad 2x + 1 = 0 \quad \text{(Principle of Zero Products)}$$

$$x = 0 \quad \text{or} \quad 2x = 1 \quad \text{or} \quad 2x = -1$$

$$x = 0 \quad \text{or} \quad x = \tfrac{1}{2} \quad \text{or} \quad x = -\tfrac{1}{2}$$

The solution set is $\{0, \tfrac{1}{2}, -\tfrac{1}{2}\}$.

Fractional Equations

A *fractional equation* is an equation that contains fractional expressions. The solution of such equations usually requires multiplying both sides of the equation by an expression with a variable. In such cases, possible solutions must be checked.

Example 8   Solve $\dfrac{x - 3}{x - 7} = \dfrac{4}{x - 7}$.

Solution

$$(x - 7) \cdot \frac{x - 3}{x - 7} = (x - 7) \cdot \frac{4}{x - 7}$$

$$\left\{\begin{array}{l}\text{Caution! Here we multiplied} \\ \text{by an expression with a} \\ \text{variable. Thus we must check.}\end{array}\right.$$

$$x - 3 = 4$$

$$x = 7$$

The possible solution is 7. We check:

$$\begin{array}{c|c} \dfrac{x - 3}{x - 7} & = & \dfrac{4}{x - 7} \\[2mm] \hline \dfrac{7 - 3}{7 - 7} & & \dfrac{4}{7 - 7} \\[2mm] \dfrac{4}{0} & & \dfrac{4}{0} \end{array}$$

Division by 0 is undefined; 7 is not a solution. The equation has no solutions. The solution set is $\emptyset$.

Example 9   Solve $\dfrac{x^2}{x - 3} = \dfrac{9}{x - 3}$.

Solution

$$(x - 3) \cdot \dfrac{x^2}{x - 3} = (x - 3) \cdot \dfrac{9}{x - 3}$$

> Caution! Here we multiplied by an expression with a variable. Thus we must check.

$$x^2 = 9$$

$$x^2 - 9 = 0$$

$$(x + 3)(x - 3) = 0$$

$$x + 3 = 0 \text{ or } x - 3 = 0$$

$$x = -3 \text{ or } \qquad x = 3$$

The possible solutions are 3 and -3. We must check since we have multiplied by an expression with a variable.

$$\text{For 3:} \quad \dfrac{x^2}{x - 3} = \dfrac{9}{x - 3}$$

$$\begin{array}{c|c} \dfrac{3^2}{3 - 3} & \dfrac{9}{3 - 3} \\[2ex] \dfrac{9}{0} & \dfrac{9}{0} \end{array} \quad \text{(3 does not check)}$$

$$\text{For } -3: \quad \dfrac{x^2}{x - 3} = \dfrac{9}{x - 3}$$

$$\begin{array}{c|c} \dfrac{(-3)^2}{-3 - 3} & \dfrac{9}{-3 - 3} \\[2ex] -\dfrac{9}{6} & -\dfrac{9}{6} \end{array} \quad (-3 \text{ does check)}$$

Thus, the solution set is $\{-3\}$.

A procedure for solving fractional equations involves multiplying by the LCM of all the denominators. It is called "clearing of fractions." Let us solve another fractional equation.

Example 10   Solve $\dfrac{14}{x + 2} - \dfrac{1}{x - 4} = 1$.

Solution   We multiply by the LCM of all the denominators: $(x + 2)(x - 4)$.

$$(x + 2)(x - 4) \cdot \frac{14}{x + 2} - (x + 2)(x - 4) \cdot \frac{1}{x - 4} = (x + 2)(x - 4) \cdot 1$$

$$14(x - 4) - (x + 2) = (x + 2)(x - 4)$$

$$14x - 56 - x - 2 = x^2 - 2x - 8$$

$$0 = x^2 - 15x + 50$$

$$0 = (x - 10)(x - 5)$$

$$x = 10 \text{ or } x = 5$$

The possible solutions are 10 and 5. These check, so the solution set is {10, 5}.

EXERCISE SET 1.7

Solve.

1. $-7x + 10 = 5x - 11$

2. $-8x + 9 = 4x - 70$

3. $5x - 17 - 2x = 6x - 1 - x$

4. $5x - 2 + 3x = 2x + 6 - 4x$

5. $x + 0.8x = 216$

6. $x + 0.5x = 210$

7. $2x^2 - 6x = 0$

8. $9x^2 + 18x = 0$

9. $3y^3 - 5y^2 - 2y = 0$

10. $3t^3 - 5t^2 + 2t = 0$

11. $(2x - 3)(3x + 2)(x - 1) = 0$

12. $(y - 4)(4y + 12)(2y + 1) = 0$

13. $(2 - 4y)(y^2 + 3y) = 0$

14. $(y^2 - 9)(y^2 - 36) = 0$

15. $\dfrac{x + 2}{2} + \dfrac{3x + 1}{5} = \dfrac{x - 2}{4}$

16. $\dfrac{2x - 1}{3} - \dfrac{x - 2}{5} = \dfrac{x}{2}$

17. $\dfrac{1}{2} + \dfrac{2}{x} = \dfrac{1}{3} + \dfrac{3}{x}$

18. $\dfrac{1}{t} + \dfrac{1}{2t} + \dfrac{1}{3t} = 5$

19. $\dfrac{4}{x^2 - 1} - \dfrac{2}{x - 1} = \dfrac{3}{x + 1}$

20. $\dfrac{3y + 5}{y^2 + 5y} + \dfrac{y + 4}{y + 5} = \dfrac{y + 1}{y}$

21. $\dfrac{1}{2t} - \dfrac{2}{5t} = \dfrac{1}{10t} - 3$

22. $\dfrac{3}{m + 2} + \dfrac{2}{m - 2} = \dfrac{4m - 4}{m^2 - 4}$

23. $1 - \dfrac{3}{x} = \dfrac{40}{x^2}$

24. $1 - \dfrac{15}{y^2} = \dfrac{2}{y}$

25. $\dfrac{11 - t^2}{3t^2 - 5t + 2} = \dfrac{2t + 3}{3t - 2} - \dfrac{t - 3}{t - 1}$

26. $\dfrac{1}{3y^2 - 10y + 3} = \dfrac{6y}{9y^2 - 1} + \dfrac{2}{1 - 3y}$

27. ▦ $3.12x^2 - 6.715x = 0$

28. ▦ $9.25x^2 + 18.03x = 0$

29. ▦ $\dfrac{2.315}{y} - \dfrac{12.6}{17.4} = \dfrac{6.71}{7} + 0.763$

30. ▦ $\dfrac{6.034}{x} - 43.17 = \dfrac{0.793}{x} + 18.15$

Solve.

31. $5x^3 + x^2 - 5x - 1 = 0$
  [*Hint:* $x^2(5x + 1) - 1(5x + 1) = 0$]

32. $3x^3 + x^2 - 12x - 4 = 0$

33. $y^3 + 2y^2 - y - 2 = 0$

34. $t^3 + t^2 - 25t - 25 = 0$

35. $x - x = 5$

36. $x + 3 = 3 + x$

1.8 FORMULAS AND APPLICATIONS

Formulas

A formula is a recipe for doing a calculation. An example is the compound interest formula (which we have already considered):

$$A = P(1 + i)^t.$$

Suppose we wanted to find P when A, i, and t were known. Our knowledge of equations allows us to get P alone on one side, or as we say, "solve the formula for P."

Example 1   Solve $A = P(1 + i)^t$, for P.

Solution

$$A = P(1 + i)^t$$

$$\dfrac{A}{(1 + i)^t} = P \qquad \left(\text{Multiplying by } \dfrac{1}{(1 + i)^t}\right)$$

Example 2   Solve $\dfrac{1}{t} = \dfrac{1}{a} + \dfrac{1}{b}$ for t.

Solution   We first multiply by the LCM, which is tab:

$$tab \cdot \dfrac{1}{t} = tab\left[\dfrac{1}{a} + \dfrac{1}{b}\right] \qquad \text{(Multiplying by } tab)$$

$$ab = tab \cdot \dfrac{1}{a} + tab \cdot \dfrac{1}{b} \qquad \text{(Distributive Law)}$$

$$ab = tb + ta \qquad \text{(Simplifying)}$$

$$ab = t(b + a) \qquad \text{(Factoring)}$$

$$\dfrac{ab}{b + a} = t$$

Applications

By an *application*, or an applied problem, we mean a situation in which mathematical techniques are used to answer some question. The following are some hints for solving such problems.

Strategy for solving applied problems:

1. Become familiar with the situation of the problem. If the problem is written, then you must read it carefully to find the facts.
2. Look for the question. This may mean making a list of known facts and a list of what you wish to find out. A drawing, if appropriate, can help in sorting out the facts.
3. Translate the problem situation to mathematical language or symbolism. Many times this means translating to an equation or an inequality.
4. Use your mathematical knowledge to find a possible solution. In algebra this usually means to solve an equation, or system of equations.
5. Check to see if your possible solution actually fits the problem situation, and is thus really a solution of the problem.

Although there is no rule for solving problems because they can be so different, it does help to consider a few different types of problems. In the final analysis, *the best way to learn to solve problems is to solve a lot of them.*

Example 3

18% of what is $990?

Translate $18\% \cdot y = 990$

Solve $0.18 \cdot y = 990$

$$y = \frac{990}{0.18} = 5500$$

Check $18\%(5500) = 0.18(5500) = 990$

Thus, 18% of $5500 is $990.

Note in Example 3 that "is" translates to $=$, the word "what" translates to a variable, and the word "of" translates to a multiplication sign.

Example 4 An investment is made at 19%, compounded annually. It grows to $6783 at the end of one year. How much was originally invested?

Solution   There is more than one way to translate the problem to mathematical language. The following is one method.

We first restate the situation as follows:

The invested amount *plus* the interest is $6783.

Now the interest is 19% of the invested amount, so we have the following, which translates directly.

$$\underbrace{\text{Invested Amount}} \; \underbrace{\text{plus}} \; \underbrace{19\%} \; \underbrace{\text{of}} \; \underbrace{\text{Invested Amount}} \; \underbrace{\text{is}} \; \underbrace{\$6783}$$

$$x \quad + \quad 19\% \; \cdot \quad x \quad = \quad 6783$$

Now we solve the equation:

$$x + 19\%x = 6783$$

$$x + 0.19x = 6783$$

$$1x + 0.19x = 6783$$

$$(1 + 0.19)x = 6783$$

$$1.19x = 6783$$

$$x = \frac{6783}{1.19} = 5700$$

The number 5700 checks, so the answer is $5700.

Work Problems

An employee can do a certain job in 5 hr. Then that same employee can do $\frac{1}{5}$ of it in 1 hr and $\frac{3}{5}$ of it in 3 hr. The basic principle for translating work problems is as follows.

If a job can be done in time *t*, then $\frac{1}{t}$ of it can be done in 1 unit of time.

Example 5   Employee A can do a certain job in 3 hr. Employee B can do the same job in 5 hr. How long would it take both, working together, to do the same job?

Solution   In this case it is of interest to make a guess at the solution. Does 4 hr seem reasonable? Sometimes our intuition can fool us. Clearly the answer is less than 3 hr because one can do the job alone in 3 hr.

A can do the job in 3 hr. Thus, $\frac{1}{3}$ of it can be done in 1 hr. Similarly, B can do $\frac{1}{5}$ of the job in 1 hr. Thus together they can do $\frac{1}{3} + \frac{1}{5}$ of it in 1 hr. Let t represent the amount of time it takes to do the job if they work together. Then together they can do $\dfrac{1}{t}$ of the job in 1 hr. Thus,

$$\frac{1}{3} + \frac{1}{5} = \frac{1}{t}$$

$$5t + 3t = 5 \cdot 3 \qquad \text{(Multiplying by the LCM, } 3 \cdot 5 \cdot t.\text{)}$$

$$8t = 15$$

$$t = \frac{15}{8}, \quad \text{or} \quad 1\frac{7}{8} \text{ hr.}$$

And, $1\frac{7}{8}$ hr checks. Thus it takes the employees $1\frac{7}{8}$ hr if they work together.

EXERCISE SET 1.8

Solve.

1. $I = Prt$, for t

2. $P = BR$, for B

3. $A = P + Prt$, for P

4. $A = P + Prt$, for t

5. $A = \dfrac{a + b + c}{3}$, for a

6. $Q = I + IOU$, for I

7. $\dfrac{1}{a} + \dfrac{1}{b} = \dfrac{1}{t}$, for b

8. $\dfrac{1}{P} = \dfrac{1}{Q} + \dfrac{1}{R}$, for P

9. $V = \dfrac{P[(1 + i)^N - 1]}{i}$, for P

10. $S = \dfrac{P[1 - (1 + i)^{-N}]}{i}$, for P

Applications.

11. $1615 is what percent of $8500?

12. What percent of $200 is $16?

13. 23% of $6500 is what?

14. 8% of what is $96?

15. An investment is made at 13%, compounded annually. It grows to $7345 at the end of one year. How much was originally invested?

16. An investment is made at 14%, compounded annually. It grows to $9120 at the end of one year. How much was originally invested?

17. One year the pilots of Pan American Airlines shook the business world by taking a pay cut of 11% to a new salary of $48,950 per year. What was their former salary?

18. One year the population of the United States increased from 215 million to 216.72 million. What was the percent of increase?

19. An employee gets an 11% raise in salary, which is $1595. What was the old salary? the new salary?

20. After a 3% increase, the population of a city is 741,600. What was the former population?

21. Employee A can do a certain job in 3 hr. Employee B can do the same job in 5 hr, and Employee C can do the same job in 7 hr. How long would it take with all three working together?

22. ▦ Employee A can do a certain job, working alone, in 3.15 hr. Employee B working with A can do the same job in 2.09 hr. How long would it take B, working alone, to do the job?

23. It takes Red Brick 9 hrs longer to build a wall than Mort Arr. If they work together, they can build the wall in 20 hr. How long would it take each, working alone, to build the wall?

24. Fran Inkfingers and Helen Huntinpeck work together and get a certain typing job completed in 4 hr. It would take Helen 6 hr longer, working alone, to do the job than it would Fran. How long would it take each working alone to do the job?

■ ────────────────────────────

25. Recently, in the state of Indiana a 4% sales tax was added on the pump reading of a gasoline purchase. One day one of your authors drove into a station and asked for $10 worth of gasoline. The attendant took 4% of $10, which was $0.40, subtracted from $10, and pumped $9.60 worth of gasoline. Something is wrong with this computation. Explain, using algebra.

26. b is 20% more than a, c is 25% more than b, and d is k% less than c. Find k such that $a = d$.

1.9 INEQUALITIES AND INTERVAL NOTATION

Inequalities

Principles for solving inequalities are similar to those for solving equations. We can add the same number on both sides of an inequality. We can also multiply on both sides by the same nonzero number; but if that number is negative, we must reverse the inequality sign. Let us see why this is necessary. Consider the true inequality

$$5 < 9. \tag{1}$$

Let us multiply both members by 2. We get another true inequality,

$$10 < 18.$$

Let us multiply both members in (1) by -3

$$-15 < -27$$

This time the inequality is false. However, if we reverse the inequality symbol (use $>$ instead of $<$), we will get a true inequality,

$$-15 > -27.$$

The following is a reformulation of the inequality-solving principles.

If the inequality $a < b$ is true, then

    i) $a + c < b + c$ **is true, for any** c,
    ii) $a \cdot c < b \cdot c$, **for any** *positive* c,
    iii) $a \cdot c > b \cdot c$, **for any** *negative* c.

Similar principles hold when $<$ is replaced by $\leq$, and $>$ is replaced by $\geq$.

Example 1   Solve $5x > 12 - 3x$.

Solution
$$5x > 12 - 3x$$
$$5x + 3x > 12 \qquad \text{(Adding } 3x\text{)}$$
$$8x > 12$$
$$\tfrac{1}{8} \cdot 8x > \tfrac{1}{8} \cdot 12 \qquad \text{(Multiplying by } \tfrac{1}{8}\text{)}$$
$$x > \tfrac{3}{2}$$

Any number greater than $\tfrac{3}{2}$ is a solution.

Example 2   Solve $17 - 8x \geq 5x - 4$.

Solution
$$17 - 8x \geq 5x - 4$$
$$-8x \geq 5x - 21 \qquad \text{(Adding } -17\text{)}$$
$$-13x \geq -21 \qquad \text{(Adding } -5x\text{)}$$
$$-\tfrac{1}{13}(-13x) \leq -\tfrac{1}{13}(-21) \qquad \text{(Multiplying by } -\tfrac{1}{13}\text{, and}$$
$$\text{reversing the inequality sign)}$$
$$x \leq \tfrac{21}{13}$$

Any number less than or equal to $\tfrac{21}{13}$ is a solution.

Example 3   Raggs, Ltd., a clothing firm, determines that its total revenue, in dollars, from the sale of x suits is

$$2x + 50.$$

Determine the number of suits the firm must sell so that its total revenue will be more than $70,000.

Solution   We translate to an inequality and solve

$$2x + 50 > 70,000$$

$$2x > 69,950 \qquad \text{(Adding } -50\text{)}$$

$$x > 34,975. \qquad \text{(Multiplying by } \tfrac{1}{2}\text{)}$$

Thus the company's total revenue will exceed $70,000 when it sells more than 34,975 suits.

Interval Notion

The set of real numbers corresponds to the set of points on a line.

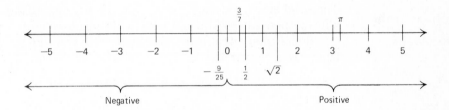

For real numbers a and b such that $a < b$ (a is to the left of b on a number line), we define the *open interval* (a, b) to be the set of numbers between, but not including, a and b. That is,

(a, b) = the set of all numbers x such that $a < x < b$.

The graph of (a, b) is shown above. The open circles and the parentheses indicate that a and b are *not* included. The numbers a and b are called *endpoints*.

The *closed* interval $[a, b]$ is the set of numbers between and including a and b. That is,

$[a, b]$ = the set of all numbers x such that $a \leqslant x \leqslant b$.

The graph of $[a, b]$ is shown above. The solid circles and the brackets indicate that a and b are included.

There are two kinds of *half-open intervals* defined as follows:

(a, b] = the set of all numbers x such that $a < x \leq b$.

The open circle and the parenthesis indicate that a is not included. The solid circle and the bracket indicate that b is included. Also,

[a, b) = the set of all numbers x such that $a \leq x < b$.

The solid circle and the bracket indicate that a is included. The open circle and the parenthesis indicate that b is not included.

Some intervals are of unlimited extent in one or both directions. In such cases we use the infinity symbol ∞. For example,

[a, ∞) = the set of all numbers x such that $x \geq a$.

Note that ∞ is not a number.

(a, ∞) = the set of all numbers x such that $x > a$.

(−∞, b] = the set of all numbers x such that $x \leq b$.

(−∞, b) = the set of all numbers x such that $x < b$.

We can name the entire set of real numbers using (−∞, ∞).

Any point in an interval which is not an endpoint is an *interior* point.

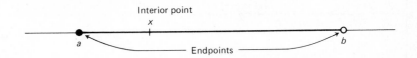

Note that all of the points in an open interval are interior points.

EXERCISE SET 1.9

Solve.

1. $3 - x \leqslant 4x + 7$

2. $x + 6 \leqslant 5x - 6$

3. $5x - 5 + x > 2 - 6x - 8$

4. $3x - 3 + 3x > 1 - 7x - 9$

5. $-7x < 4$

6. $-5x \geqslant 6$

7. $5x + 2x \leqslant -21$

8. $9x + 3x \geqslant -24$

9. $2x - 7 < 5x - 9$

10. $10x - 3 \geqslant 13x - 8$

11. $8x - 9 < 3x - 11$

12. $11x - 2 \geqslant 15x - 7$

13. $8 < 3x + 2 < 14$

14. $2 < 5x - 8 \leqslant 12$

15. $3 \leqslant 4x - 3 \leqslant 19$

16. $9 \leqslant 5x + 3 < 19$

17. $-7 \leqslant 5x - 2 \leqslant 12$

18. $-11 \leqslant 2x - 1 < -5$

Applied Problems

19. A firm determines that the total revenue, in dollars, from the sale of x units of a product is

$$3x + 1000.$$

Determine the number of units that must be sold so that its total revenue will be more than $22,000.

21. To get a B in a course a student's average must be greater than or equal to 80% (at least 80%) and less than 90%. On the first three tests the student scores 78%, 90%, and 92%. Determine the scores on the 4th test that will yield a B.

20. A firm determines that the total revenue, in dollars, from the sale of x units of a product is

$$5x + 1000.$$

Determine the number of units that must be sold so that its total revenue will be more than $22,000.

22. To get a C in a course a student's average must be greater than or equal to 70% and less than 80%. On the first three tests the student scores 65%, 83%, and 82%. Determine the scores on the 4th test that will yield a C.

Write interval notation for each graph in Exercises 23 through 30.

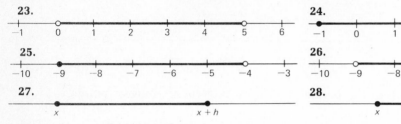

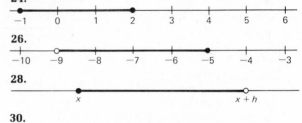

Write interval notation for Exercises 31 through 36.

31. The set of all numbers x such that $-3 \leq$ x ≤ 3.

32. The set of all numbers x such that $-4 <$ x < 4.

33. The set of all numbers x such that $-14 \leq$ x < -11.

34. The set of all numbers x such that $6 <$ x ≤ 20.

35. The set of all numbers x such that $x \leq -4$.

36. The set of all numbers x such that $x > -5$.

CHAPTER 1 REVIEW

Given the numbers

$$-25.89,\ 13,\ -4,\ -\tfrac{1}{3},\ \sqrt{3},\ \sqrt[3]{7},\ -2,\ -\tfrac{8}{5},\ 9\tfrac{4}{7},\ -39,\ 47,\ 0,$$

which are

1. integers?

2. natural numbers?

3. rational numbers?

4. real numbers?

5. irrational numbers?

6. whole numbers?

Compute.

7. $15 + (-19)$

8. $-11 + (-5)$

9. $-3.5 + (-4.5)$

10. $23 - (-9)$

11. $\dfrac{48}{-3}$

12. $(-18)(-9)$

13. $-20(10)(-5)(-4)$

14. $\tfrac{7}{12} - \left(-\tfrac{5}{8}\right)$

15. Rename without a negative exponent. e^{-k}

16. Divide. $\dfrac{e^{-5}}{e^{8}}$

Simplify.

17. $(5xy^4 - 7xy^2 + 4x^2 - 3) - (-3xy^4 + 2xy^2 - 2y + 4)$

18. $(x + t)(x^2 - xt + t^2)$ **19.** $(5x + 4b)^3$

Factor.

20. $x^3 + 2x^2 - 3x - 6$ **21.** $12a^3 - 27ab^4$

22. $24x + 144 + x^2$ **23.** $9x^3 + 35x^2 - 4x$

24. A person makes an investment at 8% compounded annually. It grows to $993.60 at the end of 1 year. How much was originally invested?

25. Simplify.
$$\frac{b - a^{-1}}{a - b^{-1}}$$

26. Divide and simplify. $\dfrac{3x^2 - 12}{x^2 + 4x + 4} \div \dfrac{x - 2}{x + 2}$

27. Subtract and simplify. $\dfrac{x}{x^2 + 9x + 20} - \dfrac{4}{x^2 + 7x + 12}$

Solve.

28. $y^2 - 3y = 18$ **29.** $3[x - 5(4 + 2x)] = 7x - 10(3x - 2)$

30. $\dfrac{5}{2x + 3} + \dfrac{1}{x - 6} = 0$ **31.** Solve $A = P(1 + i)$ for i

32. 18 is 30% of what?

33. Working together, A and B can mow a lawn in 1 hr. Working alone, A can mow the same lawn in 3 hr. How long would it take B, working alone, to mow the lawn?

34. Write interval notation for this graph.

35. Solve. $-3x < 12$

GRAPHS, FUNCTIONS, AND EQUATIONS

Graphs

Each point in the plane corresponds to an ordered pair of numbers. Note that the pair (2, 5) is different from the pair (5, 2). This is why we call (2, 5) an *ordered pair*. The first member 2 is called the *first coordinate* of the point, and the second member 5 is called the *second coordinate*. Together these are called the *coordinates of the point*. The vertical line is called the *y-axis* and the horizontal line is called the *x-axis* (see next page).

Graphs of Equations

A *solution* of an equation in two variables is an ordered pair of numbers that, when substituted alphabetically for the variables, gives a true sentence. For example, (−1, 2) is a solution of the equation $3x^2 + y = 5$, because when we substitute −1 for x and 2 for y we get a true sentence.

$$
\begin{array}{c|c}
3x^2 + y = 5 \\
\hline
3(-1)^2 + 2 & 5 \\
3 + 2 & \\
5 &
\end{array}
$$

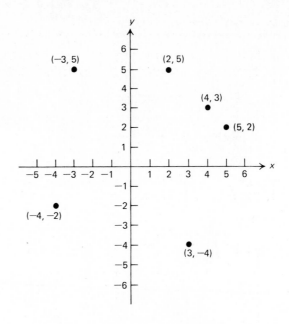

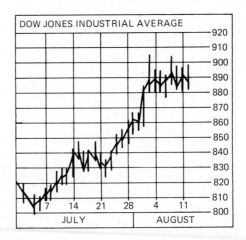

The *graph* of an equation is a geometric representation of all of its solutions. It is obtained by plotting enough ordered pairs (which are solutions) to see a pattern. The graph could be a line, curve (or curves), or some other configuration.

Example 1   Graph $y = 2x + 1$.

x	0	−1	−2	1	2
y	1	−1	−3	3	5

We choose these numbers at random (since y is expressed in terms of x).

We find these numbers by substituting in the equation.

For example, when $x = -2$, $y = 2(-2) + 1 = -3$. This yields the pair $(-2, -3)$. We plot all the pairs from the table and, in this case, draw a line to complete the graph.

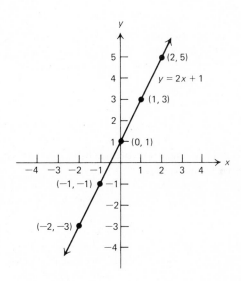

Example 2   Graph $y = x^2 - 1$.

x	0	1	2	−1	−2
y	−1	0	3	0	3

We choose these numbers at random (since y is expressed in terms of x).

We find these numbers by substituting in the equation.

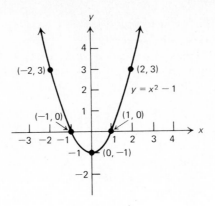

Example 3   Graph $x = y^2$.

x	0	1	4	1	4
y	0	1	2	-1	-2

We find these numbers by substituting in the equation.

This time we choose numbers at random since x is expressed in terms of y.

We plot these points, keeping in mind that x is still the first coordinate and y the second.

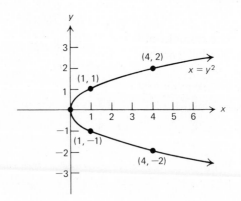

Functions

A *function* is a special kind of relation between two or more variables. Such relations are of fundamental importance in calculus.

A Function as an Input–Output Relation

DEFINITION   A *function* is a relation that assigns to each "input" number a unique "output" number. The set of all input numbers is called the *domain*. The set of all output numbers is called the *range*.

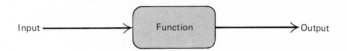

Example 4   Squaring numbers is a function. We can take any number as an input. We square that number to find the output, x^2.

Inputs	Outputs
-3	9
1.73	2.9929
k	k^2
$\sqrt{a}$	a
$1 + t$	$(1 + t)^2$, or $1 + 2t + t^2$

The domain of this function is the set of all real numbers, because any real number can be squared.

It is customary to use letters such as f and g to represent functions. Suppose f is a function and x is a number in its domain. For the input x, we can name the output as

$f(x)$, read "f of x," or "the value of f at x."

If f is the squaring function, then $f(3)$ is the output for the input 3. Thus $f(3) = 3^2 = 9$.

Example 5   The squaring function is given by

$$f(x) = x^2.$$

Find $f(-3)$, $f(1)$, $f(k)$, $f(\sqrt{k})$, $f(1 + t)$, and $f(x + h)$.

Solution
$$f(-3) = (-3)^2 = 9, \qquad f(1) = 1^2 = 1,$$
$$f(k) = k^2, \qquad f(\sqrt{k}) = (\sqrt{k})^2 = k,$$
$$f(1 + t) = (1 + t)^2 = 1 + 2t + t^2,$$
$$f(x + h) = (x + h)^2 = x^2 + 2xh + h^2.$$

To find $f(x + h)$, remember what the function does—it squares the input. Thus $f(x + h) = (x + h)^2 = x^2 + 2xh + h^2$. This amounts to replacing x on both sides of $f(x) = x^2$, by $x + h$.

Example 6   A function f subtracts the square of an input from the input. A description of f is given by

$$f(x) = x - x^2.$$

Find $f(4)$ and $f(x + h)$.

Solution   We replace the x's on both sides by the inputs. Thus

$$f(4) = 4 - 4^2 = 4 - 16 = -12,$$
$$f(x + h) = (x + h) - (x + h)^2$$
$$= x + h - (x^2 + 2xh + h^2)$$
$$= x + h - x^2 - 2xh - h^2.$$

Taking square roots is *not* a function. This is because an input can have more than one output. For example, the input 4 has two outputs 2 and -2.

Example 7   Taking principal square roots (nonnegative roots) is a function. Let g be this function. Then g can be described as

$$g(x) = \sqrt{x}.$$

(Recall from algebra that the symbol "$\sqrt{a}$" represents the nonnegative square root of a.) The domain of this function is the set of nonnegative real numbers. Find $g(0)$, $g(2)$, $g(a)$, $g(16)$, and $g(t + h)$.

Solution
$$g(0) = \sqrt{0} = 0, \qquad g(2) = \sqrt{2},$$
$$g(a) = \sqrt{a}, \qquad g(16) = \sqrt{16} = 4,$$
$$g(t + h) = \sqrt{t + h}$$

A Function as a Mapping

Another way of thinking of a function is as a "mapping" of one set to another.

> A *function* is a mapping that associates with each number x in one set (called the domain) a unique number y in another set.

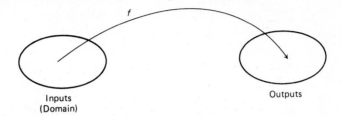

Inputs
(Domain)

Outputs

For example, the squaring function maps members of the set of real numbers to members of the set of nonnegative numbers.

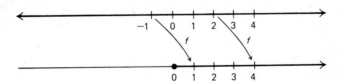

The statement

$$y = f(x)$$

means that the number x is mapped to the number y by the function f. Functions are often implicit in certain equations. For example, consider

$$xy = 2.$$

For any nonzero x there is a unique number y satisfying the equation. This yields a function which is given explicitly by

$$y = f(x) = \frac{2}{x}.$$

On the other hand, consider the equation

$$x = y^2.$$

A number x would be related to two values of y, namely $\sqrt{x}$ and $-\sqrt{x}$. Thus, this equation is not an implicit description of a function which maps inputs x to outputs y.

Graphs of Functions

Consider again the squaring function. The input 3 is associated with the output 9. The input–output pair (3, 9) is one point on the *graph* of this function.

DEFINITION

The *graph* of a function f is a geometric representation of all of its input–output pairs $(x, f(x))$. **In cases where the function is given by an equation, the graph of a function is the graph of the equation $y = f(x)$.**

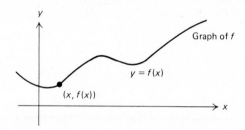

It is customary to locate input values (the domain) on the horizontal axis and output values on the vertical axis.

Example 8   Graph $f(x) = 2x + 1$.

Solution   We choose these inputs at random.

x	0	−1	−2	1	2
f(x)	1	−1	−3	3	5

We compute these outputs.

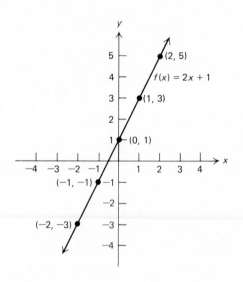

Next we plot the input–output pairs from the table and, in this case, draw a line to complete the graph.

Example 9   Graph $f(x) = x^2 - 1$.

Solution

x	0	1	2	-1	-2
$f(x)$	-1	0	3	0	3

We choose these inputs at random.

We compute these outputs.

Next we plot the input–output pairs from the table and, in this case, draw a curve to complete the graph.

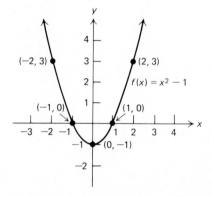

The following figure illustrates how the idea of a mapping is connected with the graph of a function.

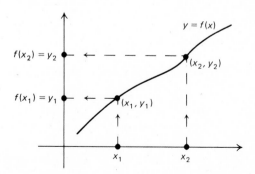

Let us now determine how we can look at a graph and decide whether it is a graph of a function. We already know that

$$x = y^2$$

does not yield a function that maps a number x to a unique number y. Look at its graph.

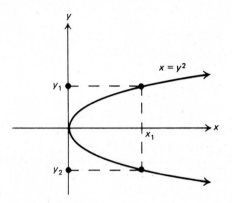

Note that there is a point x_1 that has two outputs. Equivalently, we have a vertical line that meets the graph more than once.

Vertical line test. **A graph is that of a function provided no vertical line meets the graph more than once.**

Example 10   Which of the following are graphs of functions?

a)   b)

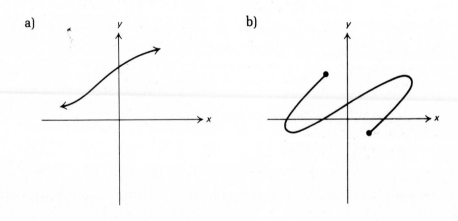

c)   d)

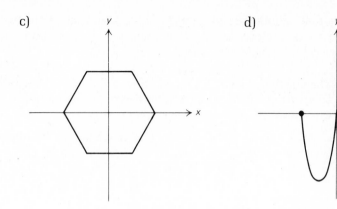

Solution   a) A function. No vertical line meets the graph more than once.

b) Not a function. A vertical line (in fact many) meets the graph more than once.

c) Not a function.

d) A function.

Increasing and Decreasing Functions

If the graph of a function rises from left to right on an interval I, it is said to be *increasing* on I. If the graph drops from left to right on an interval I, it is said to be *decreasing* on I.

Example 11

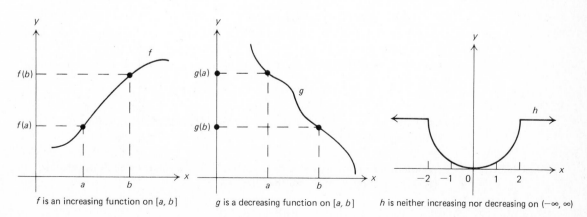

f is an increasing function on $[a, b]$ g is a decreasing function on $[a, b]$ h is neither increasing nor decreasing on $(-\infty, \infty)$

Note that while the function h is neither increasing nor decreasing on $(-\infty, \infty)$ it is decreasing on the interval $[-2, 0]$ and increasing on the interval $[0, 2]$. More formally:

> The function f is *increasing* on an interval I in its domain if $f(a) < f(b)$ whenever $a < b$ in I. Similarly, f is *decreasing* on I if $f(a) > f(b)$ whenever $a < b$ in I.

When no interval is specified, it is assumed to be the entire real line $(-\infty, \infty)$.

Some Final Remarks

Almost all of the functions in this text can be described by equations. Some functions, however, cannot. We sometimes use the terminology *y is a function of x*. This means that x is an input and y is an output. We sometimes refer to x as the *independent* variable when it represents inputs, and y as the *dependent* variable when it represents outputs. We may refer to "the function, $y = x^2$," without naming it with a letter f. We may simply refer to x^2 (alone) as a function.

Functions of Two Variables

Suppose a one-product firm produces x items of its product at a profit of $4 per item. Then its total profit P is given by

$$P(x) = 4x.$$

This is a function of *one* variable.

Suppose a two-product firm produces x_1 items of one product at a profit of $4 per item and x_2 items of a second at a profit of $6 per item. Then its total profit P is a function of the *two* variables x_1 and x_2 and is given by

$$P(x_1, x_2) = 4x_1 + 6x_2.$$

This is a function of *two* variables, which assigns to the input pair (x_1, x_2) a unique output number $4x_1 + 6x_2$.

DEFINITION   A function of *two* variables is a relation f that assigns to each input pair (x_1, x_2) a unique output number $f(x_1, x_2)$.

Example 12   For $P(x_1, x_2) = 4x_1 + 6x_2$, find $P(15, 20)$.

Solution $P(15, 20)$ is defined to be the value of the function found by substituting 15 for x_1 and 20 for x_2.

$$P(15, 20) = 4 \cdot 15 + 6 \cdot 20 = 60 + 120 = 180$$

For the two-product firm, this means that by selling 15 items of the first product and 20 items of the second, it will make a profit of $180.

Example 13   A function f is given by

$$f(x_1, x_2) = x_1^2 + x_2^2 - 2x_1x_2.$$

Find $f(-2, 3)$ and $f(8, 0)$.

Solution $$f(-2, 3) = (-2)^2 + 3^2 - 2(-2)3 = 4 + 9 + 12 = 25,$$

$$f(8, 0) = 8^2 + 0^2 - 2 \cdot 8 \cdot 0 = 64 + 0 - 0 = 64.$$

Functions can arise without a specific formula. For example, it would probably be agreed that a student's score S on a test is a function of mental ability A and the amount of time studied t, even though it may be difficult or impossible to determine a formula for S. A statistical experiment may provide an approximating formula.

EXERCISE SET 2.1

1. A function f is given by

$$f(x) = 2x + 3.$$

This function takes a number x, multiplies it by 2, and adds 3.

a) Complete this table.

Inputs	Outputs
4.1	
4.01	
4.001	
4	

b) Find $f(5)$, $f(-1)$, $f(k)$, $f(1 + t)$, and $f(x + h)$.

2. A function f is given by

$$f(x) = 3x - 1.$$

This function takes a number x, multiplies it by 3, and subtracts 1.

a) Complete this table.

Inputs	Outputs
5.1	
5.01	
5.001	
5	

b) Find $f(4)$, $f(-2)$, $f(k)$, $f(1 + t)$, and $f(x + h)$.

3. A function g is given by

$$g(x) = x^2 - 3.$$

This function takes number x, squares it, and subtracts 3. Find $g(-1)$, $g(0)$, $g(1)$, $g(5)$, $g(u)$, $g(a + h)$, and $g(1 - h)$.

5. A function f is given by

$$f(x) = (x - 3)^2.$$

This function takes a number x, subtracts 3 from it, and squares the result.

   a) Find $f(4)$, $f(-2)$, $f(0)$, $f(a)$, $f(t + 1)$, $f(t + 3)$, and $f(x + h)$.

   b) Note that f could also be given by

$$f(x) = x^2 - 6x + 9.$$

   Explain what this does to an input number x.

4. A function g is given by

$$g(x) = x^2 + 4.$$

This function takes a number x, squares it, and adds 4. Find $g(-3)$, $g(0)$, $g(-1)$, $g(7)$, $g(v)$, $g(a + h)$, and $g(1 - t)$.

6. A function f is given by

$$f(x) = (x + 4)^2.$$

This function takes a number x, adds 4 to it, and squares the result.

   a) Find $f(3)$, $f(-6)$, $f(0)$, $f(k)$, $f(t - 1)$, $f(t - 4)$, and $f(x + h)$.

   b) Note that f could also be given by

$$f(x) = x^2 + 8x + 16.$$

   Explain what this does to an input number x.

Graph the following functions.

7. $f(x) = 2x + 3$ **8.** $f(x) = 3x - 1$ **9.** $g(x) = -4x$ **10.** $g(x) = -2x$

11. $f(x) = x^2 - 1$ **12.** $f(x) = x^2 + 4$ **13.** $g(x) = x^3$ **14.** $g(x) = \frac{1}{2}x^3$

Which of the following are graphs of functions?

15. 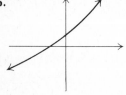   **16.**    **17.**    **18.**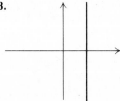

19. 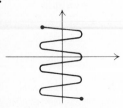   **20.** 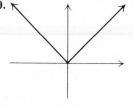   **21.** 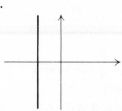   **22.**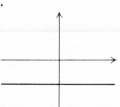

23. a) Graph $x = y^2 - 1$.
   b) Is this a function?

24. a) Graph $x = y^2 - 3$.
   b) Is this a function?

25. For $f(x) = x^2 - 3x$, find $f(x + h)$.

27. *Revenue.* Raggs, Ltd., a clothing firm, determines that its total revenue (money coming in) from the sale of x suits is given by the function

$$R(x) = 2x + 50,$$

where $R(x)$ is the revenue, in dollars, from the sale of x suits. Find $R(10)$ and $R(100)$.

26. For $f(x) = x^2 + 4x$, find $f(x + h)$.

28. *Compound interest.* The amount of money in an investment at 18% compounded annually depends on the initial investment x and is given by the function

$$A(x) = x + 18\% x,$$

where $A(x) = $ amount in the account at the end of one year. Find $A(100)$ and $A(1000)$.

Decide whether the following graphs of functions are increasing, decreasing, or neither over the interval shown.

29.

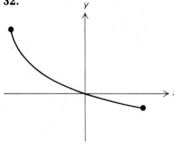

30.

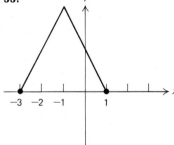

31.

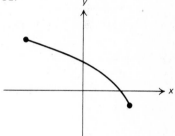

32.

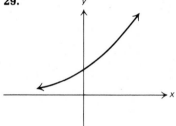

33.

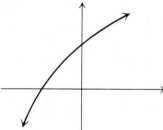

34.

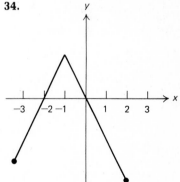

35. On what interval in Exercise 33 is the function increasing? decreasing?

37. For $f(x_1, x_2) = 3x_1 - 4x_2$, find $f(-2, 5)$, $f(4, 0)$, and $f(10, -6)$.

39. For $f(x_1, x_2) = x_2^2 + 3x_1x_2$, find $f(-2, 0)$, $f(3, 2)$, and $f(-5, 10)$.

36. On what interval in Exercise 34 is the function increasing? decreasing?

38. For $f(x_1, x_2) = 5x_1 - 2x_2$, find $f(2, -5)$, $f(0, 6)$, and $f(-4, -20)$.

40. For $f(x_1, x_2) = x_1^2 - 2x_1x_2$, find $f(0, -2)$, $f(2, 3)$, and $f(10, -5)$.

41. For $f(x_1, x_2) = x_1^2 - x_2^2$, find $f(-2, -3)$, $f(5, 0)$, and $f(0, 5)$.

42. For $f(x_1, x_2) = x_1^2 + x_2^2$, find $f(-3, -2)$, $f(7, 0)$, and $f(0, 7)$.

43. For $f(x_1, x_2) = (3x_1 + 4x_2)^2$, find $f(-1, 0)$, $f(2, 2)$, and $f(-4, 5)$.

44. For $f(x_1, x_2) = (4x_1 - x_2)^2$, find $f(-2, 0)$, $f(5, 5)$, and $f(6, -4)$.

2.2 STRAIGHT LINES AND LINEAR FUNCTIONS

Horizontal and Vertical Lines

Let us consider graphs of equations $y = b$ and $x = a$.

Example 1 a) Graph $y = 4$.

b) Decide if the relation is a function.

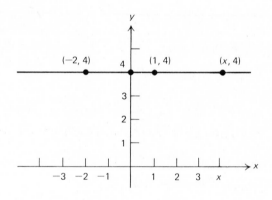

Solution a) The graph consists of all ordered pairs whose second coordinate is 4. To see how a pair such as $(-2, 4)$ could be a solution we can consider the above equation in the form

$$0x + y = 4.$$

Then $(-2, 4)$ is a solution because

$$0(-2) + 4 = 4 \text{ is true.}$$

b) The vertical line test holds. Thus, this is a function.

Example 2 a) Graph $x = -3$.

b) Decide if it is a function.

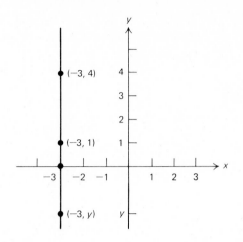

Solution   a) The graph consists of all ordered pairs whose first coordinate is -3.

b) This is *not* a function. It fails the vertical line test. The line itself meets the graph more than once, in fact, infinitely many times more.

In general,

The graph of $y = b$, a horizontal line, is the graph of a function.
The graph of $x = a$, a vertical line, is not the graph of a function.

The Equation $y = mx$

Consider the following table of numbers and look for a pattern.

x	1	-1	$-\frac{1}{2}$	2	-2	3	-7	5
y	3	-3	$-\frac{3}{2}$	6	-6	9	-21	15

Note that the ratio of the bottom number to the top one is 3. That is,

$$\frac{y}{x} = 3, \quad \text{or} \quad y = 3x.$$

Ordered pairs from the table can be used to graph the equation $y = 3x$. Note that this is a function.

The function f given by

$$y = mx \quad \text{or} \quad f(x) = mx$$

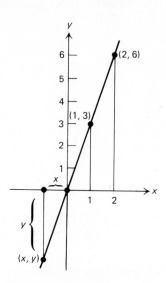

is the straight line through the origin (0, 0) and the point (1, _m_). The constant _m_ is called the _slope_ of the line.

Various graphs of y = mx for positive m are shown below in (a). Note that such graphs rise from left to right. A line with large positive slope rises faster than a line with smaller positive slope.

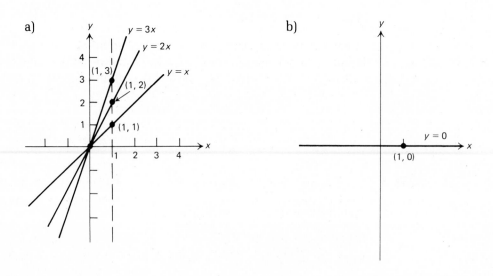

c)

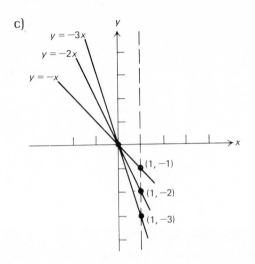

When $m = 0$, $y = 0x$, or $y = 0$. Graph (b) is a graph of $y = 0$. Note that this is the x-axis and is a horizontal line. Graphs of $y = mx$ for negative m are shown in (c). Note that such graphs fall from left to right. A line that has a small negative slope is steeper than a line with larger negative slope.

Direct Variation

There are many applications involving equations like $y = mx$, where m is some positive number. In such situations we say we have *direct variation*, and m (the slope) is called the *variation constant*, or *constant of proportionality*. Usually only positive values of x and y are considered.

> The variable **y** *varies* ***directly*** as **x** if there is some positive constant **m** such that **y** **=** **mx.** We also say that **y** is ***directly proportional to x.***

Example 3   Consumer specialists have determined that the amount F that the average family spends on food is directly proportional to its income I. A family making $19,200 will spend $4992 on food.

a) Find an equation of variation.

b) A family spends $5460 on food. How much does it make?

Solution   a) $F = kI$, so $4992 = k(19,200)$ and $k = 0.26$. Thus $F = 0.26I$.

b) To find how much a family makes when it spends $5460 on food, we substitute 5460 for F and solve for I.

$$F = 0.26I$$

$$5460 = 0.26I$$

$$\frac{5460}{0.26} = I$$

$$\$21{,}000 = I$$

Thus a family spending $5460 on food makes $21,000.

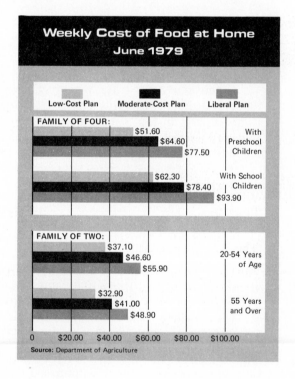

The Equation $y = mx + b$

Compare the graphs of the equations

$$y = 3x \quad \text{and} \quad y = 3x - 2.$$

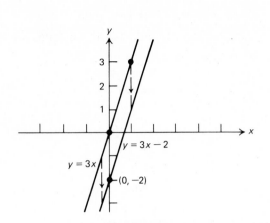

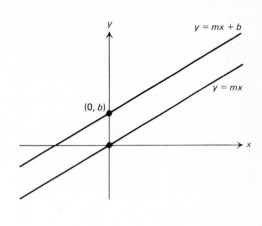

Note that $y = 3x - 2$ is a shift downward 2 units of the graph of $y = 3x$ and that $y = 3x - 2$ has y-intercept $(0, -2)$. Note also that $y = 3x - 2$ is a graph of a function.

> **A *linear function*** is given by
>
> $$y = mx + b \quad \text{or} \quad f(x) = mx + b$$
>
> **and has a graph which is the straight line parallel to $y = mx$ with y-intercept $(0, b)$. The constant m is called the *slope*.**

When $m = 0$, $y = 0x + b = b$, and we have what is known as a *constant function*. The graph of such a function is a horizontal line.

The Slope-Intercept Equation

Any nonvertical line l is uniquely determined by its slope m and its y-intercept $(0, b)$. In other words, the slope describes the "slant" of the line and the y-intercept is the point where it crosses the y-axis. Accordingly,

> $y = mx + b$ is called the *slope-intercept* equation of a line.

Example 4 Find the slope and y-intercept of $2x - 4y - 7 = 0$.

Solution We solve for y.

$$-4y = -2x + 7$$

$$y = \tfrac{1}{2}x - \tfrac{7}{4}$$

Slope: $\tfrac{1}{2}$ y-intercept: $(0, -\tfrac{7}{4})$

The Point-Slope Equation

Suppose we know the slope of a line and some point of the line other than the y-intercept. We can still find an equation of the line.

Example 5   Find an equation of the line with slope 3 containing the point $(-1, -5)$.

Solution   From the slope-intercept equation we have

$$y = 3x + b,$$

so we must determine b. Since $(-1, -5)$ is on the line, it follows that

$$-5 = 3(-1) + b,$$

so $-2 = b$ and $y = 3x - 2.$

If a point (x_1, y_1) is on the line

$$y = mx + b, \tag{1}$$

it must follow that

$$y_1 = mx_1 + b. \tag{2}$$

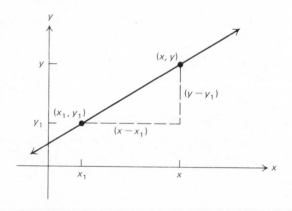

Subtracting equation (2) from (1) gets rid of the b's and we have

$$y - y_1 = (mx + b) - (mx_1 + b)$$
$$= mx + b - mx_1 - b$$
$$= mx - mx_1 = m(x - x_1).$$

Now

$y - y_1 = m(x - x_1)$ **is called the *point-slope* equation**

of a line L. This allows us to write an equation of a line given its slope and the coordinates of *any* point on it.

Example 6   Find an equation of the line with slope 3 containing the point $(-1, -5)$.

Solution   Substituting in

$$y - y_1 = m(x - x_1),$$

we get

$$y - (-5) = 3[x - (-1)].$$

Simplifying and solving for y we get the slope-intercept equation as found in Example 5.

$$y + 5 = 3(x + 1)$$
$$y = 3x + 3 - 5$$
$$y = 3x - 2$$

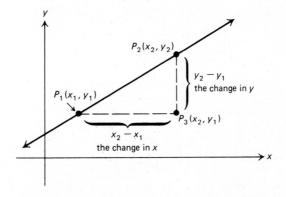

We now determine a way to compute the slope of a line when we know the coordinates of two of its points. Suppose (x_1, y_1) and (x_2, y_2) are the coordinates of two different points, P_1 and P_2, on a line that is not parallel to an axis. Consider a right triangle as shown, with legs parallel to the axes. The point P_3 with coordinates (x_2, y_1) is the third vertex of the triangle. As we move from P_1 to P_2, y changes from y_1 to y_2. The change in y is $y_2 - y_1$. Similarly, the change in x is $x_2 - x_1$. The ratio of these changes is the slope. To see this, consider the point-slope equation

$$y - y_1 = m(x - x_1).$$

Since (x_2, y_2) is on the line, it must follow that

$$y_2 - y_1 = m(x_2 - x_1).$$

Since the line is not vertical, the two x coordinates must be different, so $x_2 - x_1$ is nonzero and we can divide by it to get

$$m = \frac{y_2 - y_1}{x_2 - x_1} = \frac{\textbf{change in y}}{\textbf{change in x}} = \begin{array}{c}\textbf{slope of line containing points}\\ \textbf{(x}_1\textbf{, y}_1\textbf{) and (x}_2\textbf{, y}_2\textbf{).}\end{array}$$

Example 7   Find the slope of the line containing the points $(-2, 6)$ and $(-4, 9)$.

Solution
$$m = \frac{y_2 - y_1}{x_2 - x_1} = \frac{6 - 9}{-2 - (-4)} = \frac{-3}{2} = -\frac{3}{2}$$

Note that it does not matter which point is taken first, as long as we subtract coordinates in the same order. In this example we can also find m as follows.

$$m = \frac{9 - 6}{-4 - (-2)} = \frac{3}{-2} = -\frac{3}{2}$$

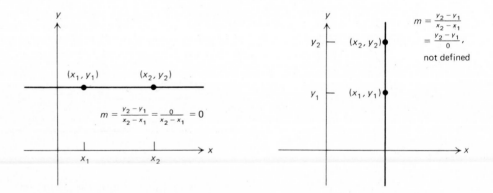

If a line is horizontal the change in y for any two points is 0. Thus a horizontal line has slope 0. If a line is vertical, the change in x for any two points is 0. Thus the slope is not defined because we cannot divide by 0. A vertical line has no slope. Thus "0 slope" and "no slope" are two very distinct concepts.

Increasing and Decreasing Linear Functions

We do not need to graph a linear function $f(x) = mx + b$ to determine whether it is increasing, decreasing, or neither. We merely look at the slope m. If $m > 0$, the function is increasing. If $m < 0$, the function is decreasing. If $m = 0$, the function is constant, so is neither increasing nor decreasing.

Example 8   Determine whether increasing, decreasing, or neither.

$$g(x) = -2x + 3, \quad f(x) = \tfrac{2}{3}x + 2, \quad h(x) = 4$$

Solution   The graphs are provided for illustration and should not be needed when doing the exercises.

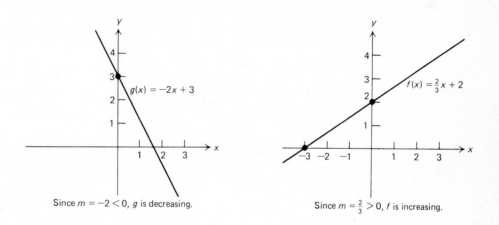

Since $m = -2 < 0$, g is decreasing.   Since $m = \tfrac{2}{3} > 0$, f is increasing.

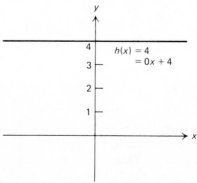

Since $m = 0$, h is neither increasing nor decreasing.

Applications of Linear Functions

Many applications are modeled by linear functions.

Example 9   *Total cost.* Raggs, Ltd., a clothing firm, has *fixed costs* of $10,000 per year. These are costs such as rent, maintenance, and so on, which must be paid no matter how much the company produces. To produce x units of a certain kind of suit it costs $20 per unit in addition to the fixed costs. That is, the *variable costs* are 20x dollars. These are costs which are directly related to production, such as material, wages, and fuel. Then the *total cost, C(x),* of producing x suits in a year is given by a function C.

$$C(x) = \text{(variable costs)} + \text{(fixed costs)} = 20x + 10{,}000$$

a) Graph the variable cost, fixed cost, and total cost functions.

b) What is the total cost of producing 100 suits? 400 suits?

c) How much more does it cost to produce 400 suits than 100 suits?

Solution   a) The variable cost and fixed cost functions appear below left; the total cost function, below right. From a practical standpoint, the domains of these functions are nonnegative integers 0, 1, 2, 3, and so on. This is because it does not make sense to make a negative number of suits or

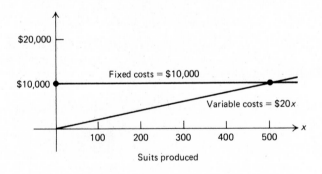

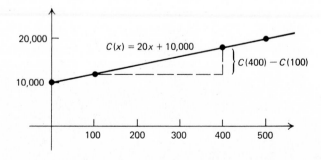

a fractional number of suits. Nevertheless, it is common practice to draw the graphs as if the domains were the entire set of nonnegative real numbers.

b) The total cost of producing 100 suits is

$$C(100) = 20 \cdot 100 + 10,000 = \$12,000.$$

The total cost of producing 400 suits is

$$C(400) = 20 \cdot 400 + 10,000 = \$18,000.$$

c) The extra cost of producing 400 rather than 100 suits is given by

$$C(400) - C(100) = \$18,000 - \$12,000 = \$6000.$$

Example 10 *Profit and loss analysis.* In reference to Example 9, Raggs, Ltd. determines that its total revenue (money coming in) from the sale of x suits is $80 per suit. That is, total revenue $R(x)$ is given by the function

$$R(x) = 80x.$$

a) Graph $R(x)$ and $C(x)$ using the same axes.

b) Total profit $P(x)$ is given by a function P.

$$P(x) = (\text{total revenue}) - (\text{total costs}) = R(x) - C(x)$$

Determine $P(x)$ and draw its graph using the same axes.

c) The company will *break even* at that value of x for which $P(x) = 0$ (that is, no profit and no loss). This is where $R(x) = C(x)$. Find the break-even value of x.

Solution a) The graphs of $R(x) = 80x$ and $C(x) = 20x + 10,000$ are shown here.

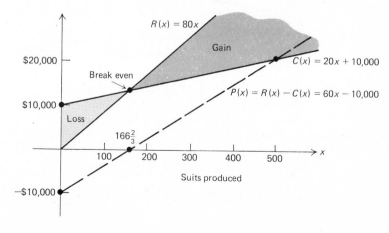

b) $P(x) = R(x) - C(x) = 80x - (20x + 10,000) = 60x - 10,000$. The graph of $P(x)$ is shown.

c) To find the break-even value we solve $R(x) = C(x)$.

$$80x = 20x + 10,000$$

$$60x = 10,000$$

$$x = 166\tfrac{2}{3}$$

How do we interpret the fractional answer, since it is not possible to produce $\tfrac{2}{3}$ of a suit? One would simply round to 167. Estimates of break-even points are usually sufficient since companies want to operate well above break-even points where profit is maximized.

Variables with Subscripts

When working with linear equations it is convenient to use a variable x_1 to represent the x, or first coordinate. The "1" is called a *subscript*. Similarly, we use x_2 to represent the y, or second coordinate. Note the connection: x_1 is the "first" coordinate and x_2 is the "second" coordinate. An equation like

$$4x - 6y = -10$$

can now be written

$$4x_1 - 6x_2 = -10.$$

Graphing is done with the axes labeled x_1 and x_2.

Example 11   Graph $2x_1 + 3x_2 = 6$.

Solution   a) Any point on the x_2-axis (the vertical axis) has first coordinate, or x_1 coordinate, 0. Therefore, to find the x_2-intercept, we substitute 0 for x_1, and solve for x_2.

$$2 \cdot 0 + 3x_2 = 6$$

$$0 + 3x_2 = 6$$

$$3x_2 = 6$$

$$x_2 = 2 \qquad \text{(The x_2-intercept is (0, 2).)}$$

b) Any point on the x_1-axis has second coordinate, or x_2 coordinate, 0. To find the x_1-intercept, then, we substitute 0 for x_2, and solve for x.

$$2x_1 + 3 \cdot 0 = 6$$

$$2x_1 + 0 = 6$$

$$2x_1 = 6$$

$$x_1 = 3 \qquad \text{(The } x_1\text{-intercept is (3, 0).)}$$

c) We plot (0, 2) and (3, 0) and draw a line through them.

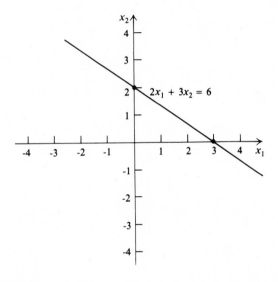

Families of Parallel Lines

Let us consider

$$2x_1 - x_2 = c$$

for various values of c.

Example 12   Using the same set of axes, graph

$$2x_1 - x_2 = 1,$$

$$2x_1 - x_2 = 0,$$

$$2x_1 - x_2 = -3.$$

Solution

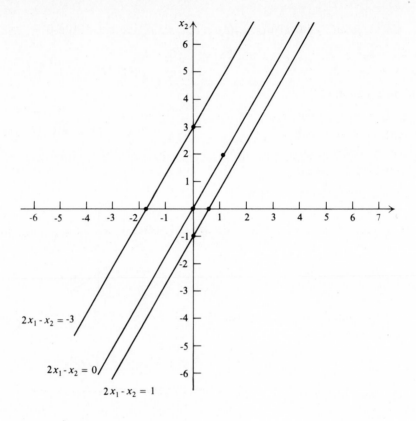

$2x_1 - x_2 = -3$

$2x_1 - x_2 = 0$

$2x_1 - x_2 = 1$

Note that the lines are parallel. In general, if we consider graphs of

$$ax_1 + bx_2 = c,$$

where a and b are fixed and c varies, the graphs form a *family* of parallel lines.

EXERCISE SET 2.2

Graph.

1. $y = -4$ **2.** $y = -3.5$ **3.** $x = 4.5$ **4.** $x = 10$

Graph. Find the slope and y-intercept.

5. $y = -3x$ **6.** $y = -0.5x$ **7.** $y = 0.5x$ **8.** $y = 3x$

9. $y = -2x + 3$ **10.** $y = -x + 4$ **11.** $y = -x - 2$ **12.** $y = -3x + 2$

Find the slope and y-intercept.

13. $2x + y - 2 = 0$

14. $2x - y + 3 = 0$

15. $2x + 2y + 5 = 0$

16. $3x - 3y + 6 = 0$

Find an equation of the line:

17. with $m = -5$, containing $(1, -5)$.

18. with $m = 7$, containing $(1, 7)$.

19. with $m = -2$, containing $(2, 3)$.

20. with $m = -3$ containing $(5, -2)$.

21. with y-intercept $(0, -6)$ and slope $\frac{1}{2}$.

22. with y-intercept $(0, 7)$ and slope $\frac{4}{3}$.

23. with slope 0, containing $(2, 3)$.

24. with slope 0, containing $(4, 8)$.

Find the slope of the line containing each pair of points.

25. $(-4, -2)$, $(-2, 1)$

26. $(-2, 1)$, $(6, 3)$

27. $(2, -4)$, $(4, -3)$

28. $(-5, 8)$, $(5, -3)$

29. $(3, -7)$, $(3, -9)$

30. $(-4, 2)$, $(-4, 10)$

31. $(2, 3)$, $(-1, 3)$

32. $(-6, \frac{1}{2})$, $(-7, \frac{1}{2})$

33. $(x, 3x)$, $(x + h, 3(x + h))$

34. $(x, 4x)$, $(x + h, 4(x + h))$

35. $(x, 2x + 3)$, $(x + h,$ $2(x + h) + 3)$

36. $(x, 3x - 1)$, $(x + h,$ $3(x + h) - 1)$

The two-point equation. **An equation of the nonvertical line containing the points (x_1, y_1) and (x_2, y_2) is given by**

$$y - y_1 = \frac{y_2 - y_1}{x_2 - x_1} (x - x_1). \qquad \textit{Two-point equation}$$

This can be proved by replacing m in the point-slope equation $y - y_1 = m(x - x_1)$ by $\dfrac{y_2 - y_1}{x_2 - x_1}.$

37.–48. Find an equation of the line containing each pair of points in Exercises 25 through 36.

Without graphing, decide whether each function is increasing, decreasing, or neither.

49. $f(x) = 43$

50. $f(x) = -27$

51. $f(x) = -4x + 3$

52. $f(x) = -3x - 7$

53. $f(x) = 0.2x + 170$

54. $f(x) = 0.1x + 50,000$

55. *Profit and loss analysis.* A ski manufacturer is planning a new line of skis. For the first year, the fixed costs for setting up the new production line are $22,500. Variable costs for producing each pair of skis are estimated to be $40. The sales department projects that 3000 pairs can be sold during the first year at $85 per pair.

a) Formulate a function $C(x)$ for the total cost of producing x pairs of skis.

b) Formulate a function $R(x)$ for the total revenue from the sale of x pairs of skis.

c) Formulate a function $P(x)$ for the total profit from the production and sale of x pairs of skis.

d) What profit or loss will the company realize if expected sales of 3000 pairs occur?

e) How many pairs must the company sell to break even?

56. *Profit and loss analysis.* Boxowitz, Inc., a computer firm, is planning to sell a new mini-calculator. For the first year, the fixed costs for setting up the new production line are $100,000. Variable costs for producing each calculator are estimated to be $20. The sales department projects that 150,000 calculators can be sold during the first year at a price of $45 each.

   a) Formulate a function $C(x)$ for the total cost of producing x calculators.

   b) Formulate a function $R(x)$ for the total revenue from the sale of x calculators.

   c) Formulate a function $P(x)$ for the total profit from the production and sale of x calculators.

   d) What profit or loss will the firm realize if the expected sales of 150,000 calculators occur?

   e) How many calculators must the firm sell to break even?

58. *Investments.* A person makes an investment of P dollars at 18%. After 1 year it grows to an amount, A.

   a) Show that A is directly proportional to P.

   b) Find A when P = $100.

   c) Find P when A = $283.20.

57. *Sales commissions.* A person applying for a sales position is offered alternative salary plans:

Plan A: A base salary of $600 per month plus a commission of 4% of the gross sales for the month.

Plan B: A base salary of $700 per month plus a commission of 6% of the gross sales for the month in excess of $10,000.

   a) For each plan formulate a function that expresses monthly earnings as a function of gross sales x.

   b) For what gross sales values is Plan B preferable?

Graph.

59. $4x_1 + 5x_2 = 20$ **60.** $4x_1 - 5x_2 = 20$ **61.** $2x_1 - x_2 = 4$ **62.** $2x_1 + x_2 = 4$

63. $3x_2 + 4x_1 = 12$ **64.** $4x_2 - 3x_1 = 12$ **65.** $x_2 - x_1 = 0$ **66.** $x_2 + x_1 = 0$

67. $2x_1 + 3x_2 = 5$ **68.** $2x_1 - 3x_2 = 5$ **69.** $x_2 = 5$ **70.** $x_2 = 4$

71. $x_1 = -2$ **72.** $x_1 = -1$ **73.** $x_2 = 0$ **74.** $x_1 = 0$

75. $x_2 = -3.5$ **76.** $x_1 = 4.5$

77. Using the same set of axes, graph each equation.

$$x_2 - x_1 = 0$$

$$x_2 - x_1 = 2$$

$$x_2 - x_1 = -3$$

78. Using the same set of axes, graph each equation.

$$x_2 + 2x_1 = 0$$

$$x_2 + 2x_1 = 3$$

$$x_2 + 2x_1 = -2$$

2.3 SYSTEMS OF EQUATIONS IN TWO VARIABLES —GRAPHICAL SOLUTION

Systems of Equations in Two Variables

A pair of linear equations,

$$a_1x_1 + b_1x_2 = c_1,$$

$$a_2x_1 + b_2x_2 = c_2,$$

is called a *system* of two linear equations in two variables. A *solution* of a system is an ordered pair which is a solution of *both* equations.

Example 1 Decide whether (2, 3) is a solution of the system

$$x_1 - x_2 = -1,$$

$$4x_1 + 4x_2 = 14.$$

Solution We substitute 2 for x_1 and 3 for x_2 in each equation.

$x_1 - x_2 = -1$		$4x_1 + 2x_2 = 14$	
$2 - 3$	-1	$4 \cdot 2 + 2 \cdot 3$	14
-1		$8 + 6$	
		14	

We see that (2, 3) is a solution of both equations, so it is a solution of the system.

The graph of each equation in a system is a line. Given two lines, the following can happen:

1. The lines have no point in common—they are parallel.

2. The lines have exactly one point in common.

3. The lines are the same—they have infinitely many points in common.

A system of two linear equations in two variables is

> *Consistent* if it has one or more solutions.
> *Inconsistent* if it has *no* solution.
> *Linearly dependent* if it is possible to multiply one equation by a constant and obtain the other.
> *Linearly independent* if it is not possible to multiply one equation by a constant and obtain the other equation.

Let us look at the three possibilities for lines to intersect, and describe the system in terms of the preceding terminology.

Example 2   The graph of the system

$$x_2 = 2x_1 - 1,$$

$$x_2 = 2x_1 + 1$$

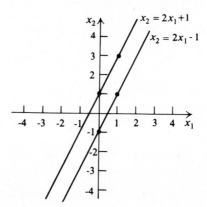

is shown above. Note that the lines are parallel. Thus the system has no solution—it is inconsistent. There is no way to obtain one equation from the other by multiplying by a constant, so the system is independent.

Example 3   The graph of the system

$$x_2 = 2x_1 - 1,$$

$$3x_2 = 6x_1 - 3$$

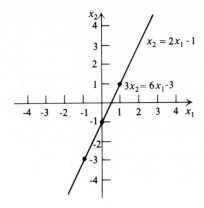

is shown above. Note that the lines are the same. Thus the system has infinitely many solutions—it is consistent. We obtain the second equation from the first by multiplying by 3. Thus the system is dependent.

Example 4 The graph of the system

$$x_1 - 2x_2 = 0,$$

$$-2x_1 + x_2 = 2$$

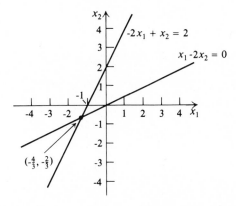

is shown above. Note that the lines intersect at exactly one point—it is consistent. There is no way to obtain one equation from the other by multiplying by a constant, so the system is independent.

Graphical Solution of Systems of Linear Equations

We can solve systems of equations graphically.

Example 5   Solve graphically

$$x_2 - x_1 = 1,$$

$$x_2 + x_1 = 5.$$

Solution   We graph the two equations. The point of intersection appears to be $(2, 3)$. We can check this as follows.

$x_2 - x_1 = 1$		$x_2 + x_1 = 5$	
$3 - 2$	1	$3 + 2$	5
1		5	

Thus, the solution is $(2, 3)$. Note that this procedure is subject to error, especially when fractional solutions are involved (see Example 4). Algebraic procedures will be developed in the next section and in Chapter 3 for obtaining exact answers.

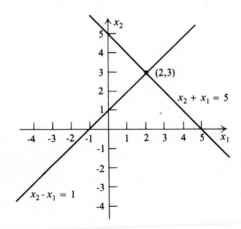

Decide whether $(3, -2)$ is a solution of each system.

1. $x_1 + x_2 = 1$
   $x_1 - x_2 = 6$

2. $2x_1 + x_2 = 4$
   $x_1 - 2x_2 = 7$

Graph each system and classify it as consistent or inconsistent, dependent or independent.

3. $x_1 + x_2 = 1$
$x_1 - x_2 = 6$

4. $x_2 - 2x_1 = 1$
$x_2 - 2x_1 = 3$

5. $2x_1 + 3x_2 = 1$
$-x_1 - 1.5x_2 = -\frac{1}{2}$

6. $2x_1 - 4x_2 = 8$
$-\frac{1}{2}x_1 + x_2 = -2$

7. $x_1 + 3x_2 = 4$
$x_1 + 3x_2 = 6$

8. $2x_1 + x_2 = 4$
$x_1 - 2x_2 = 7$

Solve graphically.

9. $x_2 + 3x_1 = 5$
$2x_2 - x_1 = -4$

10. $2x_1 - x_2 = 4$
$5x_1 - x_2 = 13$

11. $2x_1 - 4x_2 = 7$
$x_1 = 2x_2 - 5$

12. $3x_2 - 6x_1 = 10$
$x_2 - 2x_1 = -1$

13. $x_2 - 4 = 0$
$x_1 + 5 = 0$

14. $x_1 + 3 = 0$
$x_2 - 1 = 0$

2.4 SYSTEMS OF EQUATIONS IN TWO VARIABLES —ALGEBRAIC SOLUTION

Here we consider algebraic procedures (using algebra) for finding exact solutions to systems of equations.

The Substitution Method

Substitution method. **Solve one of the equations for one of the variables. Then substitute the resulting expression in the other equation and solve for the second variable.**

Example 1 Solve

$$x_1 - 2x_2 = 0, \qquad (1)$$

$$-2x_1 + x_2 = 2. \qquad (2)$$

Solution Since Eq. (2) has x_2 with coefficient 1, it is easiest to solve that equation for x_2.

$$x_2 = 2 + 2x_1 \qquad (3)$$

Now we substitute $2 + 2x_1$ for x_2 in Eq. (1).

$$x_1 - 2(2 + 2x_1) = 0$$

We now have an equation in one variable, x_1. We solve for x_1 using the addition and multiplication principles.

$$x_1 - 4 - 4x_1 = 0$$

$$-4 - 3x_1 = 0$$

$$-3x_1 = 4$$

$$x_1 = -\tfrac{4}{3}$$

We now substitute $-\tfrac{4}{3}$ for x_1 in Eq. (3) to find x_2. We could also substitute in either of the original equations, but it is faster to use Eq. (3) since x_2 has coefficient 1 on one side.

$$x_2 = 2 + 2(-\tfrac{4}{3}) = 2 - \tfrac{8}{3} = -\tfrac{2}{3}$$

The solution is $(-\tfrac{4}{3}, -\tfrac{2}{3})$. The reader should check this.

Always check! It is very easy to do with systems of linear equations.

The Addition Method

The *addition method* for solving systems of equations makes use of the *addition* and *multiplication principles* for solving equations. The idea, just as with substitution, is to obtain an equation with one variable.

Example 2 Solve

$$3x_2 + 5x_1 = 17, \tag{1}$$

$$2x_2 - 5x_1 = 3. \tag{2}$$

Solution We add the equations as follows.

$$\begin{array}{l} 3x_2 + 5x_1 = 17 \\ \underline{2x_2 - 5x_1 = 3} \end{array}$$

$$\begin{aligned} 5x_2 \quad\;\; &= 20 \\ 5x_2 &= 20 \\ x_2 &= 4 \end{aligned}$$ (Adding the "sides" of the equations, using the addition principle)

We substitute in Eq. (1) to find x_1. (We could use Eq. (2) also.)

$$3 \cdot 4 + 5x_1 = 17$$

$$12 + 5x_1 = 17$$

$$5x_1 = 5$$

$$x_1 = 1$$

The solution is (1, 4). The reader should check this.

Note in Example 2 that the term $5x_1$ of Eq. (1) and the term $-5x_1$ of Eq. (2) add to 0. Thus when we added we eliminated x_1. In the following examples, we first multiply one or both of the equations in order to create a situation like Example 2.

Example 3 Solve

$$9x_1 - 2x_2 = -4, \tag{1}$$

$$3x_1 + 4x_2 = 1. \tag{2}$$

Solution We first multiply Eq. (1) by 2, then add.

$$
\begin{array}{ll}
18x_1 - 4x_2 = -8 & \text{(Multiplying by 2, using the} \\
\underline{3x_1 + 4x_2 = 1} & \text{multiplication principle)} \\
21x_1 \qquad\quad = -7 & \text{(Adding, using the addition} \\
21x_1 = -7 & \text{principle)} \\
x_1 = \dfrac{-7}{21} = -\dfrac{1}{3} &
\end{array}
$$

We substitute $-\frac{1}{3}$ for x_1 in Eq. (2) and solve for x_2.

$$3(-\tfrac{1}{3}) + 4x_2 = 1$$

$$-1 + 4x_2 = 1$$

$$4x_2 = 2$$

$$x_2 = \tfrac{2}{4} = \tfrac{1}{2}$$

The solution is $(-\tfrac{1}{3}, \tfrac{1}{2})$.

Example 4   Solve

$$3x_1 + 5x_2 = 7, \tag{1}$$

$$5x_1 + 3x_2 = -23. \tag{2}$$

Solution   We multiply Eq. (1) by 5 and Eq. (2) by -3.

$$
\begin{array}{ll}
15x_1 + 25x_2 = 35 & \text{(Multiplying by 5)} \\
-15x_1 - 9x_2 = 69 & \text{(Multiplying by } -3)
\end{array}
$$

$$
\begin{aligned}
16x_2 &= 104 \\
x_2 &= \tfrac{104}{16} = \tfrac{13}{2}
\end{aligned}
$$

We substitute $\tfrac{13}{2}$ for x_2 in Eq. (1) and solve for x_1.

$$3x_1 + 5(\tfrac{13}{2}) = 7$$

$$3x_1 + \tfrac{65}{2} = 7$$

$$3x_1 = 7 - \tfrac{65}{2}$$

$$3x_1 = \tfrac{14}{2} - \tfrac{65}{2}$$

$$3x_1 = -\tfrac{51}{2}$$

$$x_1 = (-\tfrac{51}{2})\tfrac{1}{3} = -\tfrac{17}{2}$$

The solution is $(\tfrac{13}{2}, -\tfrac{17}{2})$.

Example 5   Solve

$$4x_1 + 6x_2 = -8, \tag{1}$$

$$-2x_1 - 3x_2 = 4. \tag{2}$$

Solution   We multiply Eq. (2) by 2 and add.

$$
\begin{array}{ll}
4x_1 + 6x_2 = -8 & \\
-4x_1 - 6x_2 = 8 & \text{(Multiplying by 2)}
\end{array}
$$

$$
0 = 0 \quad \text{(Adding)}
$$

We get the true equation $0 = 0$. This will happen for any ordered pair that is a solution of one of the equations. Thus we have an infinite number of solutions. If we had multiplied Eq. (2) by -2, we would have gotten Eq. (1), which is another way of verifying that we have an infinite number of solutions, because the system is dependent.

Example 6 Solve

$$3x_2 + x_1 = 10,$$

$$6x_2 + 2x_1 = 23.$$

Solution We multiply Eq. (1) by -2 and add.

$$\begin{array}{rl} -6x_2 - 2x_1 = -20 & \text{(Multiplying by } -2) \\ 6x_2 + 2x_1 = 23 & \\ \hline 0 = 3 & \text{(Adding)} \end{array}$$

Since we get the false equation $0 = 3$, the system has no solution. We could check this by graphing the system—the lines would be *parallel*.

The substitution and addition methods, when applied correctly, will yield the solution(s). Overall, the fastest method is usually the addition method, which is the basis for other procedures that we will develop later in the text. For this reason, it is better to practice using it more than the substitution method.

EXERCISE SET 2.4

Solve, using the substitution method.

1. $\quad x_2 + 4x_1 = 5$
$\quad -3x_2 + 2x_1 = 13$

2. $4x_2 + x_1 = 8$
$\quad 5x_2 + 3x_1 = 3$

3. $5x_1 + x_2 = 8$
$\quad 3x_1 - 4x_2 = 14$

4. $2x_1 - 3x_2 = 8$
$\quad 4x_1 + x_2 = 2$

Solve, using the addition method.

5. $3x_1 + 5x_2 = 28$
$\quad 5x_1 - 3x_2 = 24$

6. $4x_1 + 3x_2 = 17$
$\quad 6x_1 + 5x_2 = 27$

7. $5x_1 - 4x_2 = -3$
$\quad 7x_1 + 2x_2 = 6$

8. $-2x_1 + 4x_2 = 3$
$\quad 3x_1 - 7x_2 = 1$

9. $4x_1 + 2x_2 = 11$
$\quad 3x_1 - x_2 = 2$

10. $5x_1 - 3x_2 = -2$
$\quad 4x_1 + 2x_2 = 5$

11. $9x_1 - 2x_2 = 5$
$\quad 3x_1 - 3x_2 = 11$

12. $3x_1 + 4x_2 = 7$
$\quad -5x_1 + 2x_2 = 10$

13. $3x_2 - 6x_1 = 15$
$\quad 4x_2 - 8x_1 = 20$

14. $8x_1 + 4x_2 = 20$
$\quad 6x_1 + 3x_2 = 14$

15. $5x_1 + 10x_2 = 20$
$\quad 2x_1 + 4x_2 = 9$

16. $2x_1 - 4x_2 = 8$
$\quad 5x_1 - 10x_2 = 20$

17. Eight times a certain number added to five times a second number is 184. The first number minus the second number is -3. Find the numbers.

18. One number is 4 times another number. Their sum is 175. Find the numbers.

19. One day a business sold 20 pairs of gloves. The cloth gloves brought $4.95 per pair and the pigskin gloves sold for $7.50 per pair. The business took in $137.25. How many of each kind were sold?

20. A store sold 30 sweatshirts. They sold white ones for $8.95 and red ones for $9.50. They took in $272.90. How many of each color did they sell?

21. Solution A is 2% acid. Solution B is 6% acid. A lab technician wants to mix the two to get 60 liters of a solution that is 3.2% acid. How many liters of each should the owner use?

22. A gardener has two kinds of solutions containing weedkiller and water. One is 5% weedkiller and the other is 15% weedkiller. The gardener needs 100 liters of a 12% solution and wants to make it by mixing. How much of each solution should be used?

Recall the formula for simple interest $I = Prt$, where I is interest, P is principal, r is rate, and t is time in years.

23. Two investments are made totaling $4800. In the first year they yield $604 in simple interest. Part of the money is invested at 12% and the rest at 13%. Find the amount invested at each rate of interest.

24. For a certain year $9500 is received in interest from two investments. A certain amount is invested at 13% and $10,000 more than this is invested at 14%. Find the amount invested at each rate.

■ ────────────────────────────────

25. Solve for (x, y).
$$ax - by = a^2$$
$$bx + ay = ab$$

26. ▦ Solve.
$$4.83x + 9.06y = -39.42$$
$$-1.35x + 6.67y = -33.99$$

2.5 OTHER TYPES OF FUNCTIONS

Quadratic Functions

A *quadratic function f* is given by

$$f(x) = ax^2 + bx + c, \text{ where } a \neq 0.$$

We have already considered some such functions, for example $f(x) = x^2$ and $g(x) = x^2 - 1$. Graphs of quadratic functions are always cup-shaped, like those in Example 1. Each has a dashed line of symmetry.

Example 1   Graph $y = x^2 - 2x - 3$ and $y = -2x^2 + 4x + 1$.

Solutions $y = x^2 - 2x - 3$

x	0	1	2	3	4	−1	−2
y	−3	−4	−3	0	5	0	5

$y = -2x^2 + 4x + 1$

x	0	1	2	3	−1
y	1	3	1	−5	−5

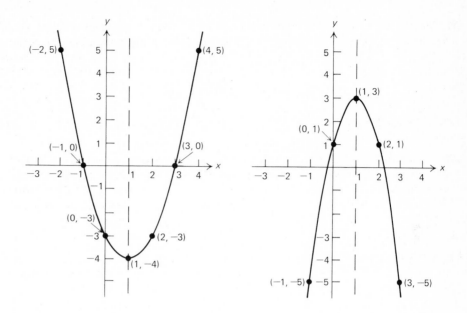

If the coefficient a is positive, the graph opens upward. If a is negative, the graph opens downward.

First coordinates of points where a quadratic function intersects the x-axis (x-intercepts), if they exist, can be found by solving the quadratic equation $ax^2 + bx + c = 0$. If real number solutions exist, they can be found using the quadratic formula.

> **The quadratic formula.** The solutions of any quadratic equation $ax^2 + bx + c = 0$, $a \neq 0$, are given by*
>
> $$x = \frac{-b \pm \sqrt{b^2 - 4ac}}{2a}.$$

Example 2 Solve $3x^2 - 4x = 2$.

---

* In the quadratic formula the expression $b^2 - 4ac$ is called the *discriminant*. If the discriminant is less than 0, the equation has no real number solutions. Such solutions lie in an expanded number system, called the complex numbers.

Solution First find standard form $ax^2 + bx + c = 0$, and determine a, b, and c.

$$3x^2 - 4x - 2 = 0,$$

$$a = 3, \quad b = -4, \quad c = -2$$

Then use the quadratic formula

$$x = \frac{-b \pm \sqrt{b^2 - 4ac}}{2a} = \frac{-(-4) \pm \sqrt{(-4)^2 - 4(3)(-2)}}{2 \cdot 3}$$

$$= \frac{4 \pm \sqrt{16 + 24}}{6} = \frac{4 \pm \sqrt{40}}{6}$$

$$= \frac{4 \pm \sqrt{4 \cdot 10}}{6} = \frac{4 \pm 2\sqrt{10}}{6}$$

$$= \frac{2(2 \pm \sqrt{10})}{2 \cdot 3} = \frac{2 \pm \sqrt{10}}{3}.$$

The solutions are $\dfrac{2 + \sqrt{10}}{3}$ and $\dfrac{2 - \sqrt{10}}{3}$.

Polynomial Functions

Linear and quadratic functions are part of a general class of polynomial functions.

A *polynomial function f* is given by

$$f(x) = a_n x^n + a_{n-1} x^{n-1} + \cdots + a_2 x^2 + a_1 x^1 + a_0,$$

where *n* is a nonnegative integer, and a_n, a_{n-1}, ..., a_1, a_0, are real numbers.

The following are some examples:

$$f(x) = -5 \qquad \text{(A constant function)}$$
$$f(x) = 4x + 3 \qquad \text{(A linear function)}$$
$$f(x) = -x^2 + 2x + 3 \qquad \text{(A quadratic function)}$$
$$f(x) = 2x^3 - 4x^2 + x + 1 \qquad \text{(A cubic function)}$$

In general, graphing polynomial functions other than linear and quadratic is difficult. Some *power* functions, such as

$$y = ax^n,$$

are relatively easy to graph.

Example 3 Using the same set of axes, graph $y = x^2$ and $y = x^3$.

Solution

x	-2	-1	$-\frac{1}{2}$	0	$\frac{1}{2}$	1	2
x^2	4	1	$\frac{1}{4}$	0	$\frac{1}{4}$	1	4
x^3	-8	-1	$-\frac{1}{8}$	0	$\frac{1}{8}$	1	8

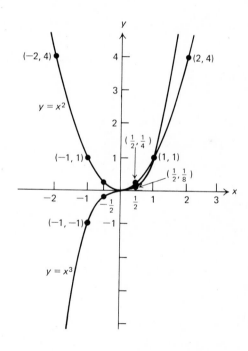

Rational Functions

Functions given by the ratio of two polynomials are called *rational*.

The following are examples of rational functions.

$$f(x) = \frac{x^2 - 9}{x - 3}, \quad g(x) = \frac{x^2 - 16}{x + 4}, \quad h(x) = \frac{x - 3}{x^2 - x - 2}$$

The domain of a rational function is restricted to those input values that do not result in division by 0. Thus for f the domain consists of all real numbers except 3. To determine the domain of h, we set the denominator equal to 0 and solve.

$$x^2 - x - 2 = 0$$

$$(x + 1)(x - 2) = 0$$

$$x = -1 \quad \text{or} \quad x = 2$$

Thus -1 and 2 are not in the domain. The domain consists of all real numbers except -1 and 2.

> **A function f is *not defined* for the number a when for that input a it is not possible to obtain an output value of the function $f(a)$.**

Thus for h above, the function is not defined at -1 and 2. The function f, given by $f(x) = \sqrt{x}$, is not defined for any negative number. Its domain is the set of all numbers x for which $x \geq 0$.

One important class of rational functions is given by $y = \dfrac{k}{x}$.

Example 4   Graph $y = \dfrac{1}{x}$.

Solution

x	-3	-2	-1	$-\frac{1}{2}$	$-\frac{1}{4}$	$\frac{1}{4}$	$\frac{1}{2}$	1	2	3
y	$-\frac{1}{3}$	$-\frac{1}{2}$	-1	-2	-4	4	2	1	$\frac{1}{2}$	$\frac{1}{3}$

Note that 0 is not in the domain of this function since it would yield a 0 denominator. This function is decreasing over the intervals $(-\infty, 0)$ and $(0, \infty)$. It is an example of inverse variation. That is,

> *y varies inversely* as x if there is some positive number k such that $y = k/x$. We also say that *y* is *inversely proportional* to *x*.

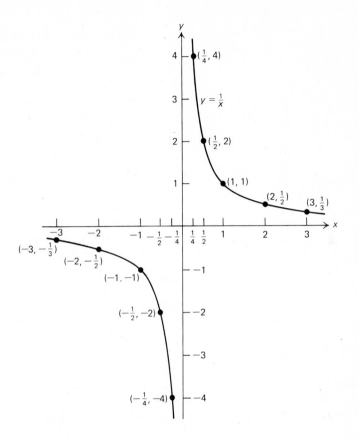

Example 5   *Stocks and Gold.* Certain economists theorize that stock prices are inversely proportional to the price of gold. That is, when the price of gold goes up, the prices of stock go down; and when the price of gold goes down, the prices of stock go up. Let us assume that the Dow-Jones Industrial Average, D, an index of the overall price of stock, is inversely proportional to the price of gold, G, in dollars per ounce. One day the Dow-Jones was 818 and the price of gold was $520 per ounce. What will the Dow-Jones be if the price of gold drops to $490?

Solution   a) $D = \dfrac{k}{G}$, so $818 = \dfrac{k}{520}$ and $k = 425{,}360$. Thus $D = \dfrac{425{,}360}{G}$.

   b) We substitute 490 for G and compute D.

$$D = \frac{425{,}360}{490} \approx 868.1$$

WARNING! Do not put too much "stock" in the equation of Example 5. It is meant to give us an idea of economic relationships. An equation to accurately predict the stock market has not been found.

Absolute Value Functions

The following is an example of an absolute value function and its graph. The absolute value of a number is its distance from 0.

Example 6 Graph $y = |x|$.

Solution

x	−3	−2	−1	0	1	2	3
y	3	2	1	0	1	2	3

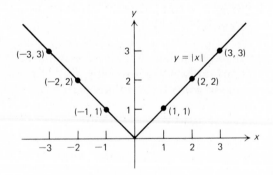

Square Root Functions

The following is an example of a square root function and its graph.

Example 7   Graph $y = -\sqrt{x}$.

Solution   The domain of this function is just the nonnegative numbers—the interval $[0, \infty)$. Table 1 at the back of the book contains approximate values of square roots of certain numbers.

x	0	1	2	3	4	5	10
$-\sqrt{x}$	0	-1	-1.4	-1.7	-2	-2.2	-3.2

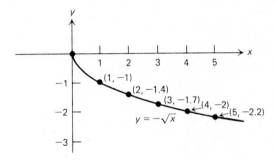

Power Functions with Fractional Exponents

We are motivated to define fractional exponents so that the same laws of Section 1.1 still hold. For example, if the laws of exponents are to hold, we would have

$$a^{1/2} \cdot a^{1/2} = a^{1/2+1/2} = a^1 = a.$$

Thus we are led to define $a^{1/2}$ to be $\sqrt{a}$. Similarly, we are led to define $a^{1/3}$ to be the cube root of a, $\sqrt[3]{a}$. In general,

$$a^{1/n} = \sqrt[n]{a}.$$

Again, if the laws of exponents are to hold, we would have

$$\sqrt[n]{a^m} = (a^m)^{1/n} = (a^{1/n})^m = a^{m/n}.$$

An expression $a^{-m/n}$ is defined by

$$a^{-m/n} = \frac{1}{a^{m/n}} = \frac{1}{\sqrt[n]{a^m}}.$$

Convert to fractional exponents.

Example 8 $\sqrt[3]{x^2} = x^{2/3}$

Example 9 $\sqrt[4]{y} = y^{1/4}$

Example 10 $\dfrac{1}{\sqrt[3]{b^5}} = \dfrac{1}{b^{5/3}} = b^{-5/3}$

Example 11 $\dfrac{1}{\sqrt{x}} = \dfrac{1}{x^{1/2}} = x^{-1/2}$

Example 12 $\sqrt{x^8} = x^{8/2}$, or x^4

Convert to radical notation.

Example 13 $x^{1/3} = \sqrt[3]{x}$

Example 14 $t^{6/7} = \sqrt[7]{t^6}$

Example 15 $x^{-2/3} = \dfrac{1}{x^{2/3}} = \dfrac{1}{\sqrt[3]{x^2}}$

Example 16 $e^{-1/4} = \dfrac{1}{e^{1/4}} = \dfrac{1}{\sqrt[4]{e}}$

Simplify.

Example 17 $8^{5/3} = (8^{1/3})^5 = (\sqrt[3]{8^5}) = 2^5 = 32$

Example 18 $81^{3/4} = (81^{1/4})^3 = (\sqrt[4]{81^3}) = 3^3 = 27$

Supply and Demand Functions

Supply and demand in economics are modeled by increasing and decreasing functions. While specific scientific formulas for these concepts are not usually known, the notions of increasing and decreasing yield understanding of the ideas.

Demand Functions

Look at the following table.

Demand schedule	
Quantity (x) (number of 5-lb bags in millions)	Price (p) (per bag)
4	$5
5	4
7	3
10	2
15	1

The table shows the relationship between the price p per bag of sugar and the quantity x of 5-lb bags that the consumer will buy at that price. Note that as price per bag increases, the quantity demanded by the consumer decreases; and as price per bag decreases, the quantity demanded by the consumer increases. Thus it is natural to think of x as a function of p. In our later work it will be more convenient to think of p as a function of x. Thus, for a *demand* function, D, D(x) is the price per unit of an item when x units are demanded by the consumer. The following figure is the graph of a demand function for sugar (using the preceding table).

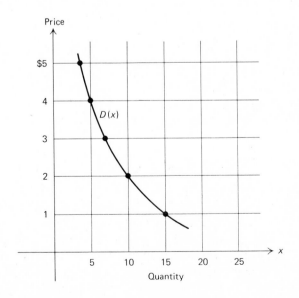

Supply Functions

Look at the following table.

Supply schedule	
Quantity (x) (number of 5-lb bags in millions)	Price (p) (per bag)
24	$5
20	4
15	3
10	2
0	1

The table shows the relationship between the price p per bag of sugar and the quantity x of 5-lb bags that the seller is willing to supply at that price. Note that as the price per bag increases, the more the seller is willing to supply; and as the price per bag decreases, the less the seller is willing to supply. Again, it is natural to think of x as a function of p, but for our later work it is more convenient to think of p as a function of x. Thus, for a *supply* function S, S(x) is the price per unit of an item at which the seller is willing to supply x units of a product to the consumer. The following figure is the graph of a supply function for sugar (using the preceding table).

Let us now look at these curves together. Note that as supply increases demand decreases, and as supply decreases demand increases. The point of intersection of the two curves (x_E, p_E) is called the *equilibrium point*. The equilibrium price, p_E (in this case $2 per bag), is where the amount, x_E (in this case 10 million bags), that the seller willingly supplies is the same as the amount that the consumer willingly demands. The situation is analogous to a buyer and seller haggling over the sale of an item. The equilibrium point or selling price is what they finally agree on.

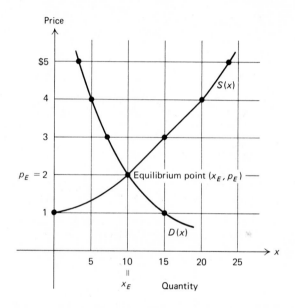

Example 19   Find the equilibrium point for the demand and supply functions

$$D(x) = (x - 6)^2 \quad \text{and} \quad S(x) = x^2 + x + 10.$$

Solution   To find the equilibrium point we set $D(x) = S(x)$ and solve.

$$(x - 6)^2 = x^2 + x + 10$$

$$x^2 - 12x + 36 = x^2 + x + 10$$

$$-12x + 36 = x + 10$$

$$-13x = -26$$

$$x = \frac{-26}{-13}$$

$$x = 2$$

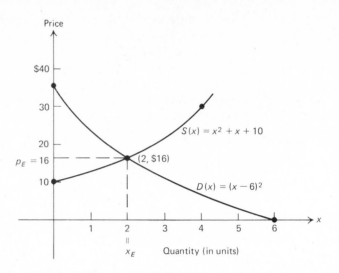

Thus $x_E = 2$(units). To find p_E we substitute x_E into either $D(x)$ or $S(x)$. We use $D(x)$. Then

$$p_E = D(x_E) = D(2) = (2 - 6)^2 = (-4)^2 = \$16.$$

Thus the equilibrium price is $16 per unit and the equilibrium point is (2, $16).

EXERCISE SET 2.5

Using the same set of axes, graph each pair of equations.

1. $y = \frac{1}{2}x^2$, $y = -\frac{1}{2}x^2$
2. $y = \frac{1}{4}x^2$, $y = -\frac{1}{4}x^2$
3. $y = x^2$, $y = (x - 1)^2$

4. $y = x^2$, $y = (x - 3)^2$
5. $y = x^2$, $y = (x + 1)^2$
6. $y = x^2$, $y = (x + 3)^2$

7. $y = |x|$, $y = |x + 3|$
8. $y = |x|$, $y = |x + 1|$
9. $y = x^3$, $y = x^3 + 1$

10. $y = x^3$, $y = x^3 - 1$
11. $y = \sqrt{x}$, $y = \sqrt{x + 1}$
12. $y = \sqrt{x}$, $y = \sqrt{x - 2}$

Graph.

13. $y = x^2 - 4x + 3$
14. $y = x^2 - 6x + 5$
15. $y = -x^2 + 2x - 1$

16. $y = -x^2 - x + 6$
17. $y = \dfrac{2}{x}$
18. $y = \dfrac{3}{x}$

19. $y = \dfrac{-2}{x}$
20. $y = \dfrac{-3}{x}$
21. $y = \dfrac{1}{x^2}$

22. $y = \dfrac{1}{x-1}$

23. $y = \sqrt[3]{x}$

[*Hint:* ■ or use Table 1 at the end of the book]

24. $y = \dfrac{1}{|x|}$

Solve.

25. $x^2 - 2x = 2$

26. $x^2 - 2x + 1 = 5$

27. $x^2 + 6x = 1$

28. $x^2 + 4x = 3$

29. $4x^2 = 4x + 1$

30. $-4x^2 = 4x - 1$

31. $3y^2 + 8y + 2 = 0$

32. $2p^2 - 5p = 1$

Convert to fractional exponents.

33. $\sqrt{x^3}$

34. $\sqrt{x^5}$

35. $\sqrt[5]{a^3}$

36. $\sqrt[4]{b^2}$

37. $\sqrt[7]{t}$

38. $\sqrt[8]{c}$

39. $\dfrac{1}{\sqrt[3]{t^4}}$

40. $\dfrac{1}{\sqrt[5]{b^6}}$

41. $\dfrac{1}{\sqrt{t}}$

42. $\dfrac{1}{\sqrt{m}}$

43. $\dfrac{1}{\sqrt{x^2 + 7}}$

44. $\sqrt{x^3 + 4}$

Convert to radical notation.

45. $x^{1/5}$

46. $t^{1/7}$

47. $y^{2/3}$

48. $t^{2/5}$

49. $t^{-2/5}$

50. $y^{-2/3}$

51. $b^{-1/3}$

52. $b^{-1/5}$

53. $e^{-17/6}$

54. $m^{-19/6}$

55. $(x^2 - 3)^{-1/2}$

56. $(y^2 + 7)^{-1/4}$

Simplify.

57. $9^{3/2}$

58. $16^{5/2}$

59. $64^{2/3}$

60. $8^{2/3}$

61. $16^{3/4}$

62. $25^{5/2}$

Determine the domain of each function.

63. $f(x) = \dfrac{x^2 - 25}{x - 5}$

64. $f(x) = \dfrac{x^2 - 4}{x + 2}$

65. $f(x) = \dfrac{x^3}{x^2 - 5x + 6}$

66. $f(x) = \dfrac{x^4 + 7}{x^2 + 6x + 5}$

67. $f(x) = \sqrt{5x + 4}$

68. $f(x) = \sqrt{2x - 6}$

Find the equilibrium point for the following demand and supply functions.

69. $D(x) = -2x + 8$, $S(x) = x + 2$

70. $D(x) = -\frac{5}{8}x + 10$, $S(x) = \frac{1}{2}x + 2$

71. $D(x) = (x - 3)^2$, $S(x) = x^2 + 2x + 1$

72. $D(x) = (x - 4)^2$, $S(x) = x^2 + 2x + 6$

73. $D(x) = (x - 4)^2$, $S(x) = x^2$

74. $D(x) = (x - 6)^2$, $S(x) = x^2$

75. *Demand.* The price p of a certain kind of radio is found to be inversely proportional to the number sold, x. It was found that 240 thousand radios will be sold when the price per radio is $12.50. How many will be sold if the price is $18.75?

76. ▦ It is theorized that the dividends paid on utilities stocks are inversely proportional to the prime (interest) rate. Recently, the dividends, D, on the stock of Indianapolis Power and Light were $2.09 per share and the prime rate was 19%. The prime rate, R, dropped to 17.5%. What dividends would be paid if the assumption of inverse proportionality is correct?

77. *Compound Interest.* $2560 is invested at interest rate i, compounded annually. In 2 years it grows to $3240. What is the interest rate?

78. *Compound Interest.* $2560 is invested at interest rate i, compounded annually. In 2 years it grows to $3610. What is the interest rate?

The following formulas will be helpful in Exercises 79 through 82:

$$T = cN$$

Total cost = (Cost per item) · (Number of items)

Total cost = (Cost per person) · (Number of persons)

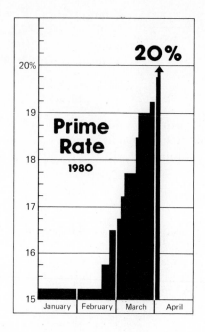

79. A group of students share equally in the $140 cost of a boat rental. In the last minute 3 students drop out and this raises the share of each remaining student $15. How many students were in the group at the outset?

80. An investor bought a group of lots for $4800. All but 4 of them were later sold by the investor for the same price of $4800. The selling price for each lot was $350 greater than the cost. How many lots were bought?

81. An investor buys some stock for $720. If each share had cost $15 less, 4 more shares could have been bought for the same $720. How many shares of stock were bought?

82. A sorority is going to spend $112 for a party. When 14 new pledges join the sorority, this reduces the cost by $4. How much did it cost each student before?

2.6   RADICAL EQUATIONS

A *radical equation* is an equation in which variables occur underneath radical signs. For example, $\sqrt[3]{x} + \sqrt[3]{4x - 7} = 2$. To solve such equations we need a new principle.

> **The Principle of Powers.** For any number n, if an equation $a = b$ is true, then the equation $a^n = b^n$ is true.

If an equation $a^n = b^n$ is true, it *may not* be true that $a = b$ is true. That is, the principle of powers does *not* always yield equations with the same solution sets-equivalent equations. For example, the solution of $x = 3$ is 3. If we square both sides we get $x^2 = 9$, which has two solutions, 3 and -3. We resolve this difficulty by being certain to check possible solutions.

Example 1   Solve $x = \sqrt{x + 7} + 5$.

Solution

$$x = \sqrt{x + 7} + 5$$

$$x - 5 = \sqrt{x + 7} \quad \text{(Adding } -5 \text{ to isolate the radical term)}$$

$$(x - 5)^2 = (\sqrt{x + 7})^2 \quad \text{(Principle of powers; squaring both sides)}$$

$$x^2 - 10x + 25 = x + 7$$

$$x^2 - 11x + 18 = 0$$

$$(x - 9)(x - 2) = 0 \quad \text{(Factoring)}$$

$$x - 9 = 0 \quad \text{or} \quad x - 2 = 0 \quad \text{(Principle of zero products)}$$

$$x = 9 \quad \text{or} \quad x = 2$$

The possible solutions are 9 and 2. Let us check:

$$\textit{For 9:} \quad x = \sqrt{x + 7} + 5 \qquad\qquad \textit{For 2:} \quad x = \sqrt{x + 7} + 5$$

9	$\sqrt{9 + 7} + 5$
	$\sqrt{16} + 5$
	$4 + 5$
	9

2	$\sqrt{2 + 7} + 5$
	$\sqrt{9} + 5$
	$3 + 5$
	8

Since 9 checks but 2 does not, the only solution is 9.

Example 2   Solve $\sqrt[3]{4x^2 + 1} = 5$.

$$(\sqrt[3]{4x^2 + 1})^3 = 5^3 \quad \text{(Principle of powers; cubing both sides)}$$

$$4x^2 + 1 = 125$$

$$4x^2 = 124$$

$$x^2 = 31$$

$$x = \pm\sqrt{31}$$

Both $\sqrt{31}$ and $-\sqrt{31}$ check. These are the solutions.

Sometimes we have to use the principle of powers more than once.

Example 3   Solve $\sqrt{2x - 5} = 1 + \sqrt{x - 3}$.

$$(\sqrt{2x - 5})^2 = (1 + \sqrt{x - 3})^2$$

$$2x - 5 = 1 + 2\sqrt{x - 3} + (x - 3)$$

$$x - 3 = 2\sqrt{x - 3}$$

$$(x - 3)^2 = (2\sqrt{x - 3})^2 \qquad \text{(Get the radical alone, then square.)}$$

$$x^2 - 6x + 9 = 4(x - 3)$$

$$x^2 - 6x + 9 = 4x - 12$$

$$x^2 - 10x + 21 = 0$$

$$(x - 7)(x - 3) = 0$$

$$x = 7 \quad \text{or} \quad x = 3$$

The numbers 7 and 3 check. Thus the solutions are 7 and 3.

EXERCISE SET 2.6

Solve.

1. $\sqrt{3x - 4} = 1$

2. $\sqrt[3]{2x + 1} = -5$

3. $\sqrt[4]{x^2 - 1} = 1$

4. $\sqrt{m + 1} - 5 = 8$

5. $\sqrt{y - 1} + 4 = 0$

6. $5 + \sqrt{3x^2 + \pi} = 0$

7. $\sqrt{x - 3} + \sqrt{x + 5} = 4$

8. $\sqrt{x} - \sqrt{x - 5} = 1$

9. $\sqrt{3x - 5} + \sqrt{2x + 3} + 1 = 0$

10. $\sqrt{2m - 3} = \sqrt{m + 7} - 2$

11. $\sqrt[3]{6x + 9} + 8 = 5$

12. $\sqrt[5]{3x + 4} = 2$

13. $\sqrt{6x + 7} = x + 2$

14. $\sqrt{6x + 7} - \sqrt{3x + 3} = 1$

15. $\sqrt{20 - x} = \sqrt{9 - x} + 3$

16. $\sqrt{n + 2} + \sqrt{3n + 4} = 2$

17. $(x - 5)^{2/3} = 2$

18. $(x - 3)^{2/3} = 2$

19. $\dfrac{x + \sqrt{x + 1}}{x - \sqrt{x + 1}} = \dfrac{5}{11}$

20. $\sqrt{\sqrt{x + 25} - \sqrt{x}} = 5$

21. $\sqrt{x + 2} - \sqrt{x - 2} = \sqrt{2x}$

22. $2\sqrt{x + 3} = \sqrt{x} + \sqrt{x + 8}$

23. $\sqrt[4]{x + 2} = \sqrt{3x + 1}$

24. $\sqrt[3]{2x - 1} = \sqrt[6]{x + 1}$

25. The demand function for a product is given by

$$p = \sqrt{500 - x}.$$

Find the number of units x sold when the price is $20 per unit, $17 per unit.

26. The demand function for a product is given by

$$p = \sqrt[3]{800 - x}.$$

Find the number of units x sold when the price is $8 per unit, $6.50 per unit.

2.7   EQUATIONS QUADRATIC IN FORM

Look for a pattern.

a) $x + 3\sqrt{x} - 10 = 0$, let $u = \sqrt{x}$.
Then $u^2 + 3u - 10 = 0$.

b) $x^4 - 6x^2 + 7 = 0$, let $u = x^2$.
Then $u^2 - 6u + 7 = 0$.

c) $(x^2 - x)^2 - 14(x^2 - x) + 24 = 0$, let $u = x^2 - x$.
Then $u^2 - 14u + 24 = 0$.

The original equations are not quadratic, but after an appropriate substitution of an expression in another variable, we get a quadratic equation. Equations like the original ones are said to be *quadratic in form*.

> **To solve equations quadratic in form we first make a substitution, solve for the new variable, then solve for the original variable.**

Example 1   Solve $x + 3\sqrt{x} - 10 = 0$.

Solution   Let $u = \sqrt{x}$. Then we solve the equation resulting from substituting u for $\sqrt{x}$:

$$u^2 + 3u - 10 = 0$$

$$(u + 5)(u - 2) = 0$$

$$u = -5 \quad \text{or} \quad u = 2$$

Now we substitute $\sqrt{x}$ for u and solve these equations:

$$\sqrt{x} = -5 \quad \text{or} \quad \sqrt{x} = 2$$

$$\text{(no solution)} \quad \text{or} \quad x = 4$$

The solution is 4.

Example 2   Solve $x^4 - 6x^2 + 7 = 0$.

Solution   Let $u = x^2$. Then we solve the equation resulting from substituting u for x^2.

$$u^2 - 6u + 7 = 0$$

$$a = 1, b = -6, c = 7$$

$$u = \frac{-b \pm \sqrt{b^2 - 4ac}}{2a}$$

$$= \frac{-(-6) \pm \sqrt{(-6)^2 - 4 \cdot 1 \cdot 7}}{2 \cdot 1}$$

$$u = \frac{6 \pm \sqrt{8}}{2} = \frac{2 \cdot 3 \pm 2\sqrt{2}}{2 \cdot 1} = 3 \pm \sqrt{2}$$

Now we substitute x^2 for u and solve for x:

$$x^2 = 3 + \sqrt{2} \qquad \text{or} \quad x^2 = 3 - \sqrt{2}$$

$$x = \pm \sqrt{3 + \sqrt{2}} \quad \text{or} \quad x = \pm \sqrt{3 - \sqrt{2}}$$

Thus we have the four solutions: $\sqrt{3 + \sqrt{2}}, -\sqrt{3 + \sqrt{2}}, \sqrt{3 - \sqrt{2}}$, and $-\sqrt{3 - \sqrt{2}}$.

Example 3   Solve $(x^2 - x)^2 - 14(x^2 - x) + 24 = 0$.

Solution   Let $u = x^2 - x$. Then we solve the equation resulting from substituting u for $x^2 - x$:

$$u^2 - 14u + 24 = 0$$

$$(u - 12)(u - 2) = 0$$

$$u = 12 \quad \text{or} \quad u = 2.$$

Now we substitute $x^2 - x$ for u and solve:

$$
\begin{array}{ccc}
x^2 - x = 12 & \text{or} & x^2 - x = 2 \\
x^2 - x - 12 = 0 & \text{or} & x^2 - x - 2 = 0 \\
(x - 4)(x + 3) = 0 & \text{or} & (x - 2)(x + 1) = 0 \\
x = 4 \quad \text{or} \quad x = -3 & \text{or} & x = 2 \quad \text{or} \quad x = -1.
\end{array}
$$

The solutions are $4, -3, 2, -1$.

Example 4   Solve $t^{2/5} - t^{1/5} - 2 = 0$.

Solution   Let $u = t^{1/5}$. Then we solve the equation resulting from substituting u for $t^{1/5}$:

$$u^2 - u - 2 = 0$$

$$(u - 2)(u + 1) = 0$$

$$u = 2 \quad \text{or} \quad u = -1$$

Now we substitute $t^{1/5}$ for u and solve:

$$t^{1/5} = 2 \quad \text{or} \quad t^{1/5} = -1 \qquad \text{(Principles of powers;}$$
$$t = 32 \quad \text{or} \quad t = -1 \qquad \text{raising to the 5th power)}$$

The solutions are 32 and -1.

EXERCISE SET 2.7

Solve.

1. $x - 10\sqrt{x} + 9 = 0$

2. $2x - 9\sqrt{x} + 4 = 0$

3. $x^4 - 10x^2 + 25 = 0$

4. $x^4 - 3x^2 + 2 = 0$

5. $t^{2/3} + t^{1/3} - 6 = 0$

6. $w^{2/3} - 2w^{1/3} - 8 = 0$

7. $z^{1/2} = z^{1/4} + 2$

8. $6 = m^{1/3} - m^{1/6}$

9. $(x^2 - 6x)^2 - 2(x^2 - 6x) - 35 = 0$

10. $(1 + \sqrt{x})^2 + (1 + \sqrt{x}) - 6 = 0$

11. $(y^2 - 5y)^2 + (y^2 - 5y) - 12 = 0$

12. $(2t^2 + t)^2 - 4(2t^2 + t) + 3 = 0$

13. $w^4 - 4w^2 - 2 = 0$

14. $t^4 - 5t^2 + 5 = 0$

15. $x^{-2} - x^{-1} - 6 = 0$

16. $4x^{-2} - x^{-1} - 5 = 0$

17. $2x^{-2} + x^{-1} = 1$

18. $10 - 9m^{-1} = m^{-2}$

19. $\left(\dfrac{x^2 - 2}{x}\right)^2 - 7\left(\dfrac{x^2 - 2}{x}\right) - 18 = 0$

20. $\left(\dfrac{x^2 + 1}{x}\right)^2 - 8\left(\dfrac{x^2 + 1}{x}\right) + 15 = 0$

21. $\dfrac{x}{x - 1} - 6\sqrt{\dfrac{x}{x - 1}} - 40 = 0$

22. $\dfrac{2x + 1}{x} + 30 = 7\sqrt{\dfrac{2x + 1}{x}}$

23. $5\left(\dfrac{x + 2}{x - 2}\right)^2 = 3\left(\dfrac{x + 2}{x - 2}\right) + 2$

24. $\left(\dfrac{x + 1}{x + 3}\right)^2 + \left(\dfrac{x + 1}{x + 3}\right) - 6 = 0$

Solve. Check possible solutions by substituting into the original equation.

25. 🔳 $6.75x = \sqrt{35x} + 5.36$

26. 🔳 $\pi x^4 - \sqrt{99.3} = \pi^2 x^2$

Solve.

27. $9x^{3/2} - 8 = x^3$

28. $\sqrt[3]{2x + 3} = \sqrt[6]{2x + 3}$

■ ───────────────────────────────

Solve.

29. $\dfrac{2x + 1}{x} = 3 + 7\sqrt{\dfrac{2x + 1}{x}}$

CHAPTER 2 REVIEW

A function is given by $f(x) = x^2 + x$. Find:

1. $f(-3)$ **2.** $f(x + h)$

3. For $f(x_1, x_2) = 10x_1 - 3x_2$, find $f(-5, 20)$.

4. What is the slope and y-intercept of
$$y = -3x + 2?$$

5. Find an equation of the line with slope $\frac{1}{4}$, containing the point $(8, -5)$.

6. Find the slope of the line containing the points $(-2, 3)$ and $(-4, -9)$.

7. A record company has fixed costs of $10,000 for producing a record master. Thereafter, the variable costs are $0.50 per record for duplicating from the record master. Revenue from each record is expected to be $1.30.

a) Formulate a function

     i) $C(x)$ for the total cost of producing x records.

     ii) $R(x)$ for the total revenue from the sale of x records.

     iii) $P(x)$ for the total profit from the production and sale of x records.

b) How many records must the company sell to break even?

8. Determine whether this function is increasing, decreasing, or neither.
$$f(x) = -0.2x + 7$$

9. Find the equilibrium point for the demand and supply functions
$$D(x) = (x - 7)^2 \quad \text{and} \quad S(x) = x^2 + x + 4.$$

10. Graph $y = \dfrac{4}{x}$.

11. Convert to fractional exponents.
$$\frac{1}{\sqrt{t}}$$

12. Convert to radical notation.
$$t^{-3/5}$$

Determine the domain of each function.

13. $f(x) = \dfrac{x^2 + 20}{(x - 2)(x + 7)}$

14. $f(x) = \sqrt{5x + 10}$

Solve using the addition method.

15. $3x_1 - x_2 = 2$
$4x_1 + 2x_2 = 11$

16. $5x_1 + 10x_2 = 15$
$3x_1 + 6x_2 = 9$

Solve.

17. $\sqrt{x - 1} - \sqrt{x - 4} = 1$

18. $\sqrt{5x + 1} - 1 = \sqrt{3x}$

19. $y^4 - 3y^2 + 1 = 0$

20. $x = 2\sqrt{x} - 1$

21. $(x^2 - 1)^2 - (x^2 - 1) - 2 = 0$

22. $t^{2/3} - 10 = 3t^{1/3}$

23. The time t required to do a certain job varies inversely as the number of people P who work on the job (assuming that all do the same amount of work). It takes 5 hours for 12 people to take an advertising survey. How long would it take 3 people to do the same job?

THE ECHELON METHOD AND MATRICES

3.1 THE ECHELON METHOD—UNIQUE SOLUTIONS

In your experience with solving a system such as

$$2x_1 + 6x_2 = 26,$$

$$8x_1 - 3x_2 = -31,$$

you may have noticed that one actually works with the coefficients, or constants, and not the variables. It is helpful to just list the constants in what is called an *echelon* tableau*.

x_1	x_2	1
2	6	26
8	−3	−31

---

* The word "echelon" is a French word meaning "a series of steps."

The *rows* of a tableau are horizontal. The *columns* are vertical.

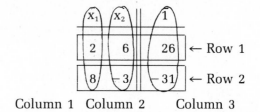

Column 1   Column 2   Column 3

Note that the first column is labeled with the variable x_1, the second with the variable x_2, and the third with a 1. The double vertical lines correspond to "$=$." To see how to translate from a tableau to the corresponding system, we multiply the elements of each row by the column headings and add.

$$
\begin{array}{ccc}
x_1 & x_2 & 1 \\
2 & 6 & 26 \\
8 & -3 & -31
\end{array}
\quad
\begin{array}{l}
\longrightarrow 2x_1 + 6x_2 = 26 \\
\longrightarrow 8x_1 - 3x_2 = -31
\end{array}
$$

The *echelon method*† for solving systems uses certain operations that correspond to operations on equations. We will carry out these operations in a way that may seem odd at first, but the reason for it will become apparent later. Before we formalize the method, let us consider an example. Compare each operation with the corresponding operation with the equations.

Example 1   Solve.

$$2x_1 + 6x_2 = 26$$
$$8x_1 - 3x_2 = -31$$

Solution   **Addition Method**   **Echelon Method**

x_1	x_2	1

$$
\begin{array}{l}
2x_1 + 6x_2 = 26 \\
8x_1 - 3x_2 = -31
\end{array}
$$

x_1	x_2	1
2	6	26
8	-3	-31

Our first goal is to get a 1 in the first row and first column.

----

† Short for *reduced row echelon method.*

1. Multiply the first equation by $\frac{1}{2}$.

1. Multiply the first row by $\frac{1}{2}$.

x_1	x_2	1
1*	3	13
8	−3	−31

$$x_1 + 3x_2 = 13$$
$$8x_1 - 3x_2 = -31$$

In the tableau we put a star (*) on the 1. It is called a *pivot* element. Our goal will always be to get 0's in the rest of a column where a pivot element occurs. To do this here, we multiply the first (pivot) row by -8 and add.

2. Multiply the first equation by -8 and add to the second. We leave the first equation as is: we are simply adding a multiple of it to the second equation.

2. Multiply the first (pivot) row by -8 and add to the second. We leave the first row as is in the tableau. We are simply adding a multiple of the pivot row to the second row.

x_1	x_2	1
1	3	13
0	−27	−135

$$x_1 + 3x_2 = 13$$
$$- 27x_2 = -135$$

Our next goal is to get a 1 in the second row and second column; this will be a new pivot element.

3. Multiply the second equation by $-\frac{1}{27}$.

3. Multiply the second row by $-\frac{1}{27}$.

x_1	x_2	1
1	3	13
0	1*	5

$$x_1 + 3x_2 = 13$$
$$x_2 = 5$$

We put a star on the 1 to indicate that this is the new pivot element. Remember that we always want to get 0's in the rest of a column where a pivot element occurs. To do this here, we multiply the second (pivot) row by -3 and add.

4. Multiply the second equation by -3 and add to the first.

4. Multiply the second (pivot) row by -3 and add to the first.

x_1	x_2	1
1	0	−2
0	1	5

$$x_1 = -2$$
$$x_2 = 5$$

The solution is $(-2, 5)$. We can obtain this directly from the tableau by translating to the corresponding system of equations shown on the left.

The echelon method. In carrying out the echelon method, we obtain pivot elements of 1 diagonally from upper left to lower right. Then we get 0's in the rest of each column by adding multiples of the pivot row to the other rows. We use any of these operations in carrying out this procedure:

   i) **Interchange any two rows.**

  ii) **Interchange any two variable columns, provided we interchange the headings.**

 iii) **Multiply any row by a nonzero constant.**

 iv) **Add a multiple of the pivot row to another row.**

It is important to note that we can add *rows* only. We cannot add columns since this would mean adding unlike terms in the equations.

Example 2 Solve using the echelon method.

$$3x_1 - 4x_2 = -1$$

$$-3x_1 + 2x_2 = 0$$

Solution   **1.** We first obtain a tableau.

x_1	x_2	1
3	-4	-1
-3	2	0

2. We obtain the pivot element 1 in the first row and first column (upper left) by multiplying the first row by $\frac{1}{3}$.

x_1	x_2	1
1^*	$-\frac{4}{3}$	$-\frac{1}{3}$
-3	2	0

3. Next we *pivot*; that is, we obtain 0's in the rest of the first column. To do this we multiply the first (pivot) row by 3 and add to the second.

x_1	x_2	1
1	$-\frac{4}{3}$	$-\frac{1}{3}$
0	-2	-1

Based on your experience with the addition method, you may have been tempted at the outset to just add the first row to the second. While this is not incorrect, remember that we are proceeding in a special way to ease and anticipate later work.

4. We obtain the next pivot element by multiplying the second row by $-\frac{1}{2}$.

x_1	x_2	1
1	$-\frac{4}{3}$	$-\frac{1}{3}$
0	1^*	$\frac{1}{2}$

5. We pivot again, multiplying the second (pivot) row by $\frac{4}{3}$ and adding to the first.

x_1	x_2	1
1	0	$\frac{1}{3}$
0	1	$\frac{1}{2}$

The solution is $(\frac{1}{3}, \frac{1}{2})$, found by translating from the tableau to the system of equations $x_1 = \frac{1}{3}$ and $x_2 = \frac{1}{2}$.

It might be noted that as long as columns are not interchanged, we could drop the headings to ease the writing.

Now let us solve a system with three variables.

Example 3 Solve, using the echelon method.

$$2x_1 - x_2 + x_3 = -1$$
$$x_1 - 2x_2 + 3x_3 = 4$$
$$4x_1 + x_2 + 2x_3 = 4$$

Solution **1.** We first write the tableau.

x_1	x_2	x_3	1
2	-1	1	-1
1	-2	3	4
4	1	2	4

2. We obtain a pivot element 1 in the first row and first column. We could do this by multiplying the first equation by $\frac{1}{2}$, but this would introduce fractions. An easier way to get the pivot element is to interchange the first and second rows.

x_1	x_2	x_3	1
1^*	-2	3	4
2	-1	1	-1
4	1	2	4

3. Next we pivot to obtain 0's in the rest of the first column. We first multiply the first (pivot) row by -2 and add to the second row.

x_1	x_2	x_3	1
1^*	-2	3	4
0	3	-5	-9
4	1	2	4

4. To complete the pivot, we multiply the first (pivot) row by -4 and add to the third row. (We usually work down the column in this way.)

x_1	x_2	x_3	1
1	-2	3	4
0	3	-5	-9
0	9	-10	-12

5. To obtain the next pivot element, we multiply the second row by $\frac{1}{3}$.

x_1	x_2	x_3	1
1	-2	3	4
0	1^*	$-\frac{5}{3}$	-3
0	9	-10	-12

6. We pivot on the starred 1. We first multiply the second (pivot) row by 2 and add to the first.

x_1	x_2	x_3	1
1	0	$-\frac{1}{3}$	-2
0	1^*	$-\frac{5}{3}$	-3
0	9	-10	-12

7. To complete the pivot, we multiply the second (pivot) row by -9 and add to the third.

x_1	x_2	x_3	1
1	0	$-\frac{1}{3}$	-2
0	1	$-\frac{5}{3}$	-3
0	0	5	15

8. To obtain the last pivot element, we multiply the third row by $\frac{1}{5}$.

x_1	x_2	x_3	1
1	0	$-\frac{1}{3}$	-2
0	1	$-\frac{5}{3}$	-3
0	0	1^*	3

9. We pivot on the starred 1. We first multiply the third (pivot) row by $\frac{1}{3}$ and add to the first.

x_1	x_2	x_3	1
1	0	0	-1
0	1	$-\frac{5}{3}$	-3
0	0	1^*	3

10. To complete the pivot, we multiply the third (pivot) row by $\frac{5}{3}$ and add to the second.

x_1	x_2	x_3	1
1	0	0	-1
0	1	0	2
0	0	1	3

The solution is found by translating from the tableau to the system of equations

$$x_1 = -1,$$

$$x_2 = 2,$$

$$x_3 = 3.$$

We can also say that the solution is the ordered triple $(-1, 2, 3)$.

Application

Example 4   *Interest Problem.* Two investments are made that total $4800. For a certain year, these investments yield $412 in simple interest. Part of the $4800 is invested at 8% and the other part at 9%. Find the amount invested at each rate.

Solution   Recall the formula for simple interest

$$I = Prt.$$

Interest I is principal P times rate r times time t.

a) Let x_1 represent the amount invested at 8% and x_2 the amount invested at 9%. Then the interest from x_1 is 8% x_1, and the interest from x_2 is 9% x_2. Thus the $412 total interest is given by

$$8\% \ x_1 + 9\% \ x_2 = 412,$$

or

$$0.08x_1 + 0.09x_2 = 412.$$

b) Considering the total amount invested, we have

$$x_1 + x_2 = 4800.$$

c) We now have a system of equations.

$$0.08x_1 + 0.09x_2 = \ \ 412$$

$$x_1 + x_2 = 4800$$

We translate this system to an echelon tableau and solve.

x_1	x_2	1
0.08	0.09	412
1	1	4800

We first multiply the first row by 100 to clear the decimals.

x_1	x_2	1
8	9	41200
1	1	4800

To get the pivot element 1 in the first row, first column, we interchange the rows.

x_1	x_2	1
1*	1	4800
8	9	41200

We multiply the first row by -8 and add to the second.

x_1	x_2	1
1	1	4800
0	1*	2800

We already have a pivot element 1 in the second row, second column. We complete the pivot by multiplying the second row by -1 and adding to the first row.

x_1	x_2	1
1	0	2000
0	1	2800

Thus the solution is

$$x_1 = 2000,$$

$$x_2 = 2800,$$

so $2000 is invested at 8% and $2800 is invested at 9%.

EXERCISE SET 3.1

Solve, using the echelon method. Interchange rows and/or columns to avoid fractions when possible.

1.
$$x_1 + 4x_2 = 5$$
$$-3x_1 + 2x_2 = 13$$

2.
$$x_1 + 4x_2 = 8$$
$$3x_1 + 5x_2 = 3$$

3.
$$-x_1 + 3x_2 = 2$$
$$2x_1 - x_2 = 11$$

4.
$$9x_1 - 2x_2 = 5$$
$$3x_1 - 3x_2 = 11$$

5.
$$2x_1 - 5x_2 = 10$$
$$4x_1 + 3x_2 = 7$$

6.
$$5x_1 - 3x_2 = -2$$
$$4x_1 + 2x_2 = 5$$

7.
$$x_1 + x_2 + x_3 = 9$$
$$x_1 - x_2 - x_3 = -15$$
$$x_1 + x_2 - x_3 = -5$$

8.
$$x_1 + x_2 + x_3 = 1$$
$$x_1 + 2x_2 + 3x_3 = 4$$
$$x_1 + 3x_2 + 7x_3 = 13$$

9.
$$x_1 - x_2 + 2x_3 = 0$$
$$x_1 - 2x_2 + 3x_3 = -1$$
$$2x_1 - 2x_2 + x_3 = -3$$

10.
$$x_1 + 2x_2 - 3x_3 = 9$$
$$2x_1 - x_2 + 2x_3 = -8$$
$$3x_1 - x_2 - 4x_3 = 3$$

11.
$$3x_1 + 2x_2 + 2x_3 = 3$$
$$2x_1 + 4x_2 - x_3 = 8$$
$$2x_1 - 4x_2 + x_3 = 0$$

12.
$$4x_1 - x_2 - 3x_3 = 1$$
$$8x_1 + x_2 - x_3 = 5$$
$$2x_1 + x_2 + 2x_3 = 5$$

13.
$$2x_1 - 3x_2 + x_3 - x_4 = -8$$
$$x_1 + x_2 - x_3 - x_4 = -4$$
$$x_1 - x_2 - x_3 - x_4 = -14$$
$$x_1 + x_2 + x_3 + x_4 = 22$$

14.
$$3x_1 - 2x_2 + 2x_3 + x_4 = -6$$
$$x_1 - x_2 + 4x_3 + 3x_4 = -2$$
$$x_1 + x_2 + x_3 + x_4 = -5$$
$$2x_1 + 2x_2 - 2x_3 - 2x_4 = -10$$

15. Two investments are made that total $8800. For a certain year, these investments yield $663 in simple interest. Part of the $8800 is invested at 7% and part at 8%. Find the amount invested at each rate.

16. Two investments are made that total $15,000. For a certain year, these investments yield $1432 in simple interest. Part of the $15,000 is invested at 9% and part at 10%. Find the amount invested at each rate.

17. For a certain year $3900 is received in interest from two investments. A certain amount is invested at 5%, and $10,000 more than this is invested at 6%. Find the amount invested at each rate. [*Hint:* Express each equation in standard form $ax_1 + bx_2 = c$.]

18. For a certain year $876 is received in interest from two investments. A certain amount is invested at 7%, and $1200 more than this is invested at 8%. Find the amount invested at each rate.

19. One day a campus bookstore sold 30 sweatshirts. White ones cost $9.95 and yellow ones cost $10.50. In dollars, $310.60 worth of sweatshirts were sold. How many of each color were sold?

20. One week a business sold 40 scarves. White ones cost $4.95 and designed ones cost $7.95. In dollars, $282 worth of scarves were sold. How many of each kind were sold?

21. Soybean meal is 16% protein; corn meal is 9% protein. How many pounds of each should be mixed together to get 350 pounds of a mixture that is 12% protein?

22. A chemist has one solution of acid and water that is 25% acid and a second that is 50% acid. How many gallons of each should be mixed together to get 10 gallons of a solution that is 40% acid?

23. A person receives $212 per year in simple interest from three investments totalling $2500. Part is invested at 7%, part at 8%, and part at 9%. There is $1100 more invested at 9% than at 8%. Find the amount invested at each rate.

24. A person receives $306 per year in simple interest from three investments totalling $3200. Part is invested at 8%, part at 9%, and part at 10%. There is $1800 more invested at 10% than at 8%. Find the amount invested at each rate.

3.2   THE ECHELON METHOD—SPECIAL CASES

In the preceding section, each system had exactly one solution and the final tableau had a form like the following.

x_1	x_2	x_3	1
1	0	0	p
0	1	0	q
0	0	1	r

This is called the *reduced row echelon form,* or *echelon form,* for short. Here we consider special cases where systems have no solution, or infinitely many solutions, or the number of variables is not the same as the number of equations. All these cases can be analyzed in the same general way.*

Example 1   Solve

$$6x_1 - 3x_2 = 21,$$
$$4x_1 - 2x_2 = 19.$$

Solution   We translate to the echelon tableau, multiply the first row by $\frac{1}{6}$, and obtain

x_1	x_2	1
1^*	$-\frac{1}{2}$	$\frac{7}{2}$
4	-2	19

We carry out the pivot by multiplying the pivot row by -4 and adding to the second row.

x_1	x_2	1
1	$-\frac{1}{2}$	$\frac{7}{2}$
0	0	5

The pivoting is considered to be complete here even though we do not have 1's down the main diagonal.

Earlier we found the solution by translating back to a system of equations. If we do that here, we obtain

$$x_1 - \tfrac{1}{2}x_2 = \tfrac{7}{2},$$
$$0 = 5.$$

But the second equation is false. Thus the system is inconsistent. It has *no solution*.

Example 2   Solve

$$6x_1 - 3x_2 = 21,$$
$$4x_1 - 2x_2 = 14.$$

---

* Homogeneous equations, that is, equations whose constant terms (right-hand sides) are zero, require *no* special consideration.

Solution We translate to the echelon tableau, multiply the first row by $\frac{1}{8}$, and obtain

x_1	x_2	$\parallel$	1
1^*	$-\frac{1}{2}$	$\parallel$	$\frac{7}{2}$
4	-2	$\parallel$	14

We carry out the pivot by multiplying the pivot row by -4 and adding to the second row.

x_1	x_2	$\parallel$	1
1	$-\frac{1}{2}$	$\parallel$	$\frac{7}{2}$
0	0	$\parallel$	0

Translating back to a system of equations we obtain

$$x_1 - \tfrac{1}{2}x_2 = \tfrac{7}{2},$$

$$0 = 0.$$

We know from previous work that this system is consistent and the second equation is linearly dependent upon the first. The system has infinitely many solutions. Every point on the line $x_1 - \frac{1}{2}x_2 = \frac{7}{2}$ is a solution. We can describe this by solving the equation for x_1. Then the solutions can be described by

$$x_1 = \tfrac{7}{2} + \tfrac{1}{2}x_2,$$

$$x_2 = \text{any number}.$$

By selecting arbitrary values of x_2 and computing x_1 we find the following as some solutions.

$x_2 = 0$	$x_2 = 1$	$x_2 = -3$
$x_1 = \frac{7}{2}$	$x_1 = \frac{7}{2} + \frac{1}{2} = 4$	$x_1 = \frac{7}{2} - \frac{3}{2} = 2$

Example 3 Suppose we are trying to solve a system with 3 equations and 4 variables, and we reach this stage in the tableau.

x_1	x_2	x_3	x_4	$\parallel$	1
1^*	0	-2	0	$\parallel$	2
2	1	2	0	$\parallel$	1
3	0	-6	5	$\parallel$	26

The pivot element is in the first row and first column. We carry out the pivoting by multiplying the first row by -2 and adding to the second and multiplying the first row by -3 and adding to the third. We obtain

x_1	x_2	x_3	x_4	1
1	0	-2	0	2
0	1	6	0	-3
0	0	0	5	20

Note that the pivot in the second row, second column is also complete.

Consider now the third row and third column, where we have a 0. The only way to get a 1 there is to interchange the third and fourth columns and multiply by a constant. Instead of doing this we simply move on to the third row and fourth column. We multiply by $\frac{1}{5}$ and obtain

x_1	x_2	x_3	x_4	1
1	0	-2	0	2
0	1	6	0	-3
0	0	0	1^*	4

Since the rest of the fourth column already has 0's, the pivoting is complete. This is a more general example of the *echelon form*. The solutions are found by translating back to a system of equations. We obtain

$$x_1 - 2x_3 = 2,$$
$$x_2 + 6x_3 = -3,$$
$$x_4 = 4.$$

The solutions can be described by

$$x_1 = 2 + 2x_3,$$
$$x_2 = -3 - 6x_3,$$
$$x_3 = \text{any number},$$
$$x_4 = 4.$$

Here are some solutions obtained by picking arbitrary values of x_3.

$x_1 =$	2	$x_1 =$	4	$x_1 =$	0
$x_2 =$	-3	$x_2 =$	-9	$x_2 =$	3
$x_3 =$	0	$x_3 =$	1	$x_3 =$	-1
$x_4 =$	4	$x_4 =$	4	$x_4 =$	4

The echelon form has a general "staircase" description like any of those shown here where # means that any type of number can be in that location.

x_1	x_2	x_3	x_4	x_5	1
1	0	#	0	#	#
0	1	#	0	#	#
0	0	0	1	#	#

x_1	x_2	x_3	1
1	0	0	#
0	1	0	#
0	0	1	#

x_1	x_2	x_3	1
1	0	0	#
0	1	0	#
0	0	0	#

These do not show all possibilities, but they give the general idea.

The following discussion concerns those situations where there is a row with all 0's to the left of the double vertical line.

i) Any time we have a row with all 0's to the left of the double vertical line and a nonzero number to the right, the system has no solution.

$$0 \quad 0 \quad 0 \quad 0 \ \| \ k \qquad \text{(where } k \neq 0)$$

ii) For a row of *all* 0's, we cannot determine the nature of the solutions without further analysis.

$$0 \quad 0 \quad 0 \quad 0 \ \| \ 0$$

This row corresponds to an equation that is linearly dependent. So up to this point the system would seem to be consistent. We shift that row to the bottom of the tableau and make further analysis of the upper part of the tableau. We may have exactly one solution, infinitely many solutions, or no solution, should Case (i) later occur.

Example 4   Suppose we are trying to solve a system of 4 equations in 3 variables, and we reach this stage in the tableau.

x_1	x_2	x_3	1
1	0	5	8
0	1	$-\frac{1}{4}$	-2
0	0	0	$-\frac{1}{2}$
0	0	-3	6

Because the third row has all 0's to the left of the double vertical line and a nonzero number to the right, the system has *no solution*. No further analysis is necessary.

Example 5 Suppose we are trying to solve a system of 4 equations in 3 variables and we reach this stage in the tableau.

x_1	x_2	x_3	1
1	0	5	8
0	1	$-\frac{1}{4}$	-2
0	0	0	0
0	0	-3	6

Since we have a row with all 0's, we interchange it with the fourth row.

x_1	x_2	x_3	1
1	0	5	8
0	1	$-\frac{1}{4}$	-2
0	0	-3	6
0	0	0	0

The pivot element is in the third row and third column. We multiply the third row by $-\frac{1}{3}$.

x_1	x_2	x_3	1
1	0	5	8
0	1	$-\frac{1}{4}$	-2
0	0	1^*	-2
0	0	0	0

Now we pivot. We multiply the third row by $\frac{1}{4}$ and add to the second, and we multiply the third row by -5 and add to the first, obtaining

x_1	x_2	x_3	1
1	0	0	18
0	1	0	$-\frac{5}{2}$
0	0	1	-2
0	0	0	0

We now find the solution by translating back to a system of equations:

$$x_1 = 18,$$

$$x_2 = -\tfrac{5}{2},$$

$$x_3 = -2,$$

$$0 = 0.$$

The last equation plays no role here. The solution can be stated as an ordered triple $(18, -\frac{5}{2}, -2)$.

The original system of equations was consistent and *linearly dependent*. If we have a system of more than two equations that is consistent and linearly dependent, then one of the equations is a multiple of the others or a sum of multiples of the others.

(Optional) All-Integer Method for Solving Linear Algebraic Systems.

In the course of solution of linear algebraic systems, fractions frequently arise which often become a source of woe to students. To avoid encountering fractions in the course of solution (but not necessarily in the solution itself), one of the authors (JCC) developed an all-integer method based on a new theorem.* In essence, this theorem states that if we start with an all-integer tableau and use the all-integer method, then all tableaux will be all integer.

First, we shall state the all-integer method. Then we shall give a detailed example of its use.

The All-Integer Method

1. **Start with an all-integer tableau with entries a_{ij} (and $b_i = a_{i0}$) and set the old pivot element, $p_0 = 1$.**

2. **Leave the pivot row ($i = r$) unchanged in the new tableau.**

For each row other than the pivot row, in turn:

3. **Multiply the ith row by the pivot element, $p = a_{rk} \neq 0$.**

4. **Multiply the pivot row ($i = r$) by $-a_{ik}$, the negative of the ith element in the pivot column ($j = k$).**

5. **Add (3) and (4).**

6. **Divide (5) by the old pivot element, p_0. (The old pivot element, p_0, is the pivot element, p, from the *preceding* tableau. Initially, there is no preceding tableau, so we set $p_0 = 1$.)**

Formally, we obtain for the elements of the new tableau

$$a'_{rj} = a_{rj}$$

---

*J. C. Crown. "Solution of Linear Algebraic Systems Using All-Integer Tableaux." To be published.

and

$$a'_{ij} = \frac{1}{p_0}(a_{rk}a_{ij} - a_{ik}a_{rj}), \quad \text{for all } i \neq r$$

or, in determinant form (see Section 3.5),

$$a'_{ij} = \frac{1}{p_0}\begin{vmatrix} a_{rk} & a_{rj} \\ a_{ik} & a_{ij} \end{vmatrix}, \quad \text{for all } i \neq r.$$

If any a'_{ij} is not found to be integer, then a computation mistake has been made.

Example 6   Solve using the all-integer method:

$$3x_1 + 4x_2 + 5x_3 = 1,$$
$$4x_1 - 2x_2 + 7x_3 = 2,$$
$$7x_1 + 5x_2 - 3x_3 = 3.$$

Solution   First, we put this set of equations into an echelon tableau.

x_1	x_2	x_3	1	
3*	4	5	1	$p_0 = 1$
4	-2	7	2	$p = 3$
7	5	-3	3	

Here we *set* $p_0 = 1$ and obtain the pivot element, p, in the *usual* manner. Thus, here $p = 3$. Pivoting, we obtain

x_1	x_2	x_3	1	
3	4	5	1	$p_0 = 3$
0	-22*	1	2	$p = -22$
0	-13	-44	2	

Note that rather than have an l as the first element of the main diagonal, we have p. Now p_0 takes on the value of the previous p, that is $p_0 = 3$. The new p is the next element along the main diagonal, so $p = -22$.* Pivoting

---

*If desired, negative pivot elements can be avoided by simply multiplying the pivot row by ± 1 so that $p > 0$.

a second time, we obtain

x_1	x_2	x_3		1	
-22	0	-38		-10	$p_0 = -22$
0	-22	1		2	$p = 327$
0	0	327^*		-6	

We still have p along (part of) the main diagonal, but for this tableau $p = -22$, while in the preceding tableau $p = 3$. Pivoting a third and last time, we obtain

x_1	x_2	x_3		1	
327	0	0		159	$p_0 = 327$
0	327	0		-30	
0	0	327		-6	

Reading off the solution, we have

$$x_1 = \frac{159}{327}, x_2 = -\frac{30}{327}, x_3 = -\frac{6}{327}$$

or, simplifying fractions,

$$x_1 = \frac{53}{109}, x_2 = -\frac{10}{109}, x_3 = -\frac{2}{109}.$$

EXERCISE SET 3.2

Solve, using the echelon method. Interchange rows and/or columns to avoid fractions when possible.

1. $\begin{aligned} x_1 - 3x_2 &= 2 \\ -2x_1 + 6x_2 &= -4 \end{aligned}$

2. $\begin{aligned} 3x_1 + 6x_2 &= 9 \\ x_1 + 2x_2 &= 3 \end{aligned}$

3. $\begin{aligned} x_1 - 3x_2 &= 2 \\ -2x_1 + 6x_2 &= -3 \end{aligned}$

4. $\begin{aligned} 3x_1 + 6x_2 &= 8 \\ x_1 + 2x_2 &= 3 \end{aligned}$

5. $\begin{aligned} 4x_1 + 12x_2 + 16x_3 &= 4 \\ 3x_1 + 4x_2 + 7x_3 &= 3 \\ x_1 + 8x_2 + 9x_3 &= 1 \end{aligned}$

6. $\begin{aligned} 2x_1 - 3x_2 + 7x_3 &= 2 \\ x_1 - 4x_2 + x_3 &= 6 \\ 4x_1 - 16x_2 + 4x_3 &= 24 \end{aligned}$

7. $\begin{aligned} 4x_1 + 12x_2 + 16x_3 &= 0 \\ 3x_1 + 4x_2 + 5x_3 &= 0 \\ x_1 + 8x_2 + 11x_3 &= 0 \end{aligned}$

8. $\begin{aligned} 2x_1 + x_2 - 3x_3 &= 0 \\ x_1 - 4x_2 + x_3 &= 0 \\ 4x_1 - 16x_2 + 4x_3 &= 0 \end{aligned}$

9. $\begin{aligned} x_1 + x_2 + 13x_3 &= 0 \\ x_1 - x_2 - 6x_3 &= 0 \end{aligned}$

10. $\begin{aligned} x_1 + x_2 - x_3 &= -3 \\ x_1 + 2x_2 + 2x_3 &= -1 \end{aligned}$

11. $\begin{aligned} 3x_1 - 9x_3 &= 3 \\ 2x_1 + x_2 - x_3 &= 6 \\ x_1 + 2x_2 + 7x_3 + x_4 &= 7 \end{aligned}$

12.
$$x_1 + x_2 + 12x_3 + 2x_4 = 20$$
$$-2x_1 - x_2 - 20x_3 - 3x_4 = -31$$
$$3x_1 + 4x_2 + 40x_3 + 7x_4 = 69$$

13.
$$2x_1 - 2x_2 + 18x_3 = -14$$
$$x_1 - 2x_2 + 13x_3 = -4$$
$$-2x_2 + 8x_3 = 4$$
$$2x_1 + x_2 + 36x_3 = 7$$

14.
$$-2x_1 - 3x_2 - 4x_3 = -13$$
$$x_1 + 2x_3 = 3$$
$$x_1 + x_2 + 2x_3 = 8$$
$$x_1 + 3x_3 = 5$$

Complete the solution using the echelon method.

15.

x_1	x_2	x_3	x_4	1
1	2	-4	8	7
0	-3	9	12	18
0	3	-9	-12	-18

16.

x_1	x_2	x_3	x_4	1
1	0	5	0	6
0	1	-3	0	4
0	0	0	-2	10

17.

x_1	x_2	x_3	1
1	-1	-2	-5
0	0	0	0
0	0	0	0
0	-2	4	-8

18.

x_1	x_2	x_3	1
1	-2	9	6
0	0	0	0
0	0	0	0
0	3	4	5

12.

x_1	x_2	x_3	x_4	x_5	1
1	0	8	-3	0	6
0	1	4	2	0	4
0	0	0	0	-2	10

20.

x_1	x_2	x_3	x_4	x_5	1
1	0	8	-3	0	6
0	1	4	2	0	4
0	0	0	0	3	-6

3.3 BASIC MATRIX PROPERTIES

A company makes two types of stereos. Type I requires 65 transistors, 50 capacitors, and 4 dials. Type II requires 85 transistors, 42 capacitors, and 6 dials. We can represent this information as follows. This table forms a rectangular array of numbers called a *matrix*.

	Transistors	Capacitors	Dials
Type I	65	50	4
Type II	85	42	6

A matrix is a rectangular array of numbers. The elements of a matrix are enclosed in brackets.

We can also think of a matrix being formed from the coefficients and constants in a system of equations. Thus, from the system

$$-2x_1 + 8x_2 = 3,$$

$$\tfrac{1}{2}x_1 + 16x_2 = 5,$$

we get the matrix

$$\begin{bmatrix} -2 & 8 & 3 \\ \tfrac{1}{2} & 16 & 5 \end{bmatrix}.$$

This matrix has 2 *rows* and 3 *columns*.

> A matrix with *m* rows and *n* columns has *dimensions m × n*, read "*m* by *n*."

Example 1 Find the dimensions of each matrix.

a) $[-2 \quad 3 \quad 4 \quad \tfrac{1}{4}]$ 　　b) $\begin{bmatrix} 6 \\ 7 \\ -3 \\ -\tfrac{1}{2} \end{bmatrix}$ 　　c) $\begin{bmatrix} -2 & \tfrac{1}{4} & 8 \\ 0 & 1 & 5 \\ -8 & 6 & 4 \end{bmatrix}$ 　　d) $[8]$

Solution a) The dimensions are 1 × 4.

b) The dimensions are 4 × 1.

c) The dimensions are 3 × 3. Such a matrix is called a *square* matrix since it has the same number of rows as columns.

d) The dimensions are 1 × 1.

We will usually drop the brackets from a 1 × 1 matrix. That is,

$$[8] = 8.$$

We will use capital letters to represent matrices. The elements of a matrix will be denoted by lower-case letters with subscripts. For example, with

$$A = \begin{bmatrix} a_{11} & a_{12} & a_{13} \\ a_{21} & a_{22} & a_{23} \end{bmatrix},$$

the element in the *i*th row and *j*th column is given by a_{ij}. The above is a

2×3 matrix. We may also denote it

$$A = [a_{ij}]_{2 \times 3}, \quad \text{or} \quad [a_{ij}].$$

Two matrices are *equal* if and only if they have the same dimensions and corresponding elements are equal. Formally if $A = [a_{ij}]_{m \times n}$ and $B = [b_{ij}]_{m \times n}$, then $A = B$ if and only if $a_{ij} = b_{ij}$ for each i and j, where i ranges from 1 to m and j ranges from 1 to n.

Examples

a) $\begin{bmatrix} 2^3 & 0 \\ 1-5 & 9 \end{bmatrix} = \begin{bmatrix} 8 & 0 \\ -4 & 9 \end{bmatrix}$

b) $\begin{bmatrix} -2 & 4 & 7 \\ 0 & 1 & 5 \end{bmatrix} \neq \begin{bmatrix} -2 & 4 \\ 0 & 1 \end{bmatrix}$

c) $\begin{bmatrix} 8 & -9 \\ -6 & 7 \end{bmatrix} \neq \begin{bmatrix} 8 & -9 \\ 6 & 7 \end{bmatrix}$

Example 2 Solve for p and r.

$$\begin{bmatrix} -6 & 3r-5 \\ 0 & p \end{bmatrix} = \begin{bmatrix} -6 & 14 \\ 0 & -9 \end{bmatrix}$$

Solution Since the matrices are equal, $p = -9$, and $3r - 5 = 14$, or $r = \frac{19}{3}$.

A $1 \times n$ matrix is often referred to as a *row vector,* and an $m \times 1$ matrix is often referred to as a *column vector.*

Example 3 Which are row vectors and which are column vectors?

$$A = [5 \quad -3 \quad 0], \quad B = \begin{bmatrix} 7 \\ -4 \\ 3 \end{bmatrix}, \quad C = [-8 \quad 9 \quad 10 \quad 0 \quad \tfrac{1}{4}], \quad D = \begin{bmatrix} -3 \\ 1 \end{bmatrix}$$

Solution The row vectors are A and C. The column vectors are B and D.

The Transpose of a Matrix

The *transpose* of a matrix A, denoted A^T, is found by interchanging the rows and columns of A. That is, if $A = [a_{ij}]$, then $A^T = [a_{ji}]$.

Example 4   Find A^T, B^T, C^T, and D^T.

$$A = \begin{bmatrix} 2 & 4 & 6 \\ 9 & 8 & -2 \\ 0 & -1 & 4 \end{bmatrix}, \quad B = \begin{bmatrix} -3 & 0 & 4 \\ 7 & 1 & 6 \end{bmatrix},$$

$$C = \begin{bmatrix} -4 \\ 3 \\ 2 \end{bmatrix}, \quad D = [-1 \quad 2 \quad 3 \quad 0].$$

Solution

$$A^T = \begin{bmatrix} 2 & 9 & 0 \\ 4 & 8 & -1 \\ 6 & -2 & 4 \end{bmatrix}, \quad B^T = \begin{bmatrix} -3 & 7 \\ 0 & 1 \\ 4 & 6 \end{bmatrix},$$

$$C^T = [-4 \quad 3 \quad 2], \quad D^T = \begin{bmatrix} -1 \\ 2 \\ 3 \\ 0 \end{bmatrix}.$$

You have probably discovered in the margin exercises and Example 4 that if the dimensions of A are $m \times n$, then the dimensions of A^T are $n \times m$. Also, the transpose of a row vector is a column vector, and the transpose of a column vector is a row vector. The latter is a convenient method of saving space. That is, instead of writing

$$A = \begin{bmatrix} x_1 \\ x_2 \\ x_3 \end{bmatrix}$$

we may write

$$A^T = [x_1 \quad x_2 \quad x_3], \quad \text{or} \quad A = [x_1 \quad x_2 \quad x_3]^T.$$

Addition of Matrices

The *sum* of two matrices of the same dimensions is the matrix whose elements are the sums of corresponding elements of the given matrices. Formally, if $A = [a_{ij}]$ and $B = [b_{ij}]$, then $A + B = [a_{ij} + b_{ij}]$.

Note that matrix addition is defined only for matrices of the same dimensions.

Example 5   Find $A + B$ and $B + A$.

$$A = \begin{bmatrix} -4 & 0 \\ 3 & \frac{1}{4} \end{bmatrix}, \quad B = \begin{bmatrix} 7 & -5 \\ 2 & \frac{1}{2} \end{bmatrix}.$$

Solution

$$A + B = \begin{bmatrix} -4 + 7 & 0 + (-5) \\ 3 + 2 & \frac{1}{4} + \frac{1}{2} \end{bmatrix} = \begin{bmatrix} 3 & -5 \\ 5 & \frac{3}{4} \end{bmatrix},$$

$$B + A = \begin{bmatrix} 7 + (-4) & -5 + 0 \\ 2 + 3 & \frac{1}{2} + \frac{1}{4} \end{bmatrix} = \begin{bmatrix} 3 & -5 \\ 5 & \frac{3}{4} \end{bmatrix}.$$

For any matrices **A, B,** and **C,** of the same dimensions,

$A + B = B + A$ (Addition of matrices is commutative)

$A + (B + C) = (A + B) + C$ (Addition of matrices is associative)

We give a proof of the commutative law,

$$A + B = [a_{ij}] + [b_{ij}]$$

$$= [a_{ij} + b_{ij}] \qquad \text{(Definition of matrix addition)}$$

$$= [b_{ij} + a_{ij}] \qquad \text{(Addition of real numbers is commutative)}$$

$$= [b_{ij}] + [a_{ij}] \qquad \text{(Reverse of matrix addition)}$$

$$= B + A$$

A *zero matrix* is denoted by the capital letter O and is a matrix with all zero elements. If A and O are the same dimensions, then

$$A + O = O + A = A. \quad (O \text{ is the } \textit{additive identity})$$

The product of a constant and a matrix, a *scalar product*, is defined as follows.

The *scalar product* of a number c (sometimes called a *scalar*) and a matrix A is the matrix obtained by multiplying the elements of A by c. Formally, if $A = [a_{ij}]$, then $cA = [ca_{ij}]$.

Example 6   Find $4A$ and $(-1)A$.

$$A = \begin{bmatrix} -2 & 0 \\ 1 & 5 \end{bmatrix}$$

Solution

$$4A = \begin{bmatrix} 4(-2) & 4 \cdot 0 \\ 4 \cdot 1 & 4 \cdot 5 \end{bmatrix} = \begin{bmatrix} -8 & 0 \\ 4 & 20 \end{bmatrix},$$

$$(-1)A = \begin{bmatrix} -1(-2) & -1 \cdot 0 \\ -1 \cdot 1 & -1 \cdot 5 \end{bmatrix} = \begin{bmatrix} 2 & 0 \\ -1 & -5 \end{bmatrix}.$$

For real numbers we know that $-a$ represents the number we add to a to get 0. We call $-a$ the *additive inverse* of a. For matrices, $-A$ is the matrix we add to A to get the zero matrix O. Thus

$$A + (-1)A = (-1)A + A = O$$

(The additive inverse of A, $-A$, is $(-1)A$).

We subtract as follows.

The difference $A - B = A + (-1)B$. We subtract B from A by adding the additive inverse of B.

Note that A and B must be of the *same dimensions* in order to subtract one from the other.

Example 7   Find $A - B$.

$$A = \begin{bmatrix} -3 & 5 \\ 4 & 8 \end{bmatrix}, \quad B = \begin{bmatrix} 11 & -2 \\ 6 & 7 \end{bmatrix}.$$

$$A - B = A + (-1)B = \begin{bmatrix} -3 & 5 \\ 4 & 8 \end{bmatrix} + (-1)\begin{bmatrix} 11 & -2 \\ 6 & 7 \end{bmatrix}$$

$$= \begin{bmatrix} -3 & 5 \\ 4 & 8 \end{bmatrix} + \begin{bmatrix} -11 & 2 \\ -6 & -7 \end{bmatrix}$$

$$= \begin{bmatrix} -14 & 7 \\ -2 & 1 \end{bmatrix}.$$

Note that $A - B$ can be found directly by subtracting corresponding elements of B from those of A.

EXERCISE SET 3.3

Consider

$$A = \begin{bmatrix} 1 & 3 \\ 4 & 2 \end{bmatrix}, \quad B = \begin{bmatrix} -2 & 0 \\ -2 & -1 \end{bmatrix}, \quad C = \begin{bmatrix} -1 & -2 & -3 \\ 3 & 2 & 1 \end{bmatrix}, \quad \text{and} \quad D = \begin{bmatrix} 0 & 8 & -4 \\ 1 & 0 & -1 \end{bmatrix}.$$

Find:

1. The dimensions of A   **2.** The dimensions of B

3. The dimensions of C   **4.** The dimensions of D

5. $A + B$ **6.** $B + A$ **7.** $C + D$ **8.** $D + C$

9. $3A$ **10.** $3B$ **11.** $-5C$ **12.** $-6D$

13. $A - B$ **14.** $B - A$ **15.** $C - D$ **16.** $D - C$

17. $A + C$ **18.** $A + D$ **19.** kC **20.** kD

21. $A + O$ **22.** $O + D$ **23.** A^T **24.** B^T

25. C^T **26.** D^T **27.** $A^T + B^T$ **28.** $C^T + D^T$

29. For $[a_{ij}] = \begin{bmatrix} -4 & 5 \\ 0 & 9 \\ 1 & 3 \end{bmatrix}$, find a_{11}, a_{12}, a_{31}, a_{22}, a_{32}, and a_{21}.

30. For $[b_{ij}] = \begin{bmatrix} -2 & -3 & 0 \\ \frac{1}{4} & \frac{1}{2} & 1 \end{bmatrix}$, find b_{11}, b_{21}, b_{23}, b_{22}, b_{13}, and b_{12}.

31. Find X^T where $X = \begin{bmatrix} x_1 \\ x_2 \\ x_3 \\ x_4 \end{bmatrix}$.

32. Find Y^T where $Y = \begin{bmatrix} y_1 \\ y_2 \\ y_3 \\ y_4 \end{bmatrix}$.

3.4 MATRIX MULTIPLICATION

Summation Notation

Consider this sum.

$$a_1 + a_2 + a_3 + a_4$$

We can denote this sum using *summation notation,* which utilizes the Greek capital letter Σ (sigma).

$$\sum_{i=1}^{4} a_i$$

This is read "the sum of the numbers a_i from $i = 1$ to $i = 4$." To recover the original sum, substitute the numbers 1 through 4 successively into a_i and write plus signs between the results.

Example 1 Write summation notation for $2 + 4 + 6 + 8 + 10$.

Solution $$2 + 4 + 6 + 8 + 10 = \sum_{i=1}^{5} 2i$$

Example 2 Write summation notation for

$$a_1 + a_2 + a_3 + a_4 + \cdots + a_{19}.$$

The dots indicate that we are not writing all the terms in between.

Solution
$$a_1 + a_2 + a_3 + a_4 + \cdots + a_{19} = \sum_{i=1}^{19} a_i$$

Example 3   Express $\displaystyle\sum_{i=1}^{4} 3^i$ without using summation notation.

Solution
$$\sum_{i=1}^{4} 3^i = 3^1 + 3^2 + 3^3 + 3^4$$

Example 4   Express $\displaystyle\sum_{i=1}^{30} a_i b_i$ without using summation notation.

Solution
$$\sum_{i=1}^{30} a_i b_i = a_1 b_1 + a_2 b_2 + \cdots + a_{30} b_{30}$$

Matrix Multiplication

The product of two matrices A and B will *not* be defined as the matrix whose elements are products of corresponding elements of A and B. Some motivation for the definition of matrix multiplication is based on converting an equation such as

$$2x_1 - 4x_2 + 7x_3 = 8$$

to a product of a row vector and a column vector.

$$[2 \quad -4 \quad 7]\begin{bmatrix} x_1 \\ x_2 \\ x_3 \end{bmatrix} = [8], \quad \text{or} \quad 8$$

The *product* of a row vector A, a matrix of dimensions $1 \times n$, and a column vector B, a matrix of dimensions $n \times 1$, is the 1×1 matrix (or scalar) whose element is the sum of products of corresponding elements of A and B. Formally, if

$$A = [a_1 \quad a_2 \quad a_3 \cdots a_n] \quad \text{and} \quad B = \begin{bmatrix} b_1 \\ b_2 \\ b_3 \\ \vdots \\ b_n \end{bmatrix},$$

then

$$AB = a_1 b_1 + a_2 b_2 + a_3 b_3 + \cdots + a_n b_n$$

or, using summation notation,

$$AB = \sum_{i=1}^{n} a_i b_i.$$

Find the product for each of the following.

Example 5 $\begin{bmatrix} 2 & -4 & 7 \end{bmatrix} \begin{bmatrix} -1 \\ 0 \\ 5 \end{bmatrix} = [2(-1) - 4 \cdot 0 + 7 \cdot 5] = [33]$, or 33

Example 6 $\begin{bmatrix} \frac{1}{4} & -8 \end{bmatrix} \begin{bmatrix} 12 \\ 1 \end{bmatrix} = [\frac{1}{4} \cdot 12 - 8 \cdot 1] = [-5]$, or -5

Example 7 $\begin{bmatrix} -2 & 1 & 4 & -5 \end{bmatrix} \begin{bmatrix} x_1 \\ x_2 \\ x_3 \\ x_4 \end{bmatrix} = [-2x_1 + x_2 + 4x_3 - 5x_4]$, or

$$-2x_1 + x_2 + 4x_3 - 5x_4$$

To multiply the row vector A and the column vector B, the number of elements in A must be the same as the number of elements in B. The following illustration should help you remember this.

$$\begin{array}{cc} A & B \\ 1 \times n & m \times 1 \\ \end{array}$$
$$\llcorner \, n = m \, \lrcorner$$

Before we define multiplication of more general matrices, let us reconsider an example given earlier. A company makes two types of stereos. Type I requires 65 transistors, 50 capacitors, and 4 dials. Type II requires 85 transistors, 42 capacitors, and 6 dials. We can represent this information using a matrix.

	Transistors	Capacitors	Dials
Type I	65	50	4
Type II	85	42	6

Suppose the company wanted to make 20 stereos of Type I and 30 stereos of Type II. It would determine the number of transistors needed as follows:

$$20 \cdot 65 + 30 \cdot 85 = 3850.$$

It would determine the number of capacitors needed as follows:

$$20 \cdot 50 + 30 \cdot 42 = 2260.$$

It would determine the dials needed as follows:

$$20 \cdot 4 + 30 \cdot 6 = 260.$$

The entire procedure could be done using matrices as follows:

$$[20 \quad 30] \cdot \begin{bmatrix} 65 & 50 & 4 \\ 85 & 42 & 6 \end{bmatrix}$$

$$= [20 \cdot 65 + 30 \cdot 85 \quad 20 \cdot 50 + 30 \cdot 42 \quad 20 \cdot 4 + 30 \cdot 6]$$

$$= [3850 \quad 2260 \quad 260].$$

Some further motivation for multiplication of matrices is based on converting a system of equations such as

$$2x_1 - 3x_2 = 7$$
$$4x_1 + 5x_2 = 9,$$

to matrix form:

$$\begin{bmatrix} 2 & -3 \\ 4 & 5 \end{bmatrix} \begin{bmatrix} x_1 \\ x_2 \end{bmatrix} = \begin{bmatrix} 7 \\ 9 \end{bmatrix}.$$

Multiplying these matrices, we obtain the original equations. Note the similarity with the echelon tableau, Section 3.1.

> The *product* of two matrices A and B is the matrix $C = [c_{ij}]$, where c_{ij} is obtained by multiplying the ith row of A (as a vector) by the jth column of B (as a vector).

Example 8 Multiply.

$$[2 \quad 3] \begin{bmatrix} x & a \\ y & b \end{bmatrix} = [2x + 3y \quad 2a + 3b]$$

Mentally this product is found in two steps:

$$[\text{①} \quad \text{②}]$$

where

$$\text{①} \quad \text{is} \quad [\blacksquare\!\!\!\!\!\!\!] \begin{bmatrix} | \\ | \end{bmatrix},$$

and

$$\text{②} \quad \text{is} \quad [\blacksquare\!\!\!\!\!\!\!] \begin{bmatrix} & | \\ & | \end{bmatrix},$$

Example 9 Multiply.

$$[2 \quad 3]\begin{bmatrix} 1 & -2 \\ -8 & 4 \end{bmatrix} = [2 \cdot 1 + 3(-8) \quad 2(-2) + 3 \cdot 4] = [-22 \quad 8]$$

Example 10 Multiply.

$$\begin{bmatrix} 2 & 3 \\ -6 & 7 \end{bmatrix}\begin{bmatrix} x & a \\ y & b \end{bmatrix} = \begin{bmatrix} 2x + 3y & 2a + 3b \\ -6x + 7y & -6a + 7b \end{bmatrix}$$

Mentally this product is found in four steps:

$$\begin{bmatrix} ① & ② \\ ③ & ④ \end{bmatrix};$$

① $\begin{bmatrix} ▬ \end{bmatrix}\begin{bmatrix} ▮ \end{bmatrix}$, ② $\begin{bmatrix} ▬ \end{bmatrix}\begin{bmatrix} ▮ \end{bmatrix}$,

③ $\begin{bmatrix} ▬ \end{bmatrix}\begin{bmatrix} ▮ \end{bmatrix}$, ④ $\begin{bmatrix} ▬ \end{bmatrix}\begin{bmatrix} ▮ \end{bmatrix}$.

Example 11 Multiply.

$$\begin{bmatrix} 2 & 3 \\ -6 & 7 \end{bmatrix}\begin{bmatrix} 1 & -2 \\ -8 & 4 \end{bmatrix} = \begin{bmatrix} 2 \cdot 1 + 3(-8) & 2(-2) + 3 \cdot 4 \\ -6 \cdot 1 + 7(-8) & -6(-2) + 7 \cdot 4 \end{bmatrix}$$

$$= \begin{bmatrix} -22 & 8 \\ -62 & 40 \end{bmatrix}$$

So that we can carry out the multiplication of the rows of A and the columns of B, the number of columns in A must be the same as the number of rows in B. That is, if A has dimensions $m \times n$ and B has dimensions $p \times q$, then in order to multiply we must have $n = p$. In such a case we say that the matrices are *conformable*. The product matrix has dimensions $m \times q$. The following may help you remember this.

$$
\begin{array}{ccc}
A & & B \\
m \times n & & p \times q \\
& n = p &
\end{array}
$$

$$m \times q$$

(The dimensions of AB)

Example 12   Find AB and BA, if possible.

$$A = \begin{bmatrix} -2 & 1 \\ 4 & 0 \\ -3 & -5 \end{bmatrix}, \quad B = \begin{bmatrix} 2 & -1 & 0 & -7 \\ 4 & -3 & -1 & 0 \end{bmatrix}$$

Solution

$$AB = \begin{bmatrix} -2 \cdot 2 + 1 \cdot 4 & -2(-1) + 1(-3) & -2 \cdot 0 + 1(-1) & -2(-7) + 1 \cdot 0 \\ 4 \cdot 2 + 0 \cdot 4 & 4(-1) + 0(-3) & 4 \cdot 0 + 0(-1) & 4(-7) + 0 \cdot 0 \\ -3 \cdot 2 - 5 \cdot 4 & -3(-1) - 5(-3) & -3 \cdot 0 - 5(-1) & -3(-7) - 5 \cdot 0 \end{bmatrix}$$

$$= \begin{bmatrix} 0 & -1 & -1 & 14 \\ 8 & -4 & 0 & -28 \\ -26 & 18 & 5 & 21 \end{bmatrix}$$

BA cannot be found because B and A are not conformable; that is, the number of columns in B is not the same as the number of rows in A.

The products AB and BA of a row matrix A and a column matrix B are of special interest.

Example 13   Find AB and BA, if possible.

$$A = [-1 \quad 2 \quad -5], \quad B = \begin{bmatrix} 4 \\ 0 \\ -2 \end{bmatrix}$$

Solution A is a 1×3 matrix and B is a 3×1 matrix. Thus the product AB is a 1×1 matrix given by

$$AB = [-1 \quad 2 \quad -5] \begin{bmatrix} 4 \\ 0 \\ -2 \end{bmatrix} = [-1 \cdot 4 + 2 \cdot 0 - 5(-2)] = [6], \quad \text{or} \quad 6.$$

B is a 3×1 matrix and A is a 1×3 matrix. Thus the product BA is a 3×3 matrix given by

$$BA = \begin{bmatrix} 4 \\ 0 \\ -2 \end{bmatrix} [-1 \quad 2 \quad -5] = \begin{bmatrix} 4(-1) & 4 \cdot 2 & 4(-5) \\ 0(-1) & 0 \cdot 2 & 0(-5) \\ -2(-1) & -2 \cdot 2 & -2(-5) \end{bmatrix}$$

$$= \begin{bmatrix} -4 & 8 & -20 \\ 0 & 0 & 0 \\ 2 & -4 & 10 \end{bmatrix}.$$

Note that each element of BA is the product of two numbers.

We have seen that matrix multiplication is not commutative. In some cases, there are matrices A and B such that $AB = BA$. In such cases we say that the matrices *commute*.

The notion of *conformability* is often used in many contexts with matrices. For example, matrices A and B are *equality conformable* if A and B have the same dimensions. A and B are *addition conformable* if A and B have the same dimensions. A and B are *multiplication conformable* if the number of columns in A is the same as the number of rows in B.

For any conformable matrices A, B, and C,

$$(AB)C = A(BC) = ABC \qquad \text{(Multiplication of matrices is associative)}$$

$$A(B+C) = AB + AC \qquad \text{(Multiplication of matrices is distributive)}$$

Identity Matrices

The letter I is used to represent square matrices such as

$$I = \begin{bmatrix} 1 & 0 \\ 0 & 1 \end{bmatrix}, \quad \text{and} \quad I = \begin{bmatrix} 1 & 0 & 0 \\ 0 & 1 & 0 \\ 0 & 0 & 1 \end{bmatrix}.$$

These square matrices have 1's extending from the upper left down to the lower right along what is called the *main diagonal*. The rest of the elements are 0.

For any square matrix A of dimensions $n \times n$,

$$AI = IA = A \quad \text{(I is a multiplicative identity)},$$

where I is the square matrix, described above, of dimensions $n \times n$.

We also have the following.

For any matrix A with exactly n rows,

$$IA = A,$$

where I is the square matrix, described above, of dimensions $n \times n$.

Matrix Inverses

The equation in real numbers, or *scalar* equation,

$$ax = b, \text{ where } a \text{ is real,}$$

can be solved for x by multiplying both sides of the equation by a^{-1}, the inverse of a:

$$a^{-1}ax = a^{-1}b.$$

Since $a^{-1}a = aa^{-1} = 1$, the multiplicative identity element such that $1x = x$, we obtain

$$x = a^{-1}b.$$

For scalar numbers

$$a^{-1} = \frac{1}{a}, \text{ for } a \neq 0,$$

so that

$$x = \frac{b}{a}.$$

Let us see how we can use matrices to represent and solve systems of equations. Consider the system

$$3x_1 + 2x_2 = 1,$$

$$5x_1 + 3x_2 = -2.$$

We first express this system as a matrix equation.

$$\begin{bmatrix} 3 & 2 \\ 5 & 3 \end{bmatrix} \begin{bmatrix} x_1 \\ x_2 \end{bmatrix} = \begin{bmatrix} 1 \\ -2 \end{bmatrix}$$

To see that this is correct, multiply the matrices on the left and use the fact that matrices are equal if corresponding elements are equal. We let

$$A = \text{the } coefficient \text{ } matrix = \begin{bmatrix} 3 & 2 \\ 5 & 3 \end{bmatrix}, \quad X = \begin{bmatrix} x_1 \\ x_2 \end{bmatrix}, \quad \text{and} \quad B = \begin{bmatrix} 1 \\ -2 \end{bmatrix}.$$

Then

$$AX = B.$$

The solution of this *matrix* equation *cannot* be written as the quotient

$$X = \frac{B}{A}.$$

Multiplying this equation by A on the *left*, yields

$$AX = B,$$

while multiplying the same equation by A on the *right*, yields

$$XA = B.$$

This implies that the two products AX and XA commute, that is,

$$AX = XA.$$

This is not always true. As an example, consider

$$AX = B,$$

where

$$A = \begin{bmatrix} 3 & 2 \\ 5 & 3 \end{bmatrix}, \quad X = \begin{bmatrix} x_1 \\ x_2 \end{bmatrix}, \quad \text{and} \quad B = \begin{bmatrix} 1 \\ -2 \end{bmatrix}.$$

Then

$$AX = \begin{bmatrix} 3 & 2 \\ 5 & 3 \end{bmatrix}\begin{bmatrix} x_1 \\ x_2 \end{bmatrix} = \begin{bmatrix} 3x_1 + 2x_2 \\ 5x_1 + 3x_2 \end{bmatrix} = \begin{bmatrix} 1 \\ -2 \end{bmatrix}.$$

On the other hand

$$XA = \begin{bmatrix} x_1 \\ x_2 \end{bmatrix}\begin{bmatrix} 3 & 2 \\ 5 & 3 \end{bmatrix}$$

is not possible since the matrices X and A in the product XA are not conformable. Thus, **division by a matrix is not possible.**

However, we can replace division by multiplication by the **matrix inverse.** For example, consider solving

$$AX = B$$

for X as we solved $ax = b$ for x. To do this we define the **multiplicative inverse,** or simply the **inverse,** of a square matrix A to be the square matrix A^{-1} with the property that (as for the scalar a)

$$A^{-1}A = AA^{-1} = I,$$

where I is the multiplicative identity element previously defined.

Now we multiply both sides of $AX = B$ by A^{-1} on the left and obtain

$$A^{-1}AX = A^{-1}B.$$

Since $A^{-1}A = I$ and $IX = X$, we obtain

$$X = A^{-1}B.$$

If we knew the inverse matrix A^{-1}, then we could find the solution of the system of equations by computing the product $A^{-1}B$.

In the present example, we give A^{-1} without explaining how we found it:

$$A^{-1} = \begin{bmatrix} -3 & 2 \\ 5 & -3 \end{bmatrix}.$$

(A procedure for computing matrix inverses will be developed in Section 3.8.)

Compare the following:

$$AX = B \qquad \begin{bmatrix} 3 & 2 \\ 5 & 3 \end{bmatrix}\begin{bmatrix} x_1 \\ x_2 \end{bmatrix} = \begin{bmatrix} 1 \\ -2 \end{bmatrix},$$

$$X = A^{-1}B \qquad \begin{bmatrix} x_1 \\ x_2 \end{bmatrix} = \begin{bmatrix} -3 & 2 \\ 5 & -3 \end{bmatrix}\begin{bmatrix} 1 \\ -2 \end{bmatrix}$$

$$= \begin{bmatrix} -7 \\ 11 \end{bmatrix}.$$

From equality of matrices we can read off the solution. That is,

$$x_1 = -7 \quad \text{and} \quad x_2 = 11,$$

or, simply, the solution is $(-7, 11)$.

Let us relate this procedure to the echelon method. We consider the echelon tableau for the previous system.

x_1	x_2	1
3	2	1
5	3	-2

The entries to the left of the double vertical line make up the coefficient matrix A. The entries to the right make up the matrix B. When the echelon method is completed we have the following tableau.

x_1	x_2	1
1	0	-7
0	1	11

The entries to the left of the double vertical line make up the identity matrix I. Those to the right make up the solution matrix. The steps of the echelon method have the same effect as multiplying by A^{-1} without actually knowing what it is.

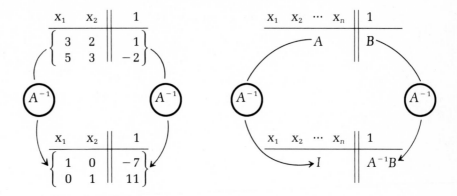

It is important to know the meaning and notation of matrix inverses. It is less important to know how to compute the inverse although the preceding is the basis for such a method.

Augmented Matrices

For later purposes we need some additional notation. Let

$$X = [x_1 \quad x_2] \quad \text{and} \quad Y = [y_1 \quad y_2].$$

Then we can form the *augmented* matrix

$$[X \quad Y] = [x_1 \quad x_2 \mid y_1 \quad y_2].$$

An augmented matrix is simply a particular way of putting two matrices together to form a new matrix. Sometimes, as above, a dashed line is used to indicate that $[X \quad Y]$ can be *partitioned* into X and Y.

Since the matrices X and Y have the same dimensions, we can also form the augmented matrix

$$\begin{bmatrix} X \\ Y \end{bmatrix} = \begin{bmatrix} x_1 & x_2 \\ y_1 & y_2 \end{bmatrix}.$$

When forming augmented matrices, the resulting array must be rectangular; that is, the matrices must conform. Thus, if $Z = [z_1 \quad z_2 \quad z_3]$, we can form the augmented matrix $[X \quad Z]$ but not $[\begin{smallmatrix} X \\ Z \end{smallmatrix}]$.

Suppose

$$A = \begin{bmatrix} 3 & 5 \\ 1 & -2 \end{bmatrix} \quad \text{and} \quad I = \begin{bmatrix} 1 & 0 \\ 0 & 1 \end{bmatrix}.$$

Then we can define an augmented matrix A' by

$$A' = [A \quad I] = \begin{bmatrix} 3 & 5 & \vdots & 1 & 0 \\ 1 & -2 & \vdots & 0 & 1 \end{bmatrix}$$

and another augmented matrix A'' by

$$A'' = \begin{bmatrix} A \\ I \end{bmatrix} = \begin{bmatrix} 3 & 5 \\ 1 & -2 \\ \hline 1 & 0 \\ 0 & 1 \end{bmatrix}.$$

Sometimes it is necessary to find the *transpose* of an augmented matrix. To do that, *first* form the augmented matrix and *then* form the transpose in the usual manner. Thus,

$$[X \quad Y]^T = \begin{bmatrix} x_1 \\ x_2 \\ \cdots \\ y_1 \\ y_2 \end{bmatrix} \quad \text{and} \quad \begin{bmatrix} X \\ Y \end{bmatrix}^T = \begin{bmatrix} x_1 & \vdots & y_1 \\ x_2 & \vdots & y_2 \end{bmatrix}.$$

EXERCISE SET 3.4

Find AB and BA, if possible.

1. $A = [-2 \quad 1]$, $B = \begin{bmatrix} 3 \\ -4 \end{bmatrix}$

2. $A = [-1 \quad -2]$, $B = \begin{bmatrix} 6 \\ -7 \end{bmatrix}$

3. $A = [2 \quad 0 \quad -4]$, $B = \begin{bmatrix} 9 \\ -5 \\ \frac{1}{4} \end{bmatrix}$

4. $A = [-3 \quad 6 \quad 8]$, $B = \begin{bmatrix} 5 \\ \frac{1}{2} \\ 1 \end{bmatrix}$

5. $A = \begin{bmatrix} 1 & 2 & 0 \\ -1 & 0 & 4 \\ 2 & 5 & 6 \end{bmatrix}$, $B = \begin{bmatrix} 3 & -4 & 1 \\ 2 & -1 & 0 \\ -3 & 2 & 1 \end{bmatrix}$

6. $A = \begin{bmatrix} -1 & 0 & 0 \\ 0 & -1 & 0 \\ 0 & 0 & -1 \end{bmatrix}$, $B = \begin{bmatrix} 2 & -5 & 1 \\ -4 & 4 & 3 \\ 5 & 6 & 9 \end{bmatrix}$

7. $A = [-4 \quad 1 \quad 3]$, $B = \begin{bmatrix} -4 & 2 \\ 1 & 0 \\ 6 & -9 \end{bmatrix}$

8. $A = \begin{bmatrix} -2 & 3 \\ 1 & 0 \\ -5 & 4 \end{bmatrix}$, $B = \begin{bmatrix} 2 \\ 3 \end{bmatrix}$

9. Find AB.

$$A = \begin{bmatrix} 1 & 0 & 2 \\ 5 & 0 & 1 \\ -1 & 0 & 4 \end{bmatrix}, \quad B = \begin{bmatrix} 0 & 0 & 0 \\ 1 & 3 & 7 \\ 0 & 0 & 0 \end{bmatrix}.$$

10. Find two matrices A and B each of dimensions 2×2, such that $A \neq 0$ and $B \neq 0$ but $AB = 0$. [*Hint.* See Exercise 9.]

11. Write the system of equations of Exercise 17 in matrix form.

12. Write the system of equations of Exercise 18 in matrix form.

13. Write the system of equations of Exercise 21 in matrix form.

14. Write the system of equations of Exercise 22 in matrix form.

Write as separate equations:

15. $\begin{bmatrix} 1 & 2 \\ 4 & -3 \end{bmatrix} \begin{bmatrix} x_1 \\ x_2 \end{bmatrix} = \begin{bmatrix} -1 \\ 2 \end{bmatrix}$

16. $\begin{bmatrix} 2 & 4 \\ 3 & 5 \end{bmatrix} \begin{bmatrix} x_1 \\ x_2 \end{bmatrix} = \begin{bmatrix} -2 \\ -4 \end{bmatrix}$

In Exercises 17 through 22, a system of equations is given, together with the inverse of the coefficient matrix. Use the matrix inverse to solve the system.

17. $\begin{aligned} 11x_1 + 3x_2 &= -4, \\ 7x_1 + 2x_2 &= 5 \end{aligned}$ $A^{-1} = \begin{bmatrix} 2 & -3 \\ -7 & 11 \end{bmatrix}$

18. $\begin{aligned} 8x_1 + 5x_2 &= -6, \\ 5x_1 + 3x_2 &= 2 \end{aligned}$ $A^{-1} = \begin{bmatrix} -3 & 5 \\ 5 & -8 \end{bmatrix}$

19. $\begin{aligned} 4x_1 - 3x_2 &= 2, \\ x_1 + 2x_2 &= -1 \end{aligned}$ $A^{-1} = \frac{1}{11} \begin{bmatrix} 2 & 3 \\ -1 & 4 \end{bmatrix}$

20. $\begin{aligned} 3x_1 + 5x_2 &= -4, \\ 2x_1 + 4x_2 &= -2 \end{aligned}$ $A^{-1} = \frac{1}{2} \begin{bmatrix} 4 & -5 \\ -2 & 3 \end{bmatrix}$

21. $\begin{aligned} 3x_1 + x_2 &= 2, \\ x_1 - x_2 + 2x_3 &= -4 \\ x_1 + x_2 + x_3 &= 5 \end{aligned}$

$A^{-1} = \frac{1}{8} \begin{bmatrix} 3 & 1 & -2 \\ -1 & -3 & 6 \\ -2 & 2 & 4 \end{bmatrix}$

22. $\begin{aligned} x_1 + x_3 &= -4, \\ 2x_1 + x_2 &= -3 \\ x_1 - x_2 + x_3 &= 1 \end{aligned}$

$A^{-1} = -\frac{1}{2} \begin{bmatrix} 1 & -1 & -1 \\ -2 & 0 & 2 \\ -3 & 1 & 1 \end{bmatrix}$

Consider

$$A = \begin{bmatrix} 0 & -1 \\ 1 & 2 \end{bmatrix} \quad \text{and} \quad B = \begin{bmatrix} -1 & 1 \\ 3 & 0 \end{bmatrix}.$$

23. Show that $(A + B)(A + B) \neq A^2 + 2AB + B^2$ where $AA = A^2$ and $BB = B^2$.

24. Show that $(A - B)(A + B) \neq A^2 - B^2$.

25. For $X = \begin{bmatrix} a \\ b \\ c \end{bmatrix}$ and $Y = \begin{bmatrix} e \\ f \\ g \end{bmatrix}$, find $\begin{bmatrix} X \\ Y \end{bmatrix}^T$.

26. For $A = [-2 \quad 3 \quad 7]$ and $O = [0 \quad 0 \quad 0]$, find $[A \quad O]$.

Given

$$A = \begin{bmatrix} 2 & -1 & 3 \\ 4 & 1 & 0 \end{bmatrix} \quad \text{and} \quad B = \begin{bmatrix} 0 & 1 & -2 \\ 1 & -3 & 7 \end{bmatrix}.$$

27. Find $[A \quad B]$ and $[A \quad B]^T$.

28. Find $\begin{bmatrix} A \\ B \end{bmatrix}$ and $\begin{bmatrix} A \\ B \end{bmatrix}^T$.

29. Find $\begin{bmatrix} A^T \\ B^T \end{bmatrix}$. Is $[A \quad B]^T = \begin{bmatrix} A^T \\ B^T \end{bmatrix}$?

30. Find $[A^T \quad B^T]$. Is $\begin{bmatrix} A \\ B \end{bmatrix}^T = [A^T \quad B^T]$?

3.5 DETERMINANTS AND CRAMER'S RULE

With every square matrix is associated a number called its determinant, defined as follows for 2×2 matrices.

DEFINITION   The determinant of the matrix $\begin{bmatrix} a & c \\ b & d \end{bmatrix}$ is denoted $\begin{vmatrix} a & c \\ b & d \end{vmatrix}$ and is defined as follows:

$$\begin{vmatrix} a & c \\ b & d \end{vmatrix} = ad - bc.$$

Example 1   Evaluate $\begin{vmatrix} \sqrt{2} & -3 \\ -4 & -\sqrt{2} \end{vmatrix}$.

$$\begin{vmatrix} \sqrt{2} & -3 \\ -4 & -\sqrt{2} \end{vmatrix} \qquad \text{(The arrows indicate the products involved.)}$$

$$= \sqrt{2}(-\sqrt{2}) - (-4)(-3) = -2 - 12 = -14$$

Determinants have many uses. One of these is in solving systems of non-homogeneous linear equations, where the number of variables is the same as the number of equations. Let us consider a system of two equations:

$$a_1 x + b_1 y = c_1$$
$$a_2 x + b_2 y = c_2.$$

Using the methods of the preceding sections we can solve. We obtain

$$x = \frac{c_1 b_2 - c_2 b_1}{a_1 b_2 - a_2 b_1},$$

$$y = \frac{a_1 c_2 - a_2 c_1}{a_1 b_2 - a_2 b_1}.$$

The numerators and denominators of the expressions for x and y are determinants:

$$x = \frac{\begin{vmatrix} c_1 & b_1 \\ c_2 & b_2 \end{vmatrix}}{\begin{vmatrix} a_1 & b_1 \\ a_2 & b_2 \end{vmatrix}}, \quad y = \frac{\begin{vmatrix} a_1 & c_1 \\ a_2 & c_2 \end{vmatrix}}{\begin{vmatrix} a_1 & b_1 \\ a_2 & b_2 \end{vmatrix}}.$$

The above equations make sense only if the denominator determinant is not 0. If the denominator *is* 0, then one of two things happens.

1. If the denominator is 0 and the other two determinants are also 0, then the system of equations is dependent.
2. If the denominator is 0 and at least one of the other determinants is not 0, then the system is inconsistent.

The equations with determinants above describe *Cramer's rule* for solving systems of equations. To use this rule, we compute the three determinants and compute x and y as shown above. Note that the denominator in both cases contains the coefficients of x and y, in the same position as in the original equations. For x the numerator is obtained by replacing the x-coefficients (the a's) by the c's. For y, the numerator is obtained by replacing the y-coefficients (the b's) by the c's.

Example 2   Solve, using Cramer's rule.

$$2x + 5y = 7$$

$$5x - 2y = -3$$

Solution

$$x = \frac{\begin{vmatrix} 7 & 5 \\ -3 & -2 \end{vmatrix}}{\begin{vmatrix} 2 & 5 \\ 5 & -2 \end{vmatrix}} = \frac{7(-2) - (-3)5}{2(-2) - 5 \cdot 5} = -\frac{1}{29}$$

$$y = \frac{\begin{vmatrix} 2 & 7 \\ 5 & -3 \end{vmatrix}}{\begin{vmatrix} 2 & 5 \\ 5 & -2 \end{vmatrix}} = \frac{2(-3) - 5 \cdot 7}{-29} = \frac{41}{29}$$

The solution is $\left(-\dfrac{1}{29}, \dfrac{41}{29} \right)$.

Three-by-Three Determinants

DEFINITION   The *determinant* of a three-by-three matrix is defined as follows:

$$\begin{vmatrix} a_1 & b_1 & c_1 \\ a_2 & b_2 & c_2 \\ a_3 & b_3 & c_3 \end{vmatrix} = a_1 \cdot \begin{vmatrix} b_2 & c_2 \\ b_3 & c_3 \end{vmatrix} - a_2 \cdot \begin{vmatrix} b_1 & c_1 \\ b_3 & c_3 \end{vmatrix} + a_3 \cdot \begin{vmatrix} b_1 & c_1 \\ b_2 & c_2 \end{vmatrix}.$$

The two-by-two determinants on the right can be found by crossing out the row and column in which the a coefficient occurs.

Example 3   Evaluate.

$$\begin{vmatrix} -1 & 0 & 1 \\ -5 & 1 & -1 \\ 4 & 8 & 1 \end{vmatrix} = -1\begin{vmatrix} 1 & -1 \\ 8 & 1 \end{vmatrix} - (-5)\cdot\begin{vmatrix} 0 & 1 \\ 8 & 1 \end{vmatrix} + 4\cdot\begin{vmatrix} 0 & 1 \\ 1 & -1 \end{vmatrix}$$

$$= -1(1 + 8) + 5(-8) + 4(-1)$$

$$= -9 - 40 - 4 = -53$$

Let us consider three equations in three variables. Consider

$$a_1x + b_1y + c_1z = d_1,$$

$$a_2x + b_2y + c_2z = d_2,$$

$$a_3x + b_3y + c_3z = d_3,$$

and the following determinants:

$$D = \begin{vmatrix} a_1 & b_1 & c_1 \\ a_2 & b_2 & c_2 \\ a_3 & b_3 & c_3 \end{vmatrix}, \quad D_x = \begin{vmatrix} d_1 & b_1 & c_1 \\ d_2 & b_2 & c_2 \\ d_3 & b_3 & c_3 \end{vmatrix},$$

$$D_y = \begin{vmatrix} a_1 & d_1 & c_1 \\ a_2 & d_2 & c_2 \\ a_3 & d_3 & c_3 \end{vmatrix}, \quad D_z = \begin{vmatrix} a_1 & b_1 & d_1 \\ a_2 & b_2 & d_2 \\ a_3 & b_3 & d_3 \end{vmatrix}.$$

If we solve the system of equations, we obtain the following:

$$x = \frac{D_x}{D}, \quad y = \frac{D_y}{D}, \quad z = \frac{D_z}{D}.$$

Note that we obtain the determinant D_x in the numerator for x from D by replacing the x-coefficients by d_1, d_2, and d_3. A similar thing happens with D_y and D_z. We have thus extended *Cramer's rule* to solve systems of three equations in three variables. As before, when $D = 0$, Cramer's rule cannot be used. If $D = 0$, and D_x, D_y, and D_z are 0, the system is dependent. If $D = 0$ and one of D_x, D_y, or D_z is not zero, then the system is inconsistent.

Example 4   Solve, using Cramer's rule.

$$x - 3y + 7z = 13$$

$$x + y + z = 1$$

$$x - 2y + 3z = 4$$

Solution

$$D = \begin{vmatrix} 1 & -3 & 7 \\ 1 & 1 & 1 \\ 1 & -2 & 3 \end{vmatrix} = -10, \qquad D_x = \begin{vmatrix} 13 & -3 & 7 \\ 1 & 1 & 1 \\ 4 & -2 & 3 \end{vmatrix} = 20,$$

$$D_y = \begin{vmatrix} 1 & 13 & 7 \\ 1 & 1 & 1 \\ 1 & 4 & 3 \end{vmatrix} = -6, \qquad D_z = \begin{vmatrix} 1 & -3 & 13 \\ 1 & 1 & 1 \\ 1 & -2 & 4 \end{vmatrix} = -24.$$

Then

$$x = \frac{D_x}{D} = \frac{20}{-10} = -2, \qquad y = \frac{D_y}{D} = \frac{-6}{10} = \frac{3}{5}, \qquad z = \frac{D_z}{D} = \frac{-24}{-10} = \frac{12}{5}.$$

The solution is $(-2, \frac{3}{5}, \frac{12}{5})$. In practice, it is not necessary to evaluate D_z. When we have found values for x and y we can substitute them into one of the equations and find z.

EXERCISE SET 3.5

Evaluate.

1. $\begin{vmatrix} -2 & -\sqrt{5} \\ -\sqrt{5} & 3 \end{vmatrix}$
2. $\begin{vmatrix} \sqrt{5} & -3 \\ 4 & 2 \end{vmatrix}$
3. $\begin{vmatrix} x & 4 \\ x & x_2 \end{vmatrix}$
4. $\begin{vmatrix} y^2 & -2 \\ y & 3 \end{vmatrix}$

5. $\begin{vmatrix} 3 & 1 & 2 \\ -2 & 3 & 1 \\ 3 & 4 & -6 \end{vmatrix}$
6. $\begin{vmatrix} 3 & -2 & 1 \\ 2 & 4 & 3 \\ -1 & 5 & 1 \end{vmatrix}$
7. $\begin{vmatrix} x & 0 & -1 \\ 2 & x & x^2 \\ -3 & x & 1 \end{vmatrix}$
8. $\begin{vmatrix} x & 1 & -1 \\ x^2 & x & x \\ 0 & x & 1 \end{vmatrix}$

Solve, using Cramer's rule.

9. $-2x + 4y = 3$
$3x - 7y = 1$

10. $5x - 4y = -3$
$7x + 2y = 6$

11. $\sqrt{3}\,x + \pi y = -5$
$\pi x - \sqrt{3}\,y = 4$

12. $\pi x - \sqrt{5}\,y = 2$
$\sqrt{5}\,x + \pi y = -3$

13. $3x + 2y - z = 4$
$3x - 2y + z = 5$
$4x - 5y - z = -1$

14. $3x - y + 2z = 1$
$x - y + 2z = 3$
$-2x + 3y + z = 1$

15. $6y + 6z = -1$
$8x + 6z = -1$
$4x + 9y = 8$

16. $3x + 5y = 2$
$2x - 3z = 7$
$4y + 2z = -1$

■ ──

Solve

17. $\begin{vmatrix} x & 5 \\ -4 & x \end{vmatrix} = 24$
18. $\begin{vmatrix} y & 2 \\ 3 & y \end{vmatrix} = y$
19. $\begin{vmatrix} x & -3 \\ -1 & x \end{vmatrix} \geqslant 0$

20. $\begin{vmatrix} y & -5 \\ -2 & y \end{vmatrix} < 0$
21. $\begin{vmatrix} x+3 & 4 \\ x-3 & 5 \end{vmatrix} = -7$
22. $\begin{vmatrix} m+2 & -3 \\ m+5 & -4 \end{vmatrix} = 3m - 5$

23. $\begin{vmatrix} 2 & x & 1 \\ 1 & 2 & -1 \\ 3 & 4 & -2 \end{vmatrix} = -6$ **24.** $\begin{vmatrix} x & 2 & x \\ 3 & -1 & 1 \\ 1 & -2 & 2 \end{vmatrix} = -10$

Rewrite each expression using determinants. Answers may vary.

25. $2L + 2W$ **26.** $\pi r + \pi h$ **27.** $a^2 + b^2$

28. $\frac{1}{2}h(a + b)$ **29.** $2\pi r^2 + 2\pi rh$ **30.** $x^2y^2 - Q^2$

3.6 MORE ON DETERMINANTS: DETERMINANTS OF HIGHER ORDER

Minors

We want to give a definition of the determinant of any square matrix. We shall restrict our attention to square matrices throughout this section.

DEFINITION   **In a matrix $[a_{ij}]$, the *minor* M_{ij} of an element a_{ij} is the determinant of the matrix found by deleting the *i*th row and *j*th column.**

Example 1   Find M_{11} and M_{23} for the matrix

$$\begin{bmatrix} -8 & 0 & 6 \\ 4 & -6 & 7 \\ -1 & -3 & 5 \end{bmatrix}.$$

Solution   To find M_{11} we delete the first row and the first column.

$$\begin{bmatrix} -8 & 0 & 6 \\ 4 & -6 & 7 \\ -1 & -3 & 5 \end{bmatrix}$$

We calculate the determinant of the matrix formed by the remaining elements.

$$M_{11} = \begin{vmatrix} -6 & 7 \\ -3 & 5 \end{vmatrix} = (-6) \cdot 5 - (-3) \cdot 7 = -30 - (-21) = -30 + 21 = -9$$

To find M_{23} we delete the second row and the third column.

$$\begin{bmatrix} -8 & 0 & 6 \\ 4 & -6 & 7 \\ -1 & -3 & 5 \end{bmatrix}$$

We calculate the determinant of the matrix formed by the remaining elements.

$$M_{23} = \begin{vmatrix} -8 & 0 \\ -1 & -3 \end{vmatrix} = -8(-3) - (-1)0 = 24$$

DEFINITION   In a matrix $[a_{ij}]$, the *cofactor* of an element a_{ij} is denoted A_{ij} and is given by

$$A_{ij} = (-1)^{i+j}M_{ij},$$

where M_{ij} is the minor of a_{ij}. In other words, to find the cofactor of an element, find its minor and multiply it by $(-1)^{i+j}$.

Note that $(-1)^{i+j}$ is 1 if $i + j$ is even and is -1 if $i + j$ is odd. Thus in calculating a cofactor, find the minor. Then add the number of the row and the number of the column, $i + j$. If this number is odd, change the sign of the minor. If this number is even, leave the minor as is.*

Example 2   In the matrix of Example 1, find A_{11} and A_{23}.

Solution   In Example 1, we found that $M_{11} = -9$. In A_{11} the sum of the subscripts is even, so

$$A_{11} = -9.$$

In Example 1, we found that $M_{23} = 24$. In A_{23} the sum of the subscripts is odd, so

$$A_{23} = -24.$$

Evaluating Determinants Using Cofactors

Consider the matrix A given by

$$A = \begin{bmatrix} a_{11} & a_{12} & a_{13} \\ a_{21} & a_{22} & a_{23} \\ a_{31} & a_{32} & a_{33} \end{bmatrix}.$$

The determinant of the matrix, denoted $|A|$ can be found as follows.

$$|A| = a_{11}A_{11} + a_{21}A_{21} + a_{31}A_{31}$$

That is, multiply each element of the first column by its cofactor and add.

---

*$(-1)^{i+j}$ can also be found by counting through the matrix horizontally and/or vertically, starting with a_{11} and $(+)$, saying $+, -, +, -$, and so on, until you come to a_{ij}.
   Start here $(+)$.

$$\begin{bmatrix} a_{11}^{+} \rightarrow^{-} \rightarrow^{+} \rightarrow & \downarrow^{-} \\ & \downarrow^{+} \\ & \downarrow^{-} \\ \leftarrow \leftarrow & a_{ij}^{+} \end{bmatrix}$$ The path does not matter.

This can be expressed as follows.

$$|A| = a_{11} \cdot \begin{vmatrix} a_{22} & a_{23} \\ a_{32} & a_{33} \end{vmatrix} - a_{21} \cdot \begin{vmatrix} a_{12} & a_{13} \\ a_{32} & a_{33} \end{vmatrix} + a_{31} \cdot \begin{vmatrix} a_{12} & a_{13} \\ a_{22} & a_{23} \end{vmatrix}$$

The last line is equivalent to the definition on p. 155. It can be shown that $|A|$ can be found by picking *any* row or column, multiplying each element by its cofactor, and adding. This is called *expanding* the determinant about a row or column. We just expanded $|A|$ about the first column. We now define the determinant of any square matrix.

> For any $n \times n$, $n > 1$, square matrix A we define the determinant of A, denoted $|A|$, to be that number found as follows. Pick any row or column. Multiply each element in that row or column by its cofactor and add the results. The determinant of a 1×1 matrix is simply the element of the matrix.

The value of a determinant will be the same no matter how it is evaluated.

Example 3 Consider the matrix A of Example 1. Find $|A|$ by expanding about the third row.

Solution $|A| = (-1)A_{31} + (-3)A_{32} + 5A_{33}$

$$= (-1)(-1)^{3+1} \cdot \begin{vmatrix} 0 & 6 \\ -6 & 7 \end{vmatrix} + (-3)(-1)^{3+2} \cdot \begin{vmatrix} -8 & 6 \\ 4 & 7 \end{vmatrix}$$

$$+ 5(-1)^{3+3} \cdot \begin{vmatrix} -8 & 0 \\ 4 & -6 \end{vmatrix}$$

$$= (-1) \cdot 1 \cdot [0 \cdot 7 - (-6)6] + (-3)(-1)[-8 \cdot 7 - 4 \cdot 6]$$

$$+ 5 \cdot 1 \cdot [-8(-6) - 4 \cdot 0]$$

$$= -[36] + 3[-80] + 5[48]$$

$$= -36 - 240 + 240$$

$$= -36$$

Properties of Determinants

We can simplify the evaluation of determinants using the following properties.

THEOREM 1   If a row (or column) of a matrix A has all elements 0, then $|A| = 0$.

Proof. Just expand the determinant about the row (or column) that has all 0's.

Example 4 Evaluate.

$$\begin{vmatrix} 0 & 6 \\ 0 & 7 \end{vmatrix} = 0$$

Example 5 Evaluate.

$$\begin{vmatrix} 4 & 5 & -7 \\ 0 & 0 & 0 \\ -3 & 9 & 6 \end{vmatrix} = 0$$

THEOREM 2 If two rows (or columns) of a matrix A are interchanged to obtain a new matrix B, then $|A| = -|B|$.

Proof. Pick one of the rows (or columns) to be interchanged and expand $|A|$ about that row. Use that same row to expand $|B|$. For that row each $(-1)^{i+j}$ has changed signs, so $|A| = -|B|$.

Example 6

$$\begin{vmatrix} 6 & 7 & 8 \\ 4 & 1 & 2 \\ 2 & 9 & 0 \end{vmatrix} = -1 \cdot \begin{vmatrix} 6 & 8 & 7 \\ 4 & 2 & 1 \\ 2 & 0 & 9 \end{vmatrix}$$

Example 7

$$\begin{vmatrix} -6 & 8 \\ 4 & -3 \end{vmatrix} = -1 \cdot \begin{vmatrix} 4 & -3 \\ -6 & 8 \end{vmatrix}$$

THEOREM 3 If two rows (or columns) of a matrix A are the same, then $|A| = 0$.

Proof. Interchanging the rows (or columns) does not change A. Thus by Theorem 2, $|A| = -|A|$. The only way this can happen is when $|A| = 0$. That is, if $a = -a$, $a + a = 0$, $2a = 0$, so $a = 0$.

Example 8 Evaluate.

$$\begin{vmatrix} 6 & 7 & 8 \\ -2 & 6 & 5 \\ -2 & 6 & 5 \end{vmatrix} = 0$$

Example 9 Evaluate.

$$\begin{vmatrix} -5 & 4 & -5 \\ 3 & 7 & 3 \\ 0 & 12 & 0 \end{vmatrix} = 0$$

THEOREM 4 If all the elements of a row (or column) of a matrix A are multiplied by k, $|A|$ is multiplied by k. Or, if all the elements of a row (or column) of A have a common factor, we can factor it out of the determinant of A.

Example 10

$$\begin{vmatrix} 2 & 4 & 6 \\ -2 & 5 & 9 \\ 4 & -1 & -3 \end{vmatrix} = 3 \cdot \begin{vmatrix} 2 & 4 & 2 \\ -2 & 5 & 3 \\ 4 & -1 & -1 \end{vmatrix}$$

Example 11

$$\begin{vmatrix} 10 & 25 \\ -4 & -7 \end{vmatrix} = 5 \cdot \begin{vmatrix} 2 & 5 \\ -4 & -7 \end{vmatrix}$$

Proof of Theorem 4.   Expand the determinants about the row (or column) in question. The cofactors are the same and the k can be factored out. Consider the case of a 3 × 3 matrix and the second column. Let

$$A = \begin{bmatrix} a_{11} & a_{12} & a_{13} \\ a_{21} & a_{22} & a_{23} \\ a_{31} & a_{32} & a_{33} \end{bmatrix},$$

and

$$B = \begin{bmatrix} a_{11} & ka_{12} & a_{13} \\ a_{21} & ka_{22} & a_{23} \\ a_{31} & ka_{32} & a_{33} \end{bmatrix}.$$

Then

$$|B| = ka_{12}A_{12} + ka_{22}A_{22} + ka_{32}A_{32}$$

$$= k(a_{12}A_{12} + a_{22}A_{22} + a_{32}A_{32})$$

$$= k|A|.$$

Example 12   Without expanding, find $|A|$.

$$A = \begin{bmatrix} -6 & 3 & 8 \\ 15 & -9 & -20 \\ -9 & -1 & 12 \end{bmatrix}$$

$$|A| = (-3) \cdot \begin{vmatrix} 2 & 3 & 8 \\ -5 & -9 & -20 \\ 3 & -1 & 12 \end{vmatrix} \qquad \text{(Factoring } -3 \text{ out of the first column)}$$

$$= (-3)(4) \cdot \begin{vmatrix} 2 & 3 & 2 \\ -5 & -9 & -5 \\ 3 & -1 & 3 \end{vmatrix} \qquad \text{(Factoring 4 out of the third column)}$$

$$= 0 \qquad \text{(By Theorem 3)}$$

THEOREM 5   **If each element in a row (or column) is multiplied by a number k, and the products are added to the corresponding elements of another row (or column), we still get the same determinant.**

Example 13 Find a determinant equal to the one on the left by adding three times the second column to the first column.

$$\begin{vmatrix} 0 & 1 & 2 \\ 4 & 5 & 6 \\ 7 & 8 & 9 \end{vmatrix} = \begin{vmatrix} 0 + 3(1) & 1 & 2 \\ 4 + 3(5) & 5 & 6 \\ 7 + 3(8) & 8 & 9 \end{vmatrix} = \begin{vmatrix} 3 & 1 & 2 \\ 19 & 5 & 6 \\ 31 & 8 & 9 \end{vmatrix}$$

Example 14 Find a determinant equal to the one on the left by adding two times the third row to the first row.

$$\begin{vmatrix} 0 & 1 & 2 \\ 4 & 5 & 6 \\ 7 & 8 & 9 \end{vmatrix} = \begin{vmatrix} 0 + 2(7) & 1 + 2(8) & 2 + 2(9) \\ 4 & 5 & 6 \\ 7 & 8 & 9 \end{vmatrix} = \begin{vmatrix} 14 & 17 & 20 \\ 4 & 5 & 6 \\ 7 & 8 & 9 \end{vmatrix}$$

We can use the properties of determinants to simplify their evaluation. We try to find another determinant where in a particular row or column one element is 1 and the rest are 0.

Example 15 Evaluate by first simplifying to a determinant where in one row or column one element is 1 and the rest are 0.

$$\begin{vmatrix} 6 & 2 & 3 \\ 6 & -1 & 5 \\ -2 & 3 & 1 \end{vmatrix}$$

We will try to get two 0's and a 1 in the third row. It already has a 1; that is why we picked the third row. We first factor a 2 out of Column 1.

$$2 \cdot \begin{vmatrix} 3 & 2 & 3 \\ 3 & -1 & 5 \\ -1 & 3 & 1 \end{vmatrix} \qquad \text{(Theorem 4)}$$

Now multiply each element of Column 3 by -3 and add the corresponding elements to Column 2.

$$2 \cdot \begin{vmatrix} 3 & -7 & 3 \\ 3 & -16 & 5 \\ -1 & 0 & 1 \end{vmatrix} \qquad \text{(Theorem 5)}$$

Now add the elements of Column 3 to the corresponding elements of Column 1 (Theorem 5).

$$2 \cdot \begin{vmatrix} 6 & -7 & 3 \\ 8 & -16 & 5 \\ 0 & 0 & 1 \end{vmatrix}$$

Now evaluate the determinant about the last row.

$$2 \cdot \left(\boxed{0} - \boxed{0} + \boxed{1} \cdot \begin{vmatrix} 6 & -7 \\ 8 & -16 \end{vmatrix} \right) = 2 \cdot [6(-16) - 8(-7)] = -80$$

EXERCISE SET 3.6

Use the following matrix for Exercises 1 through 10.

$$A = \begin{bmatrix} 7 & -4 & -6 \\ 2 & 0 & -3 \\ 1 & 2 & -5 \end{bmatrix}$$

1. Find a_{11}, a_{32}, and a_{22}.

2. Find a_{13}, a_{31}, and a_{23}.

3. Find M_{11}, M_{32}, and M_{22}.

4. Find M_{13}, M_{31}, and M_{23}.

5. Find A_{11}, A_{32}, and A_{22}.

6. Find A_{13}, A_{31}, and A_{23}.

7. Expand $|A|$ about the second row.

8. Expand $|A|$ about the second column.

9. Expand $|A|$ about the third column.

10. Expand $|A|$ about the first row.

Use the following matrix for Exercises 11 through 16.

$$A = \begin{bmatrix} 1 & 0 & 0 & -2 \\ 4 & 1 & 0 & 0 \\ 5 & 6 & 7 & 8 \\ -2 & -3 & -1 & 0 \end{bmatrix}$$

11. Find M_{41} and M_{33}.

12. Find M_{12} and M_{44}.

13. Find A_{24} and A_{43}.

14. Find A_{22} and A_{34}.

15. Expand $|A|$ about the first row.

16. Expand $|A|$ about the third column.

Evaluate.

17.
$$\begin{vmatrix} 5 & -4 & 2 & -2 \\ 3 & -3 & -4 & 7 \\ -2 & 3 & 2 & 4 \\ -8 & 9 & 5 & -5 \end{vmatrix}$$

18.
$$\begin{vmatrix} x & p & q & r \\ 0 & y & s & t \\ 0 & 0 & z & u \\ 0 & 0 & 0 & w \end{vmatrix}$$

19. For the matrices below, find $|A|$ and $|B|$ and compare.

$$A = \begin{bmatrix} -2 & 3 \\ 4 & -1 \end{bmatrix} \quad B = \begin{bmatrix} 3 & -2 \\ -1 & 4 \end{bmatrix}$$

20. For the matrices below, find $|A|$ and $|B|$ and compare.

$$A = \begin{bmatrix} -1 & -2 \\ -6 & 5 \end{bmatrix} \quad B = \begin{bmatrix} 2 & 4 \\ 12 & -10 \end{bmatrix}$$

21. For the matrices below, find $|A|$ and $|B|$ and compare.

$$A = \begin{bmatrix} 3 & -2 & 3 \\ -2 & 2 & -1 \\ -3 & 1 & -2 \end{bmatrix} \qquad B = \begin{bmatrix} -2 & 3 & 3 \\ 2 & -2 & -1 \\ 1 & -3 & -2 \end{bmatrix}$$

22. For the matrices below find $|C|$ and $|D|$ and compare.

$$C = \begin{bmatrix} 2 & -2 & 1 \\ -3 & 6 & 3 \\ -3 & 1 & 2 \end{bmatrix} \qquad D = \begin{bmatrix} 2 & -2 & 1 \\ 1 & -2 & -1 \\ -3 & 1 & 2 \end{bmatrix}$$

Consider the determinant below for Exercises 23 and 24.

$$|A| = \begin{vmatrix} 3 & -2 & 3 \\ 1 & 2 & -3 \\ 4 & -3 & 1 \end{vmatrix}$$

23. Find a determinant equal to $|A|$ by adding three times the first column to the second column.

24. Find a determinant equal to $|A|$ by adding three times the first row to the third row.

Evaluate by first simplifying to a determinant where in one row or column one element is 1 and the rest are 0.

25. $\begin{vmatrix} -4 & 5 \\ 6 & 10 \end{vmatrix}$

26. $\begin{vmatrix} 3 & -9 \\ -2 & 4 \end{vmatrix}$

27. $\begin{vmatrix} 2 & 1 & 1 \\ 2 & -3 & -1 \\ -4 & 5 & 2 \end{vmatrix}$

28. $\begin{vmatrix} 1 & 2 & 4 \\ 2 & 3 & 5 \\ 3 & 1 & 6 \end{vmatrix}$

29. $\begin{vmatrix} 11 & -15 & 20 \\ 16 & 24 & -8 \\ 6 & 9 & 15 \end{vmatrix}$

30. $\begin{vmatrix} 4 & -24 & 15 \\ -3 & 18 & -6 \\ 5 & -4 & 3 \end{vmatrix}$

31. $\begin{vmatrix} -3 & 0 & 2 & 6 \\ 2 & 4 & 0 & -1 \\ -1 & 0 & -5 & 2 \\ 0 & -1 & -2 & -3 \end{vmatrix}$

32. $\begin{vmatrix} -2 & 1 & 0 & 5 \\ 3 & 0 & -4 & -2 \\ 4 & -6 & -8 & -1 \\ 8 & 0 & -2 & -3 \end{vmatrix}$

Find each determinant without expanding.

33. $\begin{vmatrix} x & y & z \\ 0 & 0 & 0 \\ p & q & r \end{vmatrix}$

34. $\begin{vmatrix} 5 & 5 & 5 \\ 3 & 3 & 3 \\ 2 & -7 & 8 \end{vmatrix}$

35. $\begin{vmatrix} 2a & t & -7a \\ 2b & u & -7b \\ 2c & v & -7c \end{vmatrix}$

36. $\begin{vmatrix} a & -1 & 4a \\ b & 2 & 4b \\ x & -3 & 4x \end{vmatrix}$

Solve for x.

37. $\begin{vmatrix} -16 & 32 \\ -5 & -3 \end{vmatrix} = x \cdot \begin{vmatrix} 4 & -8 \\ -5 & -3 \end{vmatrix}$

38. $\begin{vmatrix} -3 & 12 & 2 \\ 5 & -6 & 3 \\ 0 & 18 & 5 \end{vmatrix} = x \cdot \begin{vmatrix} -3 & 2 & 2 \\ 5 & -1 & 3 \\ 0 & 3 & 5 \end{vmatrix}$

Factor.

39. $\begin{vmatrix} x^2 & x & 1 \\ y^2 & y & 1 \\ z^2 & z & 1 \end{vmatrix}$ **40.** $\begin{vmatrix} 1 & 1 & 1 \\ a & b & c \\ a^2 & b^2 & c^2 \end{vmatrix}$ **41.** $\begin{vmatrix} x & x^2 & x^3 \\ y & y^2 & y^3 \\ z & z^2 & z^3 \end{vmatrix}$ **42.** $\begin{vmatrix} 1 & 1 & 1 \\ a & b & c \\ a^3 & b^3 & c^3 \end{vmatrix}$

3.7 (Optional) CALCULATION OF THE MATRIX INVERSE

In this section we consider two ways of calculating the inverse of a square matrix, if it exists. We shall see that such inverses exist if and only if the determinant of the matrix is nonzero.

The Cofactor Method

The following is the first procedure we can use for calculating the inverse of a square matrix.

> *The Cofactor Method.* **To find the inverse A^{-1} of a square matrix A,**
> a) **Find the cofactor of each element.**
> b) **Replace each element by its cofactor.**
> c) **Find the transpose of the matrix found in step (b).**
> d) **Multiply the matrix in step (c) by $\dfrac{1}{|A|}$. This is A^{-1}.**

Example 1   Find A^{-1}.

$$A = \begin{bmatrix} 3 & 5 \\ 1 & -2 \end{bmatrix}$$

a) Find the cofactor of each element.

$A_{11} = (-1)^{1+1}(-2) = -2$

$A_{12} = (-1)^{1+2}(1) = -1$

$A_{21} = (-1)^{2+1}(5) = -5$

$A_{22} = (-1)^{2+2}(3) = 3$

(The determinant of a 1×1 matrix is just the number. For example, $\|[-2]\| = -2$. Don't confuse determinant notation with absolute value notation.)

b) Replace each element by its cofactor.

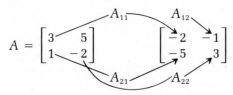

c) Find the transpose of the matrix found in step (b).

$$\text{The transpose of } \begin{bmatrix} -2 & -1 \\ -5 & 3 \end{bmatrix} \text{ is } \begin{bmatrix} -2 & -5 \\ -1 & 3 \end{bmatrix}.$$

d) Multiply by $\dfrac{1}{|A|}$.

$$|A| = 3(-2) - 1(5) = -11$$

$$A^{-1} = \frac{1}{-11} \cdot \begin{bmatrix} -2 & -5 \\ -1 & 3 \end{bmatrix} = \begin{bmatrix} \frac{2}{11} & \frac{5}{11} \\ \frac{1}{11} & -\frac{3}{11} \end{bmatrix}$$

Example 2   Find A^{-1}.

$$A = \begin{bmatrix} 2 & -1 & 1 \\ 1 & -2 & 3 \\ 4 & 1 & 2 \end{bmatrix}$$

a) Find the cofactor of each element.

$$A_{11} = (-1)^{1+1} \cdot \begin{vmatrix} -2 & 3 \\ 1 & 2 \end{vmatrix} = -7, \qquad A_{12} = (-1)^{1+2} \cdot \begin{vmatrix} 1 & 3 \\ 4 & 2 \end{vmatrix} = 10,$$

$$A_{13} = (-1)^{1+3} \cdot \begin{vmatrix} 1 & -2 \\ 4 & 1 \end{vmatrix} = 9, \qquad A_{21} = (-1)^{2+1} \cdot \begin{vmatrix} -1 & 1 \\ 1 & 2 \end{vmatrix} = 3,$$

$$A_{22} = (-1)^{2+2} \cdot \begin{vmatrix} 2 & 1 \\ 4 & 2 \end{vmatrix} = 0, \qquad A_{23} = (-1)^{2+3} \cdot \begin{vmatrix} 2 & -1 \\ 4 & 1 \end{vmatrix} = -6,$$

$$A_{31} = (-1)^{3+1} \cdot \begin{vmatrix} -1 & 1 \\ -2 & 3 \end{vmatrix} = -1, \qquad A_{32} = (-1)^{3+2} \cdot \begin{vmatrix} 2 & 1 \\ 1 & 3 \end{vmatrix} = -5,$$

$$A_{33} = (-1)^{3+3} \cdot \begin{vmatrix} 2 & -1 \\ 1 & -2 \end{vmatrix} = -3.$$

b) Replace each element by its cofactor.

$$A = \begin{bmatrix} 2 & -1 & 1 \\ 1 & -2 & 3 \\ 4 & 1 & 2 \end{bmatrix} \rightarrow \begin{bmatrix} -7 & 10 & 9 \\ 3 & 0 & -6 \\ -1 & -5 & -3 \end{bmatrix}$$

c) Find the transpose of the matrix found in step (b).

$$\text{The transpose of } \begin{bmatrix} -7 & 10 & 9 \\ 3 & 0 & -6 \\ -1 & -5 & -3 \end{bmatrix} \text{ is } \begin{bmatrix} -7 & 3 & -1 \\ 10 & 0 & -5 \\ 9 & -6 & -3 \end{bmatrix}.$$

d) Multiply by $\dfrac{1}{|A|}$.

$|A| = a_{11}A_{11} + a_{21}A_{21} + a_{31}A_{31}$ (Expanding $|A|$ about the first column)

$\quad = 2(-7) + 1(3) + 4(-1)$

$\quad = -15$

$$A^{-1} = \frac{1}{-15}\begin{bmatrix} -7 & 3 & -1 \\ 10 & 0 & -5 \\ 9 & -6 & -3 \end{bmatrix} = \begin{bmatrix} \frac{7}{15} & -\frac{1}{5} & \frac{1}{15} \\ -\frac{2}{3} & 0 & \frac{1}{3} \\ -\frac{3}{5} & \frac{2}{5} & \frac{1}{5} \end{bmatrix}.$$

If $|A|$ is 0, then $\dfrac{1}{|A|}$ is not defined and A^{-1} does not exist.

The Echelon Method

We now describe a second way to calculate a matrix inverse. We do this with an example and in the abstract. Suppose we wanted to find the inverse of the matrix

$$A = \begin{bmatrix} 2 & -1 & 1 \\ 1 & -2 & 3 \\ 4 & 1 & 2 \end{bmatrix}.$$

We are going to use an echelon tableau but a bit differently. Proceeding as if A were the coefficient matrix of some system of equations, we write the matrix A in the left side as we normally do, but on the right side we write the identity matrix and use 1's as headings:

x_1	x_2	x_3	1	1	1
2	-1	1	1	0	0
1	-2	3	0	1	0
4	1	2	0	0	1

x_1	x_2	$\cdots$	x_n	1	1 $\cdots$ 1
	A				I

Now we proceed with the echelon method, but with one exception. We *never* interchange columns. In truth, we never did interchange columns in any of the examples of Sections 3.1 and 3.2, but we could have. Thus, we use only *row operations*, performing them on the entire augmented (or lengthened) rows. From the explanation in Section 3.4, we know that carrying out the echelon method has the same effect as multiplying by A^{-1}.

But this time, when we multiply I on the right side of the tableau, we get A^{-1}.

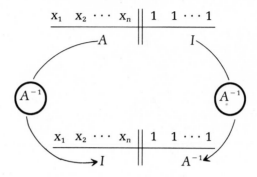

Suppose we wanted to find the inverse of the given matrix A. The procedure is to perform row operations to obtain I, or

$$\begin{bmatrix} 1 & 0 & 0 \\ 0 & 1 & 0 \\ 0 & 0 & 1 \end{bmatrix}$$

on the *left side* of the tableau. The resulting matrix appearing on the *right side* is the inverse matrix A^{-1}. We illustrate this as follows.

1. We first obtain a 1 in the first row, first column, by interchanging the first and second rows.

x_1	x_2	x_3	1	1	1
1^*	-2	3	0	1	0
2	-1	1	1	0	0
4	1	2	0	0	1

2. Next we pivot to obtain 0's in the rest of the first column. We multiply the pivot row by -2 and add to the second row. We multiply the pivot row by -4 and add to the third row.

x_1	x_2	x_3	1	1	1
1	-2	3	0	1	0
0	3	-5	1	-2	0
0	9	-10	0	-4	1

3. Next we obtain a 1 in the second row, second column. We do this by multiplying the second row by $\frac{1}{3}$.

X_1	X_2	X_3	1	1	1
1	-2	3	0	1	0
0	1^*	$-\frac{5}{3}$	$\frac{1}{3}$	$-\frac{2}{3}$	0
0	9	-10	0	-4	1

4. We pivot to obtain 0's in the rest of the second column. We multiply the pivot row by 2 and add to the first. We multiply the pivot row by -9 and add to the third.

X_1	X_2	X_3	1	1	1
1	0	$-\frac{1}{3}$	$\frac{2}{3}$	$-\frac{1}{3}$	0
0	1	$-\frac{5}{3}$	$\frac{1}{3}$	$-\frac{2}{3}$	0
0	0	5	-3	2	1

5. To get a 1 in the third row, third column, we multiply by $\frac{1}{5}$.

X_1	X_2	X_3	1	1	1
1	0	$-\frac{1}{3}$	$\frac{2}{3}$	$-\frac{1}{3}$	0
0	1	$-\frac{5}{3}$	$\frac{1}{3}$	$-\frac{2}{3}$	0
0	0	1^*	$-\frac{3}{5}$	$\frac{2}{5}$	$\frac{1}{5}$

6. We pivot to obtain 0's in the rest of the third column. We multiply the pivot row by $\frac{1}{3}$ and add to the first. We multiply the pivot row by $\frac{5}{3}$ and add to the second.

X_1	X_2	X_3	1	1	1
1	0	0	$\frac{7}{15}$	$-\frac{1}{5}$	$\frac{1}{15}$
0	1	0	$-\frac{2}{3}$	0	$\frac{1}{3}$
0	0	1	$-\frac{3}{5}$	$\frac{2}{5}$	$\frac{1}{5}$

Thus

$$A^{-1} = \begin{bmatrix} \frac{7}{15} & -\frac{1}{5} & \frac{1}{15} \\ -\frac{2}{3} & 0 & \frac{1}{3} \\ -\frac{3}{5} & \frac{2}{5} & \frac{1}{5} \end{bmatrix}.$$

The reader can check this by doing the multiplication $A^{-1}A$.

If we do not obtain the identity matrix on the left, as would be the case when the system has no solution or infinitely many solutions, then A^{-1} does not exist.

This procedure will work for any square matrix that has an inverse.

The all-integer method (see Section 3.2) can also be used to obtain the inverse of a matrix.

EXERCISE SET 3.7

Find A^{-1}, if it exists. Use the cofactor method.

1. $A = \begin{bmatrix} 3 & 2 \\ 5 & 3 \end{bmatrix}$

2. $A = \begin{bmatrix} 3 & 5 \\ 1 & 2 \end{bmatrix}$

3. $A = \begin{bmatrix} 11 & 3 \\ 7 & 2 \end{bmatrix}$

4. $A = \begin{bmatrix} 8 & 5 \\ 5 & 3 \end{bmatrix}$

5. $A = \begin{bmatrix} 4 & -3 \\ 1 & 2 \end{bmatrix}$

6. $A = \begin{bmatrix} 0 & -1 \\ 1 & 0 \end{bmatrix}$

7. $A = \begin{bmatrix} 3 & 1 & 0 \\ 1 & 1 & 1 \\ 1 & -1 & 2 \end{bmatrix}$

8. $A = \begin{bmatrix} 1 & 0 & 1 \\ 2 & 1 & 0 \\ 1 & -1 & 1 \end{bmatrix}$

9. $A = \begin{bmatrix} 1 & -1 & 2 \\ 0 & 1 & 3 \\ 2 & 1 & -2 \end{bmatrix}$

10. $A = \begin{bmatrix} 1 & -1 & 2 \\ 0 & 1 & 2 \\ 1 & -3 & -4 \end{bmatrix}$

11. $A = \begin{bmatrix} 1 & -4 & 8 \\ 1 & -3 & 2 \\ 2 & -7 & 10 \end{bmatrix}$

12. $A = \begin{bmatrix} -2 & 5 & 3 \\ 4 & -1 & 3 \\ 7 & -2 & 5 \end{bmatrix}$

13. $A = \begin{bmatrix} 1 & 2 & 3 & 4 \\ 0 & 1 & 3 & -5 \\ 0 & 0 & 1 & -2 \\ 0 & 0 & 0 & -1 \end{bmatrix}$

14. $A = \begin{bmatrix} -2 & -3 & 4 & 1 \\ 0 & 1 & 1 & 0 \\ 0 & 4 & -6 & 1 \\ -2 & -2 & 5 & 1 \end{bmatrix}$

15.–28. Find A^{-1} of each matrix in Exercises 1 through 14. Use the echelon method.

For Exercises 29 through 32, write a matrix equation equivalent to the system. Find the inverse of the coefficient matrix. Use the inverse of the coefficient matrix to solve each system.

29. $7x - 2y = -3$
$9x + 3y = 4$

30. $5x_1 + 3x_2 = -2$
$4x_1 - x_2 = 1$

31. $x_1 \quad\quad + x_3 = 1$
$2x_1 + x_2 \quad\quad = 3$
$x_1 - x_2 + x_3 = 4$

32. $x + 2y + 3z = -1$
$2x - 3y + 4z = 2$
$-3x + 5y - 6z = 4$

For Exercises 33 through 37, state the conditions under which A^{-1} exists. Then find a formula for A^{-1}.

33. $A = \begin{bmatrix} x & 0 \\ 0 & 1 \end{bmatrix}$

34. $A = [x]$

35. $A = \begin{bmatrix} x & 0 \\ 0 & y \end{bmatrix}$

36. $A = \begin{bmatrix} 0 & 0 & x \\ 0 & y & 0 \\ z & 0 & 0 \end{bmatrix}$

37. $A = \begin{bmatrix} x & 1 & 1 & 1 \\ 0 & y & 0 & 0 \\ 0 & 0 & z & 0 \\ 0 & 0 & 0 & w \end{bmatrix}$

38. Consider

$$a_{11}x + a_{12}y = c_1$$

$$a_{21}x + a_{22}y = c_2$$

Use the cofactor method and the equivalent matrix equation $AX = C$ to prove Cramer's rule.

*3.8   (Optional) LEONTIEF INPUT/OUTPUT ANALYSIS

We frequently try to explain the main aspects of our economy in terms of such factors as "supply and demand" and "wages and prices." These represent such oversimplified models of our economy that the insight they bring is largely fortuitous. In order to provide a more reliable model of our economy Wassily W. Leontief, a Professor of Economics at Harvard University, developed his *input/output analysis* and in 1973 was awarded the Nobel Prize for Economics.

Leontief's Closed Input/Output Model

A Leontief input/output model is called *closed* if *each* product is used in *both* input and output, as in the following example.

Example 1   A certain economy consists of two industries, coal and steel. Production of one ton of coal requires an *internal* consumption by the coal industry of $\frac{1}{4}$ ton of coal and $\frac{1}{3}$ ton of steel. (The coal may be used internally by the coal industry for heat or to generate electricity and the steel may be used internally by the coal industry for new track or other construction required as the network of tunnels in the mine expands.) Production of one ton of steel requires an *internal* consumption by the steel industry of 1 ton of coal and $\frac{1}{5}$ ton of steel. (The coal may be used internally by the steel industry to fuel the smelting furnaces and the steel may be used internally by the steel industry for replacement equipment or structures required to maintain production.) How many tons of coal and steel must each industry produce so that after internal consumption they have left one ton of each?

Solution We can write the given data for the *internal consumption* of product i by industry j in the following table:

Industry j / Input product i	Input to coal industry ($j=1$)	Input to steel industry ($j=2$)
Coal ($i=1$)	$\frac{1}{4}$ ton of coal per ton of coal	1 ton of coal per ton of steel
Steel ($i=2$)	$\frac{1}{3}$ ton of steel per ton of coal	$\frac{1}{5}$ ton of steel per ton of steel

Note that each element in the table is written in *units* of the amount of product i per *unit* of industry j, or *units product i per unit industry j*. Thus, the *first* unit (product i) will be the same throughout any row and the *second* unit (industry j) will be the same throughout any column. Sometimes it is convenient to use *monetary* units since they are common to all products and industries. We write K$ for $1000 (kilobucks) and M$ for $1,000,000 (megabucks).

This information can be written in matrix form.

$$A = \begin{bmatrix} \frac{1}{4} & 1 \\ \frac{1}{3} & \frac{1}{5} \end{bmatrix}$$

The matrix A is called the *input/output** matrix, or simply, I/O matrix.

In general A is an n by n matrix $[a_{ij}]$ where each element a_{ij} is the amount of *product i* used *internally* by *industry j* to produce one unit of *product j*. Each element a_{ij} must be nonnegative (since one cannot use a negative amount of a substance) and there must be at least one positive element per row (since one cannot produce something out of nothing).

Let $X = [x_1 \ x_2 \ \ldots \ x_n]^T$ be a *production* matrix whose elements x_i represent the *gross* production of industry i. In the present example $X = [x_1 \ x_2]^T$ and is to be determined.

The *internal* consumption of all products is given by AX. Thus, the coal and steel industries together consume internally

$$AX = \begin{bmatrix} \frac{1}{4} & 1 \\ \frac{1}{3} & \frac{1}{5} \end{bmatrix} \begin{bmatrix} x_1 \\ x_2 \end{bmatrix},$$

or $(\frac{1}{4}x_1 + 1x_2)$ tons of coal and $(\frac{1}{3}x_1 + \frac{1}{5}x_2)$ tons of steel.

---

* or *technological* matrix. Note: Sometimes the I/O matrix is defined as the transpose of our matrix A. The analysis carries through in a similar manner regardless.

The *net* production, or *demand*, is represented by the matrix $D = [d_1 \quad d_2 \dots d_n]^T$ whose elements d_i represent the *net* production of industry i. The *net* production D is equal to the *gross* production X minus the amount consumed internally AX:

$$D = X - AX.$$

For a net production of one ton (T) of coal and one ton of steel, $D = [1 \quad 1]^T$ and

$$1 = x_1 - (\tfrac{1}{4}x_1 + 1x_2),$$

$$1 = x_2 - (\tfrac{1}{3}x_1 + \tfrac{1}{5}x_2).$$

Alternately, we can write

$$D = (I - A)X,$$

where the unit matrix I takes on the units of A. It follows from this equation that each *diagonal* input term a_{ii} must be less than unity, so that the net output term $(1 - a_{ii})$ is positive (since there is no point in an industry that requires more as input than it has capacity for output).

Since we usually wish to know what the *gross* production X must be for a given *net* production (or demand) D, we solve this matrix equation for X and obtain

$$X = (I - A)^{-1}D,$$

provided the inverse matrix $(I - A)^{-1}$ exists. The matrix A must be such that all the elements of $(A - I)^{-1}$ are nonnegative (since to be otherwise implies that a *positive* demand could be met by a *negative* production). In the present example,

$$I - A = \begin{bmatrix} \tfrac{3}{4} & -1 \\ -\tfrac{1}{3} & \tfrac{4}{5} \end{bmatrix}.$$

Using the techniques of Section 3.7, we obtain

$$(I - A)^{-1} = \begin{bmatrix} 3 & \tfrac{15}{4} \\ \tfrac{5}{4} & \tfrac{45}{16} \end{bmatrix}.$$

For a net production, or demand, of one ton each of coal and steel, $D = [1 \quad 1]^T$ and we find that the gross production is

$$X = \begin{bmatrix} 3 & \tfrac{15}{4} \\ \tfrac{5}{4} & \tfrac{45}{16} \end{bmatrix} \begin{bmatrix} 1 \\ 1 \end{bmatrix} = \begin{bmatrix} \tfrac{27}{4} \\ \tfrac{65}{16} \end{bmatrix}.$$

Thus, for a net production of one ton of coal and one ton of steel, a gross production of $6\frac{3}{4}$ tons of coal and $4\frac{1}{16}$ tons of steel is required. It can be seen that much of the coal and steel produced is consumed internally.

Leontief's Open Input/Output Model

A Leontief input/output model is called *closed* if *each* product is used in *both* input and output. A Leontief input/output model is called *open* if there is an *extra input* (usually *labor*) that *is* involved in production but is *not* included *in the I/O matrix* either as an input to or as the product of some industry.

Example 2   In Example 1, let the production of one ton of coal require 5 work-hours of labor and one ton of steel require 8 work-hours of labor. How much labor is required for a net production of one ton each of coal and steel?

Solution   We can incorporate this new data into the table of Example 1:

Industry j / Input product i	Input to coal industry ($j=1$)	Input to steel industry ($j=2$)
Coal ($i=1$)	$\frac{1}{4}$ T of coal per T of coal	1 T of coal per T of steel
Steel ($i=2$)	$\frac{1}{3}$ T of steel per T of coal	$\frac{1}{5}$ T of steel per T of steel
Labor ($i=0$)	5 man-hours of labor per T of coal	8 man-hours of labor per T of coal

The new data can be represented by the matrix $A_0 = [a_{0j}]$. Here A_0 is given by

$$A_0 = [5 \quad 8].$$

The gross amount of labor required as input to yield a net production of one ton each of coal and steel is then given by

$$x_0 = A_0 X,$$

where the (gross) production matrix X is obtained here just as in the closed I/O model:

$$x_0 = [5 \quad 8]\begin{bmatrix} \frac{27}{4} \\ \frac{65}{16} \end{bmatrix} = 66\frac{1}{4} \text{ man-hours.}$$

EXERCISE SET 3.8

For Exercises 1 through 4:

a) Set up the I/O matrix A,

c) Determine the inverse matrix $(I - A)^{-1}$,

e) Find the production matrix X required to meet the given demand,

b) Set up the matrix A_0,

d) Find the demand matrix D,

f) Find the labor x_0 required to meet the given demand.

1. A certain economy consists of two industries, agriculture and manufacturing. Production of one bushel of agricultural produce requires an internal consumption of 0.2 bushels of produce, 0.25 lb of manufactured hardware, and 5 man-days labor. Production of one lb of hardware requires an internal consumption of 0.5 bushels of produce, 0.2 lb of hardware, and 3 man-days labor. There is a demand for 530 bushels of produce and 106 lbs of hardware.

2. A certain economy consists of two industries, agriculture and textiles. Production of one bushel of agricultural produce requires an internal consumption of 0.3 bushels of produce, 0.1 bolts of cloth, and 3 man-days labor. Production of one bolt of cloth requires an internal consumption of 0.5 bushels of produce, 0.2 bolts of cloth, and 2 man-days labor. There is a demand for 102 bushels of produce and 153 bolts of cloth.

3. A certain economy consists of three industries: mining, agriculture, and manufacturing. Production of 1 K$ of metal requires an internal consumption of 0.2 K$ metal, no produce, 0.2 K$ of manufactured hardware, and 0.4 K$ of labor. Production of 1 K$ of produce requires an internal consumption of 0.1 K$ of metal, 0.1 K$ of produce, 0.2 K$ of hardware, and 0.2 K$ of labor. Production of 1 K$ of hardware requires an internal consumption of 0.5 K$ of metal, no produce, 0.3 K$ of hardware, and 0.3 K$ of labor.

4. A certain economy consists of three industries: transportation, petroleum, and agriculture. Production of 1 M$ of transportation requires an internal consumption of 0.1 M$ of transportation, 0.9 M$ of petroleum, no produce, and 0.5 M$ of labor. Production of 1 M$ of petroleum requires an internal consumption of 0.2 M$ of transportation, 0.4 M$ of petroleum, 0.2 M$ of produce, and 0.2 M$ of labor. Production of 1 M$ of produce requires an internal consumption of 0.3 M$ of transportation, no petroleum, 0.25 M$ of produce, and 0.3 M$ of labor.

Given the following I/O matrices A and A_0 and the demand matrix D, find $(I - A)^{-1}$, the production matrix X, and the labor required x_0.

5. $A = \begin{bmatrix} 0.2 & 0.4 \\ 0.4 & 0 \end{bmatrix}$

$A_0 = [0.3 \quad 0.7]$

$D = [70 \quad 56]^T$

6. $A = \begin{bmatrix} 0.4 & 0 \\ 0.2 & 0.4 \end{bmatrix}$

$A_0 = [0.7 \quad 0.3]$

$D = [72 \quad 54]^T$

7. $A = \begin{bmatrix} 0.2 & 0.1 & 0 \\ 0 & 0.3 & 0.2 \\ 0.1 & 0 & 0.9 \end{bmatrix}$

$A_0 = [0.3 \quad 0.4 \quad 0.1]$

$D = [48 \quad 96 \quad 168]^T$

8. $A = \begin{bmatrix} 0.6 & 0 & 0.2 \\ 0.2 & 0 & 0.3 \\ 0.4 & 0.4 & 0.5 \end{bmatrix}$

$A_0 = [0.7 \quad 0.3 \quad 0.4]$

$D = [28 \quad 140 \quad 56]^T$

CHAPTER 3 REVIEW

Put in matrix form and solve using the echelon method.

1. $7x_1 + 4x_2 = -21$
$3x_1 + x_2 = -9$

2. $3x_1 - 2x_2 + 3x_3 = 24$
$x_1 + x_2 - x_3 = -7$
$2x_1 + 3x_2 - 5x_3 = -32$

Write as separate equations and solve using the echelon method.

3. $\begin{bmatrix} 4 & -8 \\ 3 & -6 \end{bmatrix} \begin{bmatrix} x_1 \\ x_2 \end{bmatrix} = \begin{bmatrix} -20 \\ -15 \end{bmatrix}$

4. $\begin{bmatrix} 8 & -4 \\ 6 & -3 \end{bmatrix} \begin{bmatrix} x_1 \\ x_2 \end{bmatrix} = \begin{bmatrix} 20 \\ 16 \end{bmatrix}$

Complete the solution using the echelon method.

5.

x_1	x_2	x_3	x_4		1
1	0	6	0		5
0	1	-2	0		3
0	0	0	-4		-8

6.

x_1	x_2	x_3		1
1	3	-2		6
0	4	-1		8
0	4	1		2
0	8	0		-10

For Exercises 7 through 10, consider

$$A = \begin{bmatrix} -3 & 2 \\ -5 & 1 \end{bmatrix} \quad \text{and} \quad B = \begin{bmatrix} 0 & -1 \\ 1 & 0 \end{bmatrix}.$$

Find:

7. $A + B$ **8.** AB **9.** $A - B$ **10.** $-4A$

11. Find C^T for

$$C = \begin{bmatrix} 2 \\ -3 \\ 4 \end{bmatrix}.$$

12. Find AB and BA, if possible.

$$A = \begin{bmatrix} 1 \\ -1 \\ 2 \end{bmatrix}, \quad B = \begin{bmatrix} 2 & -3 & 0 \\ 1 & 2 & 4 \end{bmatrix}$$

In Exercises 13 and 14, a system of equations is given, together with the inverse of the coefficient matrix. Use the matrix inverse to solve the system. Show your work.

13. $8x_1 + 3x_2 = 6,$
$4x_1 - 6x_2 = -2$

$$A^{-1} = \begin{bmatrix} \frac{1}{10} & \frac{1}{20} \\ \frac{1}{15} & -\frac{2}{15} \end{bmatrix}$$

14. $x_1 + x_2 + x_3 = 10,$
$x_1 + 2x_2 - x_3 = -5,$
$2x_1 - x_2 + 3x_3 = 20$

$$A^{-1} = \begin{bmatrix} -1 & \frac{4}{5} & \frac{3}{5} \\ 1 & -\frac{1}{5} & -\frac{2}{5} \\ 1 & -\frac{3}{5} & -\frac{1}{5} \end{bmatrix}$$

15. For $X = \begin{bmatrix} p \\ q \end{bmatrix}$ and $Y = \begin{bmatrix} t \\ u \end{bmatrix}$, find $\begin{bmatrix} X \\ Y \end{bmatrix}^T$.

16. For a certain year, $850 is received in interest from two investments. A certain amount is invested at 8%, and $1300 more than this is invested at 10%. Find the amount invested at each rate.

*17. Use the echelon method to find A^{-1}.

$$A = \begin{bmatrix} 1 & 0 & -1 \\ -1 & 1 & -1 \\ -1 & 0 & 2 \end{bmatrix}$$

Evaluate.

18. $\begin{vmatrix} -4 & \sqrt{3} \\ \sqrt{3} & 7 \end{vmatrix}$

19. $\begin{vmatrix} 1 & -1 & 2 \\ -1 & 2 & 0 \\ -1 & 3 & 1 \end{vmatrix}$

20. $\begin{vmatrix} 0 & a & b \\ -a & 0 & c \\ -b & -c & 0 \end{vmatrix}$

21. $\begin{vmatrix} 4 & -7 & 6 & 7 \\ 0 & -3 & 9 & -8 \\ 0 & 0 & -2 & 6 \\ 0 & 0 & 0 & 5 \end{vmatrix}$

22. On the basis of Exercise 16, conjecture and prove a theorem regarding determinants.

23. Without expanding, show that

$$\begin{vmatrix} 5a & 5b & 5c \\ 3a & 3b & 3c \\ d & e & f \end{vmatrix} = 0.$$

24. Factor.

$$\begin{vmatrix} 1 & a & bc \\ 1 & b & ac \\ 1 & c & ab \end{vmatrix}$$

25. Given the input/output matrices A and A_o and the demand matrix D:

$$A = \begin{bmatrix} 0.4 & 0.1 \\ 0.3 & 0.2 \end{bmatrix},$$

$$A_o = [3 \quad 7],$$
$$D = [72 \quad 81]^T.$$

Find the production matrix X and the labor required x_o.

Solve.

26. $x + y + z + w = 4$
$\quad x + y + z + w = 3$
$\quad x + y + z + w = 3$

27. $-8x + 3y + 2z + w = 0$
$\quad 5x + y - z - w = 0$
$\quad 2x + 5y \quad - w = 0$
$\quad 3x - 4y - z \quad = 0$

LINEAR PROGRAMMING—
GRAPHICAL TECHNIQUES

During World War II the Army began to formulate certain *linear optimization* problems. Their solutions were called plans or *programs*. Subsequently, many other problems, particularly economic, were found to have a similar mathematical formulation. Such problems are called linear-programming problems or *linear programs* for short.

For example, consider the manager of a department store who sends his buyer to the "market." The buyer has a budget and can spend no more than a given amount of money. Furthermore, the goods must be brought back to the store in a company truck with a maximum cargo volume and a maximum cargo weight. That is, the total *volume* of the goods bought cannot exceed the cargo *volume* limit of the truck, nor can the total *weight* of the goods bought exceed the cargo *weight* limit of the truck. Each type of item bought can be marked up a certain percent. What items should the buyer buy to *maximize* the total value of the goods bought subject to the given constraints?

Such problems are characterized by the following features:

i) The specifications of the problem are related by *inequalities*, or *constraints*, rather than by equations. For example,

$$2x_1 + 3x_2 \leq 6 \quad \text{is an inequality,}$$

while

$$2x_1 + 3x_2 = 6 \quad \text{is an equation.}$$

ii) The inequalities or constraints of the problem are linear. For example, $2x_1 + 3x_2 \leq 6$ is a linear inequality; that is, all variables are to the first power and there are no divisions by a variable. Note that

$$2x_1^2 + 9x_2^2 + \frac{1}{x_1} \leq 36 \text{ is } \textit{not} \text{ a linear inequality.}$$

iii) The *solution* of a linear program must satisfy these constraints. In addition some quantity, a *linear* function of the variables, must be maximized or minimized. For example, maximize f where $f = 3x_1 + 2x_2$, and, for short, we have written f in place of $f(x_1, x_2)$.

In the following sections we shall consider various aspects of the formulation and solution of linear programs.

4.1 GRAPHING A SYSTEM OF LINEAR CONSTRAINTS (INEQUALITIES) IN TWO VARIABLES

The first stage in the solution of a linear program is graphing the constraints (inequalities). Consider an inequality like any of the following:

$$a_1x_1 + a_2x_2 \geq b,$$

or

$$a_1x_1 + a_2x_2 \leq b,$$

or

$$a_1x_1 + a_2x_2 > b,$$

or

$$a_1x_1 + a_2x_2 < b,$$

where a_1, a_2, and b are constants.

Corresponding to any of these inequalities there is a *related equation*

$$a_1x_1 + a_2x_2 = b.$$

Its graph is a line that divides the plane into two half-planes. We graph this equation first.

For inequalities with

a) $\geq$ or $\leq$, use a solid line for the related equation;

b) $>$ or $<$, use a dashed line for the related equation.

Example 1   Graph $2x_1 + 3x_2 \leq 6$.

Solution   There are two steps. First, graph the related equation $2x_1 + 3x_2 = 6$.

Since the equality is included ($\leq$) in the present example, the line is solid in Fig. 4.1.

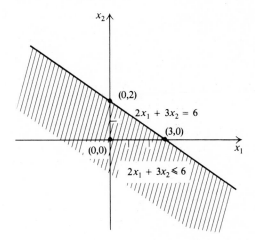

Figure 4.1

Second, having divided the plane into two half-planes, we must decide which half-plane contains the solutions of the inequality. To do this, we need consider only one test point. If *any* point on one side of the graph of the related equation satisfies the inequality, then *all* points in the same half-plane satisfy the inequality. If any point on one side of the graph of the related equation does *not* satisfy the inequality, then all points in the *opposite* half-plane satisfy the inequality.

If the graph of the related equation does not include the origin $(0, 0)$, we use the origin as a test point. In the present example, we thus ask "Is $(0, 0)$ a solution of $2x_1 + 3x_2 \leq 6$?"

We replace x_1 by 0 and x_2 by 0.

$$
\begin{array}{c|c}
2x_1 + 3x_2 & \leq 6 \\
\hline
2 \cdot 0 + 3 \cdot 0 & 6 \\
0 + \quad 0 & \\
0 &
\end{array}
$$

Because $0 \leq 6$ is true, $(0, 0)$ is a solution.

Since $(0, 0)$ is in the lower half-plane, *all* points in the lower half-plane are solutions. Thus, the shaded half-plane of Fig. 4.1 represents the solutions of the inequality.

Example 2   Graph $2x_1 - x_2 > 0$.

Solution   The related equation $2x_1 - x_2 = 0$ is graphed, using a dashed line since the line is not included in the inequality. See Fig. 4.2. Here the line passes through the origin $(0, 0)$, so we use either $(1, 0)$ or $(0, 1)$ as a test point. For $(1, 0)$ we ask "Is $(1, 0)$ a solution of $2x_1 - x_2 > 0$?"

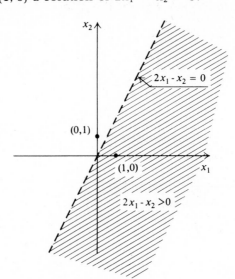

Figure 4.2

We replace x_1 by 1 and x_2 by 0.

$$2x_1 - x_2 > 0$$

$$
\begin{array}{c|c}
2 \cdot 1 - 0 & 0 \\
2 - 0 & \\
2 & \\
\end{array}
$$

Because $2 > 0$ is true, $(1, 0)$ is a solution.

Since $(1, 0)$ is in the lower half-plane, all points in the lower half-plane are solutions of the inequality.

Alternately, we could use $(0, 1)$ as a test point and ask "Is $(0, 1)$ a solution of $2x_1 - x_2 > 0$?"

We replace x_1 by 0 and x_2 by 1.

$$2x_1 - x_2 > 0$$

$$
\begin{array}{c|c}
2 \cdot 0 - 1 & 0 \\
0 - 1 & \\
-1 & \\
\end{array}
$$

Since $-1 > 0$ is false, $(0, 1)$ is not a solution.

Since $(0, 1)$ in the *upper* half-plane is *not* a solution, all points in the *lower* half-plane are solutions of the inequality.

Either case tells us the solution set is the half-plane shaded in Fig. 4.2.

It should be noted that the inequality $2x_1 - x_2 > 0$ is equivalent to $x_2 - 2x_1 < 0$, if we recall that, when both sides of an inequality are multiplied by -1, the inequality sign is *reversed*.

To graph a set, or *system*, of linear constraints, we first graph the solution set of each individual constraint using the same set of axes. The solution set of the *system* is that region, or set of ordered pairs, which satisfies *all* the constraints.

Example 3 Graph the solution set of the system of constraints

i) $\quad x_1 - 2x_2 \leqslant 0,$

ii) $-2x_1 + x_2 \leqslant 2.$

These two constraints are each graphed in Fig. 4.3. A *pair of arrows* points in the direction of the half-plane representing solutions of each inequality. The region satisfying *both* constraints is indicated by the shading.

Figure 4.3

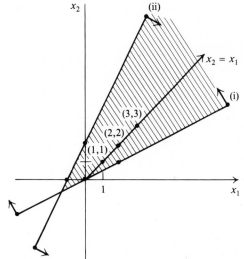

Example 4 Now let us add a third constraint to those of Example 3, so that we have

i) $\quad x_1 - 2x_2 \leqslant 0,$

ii) $-2x_1 + x_2 \leqslant 2,$

iii) $\quad x_1 + x_2 \leqslant 6.$

These are graphed in Fig. 4.4. The solution set of this system of *three* constraints is shaded. The solution set of Example 4 (Fig. 4.4) is *bounded*. This means simply that the solution set is confined to the boundary and interior of some polygon.

Not all solution sets are bounded. For example, the solution set of Example 3 (Fig. 4.3) is *unbounded*. This means that the solution set is *not* confined to the boundary and interior of some polygon. Note that in the direction of the arrow along the line $x_2 = x_1$, the boundary is *open*, so that in such a direction, given any solution one can find another solution farther out. In Example 3 any point (c, c) where $c \geq 0$ is a solution to the system of constraints (i) and (ii). The parameter c can become arbitrarily large and the point (c, c) will still be in the solution set.

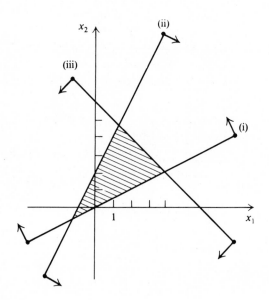

Figure 4.4

Example 5   Adding two more constraints, we have

i) $x_1 - 2x_2 \leq 0$,

ii) $-2x_1 + x_2 \leq 2$,

iii) $x_1 + x_2 \leq 6$,

iv) $x_1 \qquad \leq 2$,

v) $\qquad x_2 \leq 2$.

These are graphed in Fig. 4.5.

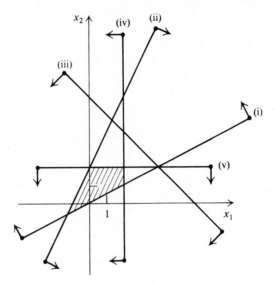

Figure 4.5

    The solution set has now been sufficiently reduced so that constraint (iii) no longer affects the solution set and hence is considered *redundant*. Redundant constraints, when identified as such, may be disregarded for present purposes.

Example 6 Now let us replace constraint (iii) by (vi), so that we have

    i) $x_1 - 2x_2 \leqslant 0,$

    ii) $-2x_1 + x_2 \leqslant 2,$

    iv) $x \quad\quad \leqslant 2,$

    v) $x_2 \leqslant 2,$

    vi) $x_1 + x_2 \leqslant 4.$

Thus, we obtain the graph in Fig. 4.6.

    The *corners* (or vertices) of the solution set are each the intersection of two lines. Thus, the coordinates of the corners can be determined by the solution of the corresponding *two* related equations. For example, point a with coordinates $(-\frac{4}{3}, -\frac{2}{3})$ is the simultaneous solution of the equations related to the *two* constraints (i) and (ii). Similarly, point b with coordinates $(2, 1)$ corresponds to the intersection of the equations related to the *two*

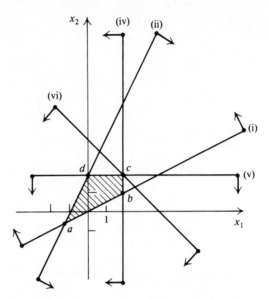

Figure 4.6

constraints (i) and (iv). Point c, on the other hand, with coordinates $(2, 2)$ is the simultaneous solution of the equations related to the *three* constraints (iv), (v), and (vi). Such points are called *degenerate* in linear programs. These degeneracies are important in later use but not here. For present purposes we consider constraint (vi) redundant. It may not be obvious from the graph which points are degenerate or which constraints are redundant. In this case, when we solved the pairs of related equations, the same solution would have occurred more than once, indicating a degeneracy.

Example 7   If constraint (vi) is replaced by (vii), so that we have

i) $x_1 - 2x_2 \leq 0,$

ii) $-2x_1 + x_2 \leq 2,$

iv) $x_1 \leq 2,$

v) $x_2 \leq 2,$

vii) $x_1 + x_2 \geq 5,$

then we obtain the graph in Fig. 4.7. In this case there is *no region common* to all constraints (i), (ii), (iv), (v), and (vii). The solution set is then *empty*. This is not the same as saying that the solution set is $(0, 0)$, because if the point $(0, 0)$ were in the solution set, it would *not* be empty. Furthermore, the empty set is bounded.

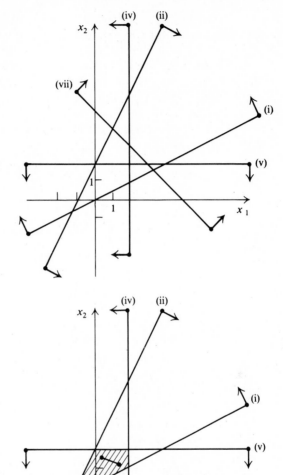

Figure 4.7

Figure 4.8

Consider two points in the solution set shown shaded in Fig. 4.8. Any point on the line segment between these two points is also in the solution set.*

---

* Any point on the line segment *between* two points is called a *convex combination* of the two points; this concept is discussed further in Section 5.4.

If the line segment between any pair of points in a set is also in the set, then such a set is called a *convex set*.

An example of a set which is not convex is the shaded region of Fig. 4.9. In this case there are two points, such as *a* and *b* in the figure, such that the line segment *between* them includes points *outside* the given set, for example, point *c*. Thus, this set is *not* convex. It can be shown that

For any system of linear constraints, the corresponding solution set must be convex.

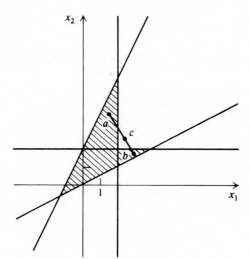

Figure 4.9

Knowing this is useful in determining the solution set of a graphed system of constraints. For example, the shaded region of Fig. 4.9 is not convex. Therefore, it could not possibly be a solution set for *any* system of linear constraints.

EXERCISE SET 4.1

Graph.

1. $5x_1 + x_2 > 10$

2. $3x_1 - 2x_2 \leq 12$

3. $3x_1 + 2x_2 \geq 6$

4. $x_1 - 4x_2 \leq 0$

5. $2x_1 + 5x_2 \leq 8$

6. $3x_1 + 7x_2 > 10$

Graph the following systems of constraints and shade the solution set.

7. $x_1 + x_2 \leqslant 6$
$x_2 \leqslant 5$
$x_1, x_2 \geqslant 0$

8. $x_1 + 2x_2 \leqslant 8$
$x_1 \leqslant 6$
$x_1, x_2 \geqslant 0$

9. $3x_1 + 2x_2 \leqslant 12$
$x_1 + x_2 \leqslant 5$
$x_1, x_2 \geqslant 0$

10. $3x_1 + 5x_2 \leqslant 15$
$3x_1 + 2x_2 \leqslant 12$
$x_1, x_2 \geqslant 0$

11. $x_1 + 2x_2 \leqslant 14$
$4x_1 + 3x_2 \leqslant 26$
$2x_1 + x_2 \leqslant 12$
$x_1, x_2 \geqslant 0$

12. $x_1 + 3x_2 \leqslant 18$
$3x_1 + 2x_2 \leqslant 19$
$2x_1 + x_2 \leqslant 12$
$x_1, x_2 \geqslant 0$

13. $3y_1 + y_2 \geqslant 9$
$y_1 + y_2 \geqslant 7$
$y_2 + 2y_2 \geqslant 8$
$y_1, y_2 \geqslant 0$

14. $2y_1 + y_2 \geqslant 8$
$4y_1 + 3y_2 \geqslant 22$
$2y_1 + 5y_2 \geqslant 18$
$y_1, y_2 \geqslant 0$

15. $2y_1 + y_2 \geqslant 9$
$4y_1 + 3y_2 \geqslant 23$
$y_1 + 3y_2 \geqslant 8$
$y_1, y_2 \geqslant 0$

16. $5y_1 + 3y_2 \geqslant 30$
$2y_1 + 3y_2 \geqslant 21$
$3y_1 + 6y_2 \geqslant 36$
$y_1, y_2 \geqslant 0$

17. $4y_1 + y_2 \geqslant 9$
$3y_1 + 2y_2 \geqslant 13$
$2y_1 + 5y_2 \geqslant 16$
$y_1, y_2 \geqslant 0$

18. $4y_1 + y_2 \geqslant 7$
$y_1 + y_2 \geqslant 4$
$2y_1 + 5y_2 \geqslant 14$
$y_1, y_2 \geqslant 0$

For the following exercises,

a) Graph the solution set of the system of constraints.

b) Is the solution set empty? nonempty?

c) Is the solution set bounded? unbounded?

d) Which constraints, if any, are redundant?

e) Which corners, if any, are degenerate?

Note. It may be difficult to answer (d) and (e) unless the equations are drawn carefully. In the next section, an alternative (algebraic) method will be used to determine the solution set more accurately.

Save your results for use at the end of the next section.

19. $x_1 + 2x_2 \leqslant 6$
$0 \leqslant x_1 \leqslant 5$
$x_2 \geqslant -2$

20. $x_1 - x_2 \geqslant -4$
$x_1 - x_2 \leqslant 6$
$-2 \leqslant x_2 \leqslant 2$

21. $x_1 \geqslant -3$
$x_1 - 2x_2 \leqslant 4$
$x_2 - 3x_1 \leqslant 9$
$3x_1 + x_2 \leqslant 10$

22. $3x_1 \geqslant x_2$
$3x_2 \geqslant x_1$
$x_1 + x_2 \geqslant 5$
$2x_1 + 3x_2 \leqslant 24$

■ ─────────────────────────

23. $-3x_1 + 2x_2 \geqslant 6$
$2x_1 + x_2 \leqslant -2$
$x_1 + x_2 \geqslant 4$
$2x_1 + 7x_2 \leqslant 21$

24. $x_1 + 4x_2 \geqslant -4$
$2x_1 + x_2 \leqslant 2$
$x_2 \geqslant 0$
$x_1 \leqslant 5$

25. $x_1 \geqslant 0$
$x_2 \geqslant 0$
$x_1 + x_2 \geqslant 2$
$x_1 - x_2 \leqslant 2$
$x_2 \leqslant 6$

26. $-3x_1 + 4x_2 \leqslant 12$
$3x_1 + 2x_2 \leqslant 24$
$x_1 \geqslant 0$
$x_2 \geqslant 0$
$x_2 \geqslant 6$

27. $x_1 + x_2 \leqslant 0$
$2x_1 - 3x_2 \leqslant 15$
$x_2 \leqslant 5$
$x_1 \geqslant 0$
$2x_1 + x_2 \geqslant 3$

28. $3x_1 + 2x_2 \geqslant 6$
$x_1 \geqslant 1$
$0 \leqslant x_2 \leqslant 6$
$2x_1 + 3x_2 \leqslant 24$
$3x_1 + x_2 \leqslant 15$

29. $x_1 \geqslant 0$
$x_2 \geqslant 0$
$5x_2 - 3x_1 \leqslant 15$
$x_1 \leqslant 4x_2$
$2x_1 - 5x_2 \leqslant 10$

30. $x_1 \geqslant 0$
$x_2 \geqslant 0$
$-7x_1 + x_2 \leqslant 7$
$4x_2 - 5x_1 \geqslant 20$
$x_1 + x_2 \leqslant 10$
$x_2 \leqslant 3$

4.2   DETERMINING THE OPTIMUM VALUE

We now find optimum values of some linear function of the variables. By this we mean the largest or smallest values of the function. The function being optimized is called the objective function. Let us again consider the solution set corresponding to constraints (i), (ii), (iv), and (v) of Example 5 of Section 4.1:

i) $x_1 - 2x_2 \leqslant 0,$

ii) $-2x_1 + x_2 \leqslant 2,$

iv) $x_1 \qquad \leqslant 2,$

v) $x_2 \leqslant 2.$

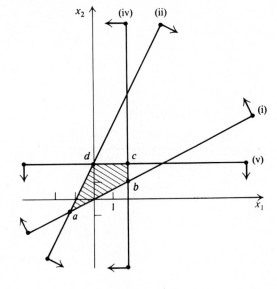

Figure 4.10

They are graphed in Fig. 4.8 and again in Fig. 4.10 where the corners have been labeled a, b, c, and d.

We need to find the coordinates of the corners. We determine them algebraically. Point a (Fig. 4.10) is the intersection of the equations related to constraints (i) and (ii):

i') $x_1 - 2x_2 = 0,$

ii') $-2x_1 + x_2 = 2.$

We find the coordinates of point a, represented by (a_1, a_2), by solving the system of equations (i') and (ii'). We use the echelon method described in Section 3.1. Other methods of solution could be used, but we are practicing the echelon method for later use.

Example 1   Solve the system of equations (i') and (ii') and determine the coordinates of point a.

Solution   The initial tableau is at the left.

x_1	x_2	1
1^*	-2	0
-2	1	2

x_1	x_2	1
1	-2	0
0	-3	2

x_1	x_2	1
1	0	$-\frac{4}{3}$
0	1^*	$-\frac{2}{3}$

Indicating the pivot by an * and pivoting (multiplying the first row by 2 and adding), we obtain the second tableau. Multiplying the second row by $-\frac{1}{3}$ to make the pivot element 1 and pivoting yields the final tableau. Thus, the coordinates of point a are $(a_1, a_2) = (-\frac{4}{3}, -\frac{2}{3})$.

By using the appropriate equations and solving algebraically (with the echelon method), we find the coordinates of the corners:

(i) and (ii) yield $(a_1, a_2) = (-\frac{4}{3}, -\frac{2}{3})$,

(i) and (iv) yield $(b_1, b_2) = (2, 1)$,

(iv) and (v) yield $(c_1, c_2) = (2, 2)$,

(ii) and (v) yield $(d_1, d_2) = (0, 2)$.

Example 2   Find the optimum (maximum and minimum) values and the points at which they are obtained, of the objective function $f(x_1, x_2) = x_1 + x_2 = f$, for short, subject to the constraints

i) $x_1 - 2x_2 \leqslant 0$,

ii) $-2x_1 + x_2 \leqslant 2$,

iv) $x_1 \qquad \leqslant 2$,

v) $x_2 \leqslant 2$.

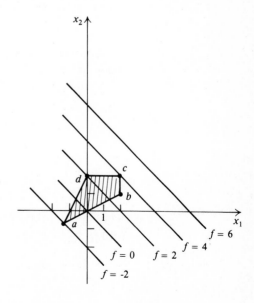

Figure 4.11

Solution To do this, let f assume various values. Thus, $f = 6$ leads to the equation

$$6 = x_1 + x_2,$$

the graph of which is a straight line.
Similarly,

$$f = \quad 4 \text{ leads to the equation} \quad 4 = x_1 + x_2,$$

$$f = \quad 2 \text{ leads to the equation} \quad 2 = x_1 + x_2,$$

$$f = \quad 0 \text{ leads to the equation} \quad 0 = x_1 + x_2,$$

$$f = -2 \text{ leads to the equation} \ -2 = x_1 + x_2.$$

The graphs of these lines are shown in Fig. 4.11 together with the solution set (shaded area).

From the figure we see that the line corresponding to $f = 6$ has no point in common with the solution set (shaded area). The lines corresponding to values of f between -2 and 4 $(-2 \leqslant f \leqslant 4)$ do have points in common with the solution set. Of all such lines $(-2 \leqslant f \leqslant 4)$, that corresponding to $f = 4$ has the maximum value of the objective function f. This maximum value is obtained at point c. Similarly, the minimum value of f is -2, obtained at point a.

> It is important to note that the optima (maximum and minimum values) were obtained at the **boundary** of the solution set and furthermore at **corner points.** For linear programs, it can be shown that the optima will always be obtained at corner points.

To determine the optima we need evaluate the objective function *only at the corner points.* In the present example,

$f(x_1, x_2)$	$= x_1 + x_2$		
$f(-\frac{4}{3}, -\frac{2}{3}) = (-\frac{4}{3}) + (-\frac{2}{3})$	$=$	-2	(minimum),
$f(2, 1)$	$=$	$2 + 1 \quad = \quad 3,$	
$f(2, 2)$	$=$	$2 + 2 \quad = \quad 4$	(maximum),
$f(0, 2)$	$=$	$0 + 2 \quad = \quad 2.$	

Note. The notation $f(2, 1)$ represents the value of $f(x_1, x_2)$ when 2 is substituted for x_1 and 1 is substituted for x_2. Thus:

$$\text{Maximum: } f(2, 2) = 4,$$

$$\text{Minimum: } f(-\tfrac{4}{3}, -\tfrac{2}{3}) = -2.$$

Example 3 Find the optimum values of the objective function

$$f(x_1, x_2) = 2x_1 - x_2,$$

subject to the constraints

i) $\quad x_1 - 2x_2 \leqslant 0,$

ii) $\quad -2x_1 + x_2 \leqslant 2,$

iv) $\quad x_1 \quad\quad \leqslant 2,$

v) $\quad\quad\quad x_2 \leqslant 2.$

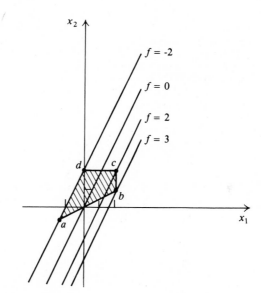

Figure 4.12

Solution As before, let f assume various values, as indicated on Fig. 4.12. The maximum value of f occurs now at point b, while the minimum occurs all along the line segment from a to d. Evaluating f at the corner points, we have

$$
\begin{array}{llll}
f(x_1, x_2) & = 2x_1 & - x_2 & \\
\hline
f(-\tfrac{4}{3}, -\tfrac{2}{3}) & = 2(-\tfrac{4}{3}) - (-\tfrac{2}{3}) & = -2 & \text{(minimum)}, \\
f(2, 1) & = 2 \cdot 2 - 1 & = 3 & \text{(maximum)}, \\
f(2, 2) & = 2 \cdot 2 - 2 & = 2, & \\
f(0, 2) & = 2 \cdot 0 - 2 & = -2 & \text{(minimum)}.
\end{array}
$$

The minimum value -2 can be seen to be attained at *more than one point*, specifically at the points a and d. It turns out that -2 is also attained for any *convex combination* of the coordinates of these two points, that is, for any point on the line segment between them.

EXERCISE SET 4.2

Find the optimum value (maximum or minimum, as indicated) for each objective function and the point at which it is obtained for each set of constraints. Save your results for later use.

1. Maximize $f(x_1, x_2) = x_1 + 2x_2$, subject to the constraints (Exercise 7, Set 4.1)

$$x_1 + x_2 \leqslant 6$$
$$x_2 \leqslant 5$$
$$x_1, x_2 \geqslant 0$$

2. Maximize $f(x_1, x_2) = x_1 + x_2$, subject to the constraints (Exercise 8, Set 4.1)

$$x_1 + 2x_2 \leqslant 8$$
$$x_1 \leqslant 6$$
$$x_1, x_2 \geqslant 0$$

3. Maximize $f(x_1, x_2) = 5x_1 + 4x_2$, subject to the constraints (Exercise 9, Set 4.1)

$$3x_1 + 2x_2 \leqslant 12$$
$$x_1 + x_2 \leqslant 5$$
$$x_1, x_2 \geqslant 0$$

4. Maximize $f(x_1, x_2) = 2x_1 + x_2$, subject to the constraints (Exercise 10, Set 4.1)

$$3x_1 + 5x_2 \leqslant 15$$
$$3x_1 + 2x_2 \leqslant 12$$
$$x_1, x_2 \geqslant 0$$

5. Maximize $f(x_1, x_2) = 3x_1 + 4x_2$, subject to the constraints (Exercise 11, Set 4.1)

$$x_1 + 2x_2 \leqslant 14$$
$$4x_1 + 3x_2 \leqslant 26$$
$$2x_1 + x_2 \leqslant 12$$
$$x_1, x_2 \geqslant 0$$

6. Maximize $f(x_1, x_2) = 5x_1 + 4x_2$, subject to the constraints (Exercise 12, Set 4.1)

$$x_1 + 3x_2 \leqslant 18$$
$$3x_1 + 2x_2 \leqslant 19$$
$$2x_1 + x_2 \leqslant 12$$
$$x_1, x_2 \geqslant 0$$

7. Minimize $f(y_1, y_2) = 3y_1 + 4y_2$, subject to the constraints (Exercise 13, Set 4.1)

$$3y_1 + y_2 \geqslant 9$$
$$y_1 + y_2 \geqslant 7$$
$$y_1 + 2y_2 \geqslant 8$$
$$y_1, y_2 \geqslant 0$$

8. Minimize $f(y_1, y_2) = 3y_1 + 4y_2$, subject to the constraints (Exercise 14, Set 4.1)

$$2y_1 + y_2 \geqslant 8$$
$$4y_1 + 3y_2 \geqslant 22$$
$$2y_1 + 5y_2 \geqslant 18$$
$$y_1, y_2 \geqslant 0$$

9. Minimize $f(y_1, y_2) = 2y_1 + 5y_2$, subject to the constraints (Exercise 15, Set 4.1)

$$2y_1 + y_2 \geqslant 9$$

$$4y_1 + 3y_2 \geqslant 23$$

$$y_1 + 3y_2 \geqslant 8$$

$$y_1, y_2 \geqslant 0$$

10. Minimize $f(y_1, y_2) = 9y_1 + 7y_2$, subject to the constraints (Exercise 16, Set 4.1)

$$5y_1 + 3y_2 \geqslant 30$$

$$2y_1 + 3y_2 \geqslant 21$$

$$3y_1 + 6y_2 \geqslant 36$$

$$y_1, y_2 \geqslant 0$$

11. Minimize $f(y_1, y_2) = 3y_1 + 5y_2$, subject to the constraints (Exercise 17, Set 4.1)

$$4y_1 + y_2 \geqslant 9$$

$$3y_1 + 2y_2 \geqslant 13$$

$$2y_1 + 5y_2 \geqslant 16$$

$$y_1, y_2 \geqslant 0$$

12. Minimize $f(y_1, y_2) = 2y_1 + 3y_2$, subject to the constraints (Exercise 18, Set 4.1)

$$4y_1 + y_2 \geqslant 7$$

$$y_1 + y_2 \geqslant 4$$

$$2y_1 + 5y_2 \geqslant 14$$

$$y_1, y_2 \geqslant 0$$

Find the optimum (maximum and minimum) values for each objective function and the points at which they are obtained subject to the constraints given.

13. $f(x_1, x_2) = x_1 - x_2$, subject to the constraints (Exercise 19, Set 4.1)

$$x_1 + 2x_2 \leqslant 6$$

$$0 \leqslant x_1 \leqslant 5$$

$$x_2 \geqslant -2$$

14. $f(x_1, x_2) = 2x_1 + 3x_2$, subject to the constraints of Exercise 13.

15. $f(x_1, x_2) = x_1 - x_2$, subject to the constraints (Exercise 21, Set 4.1)

$$x_1 \geqslant -3$$

$$x_1 - 2x_2 \leqslant 4$$

$$x_2 - 3x_1 \leqslant 9$$

$$3x_1 + x_2 \leqslant 10$$

16. $f(x_1, x_2) = x_2 - 2x_1$, subject to the constraints of Exercise 15.

17. $f(x_1, x_2) = 3x_1 - x_2$, subject to the constraints (Exercise 22, Set 4.1)

$$3x_1 \geqslant x_2$$

$$3x_2 \geqslant x_1$$

$$x_1 + x_2 \geqslant 5$$

$$2x_1 + 3x_2 \leqslant 24$$

18. $f(x_1, x_2) = 3x_2 - x_1$, subject to the constraints of Exercise 17.

19. $f(x_1, x_2) = x_1 + x_2$, subject to the constraints (Exercise 23, Set 4.1)

$$-3x_1 + 2x_2 \geqslant 6$$

$$2x_1 + x_2 \leqslant -2$$

$$x_1 + x_2 \geqslant 4$$

$$2x_1 + 7x_2 \leqslant 21$$

20. $f(x_1, x_2) = x_1 + x_2$, subject to the constraints (Exercise 24, Set 4.1)

$$x_1 + 4x_2 \geqslant -4$$

$$2x_1 + x_2 \leqslant 2$$

$$x_2 \geqslant 0$$

$$x_1 \leqslant 5$$

21. $f(x_1, x_2) = 2x_1 + 3x_2$, subject to the constraints (Exercise 29, Set 4.1)

$$x_1 \geqslant 0$$

$$x_2 \geqslant 0$$

$$5x_2 - 3x_1 \leqslant 15$$

$$x_1 \leqslant 4x_2$$

$$2x_1 - 5x_2 \leqslant 10$$

22. $f(x_1, x_2) = 3x_1 + 4x_2$, subject to the constraints (Exercise 28, Set 4.1)

$$3x_1 + 2x_2 \geqslant 6$$

$$x_1 \geqslant 1$$

$$0 \leqslant x_2 \leqslant 6$$

$$2x_1 + 3x_2 \leqslant 24$$

$$3x_1 + x_2 \leqslant 15$$

23. $f(x_1, x_2) = 4x_1 + 3x_2$, subject to the constraints (Exercise 27, Set 4.1)

$$x_1 + x_2 \leqslant 0$$

$$2x_1 - 3x_2 \leqslant 15$$

$$x_2 \leqslant 5$$

$$x_1 \geqslant 0$$

$$2x_1 + x_2 \geqslant 3$$

24. $f(x_1, x_2) = 2x_1 + 5x_2$, subject to the constraints (Exercise 30, Set 4.1)

$$x_1 \geqslant 0$$

$$x_2 \geqslant 0$$

$$-7x_1 + x_2 \leqslant 7$$

$$4x_2 - 5x_1 \geqslant 20$$

$$x_1 + x_2 \leqslant 10$$

$$x_2 \leqslant 3$$

4.3 FORMULATING MAXIMUM-TYPE LINEAR PROGRAMS AND SOLVING GRAPHICALLY

Example 1 Formulate (model) this problem.

A California vintner has available 660 lbs of Cabernet Sauvignon (CS) grapes, 1860 lbs of Pinot Noir (PN) grapes, and 2100 lbs of Barbera (B) grapes. The vintner makes a Pinot Noir (PN) wine, which contains 20% CS, 60% PN, and 20% B grapes and sells for $3 a bottle, and a Barbera (B) wine, which contains 10% CS, 20% PN, and 70% B grapes and sells for $2 a bottle. Assuming each bottle of wine requires 3 lbs of grapes, determine how many bottles of each type of wine should be produced to maximize income.

Solution This problem can be formulated using a table. The following steps show how to do this.

1. First, define the variables. Let

   x_1 = the number of bottles of Pinot Noir wine to be produced,

   x_2 = the number of bottles of Barbera wine to be produced, and

   f = the income ($) obtained from the sale of all the wine.

   Note that that the variables x_1 and x_2 are defined in terms of *bottle* units while the grape supply is given in terms of *lb* units. Since one bottle of wine requires three lbs of grapes, the available supply of grapes in lb units must be divided by three to yield the available supply of grapes in bottle units, so that consistent units are used throughout the problem. Defining the variables carefully helps prevent formulation errors.

2. Set up a table with the following general headings, which actually vary depending on the specific problem. Across the top list the *products* being manufactured and at the right write "Number of units of supply available." In the next row indicate the independent variables.

   Look ahead to see how this is done for this problem.

	Composition			Number of units of supply available
	Product 1	Product 2	$\cdots$	
Number of units	x_1	x_2	$\cdots$	
Ingredient 1 Ingredient 2 $\vdots$				
Unit value				Objective

3. In the first column list the ingredients used in making each product and at the bottom write "Unit value."

   Look at the table to see how this is done for this problem.

4. Enter into the table columnwise the data describing the composition of each product and in the bottom row its unit value.

   Note that the percents must be converted to fractions or decimals. The value, here price, could be expressed in either dollars or cents, but be consistent. See how this is done for this problem.

5. Enter into the column headed "supply available" the appropriate data for each ingredient. Indicate at the bottom of this column the "objective" of the problem.

Entering the data for this problem, we obtain the following table:

| | Composition (bottles) | | Number of bottles available |
	PN Wine	B Wine	
Number of bottles	x_1	x_2	
CS Grapes	0.20	0.10	220
PN Grapes	0.60	0.20	620
B Grapes	0.20	0.70	700
$ Price per bottle	3	2	Maximize income

6. For each ingredient the corresponding constraint can be read rowwise from the table. Note the similarity to the echelon tableau.

Noting that the supply available cannot be exceeded, we obtain

$$CS: \quad 0.20x_1 + 0.10x_2 \leqslant 220,$$

$$PN: \quad 0.60x_1 + 0.20x_2 \leqslant 620,$$

$$B: \quad 0.20x_1 + 0.70x_2 \leqslant 700.$$

7. The next two constraints are not stated *explicitly* in the problem. Rather they are *implied* by the reality of the situation. Since one cannot produce a *negative* amount of wine, we constrain the amount of wine produced to be nonnegative; that is,

$$x_1 \geqslant 0$$

and

$$x_2 \geqslant 0.$$

   The constraint that a physical quantity be realistic and hence non-negative is called the *nonnegativity constraint*.

8. Read the objective function and problem objective from the bottom row.

Here the objective is to maximize income, so that we obtain

$$\text{maximize } f, \text{ where } f = 3x_1 + 2x_2.$$

The formulation can be summarized as follows:

i) $\qquad\qquad 0.20x_1 + 0.10x_2 \leqslant 220,$

ii) $\qquad\qquad 0.60x_1 + 0.20x_2 \leqslant 620,$

iii) $\qquad\qquad 0.20x_1 + 0.70x_2 \leqslant 700,$

iv,v) $\qquad\qquad\qquad x_1, x_2 \geqslant 0$,

vi)　max f: $\quad f = \quad 3x_1 + \quad 2x_2$.

In summary, a *linear program* can be formulated, or modeled, as a system of linear inequalities, called *constraints* (both explicit and implicit), together with some linear function to be optimized—in this case maximized. That is, here we want to find the largest value of the objective function, subject to the given constraints, and the numerical values that yield it.

We can use matrices for clarification. The maximum-type linear program can be expressed in the form

$$AX \leqslant B,$$

$$X \geqslant O,$$

$$\max f: \quad f = CX,$$

where in Example 1,

$$A = \begin{bmatrix} 0.20 & 0.10 \\ 0.60 & 0.20 \\ 0.20 & 0.70 \end{bmatrix}, \quad X = \begin{bmatrix} x_1 \\ x_2 \end{bmatrix}, \quad B = \begin{bmatrix} 220 \\ 620 \\ 700 \end{bmatrix}, \quad \text{and} \quad C = [3 \quad 2].$$

The matrix A is made up of the coefficients of the constraint system. The notation $X \geqslant O$ implies that *each* component of X is nonnegative. Similarly, the notation $AX \leqslant B$ implies that each component of AX is less than or equal to the corresponding component of B.

Thus, a maximum-type linear program is composed of three parts. First, there are the linear constraints, $AX \leqslant B$, particular to each problem, and second, the nonnegativity constraints, $X \geqslant O$, which are common to most problems. Third, there is a linear objective function $f = CX$, which is to be maximized.

The linear program just formulated can be solved graphically using the techniques of the preceding sections.

A general procedure for solving linear programs in two variables is

1. **Graph the constraints;**
2. **Determine the solution set (shade this region);**
3. **Label the corner points and determine their coordinates algebraically (with the echelon method);**

    4. **Evaluate the objective function at all corner points; and**

    5. **Determine by inspection the optimum value (maximum or minimum) and where it is attained.**

Example 2   (maximum-type)   Solve graphically the linear program of Example 1.

Solution   The formulation of this linear program was found to be

$$
\begin{array}{lll}
\text{i(CS):} & 0.20x_1 + 0.10x_2 \leq 220, \\
\text{ii(PN):} & 0.60x_1 + 0.20x_2 \leq 620, \\
\text{iii(B):} & 0.20x_1 + 0.70x_2 \leq 700,
\end{array}
$$

vi, iv, v: max f: $f = 3x_1 + 2x_2$; $x_1, x_2 \geq 0$.

The constraints and solution set are shown in Fig. 4.13. Note that the nonnegativity constraints (iv, v) restrict consideration to the first quadrant. The coordinates of the corner points follow:

$$\text{iv and v\quad yield } (a_1, a_2) = (0, 0),$$

$$\text{ii and v\quad yield } (b_1, b_2) = \left(\tfrac{3100}{3}, 0\right),$$

$$\text{i and ii\quad yield } (c_1, c_2) = (900, 400),$$

$$\text{i and iii yield } (d_1, d_2) = (700, 800),$$

$$\text{iii and iv yield } (e_1, e_2) = (0, 1000).$$

Evaluating the objective function at these points, we obtain

$$
\begin{array}{lll}
f(x_1, x_2) = 3x_1 & + 2x_2, \\
f(0, 0) = 3 \cdot 0 & + 2 \cdot 0 & = 0, \\
f\left(\tfrac{3100}{3}, 0\right) = 3 \cdot \tfrac{3100}{3} & + 2 \cdot 0 & = 3100, \\
f(900, 400) = 3 \cdot 900 & + 2 \cdot 400 & = 3500, \\
f(700, 800) = 3 \cdot 700 & + 2 \cdot 800 & = 3700 \text{ (maximum)}, \\
f(0, 1000) = 3 \cdot 0 & + 2 \cdot 1000 & = 2000.
\end{array}
$$

Thus, the maximum *income* (not necessarily profit) that the vintner can obtain is \$3700 ($f = 3700$) by producing 700 bottles of PN wine ($x_1 = 700$) and 800 bottles of B wine ($x_2 = 800$). This maximum occurs at point d, so that all the CS and B grapes are used but there is an excess of PN grapes, which can be put to some other use.

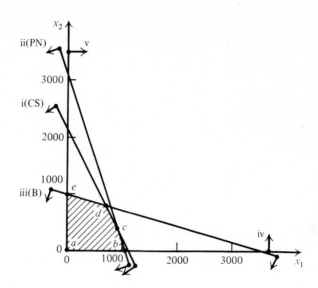

Figure 4.13

EXERCISE SET 4.3

In the following problems: (a) Formulate the model; (b) express the results in matrix form; (c) solve graphically.

1. *Maximizing income.* A clothier makes suits and dresses. Each suit requires 1 yd of polyester and 4 yds of wool while each dress requires 2 yds of polyester and 3 yds of wool. The clothier has in stock 60 yds of polyester and 120 yds of wool. If a suit sells for $120, and a dress sells for $75, how many of each should be made to maximize income?

2. *Maximizing income.* A manufacturer of hi-fi speakers makes two speaker assemblies. The inexpensive speaker assembly consists of one midrange speaker and one tweeter. It sells for $25. The expensive speaker assembly consists of one woofer, one midrange speaker, and two tweeters. This one sells for $150. The stock consists of 22 12″ woofers, 30 5″ midrange speakers, and 45 $1\frac{1}{2}$″ tweeters. How many of each type of speaker assembly should be made to maximize income?

3. *Maximizing income.* A nut dealer has 1800 lbs of peanuts, 1500 lbs of cashews, and 750 lbs of almonds, from which two mixtures will be made. Mixture I sells for $0.75 per lb and contains 60% peanuts, 30% cashews, and 10% almonds. Mixture II sells for $2.00 per lb and contains 20% peanuts, 50% cashews, and 30% almonds. How many lbs of each should be mixed to maximize income?

4. *Maximizing income.* A tea merchant has 400 lbs of cut black tea, 300 lbs of pekoe, and 240 lbs of orange pekoe tea, from which two mixtures are blended. Mixture A, selling for $1.50 per lb contains 50% cut black tea, 30% pekoe, and 20% orange pekoe. Mixture B, selling for $4.00 per lb, contains 50% pekoe and 50% orange pekoe. How many lbs of each mixture should be blended to maximize income?

5. A certain area of forest is populated by two species of animals (A1 and A2) and the forest supplies three kinds of food (F1, F2, and F3). Species A1 requires 1 unit of food F1, 2 units of food F2, and 2 units of food F3 while species A2 requires 1.2 units of food F1, 1.8 units of food F2, and 0.6 units of food F3. If the forest can normally supply a maximum of 600 units of food F1, 960 units of food F2, and 720 units of food F3, what is the maximum total numbers of these animals that the forest can support?

7. In reference to Exercise 5, if there is a wet spring, so that the maximum available supply of food becomes 720 units of food F1, 960 units of food F2, and 600 units of food F3, what maximum number of animals can now be supported? What would happen to species A1?

6. In reference to Exercise 5, if species A1 is valued at $150 and species A2 is valued at $120, how many animals of each species will maximize the value of the animal stock?

4.4 FORMULATING MINIMUM-TYPE LINEAR PROGRAMS AND SOLVING GRAPHICALLY

Example 1 Formulate (model) this problem.

Minimizing cost, Nutrition. A feed supplier mixes feed for a particular animal which requires for proper nutrition at least 160 lbs of nutrient A, at least 24 lbs of nutrient B, and at least 28 lbs of nutrient C over some period of time. The supplier has available soybean meal*, which costs $15 per ~~100-lb~~ sack and contains 40 lbs of nutrient A, 4 lbs of nutrient B, and 4 lbs of nutrient C and triticale†, which costs $10 per ~~100-lb~~ sack and contains 20 lbs of nutrient A, 4 lbs of nutrient B, and 6 lbs of nutrient C. How many sacks of each ingredient should be used to mix animal feed to satisfy the minimum requirements at minimum cost?

Solution This problem can be formulated as follows:

1. First, define the variables. Let

$$y_1 = \text{the number of 100-lb sacks of soybean meal,}$$

$$y_2 = \text{the number of 100-lb sacks of triticale, and}$$

$$f = \text{the \$ cost of the animal feed.}$$

---

* Soybean meal is made from soybeans by extracting the oil, which is then used commercially for other purposes.

† *Tri´-ti-cale:* a hybrid of wheat and rye.

2. As for maximum-type programs, set up a table with the following general headings. Across the top list the *sources* of materials and at the right write "Amount of Component Required." In the next row indicate the independent variables.

Look ahead to see how this is done for the present example.

	Composition			Amount of component required
	Source 1	Source 2	$\cdots$	
Number of units	y_1	y_2	$\cdots$	
Component 1 Component 2 $\vdots$				
Unit cost				Objective

3. In the first column list the *components* of the sources of materials and at the bottom write "Unit cost."

Look at the table and see how this is done for this example.

4. Enter into the table columnwise the data describing the composition of each source material and its unit cost in the bottom row.

See how this is done for the present example.

5. Enter into the column headed "Amount of component required" the appropriate data for each component. Indicate at the bottom of this column the "objective" of the problem.

Entering the data for this example, we obtain the following table:

	Composition (lbs per 100-lb sack)		Pounds required
	Soybean meal	Triticale	
Number of 100-lb sacks	y_1	y_2	
Nutrient A Nutrient B Nutrient C	40 4 4	20 4 6	160 24 28
$ Cost per 100-lb sack	15	10	Minimize cost

6. For each component the corresponding constraint can be read rowwise from the table by noting that the amount of the component must be at least satisfied:

$$A: \quad 40y_1 + 20y_2 \geqslant 160,$$

$$B: \quad 4y_1 + 4y_2 \geqslant 24,$$

$$C: \quad 4y_1 + 6y_2 \geqslant 28.$$

7. As for the maximum-type programs, we have the implied nonnegativity constraints:

$$y_1 \geqslant 0 \quad \text{and} \quad y_2 \geqslant 0.$$

In this Example there is another *implied* constraint. Soybean meal and triticale are sold in 100-lb sacks. Hence, their number must be *integer*. Problems with this integer constraint (which is *not* linear) are called *integer programs*. (Their solutions can be found by considering the various integer solutions neighboring the linear program solution, but this involves much extra work.) We shall *ignore* this integer constraint and accept whatever numerical values are obtained from the solution to the *linear* program.

8. Read the objective function and problem objective from the bottom row. Here the objective is to minimize the cost, so that we obtain

$$\text{minimize } f \text{ where } f = 15y_1 + 10y_2.$$

The formulation can be summarized as follows:

i(A):	$40y_1 + 20y_2 \geqslant 160,$
ii(B):	$4y_1 + 4y_2 \geqslant 24,$
iii(C):	$4y_1 + 6y_2 \geqslant 28,$
iv,v:	$y_1, y_2 \geqslant 0,$
vi:	min f: $f = 15y_1 + 10y_2$.

In matrix notation, a minimum-type linear program can be written in the form

$$AY \geqslant B,$$

$$Y \geqslant O,$$

$$\text{min } f: \quad f = CY,$$

where, in the preceding example,

$$A = \begin{bmatrix} 40 & 20 \\ 4 & 4 \\ 4 & 6 \end{bmatrix}, \quad Y = \begin{bmatrix} y_1 \\ y_2 \end{bmatrix}, \quad B = \begin{bmatrix} 160 \\ 24 \\ 28 \end{bmatrix}, \quad \text{and} \quad C = [15 \quad 10].$$

Thus, a minimum-type linear program is also composed of three parts. First, there are the linear constraints, $AY \geq B$, particular to each problem, and second, the nonnegativity constraints, $Y \geq O$, which are common to most problems. Third, there is a linear objective function $f = CY$, which is to be minimized.

For convenience, we use the word "optimum" to refer to either a "maximum" or a "minimum," whichever is appropriate. Thus, in general, a linear program consists of a system of particular (linear) constraints, plus nonnegativity constraints and a linear objective function to be optimized.

Example 2 Solve graphically the linear program of Example 1.

Solution The formulation of this linear program is

i(A): $\qquad\qquad 40y_1 + 20y_2 \geq 160,$

ii(B): $\qquad\qquad 4y_1 + 4y_2 \geq 24,$

iii(C): $\qquad\qquad 4y_1 + 6y_2 \geq 28,$

vi,iv,v: $\quad$ min f: $\quad f = 15y_1 + 10y_2;$ $\qquad y_1, y_2 \geq 0.$

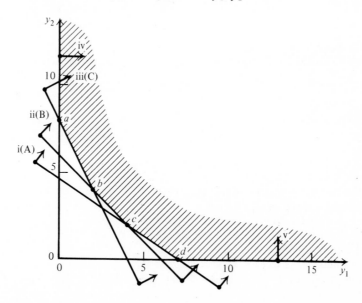

Figure 4.14

The constraints and solution set are shown in Fig. 4.14. Again, the nonnegativity constraints (iv, v) restrict consideration to the first quadrant.

The four corners a, b, c, and d of the solution set have coordinates as follows:

$$\text{(iii) and (iv) yield } (a_1, a_2) = (0, 8),$$

$$\text{(ii) and (iii) yield } (b_1, b_2) = (2, 4),$$

$$\text{(i) and (ii) yield } (c_1, c_2) = (4, 2),$$

$$\text{(i) and (v) yield } (d_1, d_2) = (7, 0).$$

Evaluating the objective function $f = 15y_1 + 10y_2$ at these points, we obtain

$$
\begin{array}{l}
f(y_1, y_2) = 15y_1 + 10y_2 \\
\hline
f(0, 8) = 15(0) + 10(8) = 80, \\
f(2, 4) = 15(2) + 10(4) = 70 \quad \text{(minimum)}, \\
f(4, 2) = 15(4) + 10(2) = 80, \\
f(7, 0) = 15(7) + 10(0) = 105.
\end{array}
$$

Thus, point b yields the minimum value of the objective function. The supplier should buy 2 sacks of soybean meal for each 4 sacks of triticale to minimize cost.

EXERCISE SET 4.4

a) Formulate (model) the following problems.

b) Express the results in matrix form.

c) Solve graphically.

1. *Minimizing cost, Nutrition.* An animal feed to be mixed from soybean meal and oats must contain at least 120 lbs of protein, 24 lbs of fat, and 10 lbs of mineral ash. Each 100-lb sack of soybean meal costs $15 and contains 50 lbs of protein, 8 lbs of fat, and 5 lbs of mineral ash. Each 100-lb sack of oats costs $5 and contains 15 lbs of protein, 5 lbs of fat, and 1 lb of mineral ash. How many sacks of each should be used to satisfy the minimum requirements at minimum cost?

2. *Minimizing cost, Nutrition.* Suppose the oats in the preceding problem were replaced by alfalfa, which costs $8 per 100 lbs and contains 20 lbs of protein, 6 lbs of fat, and 8 lbs of mineral ash. How much of each is now required to minimize the cost?

3. *Minimizing cost, Nutrition.* How is the formulation of Exercise 2 changed if the mineral requirement is doubled?

5. *Minimizing cost, Transportation.* An airline with two types of airplanes, P1 and P2, has contracted with a tour group to provide accommodations for a minimum of each of 2000 first-class, 1500 tourist, and 2400 economy-class passengers. Airplane P1 costs $12 thousand per mile to operate and can accommodate 40 first-class, 40 tourist, and 120 economy-class passengers, while airplane P2 costs $10 thousand per mile to operate and can accommodate 80 first-class, 30 tourist, and 40 economy-class passengers. How many of each type of airplane should be used to minimize the operating cost?

7. *Minimizing cost, Transportation.* If, instead of replacing P1 by P3, P2 is replaced by P3, how many of P1 and P3 should be used, to minimize the operating cost?

9. *Minimizing cost, Transportation.* If the contract requirements are changed to a minimum of 1600 first-class, 2100 tourist, and 2400 economy-class passengers, how many of airplanes P1 and P2 are now required to minimize the operating cost?

11. *Minimizing cost, Transportation.* As in Exercise 9 but with airplanes P1 and P3 . . . ?

4. *Minimizing cost, Nutrition.* How is the formulation of Exercise 2 changed if the cost of alfalfa is increased to $10?

6. *Minimizing cost, Transportation.* A new airplane P3 becomes available, having an operating cost of $15 thousand per mile, and accommodating 40 first-class, 80 tourist, and 80 economy-class passengers. If airplane P1 of Exercise 5 were replaced by airplane P3, how many of P2 and P3 would be needed to minimize the operating cost?

8. *Minimizing cost, Transportation.* If all three planes P1, P2, and P3 are used, how many of each should be used to minimize the cost? Formulate and put in matrix form only.

10. *Minimizing cost, Transportation.* As in Exercise 9, but with airplanes P2 and P3 . . . ?

12. *Minimizing cost, Transportation.* As in Exercise 9, but using all three airplanes . . . ? Formulate and put in matrix form only.

4.5 POST-OPTIMALITY ANALYSIS

Once a linear program has been solved, we are sometimes interested in knowing how much the solution is changed when the given data is changed. Such considerations are called *post-optimality* or *sensitivity analysis*.

For linear programs written in the form

$$AX \leq B, \quad X \geq 0,$$

$$\max f: \quad f = CX,$$

or

$$AY \geq B, \quad Y \geq 0,$$

$$\min f: \quad f = CY,$$

we shall consider, in turn, three kinds of changes:

1. Changes in the objective function (C),
2. Changes in the requirements (B), and
3. Changes in the composition (A).

Example 1   Consider Example 1 of Section 4.3 with the formulation

$$0.20x_1 + 0.10x_2 \leqslant 220,$$

$$0.60x_1 + 0.20x_2 \leqslant 620,$$

$$0.20x_1 + 0.70x_2 \leqslant 700,$$

$$\max f: \quad f = 3x_1 + 2x_2; \, x_1, x_2 \geqslant 0,$$

and with the solution

$$\max f = 3700 \text{ for } x_1 = 700 \text{ and } x_2 = 800.$$

How high can the price per bottle of Pinot Noir wine be raised before the production schedule ($x_1 = 700$, $x_2 = 800$) is no longer optimum?

Solution   The given objective function was

$$f_1 = 3x_1 + 2x_2$$

with f replaced by f_1. We now replace the \$3 per bottle cost of Pinot Noir wine by c_1 (\$ per bottle) and obtain a new objective function:

$$f_2 = c_1x_1 + 2x_2.$$

Consider again the graph of these constraints in Fig. 4.15 (taken from Fig. 4.13) where we have added the original objective function

$$f_1 = 3x_1 + 2x_2$$

passing through point d, which optimizes the original problem.

The shaded area represents the solution set of the constraints

$$AX \leqslant B \quad \text{and} \quad X \geqslant 0.$$

We know from Section 4.2 that the optimum value of the objective function will be realized at one or more corner points. As the cost c_1 is increased, the slope $\left(\dfrac{-c_1}{2}\right)$ of the objective function becomes more negative. To determine when point d no longer optimizes the objective function, we rotate

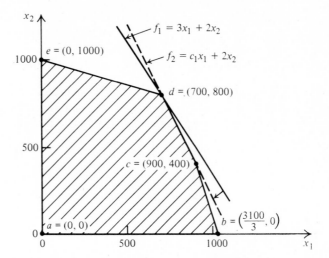

Figure 4.15

the line representing the objective function clockwise until it just passes through point c. For any further increase in c_1, we would have to rotate the objective function line clockwise about point c.

Thus, for point d, we have

$$f_2(700, 800) = 700c_1 + 1600,$$

and for point c, we have

$$f_2(900, 400) = 900c_1 + 800.$$

Equating these two expressions for f_2 and solving for c_1, we obtain

$$c_1 = 4, \text{ or } \$4 \text{ per bottle,}$$

and, correspondingly,

$$f_2 = 4400.$$

For any increase in the price of Pinot Noir wine from \$3 to less than \$4 per bottle, the optimum solution is still point d, $x_1 = 700$ and $x_2 = 800$. For an increase to more than \$4 per bottle, the solution shifts to point c, $x_1 = 900$ and $x_2 = 400$. For an increase to just \$4, the solution is any convex combination of $(700, 800)$ and $(900, 400)$.

If we had simply increased the price of PN wine, then, having previously found the coordinates of all the corner points, all we need have done was to evaluate the new objective function at each corner point to find the new optimum. The present example provides us with more information since we do not have to resolve the problem each time the cost of PN wine is changed but can tell at what critical price the optimum values of x_1, x_2 change.

This same procedure can be used for minimum-type linear programs.

Example 2   Consider again the original linear program of Example 1. How large would the supply of Cabernet Sauvignon grapes have to become before any further increase in supply would have no effect on production?

Solution   The original constraint on Cabernet Sauvignon grapes was

$$0.20x_1 + 0.10x_2 \leqslant 220.$$

We replace the supply of 220 bottles (660 lbs) by b_1 bottles ($3b_1$ lbs), so that the constraint on CS grapes becomes

$$0.20x_1 + 0.10x_2 \leqslant b_1.$$

We have in Fig. 4.16 a graph of our constraints. As b_1 is increased from 220, the line corresponding to the CS grape constraint,

$$0.20x_1 + 0.10x_2 = b_1,$$

moves up to the right, parallel to itself, enlarging the solution set. When it passes through point g, the CS grape constraint becomes redundant; that is, any further increase in b_1 does not enlarge the solution set. Point g corresponds to the intersection of the lines corresponding to the PN and B grape constraints (the *other* two constraints) and has the coordinates

$$(g_1, g_2) = \left(\frac{14700}{19}, \frac{14800}{19}\right).$$

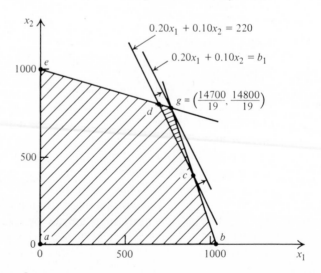

Figure 4.16

Using these coordinates, we calculate b_1:

$$b_1 = 0.20g_1 + 0.10g_2$$

$$= \tfrac{4420}{19} = 232\tfrac{12}{19} \text{ bottles,}$$

or

$$3b_1 = \tfrac{13260}{19} = 697\tfrac{17}{19} \text{ lbs.}$$

For any increase in supply from 220 to less than this value of b_1, the optimum would be at the intersection of the lines corresponding to the B and CS grape constraints.

This same procedure can be used for minimum-type linear programs.

Example 3   If in the original linear program of Example 1 the composition of PN wine is changed to 20% CS, 65% PN, and 15% B grapes, how is the optimum changed?

Solution   With the change in composition, the constraints become

$$\text{CS:}\quad 0.20x_1 + 0.10x_2 \le 220,$$

$$\text{PN:}\quad 0.65x_1 + 0.20x_2 \le 620,$$

$$\text{B:}\quad 0.15x_1 + 0.70x_2 \le 700.$$

Note that in this Example, we cannot change just one coefficient of x_1 or x_2 but, since the percentages must add to 100%, we must change at least two.

Graphing both the original constraints and the new set of constraints on Fig. 4.16, we have the result shown in Fig. 4.17 (next page). Two of the constraint equations (B and PN) have changed position while one (CS) is unchanged.

The corner points of the feasible solution set change from a, b, c, d, e to a, b', c', d', e. To determine the new optimum feasible solution, we determine the coordinates of the new corner points and the corresponding values of the objective function. Thus, we obtain the following table:

Point	x_1, x_2	$f = 3x_1 + 2x_2$
a	0, 0	0
b'	$\tfrac{12400}{13}$, 0	$\tfrac{37200}{13} = 2861\tfrac{7}{13}$
c'	720, 760	3680
d'	$\tfrac{8400}{13}$, $\tfrac{11800}{13}$	$\tfrac{48800}{13} = 3753\tfrac{11}{13}$
e	0, 1000	2000

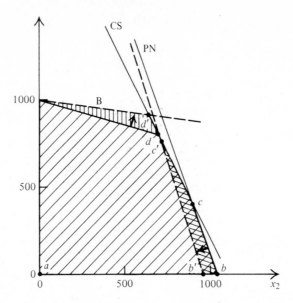

Figure 4.17

Thus, with the change in composition, the production schedule is changed from $x_1 = 700$ and $x_2 = 800$ with $f = 3700$ to $x_1 = \frac{8400}{13}$ and $x_2 = \frac{11800}{13}$ with $f = \frac{48800}{13}$.

EXERCISE SET 4.5

1. *Maximizing income.* In Exercise 1 of Set 4.3: If dresses are to be profitable, what must the minimum price of dresses be?

2. *Maximizing income.* In Exercise 2 of Set 4.3: To what value could the price of inexpensive speakers be *raised* before the production ratio of each should be changed?

3. *Maximizing income.* In Exercise 3 of Set 4.3: How many *more* lbs of cashews can the nut dealer buy and still use the same mixtures profitably without having to buy more of the other nuts?

4. *Maximizing income.* In Exercise 3 of Set 4.3: How many *fewer* lbs of peanuts can the nut dealer buy and still use the same mixtures profitably without having to buy less of the other nuts?

5. *Minimizing cost, Nutrition.* In Exercise 1 of Set 4.4: What must the price of soybean meal be *raised* to before it becomes more economical to use a mixture with less soybean meal than oats?

6. *Minimizing cost, Nutrition.* In Exercise 1 of Set 4.4: What must the price of soybean meal be *lowered* to before it becomes more economical to use all soybean meal?

7. *Minimizing cost, Transportation.* In Exercise 5 of Set 4.4: What would the operating cost of plane P2 have to be *lowered* to in order for it to be more economical to use more P2's?

8. *Minimizing cost, Transportation.* In Exercise 5 of Set 4.4: What would the operating cost of plane P2 have to be *raised* to in order for it to be more economical to use more P1's?

9. *Minimizing cost, Nutrition.* In Exercise 1 of Set 4.4: to what amount must the mineral requirement be reduced before it no longer affects the solution?

11. *Minimizing cost, Transportation.* In Exercise 5 of Set 4.4: to what number must the economy-class passenger requirement be raised before the tourist-class requirement does not affect the solution?

10. *Minimizing cost, Nutrition.* In Exercise 1 of Set 4.4: to what amount must the mineral requirement be raised before some other requirement does not affect the solution?

12. *Minimizing cost, Transportation.* In Exercise 5 of Set 4.4: to what number must the economy-class passenger requirement be lowered before it does not affect the solution?

CHAPTER 4 REVIEW

1. Graph the solution set of the system of constraints

$$\text{i)} \quad x_1 + x_2 \geq 1,$$

$$\text{ii)} \quad -x_1 + x_2 \leq 2.$$

3. As in Exercise 2, add

$$\text{iv)} \quad x_2 \leq 0, \qquad \text{v)} \quad x_2 \leq 4.$$

5. As in Exercise 2, replace constraint (vi) by

$$\text{vii)} \quad x_1 + 2 \leq 0.$$

What is the solution set?

7. Find the optima (maximum and minimum) values and the points at which they are obtained for the objective function

$$f(x_1, x_2) = 2x_1 + 3x_2,$$

subject to the same constraints as in Example 2 of Section 4.2:

$$\text{i)} \quad x_1 - 2x_2 \leq 0,$$
$$\text{ii)} \quad -2x_1 + x_2 \leq 2,$$
$$\text{iii)} \quad x_1 \qquad \leq 2,$$
$$\text{iv)} \qquad x_2 \leq 2.$$

Remember you need consider only corner points.

2. To the system of constraints of Exercise 1, add

$$\text{iii)} \quad x_1 \leq 4$$

and graph.

4. As in Exercise 2, add

$$\text{vi)} \quad x_1 \leq 2.$$

a) Determine which points (if any) are degenerate.

b) Determine which constraints (if any) are redundant.

6. Use the echelon method to solve

$$2x_1 - x_2 = 4$$

$$3x_1 + 2x_2 = 12.$$

8. Find the optimum values and the points at which they are obtained for the objective function

$$f(x_1, x_2) = 2x_2 - x_1,$$

subject to the same constraints as in Exercise 7.

9. Formulate this problem using a table.

A furniture manufacturer produces chairs and sofas. The chairs require 20 feet of wood, 1 lb of foam rubber, and 2 square yards of material. The sofas require 100 feet of wood, 50 lbs of foam rubber, and 20 square yards of material. The manufacturer has in stock 1900 feet of wood, 500 lbs of foam rubber, and 240 square yards of material. If the chairs can be sold for $20 each and the sofas for $300 each, how many of each should be made to maximize the income?

11. Solve graphically the linear program of Exercise 9.

13. Solve graphically the linear program of Exercise 12.

10. Express the results of Exercise 9 in matrix form.

12. (a) Formulate the following problem using a table and (b) express the results in matrix form.

An ore refining company has orders for 200 tons of iron, 500 tons of aluminum, and 100 tons of copper. They have available two kinds of ore. Type A has 10% iron and 2% copper and costs $10 per ton. Type B has 20% aluminum and 1% copper and costs $15 per ton. How many tons of each should be bought to minimize the cost?

14. Formulate the following problem, giving all the constraints, and write in matrix form.

A health food store manager is preparing two mixtures of breakfast cereal out of a supply of 100 lbs rolled oats, 10 lbs chopped almonds, 5 lbs chopped dried apples, 25 lbs chopped sunflower seeds, and 15 lbs monukka raisins. The first mixture contains 80% oats, 1% almonds, no dried apple, 12% sunflower seeds, and 7% raisins, and sells for $0.95 per lb. The second mixture contains 60% oats, 3% almonds, 4% dried apple, 24% sunflower seeds, and 9% raisins, and sells for $1.35 per lb. How much of each mixture should be made to maximize the income?

Given the following linear program:

i) $\qquad y_1 + 8y_2 \geq 24,$
ii) $\qquad 7y_1 + y_2 \geq 14,$
iii) $\qquad 2y_1 + 3y_2 \geq 18,$
$$\min f: \quad f = y_1 + y_2; \; y_1, y_2 \geq 0.$$

15. Graph the constraints and shade the feasible solution.

*****17.** To what value could the requirement (right-hand side) of constraint (ii) be reduced before this constraint becomes redundant?

16. Find the optimum feasible solution and explain how you found it.

LINEAR PROGRAMMING– ALGEBRAIC TECHNIQUES

The graphical method for solving linear programs, considered in Sections 4.3 and 4.4, can be used for problems with *two* variables and, with some difficulty, *three*. However, for problems where the number of variables might run into hundreds or thousands, algebraic techniques must be used. These have the advantage that they can be adapted to high-speed computers. The *simplex algorithm*** is the basic technique we consider in this chapter.

5.1 MAXIMUM-TYPE LINEAR PROGRAMS— THE SIMPLEX ALGORITHM

Standard Form of a Linear Program

In this section we will consider the algebraic solution of maximum-type linear programs, which are expressed in the following standard form,

---

* An *algorithm* is a special procedure. Here the simplex algorithm is used for solving linear programs.

a) $AX \leq B$ (This means that all constraints are in the form

$$a_1x_1 + a_2x_2 + \cdots + a_nx_n \leq b.)$$

b) $X \geq O$ (This means that all the variables $x_1, x_2, \ldots, x_n$ are nonnegative. The given variables are called *structural* variables.)

c) max x_0: $x_0 = CX$ (We are finding the maximum value of an objective function $x_0 = c_1x_1 + c_2x_2 + \cdots + c_nx_n.$)

(Here the objective function, previously denoted f, is denoted by the variable with the subscript "0", x_0.)

We place one additional provision on the standard form, and this is the positivity constraint $B > O$, that is, *all* components of B are positive. This is assumed to avoid complications.

A set of values X which satisfies the constraints $AX \leq B$ together with the corresponding value of the objective function $x_0 = CX$ is called a *solution* and can be written $X; x_0$.

A solution which also satisfies the *nonnegativity constraint*, $X \geq O$, is called a *feasible solution*.

A feasible solution which is also a *corner point* of the region defined by $AX \leq B$ and $X \geq O$ is called a *basic feasible solution*.

A basic feasible solution which also *optimizes* the value of the objective function $x_0 = CX$ is called an *optimum basic feasible solution* or simply an *optimum feasible solution*.

Briefly, solution of a maximum-type linear program by the simplex algorithm involves the following steps:

1. Adding *slack variables* to convert the inequalities into equations,

2. Setting up the *initial simplex tableau* which is similar to the echelon tableau,

3. Finding an *initial feasible solution*, since the simplex algorithm proceeds from one feasible solution to a better one until the optimum is reached,

4. Introducing *basic and nonbasic variables* as the natural way to express *basic* feasible solutions,

5. *Choosing the proper pivot* element to advance the solution and maintain the nonnegativity of all variables,

6. *Pivoting*, which is done columnwise exactly the same as in the echelon method, and

7. Continuing and recognizing when the *algorithm terminates*.

We now consider these steps in detail.

Slack Variables   The first step of the simplex algorithm is to convert the inequalities of the problem into equations.

Example 1   Convert the formulation of Example 1 of Section 4.3 from a system of inequalities to a system of equations.

Solution   The problem in question had the formulation

i) $$0.20x_1 + 0.10x_2 \leqslant 220,$$
ii) $$0.60x_1 + 0.20x_2 \leqslant 620,$$
iii) $$0.20x_1 + 0.70x_2 \leqslant 700,$$
iv) $$\max x_0: x_0 = 3.00x_1 + 2.00x_2,$$
v) $$x_1, x_2 \geqslant 0.$$

The first of these inequalities (i) can be made into an equation by adding a variable y_1 to the lefthand side. This produces the equation

$$0.20x_1 + 0.10x_2 + y_1 = 220.$$

The quantity y_1 is called a *slack variable* since it "takes up the slack" in the equation. It follows that y_1 is nonnegative, as are x_1 and x_2. To see this in an easy way, the inequality $4 + 1 \leqslant 7$ can be made into the equation $4 + 1 + 2 = 7$ where the slack is the quantity 2.

   For *each* constraint (i) through (iii), we add a *different* slack variable to the lefthand side, obtaining

i') $$0.20x_1 + 0.10x_2 + y_1 \qquad\qquad\qquad = 220,$$
ii') $$0.60x_1 + 0.20x_2 \qquad + y_2 \qquad\qquad = 620,$$
iii') $$0.20x_1 + 0.70x_2 \qquad\qquad + y_3 \qquad = 700,$$
iv') $$\max x_0: \ -3x_1 \quad -2x_2 \qquad\qquad\qquad + x_0 = 0,$$
v') $$x_1, x_2; \qquad y_1, \quad y_2, \quad y_3 \qquad \geqslant 0.$$

Note that the objective function

iv) $$x_0 = 3x_1 + 2x_2$$

has been rewritten

iv') $$-3x_1 - 2x_2 + x_0 = 0.$$

   We add a different slack variable each time, because what must be added to $0.20x_1 + 0.10x_2$ to get 220 may be different from what must be added to $0.60x_1 + 0.20x_2$ to get 620. Each *slack* variable must be nonnegative, as must the structural variables x_1 and x_2.

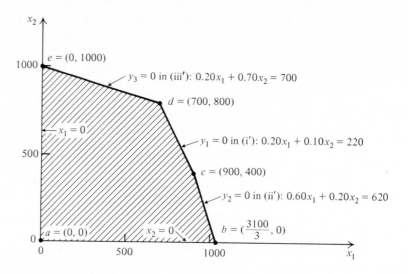

Figure 5.1

Note that the constraints (i) through (iii) can be recovered from the equations (i′) through (iii′) by setting each of the slack variables y_i, in turn, equal to 0 and replacing each $=$ sign by $\leq$.

Suppose we wanted to graph the constraints. The equations related to the constraints are obtained by setting the slack variables in the equations (i′) through (iii′) equal to 0 and maintaining the equal signs. This is shown in Fig. 5.1.

Initial Simplex Tableau

Now that we have converted the linear program from one using constraints to one using equations, we can prepare to solve it using the echelon tableau (see Sections 3.1 and 3.2). With a slight modification, the initial echelon tableau is the initial simplex tableau. See Example 2.

Example 2   Set up the initial *echelon* tableau and the initial *simplex* tableau for the problem of Example 1.

Solution   The initial *echelon* tableau for the system of equations of Example 1 is

x_1	x_2	y_1	y_2	y_3	x_0	1
0.20	0.10	1	0	0	0	220
0.60	0.20	0	1	0	0	620
0.20	0.70	0	0	1	0	700
-3	-2	0	0	0	1	0

Since the x_0 column does not change in the course of the simplex algorithm, this column is usually omitted in the simplex tableau; however, the value of x_0 will always be in the lower righthand corner in the column headed "1".

Furthermore, the objective function in the bottom row plays a special role in the simplex algorithm and hence is set off from the constraints in the other rows with a horizontal line.* Thus, we obtain the *initial simplex tableau*:

x_1	x_2	y_1	y_2	y_3	1
0.20	0.10	1	0	0	220
0.60	0.20	0	1	0	620
0.20	0.70	0	0	1	700
-3	-2	0	0	0	0

Matrix Formulation

Formally, in matrix notation, a problem with constraints of the form
$$AX \leqslant B, \qquad X \geqslant O,$$
$$\max x_0: x_0 = CX,$$
or
$$-CX + x_0 = 0,$$
is converted, by addition of slack variables Y, into one of the form†

$$[A \ \ I]\begin{bmatrix} X \\ Y \end{bmatrix} = B, \qquad \begin{bmatrix} X \\ Y \end{bmatrix} \geqslant O,$$

$$\max x_0: x_0 = [C \ \ O]\begin{bmatrix} X \\ Y \end{bmatrix}, \qquad \text{or} \qquad -[C \ \ O]\begin{bmatrix} X \\ Y \end{bmatrix} + x_0 = 0.$$

In general this can be put into an initial simplex tableau of the form

X^T	Y^T	1
A	I	B
$-C$	O	0

Note the negative sign in the bottom row.

---

* Alternately, the objective function is sometimes written in the top row. In either case it is distinguished from the constraints in the other rows by being set off with a horizontal line.

† You may need to review augmented matrices, Section 3.4.

Also the given equations can be recovered from the tableau in a straight-forward manner.

Initial Feasible Solution

Recall that a feasible solution satisfies both $AX \leq B$ and $X \geq O$.

The simplex algorithm starts with one feasible solution and then generates a better one, if possible. The *initial feasible solution* is obtained in the following manner.

Example 3   Find an initial feasible solution from the initial simplex tableau of Example 2.

Solution   In Section 4.3 we solved this linear program graphically. See Fig. 5.2.

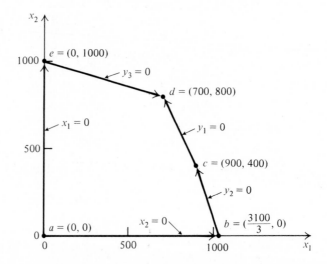

Figure 5.2

We showed previously (see Section 4.2) that the *optimum* feasible solution must occur at a *corner point*. Since we can use *any* feasible solution to start with, we choose that corner point which is simplest to find. This is the *origin* (point a) which becomes our *initial* feasible solution.

Formally, we note that our constraint equations can be written

$$[A \quad I]\begin{bmatrix} X \\ Y \end{bmatrix} = AX + IY = B.$$

Since $B > O$, for maximum-type problems we can always obtain an *initial* feasible solution by setting X (the structural variables) equal to zero and solving for Y (the slack variables):

$$X = O \quad \text{and} \quad Y = B.$$

Setting the structural variables (x_1, x_2) equal to zero in Eqs. (i′) through (iv′) of Example 1, we can determine the corresponding values of the slack variables (y_1, y_2, y_3) and the objective function (x_0):

Initial feasible solution		
Structural variables	Slack variables	Objective function
$x_1 = 0$ $x_2 = 0$	$y_1 = 220$ $y_2 = 620$ $y_3 = 700$	$x_0 = 0$

This is a *feasible solution* since *all* variables (slack and structural) are nonnegative and satisfy the given constraints. We shall take this as our *initial* feasible solution.

The simplex algorithm starts with the initial feasible solution and proceeds to other feasible solutions. In particular, it proceeds from one corner point to an *adjacent* corner point. Thus, on Fig. 5.2 the solution will proceed from point a (the *initial* feasible solution) to point d (the *optimum* feasible solution) along one of two paths: *abcd* or *aed*.

Basic Feasible Solutions

Consider the path *abcd*. In particular note that at

point a: $x_1 = x_2 = 0$, $y_1 = 220$, $y_2 = 620$, $y_3 = 700$;

point b: $x_2 = y_2 = 0$, $x_1 = \frac{3100}{3}$, $y_1 = \frac{40}{3}$, $y_3 = \frac{1480}{3}$;

point c: $y_2 = y_1 = 0$, $x_1 = 900$, $x_2 = 400$, $y_3 = 240$;

point d: $y_1 = y_3 = 0$, $x_1 = 700$, $x_2 = 800$, $y_2 = 40$.

Also for the path *aed*, we have at

point a: $x_1 = x_2 = 0$, $y_1 = 220$, $y_2 = 620$, $y_3 = 700$;

point e: $x_1 = y_3 = 0$, $x_2 = 100$, $y_1 = 120$, $y_2 = 420$;

point d: $y_3 = y_1 = 0$, $x_1 = 700$, $x_2 = 800$, $y_2 = 40$.

Note now that there are two structural variables, x_1 and x_2, and that at the origin (point a) they are both zero. As we progress from one corner to an adjacent corner, one of these variables becomes *nonzero* and a different variable becomes *zero*, so that in the present example there are always two variables that are zero in the solution at any stage.

This happens *automatically* provided we proceed along a path through adjacent corner points. Such *corner-point* solutions are important in the simplex algorithm and are called *basic* feasible solutions.

Basic and Nonbasic Variables

In general, we note that in the preceding initial feasible solution, some variables were *set to zero* and some variables were *computed*. The variables which are *computed* are called *basic* variables and the variables *set to zero* are called *nonbasic*. Basic variables can be identified from a simplex tableau as those heading a column of all zeroes except for one 1. Nonbasic variables are the rest.

The *values* of the basic variables can be read from the *simplex* tableau simply by setting the nonbasic variables to zero and reading the tableau as in the *echelon* method. Recalling that the x_0-column is omitted from the simplex tableau, we find that the value of x_0 is the bottom element in the righthand column.

Initially, the slack variables y_1, y_2, y_3 are basic and the structural variables x_1, x_2 are nonbasic.

A basic feasible solution is written using basic and nonbasic variables. If we start with an *initial* feasible solution as in Example 3, it will be a *basic* feasible solution. Furthermore, each successive step of the simplex algorithm corresponds to a basic feasible solution.*

Choosing the Pivot

The essential difference between the echelon method and the simplex algorithm is in the way one chooses the pivot element. In the simplex algorithm we choose the pivot element to increase x_0 and to maintain feasibility.

Example 4 Find a pivot element for the initial simplex tableau of Example 2.

Solution From Example 3, we see that the objective function can be written

$$x_0 = 0 + 3x_1 + 2x_2.$$

---

* The use of the terms *basic* and *nonbasic* variables simplifies the description of the simplex algorithm since each step is a *pivoting* operation (as in the echelon method) in which a *basic* variable is made *nonbasic* and a *nonbasic* variable is made *basic*. Thus, from one tableau to the next there is always a fixed number of basic variables and a fixed number of nonbasic variables. This interchanging the roles of the variables from basic to nonbasic and vice versa is done *automatically* as the pivoting is carried out and does *not* require any special consideration.

For each constraint there is a slack variable.
For each slack variable there is a basic variable.
Basic variables are *computed* and, with few exceptions, are greater than zero.

For each structural variable there is a nonbasic variable.
Nonbasic variables are *set to zero*.

Initially, $x_1 = x_2 = 0$ (nonbasic variables), so $x_0 = 0$. If either of these variables, x_1 or x_2, is increased, that is, made basic (nonzero), then x_0 will be increased. Therefore, either x_1 or x_2 could be chosen as the pivot column. When we choose either x_1 or x_2 as a pivot column and pivot, we increase the variable corresponding to that column. Another way to determine the pivot column is to examine the bottom row of the simplex tableau. The equation

$$x_0 = 0 + 3x_1 + 2x_2$$

appears in the bottom row as

$$-3x_1 - 2x_2 + x_0 = 0.$$

Note the sign changes.

The bottom row entries to the left of the double vertical line are called *indicators*.

Initially, the indicators are $-3, -2, 0, 0, 0$.

We can pick the pivot column to be any column with a *negative indicator*. When we do this, we are picking some nonbasic variable to become basic. If there is no obvious reason to do otherwise, we shall choose that column with the *most negative* indicator as the pivot column.

Having chosen the pivot column (in this case the first column), we must now determine the pivot row. The intersection of the pivot column and pivot row determines the pivot element.

All nonbasic variables except the one involved in pivoting (the one heading the pivot column) remain nonbasic, so that x_2 is zero initially and remains zero.

Consider again the set of equations (i') through (iv') with $x_2 = 0$:

$$\left.\begin{array}{l} 0.20x_1 + y_1 \qquad\qquad\qquad = 220, \\[4pt] 0.60x_1 \qquad + y_2 \qquad\qquad = 620, \\[4pt] 0.20x_1 \qquad\qquad + y_3 \qquad = 700, \\[4pt] -3.00x_1 \qquad\qquad\qquad + x_0 = 0. \end{array}\right\}(E)$$

Setting *one* of the current basic variables to zero makes it nonbasic and permits us to determine the value of the other basic variables and the objective function.

The only question remaining is *which* basic variable to set to zero (that is, to make nonbasic).

If in Equations E we set *each* basic variable to zero in turn and solve for x_1, we obtain

$$\text{for} \quad y_1 = 0, \quad x_1 = \frac{220}{0.20} = 1100,$$

$$\text{for} \quad y_2 = 0, \quad x_1 = \frac{620}{0.60} = 1033\tfrac{1}{3},$$

$$\text{for} \quad y_3 = 0, \quad x_1 = \frac{700}{0.20} = 3500.$$

The simplex tableau is usually augmented with this *quotient* column headed "q."

x_1	x_2	y_1	y_2	y_3	1	q
0.20	0.10	1	0	0	220	$1100 \left(= \dfrac{220}{0.20} \right)$
0.60*	0.20	0	1	0	620	$1033\tfrac{1}{3} \left(= \dfrac{620}{0.60} \right)$ (Minimum)
0.20	0.70	0	0	1	700	$3500 \left(= \dfrac{700}{0.20} \right)$
-3	-2	0	0	0	0	

The pivot row is the row with *minimum* quotient. Here the pivot row is the second row.

The intersection of the pivot column (here the first column) and the pivot row (here the second row) yields the pivot element, which is *starred* (*).

To summarize:

To determine the pivot row: Divide each element in the righthand column (above the bottom row) by the row-wise corresponding entry in the pivot column. The pivot row is the row with *minimum positive quotient*.

To determine the pivot element: Find the intersection of the pivot column and the pivot row. Star (*) this element.

Pivoting

The pivoting operation for one column is exactly the same in the simplex method as in the echelon method (Sections 3.1 and 3.2). The results are written in a *new tableau* with the *same* headings:

i) Divide *all* elements in the pivot row by the pivot element. Thus, the entry replacing the pivot element will be 1 and the star (*) on this element is dropped.

ii) Add some multiple of the pivot row to each other row including the bottom row (usually a different multiple for each row) to create zeroes for *all* entries of the pivot column other than the pivot element, which is now a 1. Thus, a zero is also created in the bottom row in the pivot column.

Example 5   Starting with the initial simplex tableau of Example 2, pivot until the simplex algorithm terminates.

Solution   Pivoting, we obtain the second tableau:

x_1	x_2	y_1	y_2	y_3	1	q
0	$\frac{1}{30}$*	1	$-\frac{1}{3}$	0	$\frac{40}{3}$	400 (Minimum)
1	$\frac{1}{3}$	0	$\frac{5}{3}$	0	$\frac{3100}{3}$	3100
0	$\frac{19}{30}$	0	$-\frac{1}{3}$	1	$\frac{1480}{3}$	$\frac{14800}{19} = 778\frac{18}{19}$
0	-1	0	5	0	3100	

Here the quotient column to the right of the tableau should be ignored for the present.

In the initial tableau, read horizontally from the pivot element to a column with a 1 entry in the pivot row. The basic variable heading this column becomes nonbasic (zero) through pivoting.

In this Example y_2 was basic ($= 620$) and becomes nonbasic ($= 0$) as can be seen from the second tableau.

If we *interchange* the x_1 and y_2 columns, then we obtain

y_2	x_2	y_1	x_1	y_3	1
$-\frac{1}{3}$	$\frac{1}{30}$*	1	0	0	$\frac{40}{3}$
$\frac{5}{3}$	$\frac{1}{3}$	0	1	0	$\frac{3100}{3}$
$-\frac{1}{3}$	$\frac{19}{30}$	0	0	1	$\frac{1480}{3}$
5	-1	0	0	0	3100

This tableau has the same *form* as our initial tableau provided we *reorder* the variables. However, it is *not* necessary to *physically* interchange the two columns. Solutions can be read from the tableaux in either form. Thus, it is less work simply to leave the columns in their original order and note that the *roles* of the variables have been interchanged; that is, x_1 was non-basic and became basic, while y_2 was basic and became nonbasic. Thus, we shall speak of "interchanging the roles of x_1 and y_2". This should not be confused with physically interchanging the x_1 and y_2 columns, which remain in their original location. The solution at this point is

Structural variables	Slack variables	Objective function
$x_1 = \frac{3100}{3}$, $x_2 = 0$	$y_1 = \frac{40}{3}$, $y_2 = 0$, $y_3 = \frac{1480}{3}$	$x_0 = 3100$

or

Basic variables	Nonbasic variables	Objective function
$x_1 = \frac{3100}{3}$, $y_1 = \frac{40}{3}$, $y_3 = \frac{1480}{3}$	$x_2 = 0$, $y_2 = 0$	$x_0 = 3100$

The solution is feasible (that is, it satisfies the given constraints including nonnegativity) and the objective function has been increased from a value of 0 to 3100.

Wrong Pivot

Let us examine what happens if the *wrong* pivot element is used. If, for example, we pivot using the first column and the *first* row, then we obtain

x_1	x_2	y_1	y_2	y_3	1
1	0.5	5	0	0	1100
0	-0.1	-3	1	0	-40
0	0.6	-1	0	1	480
0	-0.5	15	0	0	3300

The *negative* number in the right-hand column is a reminder that the *wrong* pivot row has been used. In this case, we obtained $y_2 = -40$. This violates the nonnegativity constraint which must be maintained.

Selecting the pivot row that corresponds to the *minimum* positive quotient guarantees that the solution does not violate the nonnegativity constraint.

Termination

Returning our attention to the correct second tableau, we find that only the second column has a negative indicator, -1. Thus, the second column will be the next pivot column and we obtain a new set of quotients, as shown augmenting the second tableau. The minimum quotient is obtained for the first row. The pivot element is starred and the 1 in the pivot row corresponds to y_1. Thus the pivoting will interchange the roles of x_2 and y_1, that is, will make x_2 basic and y_1 nonbasic ($y_1 = 0$). Performing the pivoting, we obtain

x_1	x_2	y_1	y_2	y_3	1	q
0	1	30	-10	0	400	—
1	0	-10	5	0	900	180
0	0	-19	6*	1	240	40 (Minimum)
0	0	30	-5	0	3500	

Again the quotient column here will be used to obtain the *next* tableau. The solution at this point is

$x_1 = 900,$	$y_1 = 0,$	$x_0 = 3500.$
$x_2 = 400,$	$y_2 = 0,$	
	$y_3 = 240,$	

The fourth column now has a negative indicator, -5, and thus becomes the next pivot column. The corresponding quotients are shown to the right of the tableau above. Note that the *negative* elements in the pivot column are disregarded in computing quotients. Such a pivot would make a variable *negative* and also *decrease* the value of the objective function.

Pivoting to interchange the roles of y_2 and y_3, we obtain

x_1	x_2	y_1	y_2	y_3	1
0	1	$-\frac{5}{3}$	0	$\frac{5}{3}$	800
1	0	$\frac{35}{6}$	0	$-\frac{5}{6}$	700
0	0	$-\frac{19}{6}$	1	$\frac{1}{6}$	40
0	0	$\frac{85}{6}$	0	$\frac{5}{6}$	3700

The solution at this point is

$x_1 = 700,$	$y_1 = 0,$	$x_0 = 3700.$
$x_2 = 800,$	$y_2 = 40,$	
	$y_3 = 0,$	

Since all indicators are nonnegative, there are no more possible pivot columns. Thus, the algorithm *terminates* and the current solution is *maximal*.

The path taken by the simplex algorithm can be followed in Fig. 5.2 as *abcd*. This particular path is a consequence of the choice of the initial pivot column. The alternate choice would have yielded the path *aed*.

Picking the most negative indicator to determine the pivot column is a good simple rule to minimize the number of steps required to achieve optimality but as can be seen in the present example, this is not always the best choice. Since there is no way to know beforehand the best possible pivot column, we use the "most negative" indicator as a good simple rule.

Summary

Let us summarize the steps in the simplex algorithm.

   I. **Convert the inequalities of the problem into equations by adding slack variables.**

  II. **Set up the initial simplex tableau.**

 III. **Carry out the pivoting operations as follows:**

    1. **To find the pivot column, pick the column with the most negative indicator. (Actually any column with a negative indicator will do.) If there is none, go to step IV.**

    2. **To find the pivot row, find the quotients of the entries in the righthand column by the row-wise corresponding entries in the pivot column. The pivot row is the row with the minimum positive quotient.**

    3. **Star the pivot element and carry out the pivoting operation, as in the echelon method, for this column.**

    4. **To find the feasible solution at any point in the procedure, translate the tableau to the corresponding system of equations, and let the nonbasic variables be 0. The basic variables can be identified by columns with a 1 for some element and all the other elements 0. The other columns are nonbasic.**

  IV. **Look at the bottom row of the tableau. If all the indicators are nonnegative, there are no more possible pivot columns and the algorithm terminates. The solution which can then be found using III(4) is maximal.**

To further exemplify the procedure, let us return to the previous example, but this time start by choosing the other pivot column; that is, column two. Then pivoting would proceed as follows, starting with the initial tableau:

x_1	x_2	y_1	y_2	y_3	1	q
0.20	0.10	1	0	0	220	2200
0.60	0.20	0	1	0	620	3100
0.20	0.70*	0	0	1	700	1000 (Minimum)
-3	-2	0	0	0	0	

x_1	x_2	y_1	y_2	y_3	1	q
$\frac{6}{35}$*	0	1	0	$-\frac{1}{7}$	120	700 (Minimum)
$\frac{19}{35}$	0	0	1	$-\frac{2}{7}$	420	$773\frac{13}{19}$
$\frac{2}{7}$	1	0	0	$\frac{10}{7}$	1000	3500
$-\frac{17}{7}$	0	0	0	$\frac{20}{7}$	2000	

x_1	x_2	y_1	y_2	y_3	1
1	0	$\frac{35}{6}$	0	$-\frac{5}{6}$	700
0	0	$-\frac{19}{6}$	1	$\frac{1}{6}$	40
0	1	$-\frac{5}{3}$	0	$\frac{5}{3}$	800
0	0	$\frac{85}{6}$	0	$\frac{5}{6}$	3700

At this point the algorithm terminates. Following the solution from tableau to tableau, we see that on Fig. 5.2 the solution proceeded from point *a* to point *e* to point *d*, the same optimum as before. Note that the final tableau just obtained is *not* identical to the final tableau we had previously obtained. However, it *is* *row equivalent* (there are just row interchanges) and hence has the same solution.

Usually choosing the most negative indicator will tend to yield the solution in fewer steps but, as the present example illustrates, this need not be so. Alternate choice of pivots leads to *the* optimum solution along alternate paths.

(Optional) Solution of Linear Programs Using the All-Integer Algorithm

In Section 3.2, the All-Integer Method was presented. This same algorithm can be used to solve linear programs that are all integer or can be made all integer by a linear transformation.

Example 6 Solve the following linear program using the all-integer algorithm.

$$\max x_0 \colon x_0 = 3x_1 + 7x_2 + 8x_3 \; ; \; x_1, x_2, x_3 \geq 0$$

$$3x_1 + 4x_2 + 5x_3 \leq 5$$

$$4x_1 - 2x_2 + 7x_3 \leq 8$$

$$7x_1 + 5x_2 - 3x_3 \leq 2 \, .$$

Solution To a linear program using the all-integer algorithm, we first set up the initial all-integer simplex tableau (with the objective function represented by the $i = 0$ row, so that $a_{0j} = -c_j$ and $a_{00} = 0$). The pivot elements are obtained in the usual way. Thus, using the all-integer algorithm, the following sequence of tableaux is obtained.

x_1	x_2	x_3	y_1	y_2	y_3	1	
3	4	5	1	0	0	5	$p_0 = 1$
4	-2	7	0	1	0	8	$p = 5$
7	5	-3	0	0	1	2	
-3	-7	-8	0	0	0	0	

x_1	x_2	x_3	y_1	y_2	y_3	1	
3	4	5	1	0	0	5	$p_0 = 5$
-1	-38	0	-7	5	0	5	$p = 37$
44	37	0	3	0	5	25	
9	-3	0	8	0	0	40	

x_1	x_2	x_3	y_1	y_2	y_3	1	
-13	0	37	5	0	-4	17	$p_0 = 37$
327	0	0	-29	37	38	227	
44	37	0	3	0	5	25	
93	0	0	61	0	3	311	

The solution is obtained in the usual way:

$$x_2 = \tfrac{25}{37}, \qquad x_3 = \tfrac{17}{37}, \qquad y_2 = \tfrac{227}{37}; \qquad x_0 = \tfrac{311}{37} \quad \text{(nonbasic variables} = 0).$$

Similarly, the dual solution (see Section 5.2) is

$$x_1 = \tfrac{93}{37}, \qquad y_1 = \tfrac{61}{37}, \qquad y_3 = \tfrac{3}{37}; \qquad y_0 = \tfrac{311}{37} \quad \text{(nonbasic variables} = 0).$$

EXERCISE SET 5.1

Exercises 1 through 6 are Exercises 1 through 6 from Set 4.2 where they were to be solved graphically. Here you are asked to solve these problems using the simplex algorithm and to check this solution with your graphical solution. Note that the simplex solution yields both structural and slack variables while the graphical solution yields only the structural variables.

1. Maximize $x_0(x_1, x_2) = x_1 + 2x_2$, subject to the constraints

$$x_1 + x_2 \leqslant 6,$$
$$x_2 \leqslant 5,$$
$$x_1, x_2 \geqslant 0.$$

2. Maximize $x_0(x_1, x_2) = x_1 + x_2$, subject to the constraints

$$x_1 + 2x_2 \leqslant 8,$$
$$x_1 \leqslant 6,$$
$$x_1, x_2 \geqslant 0.$$

3. Maximize $x_0(x_1, x_2) = 5x_1 + 4x_2$, subject to the constraints

$$3x_1 + 2x_2 \leqslant 12,$$
$$x_1 + x_2 \leqslant 5,$$
$$x_1, x_2 \geqslant 0.$$

4. Maximize $x_0(x_1, x_2) = 2x_1 + x_2$, subject to the constraints

$$3x_1 + 5x_2 \leqslant 15,$$
$$3x_1 + 2x_2 \leqslant 12,$$
$$x_1, x_2 \geqslant 0.$$

5. Maximize $x_0(x_1, x_2) = 3x_1 + 4x_2$, subject to the constraints

$$x_1 + 2x_2 \leqslant 14,$$
$$4x_1 + 3x_2 \leqslant 26,$$
$$2x_1 + x_2 \leqslant 12,$$
$$x_1, x_2 \geqslant 0.$$

6. Maximize $x_0(x_1, x_2) = 5x_1 + 4x_2$, subject to the constraints

$$x_1 + 3x_2 \leqslant 18,$$
$$3x_1 + 2x_2 \leqslant 19,$$
$$2x_1 + x_2 \leqslant 12,$$
$$x_1, x_2 \geqslant 0.$$

Use the simplex algorithm to solve the following problems. Check your answer by doing each problem twice, starting with different pivots, if possible.

7.
$$x_1 + 2x_2 \leqslant 60$$
$$4x_1 + 3x_2 \leqslant 140$$
max x_0: $x_0 = 120x_1 + 75x_2$; $x_1, x_2 \geqslant 0$

8.
$$4x_1 + 5x_2 \leqslant 35$$
$$3x_1 + x_2 \leqslant 18$$
max x_0: $x_0 = 3x_1 + 2x_2$; $x_1, x_2 \geqslant 0$

9.
$$3x_1 + 6x_2 \leqslant 90$$
$$5x_1 + 3x_2 \leqslant 160$$
$$x_1 + x_2 \leqslant 44$$
max x_0: $x_0 = 3x_1 + 2x_2$; $x_1, x_2 \geqslant 0$

10.
$$x_1 + 2x_2 \leqslant 16$$
$$3x_1 + 2x_2 \leqslant 20$$
$$4x_1 + x_2 \leqslant 20$$
max x_0: $x_0 = 2x_1 + x_2$; $x_1, x_2 \geqslant 0$

11.
$$5x_1 + 6x_2 \leqslant 60$$
$$x_1 + x_2 \leqslant 11$$
$$3x_1 + x_2 \leqslant 27$$
max x_0: $x_0 = 2x_1 + x_2$; $x_1, x_2 \geqslant 0$

12.
$$-x_1 + 2x_2 \leqslant 10$$
$$3x_1 + 2x_2 \leqslant 18$$
$$3x_1 + x_2 \leqslant 15$$
max x_0: $x_0 = x_1 + 2x_2$; $x_1, x_2 \geqslant 0$

13.

$$3x_1 + 4x_2 \leq 48$$
$$x_1 + x_2 \leq 13$$
$$2x_1 + x_2 \leq 22$$
$$\max x_0: x_0 = 7x_1 + 4x_2 \quad ; x_1, x_2 \geq 0$$

14.

$$x_1 + 3x_2 \leq 18$$
$$2x_1 + x_2 \leq 11$$
$$3x_1 + x_2 \leq 15$$
$$\max x_0: x_0 = 3x_1 + 4x_2 \quad ; x_1, x_2 \geq 0.$$

■ ───────────────────────────────

15.

$$3x_1 - 2x_2 + x_3 \leq 8$$
$$-4x_1 + 3x_2 + 2x_3 \leq 4$$
$$3x_1 + x_2 - 6x_3 \leq 6$$
$$\max x_0: x_0 = \quad - 2x_2 + 5x_3 \quad ; x_1, x_2, x_3 \geq 0$$

16.

$$x_1 - 4x_2 + 3x_3 \leq 12$$
$$x_1 - 2x_2 + 6x_3 \leq 4$$
$$2x_1 + 7x_2 + x_3 \leq 17$$
$$\max x_0: x_0 = 5x_1 + x_2 + 2x_3 \quad ; x_1, x_2, x_3 \geq 0$$

17.

$$2x_1 + x_2 + 4x_3 \leq 24,$$
$$x_1 + x_2 + x_3 \leq 7.$$
$$2x_1 - x_2 + 3x_3 \leq 12,$$
$$\max x_0: x_0 = x_1 + 2x_2 + 3x_3; \quad x_1, x_2, x_3 \geq 0.$$

18.

$$4x_1 + 3x_2 - 2x_3 \leq 5,$$
$$5x_1 - 2x_2 + 7x_3 \leq 11,$$
$$3x_1 - x_2 + 2x_3 \leq 3,$$
$$\max x_0: x_0 = 9x_1 - 2x_2 + 11x_3; \quad x_1, x_2, x_3 \geq 0.$$

19. *Maximizing sales, furniture.* A carpentry shop makes bookcases, desks, and tables. Each bookcase requires 5 man-hours of woodworking, 4 hours of finishing, 30 board feet of hardwood, and 15 board feet of inexpensive wood, and sells for $60. Each desk requires 10 man-hours of woodworking, 3 hours of finishing, 20 board feet of hardwood, and 20 board feet of inexpensive wood, and sells for $100. Each table requires 7 hours of woodworking, 2 hours of finishing, and 24 board feet of hardwood, and sells for $80. The available supply is 575 man-hours for woodworking, 220 man-hours for finishing, 1800 board feet of hardwood, and 1000 board feet of inexpensive wood. How many of each product should be made to maximize sales?

20. *Maximizing sales, coffee blends.* A coffee merchant has a supply of 600 lbs of Mocha coffee, 2400 lbs of Columbian coffee, and 4800 lbs of Brazilian coffee. The merchant sells 100% Mocha coffee as Turkish at $4.00 per lb; a Mocha blend consisting of 25% Mocha and 75% Columbian coffee at $2.50 per lb; a Columbian blend consisting of 10% Mocha, 60% Columbian, and 30% Brazilian coffee at $1.75 per lb; and a Brazilian blend consisting of 20% Columbian and 80% Brazilian coffee at $1.25 per lb. How many lbs of each blend should be prepared to maximize sales?

5.2   DUALITY AND MINIMUM-TYPE LINEAR PROGRAMS

Minimum-Type Linear Programs

In Section 5.1 we considered maximum-type linear programs expressed in the standard form

$$AX \leqslant B, \qquad X \geqslant O,$$

$$\max x_0 \colon x_0 = CX$$

with the positivity constraint $B > O$. Now suppose we wanted to solve a minimum-type linear program, which is expressed in the form

$$AY \geqslant B, \qquad Y \geqslant O,$$

$$\min y_0 \colon y_0 = CY.$$

One way this *might* be solved is to multiply both sides of the inequality $AY \geqslant B$ by -1. This has the effect of multiplying both sides of each constraint inequality by -1. This reverses each constraint and we obtain

$$-AY \leqslant -B.$$

Now if $-B > O$, we could proceed as in Section 5.1; that is, to find the minimum of y_0, we first find the maximum of y_0. Unfortunately, for most of the minimum-type linear programs we have formulated or will formulate, the positivity constraint $-B > O$ will not hold and another procedure must be used.* Here we shall use a procedure based on the Duality Theorem. This method has several advantages. It involves less computation, permits a check of the solution, and has an economic interpretation (which is discussed later on).

Duality

THE DUALITY RELATIONSHIP: Given a *maximum*-type linear program

$$AX \leqslant B, \qquad X \geqslant O,$$

$$\max x_0 \colon x_0 = CX,$$

its *dual*, a *minimum* type-linear program is

$$A^T Y \geqslant C^T, \qquad Y \geqslant O$$

$$\min y_0 \colon y_0 = B^T Y$$

---

* See *Finite Mathematics—A Modeling Approach*, 2d ed., by Crown-Bittinger (Reading, Massachusetts: Addison-Wesley Publishing Co., 1981).

where, as in Section 3.3, the superscript T refers to matrix transpose. Note that the dual is expressed using *new* variables Y, called dual variables.

Similarly, starting with a *minimum*-type linear program

$$AY \geqslant C, \qquad Y \geqslant O,$$

$$\min y_0 \colon y_0 = BY,$$

we can *derive* its *dual*, a *maximum-type* linear program

$$A^T X \leqslant B^T, \qquad X \geqslant O,$$

$$\max x_0 \colon x_0 = C^T X.$$

The original physical linear program, whether maximum or minimum, is often called the *primal* and the corresponding *derived* program its *dual*. The dual frequently has significance in an applied problem.

> **THE DUALITY THEOREM. For a pair of primal and dual linear programs, the objective function x_0 attains its maximum if and only if the objective function y_0 attains its minimum and, furthermore,**
>
> $$\max x_0 = \min y_0.$$

Thus, to solve a minimum-type linear program, we first obtain its dual, a maximum-type linear program. Then, as we shall illustrate, we can obtain the solution of the pair of dual programs at the same time.

When working with the simplex tableau, it is customary to call the *maximum*-type linear program the *primal* and the *minimum*-type linear program the *dual* regardless of the type of physical problem. Which meaning of primal or dual is intended can be determined from the context of its use.

Example 1   Given the maximum-type linear program of Example 1 of Section 4.3 with formulation

$$0.20x_1 + 0.10x_2 \leqslant 220,$$

$$0.60x_1 + 0.20x_2 \leqslant 620,$$

$$0.20x_1 + 0.70x_2 \leqslant 700,$$

$$\max x_0 \colon x_0 = \quad 3x_1 + \quad 2x_2; \qquad x_1, x_2 \geqslant 0,$$

find its dual.

Solution The minimum-type linear program dual to this is

$$0.20y_1 + 0.60y_2 + 0.20y_3 \geqslant 3,$$

$$0.10y_1 + 0.20y_2 + 0.70y_3 \geqslant 2,$$

$$\min y_0: y_0 = 220y_1 + 620y_2 + 700y_3; \qquad y_1, y_2, y_3 \geqslant 0.$$

Example 2 Given the minimum-type linear program (Example 1, Section 4.4) with the formulation

$$40y_1 + 20y_2 \geqslant 160,$$

$$4y_1 + 4y_2 \geqslant 24,$$

$$4y_1 + 6y_2 \geqslant 28,$$

$$\min y_0: y_0 = 15y_1 + 10y_2; \qquad y_1, y_2 \geqslant 0,$$

find its dual.

Solution The maximum-type linear program dual to this is

$$40x_1 + 4x_2 + 4x_3 \leqslant 15,$$

$$20x_1 + 4x_2 + 6x_3 \leqslant 10,$$

$$\max x_0: x_0 = 160x_1 + 24x_2 + 28x_3; \qquad x_1, x_2, x_3 \geqslant 0.$$

Example 3 Express the constraint set of Example 1 as a set of equations, set up the initial simplex tableau, and read off *both* the initial *primal* and *dual* solutions.

Solution Adding slack variables, we obtain

$$0.20x_1 + 0.10x_2 + y_1 \qquad\qquad = 220,$$

$$0.60x_1 + 0.20x_2 \qquad + y_2 \qquad = 620,$$

$$0.20x_1 + 0.70x_2 \qquad\qquad + y_3 \quad = 700,$$

$$\max x_0: \quad -3x_1 \quad - 2x_2 \qquad\qquad\qquad + x_0 = 0,$$

$$x_1, \qquad x_2; \quad y_1, \quad y_2, \quad y_3 \qquad \geqslant 0.$$

Note that we have used the same notation for the *slack* variables as we did for the *dual* variables.

The initial simplex tableau is, as before,

x_1	x_2	y_1	y_2	y_3	1
0.20	0.10	1	0	0	220
0.60	0.20	0	1	0	620
0.20	0.70	0	0	1	700
-3	-2	0	0	0	0

Recall that the x_0-column has been suppressed. As before, the initial *primal solution* is

$$x_1 = 0, \qquad y_1 = 220, \qquad x_0 = 0.$$

$$x_2 = 0, \qquad y_2 = 620,$$

$$y_3 = 700,$$

Similarly, the dual (minimum) program can be expressed as a set of equations by *subtracting* slack variables:

$$0.20y_1 + 0.60y_2 + 0.20y_3 - x_1 \qquad\qquad = 3,$$

$$0.10y_1 + 0.20y_2 + 0.70y_3 \qquad - x_2 \qquad = 2,$$

$$\min y_0: 220y_1 + 620y_2 + 700y_3 \qquad\qquad - y_0 = 0,$$

$$y_1, \qquad\quad y_2, \qquad\quad y_3; \quad x_1, \quad x_2 \qquad \geqslant 0,$$

where we have used the same notation for the dual slack variables as for the primal structural variables.

As with the primal, setting to zero the nonbasic dual variables $y_1 = y_2 = y_3 = 0$, we obtain for the basic dual variables

$$x_1 = -3, \quad \text{and} \quad y_0 = 0.$$

$$x_2 = -2,$$

Note that while the primal solution was nonnegative, the dual solution usually violates the nonnegativity constraint.

Alternately, the *dual solution* is obtained directly from the *bottom row* of the simplex tableau, so that initially

$$x_1 = -3, \qquad x_2 = -2,$$

$$y_1 = y_2 = y_3 = 0, \qquad y_0 = 0.$$

Note that $y_0 = x_0$ and that the x_0 column has been suppressed.

Note, further, that both primal and dual solutions use the same *notation* but are read off differently from the tableau.

Consider now setting up the initial simplex tableau for a minimum-type linear program.

Example 4   Given the minimum-type linear program of Example 2, find its dual. Then express this constraint set as a set of equations, set up the initial simplex tableau, and read off *both* the initial *primal* and *dual* solutions.

Solution   Starting now with the *primal*, that is, the maximum problem, we add slack variables and obtain

$$40x_1 + 4x_2 + 4x_3 + y_1 \qquad\qquad = 15,$$

$$20x_1 + 4x_2 + 6x_3 \qquad + y_2 \qquad = 10,$$

$$\text{max } x_0: -160x_1 - 24x_2 - 28x_3 \qquad\qquad + x_0 = 0,$$

$$x_1, \qquad x_2, \qquad x_3; \quad y_1, \quad y_2 \qquad \geqslant 0.$$

Again, we have purposely used the same *notation* for the *slack* variables as for the *dual* variables (in this case, the original variables).

Putting this into a simplex tableau, we obtain

x_1	x_2	x_3	y_1	y_2	1
40	4	4	1	0	15
20	4	6	0	1	10
-160	-24	-28	0	0	0

The primal solution can be read off as before:

$$x_1 = x_2 = x_3 = 0, \qquad y_1 = 15,$$

$$x_0 = 0, \qquad y_2 = 10.$$

Now, again the dual minimum program can be expressed as a set of equations by *subtracting* slack variables, obtaining

$$40y_1 + 20y_2 - x_1 \qquad\qquad = 160,$$

$$4y_1 + 4y_2 \qquad - x_2 \qquad\qquad = 24,$$

$$4y_1 - 6y_2 \qquad\qquad - x_3 \qquad = 28,$$

$$\text{min } y_0: 15y_1 + 10y_2 \qquad\qquad\qquad - y_0 = 0,$$

$$y_1, \qquad y_2; \quad x_1, \quad x_2, \quad x_3 \qquad \geqslant 0,$$

where we have used the same *notation* for the dual slack variables as for the primal variables.

As with the primal, setting the nonbasic dual variables $y_1 = y_2 = 0$, we obtain, for the basic dual variables,

$$x_1 = -160, \quad \text{and} \quad y_0 = 0.$$
$$x_2 = -24,$$
$$x_3 = -28,$$

Alternately, we can read the dual solution directly from the bottom row of the simplex tableau, obtaining

$$x_1 = -160, \quad y_1 = y_2 = 0,$$
$$x_2 = -24, \quad y_0 = 0.$$
$$x_3 = -28,$$

Thus, we see that the initial solution to the primal is

$$X = O, \qquad Y = B, \qquad x_0 = 0,$$

which is nonnegative, since we have constrained $B \geq O$. Similarly, the initial solution to the dual is

$$X = -C^T, \qquad Y = O, \qquad y_0 = 0,$$

which is generally not nonnegative.

The solution of the primal program has been considered in the preceding section. Consider now the solution to the dual.

Example 5   Solve the minimum-type problem of Example 2. The initial simplex tableau is given in Example 4.

Solution   We proceed exactly the same way as for a maximum-type problem.

The most negative number in the bottom row is -160, so that x_1 is to become basic. Using x_1, we obtain the quotients to the right of the tableau.

x_1	x_2	x_3	y_1	y_2	1	q	
40^*	4	4	1	0	15	$\frac{3}{8}$	(Minimum)
20	4	6	0	1	10	$\frac{1}{2}$	
-160	-24	-28	0	0	0		

The minimum quotient of $\frac{3}{8}$ implies that y_1 is to become nonbasic, or that the roles of x_1 and y_1 are to be interchanged. The pivot element is starred (*).

Pivoting to interchange the roles of x_1 and y_1, we obtain

x_1	x_2	x_3	y_1	y_2	1	q	
1	$\frac{1}{10}$	$\frac{1}{10}$	$\frac{1}{40}$	0	$\frac{3}{8}$	$\frac{15}{4}$	
0	2	4^*	$-\frac{1}{2}$	1	$\frac{5}{2}$	$\frac{5}{8}$	(Minimum)
-0	-8	-12	4	0	60		

The *dual* solution at this point can be read from the bottom row and is

$$y_1 = 4, \qquad x_1 = 0, \qquad y_0 = 60.$$

$$y_2 = 0, \qquad x_2 = -8,$$

$$x_3 = -12,$$

Picking x_3 (most negative indicator) to become basic leads to y_2 (minimum quotient) to become nonbasic.

Pivoting to interchange the roles of x_3 and y_2 we obtain

x_1	x_2	x_3	y_1	y_2	1	q	
1	$\frac{1}{20}$	0	$\frac{3}{80}$	$-\frac{1}{40}$	$\frac{5}{16}$	$\frac{25}{4}$	
0	$\frac{1}{2}^*$	1	$-\frac{1}{8}$	$\frac{1}{4}$	$\frac{5}{8}$	$\frac{5}{4}$	(Minimum)
0	-2	0	$\frac{5}{2}$	3	$\frac{135}{2}$		

The *dual* solution at this point is

$$y_1 = \tfrac{5}{2}, \qquad x_1 = 0, \qquad y_0 = \tfrac{135}{2}.$$

$$y_2 = 3, \qquad x_2 = -2,$$

$$x_3 = 0,$$

Pivoting now to interchange the roles of x_2 and x_3, we obtain

x_1	x_2	x_3	y_1	y_2	1
1	0	$-\frac{1}{10}$	$\frac{1}{20}$	$-\frac{1}{20}$	$\frac{1}{4}$
0	1	2	$-\frac{1}{4}$	$\frac{1}{2}$	$\frac{5}{4}$
0	0	4	2	4	70

The *dual* solution at this point is

$$y_1 = 2, \qquad x_1 = 0, \qquad y_0 = 70.$$
$$y_2 = 4, \qquad x_2 = 0,$$
$$x_3 = 4,$$

This solution is nonnegative. It is therefore also minimal and the algorithm terminates.

Note that the nonnegativity of the dual solution corresponds to optimality of the primal.

Checking Solutions

To check either a maximum- or a minimum-type linear program, we substitute *both* primal and dual solutions into their respective programs written in *equation* form.*

Example 6 Check the solution to the linear program of Example 4.

Solution First, let us restate the programs in equation form and their solutions, which can be obtained from the final tableau of Example 5.

Primal program:

$$40x_1 + 4x_2 + 4x_3 + y_1 = 15,$$
$$20x_1 + 4x_2 + 6x_3 + y_2 = 10,$$
$$\max x_0: 160x_1 + 24x_2 + 28x_3 \qquad = x_0,$$
$$x_1, x_2, x_3; y_1, y_2 \geq 0.$$

Primal solution:

$$x_1 = \tfrac{1}{4}, \qquad x_2 = \tfrac{5}{4}, \qquad x_3 = 0,$$
$$y_1 = y_2 = 0,$$
$$x_0 = 70.$$

---

* Actually, it is sufficient that if X is a primal feasible solution ($AX \leq B$, $X \geq O$) and Y is a dual feasible solution ($A^T Y \geq C^T$, $Y \geq O$), then the condition $CX = B^T Y$ ensures that both X and Y are optimal. Effecting the check in *equation* form (rather than *constraint* form as in this footnote) checks slack as well as structural variables and hence is useful in locating any errors that may exist.

Dual program:

$$40y_1 + 20y_2 - x_1 = 160,$$

$$4y_1 + 4y_2 - x_2 = 24,$$

$$4y_1 + 6y_2 - x_3 = 28,$$

$$\min y_0: 15y_1 + 10y_2 = y_0,$$

$$y_1, y_2; x_1, x_2, x_3 \geqslant 0.$$

Dual solution:

$$y_1 = 2, \ y_2 = 4,$$

$$x_1 = x_2 = 0, \ x_3 = 4,$$

$$y_0 = 70.$$

To check we first note that all variables (structural and slack) are non-negative. Next we evaluate the objective functions.

$$x_0 = 160(\tfrac{1}{4}) + 24(\tfrac{5}{4}) + 28(0) = 40 + 30 + 0 = 70, \quad \text{OK.}$$

$$y_0 = 15(2) + 10(4) = 30 + 40 = 70, \quad \text{OK.}$$

Next we substitute the primal solution into the primal equations:

$$40(\tfrac{1}{4}) + 4(\tfrac{5}{4}) + 4(0) + 0 = 10 + 5 + 0 + 0 = 15, \quad \text{OK.}$$

$$20(\tfrac{1}{4}) + 4(\tfrac{5}{4}) + 6(0) + 0 = 5 + 5 + 0 + 0 = 10, \quad \text{OK.}$$

Then we substitute the dual solution into the dual equations:

$$40(2) + 20(4) - 0 = 80 + 80 - 0 = 160, \quad \text{OK.}$$

$$4(2) + 4(4) - 0 = 8 + 16 - 0 = 24, \quad \text{OK.}$$

$$4(2) + 6(4) - 4 = 8 + 24 - 4 = 28, \quad \text{OK.}$$

All equations check. Hence the solutions are correct.

Economic Interpretation of Duality (Optional)

Example 7   Formulate the linear program dual to that of Example 1 of Section 4.4.

Minimizing cost, nutrition. A feed supplier mixes feed for a particular animal which requires at least 160 lbs of nutrient A, at least 24 lbs of nutrient B, and at least 28 lbs of nutrient C. The supplier has available soybean meal which costs $15 per 100-lb sack and contains 40 lbs of nutrient

A, 4 lbs of nutrient B, and 4 lbs of nutrient C and triticale which costs $10 per 100-lb sack and contains 20 lbs of nutrient A, 4 lbs of nutrient B, and 6 lbs of nutrient C. How many sacks of each ingredient should be used to mix animal feed which satisfies the minimum requirements at minimum cost?

Solution   The data from that problem was put into the following table:

	Composition (lbs per 100-lb sack)		Pounds required
	Soybean meal	Triticale	
Number of 100-lb sacks	y_1	y_2	
Nutrient A	40	20	160
Nutrient B	4	4	24
Nutrient C	4	6	28
$ Cost per 100-lb sack	15	10	Minimize cost

In formulating the dual we reinterpret the data. To start, we define dual variables:

x_1 = $ price per lb of nutrient A⎤
x_2 = $ price per lb of nutrient B ⎬ (if available in pure form),
x_3 = $ price per lb of nutrient C⎦

where $x_1, x_2, x_3 \geq 0$.

If we consider selling these nutrients separately (but still for animal feed), then we cannot obtain more for them than their cost combined as soybean meal or triticale, so that,

$$40x_1 + 4x_2 + 4x_3 \leq 15, \quad \text{and} \quad 20x_1 + 4x_2 + 6x_3 \leq 10.$$

We now seek to determine the prices x_1, x_2, x_3 such that we maximize our income and still satisfy the animal's requirements (at no more than the cost of the food sources):

$$\max x_0: x_0 = 160x_1 + 24x_2 + 28x_3.$$

It can be seen now that the program just formulated *is* the dual to the given program.

The optimal values of these dual variables x_1, x_2, x_3 are called *shadow prices* and are used in economic analyses.

Many other linear programs also have duals which have physical significance.

EXERCISE SET 5.2

Exercises 1 through 6 are Exercises 7 through 12 from Set 4.2 where they were solved graphically. Here you are asked to solve the problems using duality and the simplex algorithm and to check this solution with your graphical solution. Note that only the final solution checks and that intermediate solutions from the simplex tableaux have no corresponding points on the graph.

1. Exercise 7, Set 4.2:
Minimize $y_0(y_1, y_2) = 3y_1 + 4y_2$, subject to the constraints

$$
\begin{aligned}
3y_1 + y_2 &\geqslant 9, \\
y_1 + y_2 &\geqslant 7, \\
y_1 + 2y_2 &\geqslant 8, \\
y_1, y_2 &\geqslant 0.
\end{aligned}
$$

2. Exercise 8, Set 4.2:
Minimize $y_0(y_1, y_2) = 3y_1 + 4y_2$, subject to the constraints

$$
\begin{aligned}
2y_1 + y_2 &\geqslant 8, \\
4y_1 + 3y_2 &\geqslant 22, \\
2y_1 + 5y_2 &\geqslant 18, \\
y_1, y_2 &\geqslant 0.
\end{aligned}
$$

3. Exercise 9, Set 4.2:
Minimize $y_0(y_1, y_2) = 2y_1 + 5y_2$, subject to the constraints

$$
\begin{aligned}
2y_1 + y_2 &\geqslant 9, \\
4y_1 + 3y_2 &\geqslant 23, \\
y_1 + 3y_2 &\geqslant 8, \\
y_1, y_2 &\geqslant 0.
\end{aligned}
$$

4. Exercise 10, Set 4.2:
Minimize $y_0(y_1, y_2) = 9y_1 + 7y_2$, subject to the constraints

$$
\begin{aligned}
5y_1 + 3y_2 &\geqslant 30, \\
2y_1 + 3y_2 &\geqslant 21, \\
3y_1 + 6y_2 &\geqslant 36, \\
y_1, y_2 &\geqslant 0.
\end{aligned}
$$

5. Exercise 11, Set 4.2:
Minimize $y_0(y_1, y_2) = 3y_1 + 5y_2$, subject to the constraints

$$
\begin{aligned}
4y_1 + y_2 &\geqslant 9, \\
3y_1 + 2y_2 &\geqslant 13, \\
2y_1 + 5y_2 &\geqslant 16, \\
y_1, y_2 &\geqslant 0.
\end{aligned}
$$

6. Exercise 12, Set 4.2:
Minimize $y_0(y_1, y_2) = 2y_1 + 3y_2$, subject to the constraints

$$
\begin{aligned}
4y_1 + y_2 &\geqslant 7, \\
y_1 + y_2 &\geqslant 4, \\
2y_1 + 5y_2 &\geqslant 14, \\
y_1, y_2 &\geqslant 0.
\end{aligned}
$$

In Exercise Set 4.4 various minimum-type linear programs were given to be formulated and solved graphically. Here you are asked to solve these problems using duality and the simplex algorithm and to check your answer with your graphical solution.

7. Exercise 1, Set 4.4

$$
\begin{aligned}
50y_1 + 15y_2 &\geqslant 120, \\
8y_1 + 5y_2 &\geqslant 24, \\
5y_1 + y_2 &\geqslant 10, \\
\min y_0 \colon y_0 = 15y_1 + 5y_2; \quad y_1, y_2 &\geqslant 0.
\end{aligned}
$$

8. Exercise 2, Set 4.4

9. Exercise 3, Set 4.4

$$
\begin{aligned}
50y_1 + 20y_3 &\geqslant 120, \\
8y_1 + 6y_3 &\geqslant 24, \\
5y_1 + 8y_3 &\geqslant 20, \\
\min y_0 \colon y_0 = 15y_1 + 8y_3; \quad y_1, y_3 &\geqslant 0.
\end{aligned}
$$

10. Exercise 4, Set 4.4

11. Exercise 5, Set 4.4

$$40y_1 + 80y_2 \geqslant 2000,$$
$$40y_1 + 30y_2 \geqslant 1500,$$
$$120y_1 + 40y_2 \geqslant 2400,$$
$$\min y_0: y_0 = 12y_1 + 10y_2; \quad y_1, y_2 \geqslant 0.$$

12. Exercise 6, Set 4.4

13. Exercise 7, Set 4.4

$$40y_1 + 40y_3 \geqslant 2000,$$
$$40y_1 + 80y_3 \geqslant 1500,$$
$$120y_1 + 80y_3 \geqslant 2400,$$
$$\min y_0: y_0 = 12y_1 + 15y_3; \quad y_1, y_3 \geqslant 0.$$

14. Exercise 8, Set 4.4

15. Exercise 9, Set 4.4

$$40y_1 + 80y_2 \geqslant 1600,$$
$$40y_1 + 30y_2 \geqslant 2100,$$
$$120y_1 + 40y_2 \geqslant 2400,$$
$$\min y_0: y_0 = 12y_1 + 10y_2; \quad y_1, y_2 \geqslant 0.$$

16. Exercise 10, Set 4.4

17. Exercise 11, Set 4.4

$$40y_1 + 40y_3 \geqslant 1600,$$
$$40y_1 + 80y_3 \geqslant 2100,$$
$$120y_1 + 80y_3 \geqslant 2400,$$
$$\min y_0: y_0 = 12y_1 + 15y_3; \quad y_1, y_3 \geqslant 0.$$

18. Exercise 12, Set 4.4

Use duality and the simplex algorithm to solve Exercises 19 through 26 using primal and dual solutions.

19.
$$3y_1 + y_2 \geqslant 14$$
$$4y_1 + 3y_2 \geqslant 34$$
$$3y_1 + 4y_2 \geqslant 36$$
$$\min y_0: y_0 = 7y_1 + 8y_2 \quad ; y_1, y_2 \geqslant 0$$

20.
$$2y_1 + y_2 \geqslant 11$$
$$y_1 + y_2 \geqslant 9$$
$$y_1 + 2y_2 \geqslant 13$$
$$\min y_0: y_0 = 3y_1 + 2y_2 \quad ; y_1, y_2 \geqslant 0$$

21.
$$3y_1 + 2y_2 \geqslant 29$$
$$4y_1 + 5y_2 \geqslant 55$$
$$y_1 + 2y_2 \geqslant 18$$
$$\min y_0: y_0 = 5y_1 + 4y_2 \quad ; y_1, y_2 \geqslant 0$$

22.
$$5y_1 + y_2 \geqslant 15$$
$$4y_1 + 2y_2 \geqslant 24$$
$$5y_1 + 5y_2 \geqslant 35$$
$$\min y_0: y_0 = 13y_1 + 5y_2 \quad ; y_1, y_2 \geqslant 0$$

■ _____

23.
$$2x_1 + 9x_2 + 4x_3 \geqslant 6,$$
$$3x_1 + 6x_2 - 2x_3 \geqslant 8,$$
$$x_1 + x_2 + x_3 \geqslant 3,$$
$$\min x_0: x_0 = 5x_1 + 2x_2 + x_3; \quad x_1, x_2, x_3 \geqslant 0.$$

24.
$$2x_1 + x_2 + 5x_3 \geqslant 5,$$
$$2x_1 - x_2 + 2x_3 \geqslant 3,$$
$$5x_1 + 3x_2 + x_3 \geqslant 7,$$
$$\min x_0: x_0 = 6x_1 + 2x_2 + 7x_3; \quad x_1, x_2, x_3 \geqslant 0.$$

25.
$$2y_1 + 3y_2 + y_3 \geqslant 2,$$
$$5y_1 + 2y_2 - 3y_3 \geqslant 4,$$
$$7y_1 + 6y_2 + 4y_3 \geqslant 5,$$
$$\min y_0: y_0 = 8y_1 + 9y_2 + 5y_3; \quad y_1, y_2, y_3 \geqslant 0.$$

26.
$$6y_1 + 3y_2 + 4y_3 \geqslant 2,$$
$$y_1 - 2y_2 - 5y_3 \geqslant 3,$$
$$2y_1 + 9y_2 + y_3 \geqslant 8,$$
$$\min y_0: y_0 = 12y_1 + 9y_2 + 8y_3; \quad y_1, y_2, y_3 \geqslant 0.$$

27. *Minimizing cost, nutrition.* The calcium, iron, protein, and cost of various foods (per 100 g) is given in the accompanying table. Using eggs, beef, cheese, and soy beans, what is the minimum-cost diet that will satisfy the minimum daily requirements?

Food (100 g)	Calcium (mg)	Iron (mg)	Protein (g)	Cost (¢)
Eggs	54	2.7	12.8	22
Beef	7	6.6	18.6	36
Chicken	14	1.5	20.2	16
Bluefish	23	0.6	20.5	24
Whole-wheat bread	96	2.2	9.3	10
Cheddar cheese	570	0.7	20.5	32
Soy beans	260	10.0	34.9	10
Sunflower seeds	57	6.0	28.0	20
Sesame seeds	72	7.7	23.4	18
Almonds	234	4.7	18.6	48
Cashews	38	3.8	17.2	48
Filberts	209	3.4	12.6	40
Millet	20	6.8	9.9	12
Minimum daily requirement	750	10	50*	

*This is an average value. Some nutritionists recommend more, some less.

28. Using data from the table of Exercise 27, select various combinations of 3 or 4 foods (other than soy beans) and determine the minimum-cost diet that will satisfy the minimum daily requirements. Answers may vary.

29. Using data from the table of Exercise 27 for eggs, beef, and cheese, what is the minimum-cost diet that will satisfy the minimum daily requirements?

5.3 (Optional) DEGENERACIES AND OTHER SPECIAL CASES

As was shown in the graphical method of solution of linear programs, solutions may be

  i) unique,

  ii) nonunique,

iii) unbounded, or

iv) empty.

On a graph, such solutions may be easily recognized, but our present concern is with recognizing these situations from the simplex tableau.

Up to now, we have used the simplex algorithm to solve linear programs with unique solutions. We turn our attention now to those with nonunique solutions and to the related subject of degeneracies.

Degeneracies (see Section 4.1) occur when a basic variable has zero value. Thus, primal degeneracy occurs when a basic primal variable has zero value. Similarly, dual degeneracy occurs when a basic dual variable has zero value.

Degeneracies may occur in any part of the sequence of tableaux of the simplex algorithm. If primal degeneracy occurs before the final tableau has been obtained, special consideration is required in pivoting.

Degenerate Pivots

Example 1   Pivot in the following tableau:

x_1	x_2	x_3	y_1	y_2	y_3	1	q
4	-1	2	1	0	0	2	—
3	1^*	-1	0	1	0	0	0 (Minimum)
5	3	-2	0	0	1	1	$\frac{1}{3}$
4	-2	1	0	0	0	0	

Solution   In this case, the only pivot column available is the second column. The minimum quotient (to the right of the tableau) has zero value corresponding to the second row. The pivot element has been starred. Such pivots (corresponding to zero quotients) are called *degenerate pivots*. We perform the pivot operation just the same as we do with nondegenerate pivots, and obtain

x_1	x_2	x_3	y_1	y_2	y_3	1	q
7	0	1	1	1	0	2	2
3	1	-1	0	1	0	0	—
-4	0	1^*	0	-3	1	1	1 (Minimum)
10	0	-1	0	2	0	0	

Pivoting with a degeneracy permits the computation to proceed. The next pivot is nondegenerate:

x_1	x_2	x_3	y_1	y_2	y_3	1
11	0	0	1	4	-1	1
-1	1	0	0	-2	1	1
-4	0	1	0	-3	1	1
6	0	0	0	-1	1	1

This tableau contains no degeneracy and one can proceed as usual.

The degenerate pivot requires *no* modification of the rules other than noting that no modification of the rules is required.*

If there is a choice of pivots, one degenerate and one nondegenerate, choose the nondegenerate pivot, since the solution will be advanced and the degenerate pivot *may* be avoided.

Nonunique Solutions

Let us turn our attention to degeneracies in the *terminal* tableau.

Example 2   Obtain all possible solutions to the following linear program:

$$4x_1 - \ x_2 + 2x_3 \leqslant 2,$$
$$3x_1 + \ x_2 + \ x_3 \leqslant 1,$$
$$5x_1 + 3x_2 + 2x_3 \leqslant 4,$$
$$\max x_0: x_0 = 4x_1 + 3x_2 + 3x_3; \qquad x_1, x_2, x_3 \geqslant 0.$$

Solution   Starting with the second column as pivot, we obtain the following tableaux:

x_1	x_2	x_3	y_1	y_2	y_3	1	q	
4	-1	2	1	0	0	2		
3	1^*	1	0	1	0	1	1	(Minimum)
5	3	2	0	0	1	4	$\frac{4}{3}$	
-4	-3	-3	0	0	0	0		

---

* Cycling (that is, obtaining a complete set of values previously obtained) occurs so rarely that techniques to avoid cycling have been omitted.

x_1	x_2	x_3	y_1	y_2	y_3	1
7	0	3	1	1	0	3
3	1	1	0	1	0	1
−4	0	−1	0	−3	1	1
5	0	0	0	3	0	3

Thus, the primal solution is

$$y_1 = 3, \qquad x_1 = y_2 = x_3 = 0,$$

$$x_2 = 1,$$

$$y_3 = 1, \qquad x_0 = 3,$$

and the dual solution is

$$x_1 = 5, \qquad y_1 = x_2 = y_3 = 0,$$

$$y_2 = 3,$$

$$x_3 = 0, \qquad y_0 = 3.$$

Alternately, let us start pivoting with the *third* column:

x_1	x_2	x_3	y_1	y_2	y_3	1	q	
4	−1	2	1	0	0	2	1	(Minimum)
3	1	1*	0	1	0	1	1	(Minimum)
5	3	2	0	0	1	4	2	
−4	−3	−3	0	0	0	0		

x_1	x_2	x_3	y_1	y_2	y_3	1
−2	−3	0	1	−2	0	0
3	1	1	0	1	0	1
−1	1	0	0	−2	1	2
5	0	0	0	3	0	3

Thus, this primal solution is

$$y_1 = 0, \qquad x_1 = x_2 = y_2 = 0,$$

$$x_3 = 1,$$

$$y_3 = 2, \qquad x_0 = 3,$$

and the dual solution is

$$x_1 = 5, \qquad y_1 = x_3 = y_3 = 0,$$

$$x_2 = 0,$$

$$y_2 = 3, \qquad y_0 = 3.$$

It is apparent that we have obtained *two* different feasible solutions to the linear program. Each such solution of a linear program in terms of *basic* and *nonbasic* variables is called a *basic feasible solution*.

If two basic feasible solutions are represented by the vectors X_1 and X_2, then any combination

$$cX_1 + (1 - c)X_2, \qquad \text{where } 0 \leqslant c \leqslant 1,$$

is also a solution. Such a combination is called a *convex combination*.

In general, the convex combination of n points X_i can be written

$$\sum_{i=1}^{n} c_i X_i, \qquad \text{where } 0 \leqslant c_i \leqslant 1 \qquad \text{for all } i \text{ and } \sum_{i=1}^{n} c_i = 1.$$

Any convex combination of basic feasible solutions is also a solution.

How do we know whether one solution is unique? Dual degeneracy indicates primal nonuniqueness. Once we know that the solution is non-unique, we try alternative pivots until the other solutions have been obtained.

Similarly, primal degeneracy indicates dual nonuniqueness. This particular example is interesting because the terminal tableau just obtained exhibits both primal and dual degeneracies.

Let us, then, choose the other available pivot in the third column:

x_1	x_2	x_3	y_1	y_2	y_3	1	q	
4	-1	2^*	1	0	0	2	1	(Minimum)
3	1	1	0	1	0	1	1	(Minimum)
5	3	2	0	0	1	4	2	
-4	-3	-3	0	0	0	0		

x_1	x_2	x_3	y_1	y_2	y_3	1	q	
2	$-\frac{1}{2}$	1	$\frac{1}{2}$	0	0	1	—	
1	$\frac{3}{2}^*$	0	$-\frac{1}{2}$	1	0	0	0	(Minimum)
1	4	0	-1	0	1	2	$\frac{1}{2}$	
2	$-\frac{9}{2}$	0	$\frac{3}{2}$	0	0	3		

x_1	x_2	x_3	y_1	y_2	y_3	1
$\frac{7}{3}$	0	1	$\frac{1}{3}$	$\frac{1}{3}$	0	1
$\frac{2}{3}$	1	0	$-\frac{1}{3}$	$\frac{2}{3}$	0	0
$-\frac{5}{3}$	0	0	$\frac{1}{3}$	$-\frac{8}{3}$	1	2
5	0	0	0	3	0	3

This gives us, for the primal solution

$$x_3 = 1, \qquad x_1 = y_2 = y_1 = 0,$$
$$x_2 = 0,$$
$$y_3 = 2, \qquad x_0 = 3,$$

and for the dual solution

$$x_1 = 5, \qquad x_3 = x_2 = y_3 = 0,$$
$$y_2 = 3,$$
$$y_1 = 0, \qquad y_0 = 3.$$

This basic feasible solution is distinct from the previous one, allowing for *all* variables (basic and nonbasic). However, with regard to the original problem, they both yield the same solution to the original linear program,

$$x_1 = x_2 = 0, \qquad x_3 = 1;$$
$$x_0 = 3,$$

differing only in the value of the slack variables.

They both also yield the same solution to the dual program,

$$y_1 = y_3 = 0, \qquad y_2 = 3;$$
$$y_0 = 3,$$

where again the difference is in the slack variables.

Let us pivot now on the first column of the initial tableau:

x_1	x_2	x_3	y_1	y_2	y_3	1	q	
4	-1	2	1	0	0	2	$\frac{1}{2}$	
3*	1	1	0	1	0	1	$\frac{1}{3}$	(Minimum)
5	3	2	0	0	1	4	$\frac{4}{5}$	
-4	-3	-3	0	0	0	0		

x_1	x_2	x_3	y_1	y_2	y_3	1
0	$-\frac{7}{3}$	$\frac{2}{3}$	1	$-\frac{4}{3}$	0	$\frac{2}{3}$
1	$\frac{1}{3}*$	$\frac{1}{3}*$	0	$\frac{1}{3}$	0	$\frac{1}{3}$
0	$\frac{4}{3}$	$\frac{1}{3}$	0	$-\frac{5}{3}$	1	$\frac{7}{3}$
0	$-\frac{5}{3}$	$-\frac{5}{3}$	0	$\frac{4}{3}$	0	$\frac{4}{3}$

We can now pivot with either the second or third column. Doing both in turn, we obtain

x_1	x_2	x_3	y_1	y_2	y_3	1
7	0	3	1	1	0	3
3	1	1	0	1	0	1
-4	0	-1	0	-3	1	1
5	0	0	0	3	0	3

x_1	x_2	x_3	y_1	y_2	y_3	1
-2	-3	0	1	-2	0	0
3	1	1	0	1	0	1
-1	1	0	0	-2	1	2
5	0	0	0	3	0	3

Each of these basic feasible solutions has been previously obtained. Since all possible pivot choices have been exhausted, there are no more basic feasible solutions.

A complete discussion of the number of basic feasible solutions is beyond the scope of this text; however, when nonuniqueness is indicated, the student should seek *two* basic feasible solutions, unless there is evidence of more.

Unbounded Solutions

Now let us look at linear programs with unbounded solution sets. Consider the following tableau:

x_1	x_2	x_3	y_1	y_2	y_3	1
1	-4	2	1	0	0	2
3	0	4	0	1	0	9
-3	-6	2	0	0	1	5
1	-1	1	0	0	0	0

Here we must pivot on the second column, but *all* entries in this column (including the bottom one) are *nonpositive*. Thus, no pivot now can be found and the algorithm cannot be continued. The *dual* solution is clearly *infeasible*. Setting all primal nonbasic variables to zero except for that of the pivot column, we can write the basic solution as

$$y_1 = 2 + 4x_2,$$

$$y_2 = 9,$$

$$y_3 = 5 + 6x_2,$$

and

$$x_0 = 0 + x_2.$$

Thus, as x_2 increases indefinitely, the basic solution and the objective function become large without bound.

> At *any* stage of the simplex algorithm, if there is a column with *all* nonpositive entries (and the primal solution is feasible), then the primal solution is unbounded and the dual solution is infeasible.

The corresponding situation where the dual solution is unbounded and the primal solution is infeasible cannot occur with the present constraint $B \geqslant 0$, which corresponds to primal feasibility. Similarly, the possibility that both solution sets are empty, that is, that both are infeasible, also cannot occur with the constraint $B \geqslant 0$.

Example 3   Show that the solution to the following linear program is unbounded:

$$2x_1 + x_2 - 4x_3 \leqslant 2,$$

$$3x_1 - x_2 + 2x_3 \leqslant 11,$$

$$3x_1 - 2x_2 + x_3 \leqslant 8,$$

$$\max x_0\colon x_0 = 6x_1 + 4x_2 + 2x_3; \qquad x_1, x_2, x_3 \geqslant 0.$$

Solution   Setting up this program in a tableau and pivoting with the second column, we obtain

x_1	x_2	x_3	y_1	y_2	y_3	1
2	1*	−4	1	0	0	2
3	−1	2	0	1	0	11
3	−2	1	0	0	1	8
−6	−4	−2	0	0	0	0

x_1	x_2	x_3	y_1	y_2	y_3	1
2	1	−4	1	0	0	2
5	0	−2	1	1	0	13
7	0	−7	2	0	1	12
2	0	−18	4	0	0	8

Since the third column has all nonpositive entries, the primal solution is unbounded (and the dual solution infeasible.)

Let us now ask what would happen if an alternate pivot were chosen, for example, the first column. In that case, we obtain

x_1	x_2	x_3	y_1	y_2	y_3	1
2^*	1	-4	1	0	0	2
3	-1	2	0	1	0	11
3	-2	1	0	0	1	8
-6	-4	-2	0	0	0	0

x_1	x_2	x_3	y_1	y_2	y_3	1
1	$\frac{1}{2}$	-2	$\frac{1}{2}$	0	0	1
0	$-\frac{5}{2}$	8	$-\frac{3}{2}$	1	0	8
0	$-\frac{7}{2}$	7^*	$-\frac{3}{2}$	0	1	5
0	-1	-14	3	0	0	6

Pivoting on the second column to interchange x_1 and x_2 yields the same result as before. Therefore, consider pivoting the third column. Thus, we obtain

x_1	x_2	x_3	y_1	y_2	y_3	1
1	$-\frac{1}{2}$	0	$\frac{1}{14}$	0	$\frac{2}{7}$	$\frac{17}{7}$
0	$\frac{3}{2}^*$	0	$\frac{3}{14}$	1	$-\frac{8}{7}$	$\frac{16}{7}$
0	$-\frac{1}{2}$	1	$-\frac{3}{14}$	0	$\frac{1}{7}$	$\frac{5}{7}$
0	-8	0	0	0	2	16

x_1	x_2	x_3	y_1	y_2	y_3	1
1	0	0	$\frac{1}{7}$	$\frac{1}{3}$	$-\frac{2}{21}$	$\frac{67}{21}$
0	1	0	$\frac{1}{7}$	$\frac{2}{3}$	$-\frac{16}{21}$	$\frac{32}{21}$
0	0	1	$-\frac{1}{7}$	$\frac{1}{3}$	$-\frac{1}{21}$	$\frac{56}{21}$
0	0	0	$\frac{8}{7}$	$\frac{16}{3}$	$-\frac{86}{21}$	$\frac{592}{21}$

No matter which way we go, we obtain a tableau with a column of nonpositive entries. If the algorithm can be continued, we ultimately obtain a column of nonpositive entries in a tableau that cannot be continued. Under these conditions, if the primal solution is feasible, it is also unbounded.

(Optional) The Condensed Tableau

The presence of the zeros in the unit matrix in the previous, "extended" tableau takes up space unnecessarily. On a high-speed computer, the saving in space obtained by omitting these zeros can be significant for real problems with large numbers of variables and constraints. Increased insight is also provided by the "condensed" tableau.

Example 4   Condense the (extended) tableau of Example 2 of Section 5.1.

Solution

x_1	x_2	y_1	y_2	y_3	1
0.20	0.10	1	0	0	220
0.60	0.20	0	1	0	620
0.20	0.70	0	0	1	700
−3	−2	0	0	0	0

1	x_1	x_2	1
y_1	0.20	0.10	220
y_2	0.60	0.20	620
y_3	0.20	0.70	700
1	−3	−2	0

Extended tableau   Condensed tableau

The *basic* variables of the *primal* program are written in a column at the left of the condensed tableau. The *dual* program can be read directly from the condensed tableau noting that the double *horizontal* line indicates the location of the equal sign (as does the double *vertical* line for the *primal* program). The student is invited to read off the primal and dual programs from the condensed tableau and check them with the results in Section 5.3.

To illustrate the process of condensing, consider the pair of dual programs

i)
$$AX \leqslant B, \quad X \geqslant O,$$
$$\max x_0 \colon x_0 = CX$$

ii)
$$A^T Y \geqslant C^T, \quad Y \geqslant O,$$
$$\min y_0 \colon y_0 = B^T Y,$$

where, by the Duality Theorem, min y_0 = max x_0, provided these optima exist.

Adding slack variables (in the notation of dual variables), we obtain the matrix equations

$$[A \quad I]\begin{bmatrix} X \\ Y \end{bmatrix} = B; \quad X \geqslant O, \quad Y \geqslant O,$$

$$x_0 = [C \quad O]\begin{bmatrix} X \\ Y \end{bmatrix}.$$

These equations can be put into the following tableaux:

X^T	Y^T	1
A	I	B
$-C$	O	0

1	X^T	1
Y	A	B
1	$-C$	0

Extended tableau   Condensed tableau

Since the condensed tableau can be read horizontally or vertically, we can put a minimum-type linear program directly into condensed tableau form.

The actual computation of successive condensed tableaux is basically the same as for successive extended tableaux. The only difference is in the way the information is stored.

EXERCISE SET 5.3

Solve the following and indicate all such special characteristics of both the primal and dual solutions as degeneracy, nonuniqueness, unboundedness, or emptiness. If the solution is not unique, find all basic solutions.

1.
$$2x_1 + x_2 + 4x_3 \leqslant 24,$$
$$x_1 + x_2 + x_3 \leqslant 4,$$
$$2x_1 - x_2 + 3x_3 \leqslant 12,$$
$\max x_0: x_0 = \frac{11}{4}x_1 + 2x_2 + 3x_3; \quad x_1, x_2, x_3 \geqslant 0.$

2.
$$2x_1 + 5x_2 + 7x_3 \leqslant 6,$$
$$3x_1 + 2x_2 + 6x_3 \leqslant 9,$$
$$x_1 - 3x_2 + 4x_3 \leqslant 5,$$
$\max x_0: x_0 = 2x_1 + 4x_2 + 5x_3; \quad x_1, x_2, x_3 \geqslant 0.$

3.
$$x_1 - x_2 + 2x_3 \leqslant 3,$$
$$3x_1 - 4x_2 + 7x_3 \leqslant 10,$$
$$2x_1 - 3x_2 + 4x_3 \leqslant 9,$$
$\max x_0: x_0 = 2x_1 - x_2 + 5x_3; \quad x_1, x_2, x_3 \geqslant 0.$

4.
$$6x_1 + x_2 - 5x_3 \leqslant 12,$$
$$3x_1 - 4x_2 + 9x_3 \leqslant 9,$$
$$4x_1 - 5x_2 + x_3 \leqslant 8,$$
$\max x_0: x_0 = 2x_1 + 3x_2 + 8x_3; \quad x_1, x_2, x_3 \geqslant 0.$

5.
$$6x_1 + x_2 + 2x_3 \leqslant 12,$$
$$-2x_1 - x_2 + x_3 \leqslant 3,$$
$$6x_1 - x_2 + 2x_3 \leqslant 6,$$
$\max x_0: x_0 = 2x_1 - 2x_2 + 4x_3; \quad x_1, x_2, x_3 \geqslant 0.$

6.
$$3x_1 + 3x_2 - 2x_3 \leqslant 5,$$
$$5x_1 - 2x_2 + 3x_3 \leqslant 6,$$
$$3x_1 - x_2 + x_3 \leqslant 2,$$
$\max x_0: x_0 = x_1 - 2x_2 + 2x_3; \quad x_1, x_2, x_3 \geqslant 0.$

5.4 THE TRANSPORTATION PROBLEM

The transportation problem is a linear program concerned with minimizing the cost of distribution of a single product from a company's various factories (sources of supply) to its various distributors (points of demand).

Transportation problems can be solved with techniques previously described; however, the special structure of these problems permits special, more efficient, methods of solution.

Example 1 *Minimizing cost, transportation.* A company can produce 50 cases of corkscrews at one factory in Chicago and 80 cases at a second factory in Atlanta. The company sells these corkscrews through three distributors: one in New York with orders for 70 cases, a second in Denver with orders for 20 cases, and a third in San Francisco with orders for 40 cases. The unit cost of transportation from factory to distributor is given in the following table:

Factory, i	Distributor, j			Supply capacity s_i
	New York 1	Denver 2	San Francisco 3	
Chicago 1	3	7	11	50
Atlanta 2	7	9	17	80
Demand required, r_j	70	20	40	Minimize cost

● Distributor
■ Factory

The problem is to determine how many cases should be shipped from each factory to each distributor to meet the demand with the supply available at minimum cost. Set this problem up as a linear program and obtain an initial feasible solution.

Solution   To formulate this problem, let

x_{ij} = the number of cases of corkscrews shipped from factory i to distributor j.

Then, since a factory can ship *no more* than its capacity, we have

$$x_{11} + x_{12} + x_{13} \leq 50,$$

$$x_{21} + x_{22} + x_{23} \leq 80.$$

And, since each distributor must have *at least* enough stock to satisfy his orders, we have

$$x_{11} \qquad\qquad + x_{21} \qquad\qquad \geq 70,$$

$$x_{12} \qquad\qquad + x_{22} \qquad\qquad \geq 20,$$

$$x_{13} \qquad\qquad + x_{23} \geq 40.$$

Here the quantities x_{ij} are not only nonnegative

$$x_{ij} \geq 0, \qquad \text{for all } i, j$$

but also integer since only case lots can be shipped.

The cost of shipment, x_0, which is to be minimized, is given by

$$x_0 = 3x_{11} + 7x_{12} + 11x_{13} + 7x_{21} + 9x_{22} + 17x_{23}.$$

In the present example the total supply available from both factories is

$$50 + 80 = 130$$

and the total demand required by all three distributors is

$$70 + 20 + 40 = 130$$

so that the supply just equals the demand. In this case the inequalities in the preceding constraints can be replaced by equal signs yielding

$$x_{11} + x_{12} + x_{13} \qquad\qquad\qquad = 50,$$

$$x_{21} + x_{22} + x_{23} = 80,$$

and

$$x_{11} \qquad\qquad + x_{21} \qquad\qquad = 70,$$

$$x_{12} \qquad\qquad + x_{22} \qquad\qquad = 20,$$

$$x_{13} \qquad\qquad + x_{23} = 40.$$

Let

$\qquad s_i$ = supply capacity of factory i,

$\qquad r_j$ = demand requirement of distributor j, and

$\qquad c_{ij}$ = unit cost of shipping from factory i to distributor j.

Then, for the *balanced* transportation problem the supply just equals the demand:

$$\sum_i s_i = \sum_j r_j.$$

That is, the sum of the supplies from all factories equals the sum of the demands by all distributors. Thus our formulation will always have the form

$$\sum_j x_{ij} = s_i, \qquad \text{for all } i,$$

$$\sum_i x_{ij} = r_j, \qquad \text{for all } j,$$

$$x_{ij} \geq 0 \text{ and integer,} \qquad \text{for all } i \text{ and } j,$$

$$\min x_0 : x_0 = \sum_i \sum_j c_{ij} x_{ij}.$$

The integer constraint is new in our *formulation* of linear programs and such problems are called *integer* programs. They *usually* require special solution techniques; however, because of the special structure of transportation problems, we can solve them as linear programs and their solutions will *automatically* be integer. (This is not true of all integer programs.)

Equation constraints can be incorporated into the simplex algorithm; however, we can obtain the solution much more simply in the following manner. We use a modification of the table representing the given data with each cell now containing the following information:

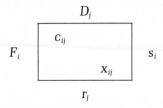

To solve the transportation problem we need an initial feasible solution, which we shall obtain by the *minimum-cost assignment* method. This will provide us with a set of basic and nonbasic values of x_{ij}. The basic values we *write in* in the lower right corner of the cell and the nonbasic values (which are zero) we indicate with a *blank* (or a dash "—").

Minimum-Cost Assignment Method for an Initial Feasible Solution

At each stage of this method we seek the *minimum* value of c_{ij} (if there are more than one with this minimum value, choose either) and assign to this x_{ij} the maximum value which will neither overdraw the supply s_i of factory i (F_i) nor oversupply r_j the distributor j (D_j).

Thus, we obtain

	D_1		D_2		D_3		
F_1	3	50	7		11		50
F_2	7	20	9	20	17	40	80
	70		20		40		

with the following assignment steps:

1. The minimum c_{ij} is $c_{11} = 3$. The maximum assignment that we can make for x_{11} without exceeding the supply $s_1 = 50$ of factory F_1 nor exceeding the requirement $r_1 = 70$ of distributor D_1 is $x_{11} = 50$ and we write this number in the lower right corner of cell $F_1 D_1$.

2. The next minimum c_{ij} is $c_{12} = c_{21} = 7$. Since the supply from F_1 has been exhausted by D_1, we cannot make an assignment for x_{12} and leave its place in its cell blank. The maximum assignment we can make for x_{21} is 20 and we write this in its cell.

3. The next minimum c_{ij} is $c_{22} = 9$. The maximum assignment we can make for x_{22} is 20 and we write this in.

4. The next minimum c_{ij} is $c_{13} = 11$ but F_1 is exhausted so no assignment can be made for x_{13} and we leave a blank.

5. The next minimum c_{ij} is $c_{23} = 17$. The maximum assignment we can make for x_{23} is 40 and we write this in.

At this point we have exhausted the supply of all the factories and met the requirements of all the distributors (but not necessarily at minimum cost) with *four* assignments.

For the balanced transportation problem (with $\Sigma_i s_i = \Sigma_j r_j$), one equation is linearly dependent on the others, so the number of linearly independent equations—which is equal to the number of basic variables (See Section 5.1)—is one less than the sum of the number of factories and distributors. In this case the number of basic variables is $2 + 3 - 1 = 4$. Since we have made four assignments, we have a *full* set of basic variables.

If we were able to make assignments which would both exhaust the supply and meet the requirements with *fewer* assignments, then we must make zero assignments until a full set of basic variables is obtained and write these zeroes into the cells.

The cost of this initial set of assignments is

$$x_0 = 3(50) + 7(20) + 9(20) + 17(40),$$

$$= 150 + 140 + 180 + 680,$$

$$= 1150.$$

Thus, from the table our initial feasible solution is

Basic variables: $x_{11} = 50$, $x_{21} = 20$, $x_{22} = 20$, $x_{23} = 40$,

Nonbasic variables: $x_{12} = x_{13} = 0$,

Objective function: $x_0 = 1150$.

Stepping-Stone Algorithm

Example 2   Solve the transportation problem of Example 1.

Solution   We solve the transportation problem using the *stepping-stone* algorithm. As in the simplex algorithm, we make one nonbasic variable basic and one basic variable nonbasic.

To determine which nonbasic variable to make basic, we consider closed paths starting with and returning to a given nonbasic cell and passing through a series of basic cells each associated rowwise or columnwise with its predecessor.

Here there are two *nonbasic* cells: F_1D_2 and F_1D_3. We consider a circuit for each:

1. F_1D_2: F_1D_2—F_2D_2—F_2D_1—F_1D_1—F_1D_2,
2. F_1D_3: F_1D_3—F_2D_3—F_2D_1—F_1D_1—F_1D_3.

For each circuit we determine the change in cost obtainable by reassigning one unit of our commodity around this circuit. To do this, we add one unit to the starting nonbasic cell and subtract one unit from the next basic cell in our circuit, then add one unit to the next basic cell and subtract one unit from the next basic cell and so on until the circuit is complete.

The change in cost obtained by doing this for each circuit is

1. F_1D_2: $c_{12} - c_{22} + c_{21} - c_{11} = 7 - 9 + 7 - 3 = 2$,
2. F_1D_3: $c_{13} - c_{23} + c_{21} - c_{11} = 11 - 17 + 7 - 3 = -2$.

Thus, for F_1D_2 the unit cost is *increased* by 2, but for F_1D_3 the unit cost is *decreased* by 2.

For each circuit representing a *decrease* in *unit* cost we now seek the *maximum* number of units that can be reassigned around this circuit without disturbing the supply and requirement balances. This is the *minimum* value of x_{ij} of those cells of the circuit with *minus* signs associated with c_{ij}.

Thus, for F_1D_3 we seek

$$\min\{x_{23}, x_{11}\} = \min\{40, 50\}$$

$$= x_{23}$$

$$= 40.$$

The *overall* change in cost for this circuit is

$$x_{23}(c_{13} - c_{23} + c_{21} - c_{11}) = 40(-2)$$

$$= -80.$$

We select that circuit which yields the maximum *overall* decrease in cost. This determines the basic variable to become nonbasic, in this case x_{23}. We modify the previous solution accordingly to obtain the next feasible solution:

	D_1		D_2		D_3		
F_1	3	10	7		11	40	50
F_2	7	60	9	20	17		80
	70		20		40		

The new value of the objective function is

$$x_0 = 3(10) + 11(40) + 7(60) + 9(20),$$

$$= 30 + 440 + 420 + 180,$$

$$= 1070,$$

or

$$x_0 = 1150 - 80,$$

$$= 1070.$$

We now have two nonbasic cells: F_1D_2 and F_2D_3. The unit change in cost for the circuits for each is

1. F_1D_2: $c_{12} - c_{11} + c_{21} - c_{13} = 7 - 3 + 7 - 9,$

$$= 2;$$

2. F_2D_3: $c_{23} - c_{21} + c_{11} - c_{13} = 17 - 7 + 3 - 11,$

$$= 2.$$

No circuit is possible which could yield a decrease in cost. Hence, the current solution is minimal:

Basic variables: $x_{11} = 10$, $x_{13} = 40$, $x_{21} = 60$, $x_{22} = 20$,

Nonbasic variables: $x_{12} = x_{23} = 0$,

Objective function: $x_0 = 1070$.

If the current solution were not minimal, we would continue as before.

EXERCISE SET 5.4

Solve the following transportation problems for the minimum cost assignment where the data is given in the format of Example 1.

1.

i	j 1	2	3	s_i
1	5	11	17	150
2	15	9	13	80
r_j	70	90	70	Min. cost

2.

i	j 1	2	3	s_i
1	3	11	9	190
2	5	8	7	130
r_j	110	90	120	Min. cost

3.

i	j 1	2	s_i
1	14	17	70
2	13	9	80
3	11	12	100
r_j	120	130	Min. cost

4.

i	j 1	2	s_i
1	21	17	80
2	13	15	90
3	19	11	70
r_j	110	130	Min. cost

5.

i	j 1	2	3	4	s_i
1	6	10	7	13	150
2	9	14	8	17	100
r_j	45	60	70	75	Min. cost

6.

i	j 1	2	3	4	s_i
1	11	17	13	21	150
2	19	14	9	15	200
r_j	70	80	90	110	Min. cost

■ ───────────────────────────────

7.

i	j 1	2	3	s_i
1	7	11	9	80
2	13	17	14	90
3	21	15	17	110
r_j	70	120	90	Min. cost

8.

i	j 1	2	3	s_i
1	11	7	13	90
2	9	17	15	70
3	17	14	21	100
r_j	80	110	70	Min. cost

Hint: If the basic cells are assigned as follows:

	1	2	3
1	x		x
2		x	x
3		x	

then for nonbasic cell 31, the appropriate route
is 31—32—22—23—13—11—31.

9.

i	j 1	2	3	4	s_i
1	11	10	8	9	100
2	13	8	16	14	125
3	14	10	12	15	150
r_j	75	100	120	80	Min. cost

10.

i	j 1	2	3	4	s_i
1	21	17	13	14	70
2	15	19	23	10	90
3	17	12	25	28	140
r_j	40	90	75	95	Min. cost

5.5 THE ASSIGNMENT PROBLEM

The assignment problem is a special case of the balanced transportation problem as is shown in the following Example.

Example 1 *Assignment of personnel.* The personnel officer of a large company seeks to fill 5 job positions each requiring a particular set of skills. There are 5 applicants for these jobs. In order to find the "best fit" of applicant to job, a test is given to each applicant. The qualifications a_{ij} for assigning applicant i to job j is given in the following table:

Applicant i	Job j				
	1	2	3	4	5
1	9	2	3	7	6
2	4	8	5	6	9
3	2	3	8	7	5
4	8	8	1	5	8
5	5	3	7	5	4

The problem is to find the "best fit" if the sum of the assigned qualifications is to be *maximized.* Show that this is a special case of the transportation problem.

Solution *Step 1:* Let x_{ij} represent the assignment of applicant i to job j, where x_{ij} = 1 if such an assignment *is* made and x_{ij} = 0 otherwise; so that,

$$x_{ij} = 0 \text{ or } 1 \quad \text{for all } i, j.$$

Since one person cannot do two jobs nor can one job have two people assigned to it, we have

a) Each person is assigned to one and only one job, or

$$\sum_j x_{ij} = 1, \quad \text{for all } i, \text{ and}$$

b) each job is filled by one and only one person, or

$$\sum_i x_{ij} = 1, \quad \text{for all } j.$$

Step 2: We could write the objective function as

$$\max a_0: a_0 = \sum_i \sum_j a_{ij} x_{ij}.$$

However, for analogy with the transportation problem and also for later use, we prefer to have this problem in *minimum* form. To do this we convert "goodness of fit," a_{ij}, to "badness of fit," b_{ij}, by subtracting each a_{ij} from $a_{i^*j^*} = \max_{i,j} a_{ij}$ (in this case, 9) obtaining

			j			
i	1	2	3	4	5	Row minimum (b_{ij^*})
1	0	7	6	2	3	0
2	5	1	4	3	0	0
3	7	6	1	2	4	1
4	1	1	8	4	1	1
5	4	6	2	4	5	2

Thus, rather than maximizing the "goodness of fit," we minimize the "badness of fit" and introduce a new objective function:

$$\min x_0 : x_0 = \sum_i \sum_j b_{ij} x_{ij}.$$

This formulation can be seen to be in the form of a transportation problem by setting

$$s_i = 1, \quad \text{for all } i, \text{ and}$$

$$r_j = 1, \quad \text{for all } j.$$

Example 2 Solve the assignment problem of Example 1.

Solution We could solve the assignment problem now as a transportation problem (see Section 5.5); however, the special structure of this problem permits a much simpler method of solution known as the *Hungarian Method* based on a theorem by the Hungarian mathematician Dénes König. Continuing with the steps of Example 1, we have

Step 3: We use a star (*) to indicate an assignment. If we can find zeroes to star (make an assignment) such that there were one and only one star in each row and in each column, then such an assignment would minimize x_0. The first two rows have exactly one zero and, hence, one star in each but the remaining rows do not.

Let b_{ij^*} be the minimum value of b_{ij} in row i. Since

$$\sum_j x_{ij} = 1,$$

if we subtract b_{ij^*} from each value of b_{ij} in row i, then x_0 changes only by the *constant* b_{ij^*} and this has no effect on the optimum assignment.[†] Thus, we subtract from each value b_{ij} in a row the minimum value b_{ij^*} in that row and do this for each row. We denote the result by b'_{ij}. This process is called *row reduction*.

Row reducing the remaining three rows, we obtain

			j		
i	1	2	3	4	5
1	0	7	6	2	3
2	5	1	4	3	0
3	6	5	0	1	3
4	0	0	7	3	0
5	2	4	0	2	3

Column minimum (b'_{i^*j}) 0   0   0   1   0

Looking at the columns, we see that there are zeroes in each column except the fourth. Let b'_{i^*j} be the minimum value of b'_{ij} in column j. Then, as for rows, we can *column-reduce* by subtracting b'_{i^*j} from each value of b'_{ij} in column j and do this for each column without changing the optimum assignment.

Column-reducing the fourth row, we obtain the row- and column-reduced table with elements c_{ij} (ignore the *'s for the present):

			j		
i	1	2	3	4	5
1	0*	7	6	1	3
2	5	1	4	2	0*
3	6	5	0	0*	3
4	0	0*	7	2	0
5	2	4	0*	1	3

Step 4: We now seek to star (*) zeroes to make assignments such that there is exactly one assignment (*) in each row and in each column.

i) Let us start by examining the first row. Since there is only one zero in this row, we star that element, c_{11}.

[†] $x_0 = \Sigma_i(\Sigma_j b_{ij} x_{ij}) = \Sigma_i[\Sigma_j(b_{ij} - b_{ij^*})x_{ij} + b_{ij^*} \cdot \Sigma_j x_{ij}] = \Sigma_i \Sigma_j (b_{ij} - b_{ij^*})x_{ij} + \Sigma_i b_{ij^*}.$

ii) Similarly, there is only one zero in the second row (c_{25}) and that zero is not in the same column as the previous zero. Thus, we star c_{25}.

iii) Similarly, there is only one zero in the fifth row (c_{53}) and that zero is not in the same column as previous starred zeroes (assignments). Thus, we star c_{53}.

iv) Looking now at columns, the first column has a starred zero. The second column has only one zero (c_{42}) and this is not in the same row as previous starred zeroes. Thus, we star c_{42}.

v) Similarly, the fourth column has only one zero (c_{34}) and this is not in the same row as previous starred zeroes. Thus, we star c_{34}.

Note: There may be some choice as to which assignment to make "next." At this point we have made five assignments with one and only one star in each row and in each column. Thus, we have found an optimum assignment.

$$x_{11} = x_{25} = x_{34} = x_{42} = x_{53} = 1,$$

$$x_{ij} = 0 \qquad \text{for all other } i, j;$$

so that,

$$a_0 = a_{11} + a_{25} + a_{34} + a_{42} + a_{53},$$

$$= 9 \quad + 9 \quad + 7 \quad + 8 \quad + 7,$$

$$= 40.$$

We can just as well column-reduce first and then row-reduce. Since these problems are frequently degenerate, the solutions are not always unique and hence column-row reduction may not yield the same assignment as row-column reduction but the value of a_0 would be the same.

It sometimes happens that an optimum assignment cannot be made from the reduced table. Consider the following example.

Example 3 Find the optimum assignment for the following *reduced* table:

			j		
i	1	2	3	4	5
1	1	7	6	0	3
2	5	0	4	2	0
3	6	5	0	0	3
4	0	0	7	2	0
5	2	4	0	1	3

Solution   Proceeding as in Step 4, we obtain the assignments

			j		
i	1	2	3	4	5
1	1	7	6	0*	3
2	5	0*	4	2	0
3	6	5	0	0	3
4	0*	0	7	2	0
5	2	4	0*	1	3

i) First row: star c_{14},
ii) Fifth row: star c_{53},
iii) First column: star c_{41},
iv) Second column: star c_{22}.

No more zero assignments can be made without having more than one zero in some row or column and no zero in some other row or column. Hence, we proceed with Step 5.

Step 5.   If an optimum assignment *cannot* be made, then it *is* possible to cover all the zeroes in the table with a number of horizontal and vertical lines *less* than the number of assignments to be made. These lines may be drawn more than one way.

   i) Starting with the greatest number of zeroes, we draw a line through Row 4.
   ii) Next we draw a line through Row 2.
   iii) Then we draw lines through Columns 3 and 4.

			j		
i	1	2	3	4	5
1	①	7	6	0	3
2	5	0	4	2	0
3	6	5	0	0	3
4	0	0	7	2	0
5	2	4	0	1	3

All zeroes are now covered with 4 lines and this number is less than the number of required assignments, 5; so that further reduction is necessary.

Note: It is not always obvious how to draw these lines and some "playing around" may be necessary.

   To obtain a better assignment, we must add or subtract some quantity to certain rows and/or columns to change the location of zeroes. This corresponds to a pivoting operation in the simplex operation. We continue with *iv*.

iv) We now seek the *smallest uncovered* element in this reduced table and call this element $c_{i^*j^*}$. Here $c_{i^*j^*} = c_{11} = 1$ and is circled. (There may be more than one element equal to $c_{i^*j^*}$ but this does not change the algorithm.)

Since we can add or subtract any constant from any row or column without changing the optimum assignment, we

v) subtract $c_{i^*j^*}$ from each c_{ij} in each *uncovered row* and

vi) add $c_{i^*j^*}$ to each c_{ij} in each *covered column*.

Alternately, it is simpler but equivalent to

v) subtract $c_{i^*j^*}$ from each *uncovered element* and

vi) add $c_{i^*j^*}$ to each *doubly-covered element*.

Doing this, we obtain

i	j 1	2	3	4	5
1	0^*	6	6	0	2
2	5	0^a	5	3	0^b
3	5	4	0	0^*	2
4	0	0^b	8	3	0^a
5	1	3	0^*	1	2

Going back to Step 4:

i) Fifth row: star c_{53},

ii) Third row: star c_{34},

iii) First row: star c_{11}.

iv) Now we have a choice:

    a) star c_{22} and c_{45}, or

    b) star c_{25} and c_{42}.

Thus, we have obtained two optimal assignments:

    a) $x_{53} = x_{34} = x_{11} = x_{22} = x_{45} = 1$, and

    b) $x_{53} = x_{34} = x_{11} = x_{25} = x_{42} = 1$,

where the value of the objective function is the same in either case but of no concern here.

If an optimal solution were *not* obtained at this point, then we would repeat Steps 5 and 4 until one is obtained.

EXERCISE SET 5.5

Solve the following assignment problems where the "goodness of fit" is given in the tables.

1.

i	\multicolumn{5}{c}{j}
	1	2	3	4	5
1	82	89	73	77	83
2	79	85	72	78	84
3	84	82	81	69	78
4	83	86	91	88	82
5	86	85	87	81	76

2.

i	\multicolumn{5}{c}{j}
	1	2	3	4	5
1	73	75	79	81	76
2	69	77	72	83	78
3	77	82	87	85	81
4	81	83	94	82	76
5	71	69	73	82	72

3.

i	\multicolumn{5}{c}{j}
	1	2	3	4	5
1	86	83	90	79	89
2	79	80	81	84	83
3	85	84	78	86	82
4	83	81	92	87	78
5	84	88	87	93	89

4.

i	\multicolumn{5}{c}{j}
	1	2	3	4	5
1	82	79	83	77	73
2	83	85	80	73	74
3	69	82	73	74	77
4	85	84	87	81	68
5	74	77	81	70	82

5.

i	\multicolumn{5}{c}{j}
	1	2	3	4	5
1	85	75	92	78	83
2	67	89	77	76	87
3	73	86	91	84	79
4	86	76	93	79	84
5	82	91	85	85	86

6.

i	\multicolumn{5}{c}{j}
	1	2	3	4	5
1	87	83	79	91	86
2	62	73	70	69	80
3	82	79	68	83	81
4	71	73	74	69	82
5	86	81	81	90	87

7.

i	\multicolumn{6}{c}{j}
	1	2	3	4	5	6
1	84	87	83	79	91	86
2	62	73	70	69	80	75
3	77	82	79	68	83	81
4	89	84	86	79	92	85
5	71	73	74	69	82	80
6	83	86	81	81	90	87

8.

i	\multicolumn{6}{c}{j}
	1	2	3	4	5	6
1	73	75	79	81	76	75
2	69	77	78	83	72	73
3	77	82	85	87	81	79
4	83	81	82	94	76	88
5	71	69	73	82	72	73
6	74	75	77	76	70	71

5.6   ACTIVITY ANALYSIS—CRITICAL PATH METHOD

The *scheduling* of the various *activities* of a *project* can be analysed by *network theory* using the *Critical Path Method*. Network theory is a *geometric* approach to the solution of certain types of linear programs.

Example 1   A contractor has the project of refinishing an apartment and has made the following assessment of the various tasks (activities):

	Task	Time required (days)	Prior tasks
A	Start	0	—
B	Inspect and determine parts needed for repair	1	A
C	Order and obtain parts	3	B
D	Clean	1	A
E	Repair work	2	C, D
F	Paint	3	B, D, E
G	Lay carpet	2	E, F
H	Finish	0	G

The rightmost column indicates which tasks must be just completed *before* the given task can be *started* (that is, the *immediate* predecessors). Draw the network to represent this project.

Solution   Let each *task* or *activity* be represented by a *point* or *node*. Thus, the initial task "start" (which is a starting "point") is represented by

$$\bullet \text{ A} \quad \text{or} \quad Ⓐ .$$

Consider two tasks, i and j. If task i must *precede* task j (that is, task i must be just *completed* before task j can be *started*), then the *line* or *arc* from node i to node j (with an *arrow* indicating direction) represents that *precedence relation*:

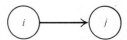

The *completion time*, or *time of performance*, of task i, t_i, is given in the "time required" column. **Assign to each arc ij a nonnegative "length" c_{ij} equal to the completion time of task i; that is, $c_{ij} = t_i$.**

Combining nodes and arcs (which may have interpretations other than the preceding), we have the following definitions:

DEFINITION   **A *graph* is a set of nodes (points) and a set of arcs (lines) connecting pairs of nodes.**

Note that it is *not* necessary for *all* nodes of a graph to be connected. An example of a graph is

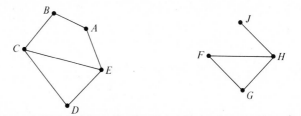

which consists of the points {A, B, C, D, E, F, G, H, J} and the lines {AB, BC, CD, CE, DE, EA, FG, FH, GH, HJ}.

Neighboring nodes are nodes separated by a *single* arc. For example, C and E are neighboring nodes but C and A are not. A *path* is a *sequence* of neighboring nodes without repetition*: there are three paths from C to A

CBA, CEA, and CDEA.

DEFINITION   **A *network* is a graph such that each node is *connected* to each other node by *some* path.**

Thus, a graph consists of one or more networks. The foregoing example of a graph consists of *two* networks: one on the left and one on the right.

DEFINITION   **An *activity network* is a network with *directed* arcs indicated by arrows.**

A *network* can be *nondirected* or *directed* and the modifier "activity" is frequently dropped when there can be no misunderstanding as to meaning, as in this section wherein all networks are directed.

A *project* can be represented by an *activity network*.

For a large project, the tasks might be represented by two or more networks, or subprojects, which can be implemented independently. We shall consider projects representable by a single network.

———————————

* Actually, this is the definition of an *elementary* path, which is all we are concerned with.

To start drawing the network, we look over the prior-task column and find that tasks B and D must be preceded by task A, the starting point, so that we must have two arcs, AB and AD, leaving node A:

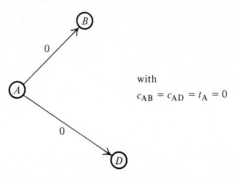

with

$$c_{AB} = c_{AD} = t_A = 0$$

Continuing, we again examine the prior-task column to seek the tasks which follow B or D. Task C follows task B (that is, task B must precede task C), so that we add node C and arc BC:

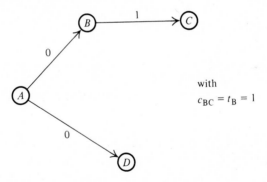

with

$$c_{BC} = t_B = 1$$

Now task E follows the *two* tasks C and D, so that we add node E and *two* arcs, CD and CE:

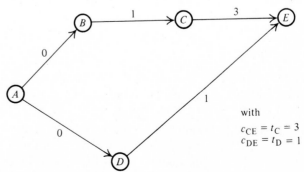

with

$$c_{CE} = t_C = 3$$
$$c_{DE} = t_D = 1$$

Now task F follows the *three* tasks B, C, and E, so that we add node F and three arcs, BF, DF, and EF:

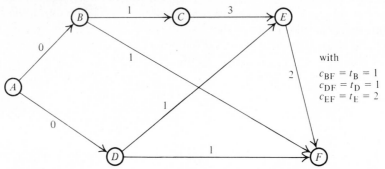

with

$c_{BF} = t_B = 1$
$c_{DF} = t_D = 1$
$c_{EF} = t_E = 2$

Now task G follows the two tasks E and F, so that we add node G and arcs EG and FG:

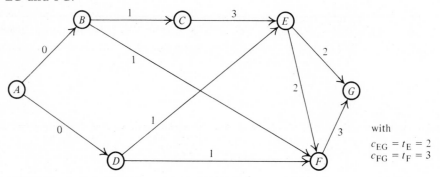

with

$c_{EG} = t_E = 2$
$c_{FG} = t_F = 3$

At last, the final task H (which is a *point* of completion) follows task G, so that we add node H and arc GH:

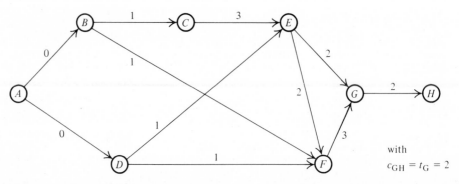

with

$c_{GH} = t_G = 2$

This completes the *representation* of the project as an activity network. Note that by drawing the nodes in different places, different, but equivalent, networks may be obtained.

Example 2   Continuing with Example 1, find the *earliest* time that each task can be *started* and the *earliest completion* time for the project.

Solution   The requirement that certain tasks be completed prior to the start of others constitutes a set of linear constraints with *time* as the independent variable. The completion time of the project is the objective function to be minimized, so that we have a linear program. We shall solve this problem using network theory which takes advantage of the special structure of the problem (representation by a network). From duality, the minimum completion time for the project corresponds to the longest (maximum) path through the network.

Let us assign to (label) each node i a time T_i and to each arc ij a time T_{ij} such that:

At the *starting* point (or node),

$$T_{\text{start}} = 0.$$

Working *forward* through the network from start to finish:

Assign to (label) each *arc* ij a time T_{ij} equal to the time assigned at the *beginning* node i, T_i, plus the arc length, c_{ij}; that is

$$T_{ij} = T_i + c_{ij}$$

and each arc is now labeled c_{ij}, T_{ij}.

Recall that $c_{ij} = t_i$, the completion time, or time of performance, of task i. Thus, if T_i is the *earliest* time task i can be *started*, then $T_{ij} = T_i + t_i$ is the *earliest* time task i can be *finished*.

Task j cannot be *started* until all tasks prior to it have been *completed*, so that T_j is the *maximum* (latest time) value of T_{ij} of all arcs ij *ending* at node j and we assign to (label) each node j a time T_j equal to this *maximum* value:

$$T_j = \max_i T_{ij}.$$

We also label node j with the value of i for which T_{ij} is maximum. This value of i represents the task which must be just completed before task j can be started.

The *earliest* time that the "finish" task can be *started* is the *minimum completion* time of the project. This we find by seeking the *longest* (timewise) path through the network.

Implementing this *forward* algorithm, in order we have

$T_A \ = 0$ and label node A with a dash "—" since there is no prior node,

$T_{AB} = T_A + c_{AB} = 0 + 0 = 0,$

$$T_{AD} = T_A + c_{AD} = 0 + 0 = 0,$$

$$T_B = T_{AB} = 0 \text{ and label node B with A,}$$

$$T_D = T_{AD} = 0 \text{ and label node D with A,}$$

$$T_{BC} = T_B + c_{BC} = 0 + 1 = 1,$$

$$T_C = T_{BC} = 1 \text{ and label node C with B,}$$

$$T_{CE} = T_C + c_{CE} = 1 + 3 = 4,$$

$$T_{DE} = T_D + c_{DE} = 0 + 1 = 1,$$

$$T_E = \max\{T_{CE}, T_{DE}\} = \max\{4, 1\} = 4 \text{ and label node E with C,}$$

$$T_{BF} = T_B + c_{BF} = 0 + 1 = 1,$$

$$T_{DF} = T_D + c_{DF} = 0 + 1 = 1,$$

$$T_{EF} = T_E + c_{EF} = 4 + 2 = 6,$$

$$T_F = \max\{T_{BF}, T_{DF}, T_{EF}\} = \max\{1, 1, 6\} = 6 \text{ and label node F}$$
with E,

$$T_{EG} = T_E + c_{EG} = 4 + 2 = 6,$$

$$T_{FG} = T_F + c_{FG} = 6 + 3 = 9,$$

$$T_G = \max\{T_{EG}, T_{FG}\} = \max\{6, 9\} = 9 \text{ and label node G with F,}$$

$$T_{GH} = T_G + c_{GH} = 9 + 2 = 11,$$

$$T_H = T_{GH} = 11 \text{ and label node H with G.}$$

Rather than make such a list, we usually simply label the nodes and arcs of the network:

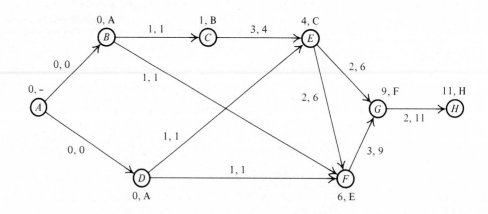

Thus, we find that the minimum completion time of the project is

$$T_{\text{finish}} = T_{\text{H}} = 11.$$

Example 3 Continuing with Example 1, find the *latest* time each task of the project can be *started*.

Solution The first pass through the network was forward from start to finish. Now we make a second pass through the network.

Working *backward* through the network from finish to start, we assign to (label) each node *i* with *another* time T_i' and each arc *ij* with *another* time T_{ij}'.

Assign a *target* time at the *finish* node:

$$T_{\text{finish}}' = T_{\text{finish}}.$$

Assign to (label) each *arc ij* a time T_{ij}' equal to the time at the *end* node *j*, T_j', minus the arc length c_{ij}; that is,

$$T_{ij}' = T_j' - c_{ij}$$

and each *arc* is now labeled c_{ij}, T_{ij}, T_{ij}'.

Recall that $c_{ij} = t_i$, the time of *performance* of task *i*. Thus, if T_j' is the *latest* time that task *j* can be *started* (for the project to be finished on time), then $T_{ij}' = T_j' - t_i$ is the *latest* time task *i* can be *finished* (for task *j* not to delay the project).

Having T_{ij}', the *latest* time task *i* can be *finished* for *each* subsequent task *j* not to delay the project, the *minimum* (earliest) value of *all* T_{ij}' with arcs *ij starting* at node *i* is the *latest* time task *i* can be *finished* for *any* subsequent task *j* not to delay the project. Thus, we assign to (label) each node *i* a time T_i' equal to this *minimum* value:

$$T_i' = \min_j T_{ij}'.$$

Each *node j* is now labeled T_j, *i*, T_j'.

Implementing this *backward* algorithm, in order we have

$$T_{\text{H}}' = T_{\text{H}} = 11,$$

$$T_{\text{GH}}' = T_{\text{H}}' - c_{\text{GH}} = 11 - 2 = 9,$$

$$T_{\text{G}}' = T_{\text{GH}}' = 9,$$

$$T_{\text{EG}}' = T_{\text{G}}' - c_{\text{EG}} = 9 - 2 = 7,$$

$$T_{\text{FG}}' = T_{\text{G}}' - c_{\text{FG}} = 9 - 3 = 6,$$

$$T'_F = T'_{FG} = 6,$$

$$T'_{EF} = T'_F - c_{EF} = 6 - 2 = 4,$$

$$T'_{DF} = T'_F - c_{DF} = 6 - 1 = 5,$$

$$T'_{BF} = T'_F - c_{BF} = 6 - 1 = 5,$$

$$T'_E = \min\{T'_{EF}, T'_{EG}\} = \min\{4, 7\} = 4,$$

$$T'_{DE} = T'_E - c_{DE} = 4 - 1 = 3,$$

$$T'_D = \min\{T'_{DE}, T'_{DF}\} = \min\{3, 5\} = 3,$$

$$T'_{CE} = T'_E - c_{CE} = 4 - 3 = 1,$$

$$T'_C = T'_{CE} = 1,$$

$$T'_{BC} = T'_C - c_{BC} = 1 - 1 = 0,$$

$$T'_B = \min\{T'_{BC}, T'_{BF}\} = \min\{0, 5\} = 0,$$

$$T'_{AB} = T'_B - c_{AB} = 0 - 0 = 0,$$

$$T'_{AD} = T'_D - c_{AD} = 3 - 0 = 3,$$

$$T'_A = \min\{T'_{AB}, T'_{AD}\} = \min\{0, 3\} = 0.$$

Or, simply adding these labels progressively to our previously labeled network, we have

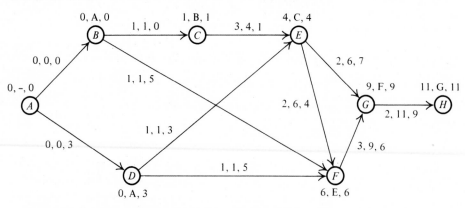

We are mainly concerned with the two times T_i and T'_i:

T_i is the *earliest* time that task i can be *started* and
T'_i is the *latest* time that task i can be *started*

for the project to be finished in *minimum* time.

Example 4 Continuing with Example 1, find the *slack* time for each task and the *critical path* through the network.

Solution We use the information gained from the *two* passes through the network.

The difference between the *late start* time, T'_i, and the *early start* time, T_i, is the *slack* time, s_i:

$$s_i = T'_i - T_i.$$

This represents the *extra* time available (that is, in addition to t_i) to complete task *i without delaying* the project.

Thus, at point C

$$s_C = T'_C - T_C = 3 - 0 = 3,$$

so that the slack time for task C is 3 days.

A task or activity is *critical* if its slack time is zero.

Thus, at point E

$$s_E = T'_E - T_E = 4 - 4 = 0,$$

so that, since the slack time for task E is zero, this task is critical.

The minimum completion time for the project equals the *sum* of the *performance* times of *all* the tasks along the *critical path*.

To find the *critical path*, we begin at the *finish* and work toward the *start* following the path indicated by the node point of the node label.

Starting at node H, we are led to node G and thence to node F and so forth. Thus, we obtain the critical path ABCEFGH indicated by the heavy line on the following diagram:

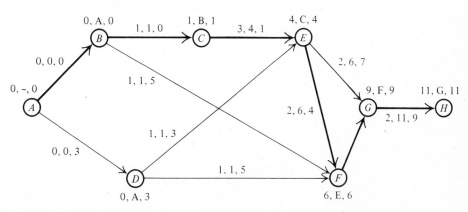

Note that the completion time of the project,

$$t_A + t_B + t_C + t_E + t_F + t_G + t_H = 0 + 1 + 3 + 2 + 3 + 2 + 0$$

$$= 11,$$

is the same as previously obtained, $T_H = 11$.

Every network must have at least one critical path (although there may be more than one). Each task along this path is critical. This means that a delay in the completion of any critical task causes a delay in the project as a whole. Similarly, if the project is to be completed ahead of schedule, then one or more critical tasks must be finished in less than the scheduled time.

EXERCISE SET 5.6

For each of the following exercises,

a) Draw the activity network,

b) Find the earliest start time for each task,

c) Find the latest start time for each task,

d) Find the slack time for each task and the critical path through the network.

1. A chef is planning a backyard barbecue and makes the following time plan:

	Task	Time required (minutes)	Prior tasks
A	Start	0	—
B	Plan dinner	30	A
C	Shop	90	B
D	Prepare fire	30	C
E	Prepare food	45	C
F	Barbecue chicken	60	D
G	Cook vegetables	40	E
H	Make salad	15	E, F
J	Set table	15	B
K	Make and chill dessert	90	C
L	Serve dinner	15	F, G, H, J
M	Finish	0	K, L

2. A family is planning to build a vacation cabin and makes the following assessment of tasks:

	Task	Time required (days)	Prior tasks
A	Start	0	—
B	Prepare land	1	A
C	Lay foundation and put in floor	3	B
D	Put up framing	4	C
E	Put in plumbing	2	C
F	Put in electrical wiring	2	D
G	Put up walls	3	D, E, F
H	Put on roof	2	D
J	Paint	2	G, H
K	Finish	0	J

3.

Task	Time required	Prior tasks
A (start)	0	—
B	2	A
C	3	A
D	5	B, C
E	4	C
F	6	B, E
G	3	C, D
H (finish)	0	C, F, G

4.

Task	Time required	Prior tasks
A (start)	0	—
B	5	A
C	3	A
D	7	A
E	6	B, C, D
F	4	B, C
G	2	D, E
H (finish)	0	E, F, G

5.

Task	Time required	Prior tasks
A (start)	0	—
B	2	A
C	3	A
D	4	B, C
E	3	B, C
F	5	B, E
G	3	D, E
H	4	C, E, F
J (finish)	0	G, H

6.

Task	Time required	Prior tasks
A (start)	0	—
B	4	A
C	3	A
D	7	B, C
E	2	C, D
F	5	B, C, E
G	6	D, F
H	1	E, F, G
J (finish)	0	G, H

7.

Task	Time required	Prior tasks
A (start)	0	—
B	3	A
C	4	A
D	7	A
E	3	B, D
F	6	C, D
G	5	E, F
H	4	D, E, G
J	2	E, G
K (finish)	0	H, J

8.

Task	Time required	Prior tasks
A (start)	0	—
B	5	A
C	3	A
D	7	B
E	4	B
F	6	C, D
G	2	C, E
H	1	E, F
J	3	E, G, H
K (finish)	0	H, J

CHAPTER 5 REVIEW

1. Adding slack variables, convert the following formulation into a system of equations and put into matrix form.

$$20x_1 + 100x_2 \leq 1900,$$
$$x_1 + 50x_2 \leq 500,$$
$$2x_1 + 20x_2 \leq 240,$$
$$x_1, x_2 \geq 0,$$
$$\max x_0 \colon x_0 = 20x_1 + 300x_2.$$

2. Set up the initial simplex tableau for the problem of Exercise 1.

3. Find an initial feasible solution from the tableau of Exercise 2.

4. Find a pivot element for the tableau of Exercise 2.

5. Starting with the initial simplex tableau of Exercise 2, pivot until the algorithm terminates. Check your solution at each step with the graphical solution of Exercise 11 of Chapter 4 Review.

6. Formulate the linear program dual to that of Exercise 1.

7. Formulate the linear program dual to

$$0.1y_1 + 0y_2 \geq 200,$$
$$0y_1 + 0.2y_2 \geq 500,$$
$$0.02y_1 + 0.01y_2 \geq 100,$$
$$\min y_0 \colon y_0 = 10y_1 + 15y_2; \qquad y_1, y_2 \geq 0.$$

8. From the initial simplex tableau of Exercise 2, read off both the initial primal and dual solutions.

9. Express the constraint set of Exercise 7 as a set of equations, set up the initial simplex tableau, and read off both the initial primal and dual solutions.

10. Solve the minimum-type linear program whose initial simplex tableau was obtained in Exercise 9.

11. Check your solution from Exercise 10 using primal and dual solutions.

12. For the following transportation problem, find an initial feasible solution.

F_i	D_j			s_i
	1	2	3	
1	7	11	4	120
2	18	9	13	70
r_j	60	50	80	Min. cost

13. Solve the transportation problem of Exercise 12.

14. Solve the assignment problem of Example 1, Section 5.5 using column reduction first and compare solutions.

15. Find the optimum assignment for the following reduced table:

i	j				
	1	2	3	4	5
1	3	7	0	6	3
2	5	0	4	2	0
3	6	5	0	3	0
4	0	0	7	2	0
5	3	4	0	2	3

16. Represent by a network the project given in the following table:

Task	Time required	Prior tasks
A (start)	0	—
B	1	A
C	2	A, B
D	4	B
E	3	B, C, D
F	2	C, E
G (finish)	0	D, F

17. For the project of Exercise 16, find the earliest start time for each task and the minimum completion time of the project.

18. For the project of Exercise 16, find the latest time that each task can be started.

19. For the project of Exercise 16, find the slack time for each task and the critical path through the network.

20. Using the simplex method, solve

$$x_1 + 2x_2 \leq 26, \quad x_1 + x_2 \leq 16, \quad 5x_1 + 3x_2 \leq 70.$$

Show all work.
$$\max x_0: x_0 = 4x_1 + 3x_2; \quad x_1, x_2 \geq 0.$$

21. Solve the following linear program:

$$y_1 + 2y_2 \geq 26,$$
$$y_1 + y_2 \geq 16,$$
$$5y_1 + 3y_2 \geq 70,$$
$$\min y_0: y_0 = 4y_1 + 3y_2; \quad y_1, y_2 \geq 0.$$

22. a) Write the linear program dual to that given in Exercise 20.

b) Read off the dual solution from the final tableau of Exercise 20.

c) Write the equations to be used in checking your solution.

d) Check your solution.

23. Pivot until the next pivot is *not* degenerate and indicate the new pivot:

x_1	x_2	x_3	y_1	y_2	y_3	1
1	5	−1	1	0	0	2
−3	1	2	0	1	0	0
−4	3	2	0	0	1	5
2	−1	1	0	0	0	0

24. Read both primal and dual solutions from the following tableaux indicating any solutions that are degenerate, nonunique, unbounded, or infeasible. Read off *all* variables.

a)

x_1	x_2	x_3	x_4	x_5	x_6	1
1	5	−1	1	0	0	2
−3	1	2	0	1	0	0
−4	3	2	0	0	1	5
2	1	1	0	0	0	10

b)

x_1	x_2	x_3	x_4	x_5	x_6	1
1	5	−1	1	0	0	2
2	1	−3	0	1	0	1
3	2	−4	0	0	1	5
2	1	−1	0	0	0	10

25. Solve the following transportation problem:

F_i	D_j 1	2	3	s_i
1	27	17	18	45
2	19	20	15	50
3	18	16	23	65
r_j	30	70	60	Min. cost

26. Solve the following assignment problem given the "goodness of fit":

i	j 1	2	3	4	5
1	9	7	3	1	4
2	8	8	7	3	4
3	7	9	6	4	5
4	7	8	7	5	6
5	8	6	7	3	5

27. Given the time plan at right:

a) Draw the activity network.

b) Find the earliest start time for each task.

c) Find the latest start time for each task.

d) Find the slack time for each task and the critical path through the network.

Task	Time required	Prior tasks
A (start)	0	—
B	3	A
C	5	A
D	4	B, C
E	6	A, B
F	7	B, E
G	2	C, E
H (finish)	0	F, G, H

SEQUENCES, SERIES, AND THE MATHEMATICS OF FINANCE

6.1 ARITHMETIC SEQUENCES*

Sequences

A *sequence* is an ordered set of numbers. Here is an example:

$$3, 5, 7, 9, 11, \ldots.$$

The dots mean that there are more and more numbers in the sequence. A sequence that does not end is called *infinite*. A sequence that does end is called *finite*.

Each number is called a *term* of the sequence. The first term is 3, the second term is 5, the third term is 7, and so on. We can describe the terms

---

* This chapter can be omitted without loss of continuity, although it is an effective introduction to calculus. A calculator with an $\boxed{x^y}$ will be quite helpful to the student.

as follows:

$$a_1 = 3,$$
$$a_2 = 5,$$
$$a_3 = 7,$$
$$a_4 = 9,$$

and so on, where the nth term is $a_n = 2n + 1$. That is, a sequence is a function whose domain is a set of consecutive natural numbers. Instead of using $a(n)$ for the nth term, we are using a_n. We also call a_n the *general term*.

Example 1   A sequence is given by

$$a_n = 2^n.$$

Find the first four terms and the 17th term.

Solution

$$a_1 = 2^1 = 2,$$
$$a_2 = 2^2 = 4,$$
$$a_3 = 2^3 = 8,$$
$$a_4 = 2^4 = 16,$$
$$\vdots$$
$$a_{17} = 2^{17} = 131{,}072.$$

Arithmetic Sequences

Consider the sequence

$$3, 5, 7, 9, 11, \ldots.$$

Note that the number 2 can be added to each term to obtain the next term. Sequences in which a certain number can be added to any term to get the next term are called *arithmetic sequences* (or *arithmetic progressions*). The number d which we add to one term to get the next is called the *common difference*. This is because we can subtract any term from the one that follows it and get d.

$$a_{k+1} - a_k = d \quad \text{for any } k \geqslant 1.$$

Examples   The following are arithmetic sequences. Identify the first term and the common difference.

Solution

Sequence	First term	Common difference
2. 3, 5, 7, 9, 11, . . .	3	2
3. 34, 27, 20, 13, 6, -1, -8, . . .	34	-7
4. $5200, $4687.50, $4175, . . .	$5200	$-$512.50

For an arithmetic sequence,

the 1st term is a_1,

the 2nd term is $a_2 = a_1 + d,$

the 3rd term is $a_3 = (a_1 + d) + d = a_1 + 2d,$

the 4th term is $a_4 = [(a_1 + d) + d] + d = a_1 + 3d,$

and so on. Generalizing, we obtain the following.

The nth term of an arithmetic sequence is given by

$$a_n = a_1 + (n - 1)d, \quad \text{for any } n \geqslant 1.$$

Example 5   Find the 15th term of the sequence 4, 7, 10, 13, ...

Solution   First note that

$$a_1 = 4, \quad d = 3, \quad \text{and } n = 15.$$

Then using the formula

$$a_n = a_1 + (n - 1)d,$$

we have

$$a_{15} = 4 + (15 - 1)3 = 4 + 14 \cdot 3 = 4 + 42 = 46.$$

We could check this by writing out 15 terms of the sequence.

Sum of the First n Terms of an Arithmetic Sequence

Suppose we add the first four terms of the sequence

$$3, 5, 7, 9, 11, ...$$

We get

$$3 + 5 + 7 + 9, \quad \text{or 24.}$$

The sum of the first n terms of a sequence is denoted S_n. Thus, for the preceding sequence, $S_4 = 24$. We want to find a formula for S_n when the sequence is arithmetic. We can denote an arithmetic sequence as

$$a_1, (a_1 + d), (a_1 + 2d), \ldots, (a_n - 2d), (a_n - d), a_n.$$

Then S_n is given by

$$S_n = a_1 + (a_1 + d) + (a_1 + 2d) + \cdots + (a_n - 2d) + (a_n - d) + a_n. \quad (1)$$

If we reverse the order of addition, we get

$$S_n = a_n + (a_n - d) + (a_n - 2d) + \cdots + (a_1 + 2d) + (a_1 + d) + a_1. \quad (2)$$

Suppose we add corresponding terms of each side of Eqs. (1) and (2). Then we get

$$2S_n = [a_1 + a_n] + [(a_1 + d) + (a_n - d)]$$
$$+ [(a_1 + 2d) + (a_n - 2d)] + \cdots$$
$$+ [(a_n - 2d) + (a_1 + 2d)]$$
$$+ [(a_n - d) + (a_1 + d)] + [a_n + a_1].$$

This simplifies to

$$2S_n = (a_1 + a_n) + (a_1 + a_n) + (a_1 + a_n) + \cdots + (a_1 + a_n).$$

Since there are n binomials $(a_1 + a_n)$ being added, it follows that $2S_n = n(a_1 + a_n)$, from which we get the following formula.

The sum of the first n terms of an arithmetic sequence is given by

$$S_n = \frac{n}{2}(a_1 + a_n).$$

Example 6   Find the sum of the first 100 natural numbers.

Solution   The sum is

$$1 + 2 + 3 + \cdots + 99 + 100.$$

This is the sum of the first 100 terms of the arithmetic sequence for which

$$a_1 = 1, \qquad a_n = 100, \qquad \text{and } n = 100.$$

Then, substituting in the formula

$$S_n = \frac{n}{2}(a_1 + a_n),$$

we get

$$S_{100} = \tfrac{100}{2}(1 + 100) = 50(101) = 5050.$$

The preceding formula is useful when we know a_1 and a_n, the first and last terms, but it often happens that a_n is not known. We thus need a formula in terms of a_1, n, and d.

Substituting $a_1 + (n - 1)d$ for a_n in the formula $S_n = \dfrac{n}{2}(a_1 + a_n)$, we get

$$S_n = \frac{n}{2}(a_1 + [a_1 + (n - 1)d]),$$

from which we get the following formula.

The sum of the first *n* terms of an arithmetic sequence is given by

$$S_n = \frac{n}{2}[2a_1 + (n - 1)d].$$

Example 7   Find the sum of the first 15 terms of the arithmetic sequence 4, 7, 10, 13, ...

Solution   Note that

$$a_1 = 4, \qquad d = 3, \qquad \text{and } n = 15.$$

Then, substituting in the formula

$$S_n = \frac{n}{2}[2a_1 + (n - 1)d],$$

we get

$$S_{15} = \tfrac{15}{2}[2 \cdot 4 + (15 - 1)3] = \tfrac{15}{2}[8 + 14 \cdot 3] = \tfrac{15}{2}[8 + 42]$$
$$= \tfrac{15}{2}[50] = 375.$$

Example 8   A family saves money in an arithmetic sequence. They save \$600 the first year, \$700 the second, and so on, for 20 years. How much do they save in all (disregarding interest)?

Solution   The amount saved is the sum

$$\$600 + \$700 + \$800 + \cdots.$$

Here the dots mean that the pattern continues, even though this is not an infinite sequence. In short, we need not bother to determine the last term.

We can find the sum by noting that

$$a_1 = \$600, \quad d = \$100, \quad \text{and } n = 20.$$

Then, substituting in the formula

$$S_n = \frac{n}{2}[2a_1 + (n - 1)d],$$

we get

$$S_{20} = \tfrac{20}{2}[2 \cdot \$600 + (20 - 1)\$100] = 10[\$1200 + 19 \cdot \$100]$$
$$= 10[\$1200 + \$1900] = 10[\$3100] = \$31,000.$$

EXERCISE SET 6.1

In each of the following sequences, the nth term is given. Find the first four terms, and the 15th term.

1. $a_n = \dfrac{n}{n + 1}$ **2.** $a_n = n + \dfrac{1}{n}$ **3.** $a_n = \dfrac{n^2 - 1}{n^3 + 1}$ **4.** $a_n = \left(-\tfrac{1}{2}\right)^n$

The following are arithmetic sequences. Identify the first term and the common difference.

5. 2, 7, 12, 17, . . .

6. 7, 3, −1, −5, . . .

7. $1.06, $1.12, $1.18, $1.24, . . .

8. $214, $211, $208, $205, . . .

9. 5, $4\frac{1}{3}$, $3\frac{2}{3}$, 3, $2\frac{1}{3}$, . . .

10. $\frac{3}{2}$, $\frac{9}{4}$, 3, $\frac{15}{4}$, . . .

11. Find the 12th term of the arithmetic sequence

$$3, 7, 11, \ldots$$

12. Find the 11th term of the arithmetic sequence

$$\$0.08, \$0.13, \$0.18, \ldots$$

13. Find the 13th term of the arithmetic sequence

$$\$1200, \$964.32, \$728.64, \ldots$$

14. Find the 10th term of the arithmetic sequence

$$\$200, \$198.32, \$196.64, \ldots$$

15. Find the sum of the first 300 natural numbers.

16. Find the sum of the first 400 natural numbers.

17. Find the sum of the first 20 terms of the sequence

$$6, 9, 12, 15, \ldots$$

18. Find the sum of the first 14 terms of the sequence

$$12, 8, 4, \ldots$$

19. Find a formula for the sum of the first n natural numbers:

$$1 + 2 + 3 + \cdots + n$$

20. Find a formula for the sum of the first n consecutive odd natural numbers starting with 1:

$$1 + 3 + 5 + \cdots + (2n - 1)$$

21. If a student saves 1¢ on October 1, 2¢ on October 2, 3¢ on October 3, etc., how much would be saved in October? (October has 31 days.)

22. If a student saves $40 on September 1, $60 on September 2, $80 on September 3, how much would be saved in September? (September has 30 days.)

23. Find the sum of the first 8 terms of the arithmetic sequence

$$\$512.50, \$1025.00, \$1537.50, \ldots$$

24. Find the sum of the first 10 terms of the arithmetic sequence

$$\$78.90, \$157.80, \$236.70, \ldots$$

6.2   GEOMETRIC SEQUENCES

Geometric Sequences

Consider the sequence

$$2, 6, 18, 54, 162, \ldots.$$

If we multiply each term by 3 we get the next term. Sequences in which each term can be multiplied by a certain number to get the next term are called *geometric*. We usually denote this number r. We refer to it as the *common ratio* because we can get r by dividing any term by the preceding term.

$$\frac{a_{k+1}}{a_k} = r, \quad \text{or} \quad a_{k+1} = ra_k, \quad \text{for any } k \geqslant 1.$$

Examples   The following are geometric sequences. Identify the common ratio.

Solution

Sequence	Common ratio
1. 3, 6, 12, 24, 48, 96, . . .	2
2. 3, −6, 12, −24, 48, −96, . . .	−2
3. $5200, $3900, $2925, $2193.75, . . .	0.75
4. $1000, $1080, $1166.40, . . .	1.08

If we let a_1 be the first term and r be the common ratio, then a_1r is the second term, a_1r^2 is the third term, and so on. Generalizing, we obtain the following.

The nth term of a geometric sequence is given by

$$a_n = a_1r^{n-1}, \quad \text{for any } n \geqslant 1.$$

Note that the exponent is one less than the number of the term.

Example 5   Find the 7th term of the geometric sequence 4, 20, 100, ...

Solution   First note that

$$a_1 = 4, \quad n = 7, \quad \text{and } r = \tfrac{20}{4}, \text{ or } 5.$$

Then, using the formula

$$a_n = a_1 r^{n-1},$$

we have

$$a_7 = 4 \cdot 5^{7-1} = 4 \cdot 5^6 = 4 \cdot 15{,}625 = 62{,}500.$$

Example 6 Find the 10th term of the geometric sequence 64, 32, 16, 8, ...

Solution First note that

$$a_1 = 64, \qquad n = 10, \qquad \text{and } r = \tfrac{32}{64}, \text{ or } \tfrac{1}{2}.$$

Then, using the formula

$$a_n = a_1 r^{n-1},$$

we have

$$a_{10} = 64 \cdot \left(\tfrac{1}{2}\right)^{10-1} = 64 \cdot \left(\tfrac{1}{2}\right)^9 = 2^6 \cdot \frac{1}{2^9} = \frac{1}{2^3} = \tfrac{1}{8}.$$

Sum of the First *n* Terms of a Geometric Sequence

We want to find a formula for the sum S_n of the first n terms of a geometric sequence

$$a_1, \; a_1 r, \; a_1 r^2, \; a_1 r^3, \; \ldots, \; a_1 r^{n-1}, \; \ldots.$$

The sum S_n is given by

$$S_n = a_1 + a_1 r + a_1 r^2 + \cdots + a_1 r^{n-2} + a_1 r^{n-1}.$$

We want a formula that allows us to find this sum without a lot of adding. If we multiply both sides of the preceding equation by r, we have

$$rS_n = a_1 r + a_1 r^2 + a_1 r^3 + \cdots + a_1 r^{n-1} + a_1 r^n.$$

When we multiply S_n by -1, we get

$$-S_n = -a_1 - a_1 r - a_1 r^2 - \cdots - a_1 r^{n-2} - a_1 r^{n-1}.$$

Then when we add rS_n and $-S_n$, we get

$$rS_n - S_n = a_1 r^n - a_1 \qquad \text{or} \qquad (r-1)S_n = a_1(r^n - 1),$$

from which we get the following formula.

The sum of the first *n* terms of a geometric sequence is given by

$$S_n = \frac{a_1(r^n - 1)}{r - 1}$$

Example 7   Find the sum of the first 7 terms of the geometric sequence 3, 15, 75, 375, ...

Solution   First note that

$$a_1 = 3, \quad n = 7, \quad \text{and } r = \tfrac{15}{3}, \text{ or } 5.$$

Then, using the formula

$$S_n = \frac{a_1(r^n - 1)}{r - 1},$$

we have

$$S_7 = \frac{3(5^7 - 1)}{5 - 1} = \frac{3(78,125 - 1)}{4} = \frac{3(78,124)}{4} = 58,593.$$

Example 8   *Doubling Your Salary.* Suppose someone offered you a job during the month of September (30 days) under the following conditions. You will be paid $0.01 for the first day, $0.02 for the second, $0.04 for the third, and so on, doubling your previous day's salary. How much would you earn? (Would you take the job? Make a decision before reading further.)

Solution   The amount earned is the sum

$$\$0.01 + \$0.01(2) + \$0.01(2^2) + \$0.01(2^3) + \cdots + \$0.01(2^{29}),$$

where

$$a_1 = \$0.01, \quad n = 30, \quad \text{and } r = 2.$$

Then, using the formula

$$S_n = \frac{a_1(r^n - 1)}{r - 1},$$

we have

$$S_{30} = \frac{\$0.01(2^{30} - 1)}{2 - 1}$$

$$\approx \$0.01(1,074,000,000 - 1) \quad \text{(Use a calculator to approximate } 2^{30}.)$$

$$\approx \$0.01(1,074,000,000)$$

$$\approx \$10,740,000.$$

Now would you take the job?

Note   One could find 2^{30} in various ways. It can be found directly on a calculator with an $\boxed{x^y}$ key or by expressing the power as, say, $2^{10} \cdot 2^{10} \cdot$

2^{10}. Then one could find 2^{10} and multiply that number by itself three times. Another way would be $2^5 \cdot 2^5 \cdot 2^5 \cdot 2^5 \cdot 2^5 \cdot 2^5$.

Infinite Geometric Series

Suppose we consider the sum of the terms of an infinite geometric sequence, such as 2, 4, 8, 16, 32, ... We get what is called an *infinite geometric series*:

$$2 + 4 + 8 + 16 + 32 + \cdots$$

As n gets larger and larger, the sum of the first n terms, S_n, gets larger and larger without bound. There are infinite series which get closer and closer to some specific number. Here is an example.

$$\frac{1}{2} + \frac{1}{4} + \frac{1}{8} + \frac{1}{16} + \cdots + \frac{1}{2^n} + \cdots$$

Let's consider S_n for some values of n.

$$S_1 = \tfrac{1}{2} \qquad\qquad\qquad\qquad = \tfrac{1}{2} = 0.5$$

$$S_2 = \tfrac{1}{2} + \tfrac{1}{4} \qquad\qquad\qquad = \tfrac{3}{4} = 0.75$$

$$S_3 = \tfrac{1}{2} + \tfrac{1}{4} + \tfrac{1}{8} \qquad\qquad = \tfrac{7}{8} = 0.875$$

$$S_4 = \tfrac{1}{2} + \tfrac{1}{4} + \tfrac{1}{8} + \tfrac{1}{16} \qquad = \tfrac{15}{16} = 0.9375$$

$$S_5 = \tfrac{1}{2} + \tfrac{1}{4} + \tfrac{1}{8} + \tfrac{1}{16} + \tfrac{1}{32} = \tfrac{31}{32} = 0.96875$$

Perhaps you have noticed that we can describe S_n as follows:

$$S_n = \frac{2^n - 1}{2^n}.$$

Note that the numerator is less than the denominator for all values of n, but as n gets larger and larger the values of S_n get closer and closer to 1. We say that 1 is the *limit* of S_n and that 1 is the *sum* of the *infinite geometric series*. The sum of an infinite series, if it exists, is denoted S_∞. It can be shown, but we will not do it here, that the sum of the terms of a geometric series exists if and only if $|r| < 1$ (that is, the absolute value of the common ratio is less than 1).

We want to find a formula for the sum of an infinite geometric series. We first consider the sum of the first n terms:

$$S_n = \frac{a_1(r^n - 1)}{r - 1} = \frac{a_1 - a_1 r^n}{1 - r}.$$

For $|r| < 1$, it follows that values of r^n get closer and closer to 0 as n gets large. (Pick a number between -1 and 1 and check this by finding larger and larger powers on your calculator). As r^n gets closer and closer to 0, so does $a_1 r^n$, so S_n gets closer and closer to $a_1/(1 - r)$.

When $|r| < 1$, the sum of an infinite geometric series is given by

$$S_\infty = \frac{a_1}{1 - r}.$$

Example 9   Determine if the following infinite geometric series has a sum. If so, find it.

$$1 + 3 + 9 + 27 + \cdots$$

Solution $|r| = |3| = 3$, and since $|r| \not< 1$ the series does *not* have a sum.

Example 10   Determine if the following infinite geometric series has a sum. If so, find it.

$$1 - \tfrac{1}{2} + \tfrac{1}{4} - \tfrac{1}{8} + \tfrac{1}{16} - \cdots$$

Solution   a) $|r| = |-\tfrac{1}{2}| = \tfrac{1}{2}$, and since $|r| < 1$ the series does have a sum.
b) The sum is given by

$$S_\infty = \frac{1}{1 - (-\tfrac{1}{2})} = \frac{2}{3}.$$

Example 11   *Economic Multiplier.* The United States banking laws require most banks to maintain a reserve equivalent to a certain proportion of their outstanding deposits. This enables such banks, when they wish and when they can find borrowers, to loan out a certain proportion of the funds that have been deposited in them. Let us assume that this proportion is 0.90 (or 90%). Now suppose a corporation deposits $1000 in a bank which, subsequently, is able to loan the maximum legally possible amount, and this loan is redeposited elsewhere, and so on. What is the total effect of the $1000 on the economy?

Solution   The total effect can be modeled as the sum of the infinite geometric series

$$\$1000 + \$1000(0.90) + \$1000(0.90)^2 + \$1000(0.90)^3 + \cdots,$$

which is given by

$$S_\infty = \frac{\$1000}{1 - 0.90} = \$10,000.$$

The sum, $10,000, is the result of what is referred to in economics as the *multiplier effect.*

EXERCISE SET 6.2

The following are geometric sequences. Identify the common ratio.

1. 7, 14, 28, 56, . . .

2. 5, −15, 45, −135, . . .

3. 12, −4, $\frac{4}{3}$, −$\frac{4}{9}$, . . .

4. 4, 2, 1, $\frac{1}{2}$, $\frac{1}{4}$, . . .

5. $5600, $5320, $5054, $4801.30, . . .

6. $780, $858, $943.80, $1038.18, . . .

7. Find the 8th term of the geometric sequence

$$1, 3, 9, \ldots$$

8. Find the 10th term of the geometric sequence

$$7, 35, 175, 875, \ldots$$

9. Find the 9th term of the geometric sequence

$$25, 5, 1, \tfrac{1}{5}, \tfrac{1}{25}, \ldots$$

10. Find the 10th term of the geometric sequence

$$64, 16, 4, 1, \tfrac{1}{4}, \tfrac{1}{16}, \ldots$$

11. Find the 12th term of the geometric sequence

$$\$1000, \$1080, \$1166.40, \ldots$$

12. Find the 9th term of the geometric sequence

$$\$1000, \$1070, \$1144.90, \ldots$$

Round to the nearest cent.

Round to the nearest cent.

13. Find the sum of the first 7 terms of the geometric sequence

$$8, 16, 32, \ldots$$

14. Find the sum of the first 8 terms of the geometric sequence

$$24, -48, 96, \ldots$$

15. Find the sum of the first 5 terms of the geometric sequence

$$\$1000, \$1000(1.08), \$1000(1.08)^2, \ldots$$

16. Find the sum of the first 6 terms of the geometric sequence

$$\$200, \$200(1.06), \$200(1.06)^2, \ldots$$

Round to the nearest cent.

Round to the nearest cent.

17. Suppose someone offered you a job during the month of February (28 days) under the following conditions. You will be paid $0.01 the first day, $0.02 the second, $0.04 the third, and so on, doubling your previous day's salary. How much would you earn?

18. In Exercise 17, how much would you earn during a February in a leap year (29 days)?

Determine if each of the following infinite geometric series has a sum. If so, find it.

19. 4 + 20 + 100 + 500 + $\cdots$

20. −6 + 18 − 54 + 162 − $\cdots$

21. 10 + 2 + $\frac{2}{5}$ + $\frac{2}{25}$ + $\frac{2}{125}$ + $\cdots$

22. 14 + 2 + $\frac{2}{7}$ + $\frac{2}{49}$ + $\frac{2}{343}$ + $\cdots$

23. 162 + 108 + 72 + 48 + $\cdots$

24. 128 + 96 + 72 + 54 + $\cdots$

25. $1000(1.08)^{-1}$ + $1000(1.08)^{-2}$ + $1000(1.08)^{-3}$ + $\cdots$

26. $500(1.02)^{-1}$ + $500(1.02)^{-2}$ + $500(1.02)^{-3}$ + $\cdots$

27. The government makes an $8,000,000,000 expenditure for a new type of aircraft. If 75% of this gets spent again, and 75% of that gets spent, and so on, what is the total effect on the economy?

28. Repeat Exercise 27 for $9,400,000,000 and 99%.

29. *Advertising Effect.* A company is marketing a new product in a city of 5,000,000 people. They plan an advertising campaign that they think will induce 40% of the people to buy the product. They then estimate that if those people like the product, they will induce 40% (of the 40% of 5,000,000) more to buy the product, and those will induce 40% more to buy the product, and so on. In all, how many people will buy the product as a result of the advertising campaign? What percentage is this of the population?

31. In a recent year the finals of the NCAA basketball tournament were held in Indianapolis. It was estimated in a local newspaper "that 20,000 people would visit the city, with each spending an average of $350, so that total economic impact on the city would be $7 million." Refute this statement and show that the effect was actually much more than $7 million.

30. Repeat Exercise 29 for 6,000,000 people and 45%.

6.3 DEPRECIATION

A company buys an office machine for $5200 on January 1 of a given year. It is expected to last for 8 years at which time its *trade-in*, or *salvage value*, will be $1100. Over its lifetime its value declines, or *depreciates*, from $5200 to $1100, or $4100. The decline in value can occur in many ways, as shown below:

	0 yrs	1	2	3	4	5	6	7	8 yrs
(1)	$5200	$4687.50	$4175.00	$3662.50	$3150.00	$2637.50	$2125.00	$1612.50	$1100
(2)	$5200	$3900.00	$2925.00	$2193.75	$1645.31	$1233.98	$1100.00	$1100.00	$1100
(3)	$5200	$4288.89	$3491.67	$2808.34	$2238.90	$1783.34	$1441.67	$1213.89	$1100

Method (1) is called the *straight-line method*, method (2) the *double-declining balance method*, and method (3) the *sum of the year's digits method*. We shall consider each of these.

Straight-Line Depreciation

Suppose, for the machine above, the company figures the decline in value to be the *same* each year, that is ⅛, or 12.5%, of $4100, which is $512.50.

After one year the *book value*, or simply *value*, is

$$\$5200 - \$512.50,$$

or

$$\$4687.50.$$

After two years it is

$$\$4687.50 - \$512.50,$$

or

$$\$4175.00.$$

After three years it is

$$\$4175.00 - \$512.50,$$

or

$$\$3662.50,$$

and so on.

For straight-line depreciation,

1. **The total depreciation = Cost − Salvage value.**

2. **The annual depreciation =** $\dfrac{\text{Cost} - \text{Salvage value}}{\text{Expected life}}$.

3. **The rate of depreciation =** $\dfrac{\text{Annual depreciation}}{\text{Total depreciation}}$.

A depreciation schedule gives a complete listing of the book values and total depreciation throughout the life of an item.

Example 1 Prepare a depreciation schedule for the following situation.
Item: Office Machine

$$\text{Cost} = \$5200,$$
$$\text{Expected life} = 8 \text{ years},$$
$$\text{Salvage value} = \$1100.$$

Solution

Year	Rate of depreciation	Annual depreciation	Book value	Total depreciation
0			$5200	
1	$\frac{1}{8}$ or 12.5%	$512.50	4687.50	$ 512.50
2	12.5%	512.50	4175.00	1025.00
3	12.5%	512.50	3662.50	1537.50
4	12.5%	512.50	3150.00	2050.00
5	12.5%	512.50	2637.50	2562.50
6	12.5%	512.50	2125.00	3075.00
7	12.5%	512.50	1612.50	3587.50
8	12.5%	512.50	1100.00	4100.00

The rate of depreciation is the same each year.

The annual depreciation is the same each year.

We find the book values by starting with the initial cost, $5200, and successively subtracting $512.50.

We find the total depreciations by starting with $512.50 after the first year and successively adding $512.50.

Why do we call this *straight-line depreciation*? If we make a graph of book values versus time (Fig. 6.1), the values lie on a straight line.

The book values V_n of an item n years after purchase form an arithmetic sequence for which

$$V_n = C - n\left(\frac{C - S}{N}\right),$$

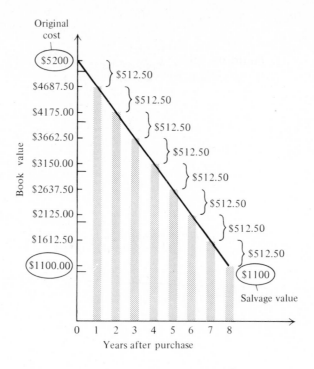

Figure 6.1

where

$$C = \text{original cost of an item,}$$
$$N = \text{years of expected life,}$$
$$S = \text{salvage value.}$$

For the machine in Example 1,

$$V_n = \$5200 - n\left(\frac{\$5200 - \$1100}{8}\right) = \$5200 - (\$512.50)n,$$

and the common difference is $-\$512.50$.

Declining Balance Depreciation

A company buys a machine for $5200. It is expected to last for 8 years at which time its salvage value will be $1100. The straight-line rate of depreciation would be $\frac{1}{8}$, or 12.5%. Depreciation can be deducted as a business expense when a business computes its taxes. When a business is starting out, it has many expenses and less income and therefore needs all the tax advantages it can get. For this, and other reasons, the Internal Revenue Service allows certain assets to be depreciated at a rate larger than the straight-line rate but *no more* than twice the straight-line rate. (Such a rate could be, for example, $1\frac{1}{4}$, $1\frac{1}{2}$, or 2 times the straight-line rate.) Suppose for the above, the rate is $2 \cdot \frac{1}{8}$, or 25%. This is called the *double-declining balance method.* Then the book value after one year is

$5200 - (25\% \times \$5200)$ (We subtract 25% of the initial book value.)

$= \$5200 - (0.25 \times \$5200)$

$= \$5200 - \$1300$

$= \$3900.$

After 2 years it is

$3900 - (0.25 \times \$3900)$ (We subtract 25% of preceding book value.)

$= \$3900 - \$975$

$= \$2925.$

After 3 years it is

$$\$2925 - (0.25 \times \$2925)$$

$$= \$2925 - \$731.25$$

$$= \$2193.75.$$

After 4 years it is

$$\$2193.75 - (0.25 \times \$2193.75)$$

$$= \$2193.75 - \$548.44 \quad \text{(Rounded to the nearest cent)}$$

$$= \$1645.31.$$

and so on.

Example 2   Prepare a depreciation schedule for the following situation. Use the double-declining balance method.

Item: Office machine

$$\text{Cost} \qquad = \$5200,$$

$$\text{Expected life} = 8 \text{ years,}$$

$$\text{Salvage value} = \$1100.$$

Solution

Year	Rate of depreciation	Annual depreciation	Book value	Total depreciation
0			$5200	
1	$\frac{2}{8}$ or 25%	$1300.00	3900.00	$1300
2	25%	975.00	2925.00	2275
3	25%	731.25	2193.75	3006.25
4	25%	548.44	1645.31	3554.69
5	25%	411.33	1233.98	3966.02
6		133.98	1100.00	4100.00
7		0	1100.00	4100.00
8		0	1100.00	4100.00

The rate of depreciation is the same each year, twice the straight-line rate.

We find the annual depreciations when we multiply each successive book value by 0.25. For example, 0.25 × $5200 = $1300, and 0.25 × $3900 = $975.

We find the book values by starting with the initial cost, $5200, and successively subtracting 0.25 times the book value. For example, $5200 − (0.25 × $5200) = $3900. Then, $3900 − (0.25 × $3900) = $2925, and so on.

The book values V_n of an item n years after purchase form a geometric sequence

$$V_n = C\left(1 - \frac{m}{N}\right)^n, \qquad 0 < m \leq 2,$$

---

* Note that

$$\$1233.98 - (0.25 \times \$1233.98) = \$1233.98 - \$308.50 = \$925.48,$$

but the book value cannot drop below the salvage value. Thus, after $1233.98, the next book value becomes $1100.00, and the annual depreciation for that year is $1233.98 − $1100.00, or $133.98.

where
$$C = \text{original cost of an item.}$$
This holds until V_n drops below the salvage value S.

Sum of the Year's Digits Depreciation

Another method of depreciation which allows larger amounts of depreciation in early years and smaller amounts in later years is the *sum of the year's digits method.* Each year a different rate of depreciation is used, which is a fraction.

Example 3 For the situation below,

    a) Find the depreciation fractions,

    b) Find the depreciation and book values after 1 year; after 2 years.

Item: Office Machine

$$\text{Cost} = \$5200,$$
$$\text{Expected life} = 8 \text{ years,}$$
$$\text{Salvage value} = \$1100.$$

Solution a) To find the depreciation we first find the sum of the year's digits:

$$8 + 7 + 6 + 5 + 4 + 3 + 2 + 1 = 36.^*$$

_____

* The sum

$$1 + 2 + 3 + \cdots + n$$

is the sum of the terms of an arithmetic sequence where $a_1 = 1$, and $a_n = n$. The sum is given by

$$S_n = \frac{n}{2}(a_1 + a_n) = \frac{n}{2}(1 + n)$$

$$= \frac{n(n + 1)}{2}$$

Thus,

$$8 + 7 + 6 + 5 + 4 + 3 + 2 + 1$$
$$= 1 + 2 + 3 + 4 + 5 + 6 + 7 + 8$$
$$= \frac{8(8 + 1)}{2} = \frac{8(9)}{2} = \frac{72}{2} = 36.$$

The number 36 will be the denominator of each fraction. We then find the depreciation fractions (rates) by dividing each number in the sum by 36:

$$\frac{8}{36}, \frac{7}{36}, \frac{6}{36}, \frac{5}{36}, \frac{4}{36}, \frac{3}{36}, \frac{2}{36}, \frac{1}{36}.$$

b) The total depreciation is $5200 − $1100, or $4100. First-year depreciation is

$$\frac{8}{36} \times \$4100 = \frac{8 \times \$4100}{36}$$

$$= \frac{\$32,800}{36}$$

$$= \$911.11. \quad \text{(Rounded to the nearest cent)}$$

The book value after one year is

$$\$5200 - \$911.11,$$

or

$$\$4288.89.$$

Second-year depreciation is

$$\frac{7}{36} \times \$4100 = \frac{7 \times \$4100}{36}$$

$$= \frac{\$28,700}{36}$$

$$= \$797.22.$$

The book value after 2 years is

$$\$4288.89 - \$797.22,$$

or

$$\$3491.67.$$

Example 4   Prepare a depreciation schedule for the following situation. Use the sum of the year's digits method.

$$\text{Cost} \quad = \$5200,$$

$$\text{Expected life} = 8 \text{ years},$$

$$\text{Salvage value} = \$1100.$$

Solution

Year	Rate of depreciation	Annual depreciation	Book value	Total depreciation
0			$5200	
1	$\frac{8}{36}$ or 22.2%	$911.11	4288.89	$ 911.11
2	$\frac{7}{36}$ or 19.4%	797.22	3491.67	1708.33
3	$\frac{6}{36}$ or 16.7%	683.33	2808.34	2391.66
4	$\frac{5}{36}$ or 13.9%	569.44	2238.90	2961.10
5	$\frac{4}{36}$ or 11.1%	455.56	1783.34	3416.66
6	$\frac{3}{36}$ or 8.3%	341.67	1441.67	3758.33
7	$\frac{2}{36}$ or 5.6%	227.78	1213.89	3986.11
8	$\frac{1}{36}$ or 2.8%	113.89	1100.00	4100.00

The rate of depreciation gets lower each year.

We find the annual depreciations first. To do this we multiply the total depreciation by each fraction. For example, $\frac{8}{36} \times \$4100 = \$911.11$, $\frac{7}{36} \times \$4100 = \$797.22$, and so on.

We find the book values by subtracting each annual depreciation in succession. For example, $5200 − $911.11 = $4288.89, $4288.89 − $797.22 = $3491.67, and so on.

EXERCISE SET 6.3

For exercises 1 through 4, use the straight-line method to

a) Prepare a depreciation schedule,
b) Find a formula for the book values V_n,
c) Find the common difference.

1. *Item:* Automobile

      Cost   = $8000,
      Expected life = 4 years,
      Salvage value = $2000,

2. *Item:* Automobile

      Cost   = $12,000
      Expected life = 3 years
      Salvage value = $4800

3. *Item:* Postage machine

      Cost   = $450
      Expected life = 8 years
      Salvage value = $0

4. *Item:* Typewriter

      Cost   = $2500
      Expected life = 6 years
      Salvage value = $0

In Exercises 5 through 8, use the double-declining balance method to

a) Prepare a depreciation schedule,

b) Find a formula for the book values V_n.

5. (See Exercise 1.)   **6.** (See Exercise 2.)   **7.** (See Exercise 3.)   **8.** (See Exercise 4.)

In Exercises 9 through 12, use the sum of the year's digits method to

a) Find the depreciation fractions,

b) Prepare a depreciation schedule.

9. (See Exercise 1.)   **10.** (See Exercise 2.)   **11.** (See Exercise 3.)   **12.** (See Exercise 4.)

6.4 SIMPLE AND COMPOUND INTEREST

Simple Interest

You put $100 in a savings account for one year. This is called *principal*. The *interest rate* is 8%. This means you get back 8% of the principal:

$$8\% \text{ of } \$100,$$

or

$$8\% \times \$100,$$

or

$$\$8.00,$$

in addition to the principal. The $8.00 is called *interest*. The *amount* you get back is

$$(\text{Principal}) + (\text{Interest}), \quad \text{or } \$100 + \$8, \quad \text{or } \$108.$$

To find interest for a fraction t of a year (or for any time t) we compute the interest for one year and multiply by t. Thus, $100 principal invested at an interest rate of 8% for $\frac{1}{4}$ of a year, yields interest of

$$(8\% \times \$100) \times \tfrac{1}{4}, \quad \text{or } \$2.00.$$

We have the following formulas.

Simple Interest. **Principal P invested at simple interest rate i for time t, in years, yields interest I given by**

$$I = P \cdot i \cdot t.$$

Amount. **The amount A to which principal P will grow at simple interest rate i, for t years, is given by**

$$A = P + Pit = P(1 + it).$$

Note that $I = Pit$ usually is written as $I = Prt$, but we are reserving the letter r for later use.

Example 1 A loan charges 18% simple interest. How much is due on $1000 left unpaid for one month?

Solution $P = \$1000$, $i = 18\%$, or 0.18, and $t = \frac{1}{12}$ yr. Then the amount due is

$$A = P(1 + it) = \$1000(1 + 0.18 \times \tfrac{1}{12}) = \$1000(1 + 0.015)$$
$$= \$1000(1.015) = \$1015.$$

Compound Interest

Suppose you invested $1000 at an interest rate of 8%, compounded annually. The amount A_1 in the account at the end of one year is given by

$$A_1 = \$1000(1 + 0.08) = \$1000(1.08) = \$1080.$$

Going into the second year you have a new principal of $1080, so by the end of the second year you would have the amount A_2, given by

$$A_2 = \$1080(1 + 0.08) = \$1080(1.08) = \$1166.40.$$

Going into the third year you have a new principal of $1166.40, so by the end of the third year you would have the amount A_3, given by

$$A_3 = \$1166.40(1 + 0.08) = \$1166.40(1.08) \approx \$1259.71.$$

Note the following:

$$A_1 = \$1000(1.08)^1,$$
$$A_2 = \$1000(1.08)^2,$$
$$A_3 = \$1000(1.08)^3.$$

The amounts A_n form a geometric sequence with common ratio 1.08. In general, suppose you invest a principal of P dollars at interest rate i, compounded annually. The amount A_1 in the account at the end of one year is given by

$$A_1 = P(1 + i) = Pr,$$

where, for convenience, $r = 1 + i$.

Going into the second year you would have a new principal of Pr dollars, so by the end of the second year you would have the amount A_2, given by

$$A_2 = A_1 \cdot r = (Pr)r = Pr^2.$$

Going into the third year you have a new principal of Pr^2, so by the end of the third year you would have the amount A_3, given by

$$A_3 = A_2 \cdot r = (Pr^2)r = Pr^3.$$

The amounts A_n form a geometric sequence with common ratio r, which is $1 + i$.

> **Interest Compounded Annually.** If principal P is invested at interest rate i, compounded annually, in t years it will grow to the amount A, given by
>
> $$A = P(1 + i)^t.$$

Example 2 Suppose $1000 is invested at 5% compounded annually. How much is in the account at the end of 3 years?

Solution We substitute $1000 for P, 0.05 for i, and 3 for t in the equation $A = P(1 + i)^t$, and get

$$A = \$1000(1 + 0.05)^3 = \$1000(1.05)^3$$

$$= \$1000(1.157625) = \$1157.625 \approx \$1157.63.$$

If interest is compounded quarterly, we can find a formula like the one above as follows:

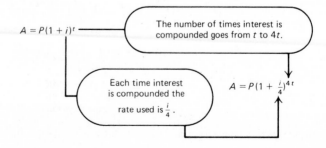

Figure 6.2

In general,

Interest Compounded n Times Per Year. If principal P is invested at interest rate i, compounded n times per year, in t years it will grow to an amount A, given by

$$A = P\left(1 + \frac{i}{n}\right)^{nt}.$$

The number nt is the total number of payment periods.

Example 3   Suppose $1000 is invested at 8%. How much is in the account at the end of 3 years if interest is

a) simple?

b) compounded annually?

c) compounded semiannually?

d) compounded quarterly?

e) compounded daily?

f) hourly?

Solution   a) $A = P(1 + it) = \$1000(1 + 0.08 \times 3) = \$1000(1 + 0.24)$

$= \$1000(1.24) = \$1240.00.$

b) $A = P(1 + i)^t = \$1000(1 + 0.08)^3 = \$1000(1.08)^3$

$= \$1000(1.259712) \approx \$1259.71.$

c) $A = P\left(1 + \dfrac{i}{n}\right)^{nt} = \$1000\left(1 + \dfrac{0.08}{2}\right)^{2 \times 3} = \$1000(1 + 0.04)^6$

$= \$1000(1.04)^6 = \$1000(1.265319) \approx \$1265.32.$

d) $A = P\left(1 + \dfrac{i}{n}\right)^{nt} = \$1000\left(1 + \dfrac{0.08}{4}\right)^{4 \times 3} = \$1000(1 + 0.02)^{12}$

$= \$1000(1.02)^{12} = \$1000(1.268242) \approx \$1268.24.$

e) $A = P\left(1 + \dfrac{i}{n}\right)^{nt} = \$1000\left(1 + \dfrac{0.08}{365}\right)^{365 \times 3}$

$= \$1000(1 + 0.000219)^{1095} = \$1000(1.000219)^{1095}$

$= \$1000(1.270967) \approx \$1270.97.$

f) $A = P\left(1 + \dfrac{i}{n}\right)^{nt} = \$1000\left(1 + \dfrac{0.08}{8760}\right)^{8760 \times 3}$

$\qquad = \$1000(1 + 0.00000913)^{26,280}$

$\qquad = \$1000(1.00000913)^{26,280}$

$\qquad = \$1000(1.271168)$

$\qquad \approx \$1271.17.$

CALCULATOR NOTE: One can find these powers on a calculator with an $\boxed{x^y}$ key, by a compound interest table, or by the method described earlier where the larger power is broken down to a product of smaller powers. The number of places on the calculator may affect the accuracy of the answer. Thus, you may occasionally find your answers do not agree with those in the answer key that have been found on a calculator with a ten-digit readout. In general, if you are using a calculator, do all your computations, and round only at the end.

Compare the amounts found in Example 3:

$\qquad$ $1240, $1259.71, $1265.32, $1268.24, $1270.97, $1271.17.

Note that as the number of periods of compounding increase within a fixed time, the greater the amount becomes, but the increase becomes less and less. If we keep using more compounding periods, the amount becomes closer and closer to an amount found by *continuous compounding*, $1271.25. We will study continuous compounding in a later chapter.

Present Value

A representative of a financial institution is often asked to solve a problem like the following.

Example 4 A parent, following the birth of a child, wants to make an initial investment P that will grow to $10,000 by the child's 20th birthday. Interest is compounded semiannually at 8%. What should the initial investment be?

Solution Using the formula

$$A = P\left(1 + \frac{i}{n}\right)^{nt},$$

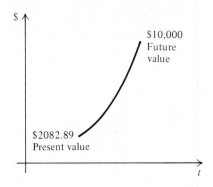

Figure 6.3

we find P such that

$$\$10,000 = P\left(1 + \frac{0.08}{2}\right)^{2 \times 20}$$

or

$$\$10,000 = P(1.04)^{40}.$$

Then

$$\$10,000 \approx P(4.801021)$$

and

$$P \approx \frac{\$10,000}{4.801021} \approx \$2082.89.$$

Thus a principal of $2082.89 would have to be invested at 8%, compounded semiannually, to grow to $10,000 in 20 years. The amount $2082.89 is called the *present value* of $10,000 for 20 years at 8% compounded semiannually. We can also say that the *future value* of $2082.89 is $10,000. By solving $A = P(1 + i)^t$ and $A = P\left(1 + \frac{i}{n}\right)^{nt}$ for P we get general formulas for present value.

> **Present Value.** The present value P of an amount A at interest rate i, compounded annually, for t years is given by
>
> $$P = A(1 + i)^{-t}.$$
>
> For interest compounded n times per year, the present value P is given by
>
> $$P = A\left(1 + \frac{i}{n}\right)^{-nt}.$$

EXERCISE SET 6.4

Suppose $2000 is invested at the simple interest rate and time given in Exercises 1 through 4. What is the amount in the account?

1. 9%, 4 months   **2.** 10%, 8 months   **3.** 14%, 2 years   **4.** 11%, 3 years

5. Suppose $2000 is invested at 7%. How much is in the account at the end of 2 years if interest is

     a) simple?
     b) compounded annually?
     c) compounded semiannually?
     d) compounded quarterly?
     e) compounded daily?

6. Suppose $1500 is invested at 10%. How much is in the account at the end of 3 years if interest is

     a) simple?
     b) compounded annually?
     c) compounded semiannually?
     d) compounded every 2 months?
     e) compounded daily?

Find the present value of

7. $1000 at 8% compounded annually for 3 years.

8. $1000 at 9% compounded annually for 4 years.

9. $1000 at 8% compounded quarterly for 3 years.

10. $1000 at 9% compounded semiannually for 4 years.

11. $10,000 at 6% compounded semiannually for 18 years.

12. $15,000 at 7% compounded semiannually for 18 years.

13. *Personal Debt.* On the average every person in this country has a debt of $1000. How much will this debt be in 2 years at 7%, compounded annually?

14. *Personal Debt.* In Exercise 13, how much will be due in 2 years at 12%, compounded annually?

15. *Inflation.* Inflation is based on what a person could buy in 1967 for $1. In 1980 what was bought for a $1 in 1967 will cost $1(1 + 0.07)^{13}$, assuming a rate of inflation of 7%. How much is that cost?

16. *Inflation.* In 1984 what was bought for $1 in 1967 will cost $1(1 + 0.07)^{17}$, assuming a rate of inflation of 7%. How much is that cost?

17. *Finding the interest rate.* $2560 is invested at interest rate i, compounded annually. In 2 years it grows to $2890. What is the interest rate?

18. *Finding the interest rate.* $1000 is invested at interest rate i, compounded annually. In 2 years it grows to $1210. What is the interest rate?

6.5   ANNUAL PERCENTAGE RATE

Effective Yield

Suppose $1000 is invested at 8%, compounded quarterly for one year. We know that this will grow to an amount

$$\$1000\left(1 + \frac{0.08}{4}\right)^4, \quad \text{or } \$1082.43,$$

which is an increase of 8.243%. This is the same as if $1000 were invested at 8.243% compounded once a year (simple interest). The 8.243% is called the *effective annual yield* or *annual percentage rate*, and the 8% is called the *nominal rate*. In general, if P is invested at interest rate i, compounded n times per year, then the effective annual yield is that number E satisfying

$$P(1 + E) = P\left(1 + \frac{i}{n}\right)^n.$$

Then

$$1 + E = \left(1 + \frac{i}{n}\right)^n,$$

and

$$E = \left(1 + \frac{i}{n}\right)^n - 1.$$

Example 1   Find the effective annual yield when the nominal interest rate is 7%, compounded semiannually.

Solution
$$E = \left(1 + \frac{i}{n}\right)^n - 1$$

$$= \left(1 + \frac{0.07}{2}\right)^2 - 1 = (1.035)^2 - 1 = 1.071225 - 1$$

$$= 0.071225 \approx 7.123\%.$$

Add-On Interest

Consider a car loan.

Situation: Car loan of $1000 at 7% for 1 year

Question: Couldn't the borrower put the $1000 in a savings account at 7.5% and make money?

Car loans are examples of what lending institutions call *add-on interest*. The nominal, or stated, interest rate is 7%. This is *not* the true rate, the *annual percentage rate*, APR. Lenders use the simple interest formula, $I = Prt$, and figure the loan will earn interest of $1000 \times 0.07 \times 1$, or $70. They "add on" the $70, so you have to pay back $1070. For simplicity, suppose you pay back the loan in 4 payments. Each payment is $1070 \div$

4, or $267.50. Your loan decreases as follows:

$$\$1070, \quad \$802.50, \quad \$535, \quad \$267.50.$$

What's the catch? The lending institution *does not* allow you the full use of the $1070 for the year. The average principal you have is

$$\frac{\$1070 + \$802.50 + \$535 + \$267.50}{4} = \$668.75.$$

How do we find APR? It is defined to be that interest rate such that

(Interest for 1st 3 months) + (Interest for 2nd 3 months)

+ (Interest for 3rd 3 months) + (Interest for 4th 3 months) = Total interest,

or

($1070 × APR × $\frac{1}{4}$) + ($802.50 × APR × $\frac{1}{4}$)

$$+ (\$535 \times APR \times \tfrac{1}{4}) + (\$267.50 \times APR \times \tfrac{1}{4}) = \$70.$$

Factoring out APR, we get

[($1070 × $\frac{1}{4}$) + ($802.50 × $\frac{1}{4}$) + ($535 × $\frac{1}{4}$) + ($267.50 × $\frac{1}{4}$)] · APR = $70,

or

$$\left[\frac{\$1070 + \$802.50 + \$535 + \$267.50}{4} \right] \cdot APR = \$70.$$

Then

$$\$668.75 \cdot APR = \$70$$

$$APR = \frac{\$70}{\$668.75} \approx 10.5\%.$$

In general,

APR = (Total interest) ÷ (Average principal).

For 12 payments in the above situation, the APR would have been 12.1%. In either case the true interest rate, or APR, is almost double the stated rate. You would not save money by putting the money in the bank. The Truth In Lending Law *requires* lenders to inform you of the APR.

EXERCISE SET 6.5

For Exercises 1 through 10, find the effective annual yield for the given nominal interest rate.

1. 8%, compounded semiannually

2. 10%, compounded semiannually

3. 9%, compounded quarterly

4. 12%, compounded quarterly

5. 8%, compounded 6 times per year

6. 10%, compounded every 2 months

7. 8%, compounded daily

8. 10%, compounded daily

9. 8%, compounded hourly

10. 10%, compounded hourly

For Exercises 11 through 14, find the APR. Assume these are car loans at the given add-on interest rate for 1 year and 12 payments.

11. Loan = $1000,
Add-on rate = 8%.

12. Loan = $1000,
Add-on rate = 6%.

13. Loan = $2000,
Add-on rate = 10%.

14. Loan = $5000,
Add-on rate = 9%.

6.6 ANNUITIES AND SINKING FUNDS

Annuities

An *annuity* is a series of equal payments made at equal time intervals. Rent payments are an example of an annuity. Fixed deposits in a savings account can also be an annuity. For example, suppose someone makes a sequence of deposits of $1000 each in a savings account on which interest is compounded annually at 8%. The total amount in the account, including interest, is called the *amount of the annuity*, or the *future value of the annuity*.

Let us find the amount of the given annuity for a period of 5 years. The following time diagram can help. Note that we do not make a deposit until the end of the first year.

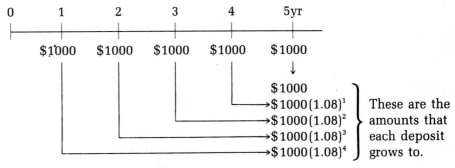

The amount of the annuity is the sum

$$\$1000 + \$1000(1.08)^1 + \$1000(1.08)^2 + \$1000(1.08)^3 + \$1000(1.08)^4.$$

This is the sum of the terms of a geometric sequence where

$$a_1 = \$1000, \quad n = 5, \quad \text{and } r = 1.08.$$

We can find this sum using the formula

$$S_n = \frac{a_1(r^n - 1)}{r - 1}.$$

We have

$$S_5 = \frac{\$1000(1.08^5 - 1)}{1.08 - 1} \approx \frac{\$1000(1.469328 - 1)}{0.08} \approx \$5866.60.$$

When equal deposits are made at equal time intervals that are the same as the periods of compounding and the first deposit is not made until the end of the first year, we have what is called an *ordinary annuity*. We shall consider only ordinary annuities.

In general, suppose we have an ordinary annuity in which P dollars are deposited each year for N years, at interest rate i, compounded annually. The first payment P, invested at the end of the first year, will be invested for $N - 1$ years and grow to

$$P(1 + i)^{N-1}.$$

The second payment will be invested for $N - 2$ years and grow to

$$P(1 + i)^{N-2},$$

and so on. The next to last payment will be invested for one year and grow to

$$P(1 + i)^1,$$

but the last payment will not have time to grow and will be

$$P.$$

Then the amount of the annuity will be the sum V given by

$$V = P + P(1 + i)^1 + P(1 + i)^2 + \cdots + P(1 + i)^{N-2} + P(1 + i)^{N-1}.$$

This is the sum of the terms of a geometric sequence where

$$a_1 = P, \qquad n = N, \qquad \text{and } r = 1 + i.$$

We can find this sum using the formula

$$S_n = \frac{a_1(r^n - 1)}{r - 1}.$$

We have

$$V = \frac{P[(1 + i)^N - 1]}{(1 + i) - 1},$$

from which we get the following formula:

> *The Amount of an Annuity.* **The amount of an annuity V, where P dollars are invested at the end of each of N years at interest rate i, compounded annually, is given by**
>
> $$V = \frac{P[(1 + i)^N - 1]}{i}.$$
>
> **If interest is compounded n times per year and deposits are being made every compounding period, the formula for V is found by replacing i by $\frac{i}{n}$ and N by nN.**

Example 1 Find the amount of an annuity where $1000 per year is being invested at 7%, compounded annually, for 15 years.

Solution
$$V = \frac{\$1000[(1 + 0.07)^{15} - 1]}{0.07} = \frac{\$1000[(1.07)^{15} - 1]}{0.07}$$

$$= \frac{\$1000[2.759032 - 1]}{0.07} \approx \$25,129.03.$$

Example 2 Find the amount of an annuity where $1000 every 3 months is being invested at 7%, compounded quarterly, for 15 years.

Solution
$$V = \frac{\$1000\left[\left(1 + \frac{0.07}{4}\right)^{60} - 1\right]}{\frac{0.07}{4}} = \frac{\$1000[(1.0175)^{60} - 1]}{0.0175}$$

$$= \frac{\$1000[2.831816 - 1]}{0.0175} \approx \$104,675.20.$$

Note that much more money is being deposited in this annuity than in Example 1.

Sinking Funds

The following is an adaptation of a problem considered before.

Example 3 Following the birth of a child, a parent wants to make a deposit on each of the child's subsequent birthdays so that $10,000 will have accumulated by the child's 20th birthday. Interest will be compounded annually at 8%. What should each deposit be?

Solution   We can use the formula

$$V = \frac{P[(1 + i)^N - 1]}{i}.$$

We know that $V = \$10,000$, $i = 0.08$, and $N = 20$. Then we substitute,

$$\$10,000 = \frac{P[(1 + 0.08)^{20} - 1]}{0.08},$$

and solve for P:

$$\$10,000(0.08) = P[(1.08)^{20} - 1],$$

$$\$800 = P[4.660957 - 1] = P[3.660957],$$

$$P = \frac{\$800}{3.660957} \approx \$218.52.$$

Each birthday after the child's birth, the parent will need to deposit $218.52.

The situation in Example 3 illustrates what is called a *sinking fund*. Any financial arrangement in which periodic payments are made for the purpose of growing to a specific future amount is called a *sinking fund*. The word "sinking" is somewhat of a misnomer in that one is making deposits to get to a future amount. The word probably comes from "sinking" the future amount back to now to consider what deposits need to be made.

EXERCISE SET 6.6

Find the amount of an annuity where

1. $1000 is being invested each year at 7%, compounded annually, for 4 years.

2. $2000 is being invested each year at 9%, compounded annually, for 5 years.

3. $1000 is being invested each year at 7%, compounded annually, for 10 years.

4. $3000 is being invested each year at 9%, compounded annually, for 10 years.

5. $2000 is being invested every 3 months at 8%, compounded quarterly, for 5 years.

6. $300 is being invested every 3 months at 6%, compounded quarterly, for 8 years.

7. $10 is being invested each month at 6%, compounded monthly, for 8 years.

8. $20 is being invested each month at 7%, compounded monthly, for 10 years.

9. A person decides to save money for retirement. $1000 is invested each year at 7.5% compounded annually. How much will be in the retirement fund at the end of 30 years?

10. A person decides to save money for retirement. $500 is invested each year at 8.5% compounded annually. How much will be in the retirement fund at the end of 40 years?

11. A family expects to buy a new car 5 years from now. They decide to put away $50 a month. At 8% interest compounded monthly how much will they have at the end of 5 years?

12. A company decides to put away money for future expansion of their business. They save $1000 a month. At 9% interest compounded monthly how much will they have at the end of 6 years?

13. Due to increased business a company expects to have to buy a $10,000 machine 8 years from now. They decide to make deposits each year at 6.5% compounded annually. What should each deposit be so the company will accumulate the $10,000?

14. A young couple wants to have a down payment of $8000 to buy a new home in 9 years. They decide to make deposits each year at 5% compounded annually. What should each deposit be so they will accumulate the $8000?

15. A family expects to pay $7000 for a car 5 years from now. They decide to make a deposit each month. Interest at 6% will be compounded monthly. What should each deposit be so they will have accumulated the $7000?

16. A family expects to pay $800 for a freezer 3 years from now. They decide to make a deposit each month. Interest at 5.5% will be compounded monthly. What should each deposit be so they will have accumulated the $800?

■ ─────────────────────────

Solve each formula for P.

17. $V = \dfrac{P[(1 + i)^N - 1]}{i}$

18. $V = \dfrac{P\left[\left(1 + \dfrac{i}{n}\right)^{nN} - 1\right]}{\dfrac{i}{n}}$

6.7   PRESENT VALUE OF AN ANNUITY AND AMORTIZATION

Present Value of an Annuity

The *present value of an annuity* is the sum of the present values of each payment of the annuity. Celebrities such as movie stars or athletes sometimes have years where they make lots of money, and then their incomes decline. Suppose a person wants to make a deposit in a lump sum right now, so that for each of the following 5 years $1000 can be drawn from the account. Interest is to be compounded annually at 8%. In effect, we can think of the deposit consisting of five different parts, the first being the amount that should be deposited now so there will be $1000 one year from now, plus the second being the amount that should be deposited now so there will be another $1000 two years from now, plus the third being the amount that should be deposited now so there will be another $1000 three years from now, and so on. Each of these is a present value of $1000 a certain number of years from now. This can be shown in the following time diagram.

These are the
present values
of each withdrawal.

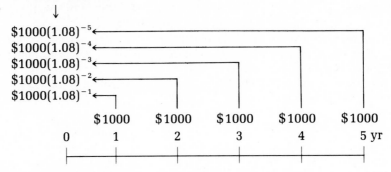

The present value of the annuity is the sum

$$\$1000(1.08)^{-1} + \$1000(1.08)^{-2} + \$1000(1.08)^{-3}$$
$$+ \$1000(1.08)^{-4} + \$1000(1.08)^{-5}.$$

This is the sum of a geometric sequence where

$$a_1 = \$1000(1.08)^{-1}, \qquad n = 5, \qquad \text{and } r = 1.08^{-1}.$$

We can find this using the formula

$$S_n = \frac{a_1(r^n - 1)}{r - 1}.$$

We have

$$S_5 = \frac{\$1000(1.08)^{-1}\,[(1.08^{-1})^5 - 1]}{1.08^{-1} - 1} = \frac{\$1000(1.08)^{-1}[(1.08)^{-5} - 1]}{1.08^{-1} - 1}.$$

Multiplying S_5 by 1 using $\dfrac{1.08}{1.08}$ will ease our calculations:

$$S_5 = \frac{1.08}{1.08} \times \frac{\$1000(1.08)^{-1}[(1.08)^{-5} - 1]}{1.08^{-1} - 1}$$

$$= \frac{\$1000[(1.08)^{-5} - 1]}{1 - 1.08} = \frac{\$1000[1 - (1.08)^{-5}]}{1.08 - 1}$$

$$= \frac{\$1000[1 - 0.680583]}{0.08} \approx \$3992.71.$$

In general, suppose a lump sum S is to be deposited now at interest rate i, compounded annually, so that P dollars can be withdrawn for each of the next N years; then S is the present value of the annuity and is given by the sum

$$P(1 + i)^{-1} + P(1 + i)^{-2} + \cdots + P(1 + i)^{-(N-1)} + P(1 + i)^{-N}.$$

We can find this sum using the formula

$$S_n = \frac{a_1(r^n - 1)}{r - 1},$$

where $a_1 = P(1 + i)^{-1}$, $n = N$, and $r = (1 + i)^{-1}$. We have

$$S = \frac{P(1 + i)^{-1}[(1 + i)^{-N} - 1]}{(1 + i)^{-1} - 1},$$

from which we get the following formula:

The Present Value of an Annuity.

$$S = \frac{P[1 - (1 + i)^{-N}]}{i}.$$

If interest is compounded n times per year and withdrawals are to be made every compounding period, the formula for S is found by replacing i by $\dfrac{i}{n}$ and N by nN.

Example 1   What lump sum would have to be deposited now at 7%, compounded annually, so that withdrawals of $1000 can be made every year for 15 years?

Solution $$S = \frac{\$1000[1 - (1.07)^{-15}]}{0.07} \approx \frac{\$1000[1 - 0.362446]}{0.07} \approx \$9107.91.$$

Example 2   What lump sum would have to be deposited now at 6%, compounded quarterly, so that withdrawals of $500 can be made every 3 months for 10 years?

Solution

$$S = \frac{\$500\left[1 - \left(1 + \dfrac{0.06}{4}\right)^{-40}\right]}{\dfrac{0.06}{4}} = \frac{\$500[1 - (1.015)^{-40}]}{0.015}$$

$$\approx \frac{\$500[1 - 0.551262]}{0.015} \approx \$14{,}957.93.$$

Amortization

In the formula for the present value of an annuity, what application is there for the situation where we know S, i, and N, and want to compute P?

Example 3 A person borrows $6000 at an interest rate of 14%, compounded monthly. The loan is to be paid off by 36 equal monthly payments over the next 3 years. How much is each payment?

Solution We can use the formula

$$S = \frac{P\left[1 - \left(1 + \dfrac{i}{n}\right)^{-nN}\right]}{\dfrac{i}{n}}.$$

We know that $S = \$6000$, $i = 0.14$, $n = 12$, and $N = 3$. Then we substitute

$$\$6000 = \frac{P\left[1 - \left(1 + \dfrac{0.14}{12}\right)^{-36}\right]}{\dfrac{0.14}{12}},$$

and solve for P:

$$\$6000\left(\frac{0.14}{12}\right) = P[1 - 0.658646],$$

$$\$70.00 = P[0.341354],$$

$$P = \frac{\$70.00}{0.341354} \approx \$205.07.$$

One might ask why we cannot use the sinking-fund formula for this problem. In a sinking fund a payment is made and then allowed to grow at a certain interest rate. The payee gets the money back at the end. When one *amortizes* a loan, as in Example 3, the money is received at the outset. In Example 3, the borrower gets the $6000 at the outset.

When financial institutions loan money they start computing interest right away. After one month a payment of $205.08 was made. In effect a part of the $6000, a present value, has grown to $205.08 during the first month and consists of principal and interest. Each monthly payment is such a payment of interest and principal; the amounts of each vary, but always total $205.08. When we amortize a loan, we know the present value of an annuity and want to find the amount of each equal payment.

EXERCISE SET 6.7

What lump sum would have to be deposited now at

1. 7%, compounded annually, so that withdrawals of $1000 can be made every year for 4 years?

2. 9%, compounded annually, so that withdrawals of $2000 can be made every year for 5 years?

3. 7%, compounded annually, so that withdrawals of $1000 can be made every year for 10 years?

4. 9%, compounded annually, so that withdrawals of $3000 can be made every year for 10 years?

5. 8%, compounded quarterly, so that withdrawals of $2000 can be made every 3 months for 5 years?

6. 6%, compounded semiannually, so that withdrawals of $300 can be made every 6 months for 8 years?

7. 6%, compounded monthly, so that withdrawals of $10 can be made every month for 8 years?

8. 7%, compounded monthly, so that withdrawals of $20 can be made every month for 10 years?

9. A family pays $4800 for a remodeling job. A down payment of $600 is made, and $4200 is borrowed at 12%, compounded monthly. The loan is to be paid off by 36 equal payments over the next 3 years. How much is each payment?

10. A family pays $10,000 for an addition to their home. A down payment of $1000 is made, and $9000 is borrowed at 10.5%, compounded monthly. The loan is to be paid off by 24 equal payments over the next 2 years. How much is each payment?

11. A family buys a house for $75,000. A down payment of $15,000 is made, and $60,000 is borrowed at 10.5%, compounded monthly. The loan is to be paid off by 360 equal payments over the next 30 years. How much is each payment?

12. A family buys a condominium for $40,000. A down payment of $10,000 is made, and $30,000 is borrowed at 11%, compounded monthly. The loan is to be paid off by 300 equal payments over the next 25 years. How much is each payment?

■ ─────────────────────────────────

Solve each formula for P.

13. $S = \dfrac{P[1 - (1 + i)^{-N}]}{i}$

14. $S = \dfrac{P\left[1 - \left(1 + \dfrac{i}{n}\right)^{-nN}\right]}{\dfrac{i}{n}}$

A *perpetuity* is an annuity in which payments will be made forever.

15. What lump sum would have to be deposited now at 8%, compounded annually, so that withdrawals of $1000 can be made every year forever? *Hint:* Use the formula for the sum of an infinite geometric series. What other method can be used?

16. A family wishes to set up at a college an endowed professorship that will pay a salary of $12,000 each year, forever. What lump sum would have to be deposited now at 7.5%, compounded annually, to provide this salary?

CHAPTER 6 REVIEW

1. The following is an arithmetic sequence. Identify the first term and the common difference.

$$5, 8, 11, \ldots$$

2. Find the 20th term of the sequence in Problem 1.

3. Find the sum of the first 20 terms of this arithmetic sequence.

$$\$1.00, \$1.06, \$1.12, \ldots$$

4. The following is a geometric sequence. Identify the common ratio.

$$\$100, \$105, \$110.25, \ldots$$

5. Find the 10th term of the geometric sequence in Problem 4. Round to the nearest cent.

6. Find the sum of the first 10 terms of the sequence in Problem 4. Round to the nearest cent.

7. Determine if the following infinite geometric series has a sum. If so, find it.

$$\$1000, \$80, \$6.40, \ldots$$

Consider this situation for Problems 8 through 10: *Item:* Automobile

$$\text{Cost} \qquad = \$8500,$$

$$\text{Expected life} \ = 4 \text{ years,}$$

$$\text{Salvage value} = \$2550.$$

8. Use the straight-line method to

   a) Prepare a depreciation schedule,

   b) Find a formula for the book values V_n,

   c) Find the common difference.

9. Use the double-declining balance method to

   a) Prepare a depreciation schedule,

   b) Find a formula for the book values V_n.

10. Use the sum of the year's digits method to

   a) Find the depreciation fractions,

   b) Prepare a depreciation schedule.

11. Suppose $1000 is invested at 6%. How much is in the account at the end of 3 years if interest is

   a) simple?

   b) compounded annually?

   c) compounded semiannually?

   d) compounded quarterly?

12. Find the effective annual yield.

   9%, compounded quarterly

13. Find the APR. Assume a car loan at the given add-on interest rate for one year and 12 payments.

   Loan = $5000,   Add-on rate = 11%.

14. Find the amount of an annuity where $2000 is being invested semiannually at 8.4%, compounded semiannually, for 7 years.

15. Due to increased business, a company expects to have to pay $8000 for a machine 6 years from now. They decide to make deposits each year at 8%, compounded annually. What should each payment be so the company will accumulate the $8000?

16. What lump sum would have to be deposited now at 5%, compounded annually, so that withdrawals of $10,000 can be made every year for 15 years?

18. Find the present value of $10,000 for 5 years at 16%, compounded quarterly.

20. Find the sum of the first 200 natural numbers.

22. Following the birth of a child, a parent wants to make a deposit on each of the child's subsequent birthdays so that $10,000 will have accumulated by the child's 10th birthday. Interest will be compounded annually at 7%. What should each deposit be?

Using the notation

$$s_{\overline{N}|k} = \frac{(1 + k)^N - 1}{k} \quad \text{and} \quad a_{\overline{N}|k} = \frac{1 - (1 + k)^N}{k}.$$

prove.

23. $\quad s_{N+\overline{M}|k} = s_{\overline{N}|k} + (1 + k)^N s_{\overline{M}|k}$

17. A family buys a condominium for $100,000. A down payment of $25,000 is made, and $75,000 is borrowed at 10%, compounded monthly. The loan is to be paid off by 240 equal payments over the next 20 years. How much is each payment?

19. The following are the first two terms of a sequence

$$\$6300, \$5953.25$$

a) Find the third term if the sequence is arithmetic.

b) Find the third term if the sequence is geometric.

21. What lump sum would have to be deposited now at 8%, compounded quarterly, so that withdrawals of $500 can be made every 3 months for 10 years?

24. $\quad a_{N+\overline{M}|k} = a_{\overline{N}|k} + (1 + k)^{-N} a_{\overline{M}|k}$

DIFFERENTIATION

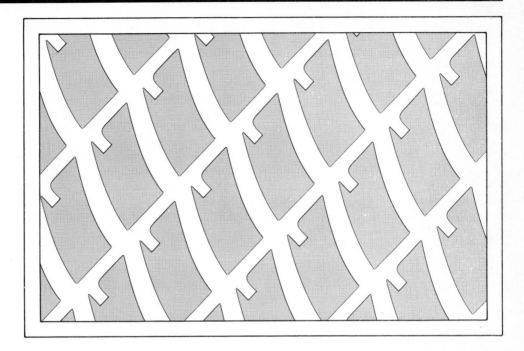

7.1 CONTINUITY AND LIMITS

In this section we give an intuitive (meaning "based on prior and present experience") treatment of two important concepts: continuity and limits.

Continuity

The following are graphs of functions that are *continuous* over the whole real line $(-\infty, \infty)$.

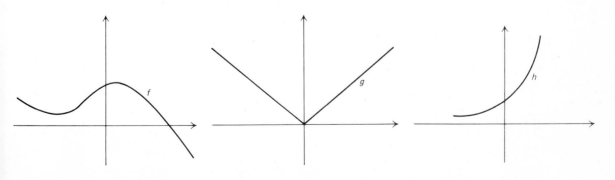

Note that there are no "jumps" or holes in the graphs. For now we will use a somewhat intuitive definition of continuity, which we will refine later. We say that a function is *continuous* over, or on, some interval of the real line if its graph can be traced without lifting a pencil from the paper. The following are graphs of functions that are *not* continuous over the whole real line.

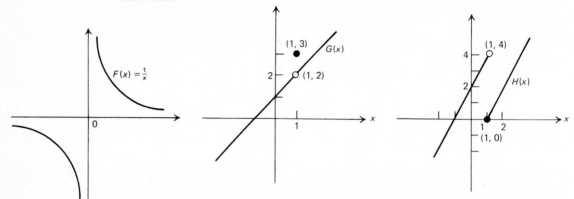

For G and H, the open circle indicates that the circled point is not part of the graph. In each case the graph *cannot* be traced without lifting the pencil from the paper. However, each case represents a different situation. Let us discuss why each case fails to be continuous over the whole real line.

The function F fails to be continuous over the *whole* real line $(-\infty, \infty)$. Since F is not defined at $x = 0$, the point $x = 0$ is not part of the domain, so $f(0)$ does not exist and there is no point $(0, f(0))$ on the graph. Thus there is no point to trace at $x = 0$. However, F is continuous on the intervals $(-\infty, 0)$ and $(0, \infty)$.

The function G is not continuous over the whole real line since it is not continuous at $x = 1$. Let us trace the graph of G to the left of $x = 1$. As x approaches 1, G(x) seems to approach 2; but at $x = 1$, G(x) *jumps* up to 3, while to the right of $x = 1$, G(x) *jumps* back to some value close to 2. Thus G is discontinuous at $x = 1$.

The function H is not continuous over the whole real line since it is not continuous at $x = 1$. Let us trace the graph of H starting to the left of $x = 1$. As x approaches 1, H(x) seems to approach 4; but at $x = 1$, H(x) *jumps* down to 0, while just to the right of $x = 1$, H(x) is close to 0. Thus H(x) is discontinuous at $x = 1$.

Limits

These notions about *continuity* can be formalized by introducing the concept of *limits*. The study of limits has application not just to continuity but throughout calculus.

Consider the function f given by

$$f(x) = 2x + 3.$$

Suppose we select input numbers x closer and closer to the number 4, and look at the output numbers $2x + 3$. Study the following tables.

R			L	
Inputs x	Outputs 2x + 3		Inputs x	Outputs 2x + 3
5	13		2	7
4.8	12.6		3.6	10.2
4.3	11.6		3.8	10.6
4.1	11.2		3.9	10.8
4.01	11.02		3.99	10.98
4.001	11.002		3.999	10.998

In Table R, the input numbers approach 4 from numbers greater than 4 or, on a graph, from numbers to the right of 4. In Table L, the input numbers approach 4 from numbers less than 4 or, on a graph, from numbers to the left of 4. In both cases the outputs approach 11. Thus we say,

As x *approaches* 4, $2x + 3$ *approaches* 11.

An arrow, $\rightarrow$, is often used for the word "approaches." Thus the above can be written

As $x \rightarrow 4$, $2x + 3 \rightarrow 11$.

The number 11 is said to be the *limit* of $2x + 3$ as x approaches 4. We can abbreviate this statement as follows:

$$\lim_{x \to 4} (2x + 3) = 11.$$

This is read, "The limit, as x approaches 4, of $2x + 3$ is 11."

DEFINITION   A function, f, has the *limit, L,* as x approaches a, written

$$\lim_{x \to a} f(x) = L,$$

if we can get $f(x)$ as close to L as we wish by restricting x to a sufficiently small interval about a but excluding a.

The limit at a point a does not depend on the function value at a, $f(a)$, should that exist. To see this more clearly, let us consider again the function G whose graph we showed as an example of a discontinuous function. G can be defined as follows:

$$G(x) = \frac{x^2 - 1}{x - 1}, \qquad x \neq 1$$

$$\left(\text{If an input } x \text{ is not 1, the output is } \frac{x^2 - 1}{x - 1}. \right)$$

$$G(x) = 3, \qquad x = 1$$

(If an input is 1, the output is 3.)

Let us set up input–output tables for $G(x)$ as x approaches 1 from the left and from the right.

R			**L**	
Inputs x	Outputs $\dfrac{x^2 - 1}{x - 1}$		Inputs x	Outputs $\dfrac{x^2 - 1}{x - 1}$
2	3		0	1
1.6	2.6		0.7	1.7
1.2	2.2		0.8	1.8
1.1	2.1		0.9	1.9
1.01	2.01		0.99	1.99
1.001	2.001		0.999	1.999

Note that as the inputs x approach 1 from either the left or right, the outputs approach 2. Thus

$$\lim_{x \to 1} G(x) = 2,$$

while the function value at $x = 1$ is

$$G(1) = 3.$$

Since these two values are not equal at $x = 1$, G is discontinuous at $x = 1$.

DEFINITION   A function f is *discontinuous at $x = a$*, if

$$\lim_{x \to a} f(x) \neq f(a).$$

Note that

$$\frac{x^2 - 1}{x - 1}$$

does not have a value at $x = 1$, but that it does have a limit, which we found using the input–output tables. Specifically, the function

$$\frac{x^2 - 1}{x - 1},$$

when factored, equals

$$\frac{(x - 1)(x + 1)}{x - 1},$$

which equals $x + 1$, provided $x \neq 1$. Accordingly, the limit as $x \to 1$ could have been found by substituting approaching inputs directly into $x + 1$.

Consider again the function H whose graph we showed as an example of a discontinuous function. H can be defined as follows.

$$H(x) = 2x + 2, \qquad x < 1$$

(If an input x is less than 1, the output is $2x + 2$.)

$$H(x) = 2x - 2, \qquad 1 \leqslant x$$

(If an input x is greater than or equal to 1, the output is $2x - 2$.)

We see that as x approaches 1 from the left, $H(x)$ approaches 4:

$$x \to 1, \qquad H(x) \to 4.$$
(from the left)

As x approaches 1 from the right, $H(x)$ approaches 0:

$$x \to 1, \qquad H(x) \to 0.$$
(from the right)

Thus the limiting values of $H(x)$ as x approaches 1 from the left and from the right are not equal: $4 \neq 0$. The limit, therefore, does *not* exist, and the function is discontinuous at this point.

DEFINITION **A function is *discontinuous* at a point, *a*, if the limit of the function as x approaches *a* from the left is not equal to the limit of the function as x approaches *a* from the right.**

In such a case, we can also say that the function is discontinuous because it does not have a limit as x approaches a.

Summarizing ideas illustrated in the foregoing examples, we obtain the following definition of continuity.

DEFINITION   A function f is *continuous* at $x = a$ if

1. $f(a)$ exists,
2. $\lim_{x \to a} f(x)$ exists, and
3. $\lim_{x \to a} f(x) = f(a)$.

A function is *continuous over an interval, I*, if it is continuous at each point in I.

We previously considered the function f given by

$$f(x) = 2x + 3.$$

This function is continuous at 4 because

1. $f(4)$ exists, $f(4) = 11$,
2. $\lim_{x \to 4} f(x)$ exists, $\lim_{x \to 4} f(x) = 11$ (as shown earlier),
3. $\lim_{x \to 4} f(x) = 11 = f(4)$.

In fact, $f(x) = 2x + 3$ is continuous at any point on the real line.

CONTINUITY   The following continuity principles, which we will not prove, allow us
PRINCIPLES   to build up continuous functions.

i. Any constant function is continuous (such a function never varies).
ii. For any positive integer n, x^n and $\sqrt[n]{x}$ are continuous. When n is even, the inputs of $\sqrt[n]{x}$ are restricted to $(0, \infty)$.
iii. If $f(x)$ and $g(x)$ are continuous, then so are $f(x) + g(x)$, $f(x) - g(x)$, and $f(x) \cdot g(x)$.
iv. If $f(x)$ is continuous, so is $1/f(x)$, as long as the inputs x are not such that the outputs $f(x) = 0$.

Let us convince ourselves that $x^2 - 3x + 2$ is continuous. Now x^2 is continuous, by (ii). The constant function 3 is continuous by (i), the function x is continuous by (ii), so the product $3x$ is continuous by (iii). Thus $x^2 - 3x$ is continuous by (iii), and since the constant 2 is continuous, we can apply (iii) again to show that $x^2 - 3x + 2$ is continuous. In similar fashion, any polynomial such as

$$f(x) = x^4 - 5x^3 + x^2 - 7$$

is continuous. A rational function is a quotient of two polynomials

$$r(x) = \frac{f(x)}{q(x)}.$$

Thus by (iv), a rational function is continuous as long as the inputs x are not such that $q(x) = 0$.

If a function is continuous at a, we can substitute to find the limit.

Example 1   Find $\lim_{x \to 2} (x^4 - 5x^3 + x^2 - 7)$.

Solution   It follows from the continuity principles that $x^4 - 5x^3 + x^2 - 7$ is continuous. Thus the limit can be found by substitution:

$$\lim_{x \to 2} (x^4 - 5x^3 + x^2 - 7) = 2^4 - 5 \cdot 2^3 + 2^2 - 7$$

$$= 16 - 40 + 4 - 7 = -27.$$

Example 2   Find $\lim_{x \to 0} \sqrt{x^2 - 3x + 2}$.

Solution   By using the continuity principles, we have shown that $x^2 - 3x + 2$ is continuous; and as long as x is restricted to values for which $x^2 - 3x + 2$ is nonnegative, it follows from principle (ii) that $\sqrt{x^2 - 3x + 2}$ is continuous. Thus, we can substitute to find the limit:

$$\lim_{x \to 0} \sqrt{x^2 - 3x + 2} = \sqrt{0^2 - 3 \cdot 0 + 2} = \sqrt{2}.$$

More on Limits

Let us consider another limit that does not exist. Consider

$$f(x) = \frac{1}{x - 1}.$$

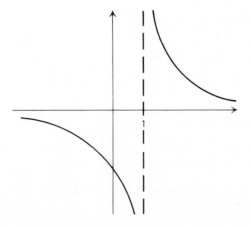

Let us try to determine

$$\lim_{x \to 1} \frac{1}{x - 1}.$$

Note that we cannot substitute 1 for x, since it would result in division by 0; that is, the function is not continuous at 1. Let us investigate the behavior of the function as x approaches 1.

R		L	
Inputs x	Outputs $\frac{1}{x-1}$	Inputs x	Outputs $\frac{1}{x-1}$
2	1	0	-1
1.6	1.667	0.7	-3.333
1.2	5.0	0.8	-5
1.1	10	0.9	-10
1.01	100	0.99	-100
1.001	1000	0.999	-1000

As x approaches 1 from the right, the outputs get larger and larger. These numbers do not approach any real number, though it might be said that "the limit from the right is ∞ (infinity)." As x approaches 1 from the left, the outputs get smaller and smaller. These numbers do not approach any real number, though it might be said that "the limit from the left is $-\infty$ (negative infinity)." Thus

$$\lim_{x \to 1} \frac{1}{x - 1}$$

does not exist.

Limit Principles

There are limit principles that correspond to the continuity principles.

If $\lim_{x \to a} f(x) = L$ and $\lim_{x \to a} g(x) = M$, then

L1. $\lim_{x \to a} c = c$. (The limit of a constant is the constant.)

L2. $\lim_{x \to a} x^n = a^n$, $\lim_{x \to a} \sqrt[n]{x} = \sqrt[n]{a}$, for any positive integer n. (When n is even, the inputs of $\sqrt[n]{x}$ must be restricted to $[0, \infty)$.)

L3. $\lim_{x \to a} [f(x) \pm g(x)] = \lim_{x \to a} f(x) \pm \lim_{x \to a} g(x) = L \pm M$. (The limit of a sum or difference is the sum or difference of the limits.)

$\lim\limits_{x\to a} [f(x) \cdot g(x)] = [\lim\limits_{x\to a} f(x)] \cdot [\lim\limits_{x\to a} g(x)] = L \cdot M$. (The limit of a product is the product of the limits.)

L4. $\lim\limits_{x\to a} \dfrac{1}{f(x)} = \dfrac{1}{\lim\limits_{x\to a} f(x)} = \dfrac{1}{L}$, provided $L \neq 0$. (The limit of a reciprocal is the reciprocal of the limit.)

Example 3   Find $\lim\limits_{x\to -3} \dfrac{x^2 - 9}{x + 3}$.

Solution   The function $(x^2 - 9)/(x + 3)$ is not continuous at $x = -3$. We use some algebraic simplification and then some limit principles.

$$\lim_{x\to -3} \frac{x^2 - 9}{x + 3} = \lim_{x\to -3} \frac{(x + 3)(x - 3)}{x + 3}$$

$$= \lim_{x\to -3} (x - 3) \text{ (assuming } x \neq -3)$$

$$= \lim_{x\to -3} x - \lim_{x\to -3} 3 \quad \text{(by L3)}$$

$$= -3 - 3 = -6$$

In the next section we encounter expressions with two variables, x and h; our interest is in limits where x is fixed as a constant and $h \to 0$.

Example 4   Find $\lim\limits_{h\to 0} (3x^2 + 3xh + h^2)$.

Solution   If we treat x as a constant, using the limit principles, it follows that

$$\lim_{h\to 0} (3x^2 + 3xh + h^2) = 3x^2 + 3x0 + 0^2 = 3x^2.$$

The reader can check any limit about which there is uncertainty by using an input–output table. Below is a table for this limit.

h	$3x^2 + 3xh + h^2$	
1	$3x^2 + 3x \cdot 1 + 1^2$, or	$3x^2 + 3x + 1$
0.8	$3x^2 + 3x(0.8) + (0.8)^2$, or	$3x^2 + 2.4x + 0.64$
0.5	$3x^2 + 3x(0.5) + (0.5)^2$, or	$3x^2 + 1.5x + 0.25$
0.1	$3x^2 + 3x(0.1) + (0.1)^2$, or	$3x^2 + 0.3x + 0.01$
0.01	$3x^2 + 3x(0.01) + (0.01)^2$, or	$3x^2 + 0.03x + 0.0001$
0.001	$3x^2 + 3x(0.001) + (0.001)^2$, or	$3x^2 + 0.003x + 0.000001$

From the pattern in the table it appears that

$$\lim_{h \to 0} (3x^2 + 3xh + h^2) = 3x^2.$$

Limits at Infinity

Sometimes we need to determine limits when the inputs get larger and larger. For example, consider

$$f(x) = 3 - \frac{1}{x}.$$

Look at the input–output table to the right. Note that as the inputs get larger and larger, the outputs get closer to 3. We say "the limit as x goes to infinity of $3 - (1/x)$ is 3." We can abbreviate this:

Inputs x	Outputs $3 - \dfrac{1}{x}$
1	2.0
10	2.9
50	2.98
100	2.99
2000	2.9995

$$\lim_{x \to \infty} \left(3 - \frac{1}{x} \right) = 3.$$

EXERCISE SET 7.1

Which functions are continuous?

1.

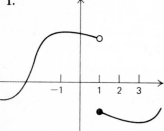

2.

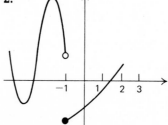

3.

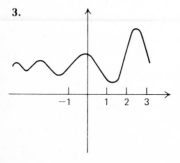

4.

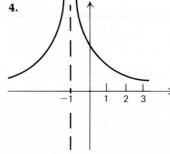

5–8. For each of Exercises 1–4, decide (a) whether the function is continuous at −1, and (b) whether the function is continuous at 1.

The Postage Function. Postal rates established in 1978 were as follows: 15¢ for the 1st ounce and 13¢ for each additional ounce or fraction thereof. Formally, if x is the weight of a letter in ounces, then p(x) is the cost of mailing the letter, where

$$p(x) = 15¢, \quad \text{if } 0 < x \leqslant 1,$$
$$p(x) = 28¢, \quad \text{if } 1 < x \leqslant 2,$$
$$p(x) = 41¢, \quad \text{if } 2 < x \leqslant 3,$$

and so on, up to 12 ounces (at which point postal cost also depends on distance). The graph of p is shown at the right.

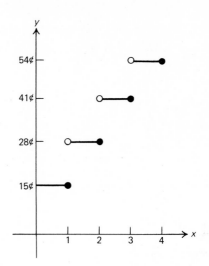

9. Is p continuous at 1? $1\frac{1}{2}$? 2? 2.53?

10. Is p continuous at 3? $3\frac{1}{4}$? 4? 3.98?

Using the graph, find each limit.

11. $\lim\limits_{x \to 1} p(x)$

12. $\lim\limits_{x \to 1/2} p(x)$

13. $\lim\limits_{x \to 2.3} p(x)$

14. $\lim\limits_{x \to 2} p(x)$

15. a) Complete.

Inputs x	Outputs $x^2 - 3$
2	
1.5	
1.2	
1.1	
1.01	
1.001	

16. a) Complete.

Inputs x	Outputs $x^2 + 4$
2	
1.4	
1.2	
1.1	
1.01	
1.001	

b) Make up and complete a table for the limit from the left.

c) Find $\lim\limits_{x \to 1} (x^2 - 3)$.

b) Make up and complete a table for the limit from the left.

c) Find $\lim\limits_{x \to 1} (x^2 + 4)$.

Find each limit, if it exists. If you have trouble, make up your own input–output table.

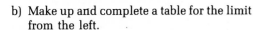

17. $\lim\limits_{x \to -5} \dfrac{x^2 - 25}{x + 5}$

18. $\lim\limits_{x \to -4} \dfrac{x^2 - 16}{x + 4}$

19. $\lim\limits_{x \to 0} \dfrac{1}{x}$

20. $\lim\limits_{x \to 0} \dfrac{3}{x}$

21. $\lim\limits_{x \to -2} \dfrac{3}{x}$

22. $\lim\limits_{x \to -4} \dfrac{1}{x}$

23. $\lim\limits_{x \to 2} \dfrac{x^3 - 8}{x - 2}$

24. $\lim\limits_{x \to 1} \dfrac{x^3 - 1}{x - 1}$

25. $\lim\limits_{x\to 1}\dfrac{x^2-1}{x^3-1}$

26. $\lim\limits_{x\to 1}\dfrac{x^3-1}{x^2-1}$

27. (▦ with $\sqrt{x}$ key.) $\lim\limits_{x\to 1}\dfrac{1-\sqrt{x}}{1-x}$

28. (▦ with $\sqrt{x}$ key.) $\lim\limits_{x\to 4}\dfrac{2-\sqrt{x}}{4-x}$

29. (▦ with $\sqrt{x}$ key.) $\lim\limits_{x\to 1}\dfrac{2-\sqrt{x+3}}{x-1}$

30. $\lim\limits_{h\to 0}\dfrac{-1}{x(x+h)}$

31. $\lim\limits_{h\to 0}(2x+h+1)$

32. a) Complete.

x	$\dfrac{2x-4}{5x}$
8	
60	
100	
400	
6000	
20,000	

33. a) Complete.

x	$\dfrac{3x+1}{4x}$
10	
80	
200	
500	
8000	
40,000	

b) Find

$$\lim_{x\to\infty}\left(\frac{2x-4}{5x}\right).$$

b) Find

$$\lim_{x\to\infty}\left(\frac{3x+1}{4x}\right).$$

Find each limit, if it exists. If you have trouble, make up your own input–output tables.

34. $\lim\limits_{x\to\infty}\dfrac{1}{x}$

35. $\lim\limits_{x\to\infty}\dfrac{2}{x}$

36. $\lim\limits_{x\to\infty}\left(2+\dfrac{1}{x}\right)$

37. $\lim\limits_{x\to\infty}\left(5-\dfrac{1}{x}\right)$

38. $\lim\limits_{x\to\infty}\dfrac{2x^2-5}{3x^2-x+7}$

39. *Depreciation.* A new conveyor system costs $10,000. In any year it depreciates 8% of its value at the beginning of that year.

a) What is the annual depreciation in each of the first five years?

b) What is the total depreciation at the end of 10 years?

c) What is the limit of the sum of the annual depreciation costs?

40. *Depreciation.* A new car costs $6000. In any year it depreciates 30% of its value at the beginning of that year.

a) What is the annual depreciation in each of the first five years?

b) What is the total depreciation at the end of 10 years?

c) What is the limit of the sum of the annual depreciation costs?

7.2 AVERAGE RATES OF CHANGE

The graph below shows the total production of suits by Raggs, Ltd. during one morning of work. Industrial psychologists háve found curves like this typical of the production of factory workers.

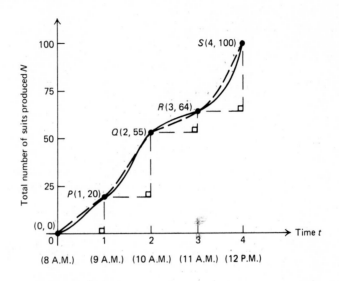

Example 1 What is the number of suits produced from 9 A.M. to 10 A.M.?

Solution At 10 A.M., 55 suits had been produced. At 9A.M., 20 suits had been produced. In the hour from 9A.M. to 10 A.M. the number of suits produced was

$$55 \text{ suits} - 20 \text{ suits, or } 35 \text{ suits.}$$

Note that this is the slope of the line from P to Q.

Example 2 What was the average number of suits produced per hour from 9 A.M. to 11 A.M.?

Solution
$$\frac{64 \text{ suits} - 20 \text{ suits}}{11 \text{ A.M.} - 9 \text{ A.M.}} = \frac{44 \text{ suits}}{2 \text{ hr}} = 22 \frac{\text{suits}}{\text{hr}} \text{ (suits per hour)}$$

This is the slope of the line from P to R. It is not shown in the graph.

Let us consider a function $y = f(x)$ and two inputs x_1 and x_2. The *change in input* or the *change in x* is

$$x_2 - x_1.$$

The *change in output* or the *change in y* is

$$y_2 - y_1.$$

The *average rate of change of y with respect to x,* as x changes from x_1 to x_2, is the ratio of the change in output to the change in input.

$$\frac{y_2 - y_1}{x_2 - x_1}.$$

If we look at a graph of the function, we see that

$$\frac{y_2 - y_1}{x_2 - x_1} = \frac{f(x_2) - f(x_1)}{x_2 - x_1}$$

and that this is the slope of the line from $P(x_1, y_1)$ to $Q(x_2, y_2)$. The line $\overleftrightarrow{PQ}$ is called a *secant* line.

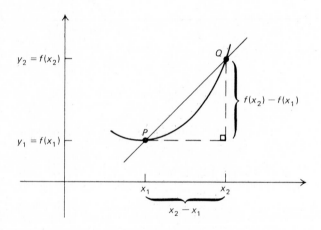

Example 3   For $y = f(x) = x^2$, find the average rates of change as

a) x changes from 1 to 3,

b) x changes from 1 to 2,

c) x changes from 2 to 3.

Solution   The following graph is not necessary to the computations, but gives us a look at the secant lines whose slopes are being computed.

a) When $x_1 = 1$, $y_1 = f(x_1) = f(1) = 1^2 = 1$, and
when $x_2 = 3$, $y_2 = f(x_2) = f(3) = 3^2 = 9$.

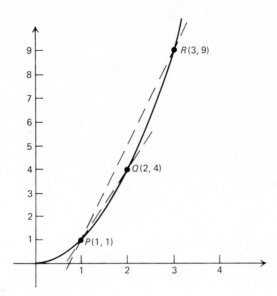

The average rate of change is

$$\frac{y_2 - y_1}{x_2 - x_1} = \frac{f(x_2) - f(x_1)}{x_2 - x_1} = \frac{9 - 1}{3 - 1} = \frac{8}{2} = 4.$$

b) When $x_1 = 1$, $y_1 = f(x_1) = f(1) = 1^2 = 1$, and
when $x_2 = 2$, $y_2 = f(x_2) = f(2) = 2^2 = 4$.

The average rate of change is

$$\frac{4 - 1}{2 - 1} = \frac{3}{1} = 3.$$

c) When $x_1 = 2$, $y_1 = f(x_1) = f(2) = 2^2 = 4$, and
when $x_2 = 3$, $y_2 = f(x_2) = f(3) = 3^2 = 9$.

The average rate of change is

$$\frac{9 - 4}{3 - 2} = \frac{5}{1} = 5.$$

For a linear function average rates of change are the same, for any choice of x_1 and x_2, being equal to the slope m of the line. A function that is not linear has average rates of change that vary with the choice of x_1 and x_2.

Difference Quotients

Let us now simplify our notation a bit, by doing away with subscripts. Instead of x_1, we will simply write x.

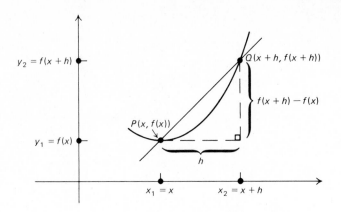

To get from x_1, or x, to x_2 we move a distance h. Thus $x_2 = x + h$. Then the average rate of change, also called a *difference quotient*, is given by

$$\frac{y_2 - y_1}{x_2 - x_1} = \frac{f(x_2) - f(x_1)}{x_2 - x_1} = \frac{f(x + h) - f(x)}{(x + h) - x} = \frac{f(x + h) - f(x)}{h}.$$

We shall be using the expression on the right.

> **The average rate of change of f with respect to x is also called the difference quotient. It is given by**
>
> $$\frac{f(x + h) - f(x)}{h}.$$
>
> **The difference quotient is equal to the slope of the line from $P(x, f(x))$ to $Q(x + h, f(x + h))$.**

Example 4   For $f(x) = x^2$, find the difference quotient when

a) $x = 5$ and $h = 3$,

b) $x = 5$ and $h = 0.1$.

Solutions   a) We substitute $x = 5$ and $h = 3$ into the formula,

$$\frac{f(x + h) - f(x)}{h} = \frac{f(5 + 3) - f(5)}{3} = \frac{f(8) - f(5)}{3}.$$

Now $f(8) = 8^2 = 64$, and $f(5) = 5^2 = 25$, and we have

$$\frac{f(8) - f(5)}{3} = \frac{64 - 25}{3} = \frac{39}{3} = 13.$$

b) We substitute $x = 5$ and $h = 0.1$ into the formula,

$$\frac{f(x + h) - f(x)}{h} = \frac{f(5 + 0.1) - f(5)}{0.1} = \frac{f(5.1) - f(5)}{0.1}.$$

Now $f(5.1) = (5.1)^2 = 26.01$ and $f(5) = 25$, and we have

$$\frac{f(5.1) - f(5)}{0.1} = \frac{26.01 - 25}{0.1} = \frac{1.01}{0.1} = 10.1.$$

For the function in Example 4, let us find a general form of the difference quotient. This will allow more efficient computations.

Example 5   For $f(x) = x^2$, find a simplified form of the difference quotient. Then find the value of the difference quotient when $x = 5$ and $h = 0.1$.

Solution
$$f(x) = x^2,$$

so

$$f(x + h) = (x + h)^2 = x^2 + 2xh + h^2.$$

Then

$$f(x + h) - f(x) = (x^2 + 2xh + h^2) - x^2 = 2xh + h^2.$$

So

$$\frac{f(x + h) - f(x)}{h} = \frac{2xh + h^2}{h} = \frac{h(2x + h)}{h} = 2x + h.$$

It is important to note that a difference quotient is defined *only* when $h \neq 0$. The simplification above is valid only for nonzero values of h.
When $x = 5$ and $h = 0.1$,

$$\frac{f(x + h) - f(x)}{h} = 2x + h = 2 \cdot 5 + 0.1 = 10 + 0.1 = 10.1.$$

Example 6   For $f(x) = x^3$ find a simplified form of the difference quotient.

Solution   Now $f(x) = x^3$, so

$$f(x + h) = (x + h)^3 = x^3 + 3x^2h + 3xh^2 + h^3.$$

This is shown on p. 26. Then

$$f(x + h) - f(x) = (x^3 + 3x^2h + 3xh^2 + h^3) - x^3$$
$$= 3x^2h + 3xh^2 + h^3.$$

So

$$\frac{f(x + h) - f(x)}{h} = \frac{3x^2h + 3xh^2 + h^3}{h}$$

$$= \frac{h(3x^2 + 3xh + h^2)}{h}$$

$$= 3x^2 + 3xh + h^2.$$

Again, this is true *only* for $h \neq 0$.

Example 7   For $f(x) = \dfrac{3}{x}$ find a simplified form of the difference quotient.

Solution   Now

$$f(x) = \frac{3}{x}, \quad \text{so} \quad f(x + h) = \frac{3}{x + h}.$$

Then

$$f(x + h) - f(x) = \frac{3}{x + h} - \frac{3}{x}$$

$$= \frac{3}{x + h} \cdot \frac{x}{x} - \frac{3}{x} \cdot \frac{x + h}{x + h} \quad \text{(Here we are multiplying by 1}$$
$$\text{to get a common denominator.)}$$

$$= \frac{3x - 3(x + h)}{x(x + h)}$$

$$= \frac{3x - 3x - 3h}{x(x + h)}$$

$$= \frac{-3h}{x(x + h)}.$$

So

$$\frac{f(x + h) - f(x)}{h} = \frac{\dfrac{-3h}{x(x + h)}}{h}$$

$$= \frac{-3h}{x(x + h)} \cdot \frac{1}{h} = \frac{-3}{x(x + h)}.$$

This is true only for $h \neq 0$.

EXERCISE SET 7.2

1. *Utility.* Utility is a type of function that arises in economics. When a consumer receives x units of a certain product, a certain amount of pleasure, or utility, U, is derived from them. Below is a typical graph of a utility function.

a) Find the average rate of change of U as x changes from 0 to 1, 1 to 2, 2 to 3, and 3 to 4.

b) Why do you think the average rates of change are decreasing?

2. *Advertising results.* The graph below shows a typical response to advertising. After an amount a is spent on advertising, the company sells $N(a)$ units of a product.

a) Find the average rate of change of N, as a changes from 0 to 1, 1 to 2, 2 to 3, and 3 to 4.

b) Why do you think the average rates of change are decreasing?

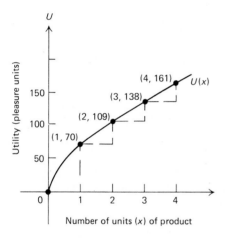

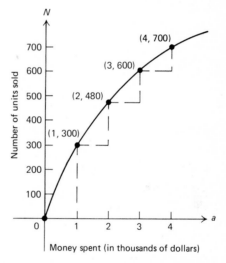

3. *Population growth.* The two curves at the right describe the number of people in each of two countries, A and B, at time t, in years.

a) Find the average rate of change of each population (number of people in the population) with respect to time t, as t changes from 0 to 4. This is often called an *average growth rate.*

b) If the calculation in (a) were the only one made, would we detect the fact that the populations were growing differently?

c) Find the average rates of change of each population as t changes from 0 to 1, 1 to 2, 2 to 3, and 3 to 4.

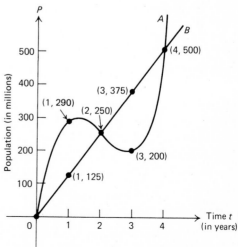

d) For which population does the statement "the population grew 125 million each year" convey the least information about what really took place?

4. *Total cost.* A firm determines that the total cost, C, of producing x units of a certain product is given by

$$C(x) = -0.05x^2 + 50x,$$

where C(x) is in dollars.

a) Find C(301).

b) Find C(300).

c) Find C(301) − C(300).

d) Find $\dfrac{C(301) - C(300)}{301 - 300}$.

6. *Average velocity.* A car is at a distance s (in miles) from its starting point in t hours, given by

$$s(t) = 10t^2.$$

a) Find s(2) and s(5).

b) Find s(5) − s(2). What does this represent?

c) Find the average rate of change of distance with respect to time as t changes from t_1 = 2 to t_2 = 5. This is known as *average velocity* or *speed*.

8. At the beginning of a trip, the odometer on a car reads 30,680 and it has a full tank of gas. At the end of the trip the odometer reads 30,970. It takes 20 gallons of gas to fill the tank again.

a) What is the average rate of consumption (rate of change of the number of miles with respect to the number of gallons)?

b) What is the average rate of change of the number of gallons with respect to the number of miles?

For functions in Exercises 10 through 21,

a) Find a simplified difference quotient,
b) Complete the table at the right.

5. *Total revenue.* A firm determines that the total revenue (money coming in) from the sale of x units of a certain product is given by

$$R(x) = -0.01x^2 + 1000x,$$

where R(x) is in dollars.

a) Find R(301).

b) Find R(300).

c) Find R(301) − R(300).

d) Find $\dfrac{X(301) - R(300)}{301 - 300}$.

7. *Average velocity.* An object is dropped from a certain height. It is known that it will fall a distance s (in feet) in t seconds, given by

$$s(t) = 16t^2.$$

a) How far will the object fall in 3 seconds?

b) How far will the object fall in the next 2 seconds?

c) What is the average rate of change of distance with respect to time during this time? This is also *average velocity* or *speed*.

9. ▦ *National debt.* On December 12, 1978 the national debt was $776,327,000,000. On January 31, 1979 the national debt was $790,116,000,000. What was the average rate of change in the national debt with respect to time?

10. $f(x) = 5x^2$ **11.** $f(x) = 7x^2$ **12.** $f(x) = -5x^2$

13. $f(x) = -7x^2$ **14.** $f(x) = 5x^3$ **15.** $f(x) = 7x^3$

16. $f(x) = \dfrac{4}{x}$ **17.** $f(x) = \dfrac{5}{x}$ **18.** $f(x) = 2x + 3$

19. $f(x) = -2x + 5$ **20.** $f(x) = x^2 + x$ **21.** $f(x) = x^2 - x$

x	h	$\dfrac{f(x + h) - f(x)}{h}$
4	2	
4	1	
4	0.1	
4	0.01	

■

Find the simplified difference quotient.

22. $f(x) = mx + b$ **23.** $f(x) = ax^2 + bx + c$ **24.** $f(x) = ax^3 + bx^2$ **25.** $f(x) = \sqrt{x}$

7.3 DIFFERENTIATION USING LIMITS

Tangent Lines

A line tangent to a circle is a line that touches the circle exactly once.

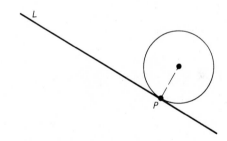

This definition becomes unworkable with other curves. For example, consider the following curve. Line L touches the curve at point P but meets the curve at other places. It will be considered a tangent line, but "touching at one point" cannot be its definition.

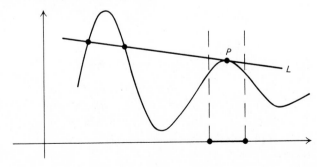

Note in the preceding figure that, over a suitably small interval containing *P*, line *L* does touch the curve exactly once. This is still not a suitable definition of *tangent line* because it allows a line like *M* in the following figure to be a tangent, which we will not accept.

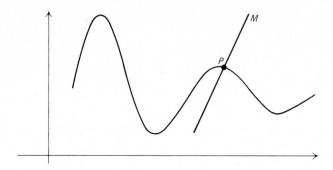

Later we will give a definition of a tangent line, but for now we will rely on intuition (experience). In the figure, L_1 and L_2 are not tangents. All the others are tangent lines.

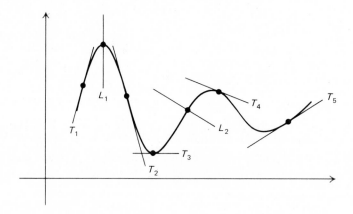

Why Do We Study Tangent Lines?

The reason for this will become evident later. To see briefly, look at the following graph of a total profit function. Note that the largest (or maximum) value of the function occurs where the graph has a horizontal tangent; that is, the tangent line has slope 0.

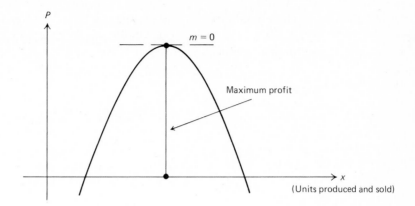

Differentiation Using Limits

We shall define *tangent* line in such a way that it makes sense for *any* curve. To do this we use the notion of limit.

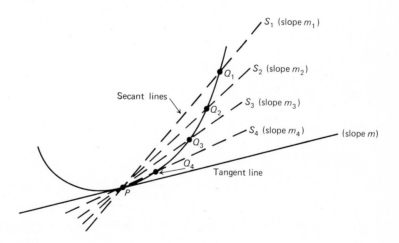

In this figure, we obtain the line tangent to the curve at point P by considering secant lines through P and neighboring points Q_1, Q_2, and so on. As the points Q approach P, the secant lines approach the tangent line. Each secant has a slope. The slopes of the secant lines approach the slope of the tangent line. In fact, we *define* the *tangent line* to be the line that contains the point P and has slope m, where m is the limit of the slopes of the secant lines as the points Q approach P.

How might we calculate the limit m? Suppose P has coordinates $(x, f(x))$. Then the first coordinate of Q is x plus some number h, or $x + h$. The coordinates of Q are $(x + h, f(x + h))$. Now from Section 7.2, we know that the slope of the secant line $\overleftrightarrow{PQ}$ is given by the difference quotient

$$\frac{f(x + h) - f(x)}{h}.$$

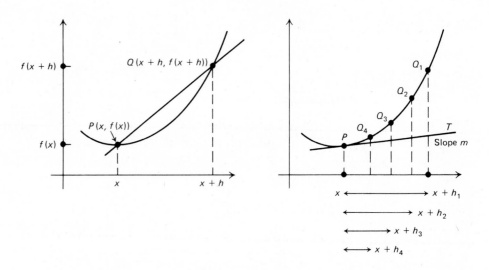

Now, as we see in the figure on the right above, as the points Q approach P, $x + h$ approaches x. That is, h approaches 0. Thus

$$\text{The slope of the tangent line } = m = \lim_{h \to 0} \frac{f(x + h) - f(x)}{h}.$$

The formal definition of the *derivative of a function f* can now be given. We will designate the derivative at x, $f'(x)$, rather than $m(x)$.

DEFINITION   **For a function $y = f(x)$, its derivative at x is defined as follows:**

$$f'(x) = \lim_{h \to 0} \frac{f(x + h) - f(x)}{h}.$$

This is the basic definition of *differential calculus*.

"Nothing in this world is so powerful as an idea whose time has come."

VICTOR HUGO

Let us now calculate some formulas for derivatives. That is, given a formula for a function f, we will be trying to find a formula for f'.

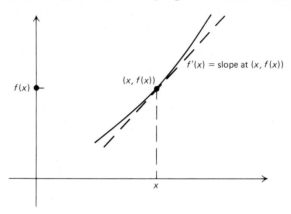

There are three steps in calculating a derivative.

a) Write down the difference quotient $\dfrac{f(x + h) - f(x)}{h}$.

b) Simplify the difference quotient.

c) Find the limit as $h \to 0$.

A formula for the derivative of a linear function

$$f(x) = mx + b$$

is

$$f'(x) = m.$$

Let us verify it using the definition.

Example 1   For $f(x) = mx + b$, find $f'(x)$.

Solution   a) $\dfrac{f(x + h) - f(x)}{h} = \dfrac{[m(x + h) + b] - (mx + b)}{h}$

b) $\dfrac{f(x + h) - f(x)}{h} = \dfrac{mx + mh + b - mx - b}{h} = \dfrac{mh}{h} = m$

c) $\lim\limits_{h \to 0} \dfrac{f(x + h) - f(x)}{h} = \lim\limits_{h \to 0} m = m,$

since m does not involve h. Thus

$$f'(x) = m.$$

Example 2 For $f(x) = x^2$, find $f'(4)$.

Solution a) $\dfrac{f(4 + h) - f(4)}{h} = \dfrac{(4 + h)^2 - 4^2}{h}$

b) $\dfrac{f(4 + h) - f(4)}{h} = \dfrac{16 + 8h + h^2 - 16}{h} = \dfrac{8h + h^2}{h}$

$$= \dfrac{h(8 + h)}{h} = 8 + h$$

c) $\lim\limits_{h \to 0} \dfrac{f(4 + h) - f(4)}{h} = \lim\limits_{h \to 0} (8 + h) = 8.$ Thus $f'(4) = 8$.

Example 3 For $f(x) = x^2$, find (the general formula) $f'(x)$.

Solution a) $\dfrac{f(x + h) - f(x)}{h} = \dfrac{(x + h)^2 - x^2}{h}$

b) In Example 5 of Section 7.2 we showed how this difference quotient can be simplified as follows:

$$\dfrac{f(x + h) - f(x)}{h} = 2x + h.$$

c) We want to find

$$\lim\limits_{h \to 0} \dfrac{f(x + h) - f(x)}{h} = \lim\limits_{h \to 0} (2x + h).$$

As $h \to 0$, we see that $2x + h \to 2x$. Thus

$$\lim\limits_{h \to 0} (2x + h) = 2x,$$

and we have

$$f'(x) = 2x,$$

which tells us, for example, that at $x = -3$, the curve has a tangent line whose slope is

$$f'(-3) = 2(-3), \quad \text{or} \quad -6.$$

We may say, simply, "The curve has slope -6."

Example 4 For $f(x) = x^3$, find $f'(x)$. Then find $f'(-1)$ and $f'(10)$.

Solution a) $\dfrac{f(x + h) - f(x)}{h} = \dfrac{(x + h)^3 - x^3}{h}$

b) In Example 6 of Section 7.2 we showed how this difference quotient can be simplified as follows:

$$\frac{f(x + h) - f(x)}{h} = 3x^2 + 3xh + h^2.$$

c) $\lim\limits_{h\to 0} \dfrac{f(x + h) - f(x)}{h} = \lim\limits_{h\to 0} (3x^2 + 3xh + h^2) = 3x^2$

An input–output table for this is shown on p. 335 of Section 7.1. Thus for $f(x) = x^3$, we have $f'(x) = 3x^2$. Then

$$f'(-1) = 3(-1)^2 = 3, \quad \text{and} \quad f'(10) = 3(10)^2 = 300.$$

Example 5 For $f(x) = \dfrac{3}{x}$, find $f'(x)$. Then find $f'(1)$ and $f'(2)$.

Solution a) $\dfrac{f(x + h) - f(x)}{h} = \dfrac{[3/(x + h)] - (3/x)}{h}$

b) In Example 7 of Section 7.2 we showed that this difference quotient can be simplified as follows:

$$\frac{f(x + h) - f(x)}{h} = \frac{-3}{x(x + h)}.$$

c) We want to find

$$\lim_{h\to 0} \frac{f(x + h) - f(x)}{h} = \lim_{h\to 0} \frac{-3}{x(x + h)}.$$

As $h \to 0$, $x + h \to x$, so we have

$$f'(x) = \lim_{h\to 0} \frac{-3}{x(x + h)} = \frac{-3}{x^2}.$$

Then

$$f'(1) = \frac{-3}{1^2} = -3, \quad \text{and} \quad f'(2) = \frac{-3}{2^2} = -\frac{3}{4}.$$

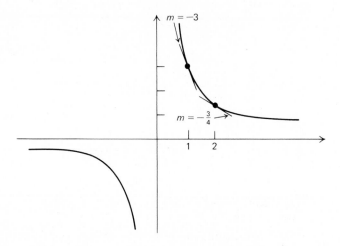

Note that $f'(0)$ does not exist because $f(0)$ does not exist. We say, "f is not differentiable at 0." When a function is not defined at a point, it is not differentiable at that point. In fact, if a function is discontinuous at a point, it is not differentiable at that point.

It can happen that a function f is defined and continuous at a point but that its derivative f' is not. The function f given by

$$f(x) = |x|$$

is an example. Note that

$$f(0) = |0| = 0,$$

so the function is defined at 0.

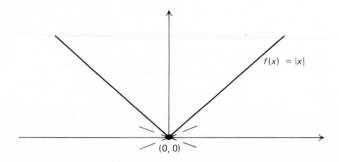

Suppose we tried to draw a tangent line at $(0, 0)$. A function like this with a corner (not smooth) would seem to have many tangents at $(0, 0)$, and hence many slopes. The derivative at such a point would not be unique. Let us try to calculate the derivative at 0.

Now

$$f'(x) = \lim_{h \to 0} \frac{|x + h| - |x|}{h}.$$

Thus at $x = 0$, we have

$$f'(0) = \lim_{h \to 0} \frac{|0 + h| - |0|}{h}$$

$$= \lim_{h \to 0} \frac{|h|}{h}.$$

h	$\dfrac{\|h\|}{h}$
2	$\dfrac{\|2\|}{2}$, or $\dfrac{2}{2}$, or 1
1	1
0.1	1
0.01	1
0.001	1

Look at the input–output tables. Note that as h approaches 0 from the right, $|h|/h$ approaches 1, but as h approaches 0 from the left, $|h|/h$ approaches -1. Thus

$$\lim_{h \to 0} \frac{|h|}{h} \text{ does not exist,}$$

so

$$f'(0) \text{ does not exist.}$$

h	$\dfrac{\|h\|}{h}$
-2	$\dfrac{\|-2\|}{-2}$, or $\dfrac{2}{-2}$, or -1
-1	-1
-0.1	-1
-0.01	-1
-0.001	-1

If a function has a "sharp point" or "corner," it will not have a derivative at that point.

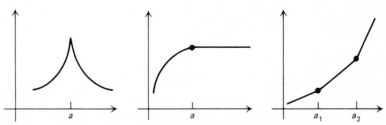

A function may also fail to be differentiable at a point by having a vertical tangent at that point. The following function has a vertical tangent at point a.

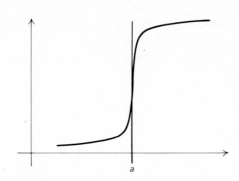

Recall that vertical lines have no slope, and hence there is no derivative at such a point.

Each of the preceding examples, including $f(x) = |x|$, is continuous at each point in an interval I but not differentiable at each point in I. That is, continuity does not imply differentiability. On the other hand, *if we know that a function is differentiable at each point in an interval I, then it is continuous over I.* The function $f(x) = x^2$ is an example. Also, *if a function is discontinuous at some point a, then it is not differentiable at a.* Thus when we know a function is differentiable over an interval, it is *smooth* in the sense that there are no "sharp points," "corners," or "breaks" in the graph.

EXERCISE SET 7.3

For each function, find $f'(x)$. Then find $f'(-2)$, $f'(-1)$, $f'(0)$, $f'(1)$, and $f'(2)$, if they exist.

1. $f(x) = 5x^2$ **2.** $f(x) = 7x^2$ **3.** $f(x) = -5x^2$ **4.** $f(x) = -7x^2$

5. $f(x) = 5x^3$ **6.** $f(x) = 7x^3$ **7.** $f(x) = 2x + 3$ **8.** $f(x) = -2x + 5$

9. $f(x) = -4x$ **10.** $f(x) = \frac{1}{2}x$ **11.** $f(x) = x^2 + x$ **12.** $f(x) = x^2 - x$

13. $f(x) = \dfrac{4}{x}$ **14.** $f(x) = \dfrac{5}{x}$ **15.** $f(x) = mx$ **16.** $f(x) = ax^2 + bx + c$

17. List the points in the graph below at which the function is not differentiable.

18. *The postage function.* Consider the postage function defined in Exercise Set 7.1. At what values is the function not differentiable?

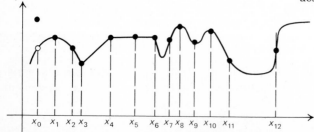

19. Consider the function f given by

$$f(x) = \frac{x^2 - 9}{x + 3}.$$

For what values is this function not differentiable?

■ ──

20. Find $f'(x)$, where $f(x) = \sqrt{x}$.

7.4   DIFFERENTIATION TECHNIQUES: POWER AND SUM-DIFFERENCE RULES

Leibniz's Notation

When y is a function of x, we will also designate the derivative, $f'(x)$, as follows

$$\frac{dy}{dx},$$

which is read "the derivative of y with respect to x." This notation was invented by the German mathematician Leibniz. It does *not* mean dy divided by dx! (That is, we cannot interpret dy/dx as a quotient until meanings are given to dy and dx, which we will not do here.) For example, if $y = x^2$, then

$$\frac{dy}{dx} = 2x.$$

We may also write

$$\frac{d}{dx} f(x)$$

to denote the derivative of f with respect to x. For example,

$$\frac{d}{dx} x^2 = 2x.$$

The value of $\frac{dy}{dx}$ when $x = 5$ can be denoted by

$$\left. \frac{dy}{dx} \right|_{x=5}.$$

Thus for $\frac{dy}{dx} = 2x$,

$$\left. \frac{dy}{dx} \right|_{x=5} = 2 \cdot 5, \text{ or } 10.$$

In general, for $y = f(x)$,

$$\frac{dy}{dx}\bigg|_{x=a} = f'(a).$$

The German mathematician and philosopher Gottfried Wilhelm von Leibniz (1646–1716) and the English mathematician, philosopher, and physicist Sir Isaac Newton (1642–1727) are both credited with the invention of the calculus, though each made the invention independent of the other. Newton used the dot notation $\dot{y}$ for dy/dt, where y is a function of time, and this notation is still used, though it is not as prevalent as Leibniz's notation.

The Power Rule

In the remainder of this section we will develop rules and techniques for efficient differentiating.

This table contains functions and derivatives that we have found in previous work. Look for a pattern.

Function	Derivative
x^2	$2x^1$
x^3	$3x^2$
x^{-1}, or $\dfrac{1}{x}$	$-1 \cdot x^{-2}$, or $-\dfrac{1}{x^2}$

Perhaps you have discovered the following.

POWER RULE   **For any real number a,**

$$\frac{d}{dx} x^a = a \cdot x^{a-1}.$$

Note that this rule holds no matter what the exponent. That is, to differentiate x^a, write down the exponent a, followed by x with an exponent 1 less than a.

① Bring down the exponent as a factor.

② Subtract 1 from the exponent.

Example 1 $\dfrac{d}{dx} x^5 = 5x^4$

Example 2 $\dfrac{d}{dx} x = 1 \cdot x^{1-1} = 1 \cdot x^0 = 1$

Example 3 $\dfrac{d}{dx} x^{-4} = -4 \cdot x^{-4-1} = -4x^{-5}$, or $-4 \cdot \dfrac{1}{x^5}$, or $-\dfrac{4}{x^5}$

The Power Rule allows us to differentiate $\sqrt{x}$.

Example 4 $\dfrac{d}{dx} \sqrt{x} = \dfrac{d}{dx} x^{1/2} = \dfrac{1}{2} \cdot x^{1/2-1} = \dfrac{1}{2} x^{-1/2}$, or $\dfrac{1}{2} \cdot \dfrac{1}{x^{1/2}}$, or $\dfrac{1}{2} \cdot \dfrac{1}{\sqrt{x}}$, or $\dfrac{1}{2\sqrt{x}}$

Example 5 $\dfrac{d}{dx} x^{-2/3} = -\dfrac{2}{3} x^{(-2/3)-1} = -\dfrac{2}{3} x^{-5/3}$, or $-\dfrac{2}{3} \dfrac{1}{x^{5/3}}$, or $-\dfrac{2}{3\sqrt[3]{x^5}}$

The Derivative of a Constant Times a Function

Look at the graph of the constant function $f(x) = c$. What is the slope at each point P on the graph? It follows that

the derivative of a constant function is 0.

Examples $\dfrac{d}{dx} 3 = 0, \quad \dfrac{d}{dx}\left(-\dfrac{1}{4}\right) = 0$

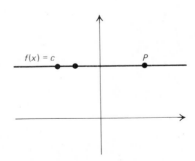

Now let us consider differentiating functions like

$$f(x) = 5x^2 \quad \text{and} \quad g(x) = -7x^4.$$

Note that we already know how to differentiate x^2 and x^4. Let us again look for a pattern in the results of Section 7.3.

Function	Derivative
$5x^2$	$10x$
$-4x$	-4
$-7x^2$	$-14x$
$5x^3$	$15x^2$

Perhaps you have discovered the following:

The derivative of a constant times a function is the constant times the derivative of the function. Using derivative notation this can be written

$$\frac{d}{dx} [c \cdot f(x)] = c \cdot f'(x).$$

Combining this rule with the Power Rule allows us to find many derivatives.

Example 6 $\dfrac{d}{dx} 5x^4 = 5\dfrac{d}{dx} x^4 = 5 \cdot 4 \cdot x^{4-1} = 20x^3$

Example 7 $\dfrac{d}{dx} - 9x = -9 \dfrac{d}{dx} x = -9 \cdot 1 = -9$

With practice you will be able to differentiate many such functions in one step.

Example 8 $\dfrac{d}{dx} \dfrac{-4}{x^2} = \dfrac{d}{dx} - 4x^{-2} = -4 \cdot \dfrac{d}{dx} x^{-2} = -4(-2)x^{-2-1} = 8x^{-3}$, or $\dfrac{8}{x^3}$

Example 9 $\dfrac{d}{dx} - x^{0.7} = -1 \cdot \dfrac{d}{dx} x^{0.7} = -1 \cdot 0.7 \cdot x^{0.7-1} = -0.7x^{-0.3}$

The Derivative of a Sum or Difference

In Exercise 11 of Exercise Set 7.3 you found that for

$$f(x) = x^2 + x$$

the derivative is

$$f'(x) = 2x + 1.$$

Note that the derivative of x^2 is $2x$, and the derivative of x is 1; and the sum of these derivatives is $f'(x)$. This illustrates the following:

**SUM–
DIFFERENCE
RULE**

a) **The derivative of a sum is the sum of the derivatives:**

$$\text{if } t(x) = f(x) + g(x), \quad \text{then } t'(x) = f'(x) + g'(x).$$

b) **The derivative of a difference is the difference of the derivatives:**

$$\text{if } t(x) = f(x) - g(x), \quad \text{then } t'(x) = f'(x) - g'(x).$$

Any function that is a sum or difference of several terms can be differentiated term by term.

Example 10 $\dfrac{d}{dx}(3x + 7) = \dfrac{d}{dx}(3x) + \dfrac{d}{dx}(7) = 3\dfrac{d}{dx}x + 0 = 3 \cdot 1 = 3$

Example 11 $\dfrac{d}{dx}(5x^3 - 3x^2) = \dfrac{d}{dx}(5x^3) - \dfrac{d}{dx}(3x^2) = 5\dfrac{d}{dx}x^3 - 3\dfrac{d}{dx}x^2$

$$= 5 \cdot 3x^2 - 3 \cdot 2x = 15x^2 - 6x$$

Example 12 $\dfrac{d}{dx}\left(24x - \sqrt{x} + \dfrac{2}{x}\right) = \dfrac{d}{dx}(24x) - \dfrac{d}{dx}(\sqrt{x}) + \dfrac{d}{dx}\left(\dfrac{2}{x}\right)$

$$= 24 \cdot \dfrac{d}{dx}x - \dfrac{d}{dx}x^{1/2} + 2 \cdot \dfrac{d}{dx}x^{-1}$$

$$= 24 \cdot 1 - \dfrac{1}{2}x^{(1/2)-1} + 2(-1)x^{-1-1}$$

$$= 24 - \dfrac{1}{2}x^{-1/2} - 2x^{-2}$$

$$= 24 - \dfrac{1}{2\sqrt{x}} - \dfrac{2}{x^2}$$

A word of caution! The derivative of

$$f(x) + c,$$

a function plus a constant, is just the derivative of the function

$$f'(x).$$

The derivative of

$$c \cdot f(x),$$

a function times a constant, is the constant times the derivative

$$c \cdot f'(x).$$

That is, for a product the constant is retained, but for a sum it is not.

It is important to be able to determine points at which the tangent line to a curve has a certain slope—that is, points at which the derivative attains a certain value.

Example 13   Find the points on the graph of $y = -x^3 + 6x^2$ at which the tangent line is horizontal.

Solution   A horizontal tangent has slope 0. Thus we seek the values of x for which $dy/dx = 0$. That is, we want to find x such that

$$-3x^2 + 12x = 0.$$

We factor and solve:

$$x(-3x + 12) = 0.$$

$$x = 0 \quad \text{or} \quad -3x + 12 = 0$$

$$x = 0 \quad \text{or} \quad -3x = -12$$

$$x = 0 \quad \text{or} \quad x = 4$$

We are to find the points *on the graph*, so we have to determine the second coordinates from the original equation $y = -x^3 + 6x^2$.

For $x = 0$, $y = -0^3 + 6 \cdot 0^2 = 0$.

For $x = 4$, $y = -(4)^3 + 6 \cdot 4^2 = -64 + 96 = 32$.

Thus the points we are seeking are $(0, 0)$ and $(4, 32)$.

Example 14   Find the points on the graph of $y = -x^3 + 6x^2$ at which the tangent has slope 6.

Solution   We want to find values of x for which $dy/dx = 6$. That is, we want to find x such that

$$-3x^2 + 12x = 6.$$

To solve, we add -6 and get

$$-3x^2 + 12x - 6 = 0.$$

We can simplify this equation by multiplying by $-\frac{1}{3}$, since each term has a common factor of -3. We get

$$x^2 - 4x + 2 = 0.$$

This is a quadratic equation, not readily factorable, so we use the quadratic formula, where $a = 1$, $b = -4$, and $c = 2$:

$$x = \frac{-b \pm \sqrt{b^2 - 4ac}}{2a} = \frac{-(-4) \pm \sqrt{(-4)^2 - 4 \cdot 1 \cdot 2}}{2 \cdot 1}$$

$$= \frac{4 \pm \sqrt{8}}{2} = \frac{2 \cdot 2 \pm 2\sqrt{2}}{2 \cdot 1}$$

$$= \frac{2}{2} \cdot \frac{2 \pm \sqrt{2}}{1} = 2 \pm \sqrt{2}.$$

The solutions are $2 + \sqrt{2}$ and $2 - \sqrt{2}$. We determine the second coordinates from the original equation. For $x = 2 + \sqrt{2}$,

$$y = -(2 + \sqrt{2})^3 + 6(2 + \sqrt{2})^2$$

$$= -[(2 + \sqrt{2})^2(2 + \sqrt{2})] + 6(4 + 4\sqrt{2} + 2)$$

$$= -[(6 + 4\sqrt{2})(2 + \sqrt{2})] + 6(6 + 4\sqrt{2})$$

$$= -[12 + 6\sqrt{2} + 8\sqrt{2} + 8] + 36 + 24\sqrt{2}$$

$$= -[20 + 14\sqrt{2}] + 36 + 24\sqrt{2}$$

$$= -20 - 14\sqrt{2} + 36 + 24\sqrt{2} = 16 + 10\sqrt{2}.$$

Similarly, for $x = 2 - \sqrt{2}$,

$$y = 16 - 10\sqrt{2}.$$

Thus the points we are seeking are

$$(2 + \sqrt{2}, 16 + 10\sqrt{2}) \quad \text{and} \quad (2 - \sqrt{2}, 16 - 10\sqrt{2}).$$

We illustrate the results of Examples 13 and 14 in the following graph. You will not be asked to sketch such graphs at this time.

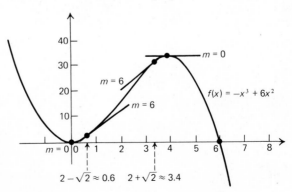

EXERCISE SET 7.4

Find $\dfrac{dy}{dx}$.

1. $y = x^7$

2. $y = x^8$

3. $y = 15$

4. $y = 78$

5. $y = 4x^{150}$

6. $y = 7x^{200}$

7. $y = x^3 + 3x^2$

8. $y = x^4 - 7x$

9. $y = 8\sqrt{x}$

10. $y = 4\sqrt{x}$

11. $y = x^{0.07}$

12. $y = x^{0.78}$

13. $y = \frac{1}{2}x^{4/5}$

14. $y = -4.8x^{1/3}$

15. $y = x^{-3}$

16. $y = x^{-4}$

17. $y = 3x^2 - 8x + 7$

18. $y = 4x^2 - 7x + 5$

19. $y = \sqrt[4]{x} - \dfrac{1}{x}$

20. $y = \sqrt[5]{x} - \dfrac{2}{x}$

Find $f'(x)$.

21. $f(x) = 0.64x^{2.5}$

22. $f(x) = 0.32x^{12.5}$

23. $f(x) = \dfrac{5}{x} - x$

24. $f(x) = \dfrac{4}{x} - x$

25. $f(x) = 4x - 7$

26. $f(x) = 7x + 11$

27. $f(x) = 4x + 9$

28. $f(x) = 7x - 14$

29. $f(x) = \dfrac{x^4}{4}$

30. $f(x) = \dfrac{x^3}{3}$

31. $f(x) = -0.01x^2 - 0.5x + 70$

32. $f(x) = -0.01x^2 + 0.4x + 50$

33. $f(x) = 3x^{-2/3} + x^{3/4} + x^{6/5} + \dfrac{8}{x^3}$

34. $f(x) = x^{-3/4} - 3x^{2/3} + x^{5/4} + \dfrac{2}{x^4}$

For each function, find the points on the graph at which the tangent line is horizontal.

35. $y = x^2$

36. $y = -x^2$

37. $y = -x^3$

38. $y = x^3$

39. $y = 3x^2 - 5x + 4$

40. $y = 5x^2 - 3x + 8$

41. $y = -0.01x^2 - 0.5x + 70$

42. $y = -0.01x^2 + 0.4x + 50$

43. $y = 2x + 4$

44. $y = -2x + 5$

45. $y = 4$

46. $y = -3$

47. $y = -x^3 + x^2 + 5x - 1$

48. $y = -\frac{1}{3}x^3 + 6x^2 - 11x - 50$

49. $y = \frac{1}{3}x^3 - 3x + 2$

50. $y = x^3 - 6x + 1$

For each function, find the points on the graph at which the tangent line has slope 1.

51. $y = 20x - x^2$

52. $y = 6x - x^2$

53. $y = -0.025x^2 + 4x$

54. $y = -0.01x^2 + 2x$

55. $y = \frac{1}{3}x^3 + 2x^2 + 2x$

56. $y = \frac{1}{3}x^3 - x^2 - 4x + 1$

57. Find the points on the graph of
$$y = x^4 - \tfrac{4}{3}x^2 - 4$$
at which the tangent line is horizontal.

58. Find the points on the graph of
$$y = 2x^6 - x^4 - 2$$
at which the tangent line is horizontal.

Find dy/dx. Each of the following can be differentiated using the rules developed in this section, but some algebra may be required beforehand.

59. $y = x(x - 1)$

60. $y = (x - 1)(x + 1)$

61. $y = (x - 2)(x + 3)$

62. $y = \dfrac{5x^2 - 8x + 3}{8}$

63. $y = \dfrac{x^5 + x}{x^2}$

64. $y = (5x)^2$

65. $y = (-4x)^3$

66. $y = \sqrt{7x}$

67. $y = \sqrt[3]{8x}$

68. $y = (x - 3)^2$

69. $y = (x + 1)^3$

70. $y = (x - 2)^3(x + 1)$

7.5 APPLICATIONS AND RATES OF CHANGE

Instantaneous Rate of Change

A car travels 100 miles in 2 hours. Its *average* speed (or velocity) is 100 mi/2 hr, or 50 mi/hr. This is the *average rate of change* of distance with respect to time. At various times during the trip the speedometer did not read 50, however. Thus we say that 50 is the *average*. A snapshot of the speedometer taken at any instant would indicate *instantaneous* speed, or rate of change.

Average rates of change are given by difference quotients. If distance s is a function of time t, then average velocity is given by

$$\text{Average velocity} = \frac{s(t + h) - s(t)}{h}.$$

Instantaneous rates of change are found by letting $h \to 0$. Thus

$$\text{Instantaneous velocity} = \lim_{h \to 0} \frac{s(t + h) - s(t)}{h} = s'(t).$$

In general, derivatives give instantaneous rates of change.

RATE OF CHANGE
If y is a function of x, then the (instantaneous) *rate of change of y with respect to x* is given by the derivative

$$\frac{dy}{dx}, \quad \text{or } f'(x).$$

Example 1   The XYZ Company makes ball bearings. The volume of a bearing changes as it is heated. The spherical volume V of a ball bearing is given by

$$V = \tfrac{4}{3}\pi r^3,$$

where r is the radius of the ball bearing, in centimeters.

a) Find the rate of change of the volume with respect to the radius.

b) Find the rate of change of volume at $r = 1.2$ cm.

Solution   a) $\dfrac{dV}{dr} = V'(r) = \frac{4}{3} \cdot 3 \cdot \pi r^2 = 4\pi r^2.$

b) $V'(1.2) = 4\pi(1.2)^2 = 5.76\pi \approx 18 \dfrac{\text{cm}^3}{\text{cm}} = 18 \text{ cm}^2.$

Example 2   The initial population of a city is 10,000. After t years the population grows to a number $P(t)$ given by

$$P(t) = 10,000(1 + 0.86t + t^2)$$

a) Find the rate of change of the population P with respect to time t. This is also known as the *growth rate*.

b) Find what the population will be after 5 years. Also find the growth rate when $t = 5$.

Solution   a) Note $P(t) = 10,000 + 8600t + 10,000t^2$. Then

$$P'(t) = 8600 + 20,000t.$$

b) The population when $t = 5$ yr is given by

$$P(5) = 10,000 + 8600 \cdot 5 + 10,000 \cdot 5^2 = 303,000.$$

The growth rate when $t = 5$ is given by

$$P'(5) = 8600 + 20,000 \cdot 5 = 108,600 \frac{\text{people}}{\text{yr}}.$$

Thus at $t = 5$, there are 303,000 people, and the population is growing at the rate of 108,600 people per year.

Rates of Change in Economics

In the study of economics we are frequently interested in how such quantities as cost, revenue, and profit change with an increase in product quantity. In particular, we are interested in what is called *marginal** cost or profit (or whatever). This term is used to signify *rate of change with respect*

---

* The word "marginal" comes from the Marginalist School of Economic Thought, which originated in Austria for the purpose of applying mathematics and statistics to the study of economics.

to quantity. Thus, if

$$C(x) = \text{the total cost of producing x units of a product}$$
(usually considered in some time period),

then

$$C'(x) = \text{the marginal cost}$$
$$= \text{the rate of change of the total cost with respect}$$
to the number of units, x, produced.

Let us think about these interpretations. The total cost of producing 5 units of a product is $C(5)$. The rate of change $C'(5)$ is the cost per unit at that stage in the production process. That this cost per unit does not include fixed costs is seen in this example.

$$C(x) = \underbrace{(x^2 + 4x)}_{\text{Variable costs}} + \underbrace{\$10,000}_{\text{Fixed costs (constant)}}$$

Then

$$C'(x) = 2x + 4.$$

This is because the derivative of a constant is 0. This verifies an economic principle that says the fixed costs of a company have no effect on marginal cost.

Following are some other marginal functions. Recall that

$$R(x) = \text{the total revenue from the sale of x units.}$$

Then

$$R'(x) = \text{the marginal revenue}$$

$$= \text{the rate of change of the total revenue with}$$
respect to the number x of units sold.

Also

$$P(x) = \text{the total profit from the production and sale}$$
of x units of a product,

$$= R(x) - C(x).$$

Then

$$P'(x) = \text{the marginal profit}$$

$$= \text{the rate of change of the total profit with}$$
respect to the number of units x produced
and sold

$$= R'(x) - C'(x).$$

Example 3   Given

$$R(x) = 50x,$$

$$C(x) = 2x^3 - 12x^2 + 40x + 10,$$

find

a) $P(x)$

b) $R(2), C(2), P(2)$

c) $R'(x), C'(x), P'(x)$

d) $R'(2), C'(2), P'(2)$

Solution   a) $P(x) = R(x) - C(x) = 50x - (2x^3 - 12x^2 + 40x + 10)$

$$= -2x^3 + 12x^2 + 10x - 10.$$

b) $R(2) = 50 \cdot 2 = \$100$ (the total revenue from the sale of the first 2 units)

$C(2) = 2 \cdot 2^3 - 12 \cdot 2^2 + 40 \cdot 2 + 10 = \$58$ (the total cost of producing the first 2 units)

$P(2) = R(2) - C(2) = \$100 - \$58 = \$42$ (the total profit from the production and sale of the first 2 units)

c) $R'(x) = 50$

$C'(x) = 6x^2 - 24x + 40$

$P'(x) = R'(x) - C'(x) = 50 - (6x^2 - 24x + 40) = -6x^2 + 24x + 10$

d) $R'(2) = \$50$ per unit

$C'(2) = 6 \cdot 2^2 - 24 \cdot 2 + 40 = \$16$ per unit

$P'(2) = \$50 - \$16 = \$34$ per unit

Note that marginal revenue is constant. No matter how much is produced and sold, the revenue per unit stays the same. This may not always be the case. Also note that $C'(2)$, or \$16 per unit, is not the average cost per unit, which is given by

$$\frac{\text{Total cost of producing 2 units}}{\text{2 units}} = \frac{\$58}{2} = \$29 \text{ per unit.}$$

In general,

$$A(x) = \text{average cost of producing } x \text{ units} = \frac{C(x)}{x}.$$

Let us look at a typical marginal cost function, C', and its associated total cost function C.

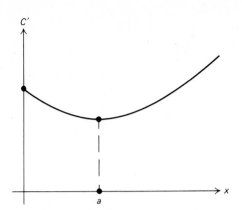

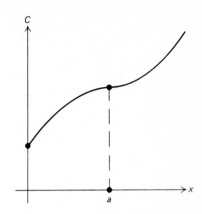

Marginal cost normally decreases as more units are produced until it reaches some minimum value at a, and then it increases. This is probably due to something like having to pay overtime or buying more machinery. Since $C'(x)$ represents slope of $C(x)$ and is positive and decreasing up to a, the graph turns downward as x goes from 0 to a. Then past a it turns upward.

EXERCISE SET 7.5

1. Given

$$R(x) = 50x - 0.5x^2,$$
$$C(x) = 4x + 10,$$

find

a) $P(x)$,

b) $R(20)$, $C(20)$, $P(20)$,

c) $R'(x)$, $C'(x)$, $P'(x)$,

d) $R'(20)$, $C'(20)$, $P'(20)$.

3. *Total Sales.* The total sales of a company are given by

$$S(t) = -0.1t^2 + 1.2t + 98.6,$$

where T is the total sales, in thousands, at time t, measured in days.

a) Find the rate of change of sales with respect to time.

b) Find the sales at $t = 2$ days.

c) Find the rate of change at $t = 2$ days.

2. Given

$$R(x) = 5x,$$
$$C(x) = 0.001x^2 + 1.2x + 60,$$

find

a) $P(x)$,

b) $R(100)$, $C(100)$, $P(100)$,

c) $R'(x)$, $C'(x)$, $P'(x)$,

d) $R'(100)$, $C'(100)$, $P'(100)$.

4. *Advertising.* A firm estimates that it will sell N units of a product after spending a dollars on advertising, where

$$N(a) = -a^2 + 300a + 6,$$

and a is measured in thousands of dollars.

a) What is the rate of change of the number of units sold with respect to the amount spent on advertising?

b) How many units will be sold after spending $10 thousand on advertising?

c) What is the rate of change at $a = 10$?

5. The Levitt Company has a salesperson cover a territory whose circumference is given by

$$C = 2\pi r,$$

where r is the radius, in miles. Find the rate of change of the circumference with respect to the radius.

6. Given

$$R(x) = 50x - 0.5x^2,$$
$$C(x) = 10x + 3,$$

find

a) $P(x)$

b) $R(40)$, $C(40)$, $P(40)$

c) $R'(x)$, $C'(x)$, $P'(x)$

d) $R'(40)$, $C'(40)$, $P'(40)$

e) Is the marginal revenue constant?

7. The LWH Company makes cardboard cartons. The volume V of a cubical carton with a side of length s, in feet, is given by

$$V = s^3.$$

a) Find the rate of change of the volume V with respect to the length s of a side.

b) Find the rate of change of volume when $s = 10$ ft.

8. The PDQ Company makes commemorative coins. The circular area A, in square centimeters, of a coin is given by

$$A = \pi r^2,$$

where r is the radius, in centimeters. Find the rate of change of the area with respect to the radius.

9. *Population growth rate.* The population of a city grows from an initial size of 100,000 to an amount P given by

$$P = 100{,}000 + 2000t^2,$$

where t is measured in years.

a) Find the growth rate.

b) Find the number of people in the city after 10 years (at $t = 10$ yr).

c) Find the growth rate at $t = 10$ yr.

10. *Percentage of the population in college.* The percentage of the population in college is given by a linear function

$$P(t) = 1.25t + 15,$$

where $P(t) = $ percentage in college the t'th year after 1940. Find the rate of change of the percentage P with respect to time t.

7.6 DIFFERENTIATION TECHNIQUES: PRODUCT AND QUOTIENT RULES

The derivative of a sum is the sum of the derivatives, but the derivative of a product is *not* the product of the derivatives. To see this, consider x^2 and x^5. The product is x^7, and the derivative of this product is $7x^6$. The individual derivatives are $2x$ and $5x^4$, and the product of these derivatives is $10x^5$, which is not $7x^6$.

The following is the rule for finding the derivative of a product.

PRODUCT RULE

If $p(x) = f(x) \cdot g(x)$, then,

$$p'(x) = f(x) \cdot g'(x) + f'(x) \cdot g(x).$$

The derivative of a product is the first factor times the derivative of the second factor, plus the derivative of the first factor times the second factor.

Let us check this for $x^2 \cdot x^5$. There are four steps.

1. Write down the first factor.
2. Multiply it by the derivative of the second factor.
3. Write the derivative of the first factor.
4. Multiply it by the second factor.

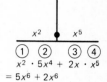

Example 1

$$\frac{d}{dx}(x^4 - 2x^3 - 7)(3x^2 - 5x) = (x^4 - 2x^3 - 7)(6x - 5)$$
$$+ (4x^3 - 6x^2)(3x^2 - 5x)$$

Note that we could have multiplied the polynomials and then differentiated, avoiding the Product Rule, but this would have been more work.

The derivative of a quotient is *not* the quotient of the derivatives. To see why, consider x^5 and x^2. The quotient x^5/x^2 is x^3, and the derivative of this quotient is $3x^2$. The individual derivatives are $5x^4$ and $2x$, and the quotient of these derivatives $5x^4/2x$ is $(5/2)x^3$, which is not $3x^2$. The rule for differentiating quotients is as follows:

QUOTIENT RULE

If $q(x) = \dfrac{f(x)}{g(x)}$, then

$$q'(x) = \frac{g(x) \cdot f'(x) - g'(x) \cdot f(x)}{[g(x)]^2}.$$

The derivative of a quotient is the denominator times the derivative of the numerator, minus the derivative of the denominator times the numerator, all divided by the square of the denominator.

Another way to remember this is shown below. It starts with squaring the denominator. The denominator is also used as the first factor of the first term above.

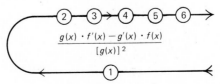

1. Square the denominator.
2. Write down the denominator.
3. Multiply the denominator by the derivative of the numerator.
4. Write a minus sign.
5. Find the derivative of the denominator.
6. Multiply it by the numerator.

Example 2   For $q(x) = x^5/x^3$, find $q'(x)$.

Solution
$$q'(x) = \frac{x^3 \cdot 5x^4 - 3x^2 \cdot x^5}{[x^3]^2} = \frac{5x^7 - 3x^7}{x^6} = \frac{2x^7}{x^6} = 2x$$

Example 3   Differentiate $\dfrac{1 + x^2}{x^3}$. This means find

$$\frac{d}{dx} f(x)$$

where $f(x)$ is given by

$$f(x) = \frac{1 + x^2}{x^3} .$$

Solution
$$\frac{d}{dx}\left(\frac{1 + x^2}{x^3}\right) = \frac{x^3 \cdot 2x - 3x^2(1 + x^2)}{(x^3)^2} = \frac{2x^4 - 3x^2 - 3x^4}{x^6}$$

$$= \frac{-x^4 - 3x^2}{x^6} = \frac{-1 \cdot x^2 \cdot x^2 - 3x^2}{x^6}$$

$$= \frac{x^2(-x^2 - 3)}{x^6} = \frac{-x^2 - 3}{x^4}$$

Example 4   Differentiate $\dfrac{x^2 - 3x}{x - 1}$.

Solution
$$\frac{d}{dx}\left(\frac{x^2 - 3x}{x - 1}\right) = \frac{(x - 1)(2x - 3) - 1(x^2 - 3x)}{(x - 1)^2}$$

$$= \frac{2x^2 - 5x + 3 - x^2 + 3x}{(x - 1)^2}$$

$$= \frac{x^2 - 2x + 3}{(x - 1)^2} .$$

It is not necessary to multiply out $(x - 1)^2$.

An Application

We discussed earlier that it is more typical for a total revenue function to vary depending on the number x of units sold. Let us see what can determine this. Recall the consumer's demand function $p = D(x)$, discussed on p. 103. It is the price p a seller must charge in order to sell exactly x units of a product. This is typically a decreasing function.

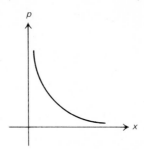

The total revenue from the sale of x units is then given by

$$R(x) = \text{(number of units sold)} \cdot \text{(price charged to sell the units)},$$

or

$$R(x) = x \cdot p = xD(x).$$

A typical graph of a revenue function is shown below.

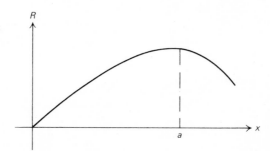

To sell more units, $D(x)$ decreases. Because we have a product $x \cdot D(x)$, the revenue typically rises for a while as x increases but tapers off as $D(x)$ gets smaller and smaller.

Using the Product Rule, one can obtain an expression for the marginal revenue $R'(x)$ in terms of x and $D'(x)$ as follows:

$$R(x) = xD(x),$$

so

$$R'(x) = 1 \cdot D(x) + x \cdot D'(x) = D(x) + xD'(x).$$

You need not memorize this. One can merely repeat the Product Rule where necessary.

EXERCISE SET 7.6

Differentiate. That is, find $\dfrac{d}{dx} f(x)$ where $f(x)$ is as follows.

1. $x^3 \cdot x^8$; two ways

2. $x^4 \cdot x^9$; two ways

3. $\dfrac{-1}{x}$; two ways

4. $\dfrac{1}{x}$; two ways

5. $\dfrac{x^8}{x^5}$; two ways

6. $\dfrac{x^9}{x^5}$; two ways

7. $(8x^5 - 3x^2 + 20)(8x^4 - 3\sqrt{x})$

8. $(7x^6 + 4x^3 - 50)(9x^{10} - 7\sqrt{x})$

9. $x(300 - x)$

10. $x(400 - x)$

11. $\dfrac{x}{300 - x}$

12. $\dfrac{x}{400 - x}$

13. $\dfrac{3x - 1}{2x + 5}$

14. $\dfrac{2x + 3}{x - 5}$

15. $\dfrac{x^2 + 1}{x^3 - 1}$

16. $\dfrac{x^3 - 1}{x^2 + 1}$

17. $\dfrac{x}{1 - x}$

18. $\dfrac{x}{3 - x}$

19. $\dfrac{x - 1}{x + 1}$

20. $\dfrac{x + 2}{x - 2}$

21. $\dfrac{1}{x - 3}$

22. $\dfrac{1}{x + 2}$

23. $\dfrac{3x^2 + 2x}{x^2 + 1}$

24. $\dfrac{3x^2 - 5x}{x^2 - 1}$

25. $\dfrac{3x^2 - 5x}{x^8}$

26. $\dfrac{3x^2 + 2x}{x^5}$

In each of Exercises 27–30, a demand function $p = D(x)$ is given. Find

a) Total revenue $R(x)$,

b) marginal revenue $R'(x)$.

27. $D(x) = 400 - x$

28. $D(x) = 500 - x$

29. $D(x) = \dfrac{4000}{x} + 3$

30. $D(x) = \dfrac{3000}{x} + 5$

31. In Section 2.5, we defined the average cost of producing x units of a product in terms of the total cost $C(x)$ by

$$A(x) = \frac{C(x)}{x}.$$

Use the Quotient Rule to find a general expression for *marginal average cost* $A'(x)$.

32. In this section we determined that

$$R(x) = xD(x).$$

Then

$$D(x) = \frac{R(x)}{x} = \text{average revenue from the sale of } x \text{ units.}$$

Use the Quotient Rule to find a general expression for *marginal average revenue* $D'(x)$.

■

Differentiate each function.

33. $f(x) = \dfrac{x^3}{\sqrt{x} - 5}$

34. $g(t) = \dfrac{1 + \sqrt{t}}{t^5 + 3}$

35. $f(v) = \dfrac{3}{1 + v + v^2}$

36. $g(z) = \dfrac{1 + z + z^2}{1 - z + z^2}$

37. $p(t) = \dfrac{t}{1 - t + t^2 - t^3}$

38. $f(x) = \dfrac{\dfrac{2}{3x} - 1}{\dfrac{3}{x^2} + 5}$

39. $h(x) = \dfrac{x^3 + 5x^2 - 2}{\sqrt{x}}$

40. $y(t) = 5t(t - 1)(2t + 3)$

41. $f(x) = x(3x^3 + 6x - 2)(3x^4 + 7)$

42. $g(x) = (x^3 - 8) \cdot \dfrac{x^2 + 1}{x^2 - 1}$

43. $f(t) = (t^5 + 3) \cdot \dfrac{t^3 - 1}{t^3 + 1}$

44. $f(x) = \dfrac{(x^2 + 3x)(x^5 - 7x^2 - 3)}{x^4 - 3x^3 - 5}$

45. $f(x) = \dfrac{(2x^2 + 3)(4x^3 - 7x + 2)}{x^7 - 2x^6 + 9}$

46. $s(t) = \dfrac{5t^8 - 2t^3}{(t^5 - 3)(t^4 + 7)}$

7.7   THE EXTENDED POWER RULE/THE CHAIN RULE

The Extended Power Rule

How do we differentiate more complicated functions such as

$$y = (1 + x^2)^3,$$
$$y = (1 + x^2)^{89},$$

or

$$y = (1 + x^2)^{1/3}?$$

For $(1 + x^2)^3$ we can expand and then differentiate, but while this could be done for $(1 + x^2)^{89}$, it would certainly be time-consuming, and such an expansion of the Power Rule would not work for $(1 + x^2)^{1/3}$. Not knowing this, we might surmise that the derivative of the function $y = (1 + x^2)^3$ is

$$3(1 + x^2)^2. \tag{1}$$

To check this, we expand $(1 + x^2)^3$ and then differentiate. From Section 1.1, $(a + h)^3 = a^3 + 3a^2h + 3ah^2 + h^3$, so

$$(1 + x^2)^3 = 1^3 + 3 \cdot 1^2 \cdot (x^2)^1 + 3 \cdot 1 \cdot (x^2)^2 + (x^2)^3$$

$$= 1 + 3x^2 + 3x^4 + x^6.$$

(We could also have done this by finding $(1 + x^2)^2$ and then multiplying again by $1 + x^2$.) It follows that

$$\frac{dy}{dx} = 6x + 12x^3 + 6x^5$$

$$= (1 + 2x^2 + x^4)6x$$

$$= 3(1 + x^2)^2 \cdot 2x. \qquad (2)$$

Comparing this with Eq. (1), we see that the Power Rule is not sufficient for such a differentiation. Note that the factor $2x$ in the actual derivative Eq. (2) is the derivative of the "inside" function, $1 + x^2$. This is consistent with the following new rule.

THE EXTENDED POWER RULE

Suppose $\boxed{}$ **is some function of x. Then**

$$\frac{d}{dx}\boxed{}^a = a\boxed{}^{a-1} \cdot \frac{d}{dx}\boxed{}.$$

More formally, if g(x) is a function of x, then

$$\frac{d}{dx}[g(x)]^a = a[g(x)]^{a-1} \cdot \frac{d}{dx}g(x).$$

Let us differentiate $(1 + x^3)^5$. There are four steps to carry out.

1. Mentally block out the "inside" function $1 + x^3$. $\qquad \boxed{}^5$

2. Differentiate the "outside" function $\boxed{}^5$. $\qquad 5\boxed{}^4$

3. Write in the "inside" function. $\qquad 5(1 + x^3)^4$

4. Multiply by the derivative of the "inside" function. $\qquad 5(1 + x^3)^4 \cdot 3x^2$
$$= 15x^2(1 + x^3)^4$$

Step 4 is most commonly overlooked. Try not to forget it!

Example 1

$$\frac{d}{dx}(1 + x^3)^{1/2}1 = \tfrac{1}{2}\boxed{1 + x^3}^{1/2-1} \cdot 3x^2$$

$$= \tfrac{1}{2}(1 + x^3)^{-1/2} \cdot 3x^2$$

$$= \frac{3x^2}{2\sqrt{1 + x^3}}$$

Example 2   Differentiate $(1 - x^2)^3 - (1 - x^2)^2$.

Solution   Here we combine the Difference Rule and the Extended Power Rule.

$$\frac{d}{dx}[(1 - x^2)^3 - (1 - x^2)^2]$$

$$= 3(1 - x^2)^2(-2x) - 2(1 - x^2)(-2x)$$

(We differentiate each term using the Extended Power Rule.)

$$= -6x(1 - x^2)^2 + 4x(1 - x^2)$$

$$= x(1 - x^2)[-6(1 - x^2) + 4]$$

(Here we factor out $x(1 - x^2)$.)

$$= x(1 - x^2)[-6 + 6x^2 + 4]$$

$$= x(1 - x^2)(6x^2 - 2) = 2x(1 - x^2)(3x^2 - 1)$$

Example 3   Differentiate $(x - 5)^4(7 - x)^{10}$.

Solution   Here we combine the Product Rule and the Extended Power Rule.

$$\frac{d}{dx}(x - 5)^4(7 - x)^{10}$$

$$= (x - 5)^4 10(7 - x)^9(-1) + 4(x - 5)^3(7 - x)^{10}$$

$$= -10(x - 5)^4(7 - x)^9 + 4(x - 5)^3(7 - x)^{10}$$

$$= (x - 5)^3(7 - x)^9[-10(x - 5) + 4(7 - x)]$$

(We factored out $(x - 5)^3(7 - x)^9$.)

$$= (x - 5)^3(7 - x)^9[-10x + 50 + 28 - 4x]$$

$$= (x - 5)^3(7 - x)^9(78 - 14x)$$

$$= 2(x - 5)^3(7 - x)^9(39 - 7x)$$

Example 4   Differentiate $\sqrt[4]{\dfrac{x + 3}{x - 1}}$.

Solution We have to use the Quotient Rule to differentiate the inside function $(x + 3)/(x - 1)$.

$$\frac{d}{dx}\sqrt[4]{\frac{x+3}{x-1}} = \frac{d}{dx}\left(\frac{x+3}{x-1}\right)^{1/4} = \frac{1}{4}\left(\frac{x+3}{x-1}\right)^{1/4-1}\left[\frac{(x-1)1 - 1(x+3)}{(x-1)^2}\right]$$

$$= \frac{1}{4}\left(\frac{x+3}{x-1}\right)^{-3/4}\left[\frac{x-1-x-3}{(x-1)^2}\right]$$

$$= \frac{1}{4}\left(\frac{x+3}{x-1}\right)^{-3/4} \cdot \frac{-4}{(x-1)^2}$$

$$= \left(\frac{x+3}{x-1}\right)^{-3/4} \cdot \frac{-1}{(x-1)^2}$$

The Chain Rule

The Extended Power Rule is a special case of a more general rule called the *Chain Rule*. Before discussing it, we shall define the *composition* of functions. Consider the following, for example.

$$f(x) = x^3 \qquad \text{(This function cubes each input.)}$$

and

$$g(x) = 1 + x^2 \qquad \text{(This function adds 1 to the square of each input.)}$$

We define a new function that first does what g does (adds 1 to the square) and then does what f does (cubes). The new function is called the *composition of f and g* and is symbolized $f(g(x))$. We can visualize the composition of functions as follows.

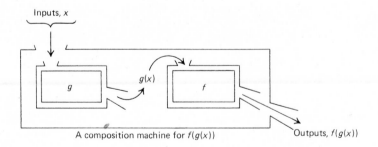

Inputs, x

$g(x)$

g f

A composition machine for $f(g(x))$

Outputs, $f(g(x))$

Example 5 Given $f(x) = x^3$ and $g(x) = 1 + x^2$, find $f(g(x))$ and $g(f(x))$.

Solution   We find $f(g(x))$ by substituting $g(x)$ for x.

$$f(g(x)) = f(1 + x^2) \qquad \text{(Substituting } 1 + x^2 \text{ for x)}$$
$$= (1 + x^2)^3$$
$$= 1 + 3x^2 + 3x^4 + x^6$$

We find $g(f(x))$ by substituting $f(x)$ for x.

$$g(f(x)) = g(x^3) \qquad \text{(Substituting } x^3 \text{ for x)}$$
$$= 1 + (x^3)^2$$
$$= 1 + x^6$$

Example 6   Given $f(x) = \sqrt{x}$ and $g(x) = x - 1$, find $f(g(x))$ and $g(f(x))$.

Solution $$f(g(x)) = f(x - 1) = \sqrt{x - 1}, \qquad g(f(x)) = g(\sqrt{x}) = \sqrt{x} - 1$$

THE CHAIN RULE   **Suppose** $\boxed{}$ **is some function of x. Then**

$$\frac{d}{dx} f\left(\boxed{}\right) = f'\left(\boxed{}\right) \cdot \frac{d}{dx} \boxed{}.$$

More formally, the derivative of the composition $f(g(x))$ is given by

$$\frac{d}{dx} f(g(x)) = f'(g(x)) \cdot \frac{d}{dx} g(x).$$

Note how the Extended Power Rule is a special case.

$$\frac{d}{dx} [g(x)]^a = a[g(x)]^{a-1} \cdot \frac{d}{dx} g(x).$$

The Chain Rule often appears in another form. Suppose $y = f(u)$ and $u = g(x)$. Then

$$\frac{dy}{dx} = \frac{dy}{du} \cdot \frac{du}{dx}.$$

For example, if $y = 2 + \sqrt{u}$ and $u = x^3 + 1$, then

$$\frac{dy}{du} = \frac{1}{2} u^{-1/2}$$

and

$$\frac{du}{dx} = 3x^2,$$

so

$$\frac{dy}{dx} = \frac{dy}{du} \cdot \frac{du}{dx}$$

$$= \frac{1}{2\sqrt{u}} \cdot 3x^2$$

$$= \frac{3x^2}{2\sqrt{x^3 + 1}} \qquad \text{(Substituting } x^3 + 1 \text{ for } u)$$

EXERCISE SET 7.7

Differentiate.

1. $(1 - x)^{55}$
2. $(1 - x)^{100}$
3. $\sqrt{1 + 8x}$
4. $\sqrt{1 - x}$

5. $\sqrt{3x^2 - 4}$
6. $\sqrt{4x^2 + 1}$
7. $(3x^2 - 6)^{-40}$
8. $(4x^2 + 1)^{-50}$

9. $x\sqrt{2x + 3}$
10. $x\sqrt{4x - 7}$
11. $x^2\sqrt{x - 1}$
12. $x^3\sqrt{x + 1}$

13. $\dfrac{1}{(3x + 8)^2}$
14. $\dfrac{1}{(4x + 5)^2}$
15. $(1 + x^3)^3 - (1 + x^3)^4$

16. $(1 + x^3)^5 - (1 + x^3)^4$
17. $x^2 + (200 - x)^2$
18. $x^2 + (100 - x)^2$

19. $(x + 6)^{10}(x - 5)^4$
20. $(x - 4)^8(x + 3)^9$
21. $(x - 4)^8(3 - x)^4$

22. $(x + 6)^{10}(5 - x)^9$
23. $-4x(2x - 3)^3$
24. $-5x(3x + 5)^6$

25. $\sqrt{\dfrac{1 - x}{1 + x}}$
26. $\sqrt{\dfrac{3 + x}{2 - x}}$

27. Consider

$$f(x) = \frac{x^2}{(1 + x)^5}.$$

a) Find $f'(x)$ using the Quotient Rule and the Extended Power Rule.

b) Note that $f(x) = x^2(1 + x)^{-5}$. Find $f'(x)$ using the Product Rule and the Extended Power Rule.

c) Compare answers to (a) and (b).

28. Consider

$$g(x) = (x^3 + 5x)^2.$$

a) Find $g'(x)$ using the Extended Power Rule.

b) Note that $g(x) = x^6 + 10x^4 + 25x^2$. Find $g'(x)$.

c) Compare answers to (a) and (b).

29. *Total cost.* A total cost function is given by

$$C(x) = 1000\sqrt{x^3 + 2}.$$

Find the marginal cost $C'(x)$.

30. *Total revenue.* A total revenue function is given by

$$R(x) = 2000\sqrt{x^2 + 3}.$$

Find the marginal revenue $R'(x)$.

31. *Compound interest.* If $1000 is invested at interest rate i, compounded annually, in 3 years it will grow to amount A given by

$$A = \$1000(1 + i)^3. \text{ (See Section 1.1.)}$$

Find the rate of change dA/di.

32. *Compound interest.* If $1000 is invested at interest rate i, compounded quarterly, in 5 years it will grow to amount A given by

$$A = \$1000\left(1 + \frac{i}{4}\right)^{20}.$$

Find the rate of change dA/di.

■ ───────────────────────────────────

Differentiate the following functions.

33. $y = \sqrt[3]{x^3 - 6x + 1}$

34. $s = \sqrt[4]{t^4 + 3t^2 + 8}$

35. $y = \dfrac{x}{\sqrt{x - 1}}$

36. $y = \dfrac{(x + 1)^2}{(x^2 + 1)^3}$

37. $u = \dfrac{(1 + 2v)^4}{v^4}$

38. $y = x\sqrt{1 + x^2}$

39. $y = \dfrac{\sqrt{1 - x^2}}{1 - x}$

40. $w = \dfrac{u}{\sqrt{1 + u^2}}$

41. $y = \left(\dfrac{x^2 - x - 1}{x^2 + 1}\right)^3$

42. $y = \sqrt{1 + \sqrt{x}}$

43. $s = \dfrac{\sqrt{t} - 1}{\sqrt{t} + 1}$

44. $y = x^{2/3} \cdot \sqrt[3]{1 + x^2}$

───────────────────────────────────

7.8 IMPLICIT DIFFERENTIATION AND RELATED RATES

Implicit Differentiation

Consider the equation

$$y^3 = x.$$

This equation *implies* that y is a function of x, for if we solve for y, we get

$$y = \sqrt[3]{x} = x^{1/3}.$$

We know from our work in this chapter that

$$\frac{dy}{dx} = \frac{1}{3}x^{-2/3}. \tag{1}$$

A method known as *implicit differentiation* allows us to find dy/dx *without* solving for y. We use the Chain Rule, treating y as a function of x. We use the Extended Power Rule, and differentiate both sides of

$$y^3 = x$$

with respect to x:

$$\frac{d}{dx}\, y^3 = \frac{d}{dx}\, x.$$

The derivative on the left side is found using the Extended Power Rule:

$$3y^2\, \frac{dy}{dx} = 1.$$

Then

$$\frac{dy}{dx} = \frac{1}{3y^2}, \qquad \text{or} \qquad \frac{1}{3}\, y^{-2}.$$

We can show that this indeed gives us the same answer as Eq. (1) by replacing y by $x^{1/3}$:

$$\frac{dy}{dx} = \frac{1}{3}\, y^{-2} = \frac{1}{3}\, (x^{1/3})^{-2} = \frac{1}{3}\, x^{-2/3}.$$

Example 1   For

$$y^3 + x^2y^5 - x^4 = 27$$

a) Find dy/dx using implicit differentiation.

b) Find the slope of the tangent line to the curve at the point $(0, 3)$.

Solution   a) The term x^2y^5 is differentiated using the Product Rule. Note that any time an expression involving y is differentiated, dy/dx must be a factor of the answer. When an expression involving just x is differentiated, there is no factor dy/dx.

$$\frac{d}{dx}\, (y^3 + x^2y^5 - x^4) = \frac{d}{dx}\, 27$$

$$\frac{d}{dx}\, y^3 + \frac{d}{dx}\, x^2y^5 - \frac{d}{dx}\, x^4 = 0$$

$$3y^2 \cdot \frac{dy}{dx} + x^2 \cdot 5y^4 \cdot \frac{dy}{dx} + 2x \cdot y^5 - 4x^3 = 0$$

$$3y^2 \cdot \frac{dy}{dx} + 5x^2y^4 \cdot \frac{dy}{dx} = 4x^3 - 2xy^5 \qquad \begin{array}{l}\text{(Get all terms}\\\text{involving } dy/dx \text{ alone}\\\text{on one side.)}\end{array}$$

$$(3y^2 + 5xy^4)\frac{dy}{dx} = 4x^3 - 2xy^5$$

$$\frac{dy}{dx} = \frac{4x^3 - 2xy^5}{3y^2 + 5xy^4} \qquad \begin{array}{l}\text{(Solve for } dy/dx.\\\text{Leave answer in}\\\text{terms of x of y.)}\end{array}$$

b) To find the slope of the tangent line to the curve at (0, 3), we replace x by 0 and y by 3:

$$\frac{dy}{dx} = \frac{4 \cdot 0^3 - 2 \cdot 0 \cdot 3^5}{3 \cdot 3^2 + 5 \cdot 0 \cdot 3^4} = 0.$$

The demand function for a product (see Sections 1.5 and 7.6) is often given implicitly.

Example 2 For the following demand equation, differentiate implicitly to find dp/dx.

$$x = \sqrt{200 - p^3}$$

Solution

$$\frac{d}{dx} x = \frac{d}{dx} (\sqrt{200 - p^3})$$

$$1 = \frac{1}{2} (200 - p^3)^{-1/2} \cdot (-3p^2) \cdot \frac{dp}{dx}$$

$$1 = \frac{-3p^2}{2\sqrt{200 - p^3}} \cdot \frac{dp}{dx}$$

$$\frac{2\sqrt{200 - p^3}}{-3p^2} = \frac{dp}{dx}$$

Related Rates

Suppose y is a function of x, say

$$y = f(x),$$

and x varies with time t (as a function of time t). Since y depends on x and x depends on t, y also depends on t. That is, y is also a function of time t. The Chain Rule gives the following:

$$\frac{dy}{dt} = \frac{dy}{dx} \cdot \frac{dx}{dt}.$$

Thus, the rate of change of y is *related* to the rate of change of x. Let us see how this comes up in problems. It helps to keep in mind that any variable can be thought of as a function of time t, even though a specific expression in terms of t may not be given.

Example 3 A restaurant supplier services the restaurants in a circular area in such a way that its radius r is increasing at the rate of 2 miles per year at the moment when r goes through the value r = 5 ft. At that moment how fast is the area increasing?

Solution   The area A and the radius r are always related by the equation for the area of a circle

$$A = \pi r^2.$$

We take the derivative of both sides with respect to t.

$$\frac{dA}{dt} = 2\pi r \cdot \frac{dr}{dt}.$$

At the moment in question, $dr/dt = 2$ mi/yr (miles per year) and $r = 5$ mi, so

$$\frac{dA}{dt} = 2\pi(5 \text{ mi})\left(2 \frac{\text{mi}}{\text{yr}}\right) = 20\pi \frac{\text{mi}^2}{\text{yr}} \approx 63 \text{ square miles per year.}$$

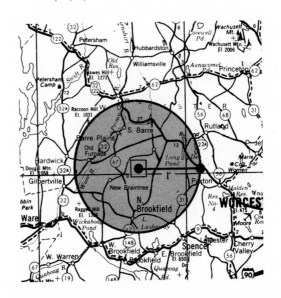

Example 4   *Rate of change of revenue, cost, and profit.* For a company making stereos, total revenue from the sale of x stereos is given by

$$R(x) = 1000x - x^2,$$

and total cost is given by

$$C(x) = 3000 + 20x.$$

Suppose the company is producing and selling stereos at the rate of 10 per day at the moment the 400th stereo is produced. At that moment, what are the (a) rate of change of total revenue, (b) cost, (c) profit?

Solution   a) $\dfrac{dR}{dt} = 1000 \cdot \dfrac{dx}{dt} - 2x \cdot \dfrac{dx}{dt}$ (Differentiating with respect to time)

$= 1000 \cdot 10 - 2(400)10$ (Substituting 10 for dx/dt and 400 for x)

$= \$2000$ per day   (Differentiating with respect to time)

b) $\dfrac{dC}{dt} = 20 \cdot \dfrac{dx}{dt} = 20(10) = \$200$ per day

c) Since $P = R - C$,

$$\dfrac{dP}{dt} = \dfrac{dR}{dt} - \dfrac{dC}{dt} \qquad = \$2000 \text{ per day} - \$200 \text{ per day}$$

$= \$1800$ per day.

EXERCISE SET 7.8

Differentiate implicitly to find $\dfrac{dy}{dx}$. Then find the slope of the curve at the given point.

1. $xy - x + 2y = 3; \; (-5, \frac{2}{3})$

2. $xy + y^2 - 2x = 0; \; (1, -2)$

3. $x^2 + y^2 = 1; \; \left(\dfrac{1}{2}, \dfrac{\sqrt{3}}{2}\right)$

4. $x^2 - y^2 = 1; \; (\sqrt{3}, \sqrt{2})$

5. $x^2y - 2x^3 - y^3 + 1 = 0; \; (2, -3)$

6. $4x^3 - y^4 - 3y + 5x + 1 = 0; \; (1, -2)$

Differentiate implicitly to find $\dfrac{dy}{dx}$.

7. $2xy + 3 = 0$

8. $x^2 + 2xy = 3y^2$

9. $x^2 - y^2 = 16$

10. $x^2 + y^2 = 25$

11. $y^5 = x^3$

12. $y^3 = x^5$

13. $x^2y^3 + x^3y^4 = 11$

14. $x^3y^2 - x^5y^3 = -19$

For the following demand equations, differentiate implicitly to find $\dfrac{dp}{dx}$.

15. $p^2 + p + 2x = 40$

16. $xp^3 = 24$

17. $(p + 4)(x + 3) = 48$

18. $1000 - 300p + 25p^2 = x$

Rates of change of total revenue, cost, and profit. Find the rates of change of total revenue, cost, and profit for

19. $R(x) = 50x - 0.5x^2$,

$C(x) = 4x + 10$,

when $x = 30$ and $\dfrac{dx}{dt} = 20$ units per day.

20. $R(x) = 50x - 0.5x^2$,

$C(x) = 10x + 3$,

when $x = 10$ and $\dfrac{dx}{dt} = 5$ units per day.

21. $R(x) = 2x$,

$C(x) = 0.01x^2 + 0.6x + 30$,

when $x = 20$ and $\dfrac{dx}{dt} = 8$ units per day.

22. $R(x) = 280x - 0.4x^2$,

$C(x) = 5000 + 0.6x^2$,

when $x = 200$ and $\dfrac{dx}{dt} = 30$ units per day.

23. Two cars start from the same point at the same time. One travels north at 25 miles per hour (mph), and the other travels east at 60 mph. How fast is the distance between them increasing at the end of 1 hr?

24. A ladder 26 ft long leans against a vertical wall. If the lower end is being moved away from the wall at the rate of 5 ft/sec, how fast is the height of the top decreasing (this will be a negative rate) when the lower end is 10 ft from the wall?

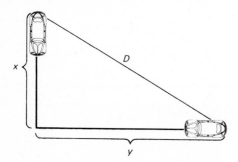

[Hint: $D^2 = x^2 + y^2$. To find D after 1 hr, solve $D^2 = 25^2 + 60^2$.]

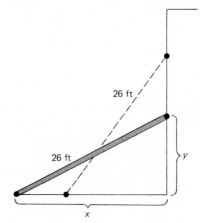

25. For a certain product a company determines that total revenue from the sale of x units is given by

$$R(x) = 200x - x^2,$$

and total cost is given by

$$C(x) = 5000 + 8x.$$

Suppose the company is producing and selling x units at the rate of 8 per day at the moment when the 100th unit is produced. At that same moment, what are the following?

a) rate of change of total revenue,

b) cost,

c) profit.

26. Two variable quantities A and B are found to be related by the equation

$$A^3 + B^3 = 9.$$

What is the rate of change dA/dt at the moment when $A = 2$ and $dB/dt = 3$?

Differentiate implicitly to find dy/dx.

27. $\sqrt{x} + \sqrt{y} = 1$

28. $\dfrac{1}{x^2} + \dfrac{1}{y^2} = 5$

29. $y^3 = \dfrac{x - 1}{x + 1}$

30. $y^2 = \dfrac{x^2 - 1}{x^2 + 1}$

31. $x^{3/2} + y^{2/3} = 1$

32. $(x - y)^3 + (x + y)^3 = x^5 + y^5$

CHAPTER 7 REVIEW

Which functions are continuous?

1.

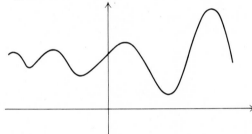

2.

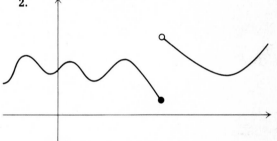

3. a) Complete.

Inputs x	Outputs $\dfrac{x^3 - 8}{x - 2}$
3	
2.5	
2.1	
2.01	
2.001	

b) Find

$$\lim_{x \to 2} \frac{x^3 - 8}{x - 2}$$

4. Find a simplified difference quotient for

$$f(x) = 3x^2 + 1.$$

5. a) Complete.

x	$\dfrac{4x - 3}{x}$
5	
80	
200	
10,000	

b) Find

$$\lim_{x \to \infty} \left(\frac{4x - 3}{x} \right).$$

Find $\dfrac{dy}{dx}$.

7. $y = x^{84}$

9. $y = \dfrac{-10}{x}$

11. $y = -0.5x^2 + 0.61x + 90$

Differentiate.

12. $\frac{1}{3}x^3 - x^2 + 2x + 4$

14. $\dfrac{x}{5 - x}$

16. $(x^5 - 4x^3 + x)^{-5}$

18. Given $R(x) = 50x$ and $C(x) = 0.001x^2 + 1.2x + 60$, find

    a) $P(x)$.

    b) $R(10)$, $C(10)$, $P(10)$.

    c) $R'(x)$, $C'(x)$, $P'(x)$.

    d) $R'(10)$, $C'(10)$, $P'(10)$.

20. Differentiate implicitly to find dy/dx. Then find the slope of the curve at the given point.

$$x^3 + y^3 = 9; \quad (1, 2)$$

6. Find the points on the graph of $y = x^3 - 3x^2$ at which the tangent is horizontal.

8. $y = 10\sqrt{x}$

10. $y = x^{5/4}$

13. $\dfrac{2x - 5}{x^4}$

15. $(x + 3)^4(7 - x)^5$

17. $x\sqrt{x^2 + 5}$

19. A company determines that the demand function for a certain product is given by

$$p = D(x) = 200 - x.$$

    a) Find an expression for total revenue $R(x)$.

    b) Find the marginal revenue $R'(x)$.

21. A board 13 ft long leans against a vertical wall. If the lower end is being moved away from the wall at the rate of 0.4 ft/sec, how fast is the upper end coming down when the lower end is 12 ft from the wall?

22. The A-One Manufacturing Company estimates that it will sell N units of its product after spending d dollars on advertising, where $N(d) = -d^2 + 80d + 15$ and d is measured in thousands of dollars.

    a) What is the rate of change of the number of units sold with respect to the amount spent on advertising?

    b) How many units will be sold after spending 20 thousand dollars on advertising (at $d = 20$)?

    c) What is the rate of change at $d = 20$?

Differentiate.

24. $y = \dfrac{1 + x}{1 - x} \cdot (3x + 2)^5$

23. Find the rates of change of total revenue, cost, and profit for

$$R(x) = 620x - x^2$$

$$C(x) = 4000 + 10x$$

when $x = 300$ and $\dfrac{dx}{dt} = 10$ units per day.

25. $y = \dfrac{x\sqrt{1 + 4x}}{1 + x^2}$

APPLICATIONS OF DIFFERENTIATION

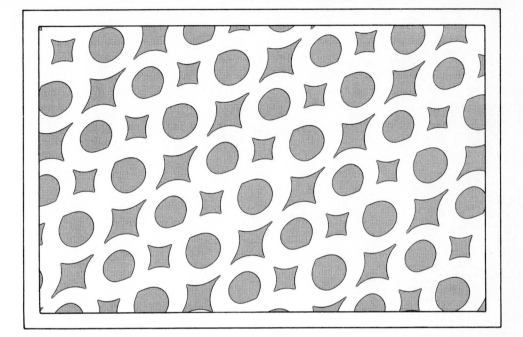

8.1 HIGHER DERIVATIVES

Consider the function given by

$$f(x) = x^5 - 3x^4 + x.$$

Its derivative f' is given by

$$f'(x) = 5x^4 - 12x^3 + 1.$$

This function f' can be differentiated. We use the notation f'' for the derivative $(f')'$. We call f'' the *second derivative of f*. It is given by

$$f''(x) = 20x^3 - 36x^2.$$

Continuing in this manner, we have

$$f'''(x) = 60x^2 - 72x, \qquad \text{(The third derivative of } f.)$$

$$f''''(x) = 120x - 72, \qquad \text{(The fourth derivative of } f.)$$

$$f'''''(x) = 120. \qquad \text{(The fifth derivative of } f.)$$

When notation, like $f''''(x)$, gets lengthy we can abbreviate it using a numeral in parentheses. Thus

$$f^{(4)}(x) = 120x - 72, \qquad f^{(5)}(x) = 120, \qquad \text{and} \qquad f^{(6)}(x) = 0.$$

Leibniz's notation for the second derivative of a function given by $y = f(x)$ is

$$\frac{d^2y}{dx^2} \qquad \text{or} \qquad \frac{d}{dx}\left(\frac{dy}{dx}\right),$$

read "the second derivative of y with respect to x." The 2s in this notation are *not* exponents. If $y = x^5 - 3x^4 + x$, then

$$\frac{d^2y}{dx^2} = 20x^3 - 36x^2.$$

Leibniz's notation for the third derivative is d^3y/dx^3, for the fourth derivative d^4y/dx^4, and so on:

$$\frac{d^3y}{dx^3} = 60x^2 - 72x, \quad \frac{d^4y}{dx^4} = 120x - 72, \quad \frac{d^5y}{dx^5} = 120.$$

Example 1 For $y = \dfrac{1}{x}$, find $\dfrac{d^2y}{dx^2}$.

Solution $y = x^{-1}$, so

$$\frac{dy}{dx} = -1 \cdot x^{-1-1} = -x^{-2}, \qquad \text{or} \qquad -\frac{1}{x^2}.$$

Then

$$\frac{d^2y}{dx^2} = (-2)(-1)x^{-2-1} = 2x^{-3}, \qquad \text{or} \qquad \frac{2}{x^3}.$$

Acceleration can be thought of as a second derivative. As an object moves, its distance from a fixed point after time t is some function of the time, say $s(t)$. Then

$$v(t) = s'(t) = \text{velocity at time } t,$$

and

$$a(t) = v'(t) = s''(t) = \text{acceleration at time } t.$$

Whenever a quantity is a function of time, the first derivative gives the rate of change with respect to time and the second derivative gives the acceleration. For example, if $y = S(t)$ gives the total sales of a corporation at time t, then $S'(t)$ gives how fast the sales are changing and $S''(t)$ gives the acceleration in the sales.

EXERCISE SET 8.1

Find $\dfrac{d^2y}{dx^2}$.

1. $y = 3x + 5$ **2.** $y = -4x + 7$ **3.** $y = -\dfrac{1}{x}$ **4.** $y = -\dfrac{3}{x}$

5. $y = x^{1/4}$ **6.** $y = \sqrt{x}$ **7.** $y = x^4 + \dfrac{4}{x}$ **8.** $y = x^3 - \dfrac{3}{x}$

9. $y = x^{-3}$ **10.** $y = x^{-4}$ **11.** $y = x^n$ **12.** $y = x^{-n}$

13. $y = x^4 - x^2$ **14.** $y = x^4 + x^3$ **15.** $y = \sqrt{x - 1}$ **16.** $y = \sqrt{x + 1}$

17. $y = ax^2 + bx + c$ **18.** $y = mx + b$

19. For $y = x^4$, find $\dfrac{d^4y}{dx^4}$.   **20.** For $y = x^5$, find $\dfrac{d^4y}{dx^4}$.

21. For $y = x^6 - x^3 + 2x$, find $\dfrac{d^5y}{dx^5}$.   **22.** For $y = x^7 - 8x^2 + 2$, find $\dfrac{d^6y}{dx^6}$.

23. For $y = x^n$, find $\dfrac{d^6y}{dx^6}$.   **24.** For $y = x^k$, find $\dfrac{d^5y}{dx^5}$.

25. If s is a distance given by $s(t) = t^3 + t^2 + 2t$, find the acceleration.

26. If s is a distance given by $s(t) = t^4 + t^2 + 3t$, find the acceleration.

27. *Total Sales.* Total sales of a corporation are given by

$$S(t) = 100{,}000(1 + 0.6t + t^2).$$

What is the acceleration in the sales?

28. The total number, $N(t)$, of employees in a company is given by

$$N(t) = 100{,}000(1 + 0.4t + t^2).$$

What is the acceleration in the number of employees?

■ ─────────────────────────────────────

Find y', y'', and y'''.

29. $y = x^{-1} + x^{-2}$ **30.** $y = \dfrac{1}{1 - x}$ **31.** $y = x\sqrt{1 + x^2}$

32. $y = 3x^5 + 8\sqrt{x}$ **33.** $y = \dfrac{3x - 1}{2x + 3}$ **34.** $y = \dfrac{1}{\sqrt{x - 1}}$

35. $y = \dfrac{x}{\sqrt{x - 1}}$ **36.** $y = \dfrac{\sqrt{x} - 1}{\sqrt{x} + 1}$

Differentiate implicitly to find $\dfrac{dy}{dx}$ and $\dfrac{d^2y}{dx^2}$.

37. $xy + x - 2y = 4$ **38.** $y^2 - xy + x^2 = 5$

39. $x^2 - y^2 = 5$ **40.** $x^3 - y^3 = 8$

8.2 THE SHAPE OF A GRAPH:
FINDING MAXIMUM AND MINIMUM VALUES

First and second derivatives give us information about the shape of a graph that may be relevant in finding the maximum and minimum values of functions. Throughout this section we will assume that the functions are continuous.

Increasing and Decreasing Functions

We have seen how the slope of a linear function determines whether it is increasing or decreasing (or neither). For a general function, the derivative yields similar information. Let us investigate how this happens in the margin exercise.

The following is how we can use derivatives to determine whether a function is increasing or decreasing.

> If $f'(x) > 0$, for all x in an interval I, then f is increasing over I.
>
> If $f'(x) < 0$, for all x in an interval I, then f is decreasing over I.

Concavity: Increasing and Decreasing Derivatives

The following figures represent two functions. The graph on the left is turning upward and the other is turning downward. Let's see if we can relate this to their derivatives.

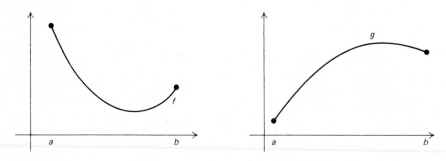

Consider the graph of f. Take a ruler, or straightedge, and move along the curve from left to right. What happens to the slopes of the tangent lines? Do the same for the graph of g. Look for a pattern.

We have the following.

1. If $f''(x) > 0$ on an interval, I, then f is turning upward on I (since f' is increasing on I). Such a graph is said to be *concave up over I.*

2. **If $f''(x) < 0$ on an interval, I, then f is turning downward on I (since f' is decreasing on I). Such a graph is said to be *concave down over I.***

The following is a helpful memory device.

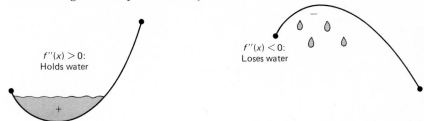

$f''(x) > 0$:
Holds water

$f''(x) < 0$:
Loses water

A *point of inflection*, or an *inflection point*, is a point across which the direction of concavity changes. For example, point P is an inflection point of the graph on the left. Points P, Q, R, and S are inflection points of the graph on the right.

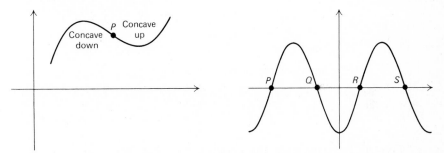

Concave
down

P Concave
up

P Q R S

Just knowing the values of f' and f'' at some specific point x_0 can yield a lot of information about the shape of the graph over some (possibly small) interval containing x_0 as an interior point (assuming f'' exists and is continuous over the interval).

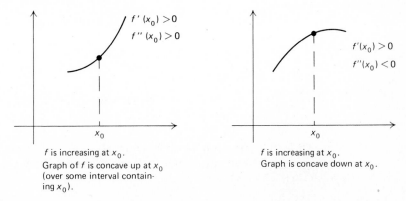

$f'(x_0) > 0$
$f''(x_0) > 0$

$f'(x_0) > 0$
$f''(x_0) < 0$

x_0

x_0

f is increasing at x_0.
Graph of f is concave up at x_0
(over some interval containing x_0).

f is increasing at x_0.
Graph is concave down at x_0.

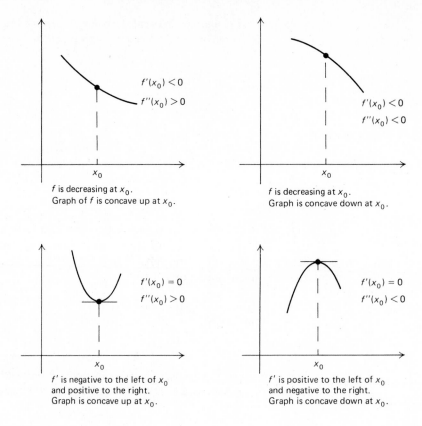

$f'(x_0) < 0$
$f''(x_0) > 0$

f is decreasing at x_0.
Graph of f is concave up at x_0.

$f'(x_0) < 0$
$f''(x_0) < 0$

f is decreasing at x_0.
Graph is concave down at x_0.

$f'(x_0) = 0$
$f''(x_0) > 0$

f' is negative to the left of x_0
and positive to the right.
Graph is concave up at x_0.

$f'(x_0) = 0$
$f''(x_0) < 0$

f' is positive to the left of x_0
and negative to the right.
Graph is concave down at x_0.

Example 1   Determine the shape of the graph of $f(x) = x^3 - x^2$ at $x = -1$.

Solution   For $f(x) = x^3 - x^2$,

$$f'(x) = 3x^2 - 2x \quad \text{and} \quad f''(x) = 6x - 2.$$

Then

$$f'(-1) = 3(-1)^2 - 2(-1)$$
$$= 3 + 2 = 5$$

and

$$f''(-1) = 6(-1) - 2$$
$$= -6 - 2 = -8.$$

Thus the function is increasing at $x = -1$ since $f'(-1) > 0$ and also concave down since $f''(-1) < 0$. This is shown below, where $f(-1) = (-1)^3 - (-1)^2 = -2$.

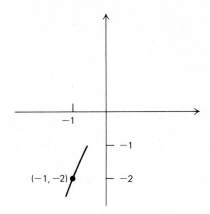

Let us take a more global look at two functions from the standpoint of the concepts we have considered. For example, consider

$$f(x) = x^2.$$

Now

$$f'(x) = 2x.$$

Note that $f'(0) = 0$. The graph has a horizontal tangent at 0. Also, when $x < 0$, $2x < 0$, so $f'(x) < 0$. Thus the function is decreasing on the interval $(-\infty, 0)$. When $x > 0$, $2x > 0$, so $f'(x) > 0$. This tells us that the function is increasing on the interval $(0, \infty)$. Check these facts on the graph.

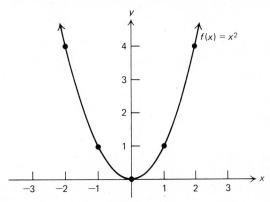

Let us look at the second derivative

$$f''(x) = 2.$$

The second derivative is positive for all values of x, since it is the constant 2; thus the graph is concave up over the entire real line. Check this on the graph.

As another example, consider

$$f(x) = x^3.$$

Now

$$f'(x) = 3x^2.$$

Note that $f'(0) = 0$. The graph has a horizontal tangent at 0. Also, when $x < 0$, $x^2 > 0$, so $3x^2 > 0$ and $f'(x) > 0$. Thus the function is increasing over the interval $(-\infty, 0)$. When $x > 0$, $x^2 > 0$, so $3x^2 > 0$ and $f'(x) > 0$. Thus the function is increasing over the interval $(0, \infty)$. In fact it is increasing over the entire real line. Check this on the graph.

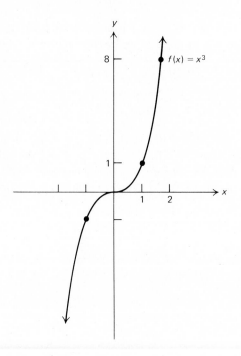

Let us look at the second derivative,

$$f''(x) = 6x.$$

When $x < 0$, $6x < 0$, so $f''(x) < 0$. Thus the graph is concave down over the interval $(-\infty, 0)$. When $x > 0$, $6x > 0$, so $f''(x) > 0$. Thus the graph is concave up over the interval $(0, \infty)$. Check this on the graph, noting also that $f''(0) = 0$ and that the graph has an inflection point $(0, 0)$.

Critical Points

A *critical point* of a function is an interior point c of its domain at which the function has a horizontal tangent, or at which the derivative does not exist. That is, c is a critical point if

$$f'(c) = 0 \qquad \text{or} \qquad f'(c) \text{ does not exist.}$$

Consider the following graph.

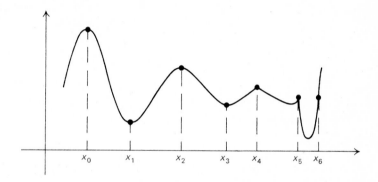

The points x_0, x_1, x_2, and x_3 are all critical points because the derivative is 0 at each of these points. The points x_4, x_5, and x_6 are all critical points because the derivative does not exist at these points.

The Shape of a Graph Between Critical Points and Endpoints

Suppose we have a continuous function defined over an interval $[a, b]$ as in the following graph.

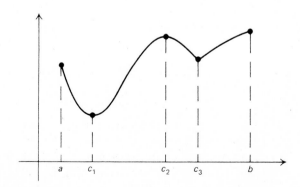

We have three critical points—c_1, c_2, and c_3. These, together with the end-points, will be referred to as *key* points. That is, the key points are

$$a, \quad b, \quad c_1, \quad c_2, \quad c_3.$$

Note, in the foregoing graph, that between any two consecutive key points the function is either increasing or decreasing.

This graph, though not a proof, exemplifies the following principle.

SHAPE
PRINCIPLE   **Suppose f is a continuous function over an interval $[a, b]$. Then between any two consecutive key points (a, b, plus critical points c_1, c_2, c_3, . . . , c_n) the function is increasing, or it is decreasing.**

Finding Maximum and Minimum Values

Consider the function f whose graph over the interval $[a, b]$ is as follows. The function value $f(c_1)$ is called a *minimum* value of the function, and $f(b)$ is called a *maximum value* of the function.

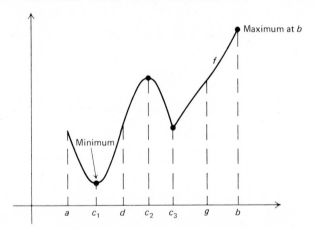

A function f on an interval $[a, b]$ has a *maximum* at x_0 if

$$f(x_0) \geqslant f(x) \quad \text{for all } x \text{ in } [a, b].$$

A function f on an interval $[a, b]$ has a *minimum* at x_0 if

$$f(x_0) \leqslant f(x) \quad \text{for all } x \text{ in } [a, b].$$

Look again at the preceding graph, but consider only the smaller interval $[d, g]$. Over that interval $f(c_2)$ is a maximum, and $f(c_3)$ is a minimum. In relation to the larger interval $[a, b]$, we sometimes call $f(c_2)$ a relative maximum and $f(c_3)$ a relative minimum, because there is a smaller interval, namely [d, g], over which they are indeed maximum and minimum values. We shall restrict our attention to finding *absolute*, or overall, *maximum* and *minimum* values.

There are two relevant theorems. The first is

THEOREM

A continuous function *f* defined on a closed interval [*a*, *b*] must have a maximum and minimum value at points in [*a*, *b*].

The second is a modification of the Shape Principle.

MAXIMUM–
MINIMUM
PRINCIPLE 1

Suppose *f* is a continuous function over an interval [*a*, *b*], with critical points $c_1, c_2, \ldots, c_n$. The key points are *a*, *b*, $c_1, c_2, \ldots, c_n$. Consider function values of the key points:

$$f(a),\ f(b),\ f(c_1),\ f(c_2),\ \ldots,\ f(c_n).$$

The largest of these is the *maximum* of *f* on the interval [*a*, *b*].
The smallest of these is the *minimum* of *f* on the interval [*a*, *b*].

This follows from the Shape Principle because between two key points the function is either increasing or decreasing. Thus whatever the maximum and minimum values are, they occur among function values of the key points.

Example 2   Find the maximum and minimum values of $f(x) = 3x^2 - x^3$ on the interval $[-\frac{1}{2}, 5]$.

Solution   a) First find $f'(x)$.

$$f'(x) = 6x - 3x^2$$

b) Determine the critical points. The derivative exists for all real numbers. Thus, the only candidates for critical points are those x's such that $f'(x) = 0$. Setting $f'(x)$ equal to 0 and solving, we get

$$f'(x) = 6x - 3x^2 = 0,$$

$$3x(2 - x) = 0,$$

$$3x = 0 \quad \text{or} \quad 2 - x = 0,$$

$$x = 0 \quad \text{or} \quad -x = -2,$$

$$x = 2.$$

The critical points are 0 and 2. The key points are $-\frac{1}{2}$, 5, 0, and 2.

c) We compute the *function* values at the key points.

$$f(-\tfrac{1}{2}) = 3(-\tfrac{1}{2})^2 - (-\tfrac{1}{2})^3 = 3 \cdot \tfrac{1}{4} + \tfrac{1}{8} \qquad\qquad = \tfrac{7}{8}$$

$$f(5) = 3 \cdot 5^2 - 5^3 = 3 \cdot 25 - 125 = 75 - 125 = -50 \quad \text{Minimum}$$

$$f(0) = 3 \cdot 0^2 - 0^3 = 0 - 0 \qquad\qquad\qquad = 0$$

$$f(2) = 3 \cdot 2^2 - 2^3 = 3 \cdot 4 - 8 \qquad\qquad\qquad = 4 \qquad \text{Maximum}$$

Thus

$$\text{Maximum} = 4 \text{ at } x = 2, \qquad \text{and} \qquad \text{Minimum} = -50 \text{ at } x = 5.$$

Example 3   Find the maximum and minimum values of $f(x) = 3x^2 - x^3$ on the interval $[7, 10]$.

Solution   As in Example 2 the derivative is 0 at 0 and 2. But neither 0 nor 2 is in the interval $[7, 10]$, so there are no critical points in this interval. Thus the maximum and minimum values occur at the endpoints.

$$f(7) = 3 \cdot 7^2 - 7^3 = 3 \cdot 49 - 343 \qquad\qquad = -196 \quad \text{Maximum}$$

$$f(10) = 3 \cdot 10^2 - 10^3 = 3 \cdot 100 - 1000 = 300 - 1000 = -700 \quad \text{Minimum}$$

Note that a maximum can be a negative number.

When there is only *one* critical point c_0 in I, it can work out that we do not need to check the endpoint values. Consider these cases.

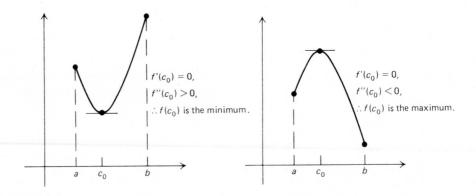

$f'(c_0) = 0,$
$f''(c_0) > 0,$
$\therefore f(c_0)$ is the minimum.

$f'(c_0) = 0,$
$f''(c_0) < 0,$
$\therefore f(c_0)$ is the maximum.

When $f'(c_0) = 0$ and $f''(c_0) > 0$, $f'(x)$ changes from negative to positive as x goes from the left of c_0 to the right. That is, the function f is decreasing to the left of c_0 and increasing to the right of c_0. It follows that $f(c_0)$ is the minimum value of f on I. Similarly, if $f'(c_0) = 0$ and $f''(c_0) < 0$, $f'(x)$ changes from positive to negative as x goes from the left of c_0 to the right. That is, the function f is increasing to the left of c_0 and decreasing to the right of c_0. It follows that $f(c_0)$ is the maximum value of f on I. The above turns out to hold no matter what the interval I—whether it is open, closed, or extends to infinity.

MAXIMUM– MINIMUM PRINCIPLE 2

Suppose f is a function such that $f'(x)$ exists for every x in an interval I, and that there is *exactly one* (critical) point c_0, interior to I, for which $f'(c_0) = 0$. Then

$$f(c_0) \text{ is the maximum value on } I \text{ if } f''(c_0) < 0$$

or

$$f(c_0) \text{ is the minimum value on } I \text{ if } f''(c_0) > 0.$$

If $f''(c_0) = 0$, we would have to use Maximum–Minimum Principle 1, or we would have to know more about the behavior of the function on the given interval.

Example 4 Find the maximum and minimum values of $f(x) = 4x - x^2$.

Solution When no interval is specified, we consider the entire domain of the function. In this case the domain is the set of all real numbers.

a) Find $f'(x)$.

$$f'(x) = 4 - 2x$$

b) Determine the critical points. The derivative exists for all real numbers. Thus we merely solve $f'(x) = 0$.

$$4 - 2x = 0$$
$$-2x = -4$$
$$x = 2$$

Since there is only one critical point, we can use the second derivative

$$f''(x) = -2.$$

Now the second derivative is constant, so $f''(2) = -2$, and since this is negative, we have the

$$\text{Maximum} = f(2) = 4 \cdot 2 - 2^2 = 8 - 4 = 4 \quad \text{at} \quad x = 2.$$

The function has no minimum, as the following graph indicates.

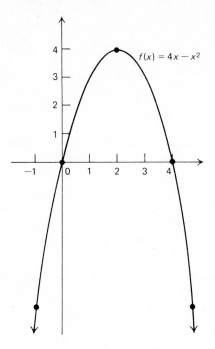

Example 5   Find the maximum and minimum values of $f(x) = 4x - x^2$ on the interval $[0, 4]$.

Solution   By the reasoning in Example 4 we know that the maximum value is $f(2)$, or 4. We know this here also, without checking the endpoints. This time we have to check for the minimum:

$$f(0) = 4 \cdot 0 - 0^2 = 0 \qquad \text{and} \qquad f(4) = 4 \cdot 4 - 4^2 = 0.$$

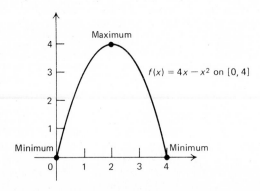

Thus the minimum is 0. It occurs twice at $x = 0$ and $x = 4$. Thus, the

$$\text{Maximum} = 4 \qquad \text{at} \qquad x = 2,$$

and the

$$\text{Minimum} = 0 \quad \text{at} \quad x = 0 \quad \text{and} \quad x = 4.$$

Example 6   Find the maximum and minimum values of $f(x) = x^3$.

Solution   a) Find $f'(x)$.

$$f'(x) = 3x^2$$

b) Find the critical points.

$$3x^2 = 0$$
$$x^2 = 0$$
$$x = 0$$

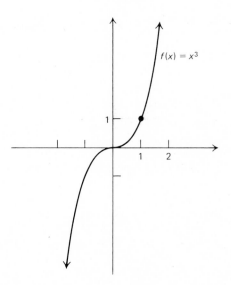

$f(x) = x^3$

Since there is only one critical point we can use the second derivative

$$f''(x) = 6x.$$

Now $f''(0) = 6 \cdot 0 = 0$, so Maximum–Minimum Principle 2 fails.

We cannot use Maximum–Minimum Principle 1 because there are no endpoints. But note that $f'(x) = 3x^2$ is never negative. Thus it is increasing everywhere but at $x = 0$, so there is no maximum or minimum.

Example 7   Find the maximum and minimum values of $f(x) = 5x + (35/x)$ on the interval $(0, \infty)$.

Solution   a) Find $f'(x)$. We first express $f(x)$ as

$$f(x) = 5x + 35x^{-1}.$$

Then

$$f'(x) = 5 - 35x^{-2} = 5 - \frac{35}{x^2}.$$

b) Now $f'(x)$ exists for all values of x in $(0, \infty)$. Thus the only critical points are those for which $f'(x) = 0$.

$$5 - \frac{35}{x^2} = 0$$

$$5 = \frac{35}{x^2}$$

$$5x^2 = 35 \quad \text{(Multiplying by } x^2, \text{ since } x \neq 0)$$

$$x^2 = 7$$

$$x = \pm\sqrt{7}$$

The only critical point in $(0, \infty)$ is $\sqrt{7}$. Thus we can use the second derivative

$$f''(x) = 70x^{-3} = \frac{70}{x^3}$$

to determine whether we have a maximum or minimum. Now $f''(x)$ is positive for all values of x in $(0, \infty)$, so $f''(\sqrt{7}) > 0$, and the

$$\text{Minimum} = f(\sqrt{7})$$

$$= 5 \cdot \sqrt{7} + \frac{35}{\sqrt{7}} \quad \text{at} \quad x = \sqrt{7}.$$

The function has no maximum value.

In general,

Suppose a function has only one critical point c in an interval that does not have endpoints or does not contain its endpoints, such as $(-\infty, \infty)$, $(0, \infty)$, or (a, b). Then, if the function has a maximum, it will have no minimum; and if it has a minimum, it will have no maximum.

See Example 4 and Example 7.

EXERCISE SET 8.2

The curves on the graph at the right show the gasoline mileage obtained when traveling at a constant speed, for an average-size car and a compact car.

1. Consider the graph for the average-size car over the interval [20, 80].

    a) Estimate the speed at which the maximum gasoline mileage is obtained.

    b) Estimate the speed at which the minimum gasoline mileage is obtained.

    c) What is the mileage obtained at 70 mph?

    d) What is the mileage obtained at 55 mph?

    e) What percent increase in mileage is there by traveling at 55 mph rather than at 70 mph?

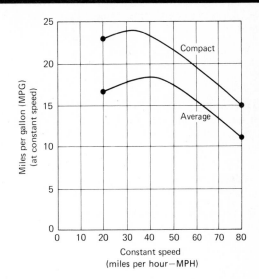

2. Answer the same questions as in Exercise 1 for the compact car.

For the following functions, find the maximum and minimum values, if they exist, over the indicated interval. When no interval is specified, use the real line $(-\infty, \infty)$.

3. $f(x) = 5 + x - x^2$; [0, 2]

4. $f(x) = 4 + x - x^2$; [0, 2]

5. $f(x) = x^3 - x^2 - x + 2$; [0, 2]

6. $f(x) = x^3 + \frac{1}{2}x^2 - 2x + 5$; [0, 1]

7. $f(x) = x^3 - x^2 - x + 2$; [-1, 0]

8. $f(x) = x^3 + \frac{1}{2}x^2 - 2x + 5$; [-2, 0]

9. $f(x) = 3x - 2$; [-1, 1]

10. $f(x) = 2x + 4$; [-1, 1]

11. $f(x) = 3x - 2$

12. $f(x) = 2x + 4$

13. $f(x) = x(70 - x)$

14. $f(x) = x(50 - x)$

15. $f(x) = 2x^2 - 40x + 400$

16. $f(x) = 2x^2 - 20x + 100$

17. $f(x) = x - \frac{4}{3}x^3$; $(0, \infty)$

18. $f(x) = 16x - \frac{4}{3}x^3$; $(0, \infty)$

19. $f(x) = 17x - x^2$

20. $f(x) = 27x - x^2$

21. $f(x) = \frac{1}{3}x^3 - 3x$; [-2, 2]

22. $f(x) = \frac{1}{3}x^3 - 5x$; [-3, 3]

23. $f(x) = -0.001x^2 + 4.8x - 60$

24. $f(x) = -0.01x^2 + 1.4x - 30$

25. $f(x) = -\frac{1}{3}x^3 + 6x^2 - 11x - 50$; (0, 3)

26. $f(x) = -x^3 + x^2 + 5x - 1$; $(0, \infty)$

27. $f(x) = 15x^2 - \frac{1}{2}x^3$; [0, 30]

28. $f(x) = 4x^2 - \frac{1}{2}x^3$; [0, 8]

29. $f(x) = 2x + \dfrac{72}{x}$; $(0, \infty)$

30. $f(x) = x + \dfrac{3600}{x}$; $(0, \infty)$

31. $f(x) = x^2 + \dfrac{432}{x}$; $(0, \infty)$

32. $f(x) = x^2 + \dfrac{250}{x}$; $(0, \infty)$

33. $f(x) = 2x^4 - x$; [-1, 1]

34. $f(x) = 2x^4 + x$; [-1, 1]

35. $f(x) = \sqrt[3]{x}$; [0, 8]

36. $f(x) = \sqrt{x}$; [0, 4]

37. $f(x) = (x + 1)^3$

38. $f(x) = (x - 1)^3$

39. See Exercise 10 in Exercise Set 7.5. What is the maximum number of units sold? What must be spent on advertising to sell that number of units?

40. See Exercise 5 in Exercise Set 7.5. Consider the function over the interval [0, 40], that is, the years 1940 to 1980.

    a) What is the maximum percentage in college and in what year does it occur?

    b) What is the minimum percentage in college and in what year does it occur?

41. At travel speed (constant velocity) x there are y accidents in daytime for every 100 million miles of travel, where y is given by

$$y = x^2 - 122.5x + 3775.$$

At what travel speed do the fewest accidents occur?

42. At travel speed (constant velocity) x, the cost y, in cents per mile, of operating a car is given by

$$y = 0.02x^2 - 1.3x + 40.$$

At what travel speed is the cost of operating a car a minimum?

■ ────────────────────────────────

Find the maximum and minimum values, if they exist, over the indicated interval. When no interval is specified, use the real line $(-\infty, \infty)$.

43. $g(x) = x\sqrt{x + 3}$; $[-3, 3]$

44. $h(x) = x\sqrt{1 - x}$; $[0, 1]$

45. $f(x) = x^{2/3}$; $[-1, 1]$

46. $g(x) = x^{2/3}$

47. $f(x) = \frac{1}{3}x^3 - x + \frac{2}{3}$

48. $f(x) = \frac{1}{3}x^3 - \frac{1}{2}x^2 - 2x + 1$

49. $f(x) = \frac{1}{3}x^3 - 2x^2 + x$; $[0, 4]$

50. $g(x) = \frac{1}{3}x^3 + 2x^2 + x$; $[-4, 0]$

51. $t(x) = x^4 - 2x^2$

52. $f(x) = 2x^4 - 4x^2 + 2$

53. Several costs in a business environment can be separated into two components: those that increase with volume and those that decrease with volume. Quality of customer service, although more expensive as it is increased, has part of its increased cost offset by customer goodwill. A firm has determined that its cost of service is the following function of "quality units,"

$$C(x) = (2x + 4) + \left(\frac{2}{x - 6}\right), \quad x > 6.$$

Find the number of "quality units" the firm should use to minimize its total cost of service.

───────────────────────────────────

8.3 MAXIMUM–MINIMUM PROBLEMS

One very important application of the differential calculus is the solving of maximum–minimum problems, that is, finding the maximum or minimum value of some varying quantity Q and the point where that maximum or minimum occurs.

Example 1   A hobby store has 20 ft of fencing to fence off a rectangular electric train area in one corner of its display room. What dimensions of the rectangle will maximize the area? What is the maximum area?

Exploratory Solution   Intuitively, one might think that it does not matter what dimensions one uses; they will all yield the same area. To show that this is not true, as well as to conjecture a possible solution, consider the exploratory exercises that follow. But, before doing those exercises let us express the area in terms of one variable. If we let x = the length of one side, and y = the length of the other, then since the sum of the lengths must be 20 ft,

$$x + y = 20, \quad \text{and} \quad y = 20 - x.$$

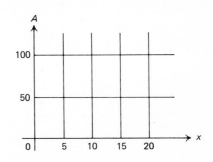

Then the area is given by

$$A = xy$$

$$A = x(20 - x) = 20x - x^2.$$

Exploratory exercises

a) Complete this table.

x	y 20 − x	A x(20 − x)
0		
4		
6.5		
8		
10		
12		
13.2		
20		

b) Make a graph of x versus A, that is, of points (x, A) from the table; and connect them with a smooth curve.

c) Does it matter what dimensions we use?

d) Make a conjecture about what the maximum might be and where it would occur.

Calculus Solution   We are trying to find the maximum value of

$$A = 20x - x^2 \text{ on the interval } (0, 20).$$

We consider the interval $(0, 20)$ because x is the length of one side and cannot be negative. Since there is only 20 ft of fencing, x cannot be greater than 20. Also, x cannot be 20 because the length of y would be 0.

a) We first find $A'(x)$, where $A(x) = 20x - x^2$.

$$A'(x) = 20 - 2x.$$

b) This derivative exists for all values of x in $(0, 20)$. Thus the only critical points are where

$$A'(x) = 20 - 2x = 0,$$
$$-2x = -20,$$
$$x = 10.$$

Since there is only one critical point in the interval, we can use the second derivative to determine whether we have a maximum. Note that

$$A''(x) = -2,$$

which is a constant. Thus $A''(10)$ is negative, so $A(10)$ is a maximum. Now

$$A(10) = 10(20 - 10) = 10 \cdot 10 = 100.$$

Thus the maximum area of 100 sq. ft is obtained using 10 ft for the length of one side, and $20 - 10$, or 10 ft, for the other. Note that while you may have conjectured this in the Exploratory Solution, the tools of calculus allowed us to prove it.

Example 2   A stereo manufacturer determines that in order to sell x units of a new stereo its price per unit must be

$$p = D(x) = 1000 - x.$$

It also determines that the total cost of producing x units is given by

$$C(x) = 3000 + 20x.$$

a) Find the total revenue $R(x)$.

b) Find the total profit $P(x)$.

c) How many units must the company produce and sell to maximize profit?

d) What is the maximum profit?

e) What price per unit must be charged to make this maximum profit?

Solution   a) $R(x)$ = Total revenue = (number of units) · (price per unit)

$$= \qquad x \qquad\qquad p$$

$$= x(1000 - x) = 1000x - x^2.$$

b) $P(x) = R(x) - C(x) = (1000 - x^2) - (3000 + 20x)$

$$= -x^2 + 980x - 3000.$$

c) To find the maximum value of $P(x)$ we first find $P'(x)$.

$$P'(x) = -2x + 980$$

This is defined for all real numbers (actually we are interested in numbers x in $[0, \infty)$ only, since we cannot produce a negative number of stereos). Thus we solve

$$P'(x) = -2x + 980 = 0$$

$$-2x = -980$$

$$x = 490.$$

Since there is only one critical point, we can try to use the second derivative to determine whether we have a maximum. Note that

$$P''(x) = -2, \text{ a constant.}$$

Thus $P''(490)$ is negative, so $P(490)$ is a maximum.

d) The maximum profit is given by

$$P(490) = -(490)^2 + 980 \cdot 490 - 3000$$

$$= \$237{,}100.$$

Thus the stereo manufacturer makes a maximum profit of \$237,100 by producing and selling 490 stereos.

e) The price per unit to make the maximum profit is

$$p = 1000 - 490 = \$510.$$

Marginal Analysis

Let us take a general look at the total profit function and its related functions.

In the first graph on the next page we have the total cost and total revenue functions. We can estimate what the maximum profit might be by looking for the widest gap between $R(x)$ and $C(x)$. Points B_0 and B_2 are "break-even" points.

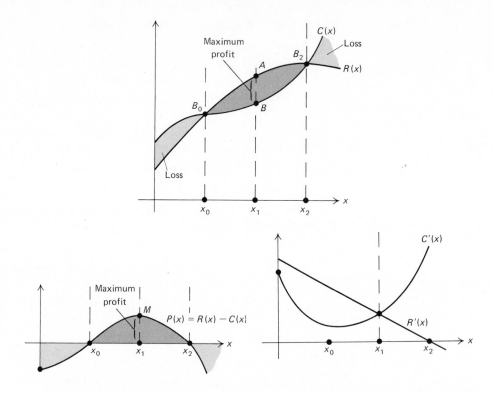

In the second graph we have the total profit function. Note that when production is too low ($<x_0$) there is a loss because of high fixed or initial costs and low revenue. When production is too high ($>x_2$), there is also a loss due to high marginal costs and low marginal revenues, as seen in the third graph.

The business operates at a profit everywhere between x_0 and x_2. Note that maximum profit occurs at a critical point x_1 of $P(x)$. If we assume that $P'(x)$ exists for all x in some interval, usually $[0, \infty)$, this critical point occurs at some number x such that

$$P'(x) = 0.$$

Since $P(x) = R(x) - C(x)$, it follows that

$$P'(x) = R'(x) - C'(x).$$

Thus the maximum profit occurs at some number x such that

$$R'(x) - C'(x) = 0,$$

or

$$R'(x) = C'(x).$$

In summary,

Maximum profit is achieved when marginal revenue equals marginal cost:

$$R'(x) = C'(x).$$

Here is a general strategy for solving maximum–minimum problems. While it may not guarantee success, it should certainly enhance one's chances.

1. Read the problem carefully. If relevant, draw a picture.

2. Label the picture with appropriate variables and constants, noting what varies and what stays fixed.

3. Translate the problem to an equation, involving a quantity Q to be maximized or minimized.

4. Try to express Q as a function of *one* variable. Use the procedures developed in Section 8.2 to determine the maximum or minimum values and the points where they occur.

Example 3   The Karma Corporation makes cardboard boxes. From a thin piece of cardboard 8 in. by 8 in., square corners are cut out so that the sides can be folded up to make a box. What dimensions will yield a box of maximum volume? What is the maximum volume?

Exploratory Solution   One might again think that it does not matter what the dimensions are, but our experience with Example 1 should lead us to think otherwise. We make a drawing as shown below.

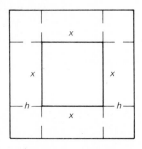
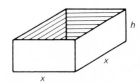

When squares of length h on a side are cut out of the corners we are left with a square base of length x. The volume of the resulting box is

$$V = lwh = x \cdot x \cdot h.$$

We want to express V in terms of one variable. Note that the overall length of a side of the cardboard is 8 in. We see from the drawing that

$$h + x + h = 8,$$

or

$$x + 2h = 8.$$

Solving for h we get

$$2h = 8 - x$$

$$h = \tfrac{1}{2}(8 - x) = \tfrac{1}{2} \cdot 8 - \tfrac{1}{2}x = 4 - \tfrac{1}{2}x.$$

Thus

$$V = x \cdot x \cdot (4 - \tfrac{1}{2}x) = x^2(4 - \tfrac{1}{2}x) = 4x^2 - \tfrac{1}{2}x^3.$$

In the following exploratory exercises you will compute some values of V.

Exploratory exercises

a) Complete this table.

x	h $\tfrac{1}{2}(8 - x)$	V $x \cdot x \cdot \tfrac{1}{2}(8 - x)$
0		
1		
2		
3		
4		
4.6		
5		
6		
6.8		
7		
8		

b) Make a graph of x versus V.

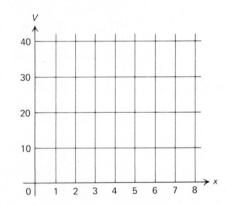

c) Make a conjecture about what the maximum might be and where it would occur.

Calculus Solution You probably noted in the exploratory exercises that it was a bit more difficult than in Example 1 to conjecture where the maximum occurs. At the least it seems reasonable that it occurs for some x between 5 and 6. Let us find out for certain, using calculus. We are trying to find the maximum value of

$$V(x) = 4x^2 - \tfrac{1}{2}x^3 \quad \text{on the interval } (0, 8).$$

We first find $V'(x)$.

$$V'(x) = 8x - \tfrac{3}{2}x^2.$$

Now $V'(x)$ exists for all x in the interval $(0, 8)$ so we set it equal to 0 to find the critical values.

$$V'(x) = 8x - \tfrac{3}{2}x^2 = 0,$$

$$x(8 - \tfrac{3}{2}x) = 0,$$

$$x = 0 \quad \text{or} \quad 8 - \tfrac{3}{2}x = 0,$$

$$x = 0 \quad \text{or} \quad -\tfrac{3}{2}x = -8,$$

$$x = 0 \quad \text{or} \quad x = -\tfrac{2}{3}(-8) = \tfrac{16}{3}.$$

The only critical point in $(0, 8)$ is $\tfrac{16}{3}$. Thus we can use second derivative

$$V''(x) = 8 - 3x$$

to determine whether we have a maximum. Since

$$V''(\tfrac{16}{3}) = 8 - 3 \cdot \tfrac{16}{3} = -8,$$

$V''(\tfrac{16}{3})$ is negative, so $V(\tfrac{16}{3})$ is a maximum, and

$$V(\tfrac{16}{3}) = 4 \cdot (\tfrac{16}{3})^2 - \tfrac{1}{2}(\tfrac{16}{3})^3 = \tfrac{1024}{27} = 37\tfrac{25}{27}.$$

The maximum volume is $37\tfrac{25}{27}$ cu. in. The dimensions that yield this maximum volume are

$$x = \tfrac{16}{3} = 5\tfrac{1}{3} \text{ in.,} \quad \text{by } x = 5\tfrac{1}{3} \text{ in.,} \quad \text{by } h = 4 - \tfrac{1}{2}(\tfrac{16}{3}) = 1\tfrac{1}{3} \text{ in.}$$

It would surely have been difficult to guess this from the exploratory exercises.

In the following problem, an open-top container of fixed volume is to be constructed. We want to determine the dimensions that will allow it to be built with the least amount of material. Such a problem could be important from an ecological standpoint.

Example 4   A container firm is designing an open-top rectangular box, with a square base, that will hold 108 cubic centimeters (cc). What dimensions yield the minimum surface area? What is the minimum surface area?

Solution   The surface area of the box is

$$S = x^2 + 4xy.$$

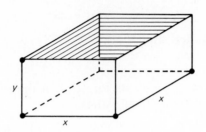

The volume must be 108 cc, and is given by

$$V = x^2 y = 108.$$

To express S in terms of one variable, we solve $x^2 y = 108$ for y:

$$y = \frac{108}{x^2}.$$

Then

$$S = x^2 + 4x\left(\frac{108}{x^2}\right) = x^2 + \frac{432}{x}.$$

Now S is defined only for positive numbers, and the problem dictates that the length x be positive, so we are minimizing S on the interval $(0, \infty)$. We first find dS/dx.

$$\frac{dS}{dx} = 2x - \frac{432}{x^2}.$$

Since dS/dx exists for all x in $(0, \infty)$, the only critical points are where $dS/dx = 0$. Thus, we solve the following equation:

$$2x - \frac{432}{x^2} = 0$$

$$x^2\left(2x - \frac{432}{x^2}\right) = x^2 \cdot 0 \qquad \text{(We multiply by } x^2 \text{ to clear of fractions.)}$$

$$2x^3 - 432 = 0$$

$$2x^3 = 432$$

$$x^3 = 216$$

$$x = 6.$$

This is the only critical point, so we can use the second derivative to determine whether we have a minimum.

$$\frac{d^2S}{dx^2} = 2 + \frac{864}{x^3}$$

Note that this is positive for all positive values of x. Thus we have a minimum at $x = 6$. When $x = 6$, it follows that $y = 3$:

$$y = \frac{108}{6^2} = \frac{108}{36} = 3.$$

Thus the surface area is minimized when $x = 6$ cm (centimeters) and $y = 3$ cm. The minimum surface area is

$$S = 6^2 + 4 \cdot 6 \cdot 3 = 108 \text{ cm}^2.$$

This, by coincidence, is the same number as the fixed volume.

Example 5   *Determining a ticket price.* Fight promoters ride a thin line between profit and loss, especially in determining the price to charge for admission to closed-circuit television showings in local theaters. By keeping records, a theater determines that, if the admission price is $20, it averages 1000 people in attendance. But, for every increase of $1, it loses 100 customers from the average. Every customer spends an average of $0.80 on concessions. What admission price should the theater charge to maximize total revenue?

Solution   Let $x = $ the amount by which the price of $20 should be increased (if x is negative the price would be decreased). We first express total revenue R as a function of x. Note that

$$R(x) = \text{(Revenue from tickets)} + \text{(Revenue from concessions)}$$

$$= \text{(Number of people)} \cdot \text{(Ticket price)}$$

$$+ \$0.80(\text{Number of people})$$

$$= (1000 - 100x)(20 + x) + 0.80(1000 - 100x)$$

$$= 20,000 - 2000x + 1000x - 100x^2 + 800 - 80x$$

$$R(x) = -100x^2 - 1080x + 20,800.$$

We are trying to find the maximum value of R over the set of all real numbers. To find x such that $R(x)$ is a maximum we first find $R'(x)$.

$$R'(x) = -200x - 1080.$$

This derivative exists for all real numbers x; thus the only critical points are where $R'(x) = 0$, so we solve that equation.

$$-200x - 1080 = 0$$

$$-200x = 1080$$

$$x = -5.4 = -\$5.40$$

Since this is the only critical point, we can use the second derivative,

$$R''(x) = -200,$$

to determine whether we have a maximum. Since $R''(-5.4)$ is negative, $R(-5.4)$ is a maximum. Thus to maximize revenue the theater should charge

$$\$20 + (-\$5.40) \qquad \text{or} \qquad \$14.60 \text{ per ticket.}$$

That is, this reduced ticket price will get more people into the theater (1000 − 100(−5.4), or 1540), and will result in maximum revenue.

EXERCISE SET 8.3

1. Of all the numbers whose sum is 50, find the two that have the maximum product. That is, maximize $Q = xy$, where $x + y = 50$.

2. Of all the numbers whose sum is 70, find the two that have the maximum product. That is, maximize $Q = xy$, where $x + y = 70$.

3. In Exercise 1, can there be a minimum product? Explain.

4. In Exercise 2, can there be a minimum product? Explain.

5. Of all numbers whose difference is 4, find the two that have the minimum product.

6. Of all numbers whose difference is 6, find the two that have the minimum product.

7. Maximize $Q = xy^2$, where x and y are positive numbers, such that $x + y^2 = 1$.

8. Maximize $Q = xy^2$, where x and y are positive numbers, such that $x + y^2 = 4$.

9. Minimize $Q = x^2 + y^2$, where $x + y = 20$.

10. Minimize $Q = x^2 + y^2$, where $x + y = 10$.

11. Maximize $Q = xy$, where x and y are positive numbers such that $(4/3)x^2 + y = 16$.

12. Maximize $Q = xy$, where x and y are positive numbers such that $x + (4/3)y^2 = 1$.

13. A rancher wants to build a rectangular fence next to a river, using 120 yd of fencing. What dimensions of the rectangle will maximize the area? What is the maximum area? Note that the rancher does not have to fence in the side next to the river.

14. A rancher wants to enclose two rectangular areas near a river, one for sheep and one for cattle. There are 240 yd of fencing available. What is the largest total area that can be enclosed?

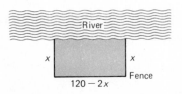

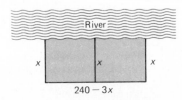

15. A carpenter is building a room with a fixed perimeter of 54 ft. What are the dimensions of the largest room that can be built? Its area?

16. Of all rectangles that have a perimeter of 34 ft, find the dimensions of the one with the largest area. What is its area?

Maximizing profit. Find the maximum profit and the number of units that must be produced and sold to yield the maximum profit.

17. $R(x) = 50x - 0.5x^2$, $C(x) = 4x + 10$

18. $R(x) = 50x - 0.5x^2$, $C(x) = 10x + 3$

19. $R(x) = 2x$, $C(x) = 0.01x^2 + 0.6x + 30$

20. $R(x) = 5x$, $C(x) = 0.001x^2 + 1.2x + 60$

21. $R(x) = 9x - 2x^2$, $C(x) = x^3 - 3x^2 + 4x + 1$; $R(x)$ and $C(x)$ are in thousands of dollars, and x is in thousands of units.

22. $R(x) = 100x - x^2$, $C(x) = \frac{1}{3}x^3 - 6x^2 + 89x + 100$; $R(x)$ and $C(x)$ are in thousands of dollars, x is in thousands of units.

23. Raggs, Ltd., a clothing firm, determines that to sell x suits its price per suit must be

$$p = D(x) = 150 - 0.5x.$$

It also determines that its total cost of producing x suits is given by

$$C(x) = 4000 + 0.25x^2.$$

a) Find the total revenue $R(x)$.

b) Find the total profit $P(x)$.

c) How many suits must the company produce and sell to maximize profit?

d) What is the maximum profit?

e) What price per suit must be charged to make this maximum profit?

24. An appliance firm is marketing a new refrigerator. It determines that to sell x refrigerators its price per refrigerator must be

$$p = D(x) = 280 - 0.4x.$$

It also determines that its total cost of producing x refrigerators is given by

$$C(x) = 5000 + 0.6x^2.$$

a) Find the total revenue $R(x)$.

b) Find the total profit $P(x)$.

c) How many refrigerators must the company produce and sell to maximize profit?

d) What is the maximum profit?

e) What price per refrigerator must be charged to make this maximum profit?

25. From a thin piece of cardboard 30 in. by 30 in., square corners are cut out so the sides can be folded up to make a box. What dimensions will yield a box of maximum volume? What is the maximum volume?

26. From a thin piece of cardboard 20 in. by 20 in. square corners are cut out so the sides can be folded up to make a box. What dimensions will yield a box of maximum volume? What is the maximum volume?

27. A container company is designing an open-top, square-based, rectangular box that will have a volume of 62.5 cubic inches. What dimensions yield the minimum surface area? What is the minimum surface area?

28. A soup company is constructing an open-top, rectangular, metal tank with a square base, that will have a volume of 32 cubic feet. What dimensions yield the minimum surface area? What is the minimum surface area?

29. A university is trying to determine what price to charge for football tickets. At $6 per ticket it averages 70,000 spectators per game. For every increase of $1 it loses 10,000 people from the average. Every person at the game spends an average of $1.50 on concessions. What price per ticket should be charged to maximize revenue? How many people will attend at that price?

30. Suppose you are the owner of a 30-unit motel. All units are occupied when you charge $20 a day per unit. For every increase of x dollars in the daily rate, there are x units vacant. Each occupied room costs $2 per day to service and maintain. What should you charge per unit to maximize profit?

31. An apple farm yields an average of 30 bushels of apples per tree when 20 trees are planted on an acre of ground. Each time 1 more tree is planted per acre, the yield decreases 1 bu. per tree due to the extra congestion. How many trees should be planted to get the highest yield?

33. The postal service places a limit of 84 inches on the combined length and girth (distance around) of a package to be sent parcel post. What dimensions of a rectangular box with square cross section will contain the largest volume that can be mailed? [*Hint:* There are two different girths.]

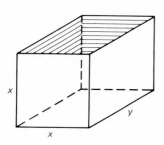

35. For what positive number is the sum of its reciprocal and five times its square a minimum?

37. A rectangular box with a volume of 320 cubic feet is to be constructed with a square base and top. The cost per square foot for the bottom is 15¢, for the top is 10¢, and for the sides is 2.5¢. What dimensions will minimize the cost?

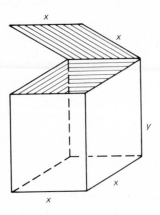

32. When a theater owner charges $3 for admission there is an average attendance of 100 people. For every $0.10 increase in admission, there is a loss of 1 customer from the average. What admission should be charged to maximize revenue?

34. A rectangular play area is to be laid out in a person's back lot and is to contain 48 square yards. The neighbor agrees to pay half the cost of the side of the play area that lines the lot. What dimensions will minimize the cost of the fence?

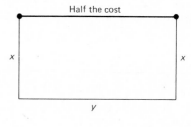

36. For what positive number is the sum of its reciprocal and four times its square a minimum?

38. A merchant who was purchasing a display sign from a salesclerk said, "I want a sign 10 ft by 10 ft." The salesclerk responded, "That's just what we'll give you; only to make it more aesthetic, why don't we change it to 7 ft by 13 ft?" Comment.

39. A Norman window is a rectangle with a semicircle on top. Suppose the perimeter of a particular Norman window is to be 24 ft. What should be its dimensions so the maximum amount of light will be allowed to enter through the window?

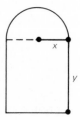

40. Solve Exercise 39, but this time the semicircle is to be stained glass, which transmits only half as much light as the semicircle in Exercise 39.

41. The amount of money deposited in a financial institution in savings accounts is directly proportional to the interest rate the financial institution pays on the money. Suppose a financial institution can loan *all* the money it takes in on its savings accounts at an interest rate of 18%. What interest rate should it pay on its savings accounts to maximize profits?

---

42. A 24-inch piece of string is cut in two pieces. One piece is used to form a circle and the other to form a square. How should the string be cut so the sum of the areas is a minimum? maximum?

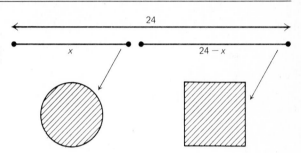

43. The total cost function for producing x units of a certain product is given by

$$C(x) = 8x + 20 + \frac{x^3}{100}.$$

a) Find the marginal cost $C'(x)$.

b) Find the average cost $A(x) = C(x)/x$.

c) Find the *marginal average cost* $A'(x)$.

d) Find the minimum of $A(x)$ and the value x_0 at which it occurs. Find the marginal cost at x_0.

e) Compare $A(x_0)$ and $C'(x_0)$.

44. Consider $A(x) = C(x)/x$.

a) Find $A'(x)$ in terms of $C'(x)$ and $C(x)$.

b) Show that $A(x)$ has a minimum at that value of x_0 such that

$$C'(x_0) = A(x_0) = \frac{C(x_0)}{x_0}.$$

This shows that when marginal cost and average cost are the same, a product is being produced at the least average cost.

8.4   BUSINESS APPLICATION: MINIMIZING INVENTORY COSTS

A retail outlet of a business is usually concerned about inventory costs. Suppose, for example, an appliance store sells 2500 tv sets per year. One way it could operate is to order all the tv sets at once. But then the owners would face the carrying costs (insurance, building space, and so on) of storing all those tv's. Thus they might make several smaller orders, say 5, so that the largest number they would ever have to store is 500. On the other hand, each time they reorder there are certain reorder costs such as paperwork, delivery charges, manpower, and so on. It would, therefore, seem that there is some balance between carrying costs and reorder costs. We will see how calculus can help to determine what that balance might be. We will be trying to minimize the following function:

$$\text{Total inventory costs} = \left(\begin{array}{c}\text{Yearly carrying}\\ \text{costs}\end{array}\right) + \left(\begin{array}{c}\text{Yearly reorder}\\ \text{costs}\end{array}\right).$$

The *lot size* x refers to the largest amount ordered each reordering period. Note the following graphs. Thus if the lot size is x, then x/2 represents the average amount held in stock over the course of the year.

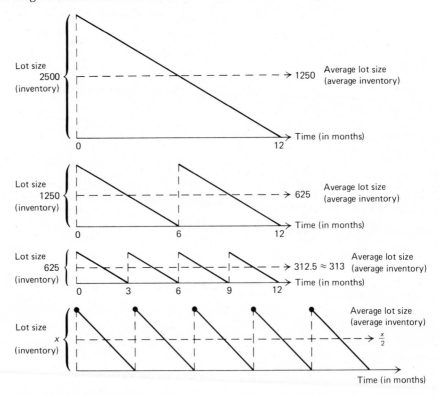

Example 1   A retail appliance store sells 2500 tv's per year. It costs $10 to store one tv for a year. To reorder tv's there is a fixed cost of $20 plus $9 for each tv. How many times per year should the store reorder tv's, and in what lot size, so that inventory costs are minimized?

Solution   Let x = the lot size. Now inventory costs are given by

$$C(x) = (\text{Yearly carrying costs}) + (\text{Yearly reorder costs}).$$

We consider each separately:

a) *Yearly carrying costs.* The average amount held in stock is $x/2$, and it costs \$10 per tv for storage. Thus

$$\text{Yearly carrying costs} = \left(\begin{array}{c}\text{Yearly cost} \\ \text{per item}\end{array}\right)\left(\begin{array}{c}\text{Average number} \\ \text{of items}\end{array}\right) = 10 \cdot \frac{x}{2}.$$

b) *Yearly reorder costs.* Now x = lot size, and suppose there are N reorders each year. Then $Nx = 2500$, and $N = 2500/x$. Thus

$$\text{Yearly reorder costs} = \left(\begin{array}{c}\text{Cost of each} \\ \text{order}\end{array}\right)\left(\begin{array}{c}\text{Number of} \\ \text{reorders}\end{array}\right) = (20 + 9x)\frac{2500}{x}.$$

c) Hence

$$C(x) = 10 \cdot \frac{x}{2} + (20 + 9x)\frac{2500}{x},$$

$$C(x) = 5x + \frac{50{,}000}{x} + 22{,}500.$$

Exploratory exercises

▦ Without a knowledge of calculus one might make a rough estimate of the lot size that will minimize total inventory costs by completing a table like the following. Complete the table and make such an estimate.

Lot size x	Number of reorders $\dfrac{2500}{x}$	Average inventory $\dfrac{x}{2}$	Carrying costs $10 \cdot \dfrac{x}{2}$	Cost of each order $20 + 9x$	Reorder costs $(20 + 9x)\dfrac{2500}{x}$	Total inventory costs $C(x)$ $10 \cdot \dfrac{x}{2} + (20 + 9x)\dfrac{2500}{x}$
2500	1	1250	\$12,500	\$22,520	\$22,520	\$35,020
1250	2	625	\$6,250	\$11,270	\$22,540	
500	5	250	\$2,500	\$4,520		
250	10	125				
167	15	84				
125	20					
100	25					
90	28					
50	50					

d) We want to find a minimum value of C on the interval $[1, 2500]$. We first find $C'(x)$:

$$C'(x) = 5 - \frac{50,000}{x^2}.$$

e) Now $C'(x)$ exists for all x in $[1, 2500]$, so the only critical points are those x such that $C'(x) = 0$. We solve $C'(x) = 0$.

$$5 - \frac{50,000}{x^2} = 0$$

$$5 = \frac{50,000}{x^2}$$

$$5x^2 = 50,000$$

$$x^2 = 10,000$$

$$x = \pm 100$$

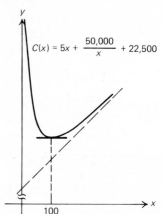

$$C(x) = 5x + \frac{50,000}{x} + 22,500$$

Now there is only one critical point in the interval $[1, 2500]$, $x = 100$, so we can use the second derivative to see if we have a maximum or minimum:

$$C''(x) = \frac{100,000}{x^3}.$$

Now $C''(x)$ is positive for all x in $[1, 2500]$, so we do have a minimum at $x = 100$. Thus, to minimize inventory costs, the store should order tv's (2500/100) or 25 times per year. The lot size is 100.

What happens in such problems when the answer is not a whole number? For functions of this type, we consider the two whole numbers closest to the answer, and substitute them into $C(x)$. The value that yields the smallest $C(x)$ is the lot size.

Example 2 Repeat Example 1, using all the data given, but change the $10 storage cost to $20. How many times per year should the store reorder tv's and in what lot size, so that inventory costs are minimized?

Solution Comparing this with Example 1, we find that the inventory cost function becomes

$$C(x) = 20 \cdot \frac{x}{2} + (20 + 9x)\frac{2500}{x} = 10x + \frac{50,000}{x} + 22,500.$$

Then we find $C'(x)$, set it equal to 0, and solve for x.

$$C'(x) = 10 - \frac{50,000}{x^2} = 0$$

$$10 = \frac{50,000}{x^2}$$

$$10x^2 = 50,000$$

$$x^2 = 5000$$

$$x = \sqrt{5000} \approx 70.7 \quad (\blacksquare \text{ or Table 1}).$$

Since it does not make sense to reorder 70.7 tv's each time, we consider the two numbers closest to 70.7, which are 70 and 71. Now

$$C(70) \approx \$23,914.29 \quad \text{and} \quad C(71) \approx \$23,204.23$$

It follows that the lot size that will minimize cost is 71. [*Note:* Such a procedure will not work for all types of functions, but will work for the type we are considering here. The number of times an order should be placed is 2500/71 ≈ 35, so there is still some estimating involved.]

The value of the lot size that minimizes total inventory costs is often referred to as the *economic ordering quantity*. There are three assumptions made in using the foregoing method to determine the economic ordering quantity. The first is that the demand for the product is the same throughout the year. For television sets this may be reasonable, but for seasonal items such as clothing or skis, this assumption may not be reasonable. The second assumption is that the time between the placing of an order and the time of its receipt should be consistent throughout the year. The third assumption is that the various costs involved, such as storage, shipping charges, and so on, do not vary. This may not be reasonable in a time of inflation, although one may account for them by anticipating what they might be and using average costs. Nevertheless, the model described above can be useful, and it allows us to analyze a seemingly difficult problem using the calculus.

EXERCISE SET 8.4

1. A sporting-goods store sells 100 pool tables per year. It costs $20 to store one pool table for one year. To reorder pool tables there is a fixed cost of $40, plus $16 for each pool table. How many times per year should the store order pool tables, and in what lot size, to minimize inventory costs?

2. A pro shop in a bowling alley sells 200 bowling balls per year. It costs $4 to store one bowling ball for one year. To reorder bowling balls there is a fixed cost of $1, plus $0.50 for each bowling ball. How many times per year should the shop order bowling balls, and in what lot size, to minimize inventory costs?

3. A retail outlet for Boxowitz Calculators sells 360 calculators per year. It costs $8 to store one calculator for one year. To reorder calculators, there is a fixed cost of $10, plus $8 for each calculator. How many times per year should the store order calculators, and in what lot size, to minimize inventory costs?

5. Repeat Exercise 3, using all the data given, but change the $8 storage charge to $9.

7. *Minimizing inventory costs—A general solution.* A store sells Q units of a product per year. It costs a dollars to store one unit for one year. To reorder units, there is a fixed cost of b dollars, plus c dollars for each unit. In what lot size should the store reorder to minimize inventory costs?

4. A sporting-goods store in southern California sells 720 surfboards per year. It costs $2 to store one surfboard for one year. To reorder surfboards there is a fixed cost of $5, plus $2.50 for each surfboard. How many times per year should the store order surfboards, and in what lot size, to minimize inventory costs?

6. Repeat Exercise 4, using all the data given, but change the $5 fixed cost to $4.

8. Use the general solution found in Exercise 7 to find how many times per year a store should reorder, and in what lot size, when $Q = 2500$, $a = \$10$, $b = \$20$, and $c = \$9$.

8.5   APPROXIMATION

Delta Notation

Recall the difference quotient,

$$\frac{f(x + h) - f(x)}{h},$$

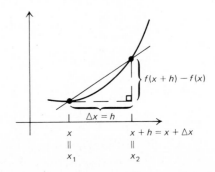

that is used to define the derivative of a function at x. The number h was considered to be a *change* in x. Another notation for such a change is Δx, read "delta x." The expression Δx is *not* the product of Δ and x but is an entity unto itself; that is, it is a new type of variable that represents the *change* in the value of x from a *first* value to a *second*. Thus

$$\Delta x = (x + h) - x = h.$$

If subscripts are used for the first and second values of x, we would have

$$\Delta x = x_2 - x_1 \quad \text{or} \quad x_2 = x_1 + \Delta x.$$

Now Δx can be positive or negative.

Examples   a) If $x_1 = 4$ and $\Delta x = 0.7$, then $x_2 = 4.7$.

b) If $x_1 = 4$ and $\Delta x = -0.7$, then $x_2 = 3.3$.

We usually omit the subscripts and use x and $x + \Delta x$.

Now suppose we have a function given by $y = f(x)$. A change in x from x to $x + \Delta x$ yields a change in y from $f(x)$ to $f(x + \Delta x)$. The change in y is given by

$$\Delta y = f(x + \Delta x) - f(x).$$

Example 1   For $y = x^2$, $x = 4$, and $\Delta x = 0.1$, find Δy.

Solution $\Delta y = (4 + 0.1)^2 - 4^2 = (4.1)^2 - 4^2 = 16.81 - 16 = 0.81.$

Example 2   For $y = x^3$, $x = 2$, and $\Delta x = -0.1$, find Δy.

Solution $\Delta y = [2 + (-0.1)]^3 - 2^3 = (1.9)^3 - 2^3 = 6.859 - 8 = -1.141.$

Using delta notation, the difference quotient

$$\frac{f(x + h) - f(x)}{h}$$

becomes

$$\frac{f(x + \Delta x) - f(x)}{\Delta x} = \frac{\Delta y}{\Delta x}.$$

We can then express the derivative as

$$\frac{dy}{dx} = \lim_{\Delta x \to 0} \frac{\Delta y}{\Delta x}.$$

Note how the delta notation resembles the Leibniz notation.

For values of Δx close to 0 we have the approximation

$$\frac{dy}{dx} \approx \frac{\Delta y}{\Delta x},$$

or

$$f'(x) \approx \frac{\Delta y}{\Delta x}.$$

Multiplying both sides of the second expression by Δx we get

$$\Delta y \approx f'(x)\, \Delta x.$$

We can see this pictorially.

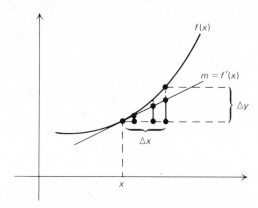

Recall that the derivative is a limit of slopes $\Delta y/\Delta x$ of secant lines. Thus as Δx gets smaller, the ratio $\Delta y/\Delta x$ gets closer to dy/dx. Note also that over small intervals the tangent line is a good approximation, linearly, to the function. Thus it is reasonable to assume that average rates of change $\Delta y/\Delta x$ of the function are approximately the same as the slope of the tangent line.

Let us use the fact that

$$\Delta y \approx f'(x) \, \Delta x$$

to make certain approximations, such as square roots.

Example 3   Approximate $\sqrt{27}$ using $\Delta y \approx f'(x) \, \Delta x$.

Solution   We first think of the number closest to 27 that is a perfect square. This is 25. What we will do is approximate how y, or $\sqrt{x}$, changes when 25 changes by $\Delta x = 2$. Let

$$y = f(x) = \sqrt{x}.$$

Then

$$\Delta y = \sqrt{x + \Delta x} - \sqrt{x} = \sqrt{x + \Delta x} - y,$$

so

$$y + \Delta y = \sqrt{x + \Delta x}.$$

Now

$$f'(x) \, \Delta x = \frac{1}{2} x^{-1/2} \, \Delta x = \frac{1}{2\sqrt{x}} \, \Delta x.$$

Let $x = 25$ and $\Delta x = 2$. Then

$$f'(x)\,\Delta x = \frac{1}{2\sqrt{25}} \cdot 2 = \frac{1}{\sqrt{25}} = \frac{1}{5} = 0.2.$$

So

$$\sqrt{27} = \sqrt{x + \Delta x} = y + \Delta y \approx \sqrt{25} + 0.2 = 5 + 0.2 = 5.2.$$

To five decimal places, $\sqrt{27} = 5.19615$. Thus our approximation is fairly good.

Suppose we have a total cost function $C(x)$. When $\Delta x = 1$, we have

$$\Delta C \approx C'(x).$$

Whether this is a good approximation depends on the function and on the values of x. Let us consider an example.

Example 4 For the total cost function

$$C(x) = 2x^3 - 12x^2 + 30x + 200.$$

a) Find ΔC and $C'(x)$ when $x = 2$ and $\Delta x = 1$.
b) Find ΔC and $C'(x)$ when $x = 100$ and $\Delta x = 1$.

Solution
a) $\Delta C = C(2 + 1) - C(2) = C(3) - C(2) = \$236 - \$228 = \$8$. Recall that $C(2)$ is the total cost of producing 2 units, and $C(3)$ is the total cost of producing 3 units, so $C(3) - C(2)$, or \$8, is the cost of the 3rd unit. Now

$$C'(x) = 6x^2 - 24x + 30, \qquad \text{so} \qquad C'(2) = \$6.$$

b) $\Delta C = C(100 + 1) - C(100) = C(101) - C(100) = \$58{,}220$. Note that this is the cost of the 101st unit. Now

$$C'(100) = \$57{,}630.$$

Note that in (a) we might not consider the approximation between ΔC and $C'(x)$ to be too good, while in (b) the approximation might be considered quite good since the numbers are so large. We have purposely used $\Delta x = 1$ to illustrate the following:

$$C'(x) \approx C(x + 1) - C(x).$$

Marginal cost is (approximately) the cost of the $(x + 1)$st, or next, unit.

This is the historical definition that economists have given to marginal cost.

Similarly,

$$R'(x) \approx R(x + 1) - R(x).$$

Marginal revenue is (approximately) the revenue from the sale of the $(x + 1)$st, or next, unit.

And

$$P'(x) \approx P(x + 1) - P(x).$$

Marginal profit is (approximately) the profit from the production and sale of the $(x + 1)$st, or next, unit.

EXERCISE SET 8.5

In Exercises 1 through 8, find Δy and $f'(x) \Delta x$.

1. For $y = f(x) = x^2$, $x = 2$, and $\Delta x = 0.01$.

2. For $y = x^3$, $x = 2$, and $\Delta x = 0.01$.

3. For $y = f(x) = x + x^2$, $x = 3$, and $\Delta x = 0.04$.

4. For $y = f(x) = x - x^2$, $x = 3$, and $\Delta x = 0.02$.

5. For $y = f(x) = 1/x^2$, $x = 1$, and $\Delta x = 0.5$.

6. For $y = f(x) = 1/x$, $x = 1$, and $\Delta x = 0.2$.

7. For $y = f(x) = 3x - 1$, $x = 4$, and $\Delta x = 2$.

8. For $y = f(x) = 2x - 3$, $x = 8$, and $\Delta x = 0.5$.

9. For the total cost function

$$C(x) = 0.01x^2 + 0.6x + 30,$$

find ΔC and $C'(x)$, when $x = 70$ and $\Delta x = 1$.

10. For the total cost function

$$C(x) = 0.01x^2 + 1.6x + 100$$

find ΔC and $C'(x)$, when $x = 80$ and $\Delta x = 1$.

11. For the total revenue function

$$R(x) = 2x,$$

find ΔR and $R'(x)$, when $x = 70$ and $\Delta x = 1$.

12. For the total revenue function

$$R(x) = 3x,$$

find ΔR and $R'(x)$, when $x = 80$ and $\Delta x = 1$.

13. a) Using $C(x)$ of Exercise 9 and $R(x)$ of Exercise 11, find the total profit $P(x)$.

   b) Find ΔP and $P'(x)$ when $x = 70$ and $\Delta x = 1$.

14. a) Using $C(x)$ of Exercise 10 and $R(x)$ of Exercise 12, find the total profit $P(x)$.

   b) Find ΔP and $P'(x)$ when $x = 80$ and $\Delta x = 1$.

Approximate, using $\Delta y \approx f'(x) \Delta x$.

15. $\sqrt{19}$ **16.** $\sqrt{10}$ **17.** $\sqrt{102}$ **18.** $\sqrt{103}$ **19.** $\sqrt[3]{10}$ **20.** $\sqrt[3]{28}$

CHAPTER 8 REVIEW

1. For $y = x^4 - 3x^2$, find $\dfrac{d^3y}{dx^3}$.

Find the maximum and minimum values, if they exist, over the indicated interval. Where no interval is specified, use the real line.

2. $f(x) = x(6 - x)$

3. $f(x) = x^3 + x^2 - x + 1; \; [-2, \frac{1}{2}]$

4. $f(x) = -x^2 + 8.6x + 10$

5. $f(x) = -2x + 5; \; [-1, 1]$

6. $f(x) = -2x + 5$

7. $f(x) = 3x^2 - x - 1$

8. $f(x) = x^2 + \dfrac{128}{x}; \; (0, \infty)$

9. Of all numbers whose difference is 8, find the two that have the minimum product.

10. Minimize $Q = x^2 + y^2$, where $x - y = 10$.

11. Find the maximum profit and the number of units that must be produced and sold to yield the maximum profit.

$$R(x) = x^2 + 110x + 60,$$

$$C(x) = 1.1x^2 + 10x + 80$$

12. From a piece of cardboard 60 in. by 60 in., square corners are cut out so the sides can be folded up to make a box. What dimensions will yield a box of maximum volume? What is the maximum volume?

13. A sporting-goods store sells 1225 tennis rackets per year. It costs $2 to store one tennis racket for one year. To reorder tennis rackets, there is a fixed cost of $1, plus $0.50 for each tennis racket. How many times per year should the sporting-goods store order tennis rackets, and in what lot size, to minimize inventory costs?

14. A company determines that in order to sell x units of a certain product its price per unit must be

$$p = D(x) = 200 - x.$$

It also determines that its total cost of producing x units is given by

$$C(x) = 5000 + 8x.$$

a) Find the total revenue $R(x)$.

b) Find the total profit $P(x)$.

c) How many units must the company produce and sell in order to maximize profit?

d) What is the maximum profit?

e) What price per unit must be charged to make this maximum profit?

15. For $y = f(x) = x^2 - 3$, $x = 5$, and $\Delta x = 0.1$, find Δy and $f'(x) \, \Delta x$.

16. Approximate $\sqrt{104}$, using $\Delta y \approx f'(x) \, \Delta x$.

17. The total cost of producing x units of a product is given by

$$C(x) = 100x + 100\sqrt{x} + \frac{\sqrt{x^3}}{100}.$$

a) Find the average cost $A(x)$.

b) Find the minimum value of $A(x)$.

EXPONENTIAL AND LOGARITHMIC FUNCTIONS

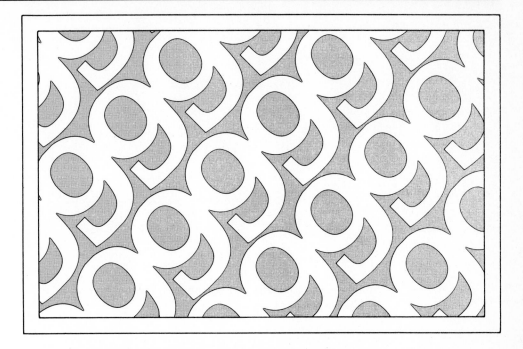

9.1 EXPONENTIAL AND LOGARITHMIC FUNCTIONS

Exponential Functions

The following are examples of exponential functions:

$$y = 2^x, \qquad y = (\tfrac{1}{2})^x, \qquad y = (0.4)^x.$$

Note, in contrast to power functions like $y = x^2$ or $y = x^3$, that the variable in an exponential function is in the exponent. Exponential functions have extensive application. Let us consider their graphs.

Example 1 Graph $y = 2^x$.

Solution a) First we find some function values.

x	0	$\frac{1}{2}$	1	2	3	-1	-2
y (or 2^x)	1	1.4	2	4	8	$\frac{1}{2}$	$\frac{1}{4}$

Note: For

$x = 0, y = 2^0 = 1$

$x = \frac{1}{2}, y = 2^{1/2} = \sqrt{2} \approx 1.4$

$x = 1, y = 2^1 = 2$

$x = 2, y = 2^2 = 4$

$x = 3, y = 2^3 = 8$

$x = -1, y = 2^{-1} = \frac{1}{2}$

$x = -2, y = 2^{-2} = \dfrac{1}{2^2} = \dfrac{1}{4}$

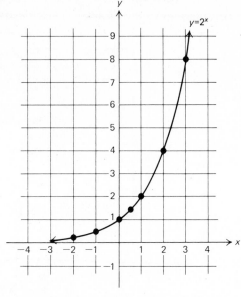

b) Next, we plot the points and connect them with a smooth curve as shown in the figure.

Example 2   Graph $y = (\frac{1}{2})^x$.

Solution   a) We first find some function values. But before we do this, we should note that

$$y = (\tfrac{1}{2})^x = (2^{-1})^x = 2^{-x}.$$

This will ease our work.

x	0	$\frac{1}{2}$	1	2	-1	-2	-3
y	1	0.7	$\frac{1}{2}$	$\frac{1}{4}$	2	4	8

Note: For,

$x = 0, y = 2^{-0} = 1$

$x = \dfrac{1}{2}, y = 2^{-1/2}$

$\quad = \dfrac{1}{\sqrt{2}} \approx \dfrac{1}{1.4} \approx 0.7$

$x = 1, y = 2^{-1} = \frac{1}{2}$

$x = 2, y = 2^{-2} = \frac{1}{4}$

$x = -1, y = 2^{-(-1)} = 2$

$x = -2, y = 2^{-(-2)} = 4$

$x = -3, y = 2^{-(-3)} = 8$

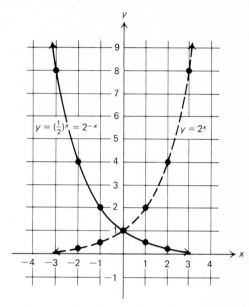

b) We plot these points and connect them with a smooth curve as shown by the solid curve in the figure. The dashed curve shows $y = 2^x$ for comparison.

Logarithmic Functions

The definition of logarithms is as follows:

$$\text{"}y = \log_a x\text{"} \qquad \textbf{means} \qquad \text{"}x = a^y\text{"}$$

The number a is called the *logarithmic base*. Thus, for logarithms base 10, $\log_{10} x$ is that number y such that $x = 10^y$. A logarithm can thus be thought of as an exponent. We can convert from a logarithmic equation to an exponential equation, and conversely, as follows.

Logarithmic equation	*Exponential equation*
$\log_a M = N$	$a^N = M$
$\log_{10} 100 = 2$	$10^2 = 100$
$\log_{10} 0.01 = -2$	$10^{-2} = 0.01$
$\log_{49} 7 = \frac{1}{2}$	$49^{1/2} = 7$

To graph a logarithmic equation, we can graph its equivalent exponential equation.

Example 3   Graph $y = \log_2 x$.

Solution   We first write the equivalent exponential equation

$$x = 2^y.$$

We select values for y and find the corresponding values of 2^y.

x (or 2^y)	1	2	4	8	$\frac{1}{2}$	$\frac{1}{4}$
y	0	1	2	3	-1	-2

Next, we plot points, remembering that x is still the first coordinate.

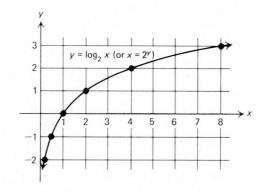

Basic Properties of Logarithms

The following are some basic properties of logarithms. The proofs are optional, but follow from properties of exponents.

PROPERTY 1. $\log_a MN = \log_a M + \log_a N$

PROPERTY 2. $\log_a \dfrac{M}{N} = \log_a M - \log_a N$

PROPERTY 3. $\log_a M^k = k \cdot \log_a M$

PROPERTY 4. $\log_a a = 1$

PROPERTY 5. $\log_a a^k = k$

PROPERTY 6. $\log_a 1 = 0$

Proof of 1 and 2 Let $X = \log_a M$ and $Y = \log_a N$. Then, writing the equivalent exponential equations, we have

$$M = a^X \quad \text{and} \quad N = a^Y.$$

Then by properties of exponents (see Section 1.1),

$$MN = a^X \cdot a^Y = a^{X+Y}, \quad \text{so} \quad \log_a MN = X + Y$$
$$= \log_a M + \log_a N,$$

$$\frac{M}{N} = a^X \div a^Y = a^{X-Y}, \quad \text{so} \quad \log_a \frac{M}{N} = X - Y$$
$$= \log_a M - \log_a N.$$

Proof of 3 Let $X = \log_a M$. Then

$$a^X = M, \quad \text{so} \quad (a^X)^k = M^k, \quad \text{or} \quad a^{Xk} = M^k.$$

Thus

$$\log_a M^k = Xk = k \cdot \log_a M.$$

Proof of 4 $\log_a a = 1$ because $a^1 = a$.

Proof of 5 $\log_a a^k = k$ because $(a^k) = a^k$.

Proof of 6 $\log_a 1 = 0$ because $a^0 = 1$.

Let us illustrate these properties.

Examples Given

$$\log_a 2 = 0.301$$
$$\log_a 3 = 0.477,$$

find each of the following.

a) $\log_a 6$.
$$\begin{aligned}\log_a 6 = \log_a (2 \cdot 3) &= \log_a 2 + \log_a 3 \qquad \text{(Property 1)}\\ &= 0.301 + 0.477\\ &= 0.778\end{aligned}$$

b) $\log_a \frac{2}{3}$.
$$\begin{aligned}\log_a \tfrac{2}{3} &= \log_a 2 - \log_a 3 \qquad \text{(Property 2)}\\ &= 0.301 - 0.477\\ &= -0.176\end{aligned}$$

c) $\log_a 81$.
$$\begin{aligned}\log_a 81 = \log_a 3^4 &= 4 \log_a 3 \qquad \text{(Property 3)}\\ &= 4(0.477)\\ &= 1.908\end{aligned}$$

d) $\log_a \frac{1}{3}$. $\log_a \frac{1}{3} = \log_a 1 - \log_a 3$ (Property 2)
$\phantom{\log_a \frac{1}{3}} = 0 - 0.477$ (Property 6)
$\phantom{\log_a \frac{1}{3}} = -0.477$

e) $\log_a \sqrt{a}$. $\log_a \sqrt{a} = \log_a a^{1/2} = \frac{1}{2}$ (Property 5)

f) $\log_a 2a$. $\log_a 2a = \log_a 2 + \log_a a$ (Property 1)
$ = 0.301 + 1$ (Property 4)
$ = 1.301$

g) $\log_a 5$.   *No way to find using these properties.*
$(\log_a 5 \neq \log_a 2 + \log_a 3)$

h) $\dfrac{\log_a 3}{\log_a 2}$. $\dfrac{\log_a 3}{\log_a 2} = \dfrac{0.477}{0.301} = 1.58$.

We simply divided, not using any of the properties.

Natural Logarithms

The number *e*, which is approximately 2.718282, has extensive application in many fields. *We will develop e thoroughly in Section 9.2.* The number $\log_e x$ is called the *natural logarithm* of x and is abbreviated ln x; that is,

$$\ln x = \log_e x.$$

The following is a restatement of the basic properties of logarithms in terms of natural logarithms.

PROPERTY 1. $\ln MN = \ln M + \ln N$

PROPERTY 2. $\ln \dfrac{M}{N} = \ln M - \ln N$

PROPERTY 3. $\ln a^k = k \cdot \ln a$

PROPERTY 4. $\ln e = 1$

PROPERTY 5. $\ln e^k = k$

PROPERTY 6. $\ln 1 = 0$

Let us illustrate these properties.

Examples   Given

$$\ln 2 = 0.6931, \quad \ln 3 = 1.0986,$$

find each of the following.

a) ln 6. $\quad$ ln 6 = ln(2 · 3) = ln 2 + ln 3 $\quad\quad$ (Property 1)
$\quad\quad\quad\quad\quad\quad\quad$ = 0.6931 + 1.0986
$\quad\quad\quad\quad\quad\quad\quad$ = 1.7917

b) ln 81. $\quad$ ln 81 = ln(3⁴) $\quad\quad\quad\quad\quad\quad$ (Property 3)
$\quad\quad\quad\quad\quad\quad$ = 4 ln 3
$\quad\quad\quad\quad\quad\quad$ = 4(1.0986)
$\quad\quad\quad\quad\quad\quad$ = 4.3944

c) ln $\frac{2}{3}$. $\quad$ ln $\frac{2}{3}$ = ln 2 − ln 3 $\quad\quad\quad\quad$ (Property 2)
$\quad\quad\quad\quad\quad$ = 0.6931 − 1.0986
$\quad\quad\quad\quad\quad$ = −0.4055

d) ln $\frac{1}{3}$. $\quad$ ln $\frac{1}{3}$ = ln 1 − ln 3 $\quad\quad\quad\quad$ (Property 2)
$\quad\quad\quad\quad\quad$ = 0 − 1.0986 $\quad\quad\quad\quad\quad$ (Property 6)
$\quad\quad\quad\quad\quad$ = −1.0986

e) ln 2e. $\quad$ ln 2e = ln 2 + ln e $\quad\quad\quad\quad$ (Property 1)
$\quad\quad\quad\quad\quad$ = 0.6931 + 1 $\quad\quad\quad\quad\quad$ (Property 4)
$\quad\quad\quad\quad\quad$ = 1.6931

f) ln $\sqrt{e^3}$. $\quad$ ln $\sqrt{e^3}$ = ln $e^{3/2}$ $\quad\quad\quad\quad$ (Property 5)
$\quad\quad\quad\quad\quad\quad\quad$ = $\frac{3}{2}$

Finding Natural Logarithms Using a Calculator If you have a $\boxed{\text{ln}}$ key on your calculator, you can find natural logarithms directly.

Examples Find each logarithm on your calculator. Round to six decimal places.

$$\text{ln } 5.24 = 1.656321, \quad \text{ln } 0.00001277 \approx -11.268412.$$

Finding Natural Logarithms Using a Table (Optional) If you do not have a calculator with a natural logarithm key, you can use Table 3. Part of Table 3 is shown below. It shows some values of ln x.

x	0.00	0.01	0.02	0.03	0.04	0.05	0.06	0.07	0.08	0.09
5.0	1.6094	1.6114	1.6134	1.6154	1.6174	1.6194	1.6214	1.6233	1.6253	1.6273
5.1	1.6292	1.6312	1.6332	1.6351	1.6371	1.6390	1.6409	1.6429	1.6448	1.6467
5.2	1.6487	1.6506	1.6525	1.6544	1.6563	1.6582	1.6601	1.6620	1.6639	1.6658
5.3	1.6677	1.6696	1.6715	1.6734	1.6752	1.6771	1.6790	1.6808	1.6827	1.6845
5.4	1.6864	1.6882	1.6901	1.6919	1.6938	1.6956	1.6974	1.6993	1.7011	1.7029

Example 4 Find ln 5.24. Use Table 3. To find ln 5.24, locate the row headed 5.2; then move across to the column headed 0.04. Note the boxed number in the table. Thus

$$\text{ln } 5.24 = 1.6563.$$

We find natural logarithms of numbers not in Table 3 as follows. We first express in scientific notation the number whose natural logarithm we are finding; that is, as a product $M \times 10^k$, where $1 \leqslant M < 10$.

Example 5   Find ln 5240. Use Table 3.

$$\ln 5240 = \ln (5.24 \times 1000)$$

$$= \ln (5.24 \times 10^3) \qquad (1000 = 10^3)$$

$$= \ln 5.24 + \ln 10^3 \qquad \text{(Property 1)}$$

$$= \ln 5.24 + 3 \ln 10 \qquad \text{(Property 3)}$$

$$= 1.6563 + 6.9078 \qquad \text{(Find ln 5.24 in the body of Table 3}$$
$$\text{and 3 ln 10 at the bottom.)}$$

$$= 8.5641$$

Example 6   Find ln 0.000524. Use Table 3.

$$\ln 0.000524 = \ln (5.24 \times 0.0001)$$

$$= \ln (5.24 \times 10^{-4}) \qquad (0.0001 = 10^{-4})$$

$$= \ln 5.24 + \ln 10^{-4} \qquad \text{(Property 1)}$$

$$= \ln 5.24 - 4 \ln 10 \qquad \text{(Property 3)}$$

$$= 1.6563 - 9.2103 \qquad \text{(Find ln 5.24 in the body of Table 3}$$
$$\text{and 3 ln 10 at the bottom.)}$$

$$= -7.554$$

A number like ln 5.243 can not be found in Table 3. In such cases we round and then use Table 3:

$$\ln 5.243 \approx \ln 5.24 \approx 1.6563.$$

Exponential Equations

An equation with a variable in the exponent we call an *exponential* equation. Logarithms can be used to manipulate or solve exponential equations.

Example 7   Solve for t: $e^t = 40$.

Solution

$$\ln e^t = \ln 40 \qquad \text{(Taking the natural logarithm on both sides)}$$

$$t = \ln 40 \qquad \text{(Property 5)}$$

$$t = 3.688879 \qquad (\blacksquare \text{ or Table 3.})$$

$$t \approx 3.7$$

It should be noted that this is an approximation for t even though an equal sign is often used.

Example 8   Solve for t: $e^{-0.04t} = 0.05$

Solution

$$\ln e^{-0.04t} = \ln 0.05 \qquad \text{(Taking the natural logarithm on both sides.)}$$

$$-0.04t = \ln 0.05 \qquad \text{(Property 5)}$$

$$t = \frac{\ln 0.05}{-0.04}$$

$$t = \frac{-2.995732}{-0.04} \qquad (\blacksquare \text{ or Table 3.})$$

$$t \approx 75$$

CALCULATOR NOTE: For purposes of space and explanation, we have rounded the value of $\ln 0.05$ to -2.995732 in an intermediate step. On a calculator you should find

$$\frac{\ln 0.05}{-0.04},$$

obtaining

$$\frac{-2.995732274}{-0.04}.$$

Divide, and round at the end. Answers in the key are found in this manner. Remember, the number of places in a table or on a calculator may affect the accuracy of the answer. Usually, your answer should agree to at least three digits.

EXERCISE SET 9.1

Graph.

1. $y = 4^x$ **2.** $y = 5^x$ **3.** $y = (0.4)^x$ **4.** $y = (0.2)^x$

5. $y = \log_4 x$ **6.** $y = \log_5 x$

Write equivalent exponential equations.

7. $\log_2 8 = 3$ **8.** $\log_3 81 = 4$ **9.** $\log_8 2 = \frac{1}{3}$ **10.** $\log_{27} 3 = \frac{1}{3}$

11. $\log_a K = J$ **12.** $\log_a J = K$ **13.** $\log_b T = v$ **14.** $\log_c Y = t$

Write equivalent logarithmic equations.

15. $e^M = b$ **16.** $e^t = p$ **17.** $10^2 = 100$ **18.** $10^3 = 1000$

19. $10^{-1} = 0.1$ **20.** $10^{-2} = 0.01$ **21.** $M^p = V$ **22.** $Q^n = T$

Given $\log_b 3 = 1.099$ and $\log_b 5 = 1.609$, find each of the following. Do not use tables.

23. $\log_b 15$ **24.** $\log_b \frac{3}{5}$ **25.** $\log_b \frac{5}{3}$ **26.** $\log_b \frac{1}{3}$

27. $\log_b \frac{1}{5}$ **28.** $\log_b \sqrt{b}$ **29.** $\log_b \sqrt{b^3}$ **30.** $\log_b 3b$

31. $\log_b 5b$ **32.** $\log_b 9$ **33.** $\log_b 25$ **34.** $\log_b 75$

Given $\ln 4 = 1.3863$ and $\ln 5 = 1.6094$, find each of the following. Do not use tables.

35. $\ln 20$ **36.** $\ln \frac{4}{5}$ **37.** $\ln \frac{5}{4}$ **38.** $\ln \frac{1}{5}$ **39.** $\ln \frac{1}{4}$ **40.** $\ln 5e$

41. $\ln 4e$ **42.** $\ln \sqrt{e^6}$ **43.** $\ln \sqrt{e^8}$ **44.** $\ln 25$ **45.** $\ln 16$ **46.** $\ln 100$

▦ Find each logarithm. Round to six decimal places.

47. $\ln 5894$ **48.** $\ln 99{,}999$ **49.** $\ln 0.0182$ **50.** $\ln 0.00087$

Using Table 3, find the following logarithms.

51. $\ln 1.88$ **52.** $\ln 18.8$ **53.** $\ln 0.0188$ **54.** $\ln 0.188$

55. $\ln 906$ **56.** $\ln 8100$ **57.** $\ln 0.011$ **58.** $\ln 0.00056$

Solve for t.

59. $e^t = 100$ **60.** $e^t = 1000$ **61.** $e^t = 60$ **62.** $e^t = 90$

63. $e^{-t} = 0.1$ **64.** $e^{-t} = 0.01$ **65.** $e^{-0.02t} = 0.06$ **66.** $e^{0.07t} = 2$

■ ────────────────────────────────────

Solve for t.   ▦ Use input–output tables. Find each limit.

67. $P = P_0 e^{kt}$ **68.** $P = P_0 e^{-kt}$ **69.** $\lim_{x \to \infty} \ln x$ **70.** $\lim_{x \to 1} \ln x$

9.2   THE EXPONENTIAL FUNCTION, BASE e

The exponential functions

$$f(x) = ce^{kx} \quad \text{and} \quad f(x) = ce^{-kx}$$

are two of the most important ones in mathematics and in the applications of mathematics.

The General Base a

In Chapter 2 we reviewed definitions of expressions of the type a^x, where x was a rational number. For example,

$$a^{2.34}, \quad \text{or} \quad a^{234/100},$$

means "raise a to the 234th power and take the 100th root."

What about expressions with irrational exponents, such as $2^{\sqrt{2}}$, 2^{π}, or $2^{-\sqrt{3}}$? An irrational number is a number named by an infinite, nonrepeating decimal. Let us consider 2^{π}. We know π is irrational with infinite, nonrepeating decimal expansion

$$3.141592654 \ldots.$$

This means that π is approached as a limit by the rational numbers

$$3, \quad 3.1, \quad 3.14, \quad 3.141, \quad 3.1415, \ldots ;$$

so it seems reasonable that 2^π should be approached as a limit by the rational powers

$$2^3, \quad 2^{3.1}, \quad 2^{3.14}, \quad 2^{3.141}, \quad 2^{3.1415}, \ldots.$$

We define 2^π to be that limit.

In general, a^x is approximated by the values of a^r for rational numbers r near x; a^x is the limit of a^r as r approaches x through rational values. In summary, for $a > 0$, the definition of a^x for rational numbers x can be extended to arbitrary real numbers x in such a way that the usual laws of exponents, such as

$$a^x \cdot a^y = a^{x+y}, \quad a^x \div a^y = a^{x-y}, \quad (a^x)^y = a^{xy}, \quad \text{and} \quad a^{-x} = \frac{1}{a^x},$$

still hold. Moreover, the function so obtained,

$$f(x) = a^x,$$

is continuous.

The following are some properties of the exponential function for various bases.

1. The function $f(x) = a^x$, where $a > 1$, is a positive, increasing, continuous function; and as x gets smaller, a^x approaches 0.

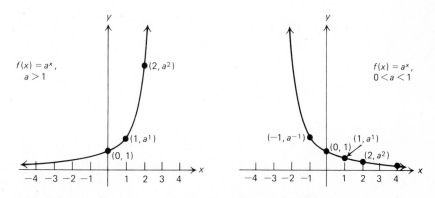

2. The function $f(x) = a^x$, where $0 < a < 1$, is a positive, decreasing, continuous function; and as x gets larger, a^x approaches 0. When $a = 1$, $f(x) = a^x = 1^x = 1$, and is a constant function.

Let us consider finding derivatives of exponential functions.

The Derivative of a^x, the Number e

Let us consider finding the derivative of the exponential function

$$f(x) = a^x.$$

The derivative is given by

$$f'(x) = \lim_{h \to 0} \frac{f(x + h) - f(x)}{h} \qquad \text{(Definition of the derivative.)}$$

$$= \lim_{h \to 0} \frac{a^{x+h} - a^x}{h} \qquad \text{(Substituting } a^{x+h} \text{ for } f(x + h) \text{ and } a^x \text{ for } f(x))$$

$$= \lim_{h \to 0} \frac{a^x \cdot a^h - a^x \cdot 1}{h}.$$

We get

$$f'(x) = a^x \cdot \lim_{h \to 0} \frac{a^h - 1}{h}. \qquad (1)$$

In particular, for $g(x) = 2^x$,

$$g'(x) = 2^x \cdot \lim_{h \to 0} \frac{2^h - 1}{h}.$$

Note that the limit does not depend on the value of x at which we are evaluating the derivative. For $g'(x)$ to exist, we must determine if

$$\lim_{h \to 0} \frac{2^h - 1}{h} \quad \text{exists.}$$

Let us investigate this question using a calculator and an input–output table.

h	$\dfrac{2^h - 1}{h}$
0.5	0.82843
0.25	0.75683
0.1	0.71773
0.01	0.69556
0.001	0.69339

The table suggests that $(2^h - 1)/h$ has a limit as h approaches 0, and that its approximate value is 0.7, so that

$$g'(x) \approx (0.7)2^x.$$

In other words, the derivative is a constant times the function value 2^x.

Similarly, for $t(x) = 3^x$,

$$t'(x) = 3^x \cdot \lim_{h \to 0} \frac{3^h - 1}{h}.$$

Again we can find an approximation for the limit which does not depend on the value of x at which we are evaluating the derivative. The student should construct an input–output table. The table should suggest that $(3^h - 1)/h$ has a limit as h approaches 0, and that its approximate value is 1.1, so that

$$t'(x) \approx (1.1)3^x.$$

In other words, the derivative is a constant times the function value 3^x.

In Fig. 1 we have graphed $g(x) = 2^x$ and $g'(x) \approx (0.7)2^x$. Note that the graph of g' lies *below* the graph of g.

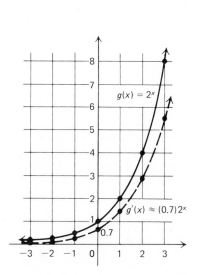

Figure 1

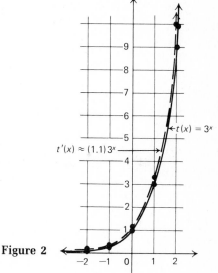

Figure 2

In Fig. 2 we have graphed $t(x) = 3^x$ and $t'(x) \approx (1.1)3^x$. Note that the graph of t' lies *above* the graph of t.

We might expect that there is exactly one base a between 2 and 3 for which a^x and its derivative have the same graph. This conjecture can be proved (though we will not do it here). We define the number e to be the unique positive real number for which

$$\lim_{h \to 0} \frac{e^h - 1}{h} = 1.$$

It follows that for the exponential function $f(x) = e^x$,

$$f'(x) = e^x \cdot \lim_{h \to 0} \frac{e^h - 1}{h} = e^x \cdot 1 = e^x.$$

Approximating e

We will now consider a way of approximating e which also happens to be an application.

The compound interest formula is

$$A = P\left(1 + \frac{i}{n}\right)^{nt},$$

where A is the amount an initial investment P will be worth after t years at interest rate i, compounded n times per year. Suppose \$1 is an initial investment at 100% interest for 1 year (no financial institution would pay this). The above formula becomes

$$A = \left(1 + \frac{1}{n}\right)^{n}.$$

Suppose we were to have the compounding periods increase indefinitely. The amount A would be growing at interest compounded continuously. Let us explore this in the following input–output table.

n	$\left(1 + \dfrac{1}{n}\right)^{n}$
1 (compounding annually)	\$2.000000
2 (compounding semiannually)	\$2.250000
3	\$2.370370
4 (compounding quarterly)	\$2.441406
5	\$2.488320
100	\$2.704814
365 (compounding daily)	\$2.714567
8760 (compounding hourly)	\$2.718121

It can be shown that the number e can be described by the limit:

$$e = \lim_{n \to \infty} \left(1 + \frac{1}{n}\right)^{n}.$$

That is, e is that number which

$$\left(1 + \frac{1}{n}\right)^n$$

approaches as n gets larger without bound. To ten decimal places e is given by

$$e = 2.7182818284 \ldots.$$

Derivatives of Exponential Functions

We have established that for the function $f(x) = e^x$, we also have $f'(x) = e^x$. Or, simply,

$$\frac{d}{dx} e^x = e^x.$$

Note that this says that the derivative (the slope of the tangent line) at any x is the same as the function value. Let us find some other derivatives.

Example 1 $\quad \dfrac{d}{dx} 3e^x = 3e^x$

Example 2 $\quad \dfrac{d}{dx} x^2 e^x = x^2 \cdot e^x + 2x \cdot e^x \qquad$ (Product Rule)

$\qquad\qquad\qquad\;\; = e^x(x^2 + 2x), \text{ or } xe^x(x + 2) \qquad$ (Factoring)

Example 3 $\quad \dfrac{d}{dx}\left(\dfrac{e^x}{x^3}\right) = \dfrac{x^3 \cdot e^x - e^x(3x^2)}{x^6} \qquad$ (Quotient Rule)

$\qquad\qquad\qquad\quad = \dfrac{x^2 e^x(x - 3)}{x^6} \qquad$ (Factoring)

$\qquad\qquad\qquad\quad = \dfrac{e^x(x - 3)}{x^4} \qquad$ (Simplifying)

The following form of the Chain Rule allows us to find many other derivatives.

$$\frac{d}{dx} e^{f(x)} = f'(x)e^{f(x)} \qquad \text{or} \qquad \frac{d}{dx} e^{\square} = \square' \cdot e^{\square}$$

The following gives us a way to remember this rule.

$$e^{x^2 - 5x}$$
$$(2x - 5)e^{x^2 - 5x}$$

Multiply the original function by the derivative of the exponent.

Example 4 $\dfrac{d}{dx} e^{3x} = 3e^{3x}$

Example 5 $\dfrac{d}{dx} e^{-x^2+4x-7} = (-2x + 4)e^{-x^2+4x-7}$

Example 6 $\dfrac{d}{dx} e^{\sqrt{x^2-3}} = \frac{1}{2}(x^2 - 3)^{-1/2} \cdot 2x \cdot e^{\sqrt{x^2-3}}$

$$= x(x^2 - 3)^{-1/2} \cdot e^{\sqrt{x^2-3}}$$

$$= \dfrac{x e^{\sqrt{x^2-3}}}{\sqrt{x^2 - 3}}$$

Graphs of e^x, e^{-x}, and $1 - e^{-kx}$

We can use a calculator or Table 4 (in the back of the book) to find approximate values of e^x and e^{-x}. With these we can draw graphs (Figures 3 and 4) of the functions.

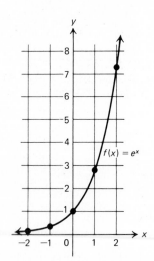

Figure 3

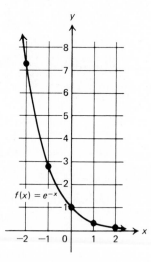

Figure 4

Note that the graph of e^{-x} is a reflection or mirror image of the graph of e^x across the y-axis.

Example 7 Graph $f(x) = 1 - e^{-2x}$, for nonnegative values of x.

Solution We obtain these values using a calculator or Table 4 at the back of the book.

x	0	$\frac{1}{2}$	1	2	3
$f(x)$	0	0.63	0.86	0.98	0.998

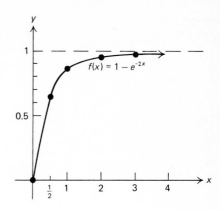

For example,

$$f(1) = 1 - e^{-2 \cdot 1}$$

$$= 1 - e^{-2}$$

$$= 1 - 0.135335 \approx 0.86.$$

In general, the graph of $f(x) = 1 - e^{-kx}$, where $k > 0$, increases from 0, since $f'(x) = ke^{-kx} > 0$, and approaches 1 as x gets larger; that is to say, $\lim_{x \to \infty} (1 - e^{-kx}) = 1$.

Application

Example 8 A company begins a radio advertising campaign in New York City to market a new product. The percentage of the "target market" that buys a product is normally a function of the length of the advertising campaign. The radio station estimates this percentage as $(1 - e^{-0.04t})$ for this type of product, where t = number of days of the campaign. The target market is estimated to be 1,000,000 people and the price per unit is $0.50. The costs of advertising are $1000 per day. Find the length of the advertising campaign that will result in maximum profit.

Solution That the percentage of the target market that buys the product can be modeled by $f(t) = 1 - e^{-0.04t}$ is justified by looking at its graph.

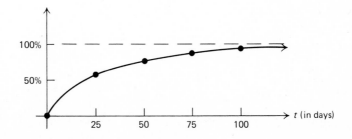

The function increases from 0(0%) towards 1(100%). The longer the advertising campaign, the larger the percentage of the market that has bought the product. (See also the discussion in Section 7.4.)

Recall the profit function (here expressed in terms of time, t):

$$\text{Profit} = \text{Revenue} - \text{Cost}$$

$$P(t) = R(t) - C(t).$$

a) Find $R(t)$.

$$R(t) = (\text{Price per unit}) \cdot (\text{Target market}) \cdot (\text{Percentage buying})$$

$$R(t) = 0.5(1{,}000{,}000)(1 - e^{-0.04t}) = 500{,}000 - 500{,}000e^{-0.04t}$$

b) Find $C(t)$

$$C(t) = (\text{Advertising costs per day}) \cdot (\text{Number of days})$$

$$C(t) = 1000t.$$

c) Find $P(t)$, and take its derivative.

$$P(t) = R(t) - C(t)$$

$$P(t) = 500{,}000 - 500{,}000e^{-0.04t} - 1000t$$

$$P'(t) = (-0.04)(-500{,}000e^{-0.04t}) - 1000$$

$$P'(t) = 20{,}000e^{-0.04t} - 1000.$$

d) Set the first derivative equal to 0 and solve.

$$20{,}000e^{-0.04t} - 1000 = 0$$

$$20{,}000e^{-0.04t} = 1{,}000$$

$$e^{-0.04t} = \frac{1{,}000}{20{,}000} = 0.05 \qquad (1)$$

$$\ln e^{-0.04t} = \ln 0.05$$

$$-0.04t = \ln 0.05$$

$$t = \frac{\ln 0.05}{-0.04}$$

$$t = \frac{-2.995732}{-0.04} \qquad (\blacksquare \text{ or Table 3.})$$

$$t \approx 75.$$

e) We have only one critical point. So we can use the second derivative to determine if we have a maximum.

$$P''(t) = -0.04(20{,}000e^{-0.04t}) = -800e^{-0.04t}.$$

Now since exponential functions are positive, $e^{-0.04t} > 0$ for all numbers t. Thus $-800e^{-0.04t} < 0$ for all numbers t. Thus $P''(t)$ is less than 0 for $t = 75$ and we have a maximum.

The length of the advertising campaign must be 75 days to result in maximum profit.

A *word of caution!* Functions of the type a^x (for example, 2^x, 3^x, and e^x) are different from functions of the type x^a (for example, x^2, x^3, $x^{1/2}$). For a^x the variable is in the exponent. For x^a the variable is in the base. The derivative of a^x is not xa^{x-1}. In particular,

$$\frac{d}{dx}e^x \neq xe^{x-1}, \quad \text{but} \quad \frac{d}{dx}e^x = e^x.$$

EXERCISE SET 9.2

Differentiate.

1. e^{3x}	**2.** e^{2x}	**3.** $5e^{-2x}$	**4.** $4e^{-3x}$	**5.** $3 - e^{-x}$	**6.** $2 - e^{-x}$
7. $-7e^x$	**8.** $-4e^x$	**9.** $\frac{1}{2}e^{2x}$	**10.** $\frac{1}{4}e^{4x}$	**11.** x^4e^x	**12.** x^5e^x
13. $\dfrac{e^x}{x^4}$	**14.** $\dfrac{e^x}{x^5}$	**15.** e^{-x^2+7x}	**16.** e^{-x^2+8x}	**17.** $e^{-x^2/2}$	**18.** $e^{x^2/2}$

19. $e^{\sqrt{x-7}}$ **20.** $e^{\sqrt{x-4}}$ **21.** $\sqrt{e^x - 1}$

22. $\sqrt{e^x + 1}$ **23.** $xe^{-2x} + e^{-x} + x^3$ **24.** $e^x + x^3 - xe^x$

25. $1 - e^{-x}$ **26.** $1 - e^{-3x}$ **27.** $1 - e^{-kx}$

28. $1 - e^{-mx}$

Graph, using Table 4.

29. $f(x) = e^{2x}$ **30.** $f(x) = e^{(1/2)x}$ **31.** $f(x) = e^{-2x}$ **32.** $f(x) = e^{-(1/2)x}$

33. $f(x) = 1 - e^{-x}$, for nonnegative values of x. **34.** $f(x) = 2(1 - e^{-x})$, for nonnegative values of x.

Applied Problems

35. Solve the advertising problem (Example 8) where the costs of advertising are $2000 per day.

36. Solve the advertising problem where the costs of advertising are $4000 per day.

37. A company's total cost, in millions of dollars, is given by

$$C(t) = 100 - 50e^{-t},$$

where t = time. Find

   a) the marginal cost $C'(t)$,

   b) $C'(0)$,

   c) $C'(4)$.

38. A company's total cost, in millions of dollars, is given by

$$C(t) = 200 - 40e^{-t},$$

where t = time. Find

   a) the marginal cost $C'(t)$,

   b) $C'(0)$,

   c) $C'(5)$.

39. *Acceptances of a new medicine.* The percentage P of doctors who accept a new medicine is given by

$$P(t) = 1 - e^{-0.2t},$$

where t = time, in months.

a) Find $P(1)$ and $P(6)$.

b) Find $P'(t)$.

c) How many months will it take for 90% of the doctors to accept the new medicine?

40. A typist learns to type W words per minute after t weeks of practice, where W is given by

$$W(t) = 100(1 - e^{-0.3t}).$$

a) Find $W(1)$ and $W(8)$.

b) Find $W'(t)$.

c) After how many weeks will the typist's speed be 95 words per minute?

41. *Growth of a stock.* The value of a stock is modeled by

$$V(t) = \$58(1 - e^{-1.1t}) + \$20,$$

where V is the value of the stock after time t, in months.

a) Find $V(1)$ and $V(12)$.

b) Find $V'(t)$.

c) After how many months will the value of the stock be $75?

42. *Marginal revenue.* The demand function for a certain product is given by

$$p = D(x) = 800e^{-0.125x}.$$

Recall that total revenue is given by $R(x) = xD(x)$.

a) Find $R(x)$.

b) Find the marginal revenue, $R'(x)$.

c) At what value of x will the revenue be maximum?

■ ――――――――――――――――――――――――――――――――

Differentiate.

43. $(e^{3x} + 1)^5$

44. $(e^{x^2} - 2)^4$

45. $\dfrac{e^{3t} - e^{7t}}{e^{4t}}$

46. $\sqrt[3]{e^{3t} + t}$

47. $\dfrac{e^x}{x^2 + 1}$

48. $\dfrac{e^x}{1 - e^x}$

49. $e^{\sqrt{x}} + \sqrt{e^x}$

50. $\dfrac{1}{e^x} + e^{1/x}$

51. $e^{x/2} \cdot \sqrt{x - 1}$

52. $\dfrac{xe^{-x}}{1 + x^2}$

53. $\dfrac{e^x - e^{-x}}{e^x + e^{-x}}$

▦ with y^x key. Each of the following is an expression for e. Find the function values that are approximations for e. Round to five decimal places.

54. $e = \lim_{t \to 0} f(t)$; $f(t) = (1 + t)^{1/t}$. Find $f(1)$, $f(0.5)$, $f(0.2)$, $f(0.1)$, and $f(0.001)$.

55. $e = \lim_{t \to 1} g(t)$; $g(t) = t^{1/(t-1)}$. Find $g(0.5)$, $g(0.9)$, $g(0.99)$, $g(0.999)$, and $g(0.9998)$.

―――――――――――――――――――――――――――――――――――

9.3   THE NATURAL LOGARITHM FUNCTION

Recall the definition of logarithms:

$$\text{``}y = \log_e x\text{''} \quad \text{means} \quad \text{``}x = e^y.\text{''}$$

Thus, for natural logarithms, $\log_e x$ is that number y such that $x = e^y$. The number $\log_e x$ is called the *natural logarithm* of x and is abbreviated ln x. That is,

$$\ln x = \log_e x.$$

There are two ways we might obtain the graph of $y = \ln x$. One is by writing its equivalent equation $x = e^y$.

Then we select values for y, and use a calculator or Table 4 to find the corresponding values of e^y. We then plot points, remembering that x still is the first coordinate.

x(or e^y)	0.4	0.1	1	2.7	7.4	20
y	−1	−2	0	1	2	3

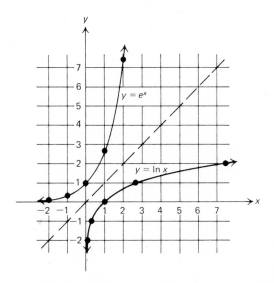

Figure 5

(How does this procedure in Fig. 5 compare with that used in plotting Fig. 3?) Note that the graph of $y = \ln x$ is a reflection, or mirror image, across the line $y = x$, of the graph of $y = e^x$.

The second way of graphing $y = \ln x$ is by using a calculator or Table 3, which is a table of natural logarithms at the back of the book. For example, $\ln 2 = 0.6931 \approx 0.7$.

These properties follow.

ln x exists only for positive number x.

ln x < 0 for 0 < x < 1.

ln x > 0 for x > 1.

The Derivative of ln x

Consider $f(x) = \ln x$. We can show that $f'(x) = 1/x$ (the slope of the tangent line at x is just the reciprocal of x). We are trying to find the derivative of

$$f(x) = \ln x. \qquad (1)$$

We first write its equivalent exponential equation

$$e^{f(x)} = x. \qquad (2)$$

Now we differentiate both sides of this equation.

$$\frac{d}{dx} e^{f(x)} = \frac{d}{dx} x \qquad \text{(This is implicit differentiation.)}$$

$$f'(x) \cdot e^{f(x)} = 1$$

$$f'(x) \cdot x = 1 \qquad \text{(Substituting x for $e^{f(x)}$ from Eq. (2))}$$

$$f'(x) = \frac{1}{x}$$

Thus

$$\frac{d}{dx} \ln x = \frac{1}{x}.$$

This is true only for positive values of x, since $\ln x$ is defined only for positive numbers. Let us find some derivatives.

Example 1 $\dfrac{d}{dx} 3 \ln x = \dfrac{3}{x}$

Example 2 $\dfrac{d}{dx} (x^2 \ln x + 5x) = x^2 \cdot \dfrac{1}{x} + 2x \cdot \ln x + 5$ (Product Rule on $x^2 \ln x$)

$$= x + 2x \cdot \ln x + 5$$

$$= x(1 + 2 \ln x) + 5 \qquad \text{(Simplifying)}$$

Example 3 $\dfrac{d}{dx} \left(\dfrac{\ln x}{x^3} \right) = \dfrac{x^3 \cdot \frac{1}{x} - (\ln x)(3x^2)}{x^6}$ (Quotient Rule)

$$= \frac{x^2 - 3x^2 \ln x}{x^6}$$

$$= \frac{x^2(1 - 3 \ln x)}{x^6} \qquad \text{(Factoring)}$$

$$= \frac{1 - 3 \ln x}{x^4} \qquad \text{(Simplifying)}$$

The following rule (a form of the Chain Rule) allows us to find many other derivatives.

$$\frac{d}{dx} \ln f(x) = f'(x) \cdot \frac{1}{f(x)}, \quad \text{or} \quad \frac{d}{dx} \ln \square = \square' \cdot \frac{1}{\square}$$

The following gives us a way of remembering this rule.

$$\ln(x^2 - 8x)$$

1. Differentiate the "inside" function.
2. Multiply by the reciprocal of the "inside" function.

$$(2x - 8) \cdot \frac{1}{x^2 - 8x}$$

Example 4 $\dfrac{d}{dx} \ln 3x = 3 \cdot \dfrac{1}{3x} = \dfrac{1}{x}$

Note that we could have done this another way using Property 1:

$$\ln 3x = \ln 3 + \ln x;$$

then

$$\frac{d}{dx} \ln 3x = \frac{d}{dx} \ln 3 + \frac{d}{dx} \ln x = 0 + \frac{1}{x} = \frac{1}{x}.$$

Example 5 $\dfrac{d}{dx} \ln(x^2 - 5) = 2x \cdot \dfrac{1}{x^2 - 5} = \dfrac{2x}{x^2 - 5}$

Example 6 $\dfrac{d}{dx} \ln(\ln x) = \dfrac{1}{x} \cdot \dfrac{1}{\ln x} = \dfrac{1}{x \ln x}$

Example 7 $\dfrac{d}{dx} \ln \left(\dfrac{x^3 + 4}{x} \right) = \dfrac{d}{dx} [\ln(x^3 + 4) - \ln x]$ (Property 2. This avoids using the Quotient Rule.)

$$= 3x^2 \cdot \frac{1}{x^3 + 4} - \frac{1}{x} = \frac{3x^2}{x^3 + 4} - \frac{1}{x}$$

$$= \frac{3x^2}{x^3 + 4} \cdot \frac{x}{x} - \frac{1}{x} \cdot \frac{x^3 + 4}{x^3 + 4}$$

$$= \frac{(3x^2)x - (x^3 + 4)}{x(x^3 + 4)}$$

$$= \frac{3x^3 - x^3 - 4}{x(x^3 + 4)}$$

$$= \frac{2x^3 - 4}{x(x^3 + 4)}$$

EXERCISE SET 9.3

Differentiate.

1. $-6 \ln x$

2. $-4 \ln x$

3. $x^4 \ln x - \frac{1}{2}x^2$

4. $x^5 \ln x - \frac{1}{4}x^4$

5. $\dfrac{\ln x}{x^4}$

6. $\dfrac{\ln x}{x^5}$

7. $\ln \dfrac{x}{4}$ $\left[Hint: \ln \dfrac{x}{4} = \ln x - \ln 4 \right]$

8. $\ln \dfrac{x}{2}$

9. $\ln (5x^2 - 7)$

10. $\ln (7x^3 + 4)$

11. $\ln (\ln 4x)$

12. $\ln (\ln 3x)$

13. $\ln \left(\dfrac{x^2 - 7}{x} \right)$

14. $\ln \left(\dfrac{x^2 + 5}{x} \right)$

15. $e^x \ln x$

16. $e^{2x} \ln x$

17. $\ln (e^x + 1)$

18. $\ln (e^x - 2)$

19. $(\ln x)^2$ [Hint: The Extended Power Rule]

20. $(\ln x)^3$

21. *Advertising.* A model for advertising response is given by

$$N(a) = 1000 + 200 \ln a, \qquad a \geq 1,$$

where

$$N(a) = \text{number of units sold}$$
$$a = \text{amount spent on advertising in thousands of dollars.}$$

a) How many units were sold after spending 1 thousand dollars $(a = 1)$ on advertising?

b) Find $N'(a)$, $N'(10)$.

c) Find maximum and minimum values, if they exist.

22. *Walking speed.* Bornstein and Bornstein found in a study that the average walking speed v of a person living in a city of population p, in thousands, is given by

$$v(p) = 0.86 \ln p + 0.05,$$

where v is in feet per second.

a) The population of Seattle is 531,000. What is the average walking speed of a person living in Seattle? Find $v(531)$.

b) The population of New York is 7,900,000. What is the average walking speed of a person living in New York?

c) Find $v'(p)$. Interpret $v'(p)$.

Differentiate.

23. $(\ln x)^{-4}$

24. $(\ln x)^n$

25. $\ln (t^3 + 1)^5$

26. $\ln (t^2 + t)^3$

27. $[\ln (x + 5)]^4$

28. $\ln [\ln (\ln 3x)]$

29. $\ln (t^3 + 3)(t^2 - 1)$

30. $\ln \dfrac{1 - t}{1 + t}$

31. $\ln \dfrac{x^5}{(8x + 5)^2}$

32. $\ln \sqrt{5 + x^2}$

33. $\dfrac{\ln t^2}{t^2}$

34. $\frac{1}{5}x^5(\ln x - \frac{1}{5})$

35. $\dfrac{x^{n+1}}{n + 1} \left(\ln x - \dfrac{1}{n + 1} \right)$

36. $\dfrac{x \ln x - x}{x^2 + 1}$

37. $\ln (t + \sqrt{1 + t^2})$

38. Find: $\lim\limits_{h \to 0} \dfrac{\ln (1 + h)}{h}$

39. ▉ Which is larger, e^{π} or π^e?

40. ▉ Find $\sqrt[e]{e}$. Compare it to other expressions of the type $\sqrt[x]{x}$, $x > 0$. What can you conclude?

9.4 APPLICATIONS:

THE UNINHIBITED GROWTH MODEL, $\dfrac{dP}{dt} = kP$

Consider the function

$$f(x) = 2e^{3x}.$$

Differentiating, we get

$$f'(x) = 3 \cdot 2e^{3x} = 3 \cdot f(x).$$

This, graphically, says that the derivative, or slope of the tangent line, is simply the constant 3 times the function value.

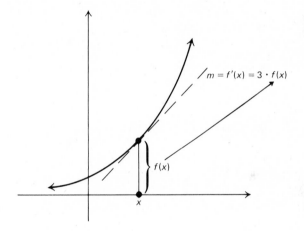

In general,

A function $y = f(x)$ satisfies the equation*

$$\frac{dy}{dx} = ky \qquad [f'(x) = k \cdot f(x)]$$

if and only if

$$y = ce^{kx} \qquad [f(x) = ce^{kx}]$$

for some constant c.

No matter what the variables, you should be able to write the solution.

Example 1   The solution of $\dfrac{dA}{dt} = kA$ is $A = ce^{kt}$, or $A(t) = ce^{kt}$.

---

*Called a *differential equation*.

Example 2   The solution of $\dfrac{dP}{dt} = kP$ is $P = ce^{kt}$, or $P(t) = ce^{kt}$.

Example 3   The solution of $f'(Q) = k \cdot f(Q)$ is $f(Q) = ce^{kQ}$.

The equation

$$\frac{dP}{dt} = kP, \qquad k > 0 \qquad [P'(t) = k \cdot P(t), \qquad k > 0]$$

is the basic model of uninhibited population growth, whether it be a population of humans, a bacteria culture, or money invested at interest compounded continuously. Neglecting special inhibiting and stimulating factors, a population normally reproduces itself at a rate proportional to its size, and this is exactly what the equation $dP/dt = kP$ says. The solution of the equation is

$$P(t) = ce^{kt}, \tag{1}$$

where t = time. At $t = 0$, we have some "initial" population $P(0)$ that we will represent by P_0. We can rewrite Eq. (1) in terms of P_0 as follows:

$$P_0 = P(0) = ce^{k \cdot 0} = ce^0 = c \cdot 1 = c.$$

Thus $P_0 = c$, so we can express $P(t)$ as

$$P(t) = P_0 e^{kt}.$$

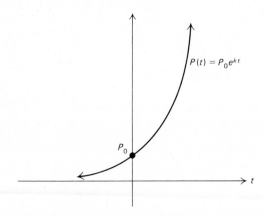

Its graph is the curve shown here, which shows how uninhibited growth results in a "population explosion."

   The constant k is called the *rate of exponential growth*, or simply the *growth rate*. This is not the rate of change of population size, which is

$$\frac{dP}{dt} = kP,$$

but the constant that P must be multiplied by to get its rate of change. It is thus a different use of the word *rate*. It is like the *interest rate* paid by a bank. If the interest rate is 7%, or 0.07, we do not mean that your bank balance P is growing at the rate of 0.07 dollars per year, but at the rate of $0.07P$ dollars per year. We therefore express the rate as 7% per year, rather than 0.07 dollars per year. We could say that the rate is 0.07 dollars *per dollar* per year. When interest is compounded continuously, the interest rate *is* a true exponential growth rate.

Example 4   *Interest compounded continuously.* Suppose an amount P_0 is invested in a savings account where interest is compounded continuously at 7% per year. That is, the balance P grows at the rate given by

$$\frac{dP}{dt} = 0.07P.$$

a) Find the solution of the equation in terms of P_0 and 0.07.

b) Suppose \$100 is invested. What is the balance after 1 year?

c) When will an investment of \$100 double itself?

Solution   a) $P(t) = P_0 e^{0.07t}$

b) $P(1) = 100e^{0.07(1)} = 100e^{0.07} = 100(1.072508)$
$\approx \$107.25$ (⊞ or Table 4.)

c) We are asking at what time T does $P(T) = \$200$. The number T is called the *doubling time*. To find T we solve the equation

$$200 = 100e^{0.07 \cdot T}$$

$$2 = e^{0.07T} \quad \text{(Multiplying by } \tfrac{1}{100}\text{)}$$

We use natural logarithms to solve this equation.

$$\ln 2 = \ln e^{0.07T}$$

$$\ln 2 = 0.07T \quad \text{(Property 5: } \ln e^k = k.\text{)}$$

$$\frac{\ln 2}{0.07} = T$$

$$\frac{0.693147}{0.07} = T \quad \text{(⊞ or Table 3.)}$$

$$9.9 \approx T$$

Thus \$100 will double itself in 9.9 years.

We can find a general expression relating the growth rate k and the doubling time T by solving the equation

$$2P_0 = P_0 e^{kT}$$

$$2 = e^{kT} \qquad \text{(Multiplying by } 1/P_0\text{)}$$

$$\ln 2 = \ln e^{kT}$$

$$\ln 2 = kT.$$

The growth rate k and the doubling time T are related by

$$kT = \ln 2 = 0.693147,$$

or

$$a)\ k = \frac{\ln 2}{T} = \frac{0.693147}{T} \qquad b)\ T = \frac{\ln 2}{k} = \frac{0.693147}{k}.$$

Note that this relationship between k and T does not depend on P_0.

Example 5   At one time in Canada a bank advertised that it would double your money in 6.6 years. What is the interest rate on such an account, assuming interest to be compounded continuously?

Solution $k = \dfrac{\ln 2}{T} = \dfrac{0.693147}{6.6} = 0.105 = 10.5\%$

Example 6   *World population growth.* The population of the world passed 4 billion on March 28, 1976. On the basis of data available at that time it was estimated that the population P was growing exponentially at the rate of 1.9% per year. That is, $dP/dt = 0.019P$, where $t =$ time, in years, from 1976. (To facilitate computations we assume the population was 4 billion at the start of 1976).

a) Find the solution of the equation assuming $P_0 = 4$ and $k = 0.019$.

b) Estimate the world population in 1986 ($t = 10$).

c) When will the population be double that in 1976?

Solution   a) $P(t) = 4e^{0.019t}$

b) $P(10) = 4e^{0.019(10)} = 4e^{0.19} = 4(1.209250) \qquad$ (▦ or Table 4.)
$$\approx 4.8 \text{ billion}$$

c) $T = \dfrac{\ln 2}{k} = \dfrac{0.693147}{0.019} \approx 36.5 \text{ yr}$

Thus, according to this model, the 1976 population will double by the year 2012. No wonder ecologists are alarmed!

The Rule of 70 The relationship between doubling time T and interest rate k is the basis of a rule often used in the investment world, called the *Rule of 70:* To estimate how long it will take to double your money at varying rates of return, divide 70 by the rate of return. To see how this works, let the interest rate $k = r\%$. Then,

$$T = \frac{\ln 2}{k} = \frac{0.693147}{r\%}$$

$$= \frac{0.693147}{r \times 0.01}$$

$$= \frac{0.693147}{r \times 0.01} \cdot \frac{100}{100}$$

$$= \frac{69.3147}{r} \approx \frac{70}{r}.$$

EXERCISE SET 9.4

1. State the solution of $\dfrac{dQ}{dt} = kQ$ in terms of Q_0.

2. State the solution of $\dfrac{dR}{dt} = kR$ in terms of R_0.

3. *Compound interest.* Suppose P_0 is invested in a savings account where interest is compounded continuously at 9% per year. That is, the balance P grows at the rate given by

$$\frac{dP}{dt} = 0.09P.$$

a) Find the solution of the equation in terms of P_0 and 0.09.

b) Suppose $1000 is invested. What is the balance after 1 year? 2 years?

c) When will an investment of $1000 double itself?

4. *Compound interest.* Suppose P_0 is invested in a savings account where interest is compounded continuously at 10% per year. That is, the balance P grows at the rate given by

$$\frac{dP}{dt} = 0.10P.$$

a) Find the solution of the equation in terms of P_0 and 0.10.

b) Suppose $20,000 is invested. What is the balance after 1 year? 2 years?

c) When will an investment of $20,000 double itself?

5. *Population growth of Central America.* The growth rate of the population of Central America is 3.5% per year (one of the highest in the world). What is the doubling time?

6. *Population growth of Europe.* The growth rate of the population of Europe is 1% per year (one of the lowest in the world). What is the doubling time?

7. *Annual interest rate.* A bank advertises that it compounds interest continuously and that it will double your money in 10 years. What is its annual interest rate?

8. *Annual interest rate.* A bank advertises that it compounds interest continuously and that it will double your money in 12 years. What is its annual interest rate?

9. *Population growth of USSR.* The population of the USSR was 209 million in 1959. It was estimated that the population P was growing exponentially at the rate of 1% per year. That is,

$$\frac{dP}{dt} = 0.01P.$$

a) Find the solution of the equation assuming $P_0 = 209$ and $k = 0.01$.

b) Estimate the population of the USSR in 1999.

c) When will the population be double that of 1959?

11. *Population growth of U.S.* The population of the United States in 1976 was 216 million. It was estimated that the population P was growing exponentially at the rate of 0.8% per year. That is,

$$\frac{dP}{dt} = 0.008P,$$

where t = time in years.

a) Find the solution of the equation assuming $P_0 = 216$ and $k = 0.008$.

b) Estimate U.S. population in 1981 ($t = 5$).

c) When will the population be double that in 1976?

10. *Population growth of Europe.* The population of Europe west of the USSR was 430 million in 1961. It was estimated that the population was growing exponentially at the rate of 1% per year. That is,

$$\frac{dP}{dt} = 0.01P.$$

a) Find the solution of the equation assuming $P_0 = 430$ and $k = 0.01$.

b) Estimate the population of Europe in 1991.

c) When will the population be double that of 1961?

12. *Electrical energy demand.* The graph shows past data on electrical energy demand in the U.S.

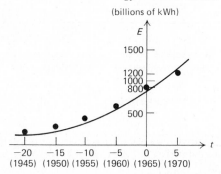

(billions of kWh)

It appears that we can fit an exponential function to the data. We accept the modeling assumption that the rate of change of electrical energy need E (in billion kilowatthours, kWh) with respect to time is given by

$$\frac{dE}{dt} = kE.$$

a) Find the solution of the equation, assuming $E_0 = 800$ billion kWh. That is, at $t = 0(1965)$, $E = 800$.

b) Find k using the data point $E(5) = 1200$ billion kWh. That is, in 1970, 1200 billion kWh were used. Round to the nearest hundredth.

c) Rewrite $E(t)$ in terms of k.

d) How much electrical energy will be needed in 1995?

13. *Franchise expansion.* A national hamburger firm is selling franchises throughout the country. The president estimates that the number of franchises N will increase at a rate of 10% per year. That is,

$$\frac{dN}{dt} = 0.10N.$$

   a) Find the solution of the equation, assuming the number of franchises at $t = 0$ is 50.

   b) How many franchises will there be in 20 years?

   c) When will the initial number of 50 franchises double?

15. *Oil demand.* The growth rate of the demand for oil in the United States is 10% per year. When will the demand be double that of 1980?

17. *Population growth of Tempe.* The population of Tempe, Arizona was 25 thousand in 1960. In 1969 it was 52 thousand. Assuming the exponential model,

   a) Find the value $k(P_0 = 25)$. Use natural logarithms. Write the equation.

   b) Estimate the population of Tempe in 1980.

19. *Wine sales in the U.S.* The total number of dollars spent on wine in the U.S. in 1934 was $90 million. In 1974 the amount spent was $1480 million. Assuming the exponential model,

   a) Find the value $k(P_0 = 90)$. Use natural logarithms. Write the equation.

   b) Estimate the amount spent on wine in 1984.

   c) When will the amount spent on wine be double that spent in 1974?

21. *Consumer price index.* The *consumer price index* compares the costs of goods and services over various years. 1967 is used as a base (P_0). The same goods and services that cost $100 in 1967 cost $184.50 in 1977. Assuming the exponential model,

14. *Franchise expansion.* Pizza, Unltd., a national pizza firm, is selling franchises throughout the country. The president estimates that the number of franchises N will increase at a rate of 15% per year. That is,

$$\frac{dN}{dt} = 0.15N.$$

   a) Find the solution of the equation, assuming the number of franchises at $t = 0$ is 40.

   b) How many franchises will there be in 20 years?

   c) When will the initial number of 40 franchises double?

16. *Coal demand.* The growth rate of the demand for coal in the world is 4% per year. When will the demand be double that of 1980?

18. *Population growth of Kansas City.* The population of Kansas City was 475 thousand in 1960. In 1970 it was 507 thousand. Assuming the exponential model,

   a) Find the value $k(P_0 = 475)$. Use natural logarithms. Write the equation.

   b) Estimate the population of Kansas City in 2000.

20. *Cost of a double-dip ice cream cone.* In 1970 the cost of a double dip ice cream cone was 52¢. In 1978 it was 66¢. Assuming the exponential model,

   a) Find the value $k(P_0 = 52)$. Use natural logarithms. Write the equation.

   b) Estimate the cost of a cone in 1986.

   c) When will the cost of a cone be twice that of 1978?

   ———————

   a) Find the value $k(P_0 = \$100)$, and write the equation.

   b) Estimate what the same goods and services will cost in 1987.

   c) When will the same goods and services cost double that of 1967?

22. *Job opportunities.* It is estimated that there were 714,000 accountants employed in 1972 and it is projected that there will be 935,000 accountants needed in 1985. Assuming the exponential model,

a) Find the value $k(P_0 = 714,000)$, and write the equation.
b) Estimate the number of accountants needed in 1990.
c) When will the need for accountants be double that of 1972?

■ ───

Effective annual yield. Suppose $100 is invested at 7% compounded continuously for 1 year. We know from Example 4 that the balance will be $107.25. This is the same as if $100 were invested at 7.25% and compounded once a year (simple interest). The 7.25% is called the "effective annual yield." In general, if P_0 is invested at $k(\%)$ compounded continuously, then the effective annual yield is that number i satisfying $P_0(1 + i) = P_0 e^k$. Then $1 + i = e^k$, or

$$\text{Effective annual yield} = i = e^k - 1.$$

23. An amount is invested at 6% per year compounded continuously. What is the effective annual yield?

24. An amount is invested at 8% per year compounded continuously. What is the effective annual yield?

25. The effective annual yield on an investment compounded continuously is 9.42%. At what rate was it invested?

26. The effective annual yield on an investment compounded continuously is 10.52%. At what rate was it invested?

27. Find an expression relating the growth rate k and the *tripling time* T_3.

28. Find an expression relating the growth rate k and the *quadrupling time* T_4.

29. Gather data concerning population growth in your city. Estimate its population in 1984, in 2000.

30. A quantity Q_1 grows exponentially with a doubling time of 1 year. A quantity Q_2 grows exponentially with a doubling time of 2 years. If the initial amounts of Q_1 and Q_2 are the same, when will Q_1 be twice the size of Q_2?

31. ▦ *Value of Manhattan Island.* Peter Minuit, of the Dutch West India Company, purchased Manhattan Island from the Indians in 1626 for $24 worth of merchandise. Assuming an exponential rate of inflation of 8%, how much would Manhattan be worth in 1984?

32. ▦ *Population growth in the Virgin Islands.* The U.S. Virgin Islands have one of the highest growth rates in the world, 9.6%. In 1970 the population was 75,150. The land area of the Virgin Islands is 3,097,600 square yards. Assuming this growth rate continues and is exponential, when will the population of the Virgin Islands be such that there's 1 person for every square yard of land?

33. ▦ *Bicentennial growth of U.S.* The population of the U.S. in 1776 was about 2,508,000. In its bicentennial year the population was about 216,000,000. Assuming the exponential model, what was the growth rate of the U.S. through its bicentennial years?

34. ▦ *Cost of a first-class postage stamp.* The cost of a first-class postage stamp in 1962 was 4¢. In 1978 it was 15¢. This was exponential growth. What was the growth rate? What will be the cost of a first-class postage stamp in 1987? 1997?

35. ▦ *Cost of a prime-rib dinner.* The average cost of a prime rib dinner in 1962 was $4.65, and was increasing at an exponential growth rate of 5.1%. What will this dinner cost in 1987? 1997?

36. ▦ *Cost of a Hershey Bar.* The cost of a Hershey Bar in 1962 was $0.05, and was increasing at an exponential growth rate of 9.7%. What will the cost of a Hershey Bar be in 1987? 1997?

9.5   APPLICATIONS: DECAY

In the equation of population growth $dP/dt = kP$ the constant k is actually given by

$$k = \text{(Birth rate)} - \text{(Death rate)}.$$

Thus a population "grows" only when the *birth rate* is greater than the *death rate*. When the birth rate is less than the death rate, k will be negative so the population will be decreasing, or "decaying," at a rate proportional to its size. The equation

$$\frac{dP}{dt} = -kP \qquad \text{(where } k > 0)$$

shows P to be *decreasing* as a function of time, and the solution

$$P(t) = P_0 e^{-kt}$$

shows it to be decreasing exponentially. This is exponential *decay*. The amount present initially at $t = 0$ is again P_0.

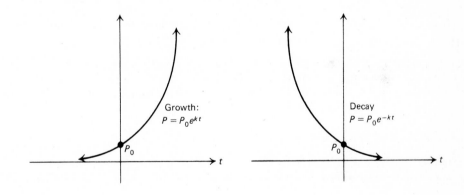

Present Value

A representative of a financial institution is often asked to solve a problem like the following

Example 1   A parent, following the birth of a child, wants to make an initial investment of P_0 that will grow to $10,000 by the child's 20th birthday. Interest is compounded continuously at 8%. What should the initial investment be?

Solution   Using the equation $P = P_0 e^{kt}$, we find P_0 such that

$$10,000 = P_0 e^{0.08 \cdot 20}, \qquad \text{or} \qquad 10,000 = P_0 e^{1.6}.$$

Now

$$\frac{10,000}{e^{1.6}} = P_0, \quad \text{or} \quad 10,000e^{-1.6} = P_0,$$

and, using a calculator or Table 4, we have

$$P_0 = 10,000e^{-1.6} = 10,000(0.201897) = \$2018.97.$$

Thus the parent must deposit $2018.97 to grow to $10,000 by the child's 20th birthday.

Economists call $2018.97 the *present value* of $10,000 due 20 years from now at 8% compounded continuously.* In general, the present value P_0 of an amount P due t years later is found by solving the following equation for P_0:

$$P_0 e^{kt} = P,$$

$$P_0 = \frac{P}{e^{kt}} = Pe^{-kt}.$$

The *present value P_0* of an amount P due t years later at interest rate k, compounded continuously, is given by

$$P_0 = Pe^{-kt}.$$

Note that this can be interpreted as exponential decay from the future back to the present.

EXERCISE SET 9.5

1. A parent, following the birth of a child, wants to make an initial investment P_0 that will grow to $5000 by the child's 20th birthday. Interest is compounded continuously at 9%. What should the initial investment be?

2. A parent, following the birth of a child, wants to make an initial investment P_0 that will grow to $5000 by the child's 20th birthday. Interest is compounded continuously at 10%. What should this initial investment be?

3. Find the present value of $60,000 due 8 years later at 12% compounded continuously.

4. Find the present value of $50,000 due 16 years later at 14% compounded continuously.

5. Find the present value of $100,000 due 30 years later at 10% compounded continuously.

6. Find the present value of $5,000,000 due 25 years later at 13.5% compounded continuously.

---

* The process of computing the present value is called *discounting*.

7. *Salvage value.* A business estimates that the salvage value V of a piece of machinery after t years is given by

$$V(t) = \$40,000e^{-t}.$$

a) What did the machinery cost initially?

b) What is the salvage value after 2 years?

9. *Population decrease of Cincinnati.* The population of Cincinnati was 503,000 in 1960 and 453,000 in 1970. Assuming the population is decreasing according to the exponential decay model,

a) Find the value k and write the equation.

b) Estimate the population of Cincinnati in 1990.

c) When will Cincinnati have just 1 person?

11. *Population of the USSR in a preceding year.* The population of the USSR was 258 million in 1980 and was growing at the rate of 1% per year. What was the population in 1970? 1940?

8. *Supply and demand.* The supply and demand for the sale of stereos by a sound company are given by

$$S(x) = e^x, \qquad D(x) = 163,000e^{-x},$$

where $S(x) =$ price at which the company is willing to supply x stereos, and $D(x) =$ demand price for a quantity of x stereos. Find the equilibrium point. For reference, see p. 105.

10. *Population decrease of Panama.* The population of Panama was 1,464,000 in 1970 and 1,260,000 in 1980. Assuming the population is decreasing according to the exponential decay model,

a) Find the value k and write the equation.

b) Estimate the population of Panama in 2000.

c) When will the population of Panama be 100,000?

12. ▦ *Consumer price index.* The consumer price index compares the costs of goods and services over various years. 1967 is used as a base. The same goods and services that cost \$100 in 1967 cost \$42 in 1940. Assuming the exponential decay model,

a) Find the value k and write the equation.

b) Estimate what the same goods and services cost in 1900.

9.6   ECONOMIC APPLICATION: ELASTICITY OF DEMAND

Suppose x represents the quantity of goods sold and p is the price per unit of the goods. Recall that x and p are related by the demand function

$$p = D(x).$$

Suppose there is a change Δx in the quantity sold. The percent change in quantity is

$$\frac{\Delta x}{x}.$$

A change in the quantity sold produces a change Δp in the price. The percent change in price is

$$\frac{\Delta p}{p}.$$

The ratio of these percents is given by

$$\frac{(\Delta x/x)}{(\Delta p/p)}, \quad \text{which can be expressed as} \quad \frac{p}{x} \cdot \frac{1}{\Delta p/\Delta x}. \tag{1}$$

For continuous functions

$$\lim_{\Delta x \to 0} \frac{\Delta p}{\Delta x} = \frac{dp}{dx},$$

and the limit as $\Delta x \to 0$ of the expression in Eq. (1) becomes

$$\frac{p}{x} \cdot \frac{1}{dp/dx} = \frac{D(x)}{x} \cdot \frac{1}{D'(x)} = \frac{1}{x} \cdot \frac{D(x)}{D'(x)}.$$

The *elasticity of demand E* is given by

$$E = -\frac{p}{x} \cdot \frac{1}{dp/dx} = -\frac{1}{x} \cdot \frac{D(x)}{D'(x)}.$$

The numbers x and p are always nonnegative. The slope of the demand curve dp/dx is always negative since the demand curve is decreasing. The minus sign makes E nonnegative and easier, for our purposes, to work with. We will find the second expression for elasticity the most useful for computations.

Example 1   A company determines that the demand function for a certain product is given by

$$p = D(x) = 200 - x.$$

Find

a) The elasticity as a function of x.

b) The elasticity at $x = 70$ and $x = 150$.

c) The value of x for which $E = 1$.

d) The total revenue function.

e) The value of x for which the revenue is a maximum.

Solution   a) To find the elasticity we first find

$$D'(x) = -1.$$

Then we substitute -1 for $D'(x)$ and $200 - x$ for $D(x)$ in the second expression for elasticity.

$$E(x) = -\frac{1}{x} \cdot \frac{D(x)}{D'(x)} = -\frac{1}{x} \cdot \frac{200 - x}{-1} = \frac{200 - x}{x}$$

b) $E(70) = \dfrac{200 - 70}{70} = \dfrac{130}{70} = \dfrac{13}{7}$, $E(150) = \dfrac{200 - 150}{150} = \dfrac{50}{150} = \dfrac{1}{3}$.

c) We set $E(x) = 1$ and solve for x.

$$\frac{200 - x}{x} = 1$$

$$200 - x = x \qquad \text{(We multiply by x assuming } x \neq 0.\text{)}$$

$$200 = 2x$$

$$100 = x$$

d) Recall that the total revenue $R(x)$ is given by $xD(x)$. Then

$$R(x) = xD(x) = x(200 - x) = 200x - x^2.$$

e) To find the value of x that maximizes total revenue, we find $R'(x)$:

$$R'(x) = 200 - 2x.$$

Now $R'(x)$ exists for all values of x in the interval $[0, \infty)$. Thus we solve

$$R'(x) = 200 - 2x = 0,$$

$$-2x = -200,$$

$$x = 100.$$

Since there is only one critical point, we can try to use the second derivative to see if we have a maximum.

$$R''(x) = -2, \text{ a constant}$$

Thus $R''(100)$ is negative, so $R(100)$ is a maximum.

Note in parts (c) and (e) of Example 1 that the value of x for which $E = 1$ is the same as the value of x for which total revenue is a maximum. This is always true.

Total revenue is a maximum at the value(s) of x for which $E = 1$.

We can prove this as follows.

$$R(x) = xD(x)$$

so

$$R'(d) = 1 \cdot D(x) + xD'(x)$$

$$= D(x)\left[1 + \frac{xD'(x)}{D(x)}\right] \qquad \text{(Check this by multiplying.)}$$

$$= D(x)\left[1 - \frac{1}{E}\right]$$

$$R'(x) = 0 \text{ when } 1 - \frac{1}{E} = 0, \text{ or } E = 1.$$

It is of benefit to look at a typical demand curve in relation to elasticity and total revenue.

The demand curve is decreasing overall. For values of x for which $E > 1$, total revenue is increasing. For values of x for which $E < 1$, total revenue is decreasing. For the value of x for which $E = 1$, total revenue is a maximum.

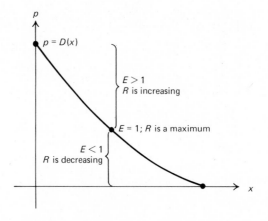

For a particular value of x, the demand is

1. **Inelastic if $E < 1$.**
2. **Elastic if $E > 1$.**
3. **Has unit elasticity if $E = 1$.**

In summary, suppose a company puts more units of a product, say a new calculator, on the market and the total revenue increases. Then we say the demand is *elastic*. If the total revenue decreases, we say the demand is *inelastic*.

EXERCISE SET 9.6

For each demand function, find: (a) the elasticity and (b) the value(s) of x for which total revenue is a maximum.

1. $p = D(x) = 400 - x$ 　　　 **2.** $p = D(x) = 500 - x$ 　　　 **3.** $p = D(x) = 200 - 4x$

4. $p = D(x) = 500 - 2x$ 　　 **5.** $p = D(x) = \dfrac{400}{x}$ 　　　 **6.** $p = D(x) = \dfrac{3000}{x}$

7. $p = D(x) = \sqrt{500 - x}$ 　　 **8.** $p = D(x) = \sqrt{300 - x}$ 　　 **9.** $p = D(x) = 100e^{-0.25x}$

10. $p = D(x) = 200e^{-0.05x}$ 　 **11.** $p = D(x) = \dfrac{100}{(x + 3)^2}$ 　 **12.** $p = D(x) = \dfrac{300}{(x + 8)^2}$

■ ──────────────────────────────────────

13. *Constant elasticity curve.*

　　a) Find the elasticity of the demand function

$$p = D(x) = \frac{k}{x^n},$$

　　where k is a positive constant and n is an integer greater than 0.

　　b) Is the value of the elasticity dependent on the quantity sold?

　　c) Does total revenue have a maximum? When?

15. Let

$$L(x) = \ln D(x).$$

Describe the elasticity in terms of $L'(x)$.

14. *Exponential demand curve.*

　　a) Find the elasticity of the demand function

$$p = D(x) = Ae^{-kx},$$

　　where A and k are positive constants.

　　b) Is the value of the elasticity dependent on the quantity sold?

　　c) Does total revenue have a maximum? At what value of x?

16. a) Find the elasticity.

$$p = D(x) = \sqrt[3]{1200 - 9x}$$

　　b) Find the value of x for which total revenue is a maximum.

CHAPTER 9 REVIEW

Differentiate.

1. e^x 　　　　　 **2.** $\ln x$ 　　　　　 **3.** e^{-x^2} 　　　　　 **4.** $\ln \dfrac{x}{7}$

5. $e^x - 5x^3$ 　　 **6.** $3e^x \ln x$ 　　 **7.** $\ln(e^x - x^3)$ 　　 **8.** $\dfrac{\ln x}{e^x}$

Given $\ln 2 = 0.6931$ and $\ln 7 = 1.9459$, find:

9. $\ln 14$ 　　　 **10.** $\ln \frac{2}{7}$ 　　　 **11.** $\ln 7e$ 　　　 **12.** State the solution of $\dfrac{dM}{dt} = kM$, in terms of M_0.

13. Suppose an amount P_0 is invested in a savings account where interest is compounded continuously at 8% per year. That is, the balance P grows at the rate given by

$$\frac{dP}{dt} = 0.08P.$$

a) Find the solution of the equation in terms of P_0 and 0.08.

b) Suppose $1000 is invested. What is the balance after 1 year?

c) When will an investment of $1000 double itself?

14. An investment is made at 6.931% per year compounded continuously. What is the doubling time?

15. The demand by airlines for fuel is increasing at the rate of 12% per year. That is,

$$\frac{dF}{dt} = 0.12F,$$

where F = amount of fuel used, and t = time in years.

a) The airlines used 3 billion gallons of fuel in 1960. Find the solution of the equation, assuming $F_0 = 3$ and $k = 0.12$.

b) How much fuel will be needed in 1986?

c) In how many years will the demand double?

16. Find the present value of $40,000 due 5 years later at 10%, compounded continuously.

17. Find

a) The elasticity of the demand function

$$p = D(x) = 400e^{-0.2x}.$$

b) The value of x for which total revenue is a maximum

18. *Business—Advertising.* A model for advertising response is given by

$$N(a) = 2000 + 500 \ln a, \quad a \geq 1,$$

where

$N(a)$ = number of units sold
a = amount spent on advertising, in thousands of dollars.

a) How many units were sold after spending 1 thousand dollars ($a = 1$) on advertising?

b) Find $N'(a)$, $N'(10)$.

c) Find maximum and minimum values, if they exist.

Differentiate.

19. $\dfrac{e^x + e^{-x}}{e^x - e^{-x}}$

20. $\ln(x + \sqrt{x^2 - 4})$

INTEGRATION

10.1 THE ANTIDERIVATIVE

We have considered several interpretations of the derivative. Some are listed below.

Function	Derivative
Distance	Velocity
Revenue	Marginal revenue
Cost	Marginal cost
Population	Rate of growth of population

For population we actually considered the derivative first and then the function. Many problems can be solved by doing the reverse of differentiation, called *antidifferentiation*.

The Antiderivative

Suppose that y is a function of x and that the derivative is the constant 8. Can we find y? It is easy to see that one such function is 8x. That is, 8x is a function whose derivative is 8. Are there other functions whose derivative is 8? Yes. Here are some examples:

$$8x + 3, \qquad 8x - 10, \qquad 8x + \sqrt{2}.$$

All of these functions are 8x plus some constant. There are no other functions having a derivative of 8 other than those of the form 8x + C. Another way of saying this is that any two functions having a derivative of 8 must differ by a constant. This is true in general.

> If two functions *F* and *G* have the same derivative on an interval, then
>
> $$F(x) = G(x) + C, \qquad \text{where } C \text{ is a constant.}$$

The reverse of differentiating is called *antidifferentiating*. The result of antidifferentiating is called an *antiderivative*. Above we found antiderivatives of the function 8. There are several of them, but they are all 8x plus some constant.

Example 1 Antidifferentiate (find the antiderivatives of) x^2.

Solution One antiderivative is $x^3/3$. All other antiderivatives differ from this by a constant, so we can denote them as follows:

$$\frac{x^3}{3} + C.$$

This is the *general form* of the antiderivative.

Integrals and Integration

The process of antidifferentiation is, in some contexts, called *integration*, and the general form of the antiderivative is referred to as an *indefinite integral*. A common notation for the indefinite integral, from Leibniz, is as follows:

$$\int f(x)\ dx.$$

The symbol $\int$ is called an *integral sign*. The symbol dx plays no apparent role at this point in our development but will be useful later. In this context, $f(x)$ is called the *integrand*. We illustrate this notation using the preceding example.

Example 2 Integrate $\int x^2 \ dx$.

Solution $\int x^2 \ dx = x^3/3 + C$

The symbol on the left is read "the integral of x^2, dx." (The "dx" is often omitted in the reading.) In this case the integrand is x^2. The constant C is called the *constant of integration*.

Example 3 Integrate $\int e^x \ dx$.

Solution $\int e^x \ dx = e^x + C$

To integrate (or antidifferentiate) we make use of differentiation formulas, in effect reading them in reverse. Below are some of these, stated in reverse, as integration formulas. These can be checked by differentiating the right-hand side and noting that the result is, in each case, the integrand.

1. $\displaystyle\int k \ dx, \ (k \text{ a constant}) = kx + C$

2. $\displaystyle\int x^r \ dx = \frac{x^{r+1}}{r+1} + C \text{ (provided } r \neq -1), \text{ or}$

$\displaystyle\int (r + 1)x^r \ dx = x^{r+1} + C$

(To integrate a power of x, other than -1, increase the power by 1 and divide by the increased power.)

3. $\displaystyle\int x^{-1} \ dx = \int \frac{1}{x} \ dx = \ln x + C$

4. $\displaystyle\int e^x \ dx = e^x + C$

The following rules allow us to find many other integrals. They are obtainable by reversing two familiar differentiation rules.

RULE A. $\int kf(x) \ dx = k \int f(x) \ dx$

(The integral of a constant times a function is the constant times the integral.)

RULE B. $\int [f(x) + g(x)]dx = \int f(x) \ dx + \int g(x) \ dx$

(The integral of a sum is the sum of the integrals.)

Example 4 $\displaystyle\int (5x + 4x^3)dx = \int 5x \ dx + \int 4x^3 \ dx$ (Rule B)

$\displaystyle = 5 \int x \ dx + \int 4x^3 \ dx$ (Rule A)

(Note that we did not factor the 4 out of the second integral. This is because we can find the antiderivative of $4x^3$ directly as x^4, as shown in the second part of formula 2.)

$$= 5 \cdot \frac{x^2}{2} + x^4 + C = \frac{5}{2}x^2 + x^4 + C.$$

(Don't forget the constant of integration!)

Note:

We can always check by differentiating.

Thus, in Example 4,

$$\frac{d}{dx}\left(\frac{5}{2}x^2 + x^4 + C\right) = 2 \cdot \frac{5}{2} \cdot x + 4x^3 = 5x + 4x^3.$$

Example 5 $\displaystyle\int (e^x - \sqrt{x})\, dx = \int e^x\, dx - \int \sqrt{x}\, dx$

$$= \int e^x\, dx - \int x^{1/2}\, dx$$

$$= e^x - \frac{x^{(1/2)+1}}{\frac{1}{2} + 1} + C$$

$$= e^x - \frac{x^{3/2}}{\frac{3}{2}} + C$$

$$= e^x - \tfrac{2}{3}x^{3/2} + C$$

Example 6 $\displaystyle\int \left(1 - \frac{3}{x} + \frac{1}{x^4}\right) dx = \int 1\, dx - 3 \int \frac{dx}{x} + \int x^{-4}\, dx$

$$= x - 3 \ln x + \frac{x^{-4+1}}{-4+1} + C$$

$$= x - 3 \ln x - \frac{x^{-3}}{3} + C$$

Another Look at Antiderivatives

The graphs of the antiderivatives of x^2 are the graphs of the functions

$$y = \int x^2\, dx = \frac{x^3}{3} + C$$

for the various values of the constant C.

As shown in the following graphs, x^2 is the derivative of each function. That is, the tangent line at the point

$$\left(a, \frac{a^3}{3} + C\right)$$

has slope a^2. The curves $(x^3/3) + C$ fill up the plane, exactly one curve going through any given point (x_0, y_0).

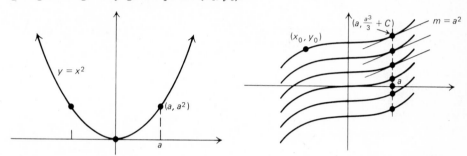

Suppose we look for an antiderivative of x^2 having a specified value at a certain point, say $f(-1) = 2$. We find that there is only one such function.

Example 7   Find the function f such that

$$f'(x) = x^2, \quad \text{and} \quad f(-1) = 2.$$

Solution   a) We find $f(x)$ by integrating.

$$f(x) = \int x^2\, dx = \frac{x^3}{3} + C.$$

b) The condition $f(-1) = 2$ allows us to find C.

$$f(-1) = \frac{(-1)^3}{3} + C = 2, \quad \text{and solving for } C \text{ we get:}$$

$$-\tfrac{1}{3} + C = 2,$$

$$C = 2 + \tfrac{1}{3}, \quad \text{or } \tfrac{7}{3}.$$

Thus $f(x) = (x^3/3) + (7/3)$.

Applied Problems

Example 8   A company determines that the marginal cost, C', of producing the xth unit of a certain product is given by

$$C'(x) = x^3 + 2x.$$

Find the total cost function C, assuming fixed costs (costs when 0 units are produced) are $45.

Solution
a) We integrate to find $C(x)$, using K for the integration constant to avoid confusion with the cost function C.

$$C(x) = \int C'(x)\, dx = \int (x^3 + 2x)\, dx = \frac{x^4}{4} + x^2 + K.$$

b) Fixed costs are $45. This means $C(0) = 45$. This allows us to determine the value of K.

$$C(0) = \frac{0^4}{4} + 0^2 + K = 45,$$

$$K = 45.$$

Thus $C(x) = \dfrac{x^4}{4} + x^2 + 45.$

EXERCISE SET 10.1

Integrate.

1. $\displaystyle\int x^6\, dx$

2. $\displaystyle\int x^7\, dx$

3. $\displaystyle\int 2\, dx$

4. $\displaystyle\int 4\, dx$

5. $\displaystyle\int x^{1/4}\, dx$

6. $\displaystyle\int x^{1/3}\, dx$

7. $\displaystyle\int (x^2 + x - 1)\, dx$

8. $\displaystyle\int (x^2 - x + 2)\, dx$

9. $\displaystyle\int (t^2 - 2t + 3)\, dt$

10. $\displaystyle\int (3t^2 - 4t + 7)\, dt$

11. $\displaystyle\int 5e^x\, dx$

12. $\displaystyle\int 3e^x\, dx$

13. $\displaystyle\int (x^3 - x^{8/7})\, dx$

14. $\displaystyle\int (x^4 - x^{6/5})\, dx$

15. $\displaystyle\int \frac{1000}{x}\, dx$

16. $\displaystyle\int \frac{500}{x}\, dx$

17. $\displaystyle\int \frac{dx}{x^2}\left(\text{or} \int \frac{1}{x^2}\, dx\right)$

18. $\displaystyle\int \frac{dx}{x^3}$

Find f.

19. $f'(x) = x - 3,\ f(2) = 9$

20. $f'(x) = x - 5,\ f(1) = 6$

21. $f'(x) = x^2 - 4,\ f(0) = 7$

22. $f'(x) = x^2 + 1,\ f(0) = 8$

Applied Problems

23. A company determines that the marginal cost, C', of producing the xth unit of a certain product is given by

$$C'(x) = x^3 - 2x.$$

Find the total cost function C, assuming fixed costs are $100.

24. A company determines that the marginal cost, C', of producing the xth unit of a certain product is given by

$$C'(x) = x^3 - x.$$

Find the total cost function C, assuming fixed costs are $200.

25. A company determines that the marginal revenue R', from selling the xth unit of a certain product is given by

$$R'(x) = x^2 - 3.$$

a) Find the total revenue function R, assuming $R(0) = 0$.

b) Why is $R(0) = 0$ a reasonable assumption?

27. *Efficiency of a machine operator.* The rate at which a machine operator's efficiency E (expressed as a percentage) changes with respect to time is given by

$$\frac{dE}{dt} = 30 - 10t,$$

where $t = $ the number of hours the operator has been at work.

a) Find $E(t)$, given that the operator's efficiency after working 2 hr is 72%. That is, $E(2) = 72$.

b) Use the answer to (a) to find operator's efficiency after 3 hr, after 5 hr.

26. A company determines that the marginal revenue R', from selling the xth unit of a certain product, is given by

$$R'(x) = x^2 - 1.$$

a) Find the total revenue function R, assuming $R(0) = 0$.

b) Why is $R(0) = 0$ a reasonable assumption?

28. *Efficiency of a machine operator.* The rate at which a machine operator's efficiency E (expressed as a percentage) changes with respect to time is given by

$$\frac{dE}{dt} = 40 - 10t,$$

where $t = $ the number of hours the operator has been at work.

a) Find $E(t)$, given that the operator's efficiency after working 2 hr is 72%. That is, $E(2) = 72$.

b) Use the answer to (a) to find the operator's efficiency after 4 hr, after 8 hr.

■ _____

Find f.

29. $f'(t) = \sqrt{t} + \dfrac{1}{\sqrt{t}}$, $f(4) = 0$ **30.** $f'(t) = t^{\sqrt{3}}$, $f(0) = 8$ **31.** $f'(t) = 3200e^{8t}$, $f(0) = 400$

Integrate.

32. $\displaystyle\int (5t + 4)^2 \, dt$

33. $\displaystyle\int (x - 1)^2 x^3 \, dx$

34. $\displaystyle\int (1 - t)\sqrt{t} \, dt$

35. $\displaystyle\int \frac{(t + 3)^2}{\sqrt{t}} \, dt$

36. $\displaystyle\int \frac{x^4 - 6x^2 - 7}{x^3} \, dx$

37. $\displaystyle\int (t + 1)^3 \, dt$

38. $\displaystyle\int \frac{1}{\ln 10} \frac{dx}{x}$

39. $\displaystyle\int be^{ax} \, dx$

40. $\displaystyle\int (3x - 5)(2x + 1) \, dx$

41. $\displaystyle\int \sqrt[3]{64x^4} \, dx$

42. $\displaystyle\int \frac{x^2 - 1}{x + 1} \, dx$

43. $\displaystyle\int \frac{t^3 + 8}{t + 2} \, dt$

10.2   AREA

In this section we consider the application of integration to finding areas of certain regions. Consider a function whose outputs are positive in an interval (the function might be 0 at one of the endpoints). We wish to find the area of the region between the graph of the function and the x-axis on that interval.

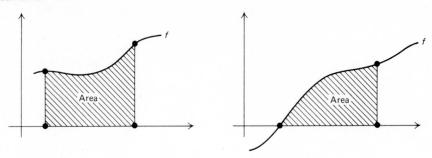

Let us first consider a constant function $f(x) = m$ on the interval from 0 to x, $[0, x]$.

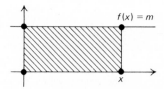

The figure formed is a rectangle, and its area is mx. Suppose we allow x to vary, giving us rectangles of different areas. The area of each rectangle is still mx. We have an area *function*,

$$A(x) = mx.$$

Its graph is shown below.

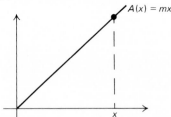

Let us next consider the linear function $f(x) = mx$ on the interval from 0 to x, $[0, x]$.

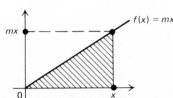

The figure formed this time is a triangle, and its area is $\frac{1}{2}$ the base times the height, $\frac{1}{2} \cdot x \cdot (mx)$, or $\frac{1}{2}mx^2$. If we allow x to vary, we again get an area function

$$A(x) = \tfrac{1}{2}mx^2.$$

Its graph is as shown below.

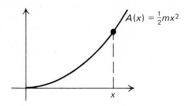

Now consider the linear function $f(x) = mx + b$ on the interval from 0 to x, [0, x].

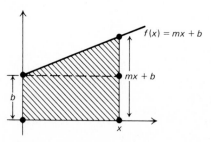

The figure formed this time is a trapezoid, and its area is $\frac{1}{2}$ the height times the sum of the lengths of its parallel sides (or, noting the dashed line, the area of the triangle plus the rectangle),

$$\tfrac{1}{2} \cdot x \cdot [b + (mx + b)], \quad \text{or } \tfrac{1}{2} \cdot x \cdot (mx + 2b), \quad \text{or } \tfrac{1}{2}mx^2 + bx.$$

If we allow x to vary, we again get an area function

$$A(x) = \tfrac{1}{2}mx^2 + bx.$$

Its graph is as shown below.

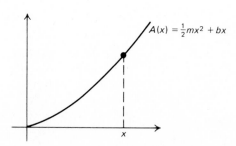

Now we consider the function $f(x) = x^2 + 1$ on the interval from 0 to x, $[0, x]$. The graph of the region in question is as shown, but it is not so easy this time to find the area function because the graph of $f(x)$ is not a straight line. Let us tabulate our previous results and look for a pattern.

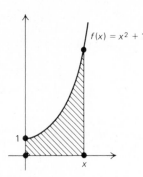

$f(x)$	$A(x)$
$f(x) = 3$	$A(x) = 3x$
$f(x) = m$	$A(x) = mx$
$f(x) = 3x$	$A(x) = \frac{3}{2}x^2$
$f(x) = mx$	$A(x) = \frac{1}{2}mx^2$
$f(x) = mx + b$	$A(x) = \frac{1}{2}mx^2 + bx$

You may have conjectured that the area function $A(x)$ is an antiderivative of $f(x)$.

THEOREM   **Let f be a positive, continuous function on an interval $[a, b]$ and let $A(x)$ be the area of the region between the graph of f and the x-axis on the interval $[a, x]$. Then $A(x)$ is a differentiable function of x and**

$$A'(x) = f(x).$$

Proof   The situation described in the theorem is shown here.

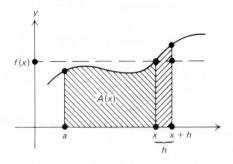

The derivative of $A(x)$ is, by definition of derivative,

$$A'(x) = \lim_{h \to 0} \frac{A(x + h) - A(x)}{h}.$$

Note, from the drawing, that $A(x + h) - A(x)$ is the area of the small, shaded, vertical strip. The area of this small strip is approximately that of a rectangle of base h and height $f(x)$, especially for small values of h. Thus we have

$$A(x + h) - A(x) \approx f(x) \cdot h.$$

Now

$$A'(x) = \lim_{h \to 0} \frac{A(x + h) - A(x)}{h}$$

$$= \lim_{h \to 0} \frac{f(x) \cdot h}{h}$$

$$= \lim_{h \to 0} f(x) = f(x),$$

since $f(x)$ does not involve h.

The theorem above also holds if $f(x) = 0$ at one or both endpoints of the interval $[a, b]$.

Since the area function A is an antiderivative of f, and since any two antiderivatives differ by a constant, we easily conclude that the area function and any antiderivative differ by a constant.

We can think of the function A as given by

$$A(x) = \text{the area on the interval } [a, x],$$

where a is some fixed point and x varies.

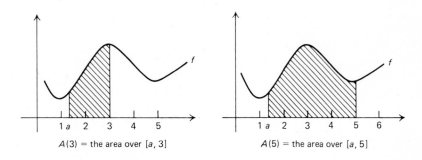

$A(3) = $ the area over $[a, 3]$ $A(5) = $ the area over $[a, 5]$

Now let us find some areas.

Example 1   Find the area under the graph of $y = x^2 + 1$ on the interval $[-1, 2]$.

Solution   a) We first make a drawing. This includes a graph of the function and the region in question.

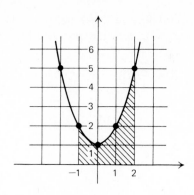 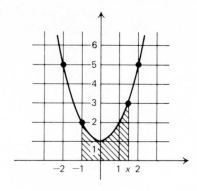

b) Second, we make a drawing showing a portion of the region from -1 to x. Now $A(x)$ is the area of this portion, that is to say, in the interval $[-1, \ x]$.

c) Now

$$A(x) = \int (x^2 + 1) \ dx = \frac{x^3}{3} + x + C,$$

where C has to be determined. Since we know that $A(-1) = 0$ (there is no area above the number -1), we can substitute for x in $A(x)$, as follows:

$$A(-1) = \frac{(-1)^3}{3} + (-1) + C = 0,$$

$$-\tfrac{1}{3} - 1 + C = 0,$$

$$C = \tfrac{4}{3}.$$

This determines that $C = \tfrac{4}{3}$, so we have

$$A(x) = \frac{x^3}{3} + x + \frac{4}{3}.$$

Then the area in the interval $[-1, 2]$ is $A(2)$. We compute $A(2)$ as follows:

$$A(2) = \frac{2^3}{3} + 2 + \frac{4}{3} = \frac{8}{3} + 2 + \frac{4}{3} = \frac{12}{3} + 2 = 6.$$

Example 2   Find the area under the graph of $y = x^3$ on the interval $[0, 5]$.

Solution   a) We first make a drawing which includes a graph of the function and the region in question.

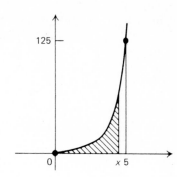

b) Second, we make a drawing showing a portion of that region from 0 to x. Now $A(x)$ is the area of this portion, that is, on the interval $[0, x]$.

c) Now

$$A(x) = \int x^3 \, dx = \frac{x^4}{4} + C,$$

where C has to be determined. Since we know that $A(0) = 0$, we can substitute 0 for x in $A(x)$, as follows:

$$A(0) = \frac{0^4}{4} + C = 0,$$

$$C = 0.$$

This determines C. So

$$A(x) = \frac{x^4}{4}.$$

Then the area in the interval $[0, 5]$ is $A(5)$. We compute $A(5)$ as follows:

$$A(5) = \frac{5^4}{4} = \frac{625}{4} = 156\tfrac{1}{4}.$$

Since the area under a curve, as in the preceding examples, is an antiderivative, area can also be associated with various kinds of functions. If, for example, we have a marginal cost function over the interval $[0, x]$, the area under the curve is the total cost of producing x units, or the accumulated cost.

Example 3   Raggs, Ltd., has a marginal cost per suit given by

$$C'(x) = 0.0003x^2 - 0.2x + 50.$$

Find the total cost of producing 400 suits. (Ignore fixed costs.)

Solution   a) First, we make a drawing. This includes a graph of the function and the region in question.

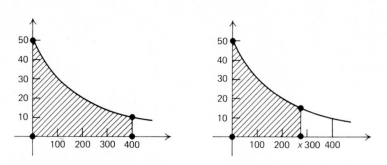

b) Second, we make a drawing showing a portion of that region from 0 to x. Now $A(x)$ is the area of that portion, that is, on the interval $[0, x]$.

c) Now,

$$C(x) = A(x) = \int (0.0003x^2 - 0.2x + 50) \, dx$$
$$= 0.0001x^3 - 0.1x^2 + 50x + K,$$

where K has to be determined. We are ignoring fixed costs, $K = 0$, and we have

$$C(x) = 0.0001x^3 - 0.1x^2 + 50x.$$

Then the area in the interval $[0, 400]$ is $A(400)$ or $C(400)$. We can compute $C(400)$ as follows:

$$C(400) = 0.0001 \cdot 400^3 - 0.1 \cdot 400^2 + 50 \cdot 400, \text{ or } \$10,400.$$

EXERCISE SET 10.2

Find the area under the given curve on the interval indicated.

1. $y = 4$; $[1, 3]$ **2.** $y = 5$; $[1, 3]$ **3.** $y = 2x$; $[1, 3]$

4. $y = x^2$; $[0, 3]$ **5.** $y = x^2$; $[0, 5]$ **6.** $y = x^3$; $[0, 2]$

7. $y = x^3$; $[0, 1]$ **8.** $y = 1 - x^2$; $[-1, 1]$ **9.** $y = 4 - x^2$; $[-2, 2]$

10. $y = e^x$; $[0, 2]$ **11.** $y = e^x$; $[0, 3]$ **12.** $y = \dfrac{1}{x}$; $[1, 2]$

13. $y = \dfrac{1}{x}$; $[1, 3]$ **14.** $y = x^2 - 4x$; $[-4, -2]$ **15.** $y = x^2 - 4x$; $[-4, -1]$

In each case give two interpretations of the shaded region.

16.

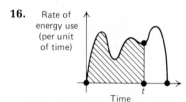

17.

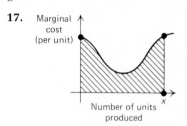

18.

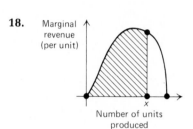

19.

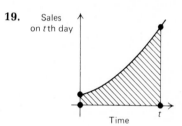

20. A sound company determines that the marginal cost of producing the xth stereo is given by

$$C'(x) = 100 - 0.2x, \qquad C(0) = 0.$$

It also determines that its marginal revenue from the sale of the xth stereo is given by

$$R'(x) = 100 + 0.2x, \qquad R(0) = 0.$$

a) Find the total cost of producing x stereos.

b) Find the total revenue of selling x stereos.

c) Find the total profit from the production and sale of x stereos.

d) Find the total profit from the production and sale of 1000 stereos.

21. A refrigeration company determines that the marginal cost of producing the xth refrigerator is given by

$$C'(x) = 50 - 0.4x, \qquad C(0) = 0.$$

It also determines that its marginal revenue from the sale of the xth refrigerator is given by

$$R'(x) = 50 + 0.4x, \qquad R(0) = 0.$$

a) Find the total cost of producing x refrigerators.

b) Find the total revenue of selling x refrigerators.

c) Find the total profit from the production and sale of x refrigerators.

d) Find the total profit from the production and sale of 1000 refrigerators.

■ _____

Find the area under the curve on the interval indicated.

22. $y = \dfrac{x^2 - 1}{x - 1}$; $[2, 3]$

23. $y = \dfrac{x^5 - x^{-1}}{x^2}$; $[1, 5]$

24. $y = (x - 1)\sqrt{x}$; $[4, 16]$

25. $y = (x + 2)^3$; $[0, 1]$

26. $y = \dfrac{\sqrt[3]{x^2} - 1}{\sqrt[3]{x}}$; $[1, 8]$

27. $y = \dfrac{x^3 + 8}{x + 2}$; $[0, 1]$

10.3   INTEGRATION ON AN INTERVAL: THE DEFINITE INTEGRAL

Let f be a positive continuous function on an interval $[a, b]$. We know that f has an antiderivative, namely $A(x)$. Let F and G be any two antiderivatives of f. Then

$$F(b) - F(a) = G(b) - G(a).$$

To understand this, recall that F and G differ by a constant. That is, $F(x) = G(x) + C$. Then

$$F(b) - F(a) = [G(b) + C] - [G(a) + C] = G(b) - G(a).$$

Thus the difference $F(b) - F(a)$ has the same value for all antiderivatives of f. It is called the *definite integral* of f from a to b.

Definite integrals are usually symbolized as follows:

$$\int_a^b f(x)\, dx.$$

This is read "the integral from a to b of $f(x)\, dx$" (the dx is sometimes omitted from the reading). From the preceding development we see that to find a definite integral $\int_a^b f(x)\, dx$ we first find an antiderivative $F(x)$. The simplest one is the one for which the constant of integration is 0. We evaluate F at b and at a and subtract.

$\int_a^b f(x)\, dx$ **is defined to be** $F(b) - F(a)$**, where** F **is any antiderivative of** f**.**

Evaluating definite integrals is called *integrating*. The numbers a and b are known as the *limits of integration*.

Example 1   Integrate $\displaystyle\int_a^b x^2\, dx.$

Solution   Using the antiderivative $F(x) = x^3/3$, we have

$$\int_a^b x^2\, dx = \frac{b^3}{3} - \frac{a^3}{3}.$$

It is convenient to use an intermediate notation

$$\int_a^b f(x)\, dx = [F(x)]_a^b = F(b) - F(a).$$

We now evaluate several definite integrals.

Example 2 $\displaystyle\int_{-1}^{2} x^2 \, dx = \left[\frac{x^3}{3}\right]_{-1}^{2} = \frac{2^3}{3} - \frac{(-1)^3}{3}$

$$= \frac{8}{3} - \left(-\frac{1}{3}\right) = \frac{8}{3} + \frac{1}{3} = 3$$

Example 3 $\displaystyle\int_{0}^{3} e^x \, dx = [e^x]_0^3 = e^3 - e^0 = e^3 - 1$

Example 4 $\displaystyle\int_{1}^{4} (x^2 - x) \, dx = \left[\frac{x^3}{3} - \frac{x^2}{2}\right]_1^4 = \left(\frac{4^3}{3} - \frac{4^2}{2}\right) - \left(\frac{1^3}{3} - \frac{1^2}{2}\right)$

$$= \left(\frac{64}{3} - \frac{16}{2}\right) - \left(\frac{1}{3} - \frac{1}{2}\right)$$

$$= \frac{64}{3} - 8 - \frac{1}{3} + \frac{1}{2} = 13\tfrac{1}{2}$$

Example 5 $\displaystyle\int_{1}^{e} \left(1 + 2x - \frac{1}{x}\right) dx = [x + x^2 - \ln x]_1^e$

$$= (e + e^2 - \ln e) - (1 + 1^2 - \ln 1)$$
$$= (e + e^2 - 1) - (1 + 1 - 0)$$
$$= e + e^2 - 1 - 1 - 1$$
$$= e + e^2 - 3$$

It is important to note that in $\int_a^b f(x) \, dx$, $a < b$. That is, the largest number is on the top!

The area under a curve can be expressed by a definite integral.

THEOREM   **Let f be a positive continuous function over the closed interval $[a, b]$. The area under the graph of f on the interval $[a, b]$ is**

$$\int_a^b f(x) \, dx.$$

Proof

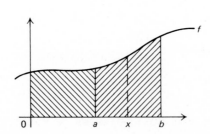

Let

$$A(x) = \text{the area of the region over } [0, x].$$

Then

$$A'(x) = f(x),$$

so $A(x)$ is an antiderivative of $f(x)$. Then

$$\int_a^b f(x)\, dx = A(b) - A(a).$$

But $A(b) - A(a)$ is the area over $[0, b]$ minus the area over $[0, a]$, which is the area over $[a, b]$.

Let us now find some areas.

Example 6   Find the area under $y = x^2 + 1$ on $[-1, 2]$.

Solution $\displaystyle\int_{-1}^{2} (x^2 + 1)\, dx = \left[\frac{x^3}{3} + x\right]_{-1}^{2}$

$$= \left(\frac{2^3}{3} + 2\right) - \left(\frac{(-1)^3}{3} + (-1)\right)$$

$$= \left(\frac{8}{3} + 2\right) - \left(-\frac{1}{3} - 1\right)$$

$$= \frac{8}{3} + 2 + \frac{1}{3} + 1 = 6$$

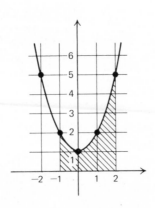

Compare this with Example 1 in Section 10.2.

Example 7 Find the area under $y = x^3$ on $[0, 5]$.

Solution $\displaystyle\int_0^5 x^3\,dx = \left[\frac{x^4}{4}\right]_0^5 = \frac{5^4}{4} - \frac{0^4}{4} = \frac{625}{4}$

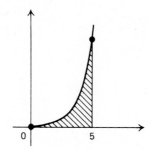

Compare this with Example 2 in Section 10.2.

Example 8 Find the area under $y = \dfrac{1}{x}$ on $[1, 4]$.

Solution $\displaystyle\int_1^4 \frac{dx}{x} = [\ln x]_1^4 = \ln 4 - \ln 1$

$= \ln 4$

≈ 1.3863 (▦ or Table 3.)

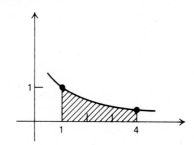

Example 9 Find the area under $y = \dfrac{1}{x^2}$ on $[1, b]$.

Solution $\displaystyle\int_1^b \frac{dx}{x^2} = \int_1^b x^{-2}\,dx = \left[\frac{x^{-2+1}}{-2+1}\right]_1^b$

$= \left[\frac{x^{-1}}{-1}\right]_1^b = \left[-\frac{1}{x}\right]_1^b = \left(-\frac{1}{b}\right) - \left(-\frac{1}{1}\right) = 1 - \frac{1}{b}.$

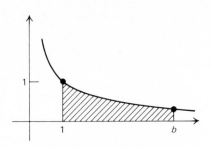

The following properties of definite integrals can be derived rather easily from the definition of definite integral and from the properties of the indefinite integral:

PROPERTY 1

$$\int_a^b k \cdot f(x)\ dx = k \cdot \int_a^b f(x)\ dx.$$

(The integral of a constant times a function is the constant times the integral of the function. That is, we can "factor out" a constant from the integrand.)

Example 10 $\int_0^5 100e^x\ dx = 100 \int_0^5 e^x\ dx = 100[e^x]_0^5 = 100(e^5 - e^0) = 100(e^5 - 1)$

PROPERTY 2

$$\int_a^b [f(x) + g(x)]\ dx = \int_a^b f(x)\ dx + \int_a^b g(x)\ dx.$$

(The integral of a sum is the sum of the integrals.)

PROPERTY 3   For $a < c < b$, $\int_a^b f(x)\ dx = \int_a^c f(x)\ dx + \int_c^b f(x)\ dx.$

(For any number c between a and b, the integral from a to b is the integral from a to c plus the integral from c to b.)

Property 3 has particular application when a function is defined in different ways over subintervals.

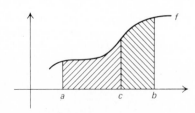

Example 11   Find the area under the graph of $y = f(x)$ from -4 to 5, where

$$f(x) = \begin{cases} 9, & \text{if } x < 3 \\ x^2 & \text{if } x \geqslant 3. \end{cases}$$

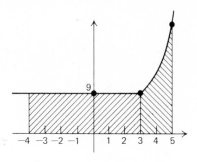

Solution $\displaystyle\int_{-4}^{5} f(x)\, dx = \int_{-4}^{3} f(x)\, dx + \int_{3}^{5} f(x)\, dx$

$\displaystyle = \int_{-4}^{3} 9\, dx + \int_{3}^{5} x^2\, dx$

$\displaystyle = 9 \int_{-4}^{2} dx + \int_{3}^{5} x^2\, dx = 9[x]_{-4}^{3} + \left[\frac{x^3}{3}\right]_{3}^{5}$

$\displaystyle = 9[3 - (-4)] + (5^3/3) - (3^3/3)$

$\displaystyle = 95\tfrac{2}{3}$

Applied Problem

Example 12   *Accumulated sales.* The sales of a company are expected to grow continuously at a rate given by the function

$$S'(t) = 100e^t,$$

where $S'(t) = $ sales rate, in dollars per day, at time t.

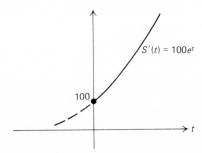

a) Find the accumulated sales for the first 7 days.

b) On what day will accumulated sales exceed \$810,000?

Solution   a) Accumulated sales through day 7 are

$$\int_0^7 S'(t)\, dt = \int_0^7 100e^t\, dt = 100 \int_0^7 e^t\, dt$$

$$= 100[e^t]_0^7 = 100(e^7 - e^0)$$

$$= 100(1096.633158 - 1)$$

$$= 100(1095.633158) \approx \$109{,}563.32.$$

b) Accumulated sales through day k are

$$\int_0^k S'(t)\, dt = \int_0^k 100e^t\, dt = 100 \int_0^k e^t\, dt$$

$$= 100[e^t]_0^k = 100(e^k - e^0) = 100(e^k - 1).$$

We set this equal to \$810,000 and solve for k.

$$100(e^k - 1) = 810{,}000$$

$$e^k - 1 = 8100$$

$$e^k = 8101$$

We solve this equation for k using natural logarithms:

$$e^k = 8101$$

$$\ln e^k = \ln 8101$$

$$k = 8.999743 \qquad (\text{▦ or Table 3})$$

$$k \approx 9$$

EXERCISE SET 10.3

Integrate.

1. $\displaystyle\int_0^1 (x - x^2)\, dx$

2. $\displaystyle\int_1^2 (x^2 - x)\, dx$

3. $\displaystyle\int_{-1}^1 (x^2 - x^4)\, dx$

4. $\displaystyle\int_0^b e^x\, dx$

5. $\displaystyle\int_a^b e^t\, dt$

6. $\displaystyle\int_0^a (ax - x^2)\, dx$

7. $\displaystyle\int_a^b 3t^2\, dt$

8. $\displaystyle\int_a^b 4t^3\, dt$

9. $\displaystyle\int_1^e \left(x + \frac{1}{x}\right) dx$

10. $\displaystyle\int_1^e \left(x - \frac{1}{x} \right) dx$

11. $\displaystyle\int_0^1 \sqrt{x}\; dx$

12. $\displaystyle\int_0^1 3\sqrt{x}\; dx$

13. $\displaystyle\int_0^1 \tfrac{10}{17} t^3\; dt$

14. $\displaystyle\int_0^1 \tfrac{12}{13} t^2\; dt$

Find the area under the graph on the interval indicated.

15. $y = x^3$; [0, 2]

16. $y = x^4$; [0, 1]

17. $y = x^2 + x + 1$; [2, 3]

18. $y = 2 - x - x^2$; [−2, 1]

19. $y = 5 - x^2$; [−1, 2]

20. $y = e^x$; [−2, 3]

21. $y = e^x$; [−1, 5]

22. $y = 2x + \dfrac{1}{x^2}$; [1, 4]

23. $y = 2x - \dfrac{1}{x^2}$; [1, 3]

Find the area under the graph on [−2, 3].

24. $f(x) = \begin{cases} x^2, & \text{if } x < 1 \\ 1, & \text{if } x \geq 1 \end{cases}$

25. $f(x) = \begin{cases} 4 - x^2, & \text{if } x < 0 \\ 4, & \text{if } x \geq 0 \end{cases}$

26. *Accumulated sales.* Raggs, Ltd. estimates that its sales will grow continuously at a rate given by the function

$$S'(t) = 10e^t,$$

where $S'(t)$ = sales rate, in dollars per day, at time t.

a) Find the accumulated sales for the first 5 days.

b) Find the sales from the second through the fifth day. This is the integral from 1 to 5.

c) On what day will accumulated sales exceed $40,000?

27. *Accumulated sales.* A company estimates that its sales will grow continuously at a rate given by the function

$$S'(t) = 20e^t,$$

where $S'(t)$ = sales rate, in dollars per day, at time t.

a) Find the accumulated sales for the first 5 days.

b) Find the sales from the second through the fifth day. This is the integral from 1 to 5.

c) On what day will accumulated sales exceed $20,000?

28. Raggs, Ltd. determines that the marginal cost per suit is given by

$$C'(x) = 0.0003x^2 - 0.2x + 50.$$

Ignoring fixed costs, find the total cost of producing the 101st through the 400th suit (integrate from $x = 100$ to $x = 400$).

29. In Exercise 28, find the cost of producing the 201st through the 400th suit (integrate from
$x = 200$ to $x = 400$).

30. A company is producing a new product. However, due to the nature of the product, it is felt that the time required to produce each unit will decrease as the workers become more familiar with the production procedure. It is determined that the function for the learning process is

$$T(x) = ax^b,$$

where

T(x) = cumulative average time to produce
      x units,
  x = number of units produced,
  a = hours required to produce 1st unit,
  b = slope of the learning curve.

a) Find an expression for the total time required to produce 100 units.

b) Suppose $a = 100$ hr and $b = -0.322$.
Find the total time required to produce
100 units. [*Hint:* $100^{0.678} \approx 22.7$.]

■ ───

Integrate.

31. $\displaystyle\int_1^2 (4x + 3)(5x - 2)\, dx$

32. $\displaystyle\int_2^5 (t + \sqrt{3})(t - \sqrt{3})\, dt$

33. $\displaystyle\int_0^1 (t + 1)^3\, dt$

34. $\displaystyle\int_1^3 \left(x - \frac{1}{x}\right)^2 dx$

35. $\displaystyle\int_1^3 \frac{t^5 - t}{t^3}\, dt$

36. $\displaystyle\int_4^9 \frac{t + 1}{\sqrt{t}}\, dt$

37. $\displaystyle\int_3^5 \frac{x^2 - 4}{x - 2}\, dx$

38. $\displaystyle\int_0^1 \frac{t^3 + 1}{t + 1}\, dt$

───

10.4   INTEGRATION TECHNIQUES: SUBSTITUTION

The following formulas provide a basis for an integration technique called
substitution.

A) $\displaystyle\int n \cdot u^{n-1}\, du = u^n + C$

B) $\displaystyle\int e^u\, du = e^u + C$

C) $\displaystyle\int \frac{1}{u}\, du = \ln u + C$

In the Leibniz notation dy/dx we did not give specific definitions of dy and
dx. Nevertheless it will be convenient to treat dy/dx as a quotient. Thus,
from

$$\frac{dy}{dx} = f'(x)$$

we can derive

$$dy = f'(x)\ dx.$$

It is possible to define dy and dx, but it is not necessary for our purposes.

Example 1 For $y = f(x) = x^3$, find dy.

Solution $\dfrac{dy}{dx} = f'(x) = 3x^2$, so $dy = f'(x)\ dx = 3x^2\ dx$.

Example 2 For $u = g(x) = \ln x$, find du.

Solution $\dfrac{du}{dx} = g'(x) = \dfrac{1}{x}$, so $du = g'(x)\ dx = \dfrac{1}{x}\ dx$, or $\dfrac{dx}{x}$.

So far the dx in

$$\int f(x)\ dx$$

has played no role in integrating, other than indicating the variable of integration. Now it will be convenient to make use of dx. Consider the integral

$$\int 2x \cdot e^{x^2}\ dx.$$

If we set

$$u = x^2,$$

then

$$du = 2x\ dx.$$

If we substitute u for x^2, and du for $2x\ dx$, the integral takes on the form

$$\int e^u\ du.$$

Since

$$\int e^u\ du = e^u + C,$$

it follows that

$$\int 2x \cdot e^{x^2}\ dx = \int e^u\ du = e^u + C = e^{x^2} + C.$$

The result can be checked by differentiation. This procedure is referred to as *substitution*, or *change of variable*. It is a *trial-and-error* procedure; that is, if we try a substitution that doesn't result in an integrand that can be easily integrated, we try another. It will not always work! It *will* work if the integrand fits one of the rules A, B, or C.

Let us consider some further examples.

Example 3

$$\int \frac{2x\ dx}{1 + x^2} = \int \frac{du}{u} \quad \text{Substitution} \quad \boxed{\text{Let } u = 1 + x^2, \\ \text{then } du = 2x\ dx.}$$

$$= \ln u + C$$

$$= \ln (1 + x^2) + C$$

Remember that this is a trial and error process. Suppose we had made the substitution

$$u = x^2.$$

Then

$$du = 2x\ dx,$$

and the integral becomes

$$\int \frac{du}{1 + u}.$$

This is still not easily integrated, so we would try another substitution.

Example 4

$$\int \frac{2x\ dx}{(1 + x^2)^2} = \int \frac{du}{u^2} \quad \text{Substitution} \quad \boxed{u = 1 + x^2, \\ du = 2x\ dx}$$

$$= -\frac{1}{u} + C = -\frac{1}{1 + x^2} + C$$

Example 5

$$\int \frac{\ln 3x\ dx}{x} = \int u\ du \quad \text{Substitution} \quad \boxed{u = \ln 3x, \\ du = \frac{1}{x}\ dx}$$

$$= \frac{u^2}{2} + C$$

$$= \frac{(\ln 3x)^2}{2} + C$$

Example 6   Integrate $\int xe^{x^2}\ dx$.

Solution Suppose we try

$$u = x^2,$$

then

$$du = 2x \, dx.$$

We don't quite have $2x \, dx$. We have only $x \, dx$ and will need to supply a 2. We do this by multiplying by $\frac{1}{2} \cdot 2$ as follows.

$$\frac{1}{2} \cdot 2 \cdot \int xe^{x^2} \, dx = \frac{1}{2} \int 2xe^{x^2} \, dx$$

$$= \frac{1}{2} \int e^{x^2}(2x \, dx)$$

$$= \frac{1}{2} \int e^u \, du$$

$$= \frac{1}{2}e^u + C$$

$$= \frac{1}{2}e^{x^2} + C$$

Example 7
$$\left.\begin{array}{l} \displaystyle\int e^{ax} \, dx = \frac{1}{a} \int ae^{ax} \, dx \\[2ex] \displaystyle\qquad = \frac{1}{a} \int e^u \, du \\[2ex] \displaystyle\qquad = \frac{1}{a} e^u + C = \frac{1}{a} e^{ax} + C \end{array}\right\} \quad \underline{\text{Substitution}} \quad \boxed{\begin{array}{l} u = ax, \\ du = a \, dx \end{array}}$$

Note that this gives us a formula for integrating e^{ax}.

Example 8
$$\int \frac{dx}{x + 3} = \int \frac{du}{u} \quad \text{Substitution} \quad \boxed{\begin{array}{l} u = x + 3, \\ du = dx \end{array}}$$

$$= \ln u + C = \ln (x + 3) + C$$

With practice, you will make certain substitutions mentally and just write down the answer. Examples 7 and 8 are good illustrations.

Example 9
$$\left.\begin{array}{l} \displaystyle\int x^2(x^3 + 1)^{10} \, dx = \frac{1}{3} \int 3x^2(x^3 + 1)^{10} \, dx \\[2ex] \displaystyle\qquad = \frac{1}{3} \int u^{10} \, du \end{array}\right\} \quad \underline{\text{Substitution}} \quad \boxed{\begin{array}{l} u = x^3 + 1 \\ du = 3x^2 \, dx \end{array}}$$

$$= \frac{1}{3} \cdot \frac{u^{11}}{11} + C = \tfrac{1}{33} (x^3 + 1)^{11} + C$$

Example 10 Evaluate.

$$\int_0^1 x^2(x^3 + 1)^{10} \, dx$$

Solution a) First find the indefinite integral (shown in Example 9).

b) Then evaluate the definite integral on [0, 1].

$$\int_0^1 x^2(x^3 + 1)^{10} \, dx = \left[\tfrac{1}{33} (x^3 + 1)^{11}\right]_0^1$$

$$= \tfrac{1}{33}[(1^3 + 1)^{11} - (0^3 + 1)^{11}]$$

$$= \tfrac{1}{33}(2^{11} - 1^{11})$$

$$= \frac{2^{11} - 1}{33}$$

EXERCISE SET 10.4

Integrate. (Be sure to check by differentiating!)

1. $\displaystyle\int \frac{3x^2 \, dx}{7 + x^3}$ **2.** $\displaystyle\int \frac{3x^2 \, dx}{1 + x^3}$ **3.** $\displaystyle\int e^{4x} \, dx$ **4.** $\displaystyle\int e^{3x} \, dx$

5. $\displaystyle\int e^{x/2} \, dx$ **6.** $\displaystyle\int e^{x/3} \, dx$ **7.** $\displaystyle\int x^3 e^{x^4} \, dx$ **8.** $\displaystyle\int x^4 e^{x^5} \, dx$

9. $\displaystyle\int t^2 e^{-t^3} \, dt$ **10.** $\displaystyle\int te^{-t^2} \, dt$ **11.** $\displaystyle\int \frac{\ln 4x \, dx}{x}$ **12.** $\displaystyle\int \frac{\ln 5x \, dx}{x}$

13. $\displaystyle\int \frac{dx}{1 + x}$ **14.** $\displaystyle\int \frac{dx}{5 + x}$ **15.** $\displaystyle\int \frac{dx}{4 - x}$ **16.** $\displaystyle\int \frac{dx}{1 - x}$

17. $\displaystyle\int t^2(t^3 - 1)^7 \, dt$ **18.** $\displaystyle\int t(t^2 - 1)^5 \, dt$ **19.** $\displaystyle\int (x^4 + x^3 + x^2)^7(4x^3 + 3x^2 + 2x) \, dx$

20. $\displaystyle\int (x^3 - x^2 - x)^9(3x^2 - 2x - 1) \, dx$ **21.** $\displaystyle\int \frac{e^x \, dx}{4 + e^x}$ **22.** $\displaystyle\int \frac{e^t \, dt}{3 + e^t}$

23. $\displaystyle\int \frac{\ln x^2}{x} \, dx$ **24.** $\displaystyle\int \frac{(\ln x)^2}{x} \, dx$ **25.** $\displaystyle\int \frac{dx}{x \ln x}$ **26.** $\displaystyle\int \frac{dx}{x \ln x^2}$

27. $\displaystyle\int \sqrt{ax + b} \, dx$ **28.** $\displaystyle\int x\sqrt{ax^2 + b} \, dx$ **29.** $\displaystyle\int be^{ax} \, dx$ **30.** $\displaystyle\int P_0 e^{kt} \, dt$

Integrate.

31. $\displaystyle\int_0^1 2xe^{x^2} \, dx$ **32.** $\displaystyle\int_0^1 3x^2 e^{x^3} \, dx$ **33.** $\displaystyle\int_0^1 x(x^2 + 1)^5 \, dx$ **34.** $\displaystyle\int_1^2 x(x^2 - 1)^7 \, dx$

35. $\int_1^3 \dfrac{dt}{1 + t}$

36. $\int_1^3 e^{2x}\, dx$

37. $\int_1^4 \dfrac{2x + 1}{x^2 + x - 1}\, dx$

38. $\int_1^3 \dfrac{2x + 3}{x^2 + 3x}\, dx$

39. $\int_0^b e^{-x}\, dx$

40. $\int_0^b 2e^{-2x}\, dx$

41. $\int_0^b me^{-mx}\, dx$

42. $\int_0^b ke^{-kx}\, dx$

43. $\int_0^4 (x - 6)^2\, dx$

44. $\int_0^3 (x - 5)^2\, dx$

45. Value of an investment. A company buys a new machine for \$250,000. The marginal revenue from the sale of products produced by the machine is projected to be

$$R'(t) = 4000t.$$

The salvage value of the machine decreases at the rate of

$$V(t) = 25{,}000e^{-0.1t}.$$

The total profit from the machine after T yrs is given by

$$P(T) = \begin{pmatrix} \text{Revenue from} \\ \text{sale of prod.} \end{pmatrix} + \begin{pmatrix} \text{Revenue from} \\ \text{sale of mach.} \end{pmatrix} - \begin{pmatrix} \text{Cost of} \\ \text{machine} \end{pmatrix}$$

$$= \int_0^T R'(t)\, dt \quad + \int_0^T V(t)\, dt \quad - \$250{,}000.$$

a) Find $P(T)$.

b) Find $P(10)$.

46. ▦ The U.S. divorce rate is approximated by

$$D(t) = 100{,}000e^{0.025t},$$

where

$D(t) =$ number of divorces occurring at time t,

$t =$ number of years measured from 1900.

That is, $t = 0$ corresponds to 1900, $t = 84\frac{9}{365}$ corresponds to January 9, 1984, and so on.

a) Find the total number of divorces from 1900 to 1984. Note that this is

$$\int_0^{84} D(t)\, dt.$$

b) Find the total number of divorces from 1980 to 1984. Note that this is $\int_{80}^{84} D(t)\, dt$.

■ ───────────────────────────────

Integrate.

47. $\int 5x\sqrt{1 - 4x^2}\, dx$

48. $\int \dfrac{dx}{ax + b}$

49. $\int \dfrac{x^2}{e^{x^3}}\, dx$

50. $\int \dfrac{e^{\sqrt{t}}}{\sqrt{t}}\, dt$

51. $\int \dfrac{e^{1/t}}{t^2}$

52. $\int \dfrac{(\ln x)^2}{x}\, dx$

53. $\int \dfrac{dx}{x(\ln x)^4}$

54. $\int (e^t + 2)e^t\, dt$

55. $\int x^2\sqrt{x^3 + 1}\, dx$

56. $\int \dfrac{t^2}{\sqrt[4]{2 + t^3}}\, dt$

57. $\int \dfrac{x - 3}{(x^2 - 6x)^{1/3}}\, dx$

58. $\int \dfrac{[(\ln x)^2 + 3(\ln x) + 4]}{x}\, dx$

59. $\int \dfrac{t^3 \ln (t^4 + 8)}{t^4 + 8}\, dt$

60. $\int \dfrac{t^2 + 2t}{(t + 1)^2}\, dt$ Hint: $\dfrac{t^2 + 2t}{(t + 1)^2} = \dfrac{t^2 + 2t + 1 - 1}{t^2 + 2t + 1} = 1 - \dfrac{1}{(t + 1)^2}$

61. $\int \dfrac{x^2 + 6x}{(x + 3)^2}\, dx$

62. $\int \dfrac{x + 3}{x + 1}\, dx$ Hint: Divide, $\dfrac{x + 3}{x + 1} = 1 + \dfrac{2}{x + 1}$

63. $\int \dfrac{t-5}{t-4}\, dt$

64. $\int \dfrac{dx}{x(\ln x)^n}$

65. $\int \dfrac{dx}{e^x+1}$ Hint: $\dfrac{1}{e^x+1} = \dfrac{e^{-x}}{1+e^{-x}}$

66. $\int \dfrac{e^x - e^{-x}}{e^x + e^{-x}}\, dx$

67. $\int \dfrac{(\ln x)^n}{x}\, dx$

10.5 INTEGRATION TECHNIQUES: INTEGRATION BY PARTS—TABLES

Recall the product rule for derivatives:

$$\frac{d}{dx}\,uv = \frac{du}{dx}\,v + \frac{dv}{dx}\,u = u\frac{dv}{dx} + v\frac{du}{dx}.$$

Integrating both sides, we get

$$uv = \int u\frac{dv}{dx}\,dx + \int v\frac{du}{dx}\,dx = \int u\,dv + \int v\,du.$$

Solving for $\int u\,dv$, we get

$$\int u\,dv = uv - \int v\,du.$$

This equation can be used as a formula for integrating in certain situations. These are situations in which an integrand is a product of two functions; one of the functions can be integrated by using the techniques we have already developed.

For example,

$$\int xe^x\,dx$$

can be considered as follows:

$$\int x(e^x\,dx) = \int u\,dv, \quad \text{where } u = x \text{ and } dv = e^x\,dx.$$

We already know how to integrate $e^x\,dx$, or dv. The simplest antiderivative is e^x. This is v. Now, since $du = dx$, the formula gives us

$$\int \overset{u}{(x)}\overset{dv}{(e^x\,dx)} = \overset{u}{(x)}\overset{v}{(e^x)} - \int \overset{v}{(e^x)}\overset{du}{(dx)}$$

$$= xe^x - e^x + C.$$

This way of integrating is called *integration by parts*, and the following formula provides the basis for it.

INTEGRATION-BY-PARTS FORMULA

$$\int u\ dv = uv - \int v\ du$$

Note that integration by parts is a trial-and-error process, as is substitution. In the preceding example, suppose we had reversed the roles of x and e^x. We would have obtained

$$u = e^x \qquad dv = x\ dx,$$

$$du = e^x\ dx \qquad v = \frac{x^2}{2},$$

and

$$\int (e^x)(x\ dx) = (e^x)\left(\frac{x^2}{2}\right) - \int \left(\frac{x^2}{2}\right)(e^x\ dx).$$

Now the integrand on the right is more difficult to integrate than the one we started with. When we can integrate *both* factors of an integrand, and thus have a choice as to how to apply the integration-by-parts formula, it can happen that only one (and maybe none) of the possibilities will work. Let us consider some further examples.

Example 1 Integrate $\int \ln x\ dx$.

Solution Note that $\int (dx/x) = \ln x + C$. However, we do not yet know how to find $\int \ln x\ dx$. Let

$$u = \ln x \qquad \text{and} \qquad dv = dx.$$

Then

$$du = \frac{1}{x}\ dx \qquad \text{and} \qquad v = x.$$

Using the integration-by-parts formula gives

$$\int \overset{u}{(\ln x)} \overset{dv}{(dx)} = \overset{u}{(\ln x)} \overset{v}{x} - \int \overset{v}{x} \overset{du}{\left(\frac{1}{x}\ dx\right)}$$

$$= x \ln x - \int dx = x \ln x - x + C.$$

Example 2 Integrate $\int x\sqrt{x+1}\ dx$.

Solution We let

$$u = x \qquad \text{and} \qquad dv = (x+1)^{1/2}\ dx.$$

Then

$$du = dx \qquad \text{and} \qquad v = \tfrac{2}{3}(x + 1)^{3/2}.$$

Note that we had to use substitution to integrate dv. Using the integration-by-parts formula gives

$$\int x\sqrt{x + 1}\, dx = x \cdot \tfrac{2}{3}(x + 1)^{3/2} - \tfrac{2}{3}\int (x + 1)^{3/2}\, dx$$

$$= \tfrac{2}{3}x(x + 1)^{3/2} - \tfrac{2}{3} \cdot \tfrac{2}{5}(x + 1)^{5/2} + C$$

$$= \tfrac{2}{3}x(x + 1)^{3/2} - \tfrac{4}{15}(x + 1)^{5/2} + C.$$

Example 3   Integrate $\int_1^2 \ln x\, dx$.

Solution   a) First find the indefinite integral (Example 1).

b) Then evaluate the definite integral.

$$\int_1^2 \ln x\, dx = [x \ln x - x]_1^2$$

$$= (2 \ln 2 - 2) - (1 \cdot \ln 1 - 1)$$

$$= 2 \ln 2 - 2 + 1$$

$$= 2 \ln 2 - 1$$

Tables of Integration Formulas

You have probably noticed that, generally speaking, integration is more difficult and "tricky" than differentiation. Because of this, integral formulas that are reasonable and/or important have been gathered into tables. Table 5 at the back of the book, though quite brief, is such an example. Entire books of integration formulas are available in libraries, and lengthy tables are also available in mathematics handbooks. Such tables are usually classified by the form of the integrand. The idea is to properly match the integral in question with a formula in the table.

Example 4   Integrate $\displaystyle\int \frac{dx}{x(3 - x)}$.

Solution   This integral fits *Formula 20* in Table 5:

$$\int \frac{1}{x(ax + b)}\, dx = \frac{1}{b} \ln\left(\frac{x}{ax + b}\right) + C.$$

In our integral, $a = -1$ and $b = 3$, so we have, by the formula,

$$\int \frac{1}{x(3-x)}\,dx = \int \frac{dx}{x(-1 \cdot x + 3)}$$

$$= \frac{1}{3}\ln\left(\frac{x}{-1 \cdot x + 3}\right) + C$$

$$= \frac{1}{3}\ln\left(\frac{x}{3-x}\right) + C.$$

EXERCISE SET 10.5

Integrate. Use integration by parts. Do not use Table 5. Check by differentiating.

1. $\int 5xe^{5x}\,dx$ **2.** $\int 2xe^{2x}\,dx$ **3.** $\int x^3(3x^2\,dx)$ **4.** $\int x^2(2x\,dx)$

5. $\int xe^{2x}\,dx$ **6.** $\int xe^{3x}\,dx$ **7.** $\int xe^{-2x}\,dx)$ **8.** $\int xe^{-x}\,dx$

9. $\int x^2 \ln x\,dx$ **10.** $\int x^3 \ln x\,dx$ **11.** $\int x \ln x^2\,dx$ **12.** $\int x^2 \ln x^3\,dx$

13. $\int \ln(x+3)\,dx$ **14.** $\int \ln(x+1)\,dx$ **15.** $\int (x+2)\ln x\,dx$

16. $\int (x+1)\ln x\,dx$ **17.** $\int (x-1)\ln x\,dx$ **18.** $\int (x-2)\ln x\,dx$

19. $\int x\sqrt{x+2}\,dx$ **20.** $\int x\sqrt{x+4}\,dx$ **21.** $\int x^3 \ln 2x\,dx$

22. $\int x^2 \ln 5x\,dx$ **23.** $\int x^2 e^x\,dx$ **24.** $\int (\ln x)^2\,dx$

25. $\int x^2 e^{2x}\,dx$ **26.** $\int x^{-5}\ln x\,dx$

Integrate. Use integration by parts. Do not use Table 5.

27. $\int_1^2 x^2 \ln x\,dx$ **28.** $\int_1^2 x^3 \ln x\,dx$ **29.** $\int_2^6 \ln(x+3)\,dx$

30. $\int_0^5 \ln(x+1)\,dx$ **31.** $\int_0^1 xe^x\,dx$ **32.** $\int_0^1 xe^{-x}\,dx$

Integrate. Use Table 5.

33. $\displaystyle\int xe^{-3x}\,dx$ **34.** $\displaystyle\int xe^{4x}\,dx$ **35.** $\displaystyle\int 5^x\,dx$ **36.** $\displaystyle\int \frac{1}{\sqrt{x^2-9}}\,dx$

37. $\displaystyle\int \frac{1}{16-x^2}\,dx$ **38.** $\displaystyle\int \frac{1}{x\sqrt{4+x^2}}\,dx$ **39.** $\displaystyle\int \frac{x}{5-x}\,dx$ **40.** $\displaystyle\int \frac{x}{(1-x)^2}\,dx$

41. $\displaystyle\int \frac{1}{x(5-x)^2}\,dx$ **42.** $\displaystyle\int \sqrt{x^2+9}\,dx$

Integrate by parts. Do not use Table 5.

43. $\int \sqrt{x} \ln x \, dx$ **44.** $\int x^n \ln x \, dx$ **45.** $\int \dfrac{te^t}{(t+1)^2} \, dt$ **46.** $\int x^2 (\ln x)^2 \, dx$

47. $\int \dfrac{\ln x}{\sqrt{x}} \, dx$ **48.** $\int x^n (\ln x)^2 \, dx$

49. a) Verify that, for any positive integer n,

$$\int x^n e^x \, dx = x^n e^x - n \int x^{n-1} e^x \, dx.$$

   b) Apply (a) repeatedly to integrate

$$\int x^3 e^x \, dx.$$

50. a) Verify that, for any positive integer n,

$$\int (\ln x)^n \, dx = x(\ln x)^n - n \int (\ln x)^{n-1} \, dx.$$

   b) Apply (a) repeatedly to integrate

$$\int (\ln x)^3 \, dx.$$

10.6   THE DEFINITE INTEGRAL AS A LIMIT OF SUMS (OPTIONAL)

We now consider approximating the area of a region by dividing it into subregions that are almost rectangles. In the next drawing $[a, b]$ has been divided into 4 subintervals, each having width Δx, or $(b - a)/4$.

The heights of the rectangles shown are

$$f(x_1), \qquad f(x_2), \qquad f(x_3), \qquad \text{and} \quad f(x_4).$$

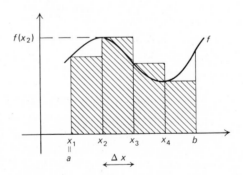

The area of the region under the curve is approximately the sum of the areas of the four rectangles,

$$f(x_1) \, \Delta x + f(x_2) \, \Delta x + f(x_3) \, \Delta x + f(x_4) \, \Delta x.$$

We can name this sum using *summation notation* which utilizes the Greek capital letter sigma, Σ,

$$\sum_{i=1}^{4} f(x_i) \, \Delta x.$$

This is read "the sum of the numbers $f(x_i) \, \Delta x$ from $i = 1$ to $i = 4$." To recover the original expression substitute the numbers 1 through 4 successively into $f(x_i) \, \Delta x$ and write plus signs between the results.

Example 1   Write summation notation for $2 + 4 + 6 + 8 + 10$.

Solution $2 + 4 + 6 + 8 + 10 = \displaystyle\sum_{i=1}^{5} 2i$

Example 2   Write summation notation for

$$g(x_1) \, \Delta x + g(x_2) \, \Delta x + \cdots + g(x_{19}) \, \Delta x.$$

Solution $g(x_1) \, \Delta x + g(x_2) \, \Delta x + \cdots + g(x_{19}) \, \Delta x = \displaystyle\sum_{i=1}^{19} g(x_i) \, \Delta x$

Example 3   Express $\displaystyle\sum_{i=1}^{4} 3^i$ without using summation notation.

Solution $\displaystyle\sum_{i=1}^{4} 3^i = 3^1 + 3^2 + 3^3 + 3^4$, or 120

Example 4   Express $\displaystyle\sum_{i=1}^{30} h(x_i) \, \Delta x$ without using summation notation.

Solution $\displaystyle\sum_{i=1}^{30} h(x_i) \, \Delta x = h(x_1) \, \Delta x + h(x_2) \, \Delta x + \cdots + h(x_{30}) \, \Delta x$

Approximation of area by rectangles becomes better as we use more rectangles and smaller subintervals, as we show in the following drawings.

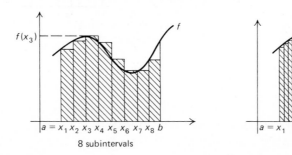

8 subintervals   24 subintervals

In general, the interval $[a, b]$ is divided into n equal subintervals, each of width $\Delta x = (b - a)/n$.

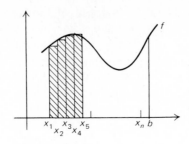

The heights of the rectangles are

$$f(x_1), f(x_2), \cdots, f(x_n).$$

The area of the region under the curve is approximated by the sum of the areas of the rectangles,

$$\sum_{i=1}^{n} f(x_i) \, \Delta x.$$

We now obtain the actual area by letting the number of intervals increase indefinitely and by taking the limit. The area is thus given by

$$A = \lim_{n \to \infty} \sum_{i=1}^{n} f(x_i) \, \Delta x.$$

The area is also given by a definite integral:

$$\int_a^b f(x) \, dx = \lim_{n \to \infty} \sum_{i=1}^{n} f(x_i) \, \Delta x.$$

The fact that we can so express the integral of a function (positive or otherwise) as a limit of a sum or in terms of an antiderivative is so important that it has a name, *The Fundamental Theorem of Integral Calculus.*

THE FUNDAMENTAL THEOREM OF INTEGRAL CALCULUS. If a function f has an antiderivative F on $[a, b]$, then

$$\int_a^b f(x) \, dx = F(b) - F(a) = \lim_{n \to \infty} \sum_{i=1}^{n} f(x_i) \, \Delta x.$$

It is interesting to envision that, as we take the limit on the right, the summation sign stretches into something reminiscent of an S (the integral sign) and the Δx becomes dx. This is also a motivation for the use of dx in the integral notation.

This result allows us to approximate the value of a definite integral by a sum, making it as good as we please by taking n sufficiently large.

Example 5   Raggs, Ltd., determines that the marginal cost per suit is

$$C'(x) = 0.0003x^2 - 0.2x + 50.$$

Approximate the total cost of producing 400 suits by computing the sum $\sum_{i=1}^{4} C'(x_i) \, \Delta x$.

Solution   The interval [0, 400] is divided into 4 subintervals, each of length $\Delta x = (400 - 0)/4 = 100$. Now x_i is varying from $x_1 = 0$ to $x_5 = 400$.

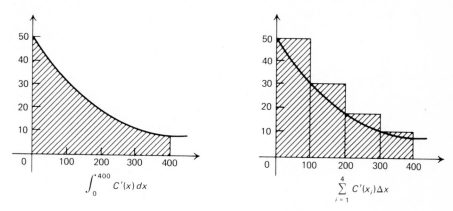

$$\int_0^{400} C'(x) \, dx \qquad\qquad \sum_{i=1}^{4} C'(x_i) \, \Delta x$$

$$\sum_{i=1}^{4} C'(x_i) \, \Delta x = C'(0) \cdot 100 + C'(100) \cdot 100 + C'(200) \cdot 100$$

$$+ \, C'(300) \cdot 100$$

$$= 50 \cdot 100 + 33 \cdot 100 + 22 \cdot 100 + 17 \cdot 100$$

$$= \$12{,}200$$

Now

$$\int_0^{400} C'(x) \, dx = \$10{,}400.$$

Thus this approximation is not too far off, even though the number of subintervals is small.

The fact that an integral can be approximated by a sum is useful when the antiderivative of a function does not have an elementary formula. For example, for the function $e^{-x^2/2}$, important in probability, there is no formula for the antiderivative. So, tables of approximate values of its integral have been computed using summation methods.

EXERCISE SET 10.6

1. a) Approximate $\int_1^7 (dx/x^2)$ by computing the area of each rectangle to four decimal places and adding.

   b) Evaluate $\int_1^7 (dx/x^2)$. Compare the answer to (a).

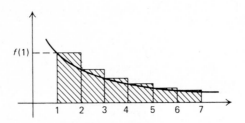

2. a) Approximate $\int_0^5 (x^2 + 1)\, dx$ by computing the area of each rectangle and adding.

   b) Evaluate $\int_0^5 (x^2 + 1)\, dx$. Compare the answer to (a).

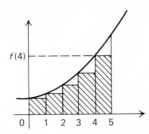

3. Referring to Example 5, find

$$\sum_{i=1}^{8} C'(x_i)\, \Delta x,$$

where the interval $[0, 400]$ is divided into 8 equal subintervals of length

$$\Delta x = \frac{400 - 0}{8} = 50.$$

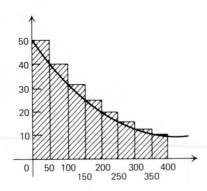

4. In graphs (a) and (b) compute the areas of each rectangle to four decimal places. Then add them to approximate the area under the curve $y = 1/x$ over $[1, 7]$.

a)

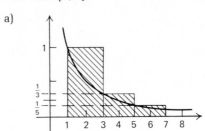

b)

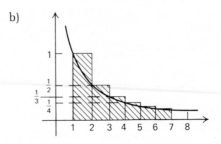

c) Evaluate

$$\int_1^7 \frac{1}{x}\, dx.$$

Find this answer in Table 3 and compare it to (a) and (b). [*Note:* Table 3 contains approximations of natural logarithms accurate to four decimal places. We could construct Table 3 using procedures like those in (a) and (b).]

CHAPTER 10 REVIEW

Integrate.

1. $\int dx$

2. $\int 1000x^4 \, dx$

3. $\int \left(e^x + \frac{1}{x} + x^{3/8} \right) dx$

Find the area under the curve on the interval indicated.

4. $y = x - x^2$; [0, 1]

5. $y = \dfrac{4}{x}$; [1, 3]

6. Give two interpretations of the shaded area.

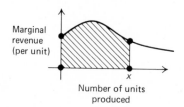

Integrate.

7. $\displaystyle\int_{-1}^{2} (2x + 3x^2) \, dx$

8. $\displaystyle\int_{0}^{1} e^{-2x} \, dx$

9. $\displaystyle\int_{a}^{b} \dfrac{dx}{x}$

Decide if $\int_a^b f(x) \, dx$ is positive, negative, or zero.

10.

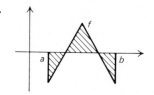

11.

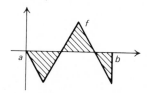

12.

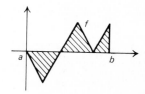

Integrate. Use substitution. Do not use Table 5.

13. $\displaystyle\int \dfrac{dx}{x + 8}$

14. $\displaystyle\int e^{-0.5x} \, dx$

15. $\displaystyle\int t^3(t^4 + 1)^9 \, dt$

Integrate. Use integration by parts. Do not use Table 5.

16. $\int xe^{5x}\, dx$

17. $\int x^3 \ln x^4\, dx$

Integrate. Use Table 5.

18. $\int 2^x\, dx$

19. $\int \dfrac{dx}{x(7 - x)}$

20. An air conditioning company determines that the marginal cost of the xth air conditioner is given by

$$C'(x) = -0.2x + 500, \qquad C(0) = 0.$$

Find the total cost of producing 100 air conditioners.

22. Pizza, Ltd. estimates that its sales will grow continuously according to the function

$$S'(t) = 3e^{2t},$$

where $S'(t)$ = sales, in dollars, on the tth day. Find the accumulated sales for the first week.

Integrate. Use any method.

23. $\int \dfrac{[(\ln x)^3 - 4(\ln x)^2 + 5]}{x}\, dx$

25. $\int \dfrac{\ln \sqrt{x}}{x}\, dx$

21. Approximate $\int_0^5 (25 - x^2)\, dx$, by computing the area of each rectangle and adding.

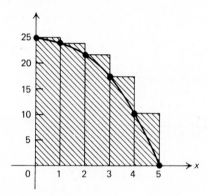

24. $\int \ln\left(\dfrac{x + 3}{x + 5}\right)\, dx$

26. $\int x^{99} \ln x\, dx$

APPLICATIONS OF INTEGRATION

11.1 ECONOMIC APPLICATION: CONSUMER'S AND PRODUCER'S SURPLUS

Recall that the consumer's demand curve $D(x)$ gives the demand price per unit that the consumer is willing to pay for x units. The producer's supply curve $S(x)$ gives the price per unit at which the producer is willing to supply x units. The equilibrium point (x_E, p_E) is the intersection of the two curves.

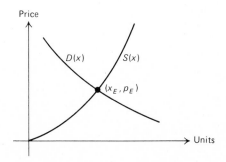

Suppose the following figure represents the supply and demand of college students for movies.

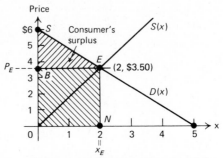

Units per week (average number of movies)

Here we might think of $6 as the price the consumer is willing to pay rather than see no movie at all, and 5 (on the x-axis) is the number of movies per week that the students would go to see if they were free. The area of rectangle *OBEN* is 2 · 3.50, or $7.00. This represents the amount the consumer pays to see 2 movies a week at $3.50 each. But the consumer actually gets utility or pleasure in terms of the area of trapezoid *OSEN* which is

$$\tfrac{1}{2} \cdot 2 \cdot (\$6 + \$3.50) \qquad \text{or} \qquad \$9.50.$$

The area of triangle *SEB* is defined to be *consumer's surplus* and is

$$\tfrac{1}{2} \cdot 2 \cdot \$2.50 \qquad \text{or} \qquad \$2.50,$$

and represents the bonus the consumer receives from living in a competitive society. The producer also benefits. The area of triangle *OBE* is defined as *producer's surplus* and is

$$\tfrac{1}{2} \cdot 2 \cdot \$3.50 \qquad \text{or} \qquad \$3.50.$$

To see this more clearly, look at the following graphs. Assume that one movie-maker is monopolizing the movies over other competitive movie-makers, and raises prices. Note how both the consumer's and producer's surplus decreases.

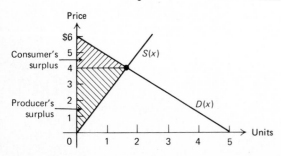

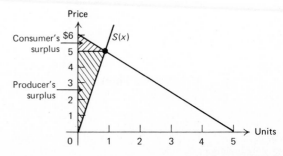

Consumer's surplus is defined as

$$\int_0^{x_E} D(x) \; dx \; - \; x_E p_E,$$

where $D(x)$ is the demand curve.

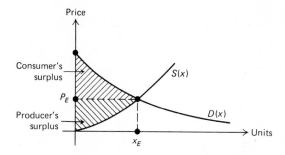

Producer's surplus is defined as

$$x_E p_E \; - \; \int_0^{x_E} S(x) \; dx,$$

where $S(x)$ is the supply curve.

Example 1   Given

$$D(x) = (x - 5)^2, \qquad S(x) = x^2 + x + 3,$$

find (a) the equilibrium point, (b) the consumer's surplus, and (c) the producer's surplus.

Solution   a) To find the equilibrium point we set $D(x) = S(x)$ and solve.

$$(x - 5)^2 = x^2 + x + 3$$
$$x^2 - 10x + 25 = x^2 + x + 3$$
$$-10x + 25 = x + 3$$
$$22 = 11x$$
$$\tfrac{22}{11} = x$$
$$2 = x$$

Thus $x_E = 2$ units. To find p_E we substitute x_E into $D(x)$ or $S(x)$. We use $D(x)$. Then

$$p_E = D(x_E) = D(2) = (2 - 5)^2 = (-3)^2 = \$9 \text{ per unit.}$$

Thus the equilibrium point is (2, $9).

b) The consumer's surplus is

$$\int_0^{x_E} D(x)\,dx - x_E p_E,$$

or

$$\int_0^2 (x-5)^2\,dx - 2\cdot 9 = \left[\frac{(x-5)^3}{3}\right]_0^2 - 18 = \frac{(2-5)^3}{3} - \frac{(0-5)^3}{3} - 18$$

$$= \frac{(-3)^3}{3} - \frac{(-5)^3}{3} - 18 = -\frac{27}{3} + \frac{125}{3} - \frac{54}{3}$$

$$= \frac{44}{3} = \$14.67$$

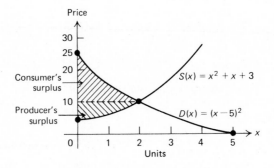

c) The producer's surplus is

$$x_E p_E - \int_0^{x_E} S(x)\,dx,$$

or

$$2\cdot 9 - \int_0^2 (x^2 + x + 3)\,dx = 2\cdot 9 - [\tfrac{1}{3}x^3 + \tfrac{1}{2}x^2 + 3x]_0^2$$

$$= 18 - [(\tfrac{1}{3}\cdot 2^3 + \tfrac{1}{2}\cdot 2^2 + 3\cdot 2) - (\tfrac{1}{3}\cdot 0^3 + \tfrac{1}{2}\cdot 0^2 + 3\cdot 0)]$$

$$= 18 - (\tfrac{8}{3} + 2 + 6) = \tfrac{22}{3} = \$7.33$$

EXERCISE SET 11.1

In each exercise find (a) the equilibrium point, (b) the consumer's surplus, and (c) the producer's surplus.

1. $D(x) = -\tfrac{5}{8}x + 10$, $S(x) = \tfrac{1}{2}x + 2$

2. $D(x) = -2x + 8$, $S(x) = x + 2$

3. $D(x) = (x - 4)^2$, $S(x) = x^2 + 2x + 6$

4. $D(x) = (x - 3)^2$, $S(x) = x^2 + 2x + 1$

5. $D(x) = (x - 6)^2$, $S(x) = x^2$

6. $D(x) = (x - 8)^2$, $S(x) = x^2$

---

7. ▦ $D(x) = e^{-x+4.5}$, $S(x) = e^{x-5.5}$

8. ▦ $D(x) = \sqrt{56 - x}$, $S(x) = x$

11.2 APPLICATIONS OF THE MODEL $\int_0^T P_0 e^{kt}\, dt$

In this chapter we will make frequent use of the integration formula

$$\int be^{ax}\, dx = \frac{b}{a} e^{ax} + C. \tag{1}$$

You should memorize it. It can be easily verified by substitution or by differentiating the right-hand side and obtaining the integrand.

Recall the basic model of exponential growth:

$$P'(t) = k \cdot P(t) \qquad \left(\text{or,} \quad \frac{dP}{dt} = kP \right).$$

The solution of the equation is

$$P(t) = P_0 e^{kt}. \tag{2}$$

Thus $P(t)$ is an antiderivative of $kP_0 e^{kt}$, as we can see by using Eq. (1):

$$\int kP_0 e^{kt}\, dt = \frac{kP_0}{k} e^{kt} = P_0 e^{kt}.$$

One application of Eq. (2) is to compute the balance of a savings account after t years, from an initial investment of P_0 at continuous interest rate k.

Example 1 Find the balance in a savings account after 3 years from an initial investment of $1000 at interest rate 8% compounded continuously.

Solution Using Eq. (2) we have

$$P(3) = 1000e^{0.08(3)} = 1000e^{0.24} = 1000(1.271249) \quad (\text{▦ or Table 4})$$

$$\approx \$1271.25.$$

The Integral $\int_0^T P_0 e^{kt}\, dt$

Consider the integral of $P_0 e^{kt}$ over the interval $[0, T]$.

$$\int_0^T P_0 e^{kt}\, dt = \left[\frac{P_0}{k} \cdot e^{kt} \right]_0^T = \frac{P_0}{k} (e^{kT} - e^{k \cdot 0}) = \frac{P_0}{k} (e^{kT} - 1)$$

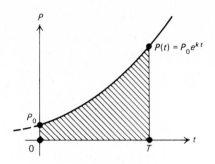

Thus

$$\int_0^T P_0 e^{kt} \, dt = \frac{P_0}{k} (e^{kT} - 1).$$ (3)

In the remainder of this section we consider two applications of this definite integral.

Business—The Amount of an Annuity

An *annuity* is a series of equal payments made at equal time intervals. Rent payments are an example of an annuity. Deposits in a savings account can also be an annuity. In Chapter 6 we studied annuities where interest is compounded n times per year. Here we study them where interest is compounded continuously. For example, suppose a person makes a deposit of $1000 annually in a savings account on which interest is compounded continuously at 8%. The amount in the account at the end of a certain time is called the *amount of the annuity*. Let us find the amount of the given annuity for a period of 5 years. The following time diagram can help. Note that deposits are made at the end of each year.

	$1000	$1000	$1000	$1000	$1000
0	1	2	3	4	5

Each $1000 grows over a different time period. The total amount in the account after 5 years, the amount of the annuity, is given by

$$1000e^{0.08(4)} + 1000e^{0.08(3)} + 1000e^{0.08(2)} + 1000e^{0.08(1)} + 1000e^{0.08(0)}$$

$$= \$1377.13 + \$1271.25 + \$1173.51 + \$1083.29 + \$1000$$

$$= \$5905.18.$$

The amount of an annuity is also the sum

$$\sum_{t=0}^{4} 1000e^{0.08t} \, \Delta t,$$

where $\Delta t = 1$, $t_0 = 0$, and $t_4 = 4$. This sum can be *approximated* by integrating the function $1000e^{0.08t}$ over the interval $[0, 5]$:

$$\int_0^5 1000e^{0.08t}\, dt = \left[\frac{1000}{0.08} e^{0.08t} \right]_0^5 = 12{,}500(e^{0.08 \cdot 5} - e^{0.08 \cdot 0})$$

$$= 12{,}500(e^{0.4} - 1)$$

$$= 12{,}500(1.491825 - 1)$$

$$\approx \$6147.81.$$

This is very close to the actual amount of the annuity. Note here that the integral provides an approximation to a sum, in contrast to a sum approximating an integral.

In general,

> The *amount of an annuity A_T*, where P_0 dollars per year is being invested at interest rate k compounded continuously over T years, is *approximated* by the expression
>
> $$A_T = \frac{P_0}{k} (e^{kT} - 1).$$

Example 2   Find the amount of an annuity where $1000 per year is being invested at 8% compounded continuously for 15 years.

Solution $$A_{15} = \frac{1000}{0.08} (e^{0.08(15)} - 1) = 12{,}500(e^{1.2} - 1)$$

$$= 12{,}500(3.320116 - 1)$$

$$\approx \$29{,}001.46$$

Example 3   What annual payment P_0 should be made so the amount of an annuity over 20 years, at interest rate 8% compounded continuously, will be $10,000?

Solution   We find P_0 such that

$$10{,}000 = \frac{P_0}{0.08} (e^{0.08(20)} - 1).$$

Solving, we get

$$800 = P_0(e^{1.6} - 1)$$

$$800 = P_0(4.953032 - 1)$$

$$800 = P_0(3.953032)$$

$$\$202.38 \approx P_0.$$

Continuous Money Flow

We have said that the integral

$$\int_0^5 1000e^{0.08t} \, dt$$

approximates the amount of an annuity that is the sum

$$\sum_{t=0}^4 1000e^{0.08t} \, \Delta t.$$

If that is the case, just what does

$$\int_0^T P_0 e^{kt} \, dt$$

represent? Consider a continuous stream or flow of money into an investment at the rate of P_0 dollars per year. If an infinitesimal (very small) amount of time dt passes, we have accumulated

$$(P_0 \cdot dt) \text{ dollars.}$$

But during this small time interval, the money has been growing at interest rate k compounded continuously, so that $(P_0 \cdot dt)$ dollars has grown to

$$(P_0 \cdot dt) \cdot e^{kt} \text{ dollars.}$$

We find the accumulation of all these amounts in time T by the integral

$$\int_0^T P_0 e^{kt} \, dt,$$

which we might call the *amount of a continuous annuity.*

If the rate of flow of money into the investment is given by some variable function of time $R(t)$, then the *amount of the continuous money flow* is given by

$$\int_0^T R(t)e^{kt} \, dt.$$

Depletion of Natural Resources

Another application of the integral of exponential growth concerns

$$P(t) = P_0 e^{kt}$$

as a model of the demand for natural resources. Suppose P_0 represents the amount of a natural resource (such as coal, oil, and so forth) used at time $t = 0$, and suppose the growth rate for the use of this resource is k. Then, assuming exponential growth (which is the case for the use of many resources), the amount to be used at time t is $P(t)$, given by

$$P(t) = P_0 e^{kt}.$$

The total amount used during an interval $[0, T]$ is given by

$$\int_0^T P_0 e^{kt}\, dt = \frac{P_0}{k}(e^{kT} - 1). \qquad (4)$$

Example 4 *The demand for copper.* In 1973 ($t = 0$) the world use of copper was

7,700,000 tons,

and the demand for it was growing exponentially at the rate of 8% per year. If the growth continues at this rate, how many tons of copper will the world use from 1973 to 1983?

Solution Using Eq. (4), we have

$$\int_0^T 7{,}700{,}000 e^{0.08t}\, dt = \frac{7{,}700{,}000}{0.08}(e^{0.08 \cdot 10} - 1)$$

$$= 96{,}250{,}000(e^{0.8} - 1)$$

$$= 96{,}250{,}000(2.225541 - 1) \quad (\blacksquare \text{ or Table 4})$$

$$= 96{,}250{,}000(1.225541)$$

$$\approx 117{,}958{,}300.$$

Thus from 1973 to 1983 the world will use 117,958,300 tons of copper.

Example 5 *The depletion of copper.* The world reserves of copper are

370,000,000 tons.

Assuming the growth rate in Example 4 continues and that no new reserves are discovered, when will the world reserves of copper be exhausted?

Solution Using Eq. (4) we want to find T such that

$$370{,}000{,}000 = \frac{7{,}700{,}000}{0.08}(e^{0.08T} - 1).$$

We solve for T as follows:

$$370{,}000{,}000 = 96{,}250{,}000(e^{0.08T} - 1)$$

$$\frac{370{,}000{,}000}{96{,}250{,}000} = e^{0.08T} - 1$$

$$3.8 = e^{0.08T} - 1 \quad \text{(Rounding to the nearest tenth)}$$

$$4.8 = e^{0.08T}$$

$$\ln 4.8 = \ln e^{0.08T} \quad \text{(Taking the natural logarithm on both sides)}$$

$$\ln 4.8 = 0.08T \quad \text{(Recall: } \ln e^k = k.)$$

$$\frac{\ln 4.8}{0.08} = T$$

$$\frac{1.568616}{0.08} = T \quad \text{(▦ or Table 3)}$$

$$20 \approx T. \quad \text{(Rounding to the nearest one)}$$

Thus 20 years from 1973 (or by 1993), the world reserves of copper will be exhausted.

EXERCISE SET 11.2

1. Find the amount in a savings account after 3 years from an initial investment of $100 at 9% compounded continuously.

2. Find the amount in a savings account after 4 years from an initial investment of $100 at 10% compounded continuously.

3. Find the amount of an annuity where $100 per year is being invested at 9% compounded continuously for 20 years.

4. Find the amount of an annuity where $100 per year is being invested at 10% compounded continuously for 20 years.

5. Find the amount of an annuity where $1000 per year is being invested at 8.5% compounded continuously for 40 years.

6. Find the amount of an annuity where $1000 per year is being invested at 7.5% compounded continuously for 40 years.

7. What annual payment should be made so that the amount of an annuity over 20 years, at interest rate 8.5% compounded continuously, will be $50,000?

8. What annual payment should be made so that the amount of an annuity over 20 years, at interest rate 7.5% compounded continuously, will be $50,000?

9. What annual payment should be made so that the amount of an annuity over 30 years, at interest rate 9% compounded continuously, will be $40,000?

10. What annual payment should be made so that the amount of an annuity over 30 years, at interest rate 10% compounded continuously, will be $40,000?

11. *The demand for aluminum ore.* In 1973 ($t = 0$) the world use of aluminum ore was

69,500,000 tons,

and the demand for it was growing exponentially at the rate of 12% per year. If the demand continues to grow at this rate, how many tons of aluminum ore will the world use from 1973 to 1983?

12. *The demand for natural gas.* In 1973 ($t = 0$) the world use of natural gas was

44,600 billion cubic feet,

and the demand for it was growing exponentially at the rate of 4% per year. If the demand continues to grow at this rate, how many cubic feet of natural gas will the world use from 1973 to 1983?

13. *The depletion of aluminum ore.* The world reserves of aluminum ore are

$$15,500,000,000 \text{ tons.}$$

Assuming the growth rate of Exercise 11 continues and that no new reserves are discovered, when will the world reserves of aluminum ore be exhausted?

14. *The depletion of natural gas.* The world reserves of natural gas are

$$1,897,000 \text{ billion cubic feet.}$$

Assuming the growth rate of Exercise 12 continues and that no new reserves are discovered, when will the world reserves of natural gas be exhausted?

15. *The demand for oil.* In 1973 $(t = 0)$ the world use of oil was

$$20,300 \text{ million barrels,}$$

and the demand for it was growing exponentially at the rate of

$$10\% \text{ per year.}$$

If the demand continues at this rate, how many barrels of oil will the world use from 1973 to 1983?

16. *The depletion of oil.* The world reserves of oil are

$$625,200 \text{ million barrels.}$$

In 1973 $(t = 0)$ the world use of oil was

$$20,300 \text{ million barrels,}$$

and the growth rate for the use of oil was 10%. Assuming this growth rate continues and that no new reserves are discovered, when will the world reserves of oil be exhausted?

∎ ————————————————————

17. Suppose that P dollars are deposited at the end of *each day* in a savings account paying 8% interest compounded continuously. Estimate, as an integral, the amount of money that will be in the account at the end of 1 year. Evaluate the integral, in general, and when $P = \$1000$. Use 365 days for 1 year.

18. Repeat Exercise 17, but estimating the amount of money that will be in the account at the end of 2 years.

Stock dividends. The total dividends on stock $D(t)$ a company pays in time T is given by

$$D(T) = \int_0^T d_0 e^{pkt}\, dt$$

where $d_0 =$ instantaneous dividend payment at time 0; $p =$ percentage of the company's earnings that it retains; and $k =$ rate of return that a company can earn on its assets if it were to invest them.

19. Find the total dividends when $d_0 = \$10$; $p = 80\%$; $k = 15\%$; and $T = 50$ years.

20. Find a general formula for $D(T)$.

Amount of a continuous money flow. The amount of a continuous money flow, as described in this section, is given by

$$\int_0^T R(t) e^{kt}\, dt.$$

Find the amount of a continuous money flow when

21. $R(t) = \$1000$, $k = 8\%$, $T = 30$ years.

22. ▤ $R(t) = t^2$, $k = 7\%$, $T = 40$ years.

11.3 APPLICATIONS OF THE MODEL $\int_0^T Pe^{-kt}\,dt$

Suppose a person owns a rental property that earns $100 a month. The current interest rate (amount being charged for loans or being paid for investments) is 9% compounded continuously. The *capital value* of the property over some time period is the sum of all the present values of the rental payments. Therefore for 6 months the capital value is found as follows:

Payment	Present value		
1	$\$100e^{-0.09(1/12)}$	$=$	$\$99.25$
2	$100e^{-0.09(2/12)}$	$=$	98.51
3	$100e^{-0.09(3/12)}$	$=$	97.78
4	$100e^{-0.09(4/12)}$	$=$	97.04
5	$100e^{-0.09(5/12)}$	$=$	96.32
6	$100e^{-0.09(6/12)}$	$=$	95.60
	Capital value $=$ $\$584.50$		

Thus the capital value is the sum

$$\sum_{i=1}^{6} 100e^{-0.09t_i},$$

where $t_i = i/12$ and i runs from 1 to 6. Now $100 = 100 \cdot (12/12) = (100 \cdot 12) \cdot (1/12) = 1200 \cdot (1/12)$. So the preceding sum can be expressed as

$$\sum_{i=1}^{6} 1200e^{-0.09t_i}\,\Delta t,$$

where

$$\Delta t = \frac{1}{12}.$$

This sum can then be approximated by integrating the function $1200e^{-0.09t}$ over the half-year interval $[0, 0.5]$. Now

$$\int_0^{0.5} 1200e^{-0.09t}\,dt = \left[\frac{1200}{-0.09}e^{-0.09t}\right]_0^{0.5}$$

$$= -13{,}333.33(e^{-0.09(0.5)} - e^{-0.09 \cdot 0})$$

$$= -13{,}333.33(0.955997 - 1)$$

$$\approx \$586.71.$$

This is very close to the actual capital value.

Suppose a rental property has an annual rent of R dollars paid in n equal payments per year. The capital value of the property over some time T is given by

$$\sum_{i=1}^{nT} \frac{R}{n} e^{-kt_i},$$

where the payment R/n is made at time t_i and the current interest rate is k, compounded continuously. This can be expressed as

$$\sum_{i=1}^{nT} Re^{-kt_i} \Delta t,$$

where

$$\Delta t = \frac{1}{n}.$$

This sum can be *approximated* by the definite integral

$$\int_0^T Re^{-kt}\,dt.$$

Evaluating this integral, we get

$$\int_0^T Re^{-kt}\,dt = \frac{R}{-k}(e^{-kT} - e^{-k \cdot 0})$$

$$= \frac{R}{k}(1 - e^{-kT}).$$

The *capital value* V_T of a property over T years is *approximated* by

$$V_T = \frac{R}{k}(1 - e^{-kT}),$$

where R is the annual rent or income, and k is the current interest rate.

Example 1   Find the capital value of a rental property over a 5-year period where the annual rent is \$2400 and the current interest rate is 8%.

Solution
$$V_5 = \frac{2400}{0.08}(1 - e^{-0.08 \cdot 5})$$

$$= 30{,}000(1 - e^{-0.4})$$

$$= 30{,}000(1 - 0.670320)$$

$$\approx \$9890.40$$

EXERCISE SET 11.3

1. Find the capital value of a rental property over a 10-year period where the annual rent is $2700 and the current interest rate is 9%.

2. Find the capital value of a rental property over a 10-year period where the annual rent is $2700 and the current interest rate is 10%.

3. An MBA accepts the position of president of a company at age 35. Assuming retirement at age 65 and an annual salary of $45,000, what is the president's capital value? The current interest rate is 8%.

4. A college dropout takes a job as a truck driver at age 25. Assuming retirement at age 65 and an annual salary of $14,000, what is the truck driver's capital value? The current interest rate is 7%.

■ ────────────────────────────────

Accumulated present values of a continuous cash flow. Suppose we know that money will flow into an investment at the rate of $R(t)$ dollars per year, from now until some time T in the future. If an infinitesimal amount of time dt passes, $R(t)\ dt$ dollars will have accumulated. The present value of that amount is $[R(t)\ dt]e^{-kt}$, where k is the current interest rate. The accumulation of all the present values is given by

$$V(T) = \int_0^T R(t)e^{-kt}\ dt$$

and is called the *accumulated present value.*

5. ▦ Find $V(T)$ when $R(t) = t$, $k = 8\%$, and $T = 20$ years.

6. ▦ Find $V(t)$ when $R(t) = e^t$, $k = 7\%$, and $T = 10$ years.

Accumulated present values of dividends. Suppose $d(t)$ represents the instantaneous dividend payment of a stock at time t. Then $d(t)e^{-mt}$ is the present value of that payment, where m is the current interest rate. The accumulation of all present values from time 0 to time T is given by

$$D_p(T) = \int_0^T d(t)e^{-mt}\ dt.$$

7. Find $D_p(T)$ when $d(t) = \$10$, $m = 8\%$, and $T = 10$ years.

8. Find $D_p(T)$ when $d(t) = t$, $m = 7\%$, and $T = 20$ years.

9. *Capital value.* U–Rent–It, Inc. expects to get P dollars a day in rent on a certain tool. Find, as an integral, the capital value of the tool over a 1-year period. Evaluate the integral, in general, and when $P = \$14$. Assume the current interest rate is 12%.

10. *Capital value.* Repeat Exercise 9, assuming a 2-year period.

11.4 IMPROPER INTEGRALS

Let us try to find the area of the region under the graph of $y = 1/x^2$ on the interval $[1, \infty)$.

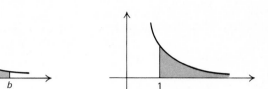

Note that this region is of infinite extent. We have not yet considered how to find the area of such a region. Let us find the area under the curve on the interval from 1 to b, and then see what happens as b gets very large. The area on $[1, b]$ is

$$\int_1^b \frac{dx}{x^2} = \left[-\frac{1}{x} \right]_1^b$$

$$= \left(-\frac{1}{b} \right) - \left(-\frac{1}{1} \right)$$

$$= -\frac{1}{b} + 1 = 1 - \frac{1}{b}.$$

Then

$$\lim_{b \to \infty} [\text{area from 1 to } b] = \lim_{b \to \infty} \left(1 - \frac{1}{b} \right).$$

Let us investigate this limit.

Note that as $b \to \infty$, $1/b \to 0$, so $[1 - (1/b)] \to 1$. Thus

$$\lim_{b \to \infty} [\text{area from 1 to } b] = \lim_{b \to \infty} \left(1 - \frac{1}{b} \right) = 1.$$

We *define* the area from 1 to ∞ to be this limit. Here we have an example of an infinitely long region with a finite area.

Such areas may not always be finite. Let us try to find the area of the region under the graph of $y = 1/x$ on the interval $[1, \infty)$.

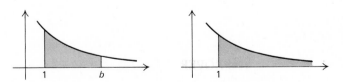

By definition, the area A from 1 to ∞ is the limit as $b \to \infty$ of the area from

1 to b, so

$$A = \lim_{b \to \infty} \int_1^b \frac{dx}{x} = \lim_{b \to \infty} [\ln x]_1^b = \lim_{b \to \infty} (\ln b - \ln 1) = \lim_{b \to \infty} \ln b.$$

On p. 433 of Chapter 9 we can see that since $\ln b$ increases indefinitely as b increases, this limit does not exist.

Thus we have an infinitely long region with an infinite area. Note that the graphs of $y = 1/x^2$ and $y = 1/x$ have similar shapes, but the region under one of them has a finite area and the other does not.

An integral such as

$$\int_a^\infty f(x)\, dx,$$

with an upper limit of ∞, is called an *improper integral*. Its value is defined to be the following limit.

$$\int_a^\infty f(x)\, dx = \lim_{b \to \infty} \int_a^b f(x)\, dx.$$

If the limit exists, then we say that the improper integral *converges*. If the limit does not exist, we say that the improper integral *diverges*. Thus

$$\int_1^\infty \frac{dx}{x^2} = 1 \text{ converges}; \quad \text{and} \quad \int_1^\infty \frac{dx}{x} = \infty \text{ diverges}.$$

Example 1

$$\int_0^\infty 2e^{-2x}\, dx = \lim_{b \to \infty} \int_0^b 2e^{-2x}\, dx = \lim_{b \to \infty} [2(-\tfrac{1}{2})e^{-2x}]_0^b$$

$$= \lim_{b \to \infty} [-e^{-2x}]_0^b$$

$$= \lim_{b \to \infty} [-e^{-2b} - (-e^{-2 \cdot 0})]$$

$$= \lim_{b \to \infty} (-e^{-2b} + 1)$$

$$= \lim_{b \to \infty} \left(1 - \frac{1}{e^{2b}}\right)$$

Now as $b \to \infty$, $e^{2b} \to \infty$ (from Chapter 9), so

$$\frac{1}{e^{2b}} \to 0 \quad \text{and} \quad \left(1 - \frac{1}{e^{2b}}\right) \to 1.$$

Thus

$$\int_0^\infty 2e^{-2x}\, dx = 1. \qquad \text{(The integral is convergent.)}$$

The following are definitions of two types of improper integrals.

$$\int_{-\infty}^{b} f(x)\,dx = \lim_{a \to -\infty} \int_{a}^{b} f(x)\,dx$$

$$\int_{-\infty}^{\infty} f(x)\,dx = \int_{-\infty}^{c} f(x)\,dx + \int_{c}^{\infty} f(x)\,dx$$

For $\int_{-\infty}^{\infty} f(x)\,dx$ to converge, both integrals on the right above must converge.

Application

In Section 11.3 we learned that the capital value of a rental property over T years is approximated by

$$A_T = \int_{0}^{T} Re^{-kt}\,dt = \frac{R}{k}(1 - e^{-kT}),$$

where R is the annual rent and k is the current interest rate. Suppose that the rent is paid perpetually. Then under this assumption the capital value over this infinite time period would be

$$\lim_{T \to \infty} A_T = \int_{0}^{\infty} Re^{-kt}\,dt$$

$$= \lim_{T \to \infty} \int_{0}^{T} Re^{-kt}\,dt$$

$$= \lim_{T \to \infty} \frac{R}{k}(1 - e^{-kT})$$

$$= \lim_{T \to \infty} \frac{R}{k}\left(1 - \frac{1}{e^{kT}}\right)$$

$$= \frac{R}{k}.$$

The capital value of a property for which the annual rent, or income, is being paid, or received, perpetually is

$$\frac{R}{k},$$

where k is the current interest rate compounded continuously.

Example 2 An annual rent of \$2000 is being paid for a property for which there is a permanent lease. The current interest rate is 8%. Find the capital value.

Solution The capital value is $\dfrac{2000}{0.08}$ or \$25,000.

EXERCISE SET 11.4

Determine whether each of the following improper integrals is convergent or divergent, and calculate its value if it is convergent.

1. $\int_{3}^{\infty} \frac{dx}{x^2}$

2. $\int_{4}^{\infty} \frac{dx}{x^2}$

3. $\int_{3}^{\infty} \frac{dx}{x}$

4. $\int_{4}^{\infty} \frac{dx}{x}$

5. $\int_{0}^{\infty} 3e^{-3x}\, dx$

6. $\int_{0}^{\infty} 4e^{-4x}\, dx$

7. $\int_{1}^{\infty} \frac{dx}{x^3}$

8. $\int_{1}^{\infty} \frac{dx}{x^4}$

9. $\int_{0}^{\infty} \frac{dx}{1+x}$

10. $\int_{0}^{\infty} \frac{4\, dx}{1+x}$

11. $\int_{1}^{\infty} 5x^{-2}\, dx$

12. $\int_{1}^{\infty} 7x^{-2}\, dx$

13. $\int_{0}^{\infty} e^{x}\, dx$

14. $\int_{0}^{\infty} e^{2x}\, dx$

15. $\int_{3}^{\infty} x^2\, dx$

16. $\int_{5}^{\infty} x^4\, dx$

17. $\int_{0}^{\infty} xe^{x}\, dx$

18. $\int_{0}^{\infty} \ln x\, dx$

19. $\int_{0}^{\infty} me^{-mx}\, dx, \quad m > 0$

20. $\int_{0}^{\infty} Qe^{-kt}\, dt, \quad k > 0$

21. *Capital value.* An annual rent of $3600 is being paid for a property for which there is a permanent lease. The current interest rate is 10%. Find the capital value.

22. *Capital value.* An annual rent of $4500 is being paid for a property for which there is a permanent lease. The current interest rate is 9%. Find the capital value.

■ ────────────────────────────────

Determine whether each of the following improper integrals is convergent or divergent, and calculate its value if it is convergent.

23. $\int_{0}^{\infty} \frac{dx}{x^{2/3}}$

24. $\int_{1}^{\infty} \frac{dx}{\sqrt{x}}$

25. $\int_{0}^{\infty} \frac{dx}{(x+1)^{3/2}}$

26. $\int_{-\infty}^{0} e^{2x}\, dx$

27. $\int_{0}^{\infty} xe^{-x^2}\, dx$

28. $\int_{-\infty}^{\infty} xe^{-x^2}\, dx$

Accumulated present values of stock dividends paid perpetually. The accumulation of all present values of dividends that are assumed to be paid perpetually is given by

$$V = \int_{0}^{\infty} d(t)e^{-mt}\, dt,$$

where $d(t)$ is the instantaneous dividend payment and m is the current interest rate.

29. Find V when $d(t) = e^{-t}$ and $m = 7\%$.

30. Find V when $d(t) = 1000 and $m = 8\%$.

11.5 DIFFERENTIAL EQUATIONS

A *differential equation* is an equation which involves derivatives or differentials. In Chapter 9 we studied one very important differential equation

$$\frac{dP}{dt} = kP,$$

where P, or $P(t)$, is the population at time t. This equation is a model of uninhibited population growth. Its solution is

$$P = P_0 e^{kt},$$

where the constant P_0 is the size of the initial population; that is, at $t = 0$. As this one equation illustrated, differential equations are rich in application.

Solving Certain Differential Equations

In this chapter we will frequently use the notation y' for a derivative— mainly because it is simple. Thus, if $y = f(x)$, then

$$y' = \frac{dy}{dx} = f'(x).$$

We have already found solutions of certain differential equations when we found antiderivatives or indefinite integrals. The differential equation

$$\frac{dy}{dx} = g(x)$$

or

$$y' = g(x),$$

has the solution

$$y = \int g(x)\, dx + C.$$

Example 1 Solve $y' = 2x$.

Solution
$$y = \int 2x\, dx + C$$

$$= x^2 + C$$

Look again at the solution to Example 1. Note the constant of integration. This solution is called a *general solution* because taking all values of C gives *all* the solutions.

Taking specific values of C gives particular solutions. For example, the following are particular solutions of $y' = 2x$:

$$y = x^2 + 3,$$

$$y = x^2,$$

$$y = x^2 - 3.$$

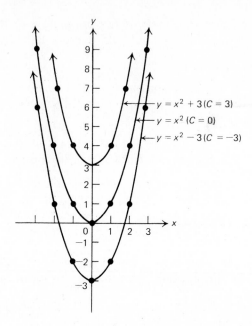

$y = x^2 + 3 (C = 3)$

$y = x^2 (C = 0)$

$y = x^2 - 3 (C = -3)$

This graph shows the curves of a few particular solutions. The general solution can be envisioned as the set of all particular solutions, a *family* of curves.

Knowing the value of a function at a particular point may allow us to select a particular solution from the general solution.

Example 2   Solve $f'(x) = e^x + 5x - x^{1/2}$, given that $f(0) = 8$.

Solution   a) First find the general solution.

$$f(x) = \int f'(x)\, dx + C = e^x + \tfrac{5}{2}x^2 - \tfrac{2}{3}x^{3/2} + C$$

b) Since $f(0) = 8$, we substitute to find C.

$$8 = e^0 + \tfrac{5}{2} \cdot 0^2 - \tfrac{2}{3} \cdot 0^{3/2} + C$$

$$8 = 1 + C$$

$$7 = C$$

Thus the solution is $f(x) = e^x + \tfrac{5}{2}x^2 - \tfrac{2}{3}x^{3/2} + 7$.

Verifying Solutions

To verify that a function is a solution of a differential equation we find the necessary derivatives and substitute.

Example 3   Show that $y = 4e^x + 5e^{3x}$ is a solution of

$$y'' - 4y' + 3y = 0.$$

Solution   a) We first find y' and y''.

$$y' = 4e^x + 15e^{3x}$$

$$y'' = 4e^x + 45e^{3x}$$

b) Then we substitute as follows in the differential equation.

$y'' - 4y' + 3y = 0$	
$(4e^x + 45e^{3x}) - 4(4e^x + 15e^{3x}) + 3(4e^x + 5e^{3x})$	0
$4e^x + 45e^{3x} - 16e^x - 60e^{3x} + 12e^x + 15e^{3x}$	
	0

Separation of Variables

Consider the differential equation

$$\frac{dy}{dx} = 2xy. \tag{1}$$

We treat dy/dx as a quotient, as we did in Chapter 5. We multiply equation (1) by dx and then by $1/y$ and get

$$\frac{dy}{y} = 2x \, dx. \tag{2}$$

We say that we have *separated the variables*, meaning that all the expressions involving y are on one side, and those involving x are on the other. We then integrate both sides of Eq. (2).

$$\int \frac{dy}{y} = \int 2x \, dx + C$$

We use only one constant because any two antiderivatives differ by a constant.

$$\ln y = x^2 + C \qquad (y > 0)$$

$$y = e^{x^2 + C} = e^{x^2} \cdot e^C$$

Thus the solution of differential Eq. (1) is

$$y = C_1 e^{x^2}, \quad \text{where } C_1 = e^C.$$

In the exercises you will be asked to show, using separation of variables, that the solution of

$$\frac{dP}{dt} = kP$$

is

$$P = P_0 e^{kt}.$$

Example 4   Solve

$$3y^2 \frac{dy}{dx} + x = 0.$$

Solution   We first separate the variables as follows,

$$3y^2 \frac{dy}{dx} = -x, \qquad 3y^2 \, dy = -x \, dx.$$

We integrate both sides.

$$\int 3y^2 \, dy = \int -x \, dx + C$$

$$y^3 = -\frac{x^2}{2} + C = C - \frac{x^2}{2}$$

$$y = \sqrt[3]{C - \frac{x^2}{2}} \qquad \text{(Taking the cube root)}$$

Example 5   Solve

$$\frac{dy}{dx} = \frac{x}{y}.$$

Solution   We first separate variables as follows.

$$y \frac{dy}{dx} = x$$

$$y \, dy = x \, dx$$

We integrate both sides:

$$\int y \, dy = \int x \, dx + C$$

$$\frac{y^2}{2} = \frac{x^2}{2} + C$$

$$y^2 = x^2 + 2C$$

$$y^2 = x^2 + C_1,$$

where $C_1 = 2C$. We make this substitution to simplify the equation. We then obtain the solutions

$$y = \sqrt{x^2 + C_1} \qquad \text{and} \qquad y = -\sqrt{x^2 + C_1}.$$

Example 6 Solve $y' = x - xy$.

Solution Before we separate variables we replace y' by $\dfrac{dy}{dx}$:

$$\frac{dy}{dx} = x - xy.$$

Now we separate variables.

$$dy = (x - xy)\, dx$$

$$dy = x(1 - y)\, dx$$

$$\frac{dy}{1 - y} = x\, dx$$

Now we integrate both sides.

$$\int \frac{dy}{1 - y} = \int x\, dx + C$$

$$-\ln(1 - y) = \frac{x^2}{2} + C \qquad (1 - y > 0)$$

$$\ln(1 - y) = -\frac{x^2}{2} - C$$

$$1 - y = e^{-x^2/2 - C}$$

$$-y = e^{-x^2/2 - C} - 1$$

$$y = -e^{-x^2/2 - C} + 1 = -e^{-x^2/2} \cdot e^{-C} + 1$$

Thus

$$y = 1 + C_1 e^{-x^2/2} \qquad (\text{where } C_1 = -e^{-C})$$

Application–Elasticity

Example 7 The elasticity of demand for a product is 1 for all $x > 0$. That is, $E(x) = 1$ for all $x > 0$. Find the demand function $p = D(x)$.

Solution Since $E(x) = 1$ for all $x > 0$,

$$1 = E(x) = -\frac{p}{x} \cdot \frac{1}{dp/dx} \qquad \text{(See Section 9.6)} \qquad (1)$$

Then

$$\frac{dp}{dx} = -\frac{p}{x}.$$

Separating variables we get

$$\frac{dp}{p} = -\frac{dx}{x}.$$

Now we integrate both sides

$$\int \frac{dp}{p} = -\int \frac{dx}{x} + C$$

$$\ln p = -\ln x + C \qquad \begin{array}{l} (p > 0 \text{ since } E(x) = 1 \text{ and } x > 0. \\ \text{See Eq. (1))} \end{array}$$

We can express $C = \ln C_1$, since any real number C is the natural logarithm of some number C_1. See Chapter 9. Then

$$\ln p = \ln C_1 - \ln x = \ln \frac{C_1}{x},$$

so

$$p = \frac{C_1}{x}.$$

This characterizes those demand functions for which the elasticity is always 1.

EXERCISE SET 11.5

Find the general solution and three particular solutions.

1. $y' = 4x^3$

2. $y' = 6x^5$

3. $y' = e^{2x} + x$

4. $y' = e^{3x} - x$

5. $y' = \frac{3}{x} - x^2 + x^5$

6. $y' = \frac{5}{x} + x^2 - x^4$

Find the particular solution determined by the given condition.

7. $y' = x^2 + 2x - 3; \quad y = 4$ when $x = 0$

8. $y' = 3x^2 - x + 5; \quad y = 6$ when $x = 0$

9. $f'(x) = x^{2/3} - x; f(1) = -6$

10. $f'(x) = x^{2/5} + x; f(1) = -7$

11. Show that $y = x \ln x + 3x - 2$ is a solution of

$$y'' - \frac{1}{x} = 0.$$

13. Show that $y = e^x + 3xe^x$ is a solution of

$$y'' - 2y' + y = 0.$$

15. Marginal cost for a certain product is $C'(x) = 2.6 - 0.02x$. Find the total cost function $C(x)$ and the average cost $A(x)$, assuming fixed costs are $120; that is, $C(0) = \$120$.

17. A firm's marginal profit P as a function of total cost C is given by

$$\frac{dP}{dC} = \frac{-200}{(C + 3)^{3/2}}.$$

   a) Find the profit function $P(C)$, if $P = \$10$ when $C = \$61$.

   b) At what cost will the firm break even $(P = 0)$?

12. Show that $y = x \ln x - 5x + 7$ is a solution of

$$y'' - \frac{1}{x} = 0.$$

14. Show that $y = -2e^x + xe^x$ is a solution of

$$y'' - 2y' + y = 0.$$

16. Marginal revenue for a certain product is $R'(x) = 300 - 2x$. Find the total revenue function $R(x)$ assuming $R(0) = 0$.

18. Solve

$$f'(x) = \frac{1}{x} - 2x + \sqrt{x}$$

given that $f(1) = 4$.

Solve.

19. $\dfrac{dy}{dx} = 4x^3y$

20. $\dfrac{dy}{dx} = 5x^4y$

21. $3y^2 \dfrac{dy}{dx} = 5x$

22. $3y^2 \dfrac{dy}{dx} = 7x$

23. $\dfrac{dy}{dx} = \dfrac{2x}{y}$

24. $\dfrac{dy}{dx} = \dfrac{x}{2y}$

25. $\dfrac{dy}{dx} = \dfrac{3}{y}$

26. $\dfrac{dy}{dx} = \dfrac{4}{y}$

27. $y' = 3x + xy$

28. $y' = 2x - xy$

29. $y' = 5y^{-2}$

30. $y' = 7y^{-2}$

31. $\dfrac{dy}{dx} = 3y$

32. $\dfrac{dy}{dx} = 4y$

33. $\dfrac{dP}{dt} = 2P$

34. $\dfrac{dP}{dt} = 4P$

35. a) Use separation of variables to solve the differential equation model of uninhibited growth.

$$\frac{dP}{dt} = kP$$

   b) Rewrite the solution in terms of the condition $P_0 = P(0)$.

36. *Domar's Capital Expansion Model* is

$$\frac{dI}{dt} = hkI$$

where I = investment, h = investment productivity (constant), k = marginal productivity to consume (constant), and t = time.

   a) Use separation of variables to solve the differential equation.

   b) Rewrite the solution in terms of the condition $I_0 = I(0)$.

37. *Utility.* The reaction R in pleasure units, by a consumer receiving S units of a product can be modeled by the differential equation

$$\frac{dR}{dS} = \frac{k}{S+1},$$

where k is a positive constant.

a) Use separation of variables to solve the differential equation.

b) Rewrite the solution in terms of the initial condition $R(0) = 0$.

c) Explain why the condition $R(0) = 0$ is reasonable.

38. The *growth rate of a certain stock* is modeled by

$$\frac{dV}{dt} = k(L - V), \qquad V = \$20 \text{ when } t = 0;$$

where

V = value of stock, per share, after time t (in months),

$L = \$24.81$, the *limiting value* of the stock,

k = constant.

Find the solution of the differential equation in terms of L and k.

Find the demand function $p = D(x)$ given the elasticity conditions.

39. $E(x) = \dfrac{200 - x}{x}$; $p = 190$ when $x = 10$.

40. $E(x) = \dfrac{4}{x}$; $p = e^{-1}$ when $x = 4$

41. $E(x) = 2$ for all $x > 0$

42. $E(x) = k$ for some constant k and all $x > 0$.

CHAPTER 11 REVIEW

1. Find the amount of an annuity where $1200 per year is being invested at 6% compounded continuously for 15 years.

2. What annual payment should be made so that the amount of an annuity over 25 years, at interest rate 6% compounded continuously, will be $20,000?

3. *The demand for iron ore.* In 1973 ($t = 0$) the world use of iron ore was 810,000 thousand tons, and the demand for it was growing exponentially at the rate of 6% per year. If the demand continues to grow at this rate, how many tons of iron ore will the world use from 1973 to 1983?

4. *The depletion of iron ore.* The world reserves of iron ore are 108,304,000 thousand tons. Assuming that the growth rate of 6% per year continues and that no new reserves are discovered, when will the world reserves of iron ore be exhausted?

5. Find the capital value of a rental property over a 20-year period where the annual rent is $3800 and the current interest rate is 11%.

6. Find the capital value of the rental property in Exercise 5 if the rent is to be paid perpetually.

Determine if each of the following improper integrals is convergent or divergent, and calculate its value if convergent.

7. $\displaystyle\int_1^\infty \frac{dx}{x^5}$

8. $\displaystyle\int_0^\infty \frac{3}{1 + x}\, dx$

Given the demand and supply functions $D(x) = (x - 7)^2$, $S(x) = x^2 + x + 4$, find:

9. the equilibrium point.   **10.** the consumer's surplus.   **11.** the producer's surplus.

12. Solve the differential equation $y' = x^2 + 3x - 5$, given the condition $y = 7$ when $x = 0$.

Solve these differential equations.

13. $\dfrac{dy}{dx} = 8x^7 y$ **14.** $\dfrac{dy}{dx} = \dfrac{9}{y}$ **15.** $\dfrac{dy}{dt} = 6y$

16. $y' = 5x^2 - x^2 y$ **17.** $\dfrac{dv}{dt} = 2v^{-3}$ **18.** $y' = 4y + xy$

19. Find the demand function given the elasticity condition,

$$E(x) = 3 \text{ for all } x > 0.$$

20. The growth rate of stock for Glamour Industries is modeled by

$$\frac{dV}{dt} = k(L - V),$$

where V = value of the stock, per share, after
         time t, in seconds.
     L = \$36, the *limiting value* of
         the stock
     k = constant

a) Write the solution $V(t)$ in terms of L and k.

b) If $V(6) = \$18$, determine k to the nearest hundredth.

c) Rewrite $V(t)$ in terms of k.

d) Use the equation in (c) to find $V(12)$, the value of the stock after 12 months.

e) In how many months will the value be \$30?

SETS AND COUNTING TECHNIQUES

12.1 SETS*

Sets form the foundation of our study of probability.

What do the following have in common?

A *flock* of birds   A *pod* of whales

A *herd* of animals   A *crowd* of people

A *school* of fish   A *host* of angels

In each case we are dealing with a collection of objects of a certain type. Rather than use a different word for each type of collection, it is convenient to denote them all by the one word "*set.*"

---

* If the appendix on Logic is to be studied, it would be most advantageous to do it just prior to this chapter.

A *set* is a collection of well-defined objects called *elements*.

One can talk about the set of all "employees" in a company since an "employee" is *well-defined*. On the other hand one cannot talk about the set of all "good" employees unless one can provide an objective way to distinguish "good" employees.

We now develop the *notation* necessary to deal with sets.

The set of vowels can be written

$$V = \{a, e, i, o, u\}$$

where the *capital letter* V denotes the *set* as do the braces enclosing the *elements*. The elements are separated by commas, read "and." Elements of sets are usually denoted by lower-case letters. This way of describing a set is known as the "roster" method.

That "a is a vowel" or "a is an element of V" can be written

$$a \in V.$$

Similarly, that "b is not a vowel," or "b is not an element of V" can be written

$$b \notin V.$$

Two sets A and B are *equal,* written A = B, if and only if each element of either set is also an element of the other set. For example

a) $\{a, e, i, o, u, a\} = \{a, e, i, o, u\}$ and

b) $\{u, o, i, e, a\} = \{a, e, i, o, u\}$,

where in (a) the *repetition* of an element does not change the set and in (b) the *order* in which we write the elements does not change the set.

Consider the set of all students in a given class. The class is not changed if some student's name is listed twice. Furthermore, the class is not changed whether the student's names are listed alphabetically, or by social security number, or any other way.

Example 1 Given $A = \{1, 2, 3, 4, 5, 6\}$, $B = \{2, 3, 4, 5, 6\}$, and $C = \{2, 3, 4, 5, 6, 1\}$.

a) Is $1 \in A$? $1 \in B$?

b) Is $A = B$? $A = C$?

Solution a) Yes, $1 \in A$; no, $1 \notin B$.

b) No, $A \neq B$, since $1 \in A$ but $1 \notin B$;
yes, $A = C$, since order of elements is immaterial.

Other Set Notation

The set containing all the integers that are greater than 1 can be written

$$\{2, 3, 4, \ldots\}.$$

The dots are read "and so forth," and indicate that the pattern of the listed elements continues. This set can also be written using words as

"The set of all integers greater than 1."

or

"The set of all x such that x is an integer and $x > 1$."

or

$$\{x | x \text{ is an integer, } x > 1\}$$

In the latter notation, the first set brace "{" is read "The set of all," and the vertical line "|" is read "such that." The entire notation is read "The set of all x such that x is an integer and x is greater than 1." This is called "set builder" notation.

Example 2   Write $C = \{1, 4, 9, \ldots\}$ using set builder notation.

Solution $$C = \{x | x \text{ is an integer and } x \text{ is a perfect square}\}$$

Answers may vary. We could have written this set

$$C = \{x | x = n^2, \quad n \text{ is an integer}, \quad n > 0\};$$

or, if we let I represent the set of all integers,

$$I = \{\ldots, -3, -2, -1, 0, 1, 2, 3, \ldots\}$$

then we could use more abbreviated notation for C.

$$C = \{x | x = n^2, \quad n \in I, \quad n > 0\}$$

Example 3   Write $E = \{x | x = 4n - 1, \quad n \in I, \quad n \geq 0\}$ using the roster method.

Solution $$E = \{-1, 3, 7, 11, 15, \ldots\}$$

The Empty Set

The set without elements is known as the *empty set*, or *null set*, and is denoted by the symbol ∅, or { }. The following is an example of the empty set:

The set of all odd numbers whose squares are even.

The notation {0} is not appropriate for the empty set, since this set has one element in it, namely the number 0. Also, {∅} is not notation for the empty set. If ∅ represents an empty set (empty paper sack), then {∅} would represent an empty sack in a sack.

Subsets

Set A is said to be a *subset* of B if and only if every element of A is an element of B. For example, if $B = \{a, b, c\}$, the subsets of B are

$$\{a\}, \quad \{b\}, \quad \{c\}, \quad \{a, b\}, \quad \{a, c\}, \quad \{b, c\}, \quad \{a, b, c\}, \quad \emptyset$$

That "A is a subset of B" is symbolized $A \subset B$, and is often read "A is *contained* in B." Thus

$$\{a\} \subset \{a, b, c\}$$

$$\{b, c\} \subset \{a, b, c\}$$

$$\{a, b, c\} \subset \{a, b, c\}$$

$$\emptyset \subset \{a, b, c\}$$

Note that, for any set A, $A \subset A$; that is, any set is a subset of itself.* Also, for any set A, $\emptyset \subset A$; that is, the empty set is a subset of every set. For example, let A be the set of all fish in a lake and C be the subset of A consisting of all fish caught by a fisherman. Thus, $C \subset A$. Now of course it is possible that the fisherman catches *nothing*. In that case, we can have $C = \emptyset$, so that $\emptyset \subset A$.

Example 4   Let $V = \{a, e, i, o, u\}$, $A = \{a, e\}$, and $B = \{a, t, s\}$.

a) Is $A \subset V$?

b) Is $B \subset V$?

Solution   a) Yes, $A \subset V$, since each element of A is also in V.

b) No, $B \not\subset V$, since the elements t and s of B are not in V.

---

*A proper subset is a subset such that $A \subset B$, but $A \neq B$. Thus $\{a, b\}$ is a proper subset of $\{a, b, c\}$, but $\{a, b, c\}$ is not a proper subset of $\{a, b, c\}$. When A is a proper subset of B, there is at least one element in B which is not in A. Some texts use $\subseteq$ to indicate a subset, and reserve the symbol $\subset$ only for a proper subset, but this distinction is not useful to us in this text.

Cardinality of a Set

The *cardinality* of a set A is the *number of distinct elements* it contains and is written $\mathcal{N}(A)$. Thus, if

$$V = \{a, e, i, o, u\},$$

then

$$\mathcal{N}(V) = 5$$

Also, $\mathcal{N}(\emptyset) = 0$; the cardinality of the empty set is 0.

Universal Sets and Complements

Any mathematical situation has a frame of reference called a *universal set.* For example, in elementary algebra the universal set is usually the set of real numbers. In plane geometry the universal set is the set of points in the plane. In probability the universal set might be, for example, the set of all possible outcomes from drawing a card from a well-shuffled deck. Usually it is clear what the universal set is, through it may have to be inferred from the context of a problem or application. We might think of the empty set as being on the low end of the frame of reference and the universal set as being on the high end. The universal set is usually denoted $\mathcal{U}$, and in any given application it must be true that for any set A, $A \subset \mathcal{U}$.

Example 5 A survey is to be made to determine the opinion of readers of the *National Observer* on a particular issue. What is the universal set?

Solution *Before* the survey is taken, the universal set consists of all readers of *National Observer.*

After the survey is taken, the universal set consists of those readers questioned in the survey. The set of readers surveyed is a subset of all the readers. The readers surveyed with opinions, pro, con, or otherwise, are all subsets of the readers surveyed.

The absolute complement, or simply, the *complement* of a set A, written A^c, is what is left in the universal set after the elements of A are removed.

Example 6 Given $A = \{a, e, i\}$ and $\mathcal{U} = \{a, e, i, o, u\}$, find A^c.

Solution $A^c = \{o, u\}.$

Note. $\mathcal{U}^c = \emptyset$ and $\emptyset^c = \mathcal{U}.$

EXERCISE SET 12.1

For Exercises 1 through 16, let $\mathcal{U} = \{x | x \in I, 0 \leq x \leq 12\}$, where I is the set of all integers, and

$A = \{x | x \in \mathcal{U}, \ 0 \leq x \leq 10\}$,

$B = \{x | x \in \mathcal{U}, \ 0 < x < 10\}$,

$C = \left\{ x | x \in \mathcal{U}, \ \dfrac{x}{2} \in A \right\}$,

$D = \{x | x \in \mathcal{U}, \ x \in A, x \notin C\}$,

$E = \left\{ x | x \in \mathcal{U}, \ \dfrac{x}{3} \in \mathcal{U} \right\}$,

$F = \{x | x \in \mathcal{U}, \ x \in E, \ x \leq 10\}$.

1. Write the sets A through C using the roster method.

2. Write the sets D through F using the roster method.

3. Determine the complements of sets A through C.

4. Determine the complements of sets D through F.

State whether each of the following is true or false.

5. $5 \in A$

6. $7 \in C$

7. $A \subset B$

8. $F \subset B$

9. $\emptyset \subset D$

10. $\emptyset \subset A$

11. $F = \{0, 6, 3, 9\}$

12. $E = \{3, 3, 6, 9, 12\}$

13. $E = \{6, 3, 12, 9\}$

14. $F = \{0, 3, 6, 3, 9\}$

15. $E \subset F$

16. $D^c \subset \mathcal{U}$

For Exercises 17 through 26, let

$$\mathcal{U} = \{a, e, i, o, u, m, n, r, t, c\}$$

and

$A = \{a, e, i, o, u\}$,

$B = \{c, m, n, r, t\}$,

$C = \{a, c, e\}$,

$D = \{m, i, n, t\}$,

$E = \{e, i\}$,

$F = \{r, t\}$.

17. Determine the complements of sets A through C.

18. Determine the complements of sets D through F.

State whether each of the following is true or false.

19. $E = \{c, e, i, o, u\}$

20. $D = \{t, i, m, e\}$

21. $\{c, e, i, o, u\} \subset \mathcal{U}$

22. $\{a, e, z\} \subset \mathcal{U}$

23. $C = \{c, a, s, e\}$

24. $F = \{t, r\}$

25. $\mathcal{N}(C) = 4$

26. $\mathcal{N}(E) = 2$

27. a) Find $\mathcal{N}(\emptyset)$.

b) List the subsets of $\emptyset$.

c) How many subsets are there?

28. a) Find $\mathcal{N}(\{a\})$.

b) List the subsets of $\{a\}$.

c) How many subsets are there?

29. a) Find $\mathcal{N}(\{a, b\})$.

b) List the subsets of $\{a, b\}$.

c) How many subsets are there?

30. a) Find $\mathcal{N}(\{a, b, c\})$.

b) List the subsets of $\{a, b, c\}$.

c) How many subsets are there?

31. On the basis of Exercises 35 through 38, complete the following table.

Cardinality of a set	0	1	2	3	4	n
Number of subsets	1					

32. Complete, based on Exercise 31.

A set with n elements has _____ subsets.

12.2   UNION AND INTERSECTION OF SETS—VENN DIAGRAMS

Union of Sets

Consider two sets A and B.

Let A be the set of all students in a Finite Mathematics class and B be the set of all students in an Economics class. The *union* of A and B, written $A \cup B$, is the set of all students taking Finite Mathematics *or* Economics *or both*.

Formally, the *union* of A and B is the set of all elements contained in *either A or B or both* and can be written

$$A \cup B = \{x \mid x \in A \qquad or \qquad x \in B\}.$$

$A \cup B$ is read "A union B."

Note.   Throughout this book, "or" will be used in the *inclusive* sense of "either or both." If the *exclusive* "or" meaning—"either but not both"—is intended, it will be specifically stated.

The union of sets can be represented geometrically by means of *Venn diagrams*. If two sets A and B are each represented by the interior of some closed curve, then the union of A and B is represented by the shaded area in the following diagram.

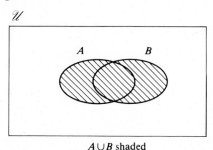

$A \cup B$ shaded

Intersection of Sets

Consider again the two sets A and B, where A is the set of all students in a Finite Mathematics class, and B is the set of all students in an Economics class.

The *intersection* of A and B, written A ∩ B, represents the set of all students taking *both* Finite Mathematics *and* Economics.

Formally, the *intersection* of A and B is the set of all elements contained in *both A and B* and can be written

$$A \cap B = \{x | x \in A \quad and \quad x \in B\}.$$

A ∩ B is read "A intersect B."

On a Venn diagram, the intersection of A and B is represented by the shaded area in the following diagram.

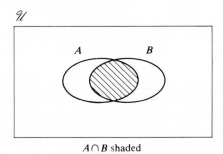

A∩B shaded

If two sets A and B have *no* elements in common, that is,

$$A \cap B = \emptyset$$

or

$$\mathcal{N}(A \cap B) = 0,$$

then A and B are said to be *disjoint*, and can be represented by the following Venn diagram;

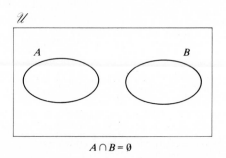

A∩B=∅

Note that A ∩ A^c = ∅ and A ∪ A^c = 𝒰. (See diagram.)

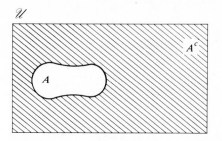

Example 1 Given $A = \{1, 2, 3, 5, 7\}$, $B = \{0, 2, 3, 6, 9\}$, what are $A \cup B$ and $A \cap B$? Represent these sets by means of a Venn diagram.

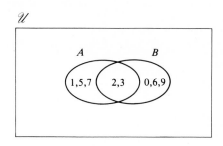

Solution

$A \cup B = \{0, 1, 2, 3, 5, 6, 7, 9\}$

$A \cap B = \{2, 3\}$

Partitions

Consider the set of all students in a Finite Mathematics class. Divide the class into groups, or subsets, such that:

i) each student in the class is in some group, and

ii) no student in the class is in more than one group.

These groups constitute a *partition* of the class.

Let A be the set of all molecules in a cookie. Break the cookie. Whatever way the cookie crumbles, the pieces are a *partition* of the cookie.

Formally, a *partition* of a set A is a division of A into subsets X_i $(i = 1, 2, \ldots, n)$ such that each element of A is contained in one and only one subset. Thus, the subsets X_i are disjoint (any two different sets have no elements in common):

$$X_i \cap X_j = \emptyset \quad \text{for all } i \neq j,$$

and their union is A:

$$X_1 \cup X_2 \cup \cdots \cup X_n = A.$$

If these conditions are satisfied, then

$$\{X_1, X_2, \ldots, X_n\}$$

expresses the statement that the X_i's are a partition of A. For example, let

$$A = \text{Set of natural numbers} = \{1, 2, 3, 4, \ldots\},$$

$$X_1 = \text{Set of odd natural numbers} = \{1, 3, 5, \ldots\}$$

$$X_2 = \text{Set of even natural numbers} = \{2, 4, 6, \ldots\}.$$

Then $\{X_1, X_2\}$ is a partition of A.

This partition can be represented by the following Venn diagram:

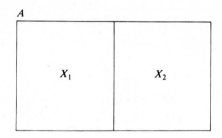

A set may be partitioned more than one way.

Example 2   Write several partitions of the set $A = \{a, e, r, s\}$ and draw the Venn diagram for each partition.

Solution

Partitions	Venn diagrams
i) $\{\{a\}, \{e\}, \{r\}, \{s\}\}$	i) $\boxed{a \mid e \mid r \mid s}$
ii) $\{\{a, e, r, s\}\}$	ii) $\boxed{a, e, r, s}$
iii) $\{\{a, e\}, \{r, s\}\}$	iii) $\boxed{a, e \mid r, s}$
iv) $\{\{a\}, \{e, r, s\}\}$	iv) $\boxed{a \mid e, r, s}$

Note that $\{\{a, e\}, \{e, r, s\}\}$ is not a partition, because the sets are not disjoint. That is, $\{a, e\} \cap \{e, r, s\} = \{e\} \neq \emptyset$. Also, $\{\{a\}, \{r, s\}\}$ is not a partition because the union of the sets is not set A.

Relative and Absolute Complements—Set Difference

The *relative complement* of a set B with respect to set A, or, simply, the *difference* of A and B, written $A - B$, is the set of all elements contained in A but *not* in B. Formally,

$$A - B = \{x | x \in A, \quad x \notin B\}.$$

The *absolute complement* of a set A, or, simply, the *complement* of A, written A^c, can now be expressed as the relative complement of set A with respect to the universal set. Formally,

$$A^c = \mathcal{U} - A,$$

or

$$A^c = \{x | x \in \mathcal{U}, \quad x \notin A\}.$$

Using Venn diagrams, we can represent $A - B$, $A \cap B$, and $B - A$ by the following diagram:

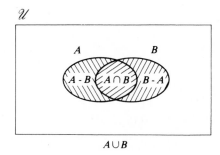

Thus, the union of two sets $A \cup B$ can always be partitioned

$$\{A - B, A \cap B, B - A\}.$$

Similarly, A and A^c can be represented by the Venn diagram:

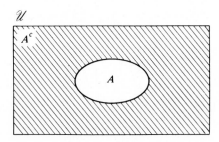

so that the universal set $\mathcal{U}$ can always be partitioned

$$\{A, A^c\}.$$

Example 3 Given $A = \{1, 2, 3, 5, 7\}$, $B = \{0, 2, 3, 6, 9\}$, and $\mathcal{U} = \{0, 1, 2, 3, 4, 5, 6, 7, 8, 9\}$ what is $A - B$, $B - A$, A^c, and $(A - B)^c$? Represent $(A - B)^c$ by a Venn diagram.

Solution
$$A - B = \{1, 5, 7\},$$
$$B - A = \{0, 6, 9\},$$
$$A^c = \{0, 4, 6, 8, 9\},$$
$$(A - B)^c = \{0, 2, 3, 4, 6, 8, 9\}$$

and is the shaded area in the figure.

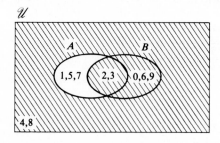

Solving Problems

Since Venn diagrams embody set concepts, they can be used to *solve* problems involving sets. It is apparent from the following Venn diagram:

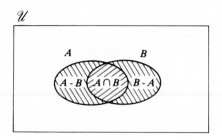

that

$$A = (A - B) \cup (A \cap B) \quad \text{and} \quad B = (B - A) \cup (A \cap B).$$

The cardinality of sets A and B is simply

$$\mathcal{N}(A) = \mathcal{N}(A - B) + \mathcal{N}(A \cap B) \tag{1}$$

and

$$\mathcal{N}(B) = \mathcal{N}(B - A) + \mathcal{N}(A \cap B). \tag{2}$$

Note that the union operation in the set relation has been replaced by the addition operation in the cardinality relation. This can be done when the components are disjoint.

Similarly, from the Venn diagram, we can write:

$$A \cup B = (A - B) \cup (A \cap B) \cup (B - A)$$

and

$$\mathcal{N}(A \cup B) = \mathcal{N}(A - B) + \mathcal{N}(A \cap B) + \mathcal{N}(B - A). \tag{3}$$

Solving for $\mathcal{N}(A - B)$ and $\mathcal{N}(B - A)$ in Eqs. (1) and (2) and substituting in Eq. (3), we obtain

$$\mathcal{N}(A \cup B) = \mathcal{N}(A) + \mathcal{N}(B) - \mathcal{N}(A \cap B).$$

This is a very important set property.

Thus, if $A = \{a, b, c, f\}$ and $B = \{a, b, c, d, e\}$, then

$$A \cup B = \{a, b, c, d, e, f\} \quad \text{and} \quad A \cap B = \{a, b, c\}.$$

Furthermore, $\mathcal{N}(A) = 4$, $\mathcal{N}(B) = 5$, $\mathcal{N}(A \cup B) = 6$, and $\mathcal{N}(A \cap B) = 3$. Substituting these quantities in

$$\mathcal{N}(A \cup B) = \mathcal{N}(A) + \mathcal{N}(B) - \mathcal{N}(A \cap B),$$

we have

$$6 = 4 + 5 - 3,$$

or

$$6 = 6,$$

which satisfies the above relation. Note that

$$\mathcal{N}(A \cup B) = \mathcal{N}(A) + \mathcal{N}(B) \quad \text{only if } A \text{ and } B \text{ are disjoint.}$$

An example more typical of the type usually solved using Venn diagrams is the following.

Example 4   Out of a sample of people surveyed,

43% smoked,

67% drank,

24% smoked and drank.

What percent neither smoked nor drank?

Solution   Let

$$\mathcal{U} = \text{The set of all people surveyed,}$$

$$S = \text{The set of all smokers (surveyed),}$$

and

$$D = \text{The set of all drinkers (surveyed).}$$

Then

$$\mathcal{N}(\mathcal{U}) = 100 \quad \text{(dropping the \% sign, for simplicity),}$$

$$\mathcal{N}(S) = 43,$$

$$\mathcal{N}(D) = 67,$$

and the number of people who smoked *and* drank is given by

$$\mathcal{N}(S \cap D) = 24.$$

We think of the set symbol "∩" as corresponding to the word "and."

We want to find the number of people in the survey who neither smoked nor drank. We can express this with sets as

$$\mathcal{U} - S - D.$$

That is, we take out the smokers and drinkers and what is left are those people who neither smoke nor drink. Thus we want

$$\mathcal{N}(\mathcal{U} - S - D).$$

The appropriate Venn diagram is as follows:

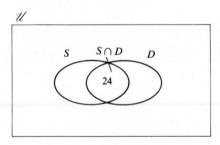

where $\mathcal{N}(S \cap D) = 24$ has been written in the area representing $S \cap D$. Now, as before, it is apparent from the Venn diagram that

$$\mathcal{N}(S - D) = \mathcal{N}(S) - \mathcal{N}(S \cap D)$$

$$= 43 - 24 = 19.$$

Similarly,

$$N(D - S) = N(D) - N(S \cap D)$$

$$= 67 - 24$$

$$= 43.$$

Writing these two numbers, 19 and 43, into the areas representing $S - D$ and $D - S$ on the Venn diagram, we obtain:

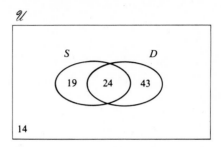

Thus, the number of people who *either* smoked or drank is

$$N(S \cup D) = N(S - D) + N(S \cap D) + N(D - S)$$

$$= 19 + 24 + 43$$

$$= 86, \quad \text{or} \quad 86\%,$$

and the number of people who *neither* smoked nor drank is

$$N(\mathcal{U} - S - D) = N(\mathcal{U}) - N(S \cup D)$$

$$= 100 - 86$$

$$= 14, \quad \text{or} \quad 14\%.$$

Here we used the Venn diagram both as a place to record the numbers representing the cardinality of various sets and also to indicate which differences to take to obtain new set cardinalities. The advantage of this approach may not be as apparent with the preceding example with two sets as it is in the next example with three sets.

Example 5   There are 220 students in a certain freshman class. Of these,

115 are taking Economics,

60 are taking Spanish,

95 are taking Mathematics,

20 are taking Economics and Spanish,

30 are taking Economics and Mathematics,

25 are taking Spanish and Mathematics,

15 are taking all three subjects.

How many students are taking only one of these three subjects?

Solution Formally, this problem may be posed in this manner:

Let $\mathcal{U}$ = set of all students in the freshman class,

E = set of all students taking Economics,

S = set of all students taking Spanish, and

M = set of all students taking Mathematics.

Then

$$\mathcal{N}(\mathcal{U}) = 220,$$

$$\mathcal{N}(E) = 115,$$

$$\mathcal{N}(S) = 60,$$

$$\mathcal{N}(M) = 95,$$

$$\mathcal{N}(E \cap S) = 20 \quad \text{(those taking Economics } and \text{ Spanish),}$$

$$\mathcal{N}(E \cap M) = 30,$$

$$\mathcal{N}(S \cap M) = 25,$$

$$\mathcal{N}(E \cap S \cap M) = 15 \quad \text{(those taking Economics } and \text{ Spanish} \\ and \text{ Mathematics).}$$

The question is then to determine

$$\mathcal{N}(E - S - M) + \mathcal{N}(S - E - M) + \mathcal{N}(M - S - E),$$

where $\mathcal{N}(E - S - M)$ is the number of students taking Economics, but not Spanish or Mathematics, and so on.

We start with information at the bottom of the data list:

$$\mathcal{N}(E \cap S \cap M) = 15 \quad \text{or} \quad (15)_1,$$

where the number 15 is being written in the Venn diagram as $(15)_1$. Here the subscript is being used to indicate the order in which the numbers are entered on the Venn diagram, to avoid redrawing it each step. Thus, $(15)_1$ is the first entry in this diagram.

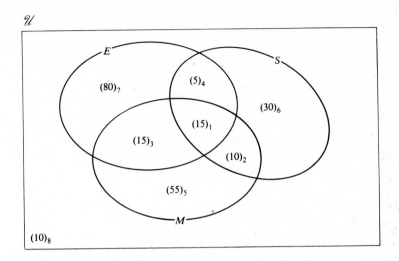

Working up the data list, we have:

$$N[(S \cap M) - E] = N(S \cap M) - N(S \cap M \cap E)$$

> (those taking Spanish and Math, but not Economics)

$$= 25 - 15 = 10, \quad \text{or} \quad (10)_2;$$

$$N[(E \cap M) - S] = 30 - 15 = 15, \quad \text{or} \quad (15)_3;$$

$$N[(E \cap S) - M] = 20 - 15 = 5, \quad \text{or} \quad (5)_4.$$

Continuing, we have

$$N(M - S - E) = 95 - 15 - 15 - 10 \quad \text{(Why?)}$$

$$= 55, \quad \text{or} \quad (55)_5.$$

That is, 40 of the elements of M are in S or E, leaving 55 elements for $M - S - E$. Similarly,

$$N(S - E - M) = 60 - 5 - 15 - 10$$

$$= 30, \quad \text{or} \quad (30)_6;$$

and

$$N(E - S - M) = 115 - 5 - 15 - 15$$

$$= 80, \quad \text{or} \quad (80)_7.$$

Thus, the number of students taking only one subject is

$$N(E - S - M) + N(S - E - M) + N(M - S - E) = 80 + 30 + 55 = 165.$$

Furthermore, the number of students taking exactly two subjects is

$$N[(E \cap S) - M] + N[(E \cap M) - S] + N[(S \cap M) - E] = 5 + 15 + 10$$

$$= 30;$$

and the number of students taking all three subjects is

$$N(E \cap S \cap M) = 15.$$

The number of students taking *at least* one subject is the sum of

$$165 + 30 + 15, \quad \text{or} \quad 210.$$

Since $N(\mathcal{U}) = 220$, there are $220 - 210 = 10$ who are not taking any of the courses mentioned. At this point the Venn diagram is completely filled out and the answer to many questions can be obtained by a simple sum.

EXERCISE SET 12.2

For Exercises 1 through 5 (as in Exercises 1 through 16, Exercise Set 12.1)

$$\mathcal{U} = \{x | x \in I, \ 0 \leq x \leq 12\},$$

where I is the set of all integers, and

$$A = \{x | x \in \mathcal{U}, \ \ 0 \leq x \leq 10\},$$

$$B = \{x | x \in \mathcal{U}, \ \ 0 < x < 10\},$$

$$C = \left\{ x | x \in \mathcal{U}, \ \ \frac{x}{2} \in A \right\},$$

$$D = \{x | x \in \mathcal{U}, \ \ x \in A, \ \ x \notin C\}$$

$$E = \left\{ x | x \in \mathcal{U}, \ \ \frac{x}{3} \in \mathcal{U} \right\},$$

$$F = \{x | x \in \mathcal{U}, \ \ x \in E, \ \ x \leq 10\}.$$

1. Determine the set indicated by each of the following:

   a) $A \cup B$

   b) $A \cap B$

   c) $A - B$

   d) $B - A$

   e) $A - A^c$

   f) $A - (D \cup E)$

   g) $(C \cup E)^c$

   h) $(A - B) \cup (C - F)$

   i) $(A - B) \cap (C - F)$

   j) $[(D - F)^c]^c$

2. Do any of the sets B, C, D, E, F partition set A? If yes, which ones?

3. Draw a Venn diagram illustrating the relationship among sets A, B, C, D, E, F.

For Exercises 4 through 6,

$\mathcal{U} = \{a, e, i, o, u, c, m, n, r, t\}$

$A = \{a, e, i, o, u\}$ $\qquad$ $C = \{a, c, e\}$ $\qquad\qquad$ $E = \{e, i\}$

$B = \{c, m, n, r, t\}$ $\qquad$ $D = \{m, i, n, t\}$ $\qquad\qquad$ $F = \{r, t\}$

4. Answer the following:

a) Is $\{C, D, F\}$ a partition of $\mathcal{U}$?

b) Are B and C disjoint?

5. Determine the set indicated by each of the following:

a) $E \cup F$ $\qquad$ e) $(A \cup B)^c$

b) $E \cap F$ $\qquad$ f) $(D - E) \cup F$

c) $B - D$ $\qquad$ g) $(D^c - E^c) \cap F$

d) $D - B$ $\qquad$ h) $(A \cap C) - (C \cap D)$

6. Draw a Venn diagram illustrating the relationship among sets A, B, C, D, E, F.

7. Of 68 people surveyed, 33 smoked, 57 drank, and 27 did both. How many did neither?

8. *Marketing analysis.* Of 87 people surveyed, 49 read *Time*, 21 read *Nation*, and 5 read both. How many read only one magazine? How many read neither magazine?

9. Of 73 men surveyed, 54 wore belts, 20 wore suspenders, and 3 wore neither. How many wore both?

10. Of 123 students, 79 could ride a bike, 53 could drive a car, and 15 could do both. How many could do neither?

11. In a recent poll of 230 people, 50 thought only the Republicans could solve our problems, 70 thought only the Democrats could, and 25 thought neither could. How many thought one could do as well as the other (that is, both)?

12. Blood can be typed as A (having Type A antigen), B (having Type B antigen), AB (having both), and O (having neither). Of 140 patients in a hospital, there were 53 with Type A blood, 47 with Type B, and 24 with Type AB. How many had Type O? *Note.* Having Type A blood implies *only* Type A antigens.

13. Of the students in a certain university,

55% took Finite Mathematics,

65% took English Composition,

35% took Spanish,

30% took Mathematics and English,

24% took Mathematics and Spanish,

18% took English and Spanish,

12% took all three.

How many students took only one of these three subjects? Only two of these three subjects? None of these courses?

14. *Marketing analysis.* Of recent car buyers,

65% bought automatic transmissions,

20% bought air conditioning,

70% bought posh seats,

50% bought automatic transmissions and posh seats,

10% bought automatic transmissions and air conditioning,

10% bought posh seats and air conditioning,

5% bought all three.

How many bought posh seats alone? No option? Posh seats but not air conditioning?

12.3   TREES—SAMPLE SPACES

In addition to Venn diagrams, *trees* are another geometric aid used in set theory. Trees can be used to illustrate the concept of *sample spaces.*

Trees and Sample Space

A set can be represented geometrically by a *tree.* A tree with all its *branches* represents the *sample space.*

Example 1   A coin is flipped. Assuming that it does not land on its edge, represent the possible outcomes of the flip by a tree. What is the sample space?

Solution   The coin must land either heads (H) or tails (T), and these two outcomes are *mutually exclusive.* Mutually exclusive events can be represented by *branches* of a tree. Thus, the tree for the outcomes of a single coin flip has two branches:

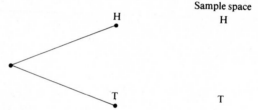

These two outcomes are the only ones possible and form the *sample space,* which can be written

$$S = \{H, T\}.$$

> **The set S of *all* possible outcomes of some action or experiment is called the *sample space* in probability and corresponds to the universal set.**

An action or experiment consisting of multiple events can also be represented by a tree.

Example 2   A coin is flipped *twice.* Draw the tree representing possible outcomes. What is the sample space?

Solution   The trees for the first and second coin flips *individually* are

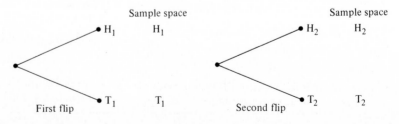

Their *individual* sample spaces are

$$S_1 = \{H_1, T_1\} \quad \text{and} \quad S_2 = \{H_2, T_2\}.$$

Combining the outcomes of *both* coin flips into a single tree, we have

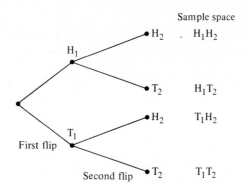

The sample space for the *combined* outcomes of both coin flips is

$$S = \{H_1H_2, H_1T_2, T_1H_2, T_1T_2\}.$$

> Each *fork* of a tree consists of a *vertex* (dot), which represents some act, and a *set of arcs* (lines leading out of the vertex), which represent all possible *mutually exclusive* outcomes of that act. A *branch* of a tree is a sequence of *connected arcs.* Following along a branch of a tree from beginning to end relates a succession of *individual* outcomes that together constitute a single *overall* outcome. A tree with all its branches represents the *sample space.*

The sample space for the outcome of flipping two coins labeled 1 and 2 (for example, a penny and a dime) is the same as in Example 2 with *time* ordering replaced by the *number* (or label) ordering. In either case, the outcomes of each *part* of the total action are *considered distinguishable.*

On the other hand, we might be interested only in *how many* heads and *how many* tails occur without regard to how each individual coin lands. In this case, the sample space is

$$S = \{HH, HT, TT\}.$$

Here the outcomes HT and TH are *considered indistinguishable* and the labels "1" and "2" dropped.

The concept of *distinguishability of outcomes* is of prime concern in probability although frequently it is stated *implicitly*, rather than explicitly, in many problems.

Cartesian Products

Cartesian products arise naturally in many situations.

Given two sets A and B, the *Cartesian product* of these sets, written $A \times B$, is the set of all ordered pairs (a, b) where $a \in A$ and $b \in B$. Formally

$$A \times B = \{(a, b) \mid a \in A, \quad b \in B\}.$$

Note that, as the name implies, the *order* of the elements in an *ordered pair* is important (although the order in which we list the ordered pairs is not important).

Example 3   Given $S_1 = \{H_1, T_1\}$ and $S_2 = \{H_2, T_2\}$ from Example 2. Find the Cartesian product of S_1 and S_2 and interpret the result.

Solution   The Cartesian product of S_1 and S_2 is

$$S = S_1 \times S_2 = \{(H_1, H_2), (H_1, T_2), (T_1, H_2), (T_1, T_2)\}.$$

This Cartesian product represents the sample space for the combined outcomes of the two coin flips.

Not all sample spaces can be represented by Cartesian products.

The foregoing is the *formally* correct way of writing Cartesian products. However, when there is no possibility for confusion, the notation may be simplified, in this case, to

$$S = \{H_1H_2, H_1T_2, T_1H_2, T_1T_2\}$$

or even

$$S = \{HH, HT, TH, TT\}.$$

Here H_1H_2 has been written HH where the first H refers to H_1 and the second H refers to H_2, and so forth.

Example 4   If $A = \{a, b\}$ and $B = \{1, 2, 3\}$, find $A \times B$, $\mathcal{N}(A)$, $\mathcal{N}(B)$, and $\mathcal{N}(A \times B)$.

Solution   The Cartesian product of A and B is

$$A \times B = \{(a, 1), (a, 2), (a, 3), (b, 1), (b, 2), (b, 3)\}, \qquad \text{or}$$

$$= \{a1, a2, a3, b1, b2, b3\}.$$

The cardinality of each set and of the Cartesian product is

$$\mathcal{N}(A) = 2 \quad \text{and} \quad \mathcal{N}(B) = 3$$

$$\mathcal{N}(A \times B) = 2 \cdot 3 = 6 \qquad \text{(as can be verified by counting)}.$$

In general, the cardinality of a Cartesian product of two sets can be found, simply by counting, to be

$$\mathcal{N}(A \times B) = \mathcal{N}(A) \cdot \mathcal{N}(B),$$

with the obvious extension to more than two sets.

EXERCISE SET 12.3

For Exercises 1 through 8 (as in Exercises 1 through 16, Exercise Set 12.1)

$$\mathcal{U} = \{x | x \in I, 0 \leqslant x \leqslant 12\},$$

where I is the set of all integers, and

$A = \{x | x \in \mathcal{U}, \quad 0 \leqslant x \leqslant 10\},$

$B = \{x | x \in \mathcal{U}, \quad 0 < x < 10\},$

$C = \left\{ x | x \in \mathcal{U}, \quad \dfrac{x}{2} \in A \right\},$

$D = \{x | x \in \mathcal{U}, \quad x \in A, \quad x \notin C\},$

$E = \left\{ x | x \in \mathcal{U}, \quad \dfrac{x}{3} \in \mathcal{U} \right\},$

$F = \{x | x \in \mathcal{U}, \quad x \in E, \quad x \leqslant 10\}.$

Answer the following.

1. $E \times F = ?$

2. $F \times E = ?$

3. Is $(E \times F) \subset (A \times B)$?

4. Is $(F \times E) \subset (A \times B)$?

5. $C \times E = ?$

6. $C \times F = ?$

7. $\mathcal{N}(C \times E) = ?$

8. $\mathcal{N}(C \times F) = ?$

9. A business manager has a problem that he discusses with each of his three assistants. Each comes up with a possible solution that looks equally acceptable. Hence, he resorts to his standard decision-maker: He tacks each to the wall and throws darts to rank them I, II, and III. The first solution is tried. If it works, then no other solution is considered further. If the first solution doesn't work, the second solution is tried, and so forth. What is the sample space for possible outcomes? Draw a tree representing them. (Nothing has been said about what happens if III fails.)

10. Stockholders are being presented with several options on which to vote. If Option I is accepted, no further options need be considered. However, if Option I is rejected, then the voters are asked to vote on which option, II or III, to consider next. That is then done, with the losing option considered last. What is the sample space? Draw the tree.

11. On any particular day the weather can be classified by temperature (above normal, normal, below normal) and sky conditions (clear, cloudy, or precipitating (rain, snow, or whatever)). What is the sample space of possible weather conditions? Draw a tree.

12. *Marketing surveys.* A survey is made to determine who buys a particular product. The people surveyed are classified by income (low, medium, or high) and education (grade school, high school, or college). What is the sample space of possible classifications? Draw a tree.

13. A political survey is made and the responders are classified by sex (male or female), marital status (single or married), or age (<18 or ⩾18). What is the sample space of the responders? Draw a tree.

14. The menu for a meal gives one the choice of (i) soup or fruit cup, (ii) fish, chicken, or meat, (iii) salad or dessert. What is the sample space of possible menus? Draw a tree.

■ ───────────────────────────────────

15. In a single elimination sports tournament consisting of *n* teams, a team is eliminated when it loses one game. How many games are required to complete the tournament?

16. In a double elimination softball tournament consisting of *n* teams, a team is eliminated when it loses two games. At most how many games are required to complete the tournament?

12.4   COUNTING TECHNIQUES—PERMUTATIONS

Trees were used in the preceding section to show the possible outcomes of an experiment. We want to develop faster counting techniques. The following example leads up to the *Fundamental Counting Principle*.

Example 1   How many 4-letter words (not necessarily meaningful or pronounceable) can be formed using the letters *P, D, Q, X without* repetition?

Solution   Such a word would have the general form

Any of the 4 letters can be used for the first letter in the word. Once this letter has been selected, the second can be selected from the 3 remaining letters, and the third from the remaining 2 letters. The fourth letter is already determined, since only 1 possible letter remains. Thus there are

$$4 \cdot 3 \cdot 2 \cdot 1, \qquad \text{or 24 words.}$$

We could, of course, have determined this by writing down all the possibilities; and even though this can be quite cumbersome in general, we list them below for reference.

PDQX   PDXQ   PQDX   PQXD   PXDQ   PXQD   DPQX   DPXQ   DQPX   DQXP   DXPQ   DXQP

QPDX   QPXD   QDPX   QDXP   QXDP   QXPD   XPDQ   XPQD   XDPQ   XDQP   XQPD   XQDP

FUNDAMENTAL COUNTING PRINCIPLE. Given a combined action, or event, in which the 1st action can be performed in n_1 ways, the 2nd action can be performed in n_2 ways, and so on, then the total number of ways the combined action can be performed is the product

$$n_1 \cdot n_2 \cdot n_3 \cdots n_k.$$

Let us demonstrate this for three actions with a tree. Assume the first action E_1 can be performed in 3 ways, the second E_2 can be performed in 4 ways, and the third E_3 in 2 ways.

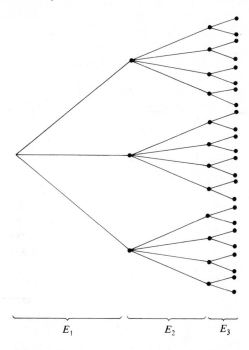

$$E_1 \qquad E_2 \qquad E_3$$

There are $3 \cdot 4 \cdot 2$, or 24 paths through the tree (count them), so there are 24 outcomes for all three actions.

Permutations

A *permutation* of a set of n objects is an ordered arrangement of all the objects. For example, consider the set of 4 objects,

$$\{P, D, Q, X\}$$

as in Example 1. There are 4 choices for the first letter, 3 choices for the second, 2 choices for the third, and 1 for the fourth. Thus, by the Fundamental Counting Principle, there are:

$$4 \cdot 3 \cdot 2 \cdot 1, \quad \text{or 24 permutations of a set of 4 objects.}$$

In general, consider a set of n objects. There are n choices for the first object, $(n-1)$ choices for the second, $(n-2)$ choices for the third, and so on. The nth object is chosen in only 1 way.

The total number of permutations of a set of *n* objects, denoted *P(n, n)*, is given by

$$P(n, n) = \underbrace{n(n - 1)(n - 2) \cdots 3 \cdot 2 \cdot 1.}_{n \text{ factors}}$$

Example 2 Find *P*(7, 7) and *P*(3, 3).

Solution
$$P(7, 7) = 7 \cdot 6 \cdot 5 \cdot 4 \cdot 3 \cdot 2 \cdot 1 = 5040,$$
$$P(3, 3) = 3 \cdot 2 \cdot 1 = 6$$

Factorial Notation

We will use products such as

$$6 \cdot 5 \cdot 4 \cdot 3 \cdot 2 \cdot 1 \quad \text{and} \quad 8 \cdot 7 \cdot 6 \cdot 5 \cdot 4 \cdot 3 \cdot 2 \cdot 1$$

so often that it is convenient to adopt a notation for them. We define

$$6 \cdot 5 \cdot 4 \cdot 3 \cdot 2 \cdot 1 = 6!, \quad \text{read "6 factorial."}$$

In general,

$$n! = n \text{ factorial} = \underbrace{n(n - 1)(n - 2) \cdots 3 \cdot 2 \cdot 1.}_{n \text{ factors}}$$

For example,

$n! = n \cdot (n - 1) \cdot (n - 2) \cdots 1$
$7! = 7 \cdot 6 \cdot 5 \cdot 4 \cdot 3 \cdot 2 \cdot 1 = 5040$
$6! = 6 \cdot 5 \cdot 4 \cdot 3 \cdot 2 \cdot 1 = 720$
$5! = 5 \cdot 4 \cdot 3 \cdot 2 \cdot 1 = 120$
$4! = 4 \cdot 3 \cdot 2 \cdot 1 = 24$
$3! = 3 \cdot 2 \cdot 1 = 6$
$2! = 2 \cdot 1 = 2$
$1! = 1 = 1$

We define

$$0! = 1$$

for consistency in formulas used later.

We can now restate the formula for the total number of permutations of n objects.

$$P(n, n) = n(n - 1)(n - 2) \cdots 3 \cdot 2 \cdot 1 = n!$$

We often use other notations for factorials. Note the following.

$$7! = 7 \cdot 6 \cdot 5 \cdot 4 \cdot 3 \cdot 2 \cdot 1 = 7 \cdot (6 \cdot 5 \cdot 4 \cdot 3 \cdot 2 \cdot 1) = 7 \cdot 6!$$

$$6! = 6 \cdot 5 \cdot 4 \cdot 3 \cdot 2 \cdot 1 = 6 \cdot (5 \cdot 4 \cdot 3 \cdot 2 \cdot 1) = 6 \cdot 5!$$

In general,

$$n! = n(n - 1)!$$

Note also that

$$7! = 7 \cdot 6!$$
$$= 7 \cdot 6 \cdot 5!$$
$$= 7 \cdot 6 \cdot 5 \cdot 4!$$

In general, for any $k < n$,

$$n! = \underbrace{\underbrace{n(n - 1)(n - 2) \cdots [n - (k - 1)]}_{k \text{ factors}} \underbrace{(n - k)!}_{(n - k) \text{ factors}}}_{n \text{ factors}}$$

Permutations of *n* Objects Taken *k* at a Time

Consider the set

$$\{P, D, Q, X, Y\}.$$

We have 5 objects. Suppose we wanted to determine the number of ordered arrangements of 3 objects taken from the set. There would be 5 choices for the first object. Then there would remain 4 choices for the second object, and 3 for the third selection. By the Fundamental Counting Principle, there would be

$5 \cdot 4 \cdot 3$, or 60 permutations of a set of 5 objects taken 3 at a time.

In general, suppose we had a set of n objects and we wanted to determine the number of permutations of these n objects taken k at a time. There would be n choices for the first object. Then there would remain $(n - 1)$ choices for the second object, $(n - 2)$ for the third, and so on. We would make k choices in all, so there will be k factors in the product.

> The total number of permutations of *n* objects taken *k* at a time, denoted *P(n, k)*, is given by
> $$P(n, k) = \underbrace{n(n - 1)(n - 2) \cdots [n - (k - 1)]}_{k \text{ factors}}.$$

An alternative symbol for $P(n, k)$ can be found by multiplying by 1, using $\dfrac{(n - k)!}{(n - k)!}$ as follows.

$$P(n, k) = n(n - 1)(n - 2) \cdots [n - (k - 1)] \cdot \frac{(n - k)!}{(n - k)!}$$

$$= \frac{n(n - 1)(n - 2) \cdots [n - (k - 1)](n - k)!}{(n - k)!}$$

$$= \frac{n!}{(n - k)!}$$

Thus,

The total number of permutations of n objects taken k at a time, is given by

$$P(n, k) = n(n - 1)(n - 2) \cdots [n - (k - 1)] \tag{1}$$

$$P(n, k) = \frac{n!}{(n - k)!} \tag{2}$$

Formula (1) is most useful in application, but formula (2) will be important in a development in Section 12.5.

Example 3 Evaluate $P(7, 3)$ using both formulas.

Solution Using formula (1), we have:

This number tells where to start.

$$P(7, 3) \;=\; \underbrace{7 \cdot 6 \cdot 5}\;=\; 210$$

This number tells how many factors.

Using formula (2) we have

$$P(7, 3) = \frac{7!}{(7 - 3)!} = \frac{7!}{4!} = \frac{7 \cdot 6 \cdot 5 \cdot 4 \cdot 3 \cdot 2 \cdot 1}{4 \cdot 3 \cdot 2 \cdot 1} = 7 \cdot 6 \cdot 5 = 210.$$

Example 4 How many ways can the letters of "organize" be arranged

a) taking 8 at a time?

b) taking 6 at a time?

c) taking 4 at a time?

d) taking 2 at a time?

Solution   a) $P(8, 8) = 8 \cdot 7 \cdot 6 \cdot 5 \cdot 4 \cdot 3 \cdot 2 \cdot 1 = 40{,}320$
b) $P(8, 6) = 8 \cdot 7 \cdot 6 \cdot 5 \cdot 4 \cdot 3 \qquad = 20{,}160$
c) $P(8, 4) = 8 \cdot 7 \cdot 6 \cdot 5 \qquad\qquad = \quad 1680$
d) $P(8, 2) = 8 \cdot 7 \qquad\qquad\qquad = \qquad 56$

Circular Permutations (Optional)

Consider arranging the 5 letters A, B, C, D, and E in a circular permutation.

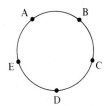

In a circle, the permutations $ABCDE$, $BCDEA$, $CDEAB$, $DEABC$, and $EABCD$ are no longer distinguishable as they would be on a line. Therefore, for each circular permutation, there would be 5 distinguishable permutations on a line. (Think of cutting the circle open and bending it out to a line.)

   Suppose we have P circular permutations. Each of these would yield $5 \cdot P$ permutations on a line, and we know there are 5! of these. Then $5 \cdot P = 5!$, so

$$P = \frac{5!}{5} = 4! = 4 \cdot 3 \cdot 2 \cdot 1 = 24.$$

In general,

> **The number of circular permutations of n objects taken n at a time is $(n - 1)!$**

Example 5   How many ways can 10 college students sit around a campfire?

Solution $(10 - 1)! = 9! = 9 \cdot 8 \cdot 7 \cdot 6 \cdot 5 \cdot 4 \cdot 3 \cdot 2 \cdot 1 = 362{,}880.$

Permutations "with Repetition" or "with Replacement"

Example 6   A standard deck of cards has 52 different cards. (For the exact makeup of the deck, see p. 581). How many 3-card permutations can be made by selecting the 3 cards without replacement? with replacement?

Solution   a) The case "without replacement" is equivalent to "without repetition," as in Example 1. This is the number of permutations of 52 things taken 3 at a time.

$$P(52, 3) = 52 \cdot 51 \cdot 50 = 132,600.$$

b) The case "with replacement" is considered by first making a selection. This can be done in 52 ways. Then the card is "replaced" and we make another selection. This can still be done 52 ways. Similarly, the third selection can be made 52 ways. Thus there are

$$52 \cdot 52 \cdot 52, \quad \text{or} \quad 140,608$$

possible permutations.

The number of permutations of n objects taken k at a time, with replacement, or with repetition, is n^k.

Mixed Counting

In the following example we carry out several types of counting.

Example 7   How many ways can 3 men and 3 women be seated in a row of 6 seats

a) with no seating restrictions?

b) if men and women must alternate?

c) if a particular couple (man–woman) must sit together?

d) if a particular couple must *not* sit together?

Solution   a) There are 6 people and 6 seats. Hence there are

$$P(6, 6) = 6! = 6 \cdot 5 \cdot 4 \cdot 3 \cdot 2 \cdot 1 = 720 \text{ possible arrangements.}$$

b) They can sit either MWMWMW or WMWMWM. These yield two possibilities. Considering the possibility MWMWMW, we think of the number of ways the *men* can be arranged within this possibility.

$$\text{MWMWMW}$$
$$\uparrow \quad \uparrow \quad \uparrow$$
$$① \quad ② \quad ③$$

This is equivalent to arranging 3 objects 3 at a time, so there are

$$P(3, 3) = 3! = 3 \cdot 2 \cdot 1 = 6 \text{ ways.}$$

Considering the same possibility MWMWMW, we think of the number of ways the *women* can be arranged within this possibility.

MWMWMW
↑ ↑ ↑
① ② ③

In all there are 6 · 6, or 36 ways within the possibility MWMWMW. Now consider the possibility WMWMWM. By a similar argument, there are 6 · 6, or 36 ways within the possibility WMWMWM. Then the total number of arrangements is 2 · 6 · 6, or 72.

c) i) The particular couple can sit MW or WM, yielding 2! or 2 possibilities.

  ii) Considering this particular couple as *one* object and the other four men and women as 4 objects, we have a total of 5 objects to be permuted (arranged 5 at a time). Then we have

$$P(5, 5) = 5! = 5 \cdot 4 \cdot 3 \cdot 2 \cdot 1 = 120 \text{ ways.}$$

  iii) The total number of arrangements, from (i) and (ii) is 2 · 120 = 240.

d) If one action can be performed in n_1 ways and another disjoint action (see p. 548) can be performed in n_2 ways, then *either* action can be performed in:

$$n_1 + n_2 \quad \text{ways.}$$

This is in contrast to the Fundamental Counting Principle where we consider *both* actions occurring and would have multiplied.

Since the couple must *either* sit together or *not* sit together, the number of arrangements with the couple sitting together (c) plus the number of arrangements with the couple not sitting together (d) must equal the number of arrangements with no seating restrictions (a). Thus, the number of arrangements with the couple not sitting together is the result of (a) minus the result of (c):

$$720 - 240 = 480.$$

EXERCISE SET 12.4

Evaluate.

1. 5!

2. 6!

3. 0!

4. 1!

5. $P(6, 6)$

6. $P(5, 5)$

7. $P(20, 2)$

8. $P(30, 2)$

9. $P(7, 5)$

10. $P(6, 4)$

11. $P(n, 3)$

12. $P(n, 2)$

13. A person can get to the airport 3 ways, fly by any of 4 airlines, and get from the airport to his final destination in 2 ways. How many different ways can a person get to his destination? (*Hint.* Use the Fundamental Counting Principle.)

14. A person driving from Boston to Los Angeles wishes to go through Washington, D.C., Atlanta, New Orleans, and Denver. If there are 6 main routes between Boston and Washington, 2 between Washington and Atlanta, 4 between Atlanta and New Orleans, 5 between New Orleans and Denver, and 7 between Denver and Los Angeles, how many possible routes can he take?

15. An office manager hires 4 secretaries, one for each of his assistants. If the secretaries are assigned at random, how many different assignments are possible? Give the solution in factorial and permutation notation. (*Hint.* See Example 1 and Example 2.)

16. An ice cream store has 6 different flavors of ice cream and room under the counter for 6 cartons of ice cream. How many different ways can the ice cream cartons be arranged under the counter? Give the solution in factorial and permutation notation.

17. As in Exercise 15, 4 secretaries apply for 2 different positions. How many ways can these two positions be filled if the secretaries are hired at random? Express the solution in permutation notation. (*Hint.* See Example 3 and Example 4.)

18. As in Exercise 16, if 8 ice cream flavors are available, in how many ways can 6 flavors be selected and arranged under the counter? Express the solution in permutation notation.

19. How many words (not necessarily meaningful or pronounceable) can be formed by rearranging the letters of the word "LOVE"? Express your answer in permutation notation. (*Hint.* See Example 4.)

20. How many 3-letter words can be formed from the letters of the word "ZORCH"? Express your answer in permutation notation.

21. How many ways can 4 people be seated at a circular bridge table? Would the answer change if the table were square? (*Hint.* See Example 5.)

22. How many ways can 8 people on a committee be seated at a circular table?

23. How many 4-number license plates can be made using digits 1, 2, 3, 4, and 5 if repetitions are permitted? not permitted? (*Hint.* See Example 6.)

24. As in Exercise 23, but the number must be even.

25. How many 3-digit numbers can be formed from the numbers 1, 2, 3, 4, and 5, if repetitions are (a) allowed, (b) not allowed?

26. As in Exercise 25, if repetitions are not allowed, how many of these are (a) larger than 300? (b) less than 500?

27. How many ways can 4 different contracts be awarded to 7 different firms? if no firm gets more than one contract?

28. How many ways can 3 people be assigned to 5 offices?

29. As in Exercise 27, but two particular contracts must be awarded to the same firm with no other restrictions.

30. As in Exercise 28, but 2 particular people want adjacent offices.

31. How many ways can 4 executives from a given company and 3 visitors from another company be seated in a row? if they must alternate host, visitor, etc.? if a member of the host company sits at each end?

32. As in Exercise 31, but (a) two particular people wish to sit together, (b) two particular people should not be seated together.

■ _____

33. A car holds three people in the front and three people in the back. How many ways can 6 people be seated in the car? if a given couple must sit together?

34. As in Exercise 33, but two particular couples must sit together.

_____

12.5   COUNTING TECHNIQUES—COMBINATIONS

We may sometimes make selections from a set without regard for order. Such selections are called *combinations*.

Example 1   How many combinations can be formed by taking elements 3 at a time from the set {A, B, C, D, E}?

Solution   The combinations are

$$\{A, B, C\}, \{A, B, D\}, \{A, B, E\}, \{A, C, D\}, \{A, C, E\},$$

$$\{A, D, E\}, \{B, C, D\}, \{B, C, E\}, \{B, D, E\}, \{C, D, E\}.$$

Note that finding all the combinations of 5 objects taken 3 at a time is the same as forming all the 3-element subsets. Thus a combination is a subset. This is consistent with our earlier work regarding sets. That is, the set, or combination, {A, C, E}, is the same as the set, or combination, {C, A, E}, because *order is not* considered when describing sets.

A *combination* containing k objects is a subset containing k objects.

The number of combinations of n objects taken k at a time, denoted $C(n, k)$, is the number of different subsets of k elements.

As in Example 1, we find that

$$C(5, 5) = 1, \qquad C(5, 2) = 10,$$

$$C(5, 4) = 5, \qquad C(5, 1) = 5,$$

$$C(5, 3) = 10, \qquad C(5, 0) = 1.$$

We can derive some general results here. First, it is always true that $C(n, n) = 1$, because a set with n objects has only 1 subset with n objects. Second, $C(n, 1) = n$ because a set with n objects has n subsets with 1 element each. Finally, $C(n, 0) = 1$, because a set with n objects has only one subset, namely the empty set Ø, with 0 elements.

We now derive a general formula for $C(n, k)$ for any $k \leq n$. Let us return to Example 1 and compare the number of combinations with the number of permutations.

Combinations	Permutations					
$\{A, B, C\} \rightarrow$	ABC	BCA	CAB	CBA	BAC	ACB
$\{A, B, D\} \rightarrow$	ABD	BDA	DAB	DBA	BAD	ADB
$\{A, B, E\} \rightarrow$	ABE	BEA	EAB	EBA	BAE	AEB
$\{A, C, D\} \rightarrow$	ACD	CDA	DAC	DCA	CAD	ADC
$\{A, C, E\} \rightarrow$	ACE	CEA	EAC	ECA	CAE	AEC
$\{A, D, E\} \rightarrow$	ADE	DEA	EAD	EDA	DAE	AED
$\{B, C, D\} \rightarrow$	BCD	CDB	DBC	DCB	CBD	BDC
$\{B, C, E\} \rightarrow$	BCE	CEB	EBC	ECB	CBE	BEC
$\{B, D, E\} \rightarrow$	BDE	DEB	EBD	EDB	DBE	BED
$\{C, D, E\} \rightarrow$	CDE	DEC	ECD	EDC	DCE	CED

Note that each combination of 3 objects, say $\{A, C, E\}$ yields $3!$, or 6, permutations, as shown above. It follows that

$$3! \cdot C(5, 3) = 60 = P(5, 3) = 5 \cdot 4 \cdot 3$$

so

$$C(5, 3) = \frac{P(5, 3)}{3!} = \frac{5 \cdot 4 \cdot 3}{\cdot 2 \cdot 1} = 10$$

In general, the number of combinations of n objects taken k at a time, $C(n, k)$, times the number of permutations of these k objects, $k!$, must equal the number of permutations of n objects taken k at a time:

$$k! \cdot C(n, k) = P(n, k)$$

so

$$C(n, k) = \frac{P(n, k)}{k!} = \frac{1}{k!} \cdot P(n, k) = \frac{1}{k!} \cdot \frac{n!}{(n - k)!} = \frac{n!}{k!(n - k)!} \qquad (1)$$

We also have

$$\mathbf{C(n, k) = \frac{n(n - 1)(n - 2) \cdots [n - (k - 1)]}{k(k - 1)(k - 2) \cdots 3 \cdot 2 \cdot 1}}. \qquad \mathbf{(2)}$$

Note that this expression for $C(n, k)$ is the quotient of two quantities, each of which has k factors.

An alternative notation, called a *Binomial Coefficient*, is also used for $C(n, k)$:

$$\mathbf{\binom{n}{k} = C(n, k).}$$

You should be able to use either notation.

Query: Why should a "combination" lock really be called a "permutation" lock?

Example 2   Evaluate $\binom{7}{5}$, using expressions (1) and (2).

Solution   a) By (1),

$$\binom{7}{5} = \frac{7!}{5!2!} = \frac{7 \cdot 6 \cdot 5 \cdot 4 \cdot 3 \cdot 2 \cdot 1}{5 \cdot 4 \cdot 3 \cdot 2 \cdot 1 \cdot 2 \cdot 1} = \frac{7 \cdot 6 \cdot 5 \cdot 4 \cdot 3}{5 \cdot 4 \cdot 3 \cdot 2 \cdot 1} = \frac{7 \cdot 6}{2 \cdot 1} = 21.$$

b) By (2),

This tells where to start

$$\binom{7}{5} = \frac{7 \cdot 6 \cdot 5 \cdot 4 \cdot 3}{5 \cdot 4 \cdot 3 \cdot 2 \cdot 1} = \frac{7 \cdot 6}{2 \cdot 1} = 21.$$

This tells how many factors in numerator and denominator, and where to start the denominator.

The method in (b), using formula (2), is easiest to carry out, but in some situations formula (1) does become useful.

Note that

$$\binom{7}{2} = \frac{7 \cdot 6}{2 \cdot 1} = 21$$

so that

$$\binom{7}{5} = \binom{7}{2}.$$

In general,

$$\binom{n}{k} = \binom{n}{n - k}.$$

This is because every set of k elements automatically determines the *set complement* with $(n - k)$ elements. So there are the same number of k-element subsets as there are $(n - k)$-element subsets. Try this with your fingers. Hold your hands up and bend down 3 fingers. This determines not only the 3-element set you turned down, but the 7-element set still up. Knowing this may ease some computation.

Example 3   For a psychology study, 4 people are chosen at random from a group of 10 people. In how many ways can this be done?

Solution   No order is implied here, nor does it seem to be important, so the number of ways the 4 people can be selected is given by

$$\binom{10}{4} = \frac{10 \cdot \overset{3}{\cancel{9}} \cdot \cancel{8} \cdot 7}{\cancel{4} \cdot \cancel{3} \cdot \cancel{2} \cdot 1} = 10 \cdot 3 \cdot 7 = 210.$$

Some problems involve repeated and/or mixed uses of combination and permutation notation.

Example 4   A university offers 5 science courses, 6 humanity courses, and 3 literature courses. How many ways can a student choose 2 science courses, 3 humanity courses, and 1 literature course?

Solution   Since the *order* of choosing the subjects is irrelevant, the student can choose 2 science courses $\binom{5}{2}$ ways, 3 humanity courses $\binom{6}{3}$ ways, and 1 literature course $\binom{3}{1}$ ways. Hence, by the Fundamental Counting Principle, the total number of choices available in the product

$$\binom{5}{2} \cdot \binom{6}{3} \cdot \binom{3}{1} = \frac{5 \cdot 4}{2 \cdot 1} \cdot \frac{6 \cdot 5 \cdot 4}{3 \cdot 2 \cdot 1} \cdot \frac{3}{1} = 600.$$

Not all solutions involve products. Some require additions.

Example 5   How many ways can 2 people be chosen out of 3 men and 4 women such that *at least* one is a man?

Solution   *Either* one or two men must be chosen to satisfy the constraints of the problem. If one man is chosen, then one woman must also be chosen. This can be done $\binom{3}{1} \cdot \binom{4}{1} = 3 \cdot 4 = 12$ ways. Two men can be chosen $\binom{3}{2} = 3$ ways. Since *either* is permitted, the total number is the sum $12 + 3 = 15$.

Some problems involve partitions.

Example 6   How many ways can 9 different books be distributed among three children so that the oldest gets 4, the middle child gets 3, and the youngest gets 2?

Solution   Here the 9 books are "partitioned" into 3 groups of 4, 3, and 2. The oldest child can "choose" his books $\binom{9}{4}$ ways. The next child can "choose" his 3 books out of the remaining $9 - 4 = 5$ books $\binom{5}{3}$ ways. The youngest child can "choose" his 2 books out of the remaining $5 - 3 = 2$ books $\binom{2}{2}$ ways. The total number of "choices" for all is the product $\binom{9}{4} \cdot \binom{5}{3} \cdot \binom{2}{2}$. Making use of the fact that

$$\binom{n}{k} = \frac{n!}{k!(n-k)!},$$

we have

$$\binom{9}{4}\binom{5}{3}\binom{2}{2} = \frac{9!}{4!5!} \cdot \frac{5!}{3!2!} \cdot \frac{2!}{2!0!}$$

$$= \frac{9!}{4!3!2!} = 9 \cdot 4 \cdot 7 \cdot 5 = 1260.$$

Verify that the same solution is obtained regardless of which child "chooses" first or second.

There is a related type of problem in which not all the elements are distinguishable in an arrangement.

Example 7 How many *distinguishable* words can be made up of all the letters of the word "MISSISSIPPI"?

Solution The word "MISSISSIPPI" has 11 letters. Thus, if all the letters were *distinguishable*, there would be

$$11! = 39,916,800 \text{ possible arrangements.}$$

However, we actually have

1 M,   4 I's,   4 S's,   2 P's.

The *different* letters are distinguishable, but the 4 I's are *indistinguishable* from each other, as are the 4 S's and the 2 P's. The 4 I's, 4 S's, and 2 P's can be made distinguishable by putting *tags* on them for the moment. Thus, we obtain "eleven" letters:

$$M, \ I_1, \ I_2, \ I_3, \ I_4, \ S_1, \ S_2, \ S_3, \ S_4, \ P_1, \ P_2.$$

Given *any* particular word, the 4 I's can be permuted $4! = 24$ ways, the 4 S's can be permuted $4! = 24$ ways, and the 2 P's can be permuted $2! = 2$ ways. Thus the I's, S's, and P's of *each* distinguishable word can be permuted $4! \cdot 4! \cdot 2! = 1152$ ways to make words distinguishable by tags, or indistinguishable when the tags are dropped. Hence, the number of *distinguishable* words is:

$$\frac{11!}{4!4!2!} = 34,650.$$

In general,

> Given a set of n objects of which n_1 are of one kind, n_2 are of a second kind, n_3 are of a third kind, and so on, where finally there are n_k of a kth kind, then the number of distinguishable arrangements is

$$\frac{n!}{n_1! \cdot n_2! \cdot n_3! \cdots n_k!}.$$

EXERCISE SET 12.5

Evaluate.

1. $C(13, 2)$

2. $C(9, 6)$

3. $\begin{pmatrix} 13 \\ 11 \end{pmatrix}$

4. $\begin{pmatrix} 9 \\ 3 \end{pmatrix}$

5. $C(7, 1)$

6. $C(8, 8)$

7. $C(n, 2)$

8. $C(n, 3)$

9. An office manager interviews 6 secretaries. If 4 are hired at random, how many ways can they be selected? (*Hint.* See Example 3.)

10. If ice cream comes in 8 flavors, in how many ways can a particular store select 6 flavors at random?

11. On a test, a student must answer any 7 of the first 10 questions, and any 5 of the second 8 questions. In how many ways can this be done? (*Hint.* See Example 4.)

12. How many committees can be formed from a set of 8 senators and 5 representatives if each committee contains 4 senators and 3 representatives?

13. From a group consisting of 6 men and 8 women, 5 are to be hired at random as sales representatives of a company. How many ways can this be done if:

    a) It does not matter how many are men and how many are women?

    b) At least 3 must be women?

    c) At least 4 must be women?

    d) At least 1 must be a woman?

14. From a group consisting of 10 smokers and 10 nonsmokers, 4 are to be chosen for a medical study. How many ways can this be done if:

    a) It does not matter how many smokers or nonsmokers there are?

    b) At least 2 must be smokers?

    c) At least 3 must be smokers?

    d) At least 1 must be a smoker?

(*Hint.* See Example 4 and Example 5.)

15. How many ways can 11 different tools be distributed among four employees if the first gets 3, the second 4, and the remaining two employees get 2 each? (*Hint.* See Example 6.)

16. How many ways can 8 different records be distributed among three students if the first gets 2, the second gets 5, and the third gets 1?

17. How many distinguishable words can be made up of all the letters in the word "CINCINNATI"? (*Hint.* See Example 7.)

18. How many distinguishable words can be made up of all the letters in the word "ABRACADABRA"?

19. A psychotic professor decides to grade his 20 students on a curve without regard to test performance. There will be 2 A's, 5 B's, 8 C's, 3 D's, and 2 F's. How many ways can this be done? (*Hint.* See Example 7.)

20. A psychotic professor decides to grade her 24 students on a curve without regard to test performance. There will be 3 A's, 5 B's, 9 C's, 4 D's, and 3 F's. How many ways can this be done?

21. How many ways can the expression $x^3y^2z^4$ be expressed without exponents?

22. How many ways can the expression $p^3q^5r^2$ be expressed without exponents?

23. From a group of 20 employees a delegation of 3 is to be selected at random.

    a) How many ways can this be done?

    b) How many ways can this be done if one of the 3 is selected at random to be spokesman?

24. For a psychological study, a group of 3 people is selected at random from a group of 4 men and 3 women.

    a) How many ways can this be done?

    b) How many ways can this be done if there must be at least 1 man and at least 1 woman in the group?

25. How many ways can a group of 3 people be selected from a group of 5 with regard to order? without regard to order?

26. How many ways can a group of 4 people be selected from a group of 6 with regard to order? without regard to order?

27. A folk-dance leader has 10 records for elementary dances and 20 records for more advanced dances.

    a) How many ways can 6 dances be selected at random for a program?

    b) How many ways can 4 elementary dances and 2 advanced dances be selected for the program?

28. How many ways can a bridge team of 4 be selected at random from 6 husband–wife pairs,

    a) If husband–wife pairs cannot be broken?

    b) If no husband or wife is on the same team as his or her spouse, but the team still consists of 2 men and 2 women?

29. How many ways can 12 work assignments be made at random, 4 to each of 3 machinists? (*Note.* Machinists are people; people are distinguishable.)

30. How many ways can 10 work assignments be made at random if one machinist gets 4 and the other two machinists 3 each?

31. As in Exercise 29, how many ways can these 12 work assignments be made on 3 work sheets *before* the work sheets are assigned to a particular machinist?

32. As in Exercise 30, how many ways can these 10 work assignments be made on 3 work sheets *before* the work sheets are assigned to particular machinists?

■ ————————————————————————

33. How many distinguishable words can be formed from the letters of ALGEBRA if each word is to contain 7 letters? 6 letters? 5 letters?

34. How many distinguishable words can be formed from the letters of PRECEDE if each word is to contain 7 letters? 6 letters? 5 letters?

35. * A class consists of 10 students of whom 4 are women of whom 3 are married to 3 of the 5 married men in the class. They all spend an evening at a motel which has 2 rooms with 2 single beds each (a double) and 2 rooms with 3 single beds each (a triple). Assuming that only one sex occupies any room except for married couples who *may* share a double, how many ways can the students distribute themselves into the rooms?

37. *Wendy's Hamburgers*, a national firm, advertizes "We Fix Hamburgers 256 Ways!" This is accomplished by various combinations of catsup, onion, mustard, pickle, mayonnaise, relish, tomato, or lettuce. Of course, one can also have a plain hamburger. Assume single portions.

a) Use combination notation to show the number of possible hamburgers.

b) Use the result of Exercise 36 to show how the expression in (a) can be evaluated quickly.

c) Interestingly, Wendy's excludes cheese from the possibilities. This may be to avoid false advertising, because then one would have a cheeseburger. Including cheese as a possibility, how many ways does Wendy's fix hamburgers?

36. In Exercises 27 through 32 of Exercise Set 12.1, we found that a set with n elements has 2^n subsets. Show that

$$2^n = \binom{n}{0} + \binom{n}{1} + \binom{n}{2} + \cdots + \binom{n}{n}$$

$$= \sum_{i=0}^{n} \binom{n}{i}.$$

(Optional) Counting Numbers of POKER Hands

In answering each problem *do not* just give the answer, provide a reasoned expression as well. Read all the problems before beginning.

38. How many different 5-card hands can be dealt from a standard 52-card deck? Note that no order is considered, even though one might "order" cards after receiving them.

39. A *royal flush* consists of a 5-card hand with A-K-Q-J-10 of the same suit. How many are there?

---

* This problem was assigned on a test by one of the authors (JCC) and subsequently submitted by the mother of one of his students to *TIME* magazine and printed with the cover letter stating that this was an example of "nonsexist mathematics," whatever that is.

A standard deck of 52 cards is made up as follows:

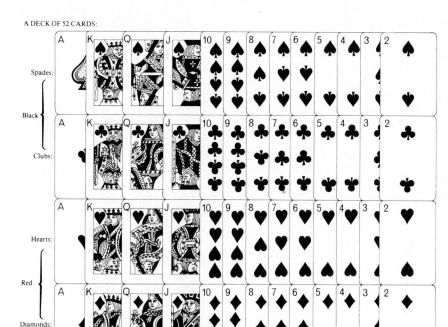

A DECK OF 52 CARDS:

40. A *straight flush* consists of five cards in sequence in the same suit, but does not include royal flushes. How many are there? (Assume an ace can be used at either the high or low end.)

42. A *full house* consists of a pair and three of a kind, such as K-K-K-7-7.

  a) How many full houses are there consisting of kings and sevens?

  b) How many full houses are there?

44. *Three of a kind* consists of a five-card hand where 3 of the cards are the same denomination and the other two cards are not the same denomination, such as K-K-K-10-3. How many are there?

46. *Two pairs* is just what it says—a hand such as Q-Q-8-8-A. How many are there?

41. *Four of a kind* is a five-card hand where 4 of the cards are the same denomination, such as 4 jacks, 4 aces, or 4 deuces. How many are there?

43. A *pair* is a five-card hand where just 2 of the cards are of the same denomination, such as Q-Q-8-A-3. How many are there?

45. A *flush* is a five-card hand where all the cards are the same suit, but not all in sequence (not a straight flush or royal flush). How many are there?

47. A *straight* is any five cards in sequence but not in the same suit. How many are there?

Exercises 48–71 provide a mixture of permutation and combination problems.

48. There are 27 people at a party. How many possible handshakes are there?

49. How many ways can 6 books be assigned to 10 students if each gets one book?

50. How many ways can 4 cars be placed in 9 garages, one car to a garage?

51. How many softball games are played in a league with 8 teams if each team plays each other team once? Twice?

52. How many games are played in a league with n teams if each team plays each other team once? Twice?

53. How many distinguishable words can be formed from all the letters of the word MATH? BUSINESS? PHILOSOPHICAL?

54. There are 8 points on a circle. How many triangles (inscribed) can be drawn with these points as vertices?

55. A money clip contains one each of the following bills: \$1, \$2, \$5, \$10, \$20, \$50, \$100. How many different sums of money can be formed using the bills?

56. How many words can be formed using 4 out of 5 letters of A, B, C, D, E if the letters

    a) are not repeated?

    b) can be repeated?

    c) are not repeated but must begin with D?

    d) are not repeated but must end with DE?

57. A state forms its license plates by first listing a number which corresponds to the county the car owner dwells in (the names of the counties are alphabetized and the number is its location in the order). Then the plate lists a letter of the alphabet and this is followed by a number from 1 to 9999. How many such plates are possible if there are 80 counties?

58. How many diagonals does a hexagon have?

59. How many diagonals does an n-agon have?

60. How many distinguishable words can be formed from all the letters of the word ORANGE? BIOLOGY? MATHEMATICS?

61. How many words can be formed using 5 out of 6 of the letters of G, H, I, J, K, L if the letters

    a) are not repeated?

    b) can be repeated?

    c) are not repeated but must begin with K?

    d) are not repeated but must end with IGH?

62. A set of 5 parallel lines crosses another set of 8 parallel lines. How many parallelograms are formed?

63. There are n points on a circle. How many quadrilaterals can be drawn with these points as vertices?

Solve for n.

64. $P(n, 5) = 7 \cdot P(n, 4)$

65. $C(n + 1, 3) = 2 \cdot C(n, 2)$

66. $\binom{n + 2}{4} = 6 \cdot \binom{n}{2}$

67. $P(n, 4) = 8 \cdot P(n - 1, 3)$

68. $C(n, n - 2) = 6$

69. $\binom{n}{3} = 2 \cdot \binom{n - 1}{2}$

70. $P(n, 5) = 9 \cdot P(n - 1, 4)$

71. $P(n, 4) = 8 \cdot P(n, 3)$

CHAPTER 12 REVIEW

1. Given $A = \{a, b, c, e, g\}$ and $B = \{b, c, e, f, s\}$. What are $A \cup B$ and $A \cap B$? Represent each of these sets by means of a Venn diagram.

3. $A = \{a, b, c, d, e, g\}$,
$\quad B = \{b, c, d, f, h\}$,
$\quad \mathcal{U} = \{a, b, c, \ldots, z\}$

Find $A - B$, $B - A$, A^c, B^c, $B^c - A^c$. Represent $B^c - A^c$ by a Venn diagram.

5. A survey of 195 people indicated that:

90 read *Time* (T),

45 read *National Review* (R),

15 read *Nation* (N),

3 read T and R,

5 read T and N,

1 read R and N,

1 read all three.

How many people read *none* of these three magazines? Use a Venn diagram.

7. Draw a tree to represent the sample space of Exercise 6.

9. How many 5-letter words can be formed using the letters P, D, Q, R, S *without* repetition?

11. A woman is going out to eat. She will put on one of 5 pantsuits, one pair out of 40 pairs of shoes, and go to one of 8 restaurants. In how many ways can she dress and eat?

13. Evaluate $P(6, 4)$ using both formulas.

15. How many ways can 6 different foods be arranged in 6 dishes *around* a Lazy Susan?

2. Write several partitions of the set $B = \{1, 2, 3, 4, 5\}$, and draw the Venn diagram for each. Answers may vary.

4. Out of a group of 240 students surveyed, 150 spent Friday night at a movie, 120 spent Saturday night at a basketball game, and 60 did both. How many students went to the basketball game, but not the movie?

6. An old sea chest contains 10 bars of silver and 5 bars of gold. If 3 bars are drawn at random, what is the sample space of possible outcomes?

8. If $A = \{a, b, c\}$ and $B = \{1, 2, 3, 4\}$, find $A \times B$ and $\mathcal{N}(A \times B)$.

10. An examination consists of ten true–false questions. How many possible different answer sheets can be turned in?

12. How many ways can 5 motorcycles be parked in a row?

14. How many ways can the letters of "soybean" be arranged,

a) taking 7 at a time?

b) taking 5 at a time?

c) taking 4 at a time?

d) taking 3 at a time?

16. How many 2-card permutations can be made by selecting 2 cards from a deck of 52,

a) without replacement?

b) with replacement?

17. The flags of five nations are to be raised on six flagpoles arranged in a row. How many ways can the flags be raised:

  a) If there are no restrictions?

  b) If all the flags must be together with no gaps between them?

  c) If three particular nations want their flags together with no separation either with an empty flagpole or another flag?

  d) If three particular nations do *not* want their flags all together, an empty flagpole being equivalent to a flag as separation?

19. Evaluate

  a) $\begin{pmatrix} 10 \\ 3 \end{pmatrix}$ b) $\begin{pmatrix} 10 \\ 7 \end{pmatrix}$

  c) $C(9, 4)$ d) $C(9, 5)$

21. How many ways can a committee of 4 men and 3 women be chosen out of a group of 7 men and 5 women?

23. How many ways can 7 different toys be distributed to 4 children with the oldest getting one and the others 2 each?

Consider these sets for Questions 25 through 30:

$$A = \{a, b, c, d, e\},$$

$$B = \{a, b, c, d, e, f, g\},$$

$$C = \{a, b, c\},$$

$$D = \{d, e\}.$$

Find:

25. $A \cup B$ **26.** $A \cap B$

29. Do sets C and D form a partition of A?

31. $P(7, 4)$ **32.** $\begin{pmatrix} 7 \\ 4 \end{pmatrix}$

35. If 3 dice of different colors are rolled simultaneously, how many ways can they land?

37. How many ways can 6 people be seated at a circular table?

18. Given the set of 4 letters

$$\{A, B, C, D\},$$

  a) Determine the number of permutations of this set, taking 3 letters at a time.

  b) List these permutations.

  c) Determine the number of combinations of this set, taking 3 letters at a time.

  d) List these combinations.

20. An examination consists of 10 questions. A student is required to answer any 8 of them. How many different ways can the student pick 8 questions to answer? (*Hint.* Is the *order* in which he answers the questions important, assuming the answers themselves are numbered?)

22. How many ways can 2 people be chosen out of 3 men and 4 women such that at least one is a woman?

24. How many distinguishable words can be made up of all the letters of the word "TENNESSEE"?

27. $C \times D$ **28.** $A - D$

30. Do sets C and D form a partition of B?

33. 6!   **34.** 1!

36. How many ways can 2 cards be drawn at random (without regard for order) from a deck of 52?

38. How many 3-digit numbers can be formed using the digits 2, 3, 5, and 7, with repetition? without repetition?

39. How many ways can 4 men and 4 women be seated in a row if men and women occupy alternate seats?

41. From a group of 12 Democrats and 9 Republicans, how many committees of 3 can be formed consisting of at least 2 Democrats?

40. How many different words can be formed from all the letters of the word JENNIFER?

42. There are 240 students in a certain freshman class. Of these

120 are taking Economics,

65 are taking Russian,

84 are taking Mathematics,

34 are taking Economics and Russian,

22 are taking Economics and Mathematics,

18 are taking Russian and Mathematics,

10 are taking all three subjects.

How many are not taking any of these subjects?

PROBABILITY: BASIC CONCEPTS

13.1 INTRODUCTION TO PROBABILITY

Suppose we toss a nickel 100 times and it comes up heads 53 times. We might say that the

Probability of getting a head is $\frac{53}{100}$, or 0.53.

Suppose we toss the same nickel another 100 times and it comes up heads 49 times. We might say that the

Probability of getting a head is $\frac{49}{100}$, or 0.49.

We might also reason about the probability of getting a head. There are 2 outcomes of tossing the nickel, heads and tails. If the coin is "fair," we might reason that the chances are 1 out of 2 of getting a head, so the probability of getting a head is $\frac{1}{2}$, or 0.50.

We call 0.53 and 0.49 *experimental probabilities*, and 0.50 *theoretical probability*. Which is correct? We really never know this. Such is the nature of probability. For example, to determine whether a coin is indeed fair, we may carry out an experiment: toss it a thousand times—or a million times.

The information gathered may lead us to reject or accept the fairness of the coin. On the other hand, it may be quite cumbersome and time-consuming to determine probabilities experimentally, so we attempt to determine them theoretically. This will be our main objective in this chapter.

We need some terminology before we continue. Suppose we perform an *experiment* such as flipping a coin, drawing a card from a deck, or checking an item off an assembly line for quality. The results of an experiment are called the *outcomes*. The set of all possible outcomes is called the *sample space*. An *event* is a set of outcomes; that is, a subset of the sample space. For example, for the experiment "flipping a coin," an *event* is "getting a head," from the *sample space* consisting of "head, tail."

We will denote the probability that an event can occur as $p(E)$, or p_E. For example, "getting a head" may be denoted by H. Then $p(H)$, or p_H, represents the probability of getting a head. When the outcomes of an experiment all have the same probability of occurring, we say that they are *equally likely*, or *equiprobable*. To see the distinction between events that are equiprobable and those that are not, consider these dartboards (executive decision-makers).

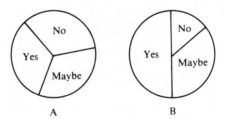

For dart board A, the events, hitting "Yes," hitting "No," hitting "Maybe," are equally likely, but for board B they are not. A sample space that can be expressed as a union of equiprobable events can allow us to calculate probabilities of other events.

BASIC PROBABILITY PRINCIPLE. If an event E can occur m ways out of n possible equiprobable outcomes of a sample space S, the probability of that event is given by

$$p(E) = p_E = \frac{m}{n}.$$

That is,

$$p(E) = \frac{\mathcal{N}(E)}{\mathcal{N}(S)}.$$

We will give many examples related to a standard bridge deck of 52 cards. Such a deck is made up as follows:

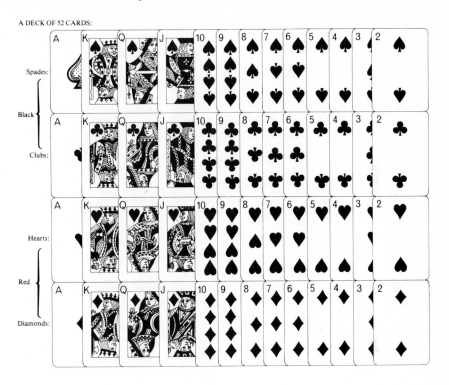

A DECK OF 52 CARDS:

Example 1 What is the probability of drawing an ace at random out of a standard deck of cards?

Solution There are 52 equally likely outcomes and there are 4 ways to get an ace, so

$$p(\text{Drawing an ace}) = \tfrac{4}{52}, \quad \text{or } \tfrac{1}{13}.$$

The wording "at random" is a way of implying that each card has the same probability of being drawn as any other card; that is, is equally likely to be drawn.

Example 2 Suppose we select, without looking, one marble from a sack containing 5 green marbles and 3 yellow marbles. What is the probability of selecting a yellow marble?

Solution   There are 8 equally likely outcomes and 3 ways to get a yellow marble, so

$$p(\text{Selecting a yellow marble}) = \tfrac{3}{8}.$$

Example 3   In Example 2, what is the probability of selecting a red marble?

Solution   There are 0 ways of selecting a red marble since there are no red marbles in the sack, so

$$p(\text{Selecting a red marble}) = \tfrac{0}{8}, \quad \text{or } 0.$$

For an event which cannot occur, $p(E) = 0$. It follows that $p(\emptyset) = 0$.

Example 4   In Example 2, what is the probability of selecting either a green marble or a yellow marble?

Solution   Since the sack contains only green and yellow marbles, there are 8 ways of selecting either one, so

$$p(\text{Selecting a green or yellow marble}) = \tfrac{8}{8}, \quad \text{or } 1.$$

For an event which is *certain* to occur, or in the case of repeated trials, will *always* occur, $p(E) = 1$. Since the sample space contains all possible events, $p(S) = 1$.

The previous examples lead us to:

The probability that an event will occur is a number from 0 to 1; that is, for any event E,

$$0 \leq p(E) \leq 1.$$

Example 5   Suppose 3 cards are drawn at random from a well-shuffled deck of cards. What is the probability that all 3 are diamonds?

Solution   The number of ways of drawing 3 cards out of a deck of 52 is

$$\binom{52}{3}.$$

Now 13 of the 52 cards are diamonds, so the number of ways of drawing the 3 diamonds is

$$\binom{13}{3}.$$

Thus,

$$p(\text{All 3 diamonds}) = \dfrac{\dbinom{13}{3}}{\dbinom{52}{3}} = \dfrac{\dfrac{13 \cdot 12 \cdot 11}{3 \cdot 2 \cdot 1}}{\dfrac{52 \cdot 51 \cdot 50}{3 \cdot 2 \cdot 1}} = \dfrac{13 \cdot 12 \cdot 11}{52 \cdot 51 \cdot 50} = \dfrac{11}{850}.$$

Example 6 For a psychology study, 2 people are selected at random from a group consisting of 8 men and 6 women. What is the probability that both are women?

Solution The number of ways of selecting 2 people from the group of 14 is $\binom{14}{2}$. The number of ways of selecting 2 women from a group of 6 is $\binom{6}{2}$. Thus,

$$p(\text{Both are women}) = \dfrac{\dbinom{6}{2}}{\dbinom{14}{2}} = \dfrac{\dfrac{6 \cdot 5}{2 \cdot 1}}{\dfrac{14 \cdot 13}{2 \cdot 1}} = \dfrac{6 \cdot 5}{14 \cdot 13} = \dfrac{3 \cdot 5}{7 \cdot 13} = \dfrac{15}{91}.$$

Example 7 For a psychology study, 3 people are selected at random from a group consisting of 8 men and 6 women. What is the probability that 1 man and 2 women are selected?

Solution The number of ways of selecting 3 people out of a group of 14 is $\binom{14}{3}$. The number of ways of selecting 1 man out of a group of 8 is $\binom{8}{1}$. The number of ways of selecting 2 women out of a group of 6 is $\binom{6}{2}$. Then, by the Fundamental Counting Principle, we know that the number of ways of selecting 1 man and 2 women is the product

$$\binom{8}{1} \cdot \binom{6}{2}.$$

Thus,

$$p(\text{1 man and 2 women}) = \dfrac{\dbinom{8}{1} \cdot \dbinom{6}{2}}{\dbinom{14}{3}} = \dfrac{\dfrac{8}{1} \cdot \dfrac{6 \cdot 5}{2 \cdot 1}}{\dfrac{14 \cdot 13 \cdot 12}{3 \cdot 2 \cdot 1}} = \dfrac{30}{91}.$$

Example 8 What is the probability of getting a total of 6 on a roll of a pair of dice?

Solution We assume the dice are different, say one white and one black. There are 6 possible outcomes on one die (singular of "dice") so, by the Fundamental

Counting Principle, there are 6 · 6, or 36 possible outcomes in the sample space for rolling two dice. We show this as follows.

White

6	(1,6)	(2,6)	(3,6)	(4,6)	(5,6)	(6,6)
5	(1,5)	(2,5)	(3,5)	(4,5)	(5,5)	(6,5)
4	(1,4)	(2,4)	(3,4)	(4,4)	(5,4)	(6,4)
3	(1,3)	(2,3)	(3,3)	(4,3)	(5,3)	(6,3)
2	(1,2)	(2,2)	(3,2)	(4,2)	(5,2)	(6,2)
1	(1,1)	(2,1)	(3,1)	(4,1)	(5,1)	(6,1)
	1	2	3	4	5	6

Black

The pairs that total 6 are enclosed in the diagram. There are 5 such pairs, so the probability of getting a total of 6 is $\frac{5}{36}$.

Complementary Events

Drawing an ace from a deck of cards is an event. *Not* drawing an ace is also an event. If E is an event, the nonoccurrence of E is expressed by the symbol E^c, read "not E." Thus, if E is the event of drawing an ace, then E^c is the event of *not* drawing an ace. E and E^c are called *complementary* events.

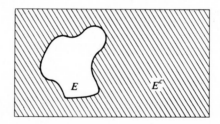

The probability that an event E will *not* occur is given by

$$p(E^c) = 1 - p(E).$$

We can demonstrate this with a Venn diagram. The total number of ways E can occur is m. Then, if there are n total outcomes, it follows that there are $(n - m)$ ways in which E does not occur, so

$$p(E^c) = \frac{n - m}{n} = \frac{n}{n} - \frac{m}{n} = 1 - p(E).$$

Example 9   Suppose $p(E) = \frac{8}{25}$. Find $p(E^c)$.

Solution $p(E^c) = 1 - \frac{8}{25} = \frac{17}{25}.$

Example 10   One card is drawn at random from a well-shuffled deck. What is the probability that it is *not* an ace?

Solution   Let $p(E)$ = probability of drawing an ace. Then $p(E^c)$ = probability that the card is not an ace. From Example 9, $p(E) = \frac{1}{13}$, so

$$p(E^c) = 1 - \tfrac{1}{13} = \tfrac{12}{13}.$$

Odds

If p is the probability for an event to occur, then, from the preceding result, we know that $(1 - p)$ is the probability for the event not to occur. The ratio

$$p{:}(1 - p)$$

is the *odds for* the event to occur. The ratio

$$(1 - p){:}p$$

is the *odds against* the occurrence.

Example 11   One card is drawn from a well-shuffled deck.

a) What are the odds for an ace to occur?

b) What are the odds against the occurrence of an ace?

Solution   From Example 10, we let p = p(getting an ace) = $\frac{1}{13}$, and $1 - p = \frac{12}{13}$. Thus,

a) The odds are 1:12 (read "1 to 12") *for* drawing an ace.

b) The odds are 12:1 *against* drawing an ace.

Probability theory came about historically as a way to calculate odds in games of chance. Today it has ever-expanding application to fields such as business, social science, behavioral science, and physics.

EXERCISE SET 13.1

One card is drawn at random from a well-shuffled deck of 52. What is the probability of drawing:

1. a queen?	**2.** a jack?	**3.** a spade?	**4.** a diamond?
5. an 8?	**6.** a 10?	**7.** a black card?	**8.** a red club?
9. a 7 or a jack?	**10.** an 8 or 10?		

Suppose we select one billiard ball from a bag containing 6 red billiard balls and 10 white ones. What is the probability of selecting:

11. a red ball?

12. a white ball?

13. a chartreuse ball?

14. a red or white ball?

15. For a sociological study, a group of 4 people are chosen from a group containing 7 men and 8 women. What is the probability that 2 men and 2 women are chosen?

16. Suppose 4 pens are selected at random from a box containing 9 yellow pens and 6 blue pens. What is the probability that 2 will be yellow and 2 will be blue?

17. What is the probability of getting a total of 9 on a roll of a pair of dice?

18. What is the probability of getting a total of 10 on a roll of a pair of dice?

19. What is the probability of getting a total of 12 ("boxcars") on a roll of a pair of dice?

20. What is the probability of getting a total of 2 ("snake eyes") on a roll of a pair of dice?

21. What is the probability of getting a total of 1 on a roll of a pair of dice?

22. What is the probability of getting a total of 13 on a roll of a pair of dice?

23. From a bag containing 7 dimes, 8 nickels, and 10 quarters, 7 coins are drawn at random. What is the probability of getting 3 dimes, 2 nickels, and 2 quarters?

24. From a sack containing 7 dimes, 5 nickels, and 10 quarters, 8 coins are drawn at random. What is the probability of getting 4 dimes, 3 nickels, and 1 quarter?

Suppose 5 cards are dealt from a well-shuffled deck of 52. What is the probability of dealing:

25. 3 sevens and 2 kings? This is a type of *full house.*

26. 2 jacks and 3 aces?

27. 4 aces and 1 five?

28. 4 kings and 1 queen?

29. 5 aces?

30. 5 kings?

31. The sales force of a business consists of 10 men and 10 women. A production unit of 4 people is set up at random. What is the probability that 2 men and 2 women are chosen?

32. A union is made up of 14 women and 7 men. A bargaining unit of 3 is chosen at random. What is the probability that 2 women and 1 man are chosen?

33. At a personal office 5 men and 3 women apply for a job. If 2 are hired at random, what is the probability that:

    a) 1 is a man and 1 is a woman?

    b) both are men?

    c) both are women?

    d) both are men *or* both are women?

34. Repeat Exercise 33, but assume that 5 men and 6 women apply for the job.

35. a) Find $p(E^c)$ if $p(E) = \frac{17}{45}$.

    b) What are the odds *for* the event E to occur?

    c) What are the odds *against* the event E occurring?

36. a) Find $p(E^c)$ if $p(E) = \frac{29}{63}$.

    b) What are the odds *for* the event E to occur?

    c) What are the odds *against* the event E occurring?

37. *Advertising, Lotteries.* In many state-run lotteries the odds *against* winning a

1. $20 prize are   200:1,
2. $500 prize are 250,000:3,
3. $1000 prize are 500,000:3.

What is the probability to win

a) $20 on one lottery ticket?
b) $500 on one lottery ticket?
c) $1000 on one lottery ticket?
d) $20 on two lottery tickets?

38. *Advertising, Lotteries.* The following is an odds chart for an actual giveaway game from a national food chain.

Prize Value	No. of Prizes	Odds for One Store Visit	Odds for 13 Store Visits	Odds for 26 Store Visits
$1000	42	147,619:1	11,355:1	5,678:1
$100	450	13,778:1	1,060:1	530:1
$20	895	6,927:1	533:1	267:1
$5	2,385	2,600:1	200:1	100:1
$2	7,450	832:1	64:1	32:1
$1	59,600	104:1	8:1	4:1
Total	70,822	88:1	7:1	3.5:1

a) What is the probability to win $1 in one store visit?
b) What is the probability to win $5 in 13 store visits?
c) What is the probability to win something in one store visit?
d) What is the probability to win something in 13 store visits?

13.2   COMPOUND EVENTS

Let us consider an experiment where two of the outcomes are E_1 and E_2. Suppose we draw one card from a well-shuffled deck. Let

$$E_1 = \text{Event of drawing an ace}$$

and

$$E_2 = \text{Event of drawing a king.}$$

The

Event of drawing an ace or a king, or both,

is denoted

$$E_1 \cup E_2, \qquad \text{or} \qquad E_1 \text{ or } E_2,$$

and is called a *disjunction*. The

Event of drawing an ace and a king

is denoted

$$E_1 \cap E_2, \qquad \text{or} \qquad E_1 \text{ and } E_2,$$

and is called a *conjunction*. The events $E_1 \cup E_2$ and $E_1 \cap E_2$ are examples of *compound events*.

Since in *one* draw of a card it is impossible to draw an ace *and* a king at the same time, the probability of drawing an ace and a king is

$$p(E_1 \cap E_2) = p(\emptyset) = 0.$$

The probability of drawing an ace or a king is

$$p(E_1 \cup E_2) = \tfrac{8}{52} = \tfrac{2}{13}.$$

If we know the probabilities $p(E_1)$, $p(E_2)$, and $p(E_1 \cap E_2)$, we can compute $p(E_1 \cup E_2)$ using the following result.

For any events E_1 and E_2,

$$\boldsymbol{p(E_1 \cup E_2) = p(E_1) + p(E_2) - p(E_1 \cap E_2).}$$

This follows from a result of Chapter 6:

$$\mathcal{N}(E_1 \cup E_2) = \mathcal{N}(E_1) + \mathcal{N}(E_2) - \mathcal{N}(E_1 \cap E_2).$$

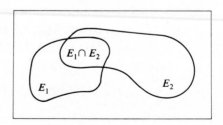

Let n = the number of elements in the sample space. Then

$$p(E_1 \cup E_2) = \frac{\mathcal{N}(E_1 \cup E_2)}{n}$$

$$= \frac{\mathcal{N}(E_1) + \mathcal{N}(E_2) - \mathcal{N}(E_1 \cap E_2)}{n}$$

$$= \frac{\mathcal{N}(E_1)}{n} + \frac{\mathcal{N}(E_2)}{n} - \frac{\mathcal{N}(E_1 \cap E_2)}{n}$$

$$= p(E_1) + p(E_2) - p(E_1 \cap E_2).$$

This result is called the *addition theorem* and will be considered in more detail later in this chapter. For now we will be more interested in the following consequences of this result.

For the event E_1 = Drawing an ace in one draw of a card and the event E_2 = Drawing a king in one draw of a card, we say that they are *mutually exclusive*, meaning that they cannot both happen at the same time. That is, $p(E_1 \cap E_2) = p(\emptyset) = 0$. Then

$$p(E_1 \cup E_2) = p(E_1) + p(E_2) - p(E_1 \cap E_2)$$

$$= p(E_1) + p(E_2) - 0$$

$$= p(E_1) + p(E_2).$$

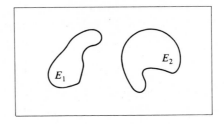

This leads us to the following.

For any events E_1 and E_2 which are mutually exclusive,

$$p(E_1 \cup E_2) = p(E_1) + p(E_2).$$

Example 1 Suppose E_1 and E_2 are mutually exclusive, and $p(E_1) = 0.45$ and $p(E_2) = 0.22$. Find $p(E_1 \cup E_2)$.

Solution $p(E_1 \cup E_2) = p(E_1) + p(E_2) = 0.45 + 0.22 = 0.67$.

Two events which are mutually exclusive can be represented as *branches* of a tree.

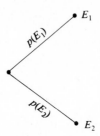

For coin-flipping, a coin cannot land both "heads up" and "tails up" at the same time, assuming the coin does not land on edge. Thus,

$$p(H \cap T) = p(\text{Heads and Tails}) = p(\emptyset) = 0,$$

so the events are mutually exclusive and

$$p(H \cup T) = p(H) + p(T) = \tfrac{1}{2} + \tfrac{1}{2} = 1.$$

Note that these events *partition* the sample space, that is, are mutually exclusive and fill the sample space.

For any events E_1 and E_2 which partition the sample space,

$$p(E_1 \cup E_2) = p(E_1) + p(E_2) = 1.$$

For any two events which partition the sample space, one event is the *complement* of the other, so

$$E_2 = E_1^c,$$

and

$$p(E_1) + p(E_2) = p(E_1) + p(E_1^c) = 1.$$

This follows from the fact that $p(E_1^c) = 1 - p(E_1)$.

Consider the example of drawing a card from a well-shuffled deck, and these 13 events:

$$E_1 = \text{drawing an ace,}$$
$$E_2 = \text{drawing a king,}$$
$$E_3 = \text{drawing a queen,}$$
$$\vdots \qquad \vdots$$
$$E_{12} = \text{drawing a three,}$$
$$E_{13} = \text{drawing a two.}$$

These events partition the sample space into 13 equiprobable subsets. That is, the sample space S consisting of all possible outcomes, is given by

$$S = E_1 \cup E_2 \cup E_3 \cup \cdots \cup E_{12} \cup E_{13},$$

and any two pairs of events are mutually exclusive. We express this as:

$$E_i \cap E_j = \emptyset, \qquad \text{for all } i \neq j,$$

or

$$p(E_i \cap E_j) = 0, \qquad \text{for all } i \neq j.$$

We can represent the events as branches of a tree:

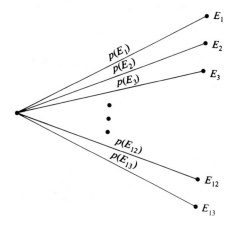

Since the events are mutually exclusive,

$$p(S) = p(E_1 \cup E_2 \cup E_3 \cup \cdots \cup E_{13})$$
$$= p(E_1) + p(E_2) + p(E_3) + \cdots + p(E_{13}).$$

The sample space S includes *all* events, so in any trial, one of them must occur, so that $p(S) = 1$. Thus

$$p(E_1) + p(E_2) + p(E_3) + \cdots + p(E_{13}) = 1,$$

where for each event $p(E_i)$, $0 \leq p(E_i) \leq 1$.

Let us use this partitioning idea in an example.

Example 2 *Manufacturing, Quality Control.* A box contains 20 transistors, 5 of which are defective. Three transistors are taken out at random. What is the probability that at least one is defective?

Solution   Let E_i be the *event* of drawing exactly i defective transistors and $p_i = p(E_i)$. Drawing different numbers of transistors are mutually exclusive events, so that

$$p_0 + p_1 + p_2 + p_3 = 1.$$

Note that no more than 3 defective transistors can be drawn. Thus, the probability of drawing at least one defective transistor, $p_{i \geqslant 1}$, is given by

$$p_{i \geqslant 1} = p_1 + p_2 + p_3 = 1 - p_0.$$

We have a choice of computing the three probabilities p_1, p_2, p_3, or the one probability p_0 and subtracting from 1. Since computing p_0 not only involves less work, but less work in turn involves less opportunity for error, we shall compute p_0.

Remember that this is a combination (unordered) rather than a permutation (ordered), since the order in which the transistors is drawn is not relevant. Thus, the number of ways 3 transistors can be drawn out of a total of 20 is $\binom{20}{3}$, and the number of ways 3 nondefective transistors can be drawn is $\binom{15}{3}$, since there are $20 - 5$ or 15 nondefective transistors. Thus, the probability p_0 is:

$$p_0 = \frac{\binom{15}{3}}{\binom{20}{3}} = \frac{\dfrac{15 \cdot 14 \cdot 13}{3 \cdot 2 \cdot 1}}{\dfrac{20 \cdot 19 \cdot 18}{3 \cdot 2 \cdot 1}} = \frac{15 \cdot 14 \cdot 13}{20 \cdot 19 \cdot 18} = \frac{91}{228}$$

and

$$p_{i \geqslant 1} = 1 - p_0 = 1 - \frac{91}{228} = \frac{137}{228}.$$

Even though it is more work, consider obtaining $p_{i \geqslant 1}$ from

$$p_{i \geqslant 1} = p_1 + p_2 + p_3.$$

Now, p_1 is the ratio of the number of ways one defective and two nondefective transistors can be drawn, or

$$p_1 = \frac{\binom{5}{1}\binom{15}{2}}{\binom{20}{3}} = \frac{105}{228}.$$

Similarly,

$$p_2 = \frac{\binom{5}{2}\binom{15}{1}}{\binom{20}{3}} = \frac{30}{228}, \quad \text{and} \quad p_3 = \frac{\binom{5}{3}\binom{15}{0}}{\binom{20}{3}} = \frac{2}{228}.$$

Thus,

$$p_{i \geqslant 1} = \frac{105}{228} + \frac{30}{228} + \frac{2}{228} = \frac{137}{228}, \qquad \text{as before.}$$

EXERCISE SET 13.2

1. a) Suppose $p(E_1) = 0.73$, $p(E_2) = 0.24$, and $p(E_1 \cap E_2) = 0.20$. Find $p(E_1 \cup E_2)$.

b) Suppose $p(E_1) = \frac{2}{7}$ and $p(E_2) = \frac{5}{14}$ and E_1 and E_2 are mutually exclusive. Find $p(E_1 \cup E_2)$.

3. Two fair dice are rolled and the sum of the numbers showing is noted. What is the probability that the sum is 7? (Express this as the union of mutually exclusive events.)

5. *Manufacturing, Quality Control.* A crate of 20 machine parts contains 3 defective parts. Two parts are drawn at random. What is the probability that:

a) Neither is defective?

b) One is defective (the other could be either defective or not defective)?

c) Only one is defective?

d) Both are defective?

7. There are 5 married couples in a room. If two people are chosen at random, what is the probability that:

a) One is a man and the other a woman?

b) They are of the same sex? (2 men or 2 women)

c) They are married (to each other)?

2. a) Suppose $p(E_1) = 0.46$, $p(E_2) = 0.50$, and $p(E_1 \cap E_2) = 0.35$. Find $p(E_1 \cup E_2)$.

b) Suppose $p(E_1) = \frac{3}{8}$ and $p(E_2) = \frac{5}{15}$ and E_1 and E_2 are mutually exclusive. Find $p(E_1 \cup E_2)$.

4. As in Exercise 3, what is the probability that the sum is even?

6. *Personnel, Public Health.* If 5 workers in a group of 25 have mononucleosis and 3 workers are chosen at random, what is the probability that:

a) None have mono?

b) All have mono?

c) Only one has mono? (1 has mono, 2 do not)

d) At least one has mono? (See Example 5 for a hint.)

8. There are 3 married couples and 3 unmarried couples in a room. If two people are chosen at random, what is the probability that:

a) They are of the opposite sex?

b) They are of the same sex?

c) They are married?

d) They are married to each other?

9. Given a standard deck of cards. Two cards are dealt from a shuffled deck. What is the probability that:

   a) Both are aces?

   b) They are a pair?

   c) Both are the same suit?

   d) They are neither a pair nor the same suit?

11. Two couples (four people) go to a theatre and find a row of six seats. If all are seated at random, what is the probability that a given couple will sit together?

13. If the letters of the word "hooch" are scrambled and reassembled by a chimpanzee (that is, randomly), what is the probability that they spell "hooch" correctly? [*Hint.* See Section 12.4, p. 570 and/or Section 12.5, p. 577. Compare methods.]

10. As in Exercise 9, what is the probability that:

   a) They are a pair but not aces?

   b) One is an ace and the other is of the same suit?

   c) Both are the same color?

   d) They are a pair of different colors?

*12. Two couples (four people) go to a restaurant and are seated at a round table with six seats. If all are seated at random, what is the probability that a given couple will sit together? [*Hint.* Look up circular permutations, Section 12.4, p. 569.]

14. A little red wagon consists of a base with four wheels and a handle. Each wheel is held on the axle with a cotter pin. The handle is attached with a larger cotter pin. If the wheels and handle are removed, what is the probability that a chimpanzee without instructions (that is, at random) will put the wagon together correctly?

13.3   INDEPENDENT EVENTS—MULTIPLICATION THEOREM

In Section 13.2 we considered, among other things, probabilities of disjunctions

$$p(E_1 \cup E_2),$$

where the joint probability $p(E_1 \cap E_2) = 0$. Such events were *mutually exclusive*. That is, we could compute the probability by adding the respective probabilities:

$$p(E_1 \cup E_2) = p(E_1) + p(E_2).$$

Now we want to consider probabilities of conjunctions

$$p(E_1 \cap E_2).$$

We shall see that, under certain conditions, we can compute these probabilities by multiplying the respective probabilities:

$$p(E_1 \cap E_2) = p(E_1) \cdot p(E_2).$$

Let us consider some examples.

Example 1   A black die and a white die are rolled. What is the probability that a 5 is obtained on the black die and an odd number is obtained on the white die?

Solution   Let E_1 = the Event of a 5 on the black die and E_2 = the Event of an odd number on the white die.

a) A 5 is obtained on the black die in 1 out of 6 outcomes, so

$$p(5 \text{ on black}) = p(E_1) = \tfrac{1}{6}.$$

b) An odd number is obtained on the white die in 3 of the 6 outcomes, so

$$p(\text{Odd on white}) = p(E_2) = \tfrac{3}{6} = \tfrac{1}{2}.$$

c) Look at the sample space in Example 8 of Section 13.1. There are 3 outcomes where a 5 on black and an odd number on white occur, so

$$p(5 \text{ on black and odd on white}) = p(E_1 \cap E_2) = \tfrac{3}{36} = \tfrac{1}{12}.$$

Note that this same result can be obtained from the product of the individual probabilities:

$$p(5 \text{ on black } and \text{ odd on white}) = p(5 \text{ on black}) \cdot p(\text{Odd on white})$$

or

$$p(E_1 \cap E_2) = p(E_1) \cdot p(E_2)$$

$$= \tfrac{1}{6} \cdot \tfrac{1}{2} = \tfrac{1}{12}.$$

In Example 1, E_1 (the event of a 5 on the black die) is *independent* of E_2 (the event of an odd number on the white die).

Not all events are independent, however. Consider the probability of rain on either of two particular days. Weather patterns being what they are, the weather on the second of two successive days is very much influenced by the weather on the preceding day.* Thus, the weather on the second day is *dependent* (to some extent) on the weather on the first day. On the other hand if the two days are sufficiently separated, say Easter and Christmas, then the weather on the second day is not likely to be influenced by the weather on the first day. Thus, in this case the weather on the second day is (essentially) *independent* of the weather on the first day. Dependent events are considered further later.

---

* In fact, if you used today's weather as a prediction of tomorrow's, you would be correct about 80% of the time.

The independence of two events usually has to be inferred from the nature of the problem. For two events E_1 and E_2 which do *not* affect each other, we have

MULTIPLICATION THEOREM FOR INDEPENDENT EVENTS   If neither of the events E_1 and E_2 affects the other, we say that the events are *independent.* Then

$$p(E_1 \cap E_2) = p(E_1) \cdot p(E_2).$$

The probability for both E_1 and E_2 to occur is the product of their individual probabilities.

Example 2   A fair coin is flipped and two fair dice are rolled. What is the probability for a tail to show on the coin *and* the total, or sum, on the dice to be 7?

Solution   The flipping of the coin does not affect the sum on the dice nor does the sum on the dice affect the flipping of the coin (unless there was some unstated strange condition, such as that the dice and coins were glued together). Thus the events

$$E_1 = \text{Getting a tail,} \qquad E_2 = \text{The total is 7}$$

are independent.

a) $p(\text{Getting a tail}) = p(E_1) = \frac{1}{2}$.

b) $p(\text{Total is 7}) = p(E_2) = \frac{1}{6}$. See the sample space in Example 8 of Section 8.1.

c) Thus,

$$p(\text{Getting a tail } and \text{ the total is 7}) = p(\text{Getting a tail}) \cdot p(\text{Total is 7})$$

or

$$p(E_1 \cap E_2) = p(E_1) \cdot p(E_2)$$
$$= \tfrac{1}{2} \cdot \tfrac{1}{6}$$
$$= \tfrac{1}{12}.$$

Sometimes we have to infer the "and" quality of an event from the wording of a problem.

Example 3   A die is rolled four times. What is the probability of getting a 5 on all four rolls?

Solution   The event

$$E = \text{Getting a 5 on all four rolls}$$

can be reexpressed with "and" as

$$E = (\text{1st roll 5}) \text{ and } (\text{2nd roll 5}) \text{ and } (\text{3rd roll 5}) \text{ and } (\text{4th roll 5}).$$

Each of these four events is independent of the others, so that from the Multiplication Theorem

$$p(E) = \tfrac{1}{6} \cdot \tfrac{1}{6} \cdot \tfrac{1}{6} \cdot \tfrac{1}{6} = \tfrac{1}{1296}.$$

Example 4   A coin is flipped five times. What is the probability that the flips come out in the order H, T, T, H, T?

Solution   The event

$$E = \text{flips come out in the order H, T, T, H, T}$$

can be expressed with "and" as

$$E = (\text{1st flip H}) \text{ and } (\text{2nd flip T}) \text{ and } (\text{3rd flip T}) \text{ and } (\text{4th flip H}) \text{ and } (\text{5th flip T}).$$

Each of these five events is independent of the others, so that from the Multiplication Theorem

$$p(E) = \tfrac{1}{2} \cdot \tfrac{1}{2} \cdot \tfrac{1}{2} \cdot \tfrac{1}{2} \cdot \tfrac{1}{2} = \tfrac{1}{32}.$$

Example 5   The probability that a man will live another 20 years is $\tfrac{1}{5}$ and the probability that his wife will live another 20 years is $\tfrac{1}{4}$. What is the probability that:

a) Both will live another 20 years?

b) Neither will live another 20 years?

c) Only one will live another 20 years?

Solution   Let

$$E_1 = \text{Event that the man lives another 20 years,}$$

$$E_2 = \text{Event that the woman lives another 20 years.}$$

a) Assuming that the longevity of each is independent (this assumption might be questioned, especially in the case of older people, where the death of one mate sometimes affects the death of the other), the joint probability that *both* will be alive in 20 years can be expressed as

$$p_{\text{Both}} = p(E_1 \text{ and } E_2) = p(E_1 \cap E_2),$$

and from the Multiplication Theorem is given by

$$p_{\text{Both}} = p(E_1 \cap E_2) = p(E_1) \cdot p(E_2) = \tfrac{1}{5} \cdot \tfrac{1}{4} = \tfrac{1}{20}.$$

b) That neither lives another 20 years can be expressed

(The man does not live another 20 years) and (The woman
does not live another 20 years)

or, in set language,

$$E_1^c \cap E_2^c.$$

Assuming these events to be independent, we have from the Multiplication Theorem

$$p_{\text{Neither}} = p(E_1^c \cap E_2^c) = p(E_1^c) \cdot p(E_2^c)$$

$$= [1 - p(E_1)] \cdot [1 - p(E_2)]$$

$$= (1 - \tfrac{1}{5})(1 - \tfrac{1}{4}) = \tfrac{4}{5} \cdot \tfrac{3}{4}$$

$$= \tfrac{3}{5}.$$

c) We look at this two ways. That only one (either) will live another 20 years can be expressed as

(The man is alive and the woman is not) or (The man is
not alive and the woman is),

or, in set language,

$$(E_1 \cap E_2^c) \cup (E_1^c \cap E_2).$$

Now the events $E_1 \cap E_2^c$ and $E_1^c \cap E_2$ are mutually exclusive—both cannot occur at the same time. Thus,

$$p_{\text{Either}} = p(E_1 \cap E_2^c) + p(E_1^c \cap E_2).$$

Now we can assume E_1 and E_2^c to be independent, and E_1^c and E_2 to be independent, so

$$p_{\text{Either}} = p(E_1 \cap E_2^c) + p(E_1^c \cap E_2)$$

$$= p(E_1) \cdot p(E_2^c) + p(E_1^c) \cdot p(E_2)$$

$$= \tfrac{1}{5} \cdot \tfrac{3}{4} + \tfrac{4}{5} \cdot \tfrac{1}{4} = \tfrac{3}{20} + \tfrac{4}{20} = \tfrac{7}{20}.$$

Considering this another way, the probability that *either* will be alive in

20 years, plus the probability that *both* will be alive, plus the probability that *neither* will be alive exhausts the possibilities, so that

$$p_{\text{Either}} + p_{\text{Both}} + p_{\text{Neither}} = 1,$$

and

$$p_{\text{Either}} = 1 - p_{\text{Both}} - p_{\text{Neither}}$$

$$= 1 - \tfrac{1}{20} - \tfrac{3}{5}$$

$$= \tfrac{7}{20}.$$

Let us solve the problem in Example 5 using trees. Since either the man lives another 20 years, or he does not, the events E_1 and E_1^c are *mutually exclusive,* so that they can be represented along different branches of a tree, as in Section 13.2.

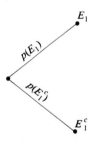

Since the events E_2 and E_2^c are also mutually exclusive whether or not the woman lives another 20 years, we can represent these events as *different branches* starting at the end of the previous branches, that is

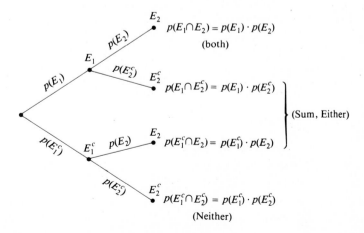

Note that since events E_1 and E_2 are independent, either event could have been written first on the tree.

From the Multiplication Theorem, the joint probability for two events (along the *same branch* of the tree) to both happen is the *product* of their individual probabilities as indicated to the right of the tree.

Using numerical values, we have:

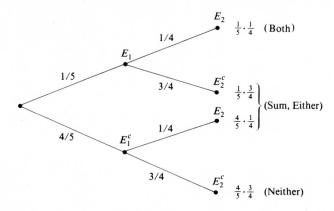

Thus, as before

$$p_{\text{Both}} = p(E_1 \cap E_2) = \tfrac{1}{5} \cdot \tfrac{1}{4} = \tfrac{1}{20},$$

$$p_{\text{Neither}} = p(E_1^c \cap E_2^c) = \tfrac{4}{5} \cdot \tfrac{3}{4} = \tfrac{3}{5},$$

and

$$p_{\text{Either}} = p(E_1 \cap E_2^c) + p(E_1^c \cap E_2) = \tfrac{1}{5} \cdot \tfrac{3}{4} + \tfrac{4}{5} \cdot \tfrac{1}{4} = \tfrac{7}{20}.$$

Example 6   *Manufacturing, Quality Control.* A box contains 20 transistors, 5 of which are defective. An inspector takes out 1 transistor at random, examines it for defects, and replaces it. After it has been replaced, another inspector does the same thing, and then so does a third inspector. What is the probability that at least one of the inspectors finds a defective transistor? (Compare with Example 2, Section 13.2.)

Solution   The probability that at least one of the inspectors finds a defective transistor, denoted $p_{i \geqslant 1}$, plus the probability that none of them finds a defective transistor, denoted p_0, sums to 1 because the events partition the sample space, so that

$$p_{i \geqslant 1} = 1 - p_0.$$

Suppose we use this fact and try to compute p_0 to then get $p_{i \geqslant 1}$. This time we must allow for *replacement*. The probability that a defective transistor is not drawn in the first trial is $\frac{15}{20}$. Since each trial is *independent* and *identical*, the probability that no defective transistors are drawn in three trials is the product

$$p_0 = \tfrac{15}{20} \cdot \tfrac{15}{20} \cdot \tfrac{15}{20} = \left(\tfrac{3}{4}\right)^3 = \tfrac{27}{64},$$

so that $p_{i \geqslant 1} = 1 - \frac{27}{64} = \frac{37}{64}$.

This problem can also be solved using a tree. If D_1 is the event that the first transistor drawn is defective and D_1^c is the event that it is not defective, then (as in Example 5) we can draw the following tree:

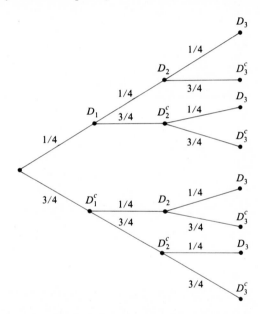

The probability that at least one defective transistor is drawn is the probability that:

(The first is defective) plus the probability that

(The first is not defective but the second is) plus the probability that

(The first and second are not defective but the third is). That is,

$$p_{i \geqslant 1} = p(D_1) + p(D_1^c \cap D_2) + p(D_1^c \cap D_2^c \cap D_3)$$

$$= \tfrac{1}{4} \quad + \tfrac{3}{4} \cdot \tfrac{1}{4} \quad + \tfrac{3}{4} \cdot \tfrac{3}{4} \cdot \tfrac{1}{4}$$

$$= \tfrac{37}{64}, \text{ as before.}$$

(Optional) The Birthday Problem

> **THE BIRTHDAY PROBLEM.** Of n people in a group, what is the probability that at least two of them have the same birthday (day and month, but not necessarily the same year)?

If $p(E)$ is the probability that at least two people have the same birthday, then $p(E^c)$ is the probability that no two people have the same birthday and

$$p(E) = 1 - p(E^c).$$

The probability $p(E^c)$ will be evaluated two ways.

i) From Section 7.1,

$$p(E^c) = \frac{N(E^c)}{N(S)}.$$

One person can have a birthday on any of 365 days (ignoring Leap Year possibilities). Two people can have birthdays on 365^2 days. Thus, in general, n people can have birthdays on 365^n days, so that

$$N(S) = 365^n.$$

Now if the second person has a birthday other than that of the first person, he has 364 possibilities. The third person has then 363 possibilities. In general, the nth person has $[365 - (n - 1)]$ possibilities, so that the n people have $N(E^c)$ possibilities, where

$$N(E^c) = 365 \cdot 364 \cdot 363 \cdots [365 - (n - 1)].$$

Thus,

$$p(E^c) = \frac{365 \cdot 364 \cdot 363 \cdots [365 - (n - 1)]}{365^n}.$$

ii) Alternately, let E_n be the event that the nth person does not have a birthday in common with the preceding $(n - 1)$ people. Thus,

$$p(E_n) = \frac{[365 - (n - 1)]}{365}.$$

(Note that $p(E_1) = 365/365 = 1$ is the probability that the first person has no common birthday with his predecessors, of which he has none.) Since each person's birthday is independent of another person's birthday, the events E_n are also independent, so that from *this* section

$$p(E^c) = p(E_1 \cap E_2 \cap \cdots \cap E_n) = p(E_1) \cdot p(E_2) \cdots p(E_n)$$

$$= \frac{365}{365} \cdot \frac{364}{365} \cdots \frac{[365 - (n - 1)]}{365},$$

which is equivalent to the first value for $p(E^c)$.

Evaluating $p(E) = 1 - p(E^c)$, we obtain the following table:

Table 1.   Probability for two or more people to have the same birthday.

n	$p(E)$	n	$p(E)$	n	$p(E)$	n	$p(E)$	n	$p(E)$
2	0.00274	16	0.284	24	0.538	32	0.753	40	0.891
5	0.0271	17	0.315	25	0.569	33	0.775	50	0.970
10	0.117	18	0.347	26	0.598	34	0.795	60	0.9951
11	0.141	19	0.379	27	0.627	35	0.814	70	0.99916
12	0.167	20	0.411	28	0.654	36	0.832	80	0.999914
13	0.194	21	0.444	29	0.681	37	0.849	90	0.999994
14	0.223	22	0.476	30	0.706	38	0.864	100	0.9999997
15	0.253	23	0.507	31	0.732	39	0.878		

For 23 or more people, the probability that two or more people will have the same birthday is greater than $\frac{1}{2}$, that is, it is more likely to occur than not!

EXERCISE SET 13.3

Given that E_1 and E_2 are independent, find $p(E_1 \cap E_2)$:

1. $p(E_1) = \frac{7}{9}$, $p(E_2) = \frac{11}{14}$.

2. $p(E_1) = \frac{4}{5}$, $p(E_2) = \frac{3}{8}$.

3. $p(E_1) = 0.48$, $p(E_2) = 0.33$.

4. $p(E_1) = 0.77$, $p(E_2) = 0.101$.

5. One card is drawn from a well-shuffled deck of 52 and replaced, and a second card is drawn. What is the probability that:

a) The first is a spade?

b) The second is an ace?

c) The first is a spade and the second is an ace?

6. As in Exercise 5, what is the probability that

a) The first is a face card?

b) The second is a king?

c) The first is a face card and the second is a king?

7. One card is drawn from a well-shuffled deck of 52, but not replaced, and a second card is drawn.

a) What is the probability that the first card is a spade?

b) What is the conditional probability that the second is a diamond, given that the first is a spade?

c) What is the probability that the first is a spade and the second a diamond?

8. As in Exercise 7,

a) What is the probability that the first card is a face card?

b) What is the conditional probability that the second card is a four, given that the first card is a face card?

c) What is the probability that the first card is a face card and the second is a four?

9. For an unfair coin, $p(H) = \frac{2}{3}$ and $p(T) = \frac{1}{3}$. The coin is flipped five times. What is the probability that the flips come out in the order T, H, H, T, H?

11. A student entering college has a $\frac{1}{3}$ probability for getting married while in college and a 0.6 probability of graduating. What is the probability that he will graduate married?

13. *Quality Control.* Candles are molded on a production line such that 10% are defective. What is the probability that a box of six are all good? All defective?

15. A class is one-third women and two-thirds men. Also, 60% are blond and 40% have dark hair. What is the probability that a person chosen at random is a blonde woman?

17. Suppose your probability of passing a test over this chapter is $\frac{3}{4}$, and the probability of your passing a psychology test the same day is $\frac{5}{8}$. Assuming the events are independent, what is the probability that you:

  a) Pass both tests?

  b) Pass one test, but not the other?

  c) Fail both tests?

19. *Quality Control.* A box contains 24 transistors, 6 of which are defective. An inspector takes out 1 transistor at random, examines it for defects, and replaces it. After it has been replaced, another inspector does the same thing, and then so does the third inspector. What is the probability that at least one of the examiners finds a defective transistor?

*21. *On the Birthday Problem.* Check an almanac for the birthdays of all the presidents of the U.S. How many presidents have there been? Do any two have the same birthday? Does this seem reasonable based on the table?

10. For an unfair coin, $p(H) = \frac{4}{5}$ and $p(T) = \frac{1}{5}$. The coin is flipped three times. What is the probability that the flips come out in the order T, H, T?

12. Two pilots are trying to communicate with each other during a severe thunderstorm. If the probability for a malfunction of either transceiver is 25%, what is the probability that they *can* communicate?

14. *Quality Control.* A vintner is making three separate batches of wine. Due to circumstances beyond his control, the probability for success is 0.9 for any one batch. What is the probability all three are successful?

16. In a lake there are several kinds of fish of which 20% are pike. Of each kind 10% is tagged. What is the probability that a fish caught at random will be a tagged pike?

18. Suppose your probability of passing a test over this chapter is $\frac{5}{8}$, and the probability of your passing a sociology test the same day is $\frac{2}{3}$. Assuming the events are independent, what is the probability that you:

  a) Pass both tests?

  b) Pass one test, but not the other?

  c) Fail both tests?

20. As in Exercise 19 but the box has 45 transistors of which 9 are defective.

*22. *On the Birthday Problem.* The probabilities regarding birthdays apply also to death dates. Check an almanac for the death dates of the U.S. presidents. Do any two have the same death date (excluding year)? Does this seem reasonable based on the table?

23. Democrats and Republicans are running for Congress (both Senate and House of Representatives). If the odds for the Democrat to win the Senate seat are 3:2 and the odds for the Republican to win the House seat are 5:4, what is the probability that both Democrats win? one Democrat and one Republican? Assume that one campaign does not affect the other. (*Hint.* Convert the odds to probabilities. For example, 3:2 converts to a probability of $\frac{3}{5}$.)

24. A baseball team is playing a doubleheader. If the odds are 4:3 to win the first game and 2:3 to win the second game, what is the probability that the team will win both games? only one game?

25. Five cards are dealt at random from a deck of 52 cards. What is the probability for:

    a) A pair?

    b) Three of a kind?

    c) Two pairs?

    d) A full house (a pair and three of a kind)?

    e) Four of a kind?

(*Hint.* See Exercises 38 through 46 of Exercise Set 12.5.)

26. As in Exercise 25 (read the whole problem for definitions), what is the probability for:

    a) A royal flush (an ace-high straight flush)?

    b) A straight flush (not including an ace as the high card)?

    c) A flush (five cards of the same suit, not all in sequence)?

    d) A straight (five cards in sequence, not all the same suit)?

(*Hint.* See Exercises 38 through 46 of Exercise Set 12.5.)

27. There are three identical urns containing purple and yellow balls. The first has 7 purple and 2 yellow, the second, 3 purple and 3 yellow, and the third, 2 purple and 4 yellow. An urn is chosen at random and a ball selected at random. What is the probability it is purple? Draw a tree.

28. As in Exercise 27, a second ball is drawn at random from a random choice of one of the two urns not selected in the first choice. What is the probability the ball is yellow?

29. A coin weighted so that heads is twice as likely as tails is to be flipped three times. What is the probability for at least two heads? Solve using a tree diagram.

13.4 THE ADDITION THEOREM

Addition Theorem—Two Events

So far we have studied

    i) *Mutually Exclusive Events:* Two events E_1 and E_2 which cannot both happen at the same time, that is, $p(E_1 \cap E_2) = 0$;

ii) *Independent Events:*   The probability of *both* occurring is the *product* of their individual probabilities (Multiplication Theorem); that is,

$$p(E_1 \cap E_2) = p(E_1) \cdot p(E_2).$$

For mutually exclusive events, the probability for *either* to happen is the *sum* of the individual probabilities; that is,

$$p(E_1 \cup E_2) = p(E_1) + p(E_2).$$

We also considered briefly $p(E_1 \cup E_2)$ for the general case. Let us reconsider such probabilities.

In Section 13.2 we developed the following result.

THE ADDITION THEOREM.   For any events E_1 and E_2,

$$p(E_1 \cup E_2) = p(E_1) + p(E_2) - p(E_1 \cap E_2).$$

The probability of either E_1 or E_2 is the probability of E_1 plus the probability of E_2 minus the probability of both E_1 and E_2.

Example 1   Suppose the probability that a student will pass a course in Finite Mathematics is 68%, or 0.68, and the probability that the student will pass an Accounting course is 70%, or 0.70. The probability that the student will pass both courses is 64%, or 0.64. What is the probability that the student will pass either Finite Mathematics or Accounting, or both?

Solution   Let

$$E_1 = \text{Event of passing Finite Mathematics,}$$

$$E_2 = \text{Event of passing Accounting.}$$

Then

$$E_1 \cap E_2 = \text{Event of passing both courses,}$$

and

$$E_1 \cup E_2 = \text{Event of passing Finite Mathematics } or \text{ Accounting (or both).}$$

We are seeking $p(E_1 \cup E_2)$, and we know $p(E_1)$, $p(E_2)$, and $P(E_1 \cap E_2)$. Thus, by the Addition Theorem, we have

$$p(E_1 \cup E_2) = p(E_1) + p(E_2) - p(E_1 \cap E_2)$$

$$= 0.68 + 0.70 - 0.64$$

$$= 0.74.$$

Note in Example 1 that the events E_1 and E_2 were not independent. That is,

$$(0.68)(0.70) = 0.476 \neq 0.64,$$

or

$$p(E_1) \cdot p(E_2) \neq p(E_1 \cap E_2).$$

Since E_1 and E_2 were *not* independent, the extra information $p(E_1 \cap E_2)$ had to be supplied.

Now let us consider a problem where events are independent.

Example 2   If the probability for rain is 0.4 on April 1, and 0.3 on November 29, what is the probability for rain on either day?

Solution   Let

$$E_1 = \text{the Event of rain on April 1}$$

and

$$E_2 = \text{the Event of rain on November 29.}$$

Then

$$E_1 \cup E_2 = \text{the Event of rain on April 1 or November 29.}$$

From the wording of the problem, we may infer that E_1 and E_2 are independent. Thus, we determine $p(E_1 \cap E_2)$ from the Multiplication Theorem and $p(E_1 \cup E_2)$ from the Addition Theorem:

$$p(E_1 \cup E_2) = p(E_1) + p(E_2) - p(E_1 \cap E_2)$$
$$= p(E_1) + p(E_2) - p(E_1) \cdot p(E_2)$$
$$= 0.4 + 0.3 - (0.4)(0.3)$$
$$= 0.58.$$

Using Trees to Solve Probability Problems

Let us see how we can use trees to facilitate solving problems.

In Example 3, we reconsider the Addition Theorem for the case where events are mutually exclusive, but now the events are themselves compound events.

Example 3   Experience shows that, with fatal accidents involving two cars, the probability that neither driver is drunk is $\frac{1}{4}$, and the probability that both are drunk is $\frac{1}{8}$. What is the probability that only one driver is drunk?

Solution   Let

$$E_1 = \text{Event that the } \textit{first} \text{ driver is drunk,}$$

and

$$E_2 = \text{Event that the } \textit{second} \text{ driver is drunk.}$$

Now the event that only one driver is drunk translates to:

(First drunk and the second not drunk) or (First not drunk and the second drunk),

or, using set language, we have

$$(E_1 \cap E_2^c) \cup (E_1^c \cap E_2).$$

This is a union of mutually exclusive events $E_1 \cap E_2^c$ and $E_1^c \cap E_2$. We are seeking the probability, p_1, of this event:

$$p_1 = p[(E_1 \cap E_2^c) \cup (E_1^c \cap E_2)] = p(E_1 \cap E_2^c) + p(E_1^c \cap E_2).$$

To find this, consider a tree.

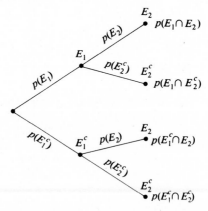

From the fact that $E_1 \cap E_2^c$ and $E_1^c \cap E_2$ represent *different* branches of the tree, we could have deduced that they are mutually exclusive events. But we also get more information from the tree, by noting that:

$$E_1 \cap E_2 = \text{the Event that both are drunk,}$$

$$E_1^c \cap E_2^c = \text{the Event that neither is drunk.}$$

Then since $E_1 \cap E_2$, $E_1 \cap E_2^c$, $E_1^c \cap E_2$, and $E_1^c \cap E_2^c$ represent *all* branches of the tree, they fill the sample space, so:

$$p(E_1 \cap E_2) + p(E_1 \cap E_2^c) + p(E_1^c \cap E_2) + p(E_1^c \cap E_2^c) = 1$$

or

$$p(E_1 \cap E_2) + p_1 + p(E_1^c \cap E_2^c) = 1,$$

so

$$p_1 = 1 - [p(E_1 \cap E_2) + p(E_1^c \cap E_2^c)]$$

$$= 1 - (\tfrac{1}{8} + \tfrac{1}{4})$$

$$= \tfrac{5}{8}.$$

Note that we never actually determined $p(E_1)$ or $p(E_2)$, nor can we from the data given (unless we assume that $p(E_1) = p(E_2)$).

We can also solve this problem using a Venn diagram.

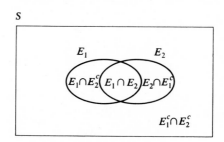

Putting in the available information, we obtain:

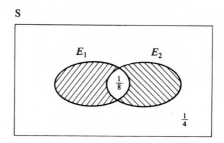

The probability that only one driver is drunk corresponds to the shaded area, and is equal to

$$p_1 = 1 - (\tfrac{1}{8} + \tfrac{1}{4})$$

$$= \tfrac{5}{8}, \qquad \text{as before.}$$

(Optional) The Addition Theorem—Three or More Events

The Addition Theorem for two events E_1 and E_2 is:

$$p(E_1 \cup E_2) = p(E_1) + p(E_2) - p(E_1 \cap E_2).$$

This theorem can be extended to three events, E_1, E_2, and E_3, by replacing E_2 in the above relation by $(E_2 \cup E_3)$, yielding

$$p(E_1 \cup E_2 \cup E_3) = p(E_1) + p(E_2 \cup E_3) - p[E_1 \cap (E_2 \cup E_3)].$$

From a Venn diagram, we can verify the relation

$$p[E_1 \cap (E_2 \cup E_3)] = p[(E_1 \cap E_2) \cup (E_1 \cap E_3)].$$

Applying the Addition Theorem for two events, we obtain the Addition Theorem for three events:

THE ADDITION THEOREM FOR THREE EVENTS.   For any events E_1, E_2, and E_3,

$$\mathbf{p(E_1 \cup E_2 \cup E_3) = p(E_1) + p(E_2) + p(E_3)}$$

$$\mathbf{- p(E_1 \cap E_2) - p(E_1 \cap E_3) - p(E_2 \cap E_3)}$$

$$\mathbf{+ p(E_1 \cap E_2 \cap E_3).}$$

For more than three events, the Addition Theorem has the same pattern as the preceding with appropriate alternating changes of sign.

Example 4   A group of n men, each with a different type of car, would like to swap cars. So they toss their keys into a pile. Each man takes out a key at random. What is the probability that at least one man gets his own car key?

Solution   Let E_i be the event that the ith man gets his own car back. Then the probability that at least one man out of n gets his own car back is

$$p_n = p(E_1 \cup E_2 \cup \cdots \cup E_n).$$

Using the Addition Theorem, this can be expanded into a series of terms representing events corresponding to one or more men getting their own cars back.

For $n = 1$, it is certain that the man will get his car back. That is, $p_1 = 1$.

Consider $n = 2$.

$$p_2 = p(E_1 \cup E_2) = p(E_1) + p(E_2) - p(E_1 \cap E_2).$$

Each man has a $\frac{1}{2}$ probability of getting his own car back; that is,

$$p(E_1) = p(E_2) = \tfrac{1}{2}.$$

But if one man gets his own car back, so must the other man, so that

$$p(E_1 \cap E_2) = \tfrac{1}{2}.$$

Thus,

$$p_2 = \tfrac{1}{2} + \tfrac{1}{2} - \tfrac{1}{2} = 1 - \tfrac{1}{2} = \tfrac{1}{2},$$

or

$$p_2 = p_1 - \tfrac{1}{2}.$$

For $n = 3$, we use the Addition Theorem for three events. The probability that any one man gets his own car back is:

$$p(E_i) = \tfrac{1}{3},$$

so that

$$p(E_1) + p(E_2) + p(E_3) = 1 = p_1.$$

Two men out of three can be chosen to get their cars back $\binom{3}{2}$ ways. A given pair can get their cars back with probability 1/3! Thus,

$$p(E_1 \cup E_2) + p(E_1 \cup E_3) + p(E_2 \cup E_3) = \binom{3}{2} \cdot \frac{1}{3!} = \frac{1}{2!}.$$

All three men can get their own cars back with probability 1/3!, so that we have

$$p_3 = 1 - \frac{1}{2!} + \frac{1}{3!} = \frac{2}{3},$$

or

$$p_3 = p_2 + \frac{1}{3!}.$$

If we keep up this process, we find that:

$$p_n = p_{n-1} + (-1)^{n-1} \cdot \frac{1}{n!},$$

or

$$p_n = 1 - \frac{1}{2!} + \frac{1}{3!} - \frac{1}{4!} + \cdots + (-1)^{n-1} \cdot \frac{1}{n!}.$$

EXERCISE SET 13.4

Find $p(E_1 \cup E_2)$, where:

1. $p(E_1) = 0.67$, $p(E_2) = 0.65$, and $p(E_1 \cap E_2) = 0.61$.

2. $p(E_1) = 0.76$, $p(E_2) = 0.57$, and $p(E_1 \cap E_2) = 0.46$.

3. Examination of fruitflies indicates that 30% have an eye defect, 60% have a color variation, and 10% have both. What is the probability that a random fly will have either an eye defect or a color variation? [*Hint.* 30% have an eye defect, so the probability of an eye defect is 0.3.]

4. *Agriculture.* A farmer finds that 24% of his corn crop has a blight, and 30% has received insufficient rain, and 8% has both. What part of the crop had either blight or insufficient rain?

Find $p(E_1 \cup E_2)$, assuming E_1 and E_2 are independent.

5. $p(E_1) = \frac{3}{5}$, $p(E_2) = \frac{1}{3}$.

6. $p(E_1) = \frac{5}{8}$, $p(E_2) = \frac{2}{5}$.

7. If the probability for snow is 0.7 and the probability of having a fire in your home is 0.0006, what is the probability of snow *or* a fire in your home?

8. If the probability for a flood is 0.0004 and the probability of passing math is 0.73, what is the probability of a flood *and* passing math?

9. *Absentee Rate.* The manager of a company is faced with the prospect of a snowstorm, which would keep 40% of the employees out, and a flu epidemic, which would keep 15% out. What percent of his employees should be expected to show up for work?

10. *Product Success.* A manufacturer is coming out with two new products. The first has a 70% chance of being successful and the second 80%. What is the probability that *either* will be successful?

11. *Automobile Seat Belts.* A survey indicates that 40% of car drivers do not wear seat belts. That is, the probability that a driver is wearing a seat belt is 0.6. In an accident between two cars what is the probability that neither driver was wearing a seat belt? just one driver? [*Hint.* Assume events independent, and draw a tree.]

12. If the probability for divorce in a marriage is $\frac{1}{3}$, what is the probability that two given couples will both stay married or both get divorced? [*Hint.* Draw a tree, assuming events independent.]

***13.** (This problem can be solved using the Addition Theorem for Three Events. It can also be solved and more simply using a Venn Diagram.) Cars can be bought with any of the following options:

    a) An engine package (higher horsepower, etc.)

    b) A suspension package (heavy duty suspension, etc.)

    c) An appointment package (vinyl seats, etc.)

If   65% buy option A,
      40% buy option B,
      40% buy option C,
      30% buy options A and B,
      20% buy options A and C,
      10% buy options B and C,
and 10% buy options A, B, and C,

what percent of the car buyers buy no options at all?

13.5   CONDITIONAL PROBABILITY—MULTIPLICATION THEOREM

In the preceding sections we considered events E_1 and E_2 as *independent*. Now let us consider events E_1 and E_2 as *dependent*. The probability that E_1 occurs *provided* that E_2 occurs is written

$$p(E_1 \text{ provided } E_2) = p(E_1|E_2).$$

Similarly, the probability that E_2 occurs *provided* that E_1 occurs is written

$$p(E_2 \text{ provided } E_1) = p(E_2|E_1).$$

Example 1   A box contains 3 red billiard balls and 2 white billiard balls. One ball is selected, but not replaced, and a second is selected. What is the probability that the second is white given that the first is red?

Solution   Let E_1 = the Event that the first ball drawn is red

and E_2 = the Event that the second ball drawn is white.

Then drawing a tree and letting the ordered pair (R, W) represent the number of red and white balls remaining in the box, we obtain

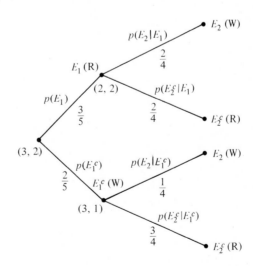

Thus, we find

$$p(\text{First red}) = p(E_1) = \tfrac{3}{5},$$

and

$$p(\text{Second white provided first red}) = p(E_2|E_1) = \tfrac{1}{2}.$$

Now consider the sample space as follows, where we label the red balls R_1, R_2, and R_3, and the white balls W_1, W_2. The first element in a pair represents the first ball selected and the second element, the second ball selected.

(R_1, R_2)	(R_1, R_3)	(R_1, W_1)	(R_1, W_2)
(R_2, R_1)	(R_2, R_3)	(R_2, W_1)	(R_2, W_2)
(R_3, R_1)	(R_3, R_2)	(R_3, W_1)	(R_3, W_2)
(W_1, R_1)	(W_1, R_2)	(W_1, R_3)	(W_1, W_2)
(W_2, R_1)	(W_2, R_2)	(W_2, R_3)	(W_2, W_1)

There are 20 equiprobable outcomes in all. Note that

$$p(\text{First red and second white}) = p(E_1 \cap E_2)$$
$$= \tfrac{6}{20} = \tfrac{3}{10}.$$

Thus, we find that

$$p(\text{First red and second white}) =$$

$$p(\text{First red}) \cdot p(\text{Second white provided first red})$$

or

$$p(E_1 \cap E_2) = p(E_1) \cdot p(E_2|E_1)$$

since

$$\tfrac{3}{10} = \tfrac{3}{5} \cdot \tfrac{1}{2}.$$

This result can be formalized as the

MULTIPLICATION THEOREM FOR ANY TWO EVENTS. If the occurrence of event E_2 depends on the occurrence of event E_1, then the probability for their joint occurrence is given by

$$p(E_1 \cap E_2) = p(E_1) \cdot p(E_2|E_1).$$

Actually, this equation is valid for any two events, dependent or independent.

Assuming $p(E_1) \neq 0$, we can divide and obtain the following alternative form of the Multiplication Theorem.

$$p(E_2|E_1) = \frac{p(E_1 \cap E_2)}{p(E_1)}.$$

Suppose S is the sample space. Then the preceding expression can be expressed as

$$p(E_2|E_1) = \frac{p(E_1 \cap E_2)}{p(E_1)} = \frac{\dfrac{\mathcal{N}(E_1 \cap E_2)}{\mathcal{N}(S)}}{\dfrac{\mathcal{N}(E_1)}{\mathcal{N}(S)}} = \frac{\mathcal{N}(E_1 \cap E_2)}{\mathcal{N}(E_1)}.$$

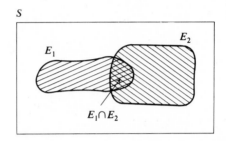

We can interpret this meaningfully by considering a Venn diagram. We can compute $p(E_2|E_1)$ by first determining how many elements are in the *reduced sample space* E_1. This is $\mathcal{N}(E_1)$. Of those elements in E_1, how many are in E_2? This is $\mathcal{N}(E_1 \cap E_2)$. The division of $\mathcal{N}(E_1 \cap E_2)$ by $\mathcal{N}(E_1)$ gives us $p(E_2|E_1)$.

Returning to Example 1, we note that

$$p(\text{First red}) = p(E_1) = \tfrac{12}{20}$$

and

$$p(\text{First red and second white}) = p(E_1 \cap E_2) = \tfrac{6}{20}.$$

It then follows that the *conditional* probability $p(E_2|E_1)$ can be obtained from the Multiplication Theorem as

$$p(\text{Second white provided first red}) = p(E_2|E_1) = \frac{p(E_1 \cap E_2)}{p(E_1)} = \frac{\tfrac{6}{20}}{\tfrac{12}{20}} = \tfrac{6}{12} = \tfrac{1}{2}.$$

Note that we can also obtain this probability by considering the reduced sample space, enclosed in the diagram. It has 12 equiprobable outcomes, of which 6 have the second ball selected as white; that is,

$$\mathcal{N}(E_1) = 12$$

and

$$\mathcal{N}(E_1 \cap E_2) = 6.$$

Thus the conditional probability is

$$p(E_2|E_1) = \frac{N(E_1 \cap E_2)}{N(E_1)} = \frac{6}{12} = \frac{1}{2}.$$

Suppose the events E_1 and E_2 are independent. Then

$$p(E_2|E_1) = \frac{p(E_1 \cap E_2)}{p(E_1)}$$

$$= \frac{p(E_1) \cdot p(E_2)}{p(E_1)}$$

$$= p(E_2),$$

which is consistent with an earlier statement regarding independent events. That is, the occurrence of E_1 does not affect E_2.

Determining Whether Events are Independent

Let us now consider an example where we try to determine whether two events are independent. That is, we will try to decide whether either $p(E_2|E_1) = p(E_2)$ or $p(E_1 \cap E_2) = p(E_1) \cdot p(E_2)$ is true.

Example 2 A medical survey of 1000 people over the age of fifty-five was made to investigate the dependence of smoking on lung cancer. Of those surveyed 500 were steady smokers. Among the smokers, 200 had some form of lung cancer, while among the nonsmokers, only 120 had lung cancer.

a) What is the probability that a person smokes?

b) What is the probability that a person has lung cancer?

c) What is the probability that a person has lung cancer provided that person smokes?

d) Are smoking and lung cancer independent events?

e) What is the probability that a person has lung cancer if that person is a nonsmoker?

Solution Let

$$S = \text{Event of smoking,}$$

$$C = \text{Event of having lung cancer.}$$

To compute the various probabilities, we first organize the data into a table in terms of the number of people involved.

	C	C^c	Total
S	200	300	500
S^c	120	380	500
Total	320	680	1000

This data can also be organized, or represented, on a Venn diagram, as follows.

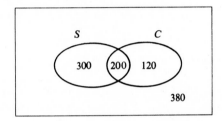

Either representation leads to the desired probabilities.

a) The probability that a person smokes is given by

$$p(S) = \tfrac{500}{1000} = 0.5.$$

b) The probability that a person has lung cancer (whether or not he smokes) is given by

$$p(C) = \tfrac{320}{1000} = 0.32.$$

c) The (conditional) probability that a person has lung cancer given that the person smokes is given by

$$p(C|S) = \frac{p(S \cap C)}{p(S)}.$$

From the table, we see that $p(S \cap C) = \tfrac{200}{1000} = 0.2$, so

$$p(C|S) = \frac{0.2}{0.5} = 0.4.$$

d) Now $p(C|S) = 0.4$ and $p(C) = 0.32$, and since

$$p(C|S) \neq p(C),$$

the events are dependent (not independent).

e) The probability that a person is a nonsmoker is given by

$$p(S^c) = \tfrac{500}{1000} = 0.50;$$

and the probability of the person being a nonsmoker and having lung cancer is given by

$$p(S^c \cap C) = \tfrac{120}{1000} = 0.12.$$

Thus, the probability that a person has lung cancer given that the person is a nonsmoker is given by

$$p(C|S^c) = \frac{p(S^c \cap C)}{p(S^c)} = \frac{0.12}{0.50} = 0.24.$$

Note that

$$p(C|S^c) = 0.24 < 0.40 = p(C|S).$$

This confirms that (from the given data) nonsmokers will have less lung cancer than will smokers.

Consider two *dependent* events E_1 and E_2. E_1 and E_1^c are mutually exclusive, as are E_2 and E_2^c, so that we can draw a tree:

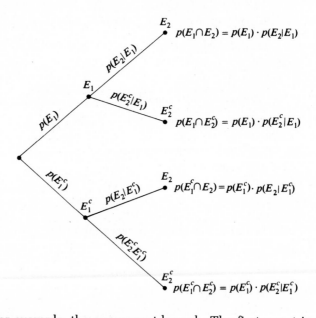

Consider, for example, the uppermost branch. The first event is E_1, and the probability that E_1 occurs is written in along the arc to E_1. If E_1 does happen, then E_2 may or may not happen. For the uppermost branch, E_2 happens, and the quantity written along the second arc represents the probability that E_2 happens provided E_1 happened, that is $p(E_2|E_1)$. From the Multiplication Theorem, the joint probability for both E_1 and E_2 to happen is the product of the two probabilities written along the arcs of the branch. Thus, trees can be used for dependent events (as here), as well as for independent events (as in the preceding section).

Trees need not be limited to two branches or two arcs. Each *branch* of a tree can consist of any number of connected arcs. If some event E_1 precedes another event E_2, then the arc corresponding to E_1 must be closer to the vertex of the tree than is that of E_2. The *joint* probability for all events represented by the connected arcs of a branch of a tree is given by the *product* of the *conditional* probabilities written in along arcs. Thus, if $E_1, E_2, E_3, \ldots, E_n$ are events corresponding to the connected arcs of a branch of a tree, then

$$p(E_1 \cap E_2 \cap E_3 \cap \cdots \cap E_n) = p(E_1) \cdot p(E_2|E_1) \cdot p(E_3|E_1 \cap E_2)$$
$$\cdots p(E_n|E_1 \cap E_2 \cap \cdots \cap E_{n-1}).$$

This is the ***Multiplication Theorem*** for n events.

Example 3   A box contains 20 transistors, 5 of which are defective. Three transistors are taken out at random. What is the probability that at least one is defective? (This is Example 2 of Section 13.2 reconsidered, using the concepts of conditional probability.)

Solution   Let D_i be the event that the ith transistor is defective. Then we obtain the following tree, where the ordered pair (d, g) represents the numbers of defective and good transistors, respectively, remaining in the box.

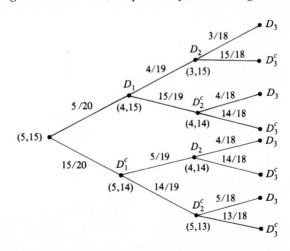

The probability for drawing at least one defective transistor is

$$p_{i \geq 1} = 1 - p_0,$$

where p_0 is the probability that none of the three transistors is defective, $p(D_i^c)$ or

$$p_0 = p(D_1^c \cap D_2^c \cap D_3^c).$$

Using the Multiplication Theorem, we obtain

$$p_0 = p(D_1^c) \cdot p(D_2^c | D_1^c) \cdot p(D_3^c | D_1^c \cap D_2^c).$$

Since there are 5 defective transistors out of a total of 20, there must be 15 nondefective transistors, so that the probability that the first transistor is not defective is

$$p(D_1^c) = \tfrac{15}{20}.$$

If the first transistor is nondefective, then there are still 5 defective transistors remaining out of a reduced total of 19. Thus, there are 14 nondefective transistors and the probability that the second transistor is not defective *provided* the first transistor is not defective is

$$p(D_2^c | D_1^c) = \tfrac{14}{19}.$$

If both the first and second transistors are not defective, then there are 13 remaining nondefective transistors out of 18, so that the conditional probability that the third is not defective, given that the first and second were not defective, is

$$p(D_3^c | D_1^c \cap D_2^c) = \tfrac{13}{18}.$$

These three probabilities

$$p(D_1^c), \qquad p(D_2^c | D_1^c), \qquad p(D_3^c | D_1^c \cap D_2^c)$$

are written in along successive arcs of the lowest branch of the tree. Their *product* is their *joint* probability,

$$p_0 = \tfrac{15}{20} \cdot \tfrac{14}{19} \cdot \tfrac{13}{18} = \tfrac{91}{228}.$$

Then

$$p_{i \geqslant 1} = 1 - p_0 = \tfrac{137}{228}, \qquad \text{as before.}$$

From the tree, it can be seen that the actual calculations involved here are quite simple, although the notation required to describe it becomes quite lengthy.

Each *fork* of a tree represents a partition of the possible outcomes. That is, the arcs out of that vertex represent mutually exclusive events which fill that sample space. Thus, all *branches* represent mutually exclusive events, so that the probability for the occurrence of *either* of several events is the *sum* of the relevant probabilities.

Example 4 Using the data and tree from Example 3, and conditional-probability concepts, what is the probability for drawing:

a) Exactly one defective transistor?

b) Either one or two defective transistors?

Solution a) The probability for drawing one defective transistor is

$$p_1 = p(D_1 \cap D_2^c \cap D_3^c) + p(D_1^c \cap D_2 \cap D_3^c) + p(D_1^c \cap D_2^c \cap D_3).$$

Each of these *joint* probabilities is, from the Multiplication Theorem, a *product* of the conditional probabilities written in along the arcs of appropriate *branches* of the tree. Since each joint event is mutually exclusive of the other, the probability for any *one* of the alternatives to occur is the *sum* of the various alternatives, as indicated by the appropriate branches,

$$p_1 = \left(\tfrac{5}{20} \cdot \tfrac{15}{19} \cdot \tfrac{14}{18}\right) + \left(\tfrac{15}{20} \cdot \tfrac{5}{19} \cdot \tfrac{14}{18}\right) + \left(\tfrac{15}{20} \cdot \tfrac{14}{19} \cdot \tfrac{5}{18}\right) = \tfrac{105}{228}, \qquad \text{as before.}$$

b) Similarly, the probability for drawing two defective transistors is the sum

$$p_2 = p(D_1 \cap D_2 \cap D_3^c) + p(D_1 \cap D_2^c \cap D_3) + p(D_1^c \cap D_2 \cap D_3).$$

Evaluating, using the Multiplication Theorem, we obtain:

$$p_2 = \left(\tfrac{5}{20} \cdot \tfrac{4}{19} \cdot \tfrac{15}{18}\right) + \left(\tfrac{5}{20} \cdot \tfrac{15}{19} \cdot \tfrac{4}{18}\right) + \left(\tfrac{15}{20} \cdot \tfrac{5}{19} \cdot \tfrac{4}{18}\right) = \tfrac{30}{228}, \qquad \text{as before.}$$

If E_i is the probability of drawing i defective transistors, then E_1 and E_2 are mutually exclusive events. The probability for *either* is the *sum*

$$p(E_1 \cup E_2) = p_1 + p_2$$

$$= \tfrac{105}{228} + \tfrac{30}{228} = \tfrac{135}{228},$$

and represents the sum of the probabilities corresponding to the branches of the tree representing one or two defective transistors.

EXERCISE SET 13.5

1. Given $p(E_1 \cap E_2) = 0.0625$ and $p(E_1) = 0.125$, find $p(E_2|E_1)$.

2. Given $p(E_1 \cap E_2) = 0.16$ and $p(E_1) = 0.64$, find $p(E_2|E_1)$.

3. Given $p(E_1 \cap E_2) = \tfrac{12}{45}$ and $p(E_1) = \tfrac{13}{45}$, find $p(E_2|E_1)$.

4. Given $p(E_1 \cap E_2) = \tfrac{16}{35}$ and $p(E_1) = \tfrac{19}{35}$, find $p(E_2|E_1)$.

5. One card is drawn from a well-shuffled deck. What is the probability that it is an ace given that it is a red card?

6. One card is drawn from a well-shuffled deck. What is the probability that it is a king given that it is a black card?

7. A sack contains 5 blue marbles and 3 yellow marbles. One marble is selected, but not replaced. A second is selected. What is the probability that

a) The second is yellow given that the first was blue?

b) The second is blue given that the first was blue?

9. The probability that Democrat A wins in the coming election is $\frac{3}{5}$; that of Democrat B winning the election for a separate seat is $\frac{2}{3}$; that for both is $\frac{1}{2}$. What is the probability that Democrat A wins provided Democrat B wins? Are their elections independent?

11. The manager of a company is faced with a snowstorm, which usually keeps 40% of his employees out, and a flu epidemic, which usually keeps 15% out. If 45% of his employees show up, is the absentee rate what should be expected if the events were independent? Or is it possible that the employees were taking advantage of the situations? If 50% show up?

13. A restaurant buyer orders some food. Due to a failure of refrigeration, 50% of the food was spoiled, and due to a fuel shortage, only 80% of the food could be transported. The buyer says she has received only 40% of her order. Is this reasonable if the two events are independent?

15. A box contains 10 candles, of which 7 are green and 3 purple. Three candles are taken out at random, one at a time. What is the probability that they alternate in color?

17. Statistics indicate that 4% of men are colorblind and 0.3% of women are colorblind. Assuming that a population is half male and half female, what is the probability that a person selected at random is color blind? Draw a tree.

19. A stockyard gets cattle from three ranches. The first ranch supplies 300 cattle, the second 500, and the third 200. An outbreak of hoof-and-mouth disease infects 10%, 15%, and 20% of the cattle, respectively. What percent of the combined stock from the first and third are infected? Overall? [*Hint.* Draw two tree diagrams.]

8. Repeat Exercise 7, where the sack contains 5 blue marbles and 2 yellow marbles.

10. A manufacturer is introducing two new products. From a survey, the first has 70% chance of success, the second 80%, and both 65%. What is the probability that the first product is successful given that the second is? Is the success of one product dependent on that of the other?

12. The manager of a sports arena knows that bad weather will reduce attendance by 30% and another game on TV will reduce attendance by 25%. Both events occur (bad weather and another game on TV) and the attendance is 60% below normal. What drop in attendance would be expected if the events were independent? Or is it possible people are using bad weather as an excuse to stay home and watch TV?

14. The manager of a shop has ordered some stock. Due to a severe rainstorm, 60% of the order was ruined; and due to a bridge washout, only 70% of the order arrived. The foreman claims that only 10% is usable. Is this reasonable if the rain damage and bridge washout are independent events? If only 30% is usable?

16. A class contains 6 men and 12 women. Four people are selected at random, one at a time. What is the probability that the first two are of the same sex and opposite to that of the last two?

18. The employees of a company are $\frac{1}{3}$ women and $\frac{2}{3}$ men. If men are twice as likely as women to have a car and a third of the women have cars, what is the probability that an employee selected at random has a car? Draw a tree.

20. Three manufacturers, A, B, and C, supply respectively, 5, 5, and 6 cases of lightbulbs. Each case contains 24 lightbulbs. Manufacturer A makes lightbulbs which are 1% defective, B 2% defective, and C 5% defective. What percent of the combined order of A and B should be defective? Of the total order? [*Hint.* Draw two tree diagrams.]

21. A person holds a two-tailed coin in one hand and a fair coin in the other. If a hand is chosen at random and that coin is flipped, what is the probability that *tails* shows? Draw a tree.

22. In an urn are three coins, of which two are fair and one is two-tailed. A person reaches in and takes out at random one in his right hand and one in his left hand. What is the probability that the two-tailed coin is in either hand? Draw a tree.

23. In an urn are three coins of which two are fair and one two-tailed. A person reaches in and takes one out in each hand at random. (See Exercise 22.) Someone selects a hand at random. The coin in the hand selected is flipped. What is the probability that tails shows? Draw a tree.

24. Two urns contain 3 and 4 fair coins, respectively. A two-tailed coin is dropped at random into one of these urns. An urn is then selected at random and a coin is taken out at random and flipped. What is the probability for tails to show? [*Hint.* How many stages does the tree have?]

25. One box contains 3 brass washers and 2 steel washers. Another box contains 4 brass washers and 3 steel ones. A box is chosen at random and a washer is taken out at random. The washer is then put into the other box (the one not chosen). A box is again chosen at random and a washer taken out at random. What is the probability it is brass? Draw a tree. What is the probability the same washer is picked both times?

26. A savings-and-loan institution classifies borrowers as AAA, AA, or A risks. AAA risks constitute 10% of the borrowers and default 5% of the time. AA risks constitute 25% and default 10% of the time. A risks constitute 65% and default 20% of the time. If a borrower is selected at random, what is the probability he will default? Draw a tree.

27. A multiple-choice exam is being given. If a student knows the answer, he gets it right. If the student doesn't know the answer, he picks at random any of the four possible answers. It is also possible he "isn't sure" but has it narrowed down to one of two answers. If a student knows 80% of the answers and does not know 10% at all, what is the probability that he will get an arbitrary question correct? Draw a tree.

28. In a certain city, registered voters are 40% Republican, 35% Democrat, and 25% independent. A Republican and a Democratic candidate are running for office. From a survey, 70% of the Republicans and 80% of the Democrats will vote for their party's candidate, while 75% of the independents will vote Democrat and the rest Republican. Which candidate has the better chance of winning, and by what odds? Draw a tree.

29. As in Exercise 28: If a voter is selected at random, what is the probability he or she will switch vote (that is, a Republican voting Democratic or a Democrat voting Republican)?

13.6   CONDITIONAL PROBABILITY—BAYES' THEOREM

In order to illustrate Bayes' Theorem, consider first:

Example 1 Three manufacturers I, II, and III supply all the calculators to a particular store. I supplies 50, with 4% defective, II supplies 60 with 1% defective, and III supplies 30 with 2% defective. If a calculator is purchased at random, what is the probability that it is defective?

Solution   Let

$$D = \text{event that the calculator is defective,}$$
$$E_1 = \text{event that it came from I,}$$
$$E_2 = \text{event that it came from II,}$$
$$E_3 = \text{event that it came from III.}$$

We first draw a tree noting that the events E_1, E_2, and E_3 are mutually exclusive. Here we use the Multiplication Theorem (Section 13.5) to rewrite the joint probabilities.

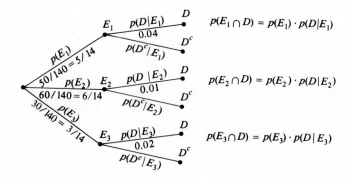

Since the outcome can be either D or D^c, the set of outcomes D is actually a *reduced sample space* which can be expressed as a union of mutually exclusive events:

$$D = (E_1 \cap D) \cup (E_2 \cap D) \cup (E_3 \cap D).$$

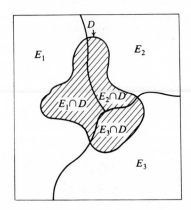

Then the probability that the calculator is defective, $p(D)$, is the sum:

$$p(D) = p(E_1 \cap D) + p(E_2 \cap D) + p(E_3 \cap D)$$

$$= p(E_1) \cdot p(D|E_1) + p(E_2) \cdot p(D|E_2) + p(E_3) \cdot p(D|E_3)$$

$$= \tfrac{5}{14}(0.04) + \tfrac{6}{14}(0.01) + \tfrac{3}{14}(0.02)$$

$$= \tfrac{5}{14} \cdot \tfrac{4}{100} + \tfrac{6}{14} \cdot \tfrac{1}{100} + \tfrac{3}{14} \cdot \tfrac{2}{100}$$

$$= \tfrac{32}{1400} = \tfrac{4}{175}.$$

Now with Example 1 in mind, consider:

Example 2   Given the data of Example 1 with a calculator purchased at random. What is the probability that if it is defective, it came from manufacturer I? II? III?

Solution   The probability that if a calculator is defective it came from manufacturer I is $p(E_1|D)$; from II, $p(E_2|D)$; from III, $p(E_3|D)$.

To determine any of these conditional probabilities, we use the reduced sample space D with probability $p(D)$. Of these $E_1 \cap D$ are defective and came from *I*. From the Multiplication Theorem (Section 8.5), we find $p(E_1|D)$:

$$p(E_1|D) = \frac{p(E_1 \cap D)}{p(D)} = \frac{p(E_1) \cdot p(D|E_1)}{p(D)}.$$

Using probabilities already computed in Example 1, we obtain:

$$p(E_1|D) = \frac{\tfrac{5}{14} \cdot \tfrac{4}{100}}{\tfrac{32}{1400}} = \tfrac{20}{32} = \tfrac{5}{8}.$$

Similarly, the probability that if the calculator is defective it came from manufacturer II, $p(E_2|D)$, is given by:

$$p(E_2|D) = \frac{p(E_2) \cdot p(D|E_2)}{p(D)} = \frac{\tfrac{6}{14} \cdot \tfrac{1}{100}}{\tfrac{32}{1400}} = \tfrac{6}{32} = \tfrac{3}{16}.$$

And the probability that if the calculator is defective it came from manufacturer III, $p(E_3|D)$, is given by

$$p(E_3|D) = \frac{p(E_3) \cdot p(D|E_3)}{p(D)} = \frac{\tfrac{3}{14} \cdot \tfrac{2}{100}}{\tfrac{32}{1400}} = \tfrac{6}{32} = \tfrac{3}{16}.$$

Alternately, using the expression for $p(D)$ from Example 1, we can write:

$$p(E_1|D) = \frac{p(E_1 \cap D)}{p(E_1 \cap D) + p(E_2 \cap D) + p(E_3 \cap D)}$$

Each of these joint probabilities can be obtained from the Multiplication Theorem, so that we can write

$$p(E_1|D) = \frac{p(E_1) \cdot p(D|E_1)}{p(E_1) \cdot p(D|E_1) + p(E_2) \cdot p(D|E_2) + p(E_3) \cdot p(D|E_3)}$$

This is Bayes' Theorem for three events.

Note that here we first calculated $p(D)$ and then $p(E_1|D)$ using the concept of reduced sample space. On the other hand Bayes' Theorem incorporates this concept implicitly so that one calculates $p(E_1|D)$ directly. Either way the result is the same but the first method may be easier to remember.

Note that the probabilities

$$p(D|E_1) = 0.04,$$
$$p(D|E_2) = 0.01,$$

and

$$p(D|E_3) = 0.02$$

represent probabilities "before" the calculator is purchased. These are sometimes called *a priori* probabilities. The probabilities, given that a calculator has been purchased,

$$p(E_1|D) = \tfrac{5}{8}, \qquad p(E_2|D) = \tfrac{3}{16}, \qquad p(E_3|D) = \tfrac{3}{16},$$

can be thought of as "after," or *a posteriori*, probabilities. That is, information known beforehand allows one to compute probabilities of what will later occur.

The general Bayes' Theorem for n events is as follows.

BAYES' THEOREM.   **For any events E_1, E_2, ..., E_n which partition a sample space, if the probability of each event is greater than 0 and if the events are conditional on some event C with $p(C) > 0$, then for each value of i ($i = 1, 2, ..., n$),**

$$p(E_i|C) = \frac{p(E_i \cap C)}{p(E_1 \cap C) + p(E_2 \cap C) + \cdots + p(E_n \cap C)}$$

$$= \frac{p(E_i) \cdot p(C|E_i)}{p(E_1) \cdot p(C|E_1) + p(E_2) \cdot p(C|E_2) + \cdots + p(E_n) \cdot p(C|E_n)}.$$

Example 3   The public relations agent for a small political party wants to convince people that more people support his party than indicated by the 10% of the vote received by the party for the past three elections. The agent chooses for a survey an issue which is supported by 75% of his party and opposed by 75% of the other parties. If a voter is selected at random, what is the probability that:

a) The voter supports the issue?

b) If the voter supports the issue, the voter also supports the party?

Solution   Let

P represent voters of the party of the PR agent,

P^c represent voters of the opposition,

S represent the voters who support the issue, and

S^c represent the voters who oppose the issue.

Then we can draw a tree to represent this situation and incorporate the data:

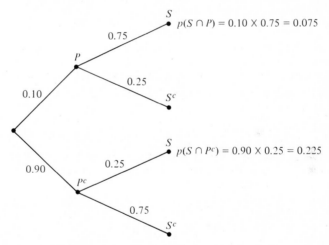

a) The probability that a voter supports the issue is

$$p(S) = p(S \cap P) + p(S \cap P^c) = 0.075 + 0.225 = 0.30.$$

b) The probability that if a voter supports the issue, he or she also supports the party is

$$p(P|S)\frac{p(S \cap P)}{p(S)} = \frac{0.075}{0.30} = \frac{1}{4} = 0.25.$$

Note how different this probability is from the probability that a voter supports the party, $p(P) = 0.10$. The results of this calculation can be used quite deceptively to make support for the party seem greater than it is.

EXERCISE SET 13.6

1. Statistics indicate that 4% of men are colorblind and 0.3% of women are colorblind. Assume that a population is half male and half female. If a person selected at random is colorblind, what is the probability the person is a woman? (See Exercise 17, Exercise Set 13.5.)

2. The employees of a company are $\frac{1}{3}$ women and $\frac{2}{3}$ men. Men are twice as likely as women to have a car and a third of the women have cars. If an employee selected at random has a car, what is the probability that the employee is a woman? (See Exercise 18, Exercise Set 13.5.)

3. A stockyard gets cattle from three ranches. The first supplies 300 cattle, the second 500, and the third 200. Due to an outbreak of hoof-and-mouth disease 10%, 15%, and 20% of the cattle, respectively, have the disease. If an animal selected at random from those shipped by the first and third ranches is infected, what is the probability it came from the third ranch? If an animal selected at random from all three ranches is infected, what is the probability it came from the third ranch? (See Exercise 19, Exercise Set 13.5.)

4. Three manufacturers A, B, and C, supply, respectively, 5, 5, and 6 cases of lightbulbs. Each case contains 24 lightbulbs. Manufacturer A makes lightbulbs that are 1% defective, B's are 2% defective, and C's are 5% defective. If a lightbulb selected at random from those provided by manufacturers A and B is defective, what is the probability it came from B? selected from all three? (See Exercise 20, Exercise Set 13.5.)

5. A person holds a two-tailed coin in one hand and a fair coin in the other. A hand is chosen at random and the coin is flipped. If tails shows, what is the probability that the coin is two-tailed? (See Exercise 21, Exercise Set 13.5.)

6. In an urn are three coins of which two are fair and one is two-tailed. A person reaches in and takes out at random one coin in each hand. A hand is then selected at random and the coin in that hand is flipped. If tails shows, what is the probability the coin is fair? (See Exercise 22, Exercise Set 13.5.)

7. Two urns contain 3 and 4 fair coins, respectively. A two-tailed coin is dropped at random into one of these urns. An urn is then selected at random and a coin is taken out at random and flipped. If tails shows, what is the probability that the coin came from the urn with the two-tailed coin? (See Exercise 24, Exercise Set 13.5.)

8. One box contains 3 brass washers and 2 steel washers. Another box contains 4 brass washers and 3 steel ones. A box is chosen at random and a washer is taken out at random and put into the other box (the one not chosen). A box is again chosen at random and a washer taken out at random. If the washer selected is brass, what is the probability that it came from the box from which a washer had been removed? (See Exercise 25, Exercise Set 13.5.)

9. A savings-and-loan institution classifies borrowers as AAA, AA, or A risks. AAA risks constitute 10% of their borrowers and default 5% of the time. AA risks constitute 25% and default 10%. A risks constitute 65% and default 20%. If a borrower defaults, what is the probability he was a AAA risk? (See Exercise 26, Exercise Set 13.5.)

10. A multiple-choice exam is being given. If a student knows the answer, he gets it right. If he doesn't know the answer, he picks at random any of the four given choices. It is also possible he "isn't sure" but has it narrowed down to one of two answers. A student knows 80% of the answers and does not know 10% at all. If he gets a question correct, what is the probability he knew the answer? (See Exercise 27, Exercise Set 13.5.)

11. In drilling for oil, it is known that terrain with geological characteristics A yields oil once in 10 strikes and constitutes 50% of available land. Terrain with characteristics B yields oil once in 5 strikes and constitutes 30% of the available land. Terrain with characteristics C yields oil once in 4 strikes and constitutes 20% of the available land. If a site is selected at random, what is the probability for an oil strike? If oil is struck, what is the probability it came from land with characteristics A?

13. A test for mononucleosis administered to students among whom 10% have the disease is 90% accurate; that is, 90% of those with the disease will have a positive reaction and vice versa. If a student has a positive reaction, what is the probability he does not have mononucleosis?

12. Patients entering a clinic have one of three (mutually exclusive) diseases A, B, or C. They also have one or more of the symptoms of fever, sore throat, or faintness. From the records of the clinic, 25% of the entering patients have disease A with symptoms of fever and sore throat, 35% disease B with symptoms of fever and faintness, and 40% disease C with all three symptoms. What is the probability that an undiagnosed patient has disease C given that he has a sore throat?

14. As in Exercise 13, how accurate must the test be such that if a student has a positive reaction, the probability he does not have mononucleosis is 0.1?

■ ──────────────────────────────────────

15. In a laboratory there are 3 boxes (numbered I, II, and III). In the first are 6 white mice, in the second 3 white and 3 black, and in the third 6 black mice. While cleaning up, an assistant bumps into one box (at random) and a mouse (at random) escapes. This mouse is then caught but the assistant doesn't know which box to put it back in. Therefore, he decides to take a mouse from each box in turn (I, II, then III). If the two mice match in color, he puts both into that box; otherwise, he goes on to the next box to try for a match. What is the probability that the mouse is put back into the box from which it escaped? Draw a tree. If the mouse is put into the third box, what is the probability it came from that box?

17. *Quality Control, Advertising.* A box of 6 clocks contains 3 defective ones. If 3 are chosen at random what is the probability that more than one is defective? In an effort to minimize the apparent number of defective clocks, if *one* or *no* clock chosen is defective, the sample is displayed. However, if more than one clock is defective, the defective clocks are replaced and that many are again drawn at random. Draw the tree. What is the probability that only one clock in the sample displayed is defective? If only one clock in the sample displayed is defective, what is the probability that some clocks had been redrawn?

16. As in Exercise 15, but two mice (instead of one) escape from the same box. If they are both white, he puts them in the first box. If they are one of each color, he puts them in the second box. If they are both black, he puts them in the third box. What is the probability that he puts them back in the correct box? Draw a tree. If he puts them in the third box, what is the probability that they came from that box?

18. As in Exercise 17, but the new clocks are redrawn *before* the old ones are replaced?

19. The winner of the National League playoffs is the first team to win three out of five games. The two teams A and B are evenly matched. What is the probability team A will win if:

a) Team A loses the first game?

b) Team A loses one of the first two games?

c) Team A loses the first two games?

d) Check a baseball almanac to compare these theoretical probabilities with the experimental probabilities you can determine from the almanac.

CHAPTER 13 REVIEW

1. Suppose 2 cards are drawn at random from a well-shuffled deck of cards. What is the probability that both are clubs?

3. Find $p(E^c)$ if

a) $p(E) = \frac{11}{34}$

b) $p(E) = 0.63$

5. Suppose

$$p(E_1) = 0.34,$$
$$p(E_2) = 0.42,$$

and

$$p(E_1 \cap E_2) = 0.13.$$

Find $p(E_1 \cup E_2)$.

7. An old sea chest contains 10 bars of silver and 5 bars of gold. If 3 bars are drawn at random, what is the probability that exactly one is gold?

2. On a roll of a pair of dice, what is the probability of getting a total of

a) 8? b) 7? c) 11? d) 14?

4. One card is drawn at random from a well-shuffled deck.

a) What are the odds for a red ace to occur?

b) What are the odds against a red ace occurring?

6. Suppose

$$p(E_1) = 0.34,$$
$$p(E_2) = 0.42,$$

and that E_1 and E_2 are mutually exclusive. Find $p(E_1 \cup E_2)$.

8. A black die and a white die are rolled.

a) What is the probability that a 2 is obtained on the black die?

b) What is the probability that an even number is obtained on the white die?

c) What is the probability that a 2 is obtained on the black die *and* an even number on the white die?

d) Does
$$p(2 \text{ on black and even on white}) =$$
$$p(2 \text{ on black}) \cdot p(\text{Even on white})?$$

9. A sack contains 4 red and 4 yellow marbles. One marble is drawn and replaced, and a second is drawn. What is the probability that the

a) first is red?

b) second is yellow?

c) first is red *and* the second is yellow?

11. A fair dime and nickel are flipped and one fair die is rolled. What is the probability that the coins show a head on the dime and a tail on the nickel and the die shows a 4?

13. A coin is flipped four times. What is the probability that the flips come out in the order H, H, T, H?

15. In Example 6, Section 13.3, what is the probability that at least two of the examiners find a defective transistor?

17. Suppose the probability that a woman lives to be 70 is 0.81 and that she will go bald is 0.37. The probability that she will live to be 70 and also go bald is 0.28. What is the probability that she will live to be 70 or go bald?

19. *Public Health.* A country is afflicted with two kinds of flu during one winter. The probability that a person will get both kinds of flu is 0.43. The probability that a person will get only one kind of flu is 0.51. What is the probability that a person will get neither kind of flu?

10. Given that E_1 and E_2 are independent, find $p(E_1 \cap E_2)$ where

a) $p(E_1) = \frac{3}{4}$, $p(E_2) = \frac{2}{9}$;

b) $p(E_1) = 0.44$, $p(E_2) = 0.3$.

12. A die is rolled three times. What is the probability of getting a 2 on all three rolls?

14. The probability that a student passes Economics is $\frac{4}{5}$ and the probability that the student passes Finite Mathematics is $\frac{2}{3}$. Assuming no dependence between passing or failing one course and passing or failing the other course, what is the probability that the student:

a) Passes both courses?

b) Passes neither course?

c) Passes one of the courses?

16. From Table 8.1, determine the probability that two or more students in your class have the same birthday. If your class is large (more than 40 students), divide the class into two groups and examine the results for each half as well as for the whole class.

18. A farmer faces a season of drought with a probability of 0.1 and an insect invasion with a probability of 0.3.

a) What is the probability that either or both events will occur?

b) What is the probability that neither event will occur? [*Hint.*

$$p(E_1^c \cap E_2^c) = p(E_1^c) \cdot p(E_2^c).]$$

20. Given

$$p(E_1 \cap E_2) = 0.125,$$

and

$$p(E_1) = 0.625,$$

find $p(E_2|E_1)$.

21. A sociological survey of 1000 people who were married at one time was made to investigate the dependence of age of marriage upon divorce. Of those surveyed 500 were divorced. Among those divorced, 280 were married as teenagers, while among those never divorced, only 190 were married as teenagers.

   a) What is the probability that a person gets divorced?

   b) What is the probability that a person was married as a teenager?

   c) What is the probability that a person was married as a teenager given that the person gets divorced?

   d) Are teenage marriages and divorce independent events?

   e) What is the probability that a person was married as a teenager given that person does not get divorced?

23. Three manufacturers A, B, and C supply all the fire alarms to a group of residences. A supplies 200 with 3% defective, B supplies 150 with 4% defective, and C supplies 100 with 5% defective. If an alarm is selected at random, what is the probability

   a) It is defective?

   b) If it is defective, it came from A? B? C?

25. Find $p(E_1 \cup E_2)$, where E_1 and E_2 are mutually exclusive, $p(E_1) = 0.34$ and $p(E_2) = 0.56$.

27. Find $p(E_1 \cup E_2)$, where E_1 and E_2 are independent, $p(E_1) = 0.11$ and $p(E_2) = 0.42$.

29. What is the probability of getting a 2 or 3 on a single roll of a die?

22. The probability that a coed passes Economics is $\frac{1}{4}$, that she passes Mathematics is $\frac{2}{3}$, and that she passes both is $\frac{3}{5}$. Are the events of passing these two courses independent? That is, does

$$p(E_1 \cap E_2) = p(E_1) \cdot p(E_2)?$$

24. a) Find $p(E^c)$ if $p(E) = \frac{23}{39}$.

   b) What are the odds *for* the event E?

   c) What are the odds *against* the event E?

26. Find $p(E_1 \cap E_2)$, where E_1 and E_2 are independent, $p(E_1) = \frac{11}{17}$ and $p(E_2) = \frac{34}{55}$.

28. a) Find $p(E_2|E_1)$, where
$$p(E_1 \cap E_2) = 0.0043$$
and $p(E_1) = 0.125$.

   b) Are the events E_1 and E_2 of (a) independent given that $p(E_2) = 0.1$?

30. A shipment of 125 stereos contains 5 defective stereos. Two stereos are selected at random. What is the probability that:

   a) Both are defective?

   b) Exactly one is defective?

   c) Neither is defective?

31. For an unfair coin, $p(H) = \frac{3}{5}$ and $p(T) = \frac{2}{5}$. The coin is flipped five times. What is the probability that the flips come out in the order H, T, T, T, H?

33. A manufacturer is introducing two new products. From a marketing survey, the first has an 80% chance of success, the second 60%, and both 48%. What is the probability that the first product is successful, given that the second is? Is the success of one product dependent on that of the other?

32. A city is afflicted with two kinds of disease during one summer. The probability that a person gets both diseases is 0.28. The probability that a person gets neither of the diseases is 0.41. What is the probability that a person gets exactly one of the diseases?

34. Three manufacturers supply all the stereos to a particular music store. A supplies 20, with 5% defective, B supplies 70 with 3% defective, and C supplies 10 with 8% defective. If a stereo is purchased at random, what is the probability that:

a) It is defective?

b) If it is defective, it came from A? from B? from C?

PROBABILITY FUNCTIONS–STATISTICS

14.1 DISCRETE RANDOM VARIABLES—PROBABILITY FUNCTIONS

It is convenient in the study of probability and statistics to introduce the concepts of "random variable" and "probability function." We shall define them formally after illustrating them.

Example 1 Two fair dice are rolled. The sum of the numbers showing is noted. What is the random variable? the probability function for this random variable?

Solution A fair die has 6 sides each of which has the same probability to show (face up). The following is a list of the 6 · 6 or 36 possible outcomes, the sample space, as developed in Example 8 of Section 13.1:

(1, 1)	(1, 2)	(1, 3)	(1, 4)	(1, 5)	(1, 6)
(2, 1)	(2, 2)	(2, 3)	(2, 4)	(2, 5)	(2, 6)
(3, 1)	(3, 2)	(3, 3)	(3, 4)	(3, 5)	(3, 6)
(4, 1)	(4, 2)	(4, 3)	(4, 4)	(4, 5)	(4, 6)
(5, 1)	(5, 2)	(5, 3)	(5, 4)	(5, 5)	(5, 6)
(6, 1)	(6, 2)	(6, 3)	(6, 4)	(6, 5)	(6, 6)

Now let us form a table listing those outcomes (a, b) whose sum $a + b$ is a particular value x:

x	2	3	4	5	6	7	8	9	10	11	12
(a, b)	(1, 1)	(1, 2) (2, 1)	(1, 3) (2, 2) (3, 1)	(1, 4) (2, 3) (3, 2) (4, 1)	(1, 5) (2, 4) (3, 3) (4, 2) (5, 1)	(1, 6) (2, 5) (3, 4) (4, 3) (5, 2) (6, 1)	(2, 6) (3, 5) (4, 4) (5, 3) (6, 2)	(3, 6) (4, 5) (5, 4) (6, 3)	(4, 6) (5, 5) (6, 4)	(5, 6) (6, 5)	(6, 6)

Counting the number of times a given sum is obtained, we obtain a table of frequencies f:

x	2	3	4	5	6	7	8	9	10	11	12
f	1	2	3	4	5	6	5	4	3	2	1

Converting these frequencies into probabilities p as in Section 13.1, we obtain the table:

x	2	3	4	5	6	7	8	9	10	11	12
p	$\frac{1}{36}$	$\frac{2}{36}$	$\frac{3}{36}$	$\frac{4}{36}$	$\frac{5}{36}$	$\frac{6}{36}$	$\frac{5}{36}$	$\frac{4}{36}$	$\frac{3}{36}$	$\frac{2}{36}$	$\frac{1}{36}$

Here we have taken the *random variable X* (upper case) to be the "sum of the numbers showing" and x (lower case) to be the *value* of the random variable. A *particular* value of the random variable is denoted by x_i.

Note that $p_1 + p_2 + \cdots + p_n = 1$, or simply,

$$\sum_{i=1}^{n} p_i = 1,$$

for probability functions.

In general, consider an experiment with n outcomes.

A *random variable X* is a *rule* (function) which assigns a numerical value x_i to each outcome.

As in the preceding Example, the outcomes of an experiment need not be equiprobable.

To each outcome we assign not only a number x_i but also a probability p_i. This set of all ordered pairs $\{(x_i, p_i)|i = 1, 2, \ldots, n\}$ for example, as

displayed in the preceding table, is called the *probability frequency function** of the random variable *X*, or simply, the *probability function.*

Many of the problems in the preceding chapter involved random drawings

  i) of objects restricted to *two* kinds,

 ii) simultaneously (in sequence and *without* replacement).

Specifically, consider the following example.

Example 2 *Quality Control.* Given a box of 20 transistors of which 5 are defective. Three are drawn at random and the number defective is noted. What is the random variable? What is the probability function for this random variable?

Solution The random variable *X* here is the number of defective transistors drawn. It takes on the values $x = 0, 1, 2, 3$. The probability of drawing a particular number x_i of defective transistors is $p(x_i)$ or p_x.

Thus, to obtain p_0 we calculate the probability of drawing 0 defective transistors out of 5 available and 3 nondefective transistors out of 15 available; that is

$$p_0 = \frac{\binom{5}{0}\binom{15}{3}}{\binom{20}{3}} = \frac{91}{228}.$$

Similarly, we obtain:

$$p_1 = \frac{\binom{5}{1}\binom{15}{2}}{\binom{20}{3}} = \frac{105}{228},$$

$$p_2 = \frac{\binom{5}{2}\binom{15}{1}}{\binom{20}{3}} = \frac{30}{228},$$

$$p_3 = \frac{\binom{5}{3}\binom{15}{0}}{\binom{20}{3}} = \frac{2}{228}.$$

---

* Or probability *density* function.

Thus, we obtain the probability function given in the following table:

x	0	1	2	3
p	$\dfrac{91}{228}$	$\dfrac{105}{228}$	$\dfrac{30}{228}$	$\dfrac{2}{228}$

Example 2 and Margin Exercise 2 just considered have certain characteristics in common. Specifically, such problems have

s objects,

m of which have a particular characteristic and

$s - m$ do not have this characteristic;

n objects are drawn at random and

r of those drawn have this characteristic.

If we take as the random variable R the number of those drawn that have this characteristic, then the values that this random variable can assume are $r = 0, 1, 2, \ldots , n$ and the probability that r have this characteristic is:

$$p_r = H(s, m; n, r) = \frac{\dbinom{m}{r}\dbinom{s - m}{n - r}}{\dbinom{s}{n}},$$

where

$$0 \leqslant r \leqslant n \leqslant s \quad \text{and} \quad 0 \leqslant r \leqslant m \leqslant s;$$

p_r is called the *hypergeometric* probability. We have already used it in Chapter 13. All we have done here is to give it a name.

EXERCISE SET 14.1

1. The sales force of a business consists of 20 people, half of whom are men and the other half women. Four people are chosen at random. What is the probability function for the number of women chosen? (See Exercise 31, Set 13.1.)

2. A union has 21 members, 14 of whom are women and the other 7 are men. Three people are chosen at random. What is the probability function for the number of women chosen? men? (See Exercise 32, Set 13.1.)

3. Eight people apply for a job, 5 men and 3 women. Four are hired at random. What is the probability function for the number of women hired?

4. Eight people apply for a job, 4 men and 4 women. Four are hired at random. What is the probability function for the number of women hired?

5. *Quality Control.* A crate of 20 machine parts contains 6 defective parts. Five parts are drawn at random. What is the probability function for the number of defective parts drawn?

7. If a party fields 3 candidates for office, each opposed by an equiprobable candidate, what is the probability function for the number of winners for the party in an election?

9. *Quality Control.* A wine rack contains 7 bottles of red wine and 2 of white wine. If 3 bottles are taken out at random, what is the probability function for the number of bottles of white wine? red wine?

11. One cage contains 3 white mice and 2 black ones and another case contains 2 white mice and 3 black ones. A cage is chosen at random and 3 mice are taken out at random. What is the probability function for the number of white mice in the sample?

13. There are 2 cages of mice as in Exercise 11. A white mouse escapes from an unidentified cage. Then a cage is chosen at random and 3 mice are taken out at random. What is the probability function for the number of white mice in the sample?

15. The winner in a World Series is the first team to win 4 out of seven games. What is the probability function for the number of games in the series if the two teams are evenly matched?

17. Two gamblers toss fair coins. One wins the toss if they match, the other if they don't. The winner of the game is the first to win two tosses in a row. What is the probability function for the number of tosses required for someone to win the game?

6. Five workers in a group of 25 have mononucleosis. Three workers are chosen at random. What is the probability distribution for the number who have mono? (See Exercise 8, Set 13.2.)

8. As in Exercise 7, but the first candidate has a probability of $\frac{1}{3}$ to win, the second $\frac{1}{2}$, and the third $\frac{2}{3}$?

10. *Quality Control.* A case of 12 bottles of wine contains 3 which have spoiled. If 3 bottles are taken out at random, what is the distribution function for the number of bottles of spoiled wine among those drawn? if the case contains 4 spoiled bottles?

12. There are 2 cages of mice as in Exercise 11. A cage is chosen at random. A mouse of unidentified color escapes from the chosen cage. Then 3 mice are taken out at random. What is the probability function for the number of white mice in the sample?

14. There are 2 cages of mice as in Exercise 11. All the mice escape and are put back at random, 5 to each cage. A cage is then selected at random and 3 mice are taken out at random. What is the probability function for the number of white mice in the sample?

16. As in Exercise 15, but the winning team must win by two games. After 7 games, one extra game is to be played if one team is winning by only one game but the series ends if there is a 4-4 tie?

18. Three gamblers each toss a fair coin. The winner of a toss is the odd man, if there is one. The winner of the game is the first one to win two tosses in a row. What is the probability function for the number of tosses required for someone to win the game?

14.2 AVERAGE AND EXPECTED VALUE

Frequently we have some data and would like some way of determining a "center" point. This is usually done by computing the *mean* or *average* value.

▦ **Example 1** The test scores for a particular class are 76, 72, 88, 90, 74, 83, 52, 79, 81, 84, and 69. What is the average score?

Solution   The mean or average value $\bar{x}$ is simply the sum of the various test scores divided by the number of test scores; that is,

$$\bar{x} = \tfrac{1}{11}(76 + 72 + 88 + 90 + 74 + 83 + 52 + 79 + 81 + 84 + 69)$$

$$= \tfrac{1}{11}(848)$$

$$= 77.09.$$

In general, if there are n data points $x_1, x_2, \ldots, x_n$, then their *average* value is:

$$\bar{x} = \frac{1}{n}(x_1 + x_2 \cdots x_n),$$

or, using summation notation,

$$\bar{x} = \frac{1}{n}\sum_{i=1}^{n} x_i.$$

Sometimes a given data point is present more than once.

▦ **Example 2**   On the fourteenth hole of the 1976 Andy Williams San Diego Open Golf Tournament, scores were obtained as given in the following table. What was the average score on this hole?

Score	Number with score
3 (Eagle)	1
4 (Birdie)	29
5 (Par)	176
6 (Bogie)	30
7 (Double bogie)	2

Solution   Here each score x_i occurs with frequency f_i (number with a particular score). The total number of scores is:

$$N = 1 + 29 + 176 + 30 + 2 = 238,$$

so that the average score is

$$\bar{x} = \tfrac{1}{238}(1 \cdot 3 + 29 \cdot 4 + 176 \cdot 5 + 30 \cdot 6 + 2 \cdot 7)$$

$$= \tfrac{1193}{238}$$

$$= 5.0126 \quad \text{(to four decimal places)}.$$

Note that the average score is quite close to par (5).

In general, if each data point x_i occurs with frequency f_i, then the total number of data points is:

$$N = f_1 + f_2 + \cdots + f_n = \sum_{i=1}^{n} f_i,$$

and the average value is given by:

$$\bar{x} = \frac{1}{N} \sum_{i=1}^{n} f_i x_i.$$

Example 3   Two fair dice are rolled. The sum of the numbers showing is noted. The random variable X corresponds to the sum.

a) Suppose we roll the dice 144 times and obtain the following frequency table.

x	2	3	4	5	6	7	8	9	10	11	12
f	4	9	12	17	21	23	19	16	13	7	3

What is the average value?

b) Suppose we roll the dice 1440 times and obtain the following frequency table.

x	2	3	4	5	6	7	8	9	10	11	12
f	38	84	119	163	207	239	193	159	122	75	41

What is the average value?

Solution   a) The average value of x is given by:

$$\bar{x} = \frac{1}{144} \sum_{i=1}^{11} x_i f_i = \frac{1}{144}(994) = 6.90278.$$

b) The average value of x is given by:

$$\bar{x} = \frac{1}{1440} \sum_{i=1}^{11} x_i f_i = \frac{1}{1440}(10{,}046) = 6.97639.$$

We might call the average values calculated in Example 3 *experimental estimates* of the "center" point. Suppose we had no data, or did not want to bother to obtain any and we wanted to determine a theoretical "center" point. Then we start with the probability distribution function, if such is available. It is. We considered it in Example 1 of the preceding section:

x	2	3	4	5	6	7	8	9	10	11	12
p	$\frac{1}{36}$	$\frac{2}{36}$	$\frac{3}{36}$	$\frac{4}{36}$	$\frac{5}{36}$	$\frac{6}{36}$	$\frac{5}{36}$	$\frac{4}{36}$	$\frac{3}{36}$	$\frac{2}{36}$	$\frac{1}{36}$

Note that the average value can be expressed as

$$\bar{x} = \frac{1}{N} \sum_{i=1}^{n} x_i f_i = \sum_{i=1}^{n} \frac{f_i}{N} x_i.$$

In the long run, after many rolls of the dice, we would expect that the probability p_i for a given outcome to be quite close to the quotient of the frequency f_i for that outcome and the total number of trials N:

$$p_i \approx \frac{f_i}{N}.$$

Thus,

$$\sum_{i=1}^{n} \frac{f_i}{N} x_i \approx \sum_{i=1}^{n} p_i x_i.$$

Then, rather than compute an *average value* from the data, we can compute an *expected value* from the probability function. This is given by:

$$E(X) = \mu = \sum_{i=1}^{n} p_i x_i,$$

where μ is the Greek letter "mu."

Here x_i are now the values of the random variable. Note that we use $\bar{x}$ to denote the average value computed from experimental data and μ to denote the expected value computed theoretically from the probability function.

The expected value of the sum of the dice is given by

$$E(X) = 2 \cdot \tfrac{1}{36} + 3 \cdot \tfrac{2}{36} + 4 \cdot \tfrac{3}{36} + 5 \cdot \tfrac{4}{36} + 6 \cdot \tfrac{5}{36}$$

$$+ 7 \cdot \tfrac{6}{36} + 8 \cdot \tfrac{5}{36} + 9 \cdot \tfrac{4}{36} + 10 \cdot \tfrac{3}{36} + 11 \cdot \tfrac{2}{36} + 12 \cdot \tfrac{1}{36},$$

$$E(X) = 7.$$

In the long run, the more we roll the dice, the closer we "expect" the average values to be to the expected value. Note in Example 3 that the average values 6.90278 and 6.97639 are getting closer to the expected value 7.

For the *hypergeometric* frequency function (see preceding section), it can be shown that the expected value is given by

$$E(X) = n \cdot p$$

where

$$p = \frac{m}{s}.$$

As before, n is the number of trials to draw a random number of objects of which m out of s have a particular characteristic, so that p represents the probability of drawing one with this characteristic *initially*.

Example 4   *Quality Control.* Given a box of 20 transistors, of which 5 are defective. Three are drawn at random and the number defective is noted. What is the expected number of defective transistors in the sample? Use both the general formula and the special one for hypergeometric probabilities. [See Example 2, Section 14.1.]

Solution   From Example 2, Section 14.1, we have the probability function

x	0	1	2	3
p	$\frac{91}{228}$	$\frac{105}{228}$	$\frac{30}{228}$	$\frac{2}{228}$

Using the general formula for expected value and the probability function previously obtained, we have

$$E(X) = 0 \cdot \tfrac{91}{228} + 1 \cdot \tfrac{105}{228} + 2 \cdot \tfrac{30}{228} + 3 \cdot \tfrac{2}{228} = \tfrac{171}{228} = \tfrac{3}{4}.$$

Using the special formula, we have

$$E(X) = 3 \cdot \tfrac{5}{20} = \tfrac{3}{4}, \qquad \text{as above.}$$

Note that the expected value $E(X)$ need not be a possible value of the random variable; that is, no value of the random variable is $\tfrac{3}{4}$.

In a game of chance, the game is said to be *favorable* or *unfavorable* to the player as the expected value is positive or negative. The game is considered fair if the expected value is zero.

Example 5   Consider a lottery in which 10,000 tickets are sold at $1 each. Five tickets are drawn at random. The first-place winner gets a $5000 car, the second-place winner gets a $700 stereo, and the next three winners get $100 each. What is the expected value of a ticket? Is the game fair?

Solution   We let the amount of winnings per ticket be the random variable. The probability function is as follows:

x	0	100	700	5000
p	$\frac{9995}{10000}$	$\frac{3}{10000}$	$\frac{1}{10000}$	$\frac{1}{10000}$

The expected value of a *ticket* is then

$$E_T = 0 \cdot \tfrac{9995}{10000} + 100 \cdot \tfrac{3}{10000} + 700 \cdot \tfrac{1}{10000} + 5000 \cdot \tfrac{1}{10000} = \tfrac{60}{100}, \quad \text{or } \$0.60.$$

Since one is paying \$1 for a ticket worth \$0.60, one would be suspicious that the game is not fair. The expected value of the *game* E_G can be obtained by identifying a new random variable X_i' with the *net* winnings; that is, total winnings minus the cost. Thus, $x_i' = x_i - 1$, so that

$$E_G = E_T - 1 = 0.60 - 1.00 = -0.40.$$

Since $E_G \neq 0$, the game is not fair. Now let c be the cost of a ticket for a fair game. The expected value of a *ticket* E_T is still \$0.60, but the expected value of the *game* is now

$$E_G = E_T - c = 0.60 - c,$$

so that $E_G = 0$ for $c = 0.60$ or \$0.60. Thus the game is fair when the cost of a ticket equals the expected value.

Example 6   You have a choice between buying one chance for \$1 in the lottery of Example 5 or 4 chances for \$0.25 each in the following lottery. There are 1000 chances being sold for \$0.25 each with a first prize of a \$100 TV set. Assuming that the prize can always be exchanged for some other article of equal value, which lottery is the better buy?

Solution   The probability function for this lottery is:

x	0	100
p	$\tfrac{999}{1000}$	$\tfrac{1}{1000}$

where the random variable is the winnings per ticket. Thus, the expected value per ticket is

$$E_T = 0 \cdot \tfrac{999}{1000} + 100 \cdot \tfrac{1}{1000} = 0.1, \quad \text{or} \quad \$0.10.$$

The expected value of 4 tickets is

$$E_{4T} = 4 \cdot E_T' = 4(0.1) = 0.4, \quad \text{or} \quad \$0.40.$$

The same answer would have been obtained had we taken the random variable as the winnings for 4 tickets. In that case:

x	0	100
p	$\tfrac{996}{1000}$	$\tfrac{4}{1000}$

and

$$E_{4T} = 0 \cdot \tfrac{996}{1000} + 100 \cdot \tfrac{4}{1000} = 0.4.$$

Thus $1 would buy four tickets in this lottery with an expected value of $0.40 compared to one ticket in the lottery of Example 5 with an expected value of $0.60, so that the better buy is from the lottery of Example 5.

(Optional) Craps

Example 7   Craps is a dice game with many variations of the basic rules. The rules used in casinos are the following: A shooter rolls two dice. If the sum of the numbers showing totals 7 or 11, he wins; if the sum totals 2, 3, or 12, he loses. If the sum is anything else (that is, 4, 5, 6, 8, 9, or 10), this becomes his "point." To win, he must roll his point before he rolls a 7, in which case he loses. What is the probability of winning? If even money is bet, what is the expected value?

Solution   First let us draw a tree and indicate for each branch the *conditional* probability of occurrence using the probabilities determined in Example 1 of Section 14.1.

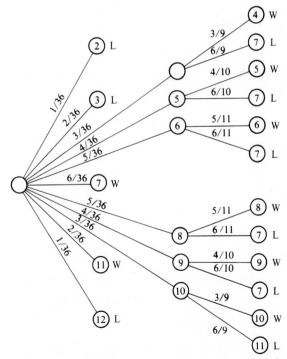

The tree has been simplified in the following respect. If, for example, the "point" is 4, then the branch of the tree for this point would be

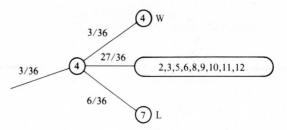

If the point 4 is obtained, the player wins and the game ends. If a 7 is obtained, the player loses and the game ends. If anything but a 4 or a 7 is obtained, the game continues until a 4 or 7 is obtained.

Using Bayes' Theorem, we can determine the probability of obtaining the point 4 provided the game ends, that is, the player gets a 4 or 7:

$$p(4|4 \text{ or } 7) = \frac{\frac{3}{36}}{\frac{3}{36} + \frac{6}{36}} = \frac{3}{9}.$$

Similarly, we can determine the probability of obtaining a 7 provided the game ends:

$$p(7|4 \text{ or } 7) = \frac{\frac{6}{36}}{\frac{3}{36} + \frac{6}{36}} = \frac{6}{9}.$$

Using only these two options, we can simplify this branch of the tree to

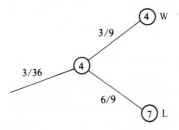

"Points" other than 4 are considered in the same manner. Thus, the probability to win p_W is:

$$p_W = \frac{3}{36} \cdot \frac{3}{9} + \frac{4}{36} \cdot \frac{4}{10} + \frac{5}{36} \cdot \frac{5}{11} + \frac{6}{36} + \frac{5}{36} \cdot \frac{5}{11}$$

$$+ \frac{4}{36} \cdot \frac{4}{10} + \frac{3}{36} \cdot \frac{3}{9} + \frac{2}{36} = \frac{244}{495}.$$

The probability to lose, p_L, is

$$p_L = 1 - p_W = \frac{251}{495},$$

Thus the odds to win are $244 : 251$. The expected value is:

$$E(X) = 1 \cdot \tfrac{244}{495} + (-1) \cdot \tfrac{251}{495} = -\tfrac{7}{495},$$

indicating that, in the long run, the *shooter* will lose.

EXERCISE SET 14.2

1. ▦ The lap speeds in the speed trials of a stock-car race were

> 90.791, 89.237, 89.108, 87.926, 86.401, 85.858, 83.271, and 79.669 mph.

What is the average lap speed?

3. ▦ In the course of an evening, a restaurant served 23 lobster dinners at $7.95, 47 steak dinners at $6.95, 53 roast beef dinners at $6.45, 33 shrimp dinners at $5.95, 29 Salisbury steak dinners at $4.95, 37 fried chicken dinners at $4.45, and 23 fish dinners at $3.75. What was the average price of a dinner?

5. A union has 21 members, 14 of whom are women and the other 7 are men. Three people are chosen at random. What is the expected number of women chosen? men? Use both formulas. (See Exercise 2, Set 14.1.)

7. Eight people apply for a job, 4 men and 4 women. Four are hired at random. What is the expected number of men hired? Use both formulas. [See Exercise 4, Set 14.1.]

9. Five workers in a group of 25 have mononucleosis. Three workers are chosen at random. What is the expected number of those chosen who have mono? [See Exercise 6, Set 14.1.]

11. If a party fields 3 candidates for office, each opposed by an equiprobable candidate, what is the expected number of winners for the party? [See Exercise 7, Set 14.1.]

13. A case of 12 bottles of wine contains 3 which have spoiled. Three bottles are taken out at random. What is the expected number of bottles of spoiled wine among those drawn? if the case contains 4 spoiled bottles? [See Exercise 10, Set 14.1.]

2. ▦ The lap speeds for a set of speed trials were

> 91.101, 90.973, 89.257, 86.118, 85.879, 82.438, 81.962, 78.113, and 78.104 mph.

What is the average lap speed?

4. ▦ A theater has 320 seats for which tickets cost $6.90, 480 seats at $5.90, 624 seats at $4.70, and 484 seats at $3.60. What is the average cost of a ticket?

6. The sales force of a business consists of 20 people, half of whom are men and the other half women. Four people are chosen at random. What is the expected number of women chosen? Use both formulas. [See Exercise 1, Set 14.1.]

8. Eight people apply for a job, 5 men and 3 women. Four are hired at random. What is the expected number of women hired? Use both formulas. [See Exercise 3, Set 14.1.]

10. A crate of 20 machine parts contains 6 defective parts. Five parts are taken out at random. What is the expected number of defective parts taken out? [See Exercise 5, Set 14.1.]

12. As in Exercise 11, but the first candidate has a probability of $\tfrac{1}{3}$ to win, the second $\tfrac{1}{2}$, and the third $\tfrac{2}{3}$? [See Exercise 8, Set 14.1.]

14. A wine rack contains 7 bottles of red wine and 2 of white wine. If 3 bottles are taken out at random, what is the expected number of bottles of white wine drawn? red wine? [See Exercise 9, Set 14.1.]

15. One cage contains 3 white mice and 2 black ones and another cage contains 2 white mice and 3 black ones. A cage is chosen at random and 3 mice are taken out at random. What is the expected number of white mice in the sample? [See Exercise 11, Set 14.1.]

16. There are two cages of mice, as in Exercise 15. A cage is chosen at random. A mouse of un-identified color escapes from the chosen cage. Then 3 mice are taken out at random. What is the expected number of white mice in the sample? [See Exercise 12, Set 14.1.]

17. There are 2 cages of mice, as in Exercise 15. A white mouse escapes from an unidentified cage. Then a cage is chosen at random and 3 mice are taken out at random. What is the expected number of white mice in the sample? [See Exercise 13, Set 14.1.]

18. There are 2 cages of mice, as in Exercise 11. All the mice escape and are put back at random, 5 to each cage. A cage is then selected at random and 3 mice are taken out at random. What is the expected number of white mice in the sample? [See Exercise 14, Set 14.1.]

19. The winner in a World Series is the first team to win 4 out of 7 games. If the two teams are evenly matched, what is the expected number of games required for one team to win the series? [See Exercise 15, Set 14.1.]

20. As in Exercise 19, but the winning team must win by two games. After 7 games one extra game is to be played if one team is winning by only one game but the series ends if there is a 4-4 tie [See Exercise 16, Set 14.1.]

21. *Craps.* From Example 7, it is apparent that one can win in the long run by betting *against* the shooter. Since this is the traditional role of the "house" in the long run a casino would lose if it accepted such bets. Since gambling casinos cannot afford to lose, they modify the rules as follows: If one bets *with* the shooter, then the same rules prevail. However, if one bets *against* the shooter, then a standoff feature is added; namely, if the initial roll is 2, the game ends with no win and no loss. What is the expectation of winning by betting against the shooter? Is it better to bet for or against the shooter?

14.3 VARIANCE AND STANDARD DEVIATION

In addition to wanting to know the mean or average value of the data or the expected value of a probability-distribution function for some random variable, we may want to know about the "spread" of the data. To do this, we use the *variance* and the *standard deviation*.

Let us consider the test scores from Example 1 of Section 14.2:

$$76, \quad 72, \quad 88, \quad 90, \quad 74, \quad 83, \quad 52, \quad 79, \quad 81, \quad 84, \quad 69.$$

In that example we found that the average value was

$$\overline{x} = 77.09.$$

We want to consider how the data *varies* from the average value. How can we do this? One way might be to consider the differences between a score and the average value

$$x_i - \bar{x}.$$

For example, $76 - 77.09 = -1.09$ represents the deviation from the mean of the score 76. If we add all of these deviations and average, we would have

$$\frac{1}{n} \sum_{i=1}^{n} (x_i - \bar{x}),$$

which is called the *average deviation from the mean*. Unfortunately, this quantity always adds to 0. Thus, it would not yield any results which would vary between different sets of data to yield information about the spread of the data. (The reader should verify that for the above set of data, the average deviation from the mean is 0.) To avoid this difficulty, we consider the *deviation squared*:

$$(x_i - \bar{x})^2.$$

The average of the deviation squared, called the *sample variance*, is given by *

$$s^2 = \frac{1}{n} \sum_{i=1}^{n} (x_i - \bar{x})^2.$$

Now calculating the variance, we obtain

$$s^2 = \tfrac{1}{11}[(76 - 77.09)^2 + (72 - 77.09)^2 + \cdots + (69 - 77.09)^2]$$

or

$$s^2 = 101.72.$$

When a probability function is known, we can find a "theoretical" variance defined as the *expected value* of the *deviation squared*:

$$\sigma^2 = E[(X - \mu)^2] = \sum_{i=1}^{n} p_i(x_i - \mu)^2.$$

■ **Example 1**   Given a box of 20 transistors, of which 5 are defective. What is the variance of the number of defective transistors?

---

* Here we consider *all* the data. If we were using only a *sample* of the data, then the n in the denominator should be replaced by $(n - 1)$, for statistical reasons which we cannot go into in this text. We need the definition of variance using n for later use.

Solution   From Example 2, Section 8.1, we have the probability function:

x	0	1	2	3
p	$\frac{91}{228}$	$\frac{105}{228}$	$\frac{30}{228}$	$\frac{2}{228}$

From Example 4, Section 14.2, we have the expected value

$$\mu = E(X) = \tfrac{3}{4}.$$

The variance is given by:

$$\sigma^2 = \tfrac{91}{228}(0 - \tfrac{3}{4})^2 + \tfrac{105}{228}(1 - \tfrac{3}{4})^2 + \tfrac{30}{228}(2 - \tfrac{3}{4})^2 + \tfrac{2}{228}(3 - \tfrac{3}{4})^2$$

$$= \tfrac{91}{228} \cdot \tfrac{9}{16} + \tfrac{105}{228} \cdot \tfrac{1}{16} + \tfrac{30}{228} \cdot \tfrac{25}{16} + \tfrac{2}{228} \cdot \tfrac{81}{16}$$

$$= 0.503.$$

Note that we started with certain units. For example, in Example 1 the test scores were measured in percentile "points." So is the average value. On the other hand, the variance is measured in the *square* of these units, or "points-squared." We can obtain a measure of the "spread" of the data in the same units as the data by using the *standard deviation* which is the square root of the variance.

■ **Example 2**   Obtain the standard deviation of the test scores of Example 1, Section 14.2.

Solution   The standard deviation is the positive square root of the variance:

$$s = +\sqrt{s^2} = \sqrt{\frac{1}{n} \sum_{i=1}^{n} (x_i - \bar{x})^2}.$$

From earlier work in this section, we know that $s^2 = 101.72$, so that $s = \sqrt{101.72} = 10.09$. (Use a square root table or hand calculator.)

In general, a small standard deviation relative to the mean indicates that the data has little spread about the mean, while a large standard deviation relative to the mean indicates a large spread about the mean.

■ **Example 3**   Find the standard deviation for the number of defective transistors of Example 1.

Solution   The standard deviation is

$$\sigma = \sqrt{\sigma^2} = \sqrt{\sum_{i=1}^{n} p_i(x_i - \mu)^2}.$$

In Example 1, we found that $\sigma^2 = 0.503$, so that

$$\sigma = \sqrt{0.503} = 0.709.$$

EXERCISE SET 14.3

1. ▦ Find the variance and standard deviation for the lap speeds of Exercise 1, Set 14.2:

> 90.791, 89.237, 89.108, 87.926, 86.401, 85.858, 83.271, and 79.669 mph.

3. ▦ Find the variance and standard deviation for the dinners of Exercise 3, Set 14.2:

> 23 at $7.95, 47 at $6.95, 53 at $6.45, 33 at $5.95, 29 at $4.95, 37 at $4.45, and 23 at $3.75.

5. A union has 21 members of whom 14 are women and 7 are men. Three people are chosen at random. What is the variance and standard deviation of the number of women chosen? [See Exercise 5, Set 14.2.]

7. Five workers in a group of 25 have mononucleosis. Three workers are chosen at random. What is the variance and standard deviation of the number with mono? [See Exercise 9, Set 14.2.]

2. ▦ Find the variance and standard deviation for the lap speeds of Exercise 2, Set 14.2:

> 91.101, 90.973, 89.257, 86.118, 85.879, 82.438, 81.962, 78.113, and 78.104 mph.

4. ▦ Find the variance and standard deviation for the tickets of Exercise 4, Set 14.2:

> 320 at $6.90, 480 at $5.90, 624 at $4.70, and 484 at $3.60.

6. The sales force of a business consists of 20 people, half of whom are men and the other half women. Four people are chosen at random. What is the variance and standard deviation of the number of women chosen? [See Exercise 6, Set 14.2.]

8. A crate of 20 machine parts contains 6 defective parts. Five parts are taken out at random. What is the variance and standard deviation of the number of defective parts taken out? [See Exercise 10, Set 14.2.]

14.4 BERNOULLI TRIALS—BINOMIAL PROBABILITY

Many experiments have outcomes which fall naturally into two disjoint sets designated simply "success" or "failure". For example,

  i) The flipping of a coin and its landing "heads" or "tails" (barring its standing on edge);

 ii) The winning or losing of an election (allowing for the ultimate resolution of a tie);

iii) The passing or failing of a manufactured article to a particular tolerance for quality control.

Experiments or trials with two possible outcomes are called *Bernoulli trials*.

Most of the problems considered so far involved repeated trials in which each trial changed the conditions of subsequent trials. In particular for hypergeometric probabilities, an object was drawn at random from a group of objects and *not* replaced before the next trial.

Now we consider trials such that whatever is removed in one trial is *replaced* before the next trial. Each trial is the same and hence *independent* of the others. Thus, we consider *repeated independent Bernoulli trials*.

Example 1   A fair coin is flipped repeatedly. What is the probability for heads to show 3 times out of 5 flips?

Solution   Here a "success" can be identified with a coin showing "heads." Since the coin is fair, the probability for either heads or tails to show is $\frac{1}{2}$. One way for heads to show 3 times out of 5 is for the first 3 flips to show heads and the last two to show tails, that is

$$\text{HHHTT.}$$

Each particular outcome (H or T) occurs with probability $\frac{1}{2}$. In the outcome HHHTT, each individual flip is independent of the others. Thus the combined outcome HHHTT will happen with a probability that is the product of the individual probabilities (Multiplication Theorem):

$$\left(\tfrac{1}{2}\right)^3\left(\tfrac{1}{2}\right)^2 = \tfrac{1}{32}.$$

There are 10 configurations in which we can get 3 heads out of 5 flips:

HHHTT	TTHHH
HHTHT	THTHH
HTHHT	THHTH
HHTTH	HTTHH
HTHTH	THHHT.

Each of these configurations is equally probable, since it is calculated exactly the same as the previous calculation for HHHTT.

Using techniques from Chapter 13, we can compute directly the number of ways 3 heads can show in 5 flips:

$$C(5, 3) = \binom{5}{3} = \frac{5 \cdot 4 \cdot 3}{1 \cdot 2 \cdot 3} = 10.$$

The probability for heads to show 3 times out of five is the product of the probability for heads to show 3 times out of five in a particular configuration times the number of different ways heads can show 3 times out of five, that is

$$p_{3H} = \tfrac{1}{32} \cdot 10 = \tfrac{10}{32}.$$

Note that the answer is the same whether *one* coin is flipped 5 times in a row or 5 coins are flipped *once* at the same time. In either case each trial is identical.

Problems of this type have a *binomial* probability. This means that for a *binomial* random variable,

i) There are two outcomes (Bernoulli trials);

ii) Each trial is independent of preceding trials;

iii) Each trial is identical to preceding trials.

Binomial probability is similar to *hypergeometric* probability in that objects in random drawings are restricted to *two* kinds, but differs in that *binomial* probability assumes *replacement* or identical trials while *hypergeometric* probability assumes *no replacement* or that successive trials differ.

Example 2   *Quality Control.* Electrical switches are manufactured with 10% being defective. Five switches are drawn at random and without replacement. What is the probability that two of these are defective?

Solution   If this problem had specified that 5 switches were to be drawn from some *fixed* number of switches, then the probability would be hypergeometric. However, a fixed number is *not* specified. Rather, switches are being manufactured, as on a production line, and continually feed into some container from which the sample of 5 is taken. Thus, within the limits of the information available to us, the trials are independent and hence the probability is binomial.

Let the *event* be the drawing of a *defective* switch. This event has a probability $p = 0.10$. The probability for drawing a nondefective switch is $q = 1 - p = 0.90$.

The probability for getting the *first two* switches defective and the *last three* switches nondefective is

$$(0.10)^2(0.90)^3.$$

The number of ways two defective switches can be drawn out of a sample of five is $\binom{5}{2}$.

Thus, the probability that there will be two defective switches in a sample of five is

$$\binom{5}{2}(0.10)^2(0.90)^3 = 10(0.01)(0.729) = 0.0729.$$

In general, if the probability is *p* that some event *will* happen in one trial and *q* = 1 − *p* that it will *not*, then the binomial probability p_k for the

event to happen k times out of n trials is given by

$$p_k = B(n, k, p) = \binom{n}{k} p^k q^{n-k}.$$

In Example 2, we have

$$p = 0.10, \qquad q = 0.90, \qquad n = 5, \qquad k = 2,$$

so that

$$p_2 = \binom{5}{2}(0.10)^2(0.90)^3 = 0.0729, \qquad \text{as before.}$$

Alternately, we may take the *event* as the drawing of a *nondefective* switch. Then we seek the probability of drawing *three nondefective* switches out of a sample of five. Thus

$$p = 0.90, \qquad q = 0.10, \qquad n = 5, \qquad k = 3,$$

and

$$p_3 = \binom{5}{3}(0.90)^3(0.10)^2 = 0.0729.$$

This is the same answer as before but with different notation. Recall that

$$\binom{n}{k} = \binom{n}{n-k}.$$

Example 3   What is the probability function for the problem of Example 2?

Solution   The probability in this case is binomial. Thus, taking the random variable K to be the number of defective switches observed in the sample, we have

k	p_k
0	$\binom{5}{0}(0.1)^0(0.9)^5 = 0.59049$
1	$\binom{5}{1}(0.1)^1(0.9)^4 = 0.32805$
2	$\binom{5}{2}(0.1)^2(0.9)^3 = 0.07290$
3	$\binom{5}{3}(0.1)^3(0.9)^2 = 0.00810$
4	$\binom{5}{4}(0.1)^4(0.9)^1 = 0.00045$
5	$\binom{5}{5}(0.1)^5(0.9)^0 = 0.00001$

In Section 14.2 the expected value of a random variable X was defined by

$$\mu = E(X) = \sum_{i=1}^{n} x_i p_i.$$

For binomial probability, the random variable is K, the number of successes in a series of trials. It takes on the values $k = 0, 1, \ldots, n$. Thus, we write

$$\mu = E(K) = \sum_{k=1}^{n} k p_k.$$

It can be shown that the expected value for the random variable with binomial probability is given by

$$\mu = E(K) = n \cdot p,$$

where n is the number of trials and p is the probability for the event to occur in one trial.

Note that the expected value for the *hypergeometric* probability function is the same as that for the *binomial* probability *provided* that, in the former case, p is taken as the probability of an *initial* success; that is, $p = m/s$, as in Section 14.2.

Example 4   Determine the expected value for the problem of Example 2 using both formulas.

Solution   Using

$$E(K) = \sum_{k=1}^{n} k p_k,$$

we have

$$E(K) = 0(0.59049) + 1(0.32805) + 2(0.07290) + 3(0.00810)$$
$$+ 4(0.00045) + 5(0.00001)$$
$$= 0.50000$$

Using $E(K) = n \cdot p$, we have $n = 5$ and $p = 0.1$, so that

$$E(K) = 5(0.1) = 0.5, \qquad \text{as above.}$$

We can also determine the variance and standard deviation for a binomial probability distribution.

▦ Example 5   Find the variance and standard deviation for the problem of Example 2.

Solution   The expected value for this problem was found in Example 4 to be

$$\mu = 0.5.$$

Thus, the variance is

$$\sigma^2 = 0.59049(0 - 0.5)^2 + 0.32805(1 - 0.5)^2 + 0.07290(2 - 0.5)^2$$
$$+ 0.00810(3 - 0.5)^2 + 0.00045(4 - 0.5)^2 + 0.00001(5 - 0.5)^2$$

or

$$\sigma^2 = 0.45000,$$

so that the standard deviation is

$$\sigma = \sqrt{0.45000} = 0.67082.$$

The variance and standard deviation for a binomial probability-distribution function can be obtained simply from the formula

$$\sigma^2 = np(1 - p).$$

In this case, $n = 5$ and $p = 0.1$ (see Example 2), so that

$$\sigma^2 = 5 \cdot 0.1(1 - 0.1), \quad \text{or} \quad \sigma^2 = 0.45, \quad \text{as before.}$$

Example 6   *Quality Control.* Given a box of 20 transistors of which 5 are defective. Three transistors are drawn at random, the number defective is noted, and the transistors are replaced. This is repeated 5 times. What is the probability that at least one is defective in at least 4 trials?

Solution   The probability p that at least one transistor is defective is the *hypergeometric* probability given by the quantity $p_{i \geq 1}$ in Example 5 of Section 14.2; that is,

$$p = \tfrac{137}{228} \quad \text{and} \quad q = 1 - p = \tfrac{91}{228}.$$

This corresponds to a "success" (that is, the event happening) in the second part of the problem. The probability for at least 4 successes is

$$p_{i \geq 4} = p_4 + p_5$$

where p_4 and p_5 are the *binomial* probabilities

$$p_4 = \binom{5}{4}\left(\tfrac{137}{228}\right)^4\left(\tfrac{91}{228}\right)^1 \quad \text{and} \quad p_5 = \binom{5}{5}\left(\tfrac{137}{228}\right)^5\left(\tfrac{91}{228}\right)^0.$$

Note that while in Example 2 the probability was given, in this Example it had to be computed. Furthermore, one problem may involve more than one type of probability, in this case both hypergeometric and binomial.

EXERCISE SET 14.4

1. Five fair coins are tossed. What is the probability function for the number of tails showing? What is the expected number of tails? What is the variance and standard deviation? Use both formulas.

2. If the birth rate for boys and girls were equal, what would be the distribution of girls in a four-child family? What is the expected number of girls? What is the variance and standard deviation? Use both formulas.

3. Half the people in a community favor a certain political stand and half oppose it. Of 6 people selected at random, what is the expected number to favor the stand? to oppose the stand? What is the probability that of these 6 people 4 or more will favor the stand or oppose it?

4. One-third of the people in a community favor a certain political stand and two thirds oppose it. Of 6 people selected at random, what is the expected number to favor the stand? to oppose the stand? What is the probability that of these 6 people at least half will oppose the issue?

5. An impostor applies for a job as a wine taster. As a test he is given 5 wines to taste to determine whether they are *vin ordinaire* or a great vintage wine. What is the probability that he gets at least 4 out of 5 correct by guessing? What is the expected number of correct evaluations? What is the variance and standard deviation?

6. As in Exercise 5, but the applicant is genuine and can distinguish the two wines 4 times out of 5. What is the probability that he fails the test (that is, fails to get at least 4 out of 5 correct)? What is the expected number of correct evaluations? What is the variance and standard deviation?

7. *Quality Control, Reliability.* A complex experiment consists of 6 components each with a reliability of 0.9 (that is, the probability for the component to work is 0.9). If the experiment is so constructed that it can be run if no more than one out of the 6 components fails to function properly, what is the probability that the experiment can be run? What is the expected number of failures? What is the variance and standard deviation?

8. *Quality Control, Reliability.* A successful flight of an exploratory space rocket requires that no more than two of the 10 components fail to function properly (due to use of interlocking fail-safe circuits). If each component has a reliability of 0.98, what is the probability for a successful flight? What is the expected number of component failures? What is the variance and standard deviation?

9. Treatment for a certain disease is effective 80% of the time. If 5 patients are sampled, what is the probability function for the number of effective treatments? What is the expected value? What is the probability that the treatment is ineffective for at least one patient?

10. If 30% of marriages end in divorce by the fifth year of marriage, what is the probability function for the number of couples out of a sample of 6 who have been divorced after no more than 5 years of marriage? What is the probability that half or more of the sample has been divorced? What is the expected number of divorced couples? the variance? the standard deviation?

11. *Quality Control.* Sparkplugs are manufactured and pass along a conveyor belt for inspection. A sample of 5 is taken at random. What is the probability function for the number of defective plugs if the defective rate is 10%? if the defective rate is 20%? if the defective rate is 30%? Which defective rate is most probable if *no* defective plugs are found in the sample? if one is found? if two are found? if three are found?

12. *Quality Control.* Machine A makes ballpoint pens with deficiency rate of 10% and machine B makes pens with a deficiency rate of 30%. Two pens are taken from each machine. What is the probability that two of the four are defective? If the pens from the two machines are mixed half and half (that is, with a deficiency rate of 20%) before a sample of 4 is taken, what is the probability that there will be two defective pens in the sample?

13. A company manufactures a type of mouse-trap which is 50% effective. They would like to claim that it is at least 80% effective. A sample of 5 traps is tested for effectiveness. What is the probability that the sample is at least 80% effective? If the testing of a sample of 5 traps is repeated 5 times, what is the expected number of trials for which the samples tested are at least 80% effective?

14. A company manufactures thermometers with a deficiency rate of 20%. A sample of 5 thermometers is tested. What is the probability that at least one thermometer is defective? If this test is repeated 5 times, what is the probability that there is at least one defective thermometer in each trial? in at least 4 out of 5 trials?

15. As in Exercise 14, what is the probability that at least two thermometers are defective? If the test is repeated 5 times, what is the probability at least two defective thermometers are found in at least 2 trials out of the five?

14.5 STANDARDIZED AND CONTINUOUS RANDOM VARIABLES— PROBABILITY DISTRIBUTIONS

The smaller the standard deviation the less spread there is in the data and the larger the standard deviation, the more spread there is. We shall pursue this concept further by converting our random variable to *standardized form* with 0 mean and a standard deviation of 1. This we do by calculating the standardized random variable Z with numerical values z:

$$z = \frac{x - \bar{x}}{s} \quad \text{or} \quad z = \frac{x - \mu}{\sigma},$$

depending on whether one is using sample or theoretical data.

▦ **Example 1**   The test scores of Example 1, Section 14.2, were 76, 72, 88, 90, 74, 83, 52, 79, 81, 84, and 69. The mean of these test scores is $\bar{x} = 77.09$ and the standard deviation is $\sigma = 10.09$. Convert a test score of 85 to standardized form.

Solution   Substituting into the preceding formula, we obtain:

$$z = \frac{85 - 77.09}{10.09} = \frac{7.91}{10.09} = 0.78.$$

▦ **Example 2**   To what test scores do $z = 1$ and $z = -1$ correspond for the data of Example 1? to what test scores do $z = 2$ and $z = -2$ correspond?

Solution   Using the standardized random variable, we have

$$z = \frac{x - 77.09}{10.09} = 1.$$

Solving for x, we obtain a test score x = 87.18.
    Similarly,

$$z = \frac{x - 77.09}{10.09} = -1$$

yields a test score x = 67.00.
    Continuing,

$$z = \frac{x - 77.09}{10.09} = 2 \qquad \text{yields} \qquad x = 97.27$$

and

$$z = \frac{x - 77.09}{10.09} = -2 \qquad \text{yields} \qquad x = 56.91.$$

Example 3   What percent of the students of Example 1 and 2 have test scores that lie within one standard deviation of the mean, that is, that lie between $z = 1$ and $z = -1$?

Solution   Out of 11 students, 8 had test scores between 67.00 ($z = -1$) and 87.18 ($z = 1$). This corresponds to $100 \cdot \frac{8}{11}$ or 73%.

So far, we have considered *discrete* random variables. Now we shall introduce *continuous* random variables and show the role played by the definite integral in the theory of probability. While in the previous sections we defined a random variable X (upper case) as a rule which assigns a numerical value x (lower case) to the outcome of an experiment, we shall use only x (lower case) for the remainder of this chapter.

Continuous Random Variables

Suppose we throw a dart at a number line in such a way that it always lands in the interval [1, 3].

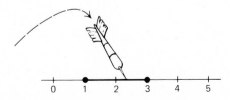

Let x be the number that the dart hits. Note that x is a quantity which can be observed (or measured) repeatedly and whose possible values consist of an entire interval of real numbers. Such a variable is called a *continuous random variable*. Suppose we throw the dart a large number of times and it lands in the subinterval [1.6, 2.8] 43% of the time; the probability, then, that the dart lands in that interval is 0.43.

Let us consider some other examples of continuous random variables.

Example 4   Suppose x is the arrival time of buses at a bus stop in a three-hour period from 2 P.M. to 5 P.M. The interval is [2, 5].

Then x is a continuous random variable distributed over the interval [2, 5].

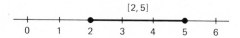

Example 5   Suppose x is the corn acreage of each farm in the U.S. and Canada. The interval is [0, a], where a is the highest acreage. Or, not knowing what the highest acreage might be, the interval might be [0, ∞) to allow for all possibilities.

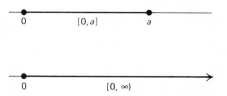

[*Note:* It might be argued that there is a value in [0, a] or [0, ∞) for which no farm has that acreage, but for practical purposes these values are often disregarded.]

Then x is a continuous random variable distributed over the interval [0, a], or [0, ∞).

Suppose, considering Example 1 on the arrival times of buses, that we wanted to know the probability that a bus will arrive between 4 P.M. and 5 P.M., as represented by

$$p([4,\ 5]),$$

or

$$p(4 \leq x \leq 5).$$

In some cases it is possible to find a function over [2, 5] such that areas over subintervals give the probabilities that a bus will arrive during these subintervals. For example, suppose we had a constant function $f(x) = \frac{1}{3}$ that will give us these probabilities. Look at its graph.

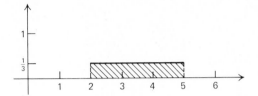

The area under the curve is $3 \cdot \frac{1}{3}$, or 1. The probability that a bus will arrive between 4 P.M. and 5 P.M. is that fraction of the large area which lies over the interval [4, 5]. That is,

$$p([4, 5]) = \frac{1}{3} = 33\tfrac{1}{3}\%.$$

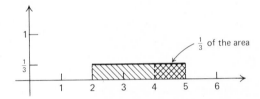

The probability that a bus will arrive between 2:00 P.M. and 4:30 P.M. is $\frac{5}{6}$ or $83\tfrac{1}{3}\%$.

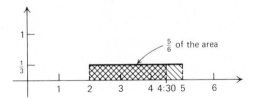

Note that any interval of length 1 has probability $\frac{1}{3}$. This may not always happen. Suppose we have a function

$$f(x) = \frac{3}{117} x^2$$

whose definite integral over the interval [4, 5] would yield the probability that a bus will arrive between 4 P.M. and 5 P.M. Then

$$P([4, 5]) = \int_4^5 f(x)\, dx = \int_4^5 \frac{3}{117} x^2\, dx$$

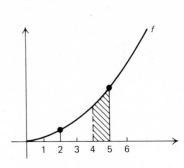

$$= \left[\frac{3}{117} \cdot \frac{1}{3} x^3 \right]_4^5$$

$$= \frac{1}{117} (5^3 - 4^3)$$

$$= \frac{61}{117} \approx 0.52.$$

Thus 52% of the time you will be able to catch a bus between 4 P.M. and 5 P.M. The function f is called a *probability density function.** Its integral over *any* subinterval gives the probability that x "lands" in that subinterval.

> **Let x be a continuous random variable distributed over some interval $[a, b]$. A function f is said to be a *probability density function* for x if**
>
> 1. **f is nonnegative over $[a, b]$, that is, $f(x) \geq 0$ for all x in $[a, b]$;**
> 2. **for any subinterval $[c, d]$ of $[a, b]$, the probability $P([c, d])$, or $P(c \leq x \leq d)$, that x lands in that subinterval is given by**
>
> $$P([c, d]) = \int_c^d f(x)\, dx;$$

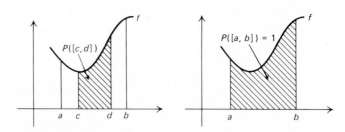

> 3. **the probability that x lands in $[a, b]$ is 1:**
>
> $$\int_a^b f(x)\, dx = 1.$$

That is, we are "certain" that x is in the interval $[a, b]$.

---

* Or probability *frequency* function.

Example 6   Verify property 3 of the above definition for

$$f(x) = \frac{3}{117} x^2.$$

Solution   The "big" interval under consideration is [2, 5]. So

$$\int_2^5 \frac{3}{117} x^2 \, dx = \left[\frac{3}{117} \cdot \frac{1}{3} x^3 \right]_2^5 = \frac{1}{117} (5^3 - 2^3) = \frac{117}{117} = 1.$$

Example 7   A company produces transistors. It determines that the life t of a transistor is from 3 to 6 years and that the probability density function for t is given by

$$f(t) = \frac{24}{t^3}, \quad \text{for} \quad 3 \le t \le 6.$$

a) Find the probability that a transistor will last no more than 4 years.
b) Find the probability that a transistor will last from 4 to 5 years.

Solution   a) The probability that a transistor will last no more than 4 years is

$$P(3 \le t \le 4) = \int_3^4 \frac{24}{t^3} \, dt = \left[24\left(-\frac{1}{2} t^{-2} \right) \right]_3^4 = \left[-\frac{12}{t^2} \right]_3^4 = -12\left(\frac{1}{4^2} - \frac{1}{3^2} \right)$$

$$= -12\left(\frac{1}{16} - \frac{1}{9} \right) = -12\left(-\frac{7}{144} \right) = \frac{7}{12} \approx 0.58.$$

b) The probability that a transistor will last from 4 to 5 years is

$$P(4 \le t \le 5) = \int_4^5 \frac{24}{t^3} \, dt = \left[24\left(-\frac{1}{2} t^{-2} \right) \right]_4^5 = \left[-\frac{12}{t^2} \right]_4^5 = -12\left(\frac{1}{5^2} - \frac{1}{4^2} \right)$$

$$= -12\left(\frac{1}{25} - \frac{1}{16} \right) = -12\left(-\frac{9}{400} \right) = \frac{27}{100} = 0.27.$$

Constructing Probability Density Functions

Suppose you have an arbitrary nonnegative function $f(x)$ whose definite integral over some interval $[a, b]$ is K. Then

$$\int_a^b f(x) \, dx = K.$$

Now multiply on both sides by $\dfrac{1}{K}$.

$$\frac{1}{K}\int_a^b f(x)\,dx = \frac{1}{K}\cdot K = 1 \qquad \text{or} \qquad \int_a^b \frac{1}{K}\cdot f(x)\,dx = 1.$$

Thus when we multiply the function $f(x)$ by $1/K$ we have a function whose area over the given interval is 1.

Example 8   Find k such that

$$f(x) = kx^2$$

is a probability density function over the interval $[2, 5]$.

Solution
$$\int_2^5 x^2\,dx = \left[\frac{x^3}{3}\right]_2^5 = \frac{5^3}{3} - \frac{2^3}{5} = \frac{125}{3} - \frac{8}{3} = \frac{117}{3}.$$

Thus $k = \dfrac{1}{(117/3)} = \dfrac{3}{117}$, and $f(x) = \dfrac{3}{117}x^2$.

Uniform Distributions

Suppose the probability density function of a continuous random variable is constant. How is it described? Consider the following graph.

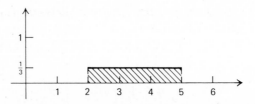

The length of the shaded rectangle is the length of the interval $[2, 5]$ which is 3. For the shaded area to be 1, the height of the rectangle must be $\frac{1}{3}$. Thus $f(x) = \frac{1}{3}$. For the general case consider the following graph.

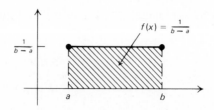

The length of the shaded rectangle is the length of the interval $[a, b]$, which is $b - a$. For the shaded area to be 1, the height of the rectangle must be $1/(b - a)$. Thus $f(x) = 1/(b - a)$.

> A continuous random variable x is said to be *uniformly distributed* over an interval $[a, b]$ if it has a probability density function f given by
>
> $$f(x) = \frac{1}{b - a}, \quad \text{for} \quad a \leqslant x \leqslant b.$$

Example 9 A number x is selected at random from the interval $[40, 50]$. The probability density function for x is given by

$$f(x) = \tfrac{1}{10}, \quad \text{for} \quad 40 \leqslant x \leqslant 50.$$

Find the probability that a number selected is in the subinterval $[42, 48]$.

Solution The probability is

$$P(42 \leqslant x \leqslant 48) = \int_{42}^{48} \tfrac{1}{10}\, dx = \tfrac{1}{10}[x]_{42}^{48} = \tfrac{1}{10}(48 - 42) = \tfrac{6}{10} = 0.6.$$

Example 10 A company produces guitars for a rock concert. The maximum loudness L of the guitars ranges from 70 to 100 decibels. The probability density for L is

$$f(L) = \tfrac{1}{30}, \quad \text{for} \quad 70 \leqslant L \leqslant 100.$$

A guitar is selected at random off the assembly line. Find the probability that its maximum loudness is from 70 to 92 decibels.

Solution The probability is

$$P(70 \leqslant L \leqslant 92) = \int_{70}^{92} \tfrac{1}{30}\, dL = \tfrac{1}{30}[L]_{70}^{92} = \tfrac{1}{30}(92 - 70) = \tfrac{22}{30} = \tfrac{11}{15} \approx 0.73.$$

Exponential Distributions

The duration of a phone call, the distance between successive cars on a highway, and the amount of time required to learn a task are all examples of exponentially distributed random variables. That is, their probability density functions are exponential.

> A continuous random variable is *exponentially distributed* if it has a probability density function given by
>
> $$f(x) = ke^{-kx}, \quad \text{over the interval } [0, \infty).$$

The function $f(x) = 2e^{-2x}$ is such a probability density function. That

$$\int_0^\infty 2e^{-2x}\, dx = 1$$

is shown in Section 6.4. The general
case

$$\int_0^\infty ke^{-kx}\, dx = 1$$

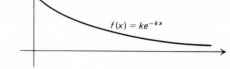

can be verified in a similar way.

Why is it reasonable to assume that distance between cars is exponentially distributed? This is because there are many more cases in which distances are small. The same argument holds for the duration of a phone call. That is, there are more short calls than long ones.

Example 11   *Transportation planning.* The distance x, in feet, between successive cars on a certain stretch of highway has probability density function

$$f(x) = ke^{-kx}, \quad \text{for} \quad 0 \leqslant x \leqslant \infty,$$

where $k = 1/a$ and a = average distance between successive cars over some period of time.

A transportation planner determines that the average distance between cars on a certain stretch of highway is 166 ft. What is the probability that the distance between cars is 50 ft or less?

Solution   We first determine k.

$$k = \tfrac{1}{166} \approx 0.006$$

The probability density function for x is

$$f(x) = 0.006e^{-0.006x}, \quad \text{for} \quad 0 \leqslant x < \infty.$$

The probability that the distance between cars is 50 ft or less is

$$P(0 \leqslant x \leqslant 50) = \int_0^{50} 0.006e^{-0.006x}\, dx$$

$$= \left[\frac{0.006}{-0.006} e^{-0.006x} \right]_0^{50}$$

$$= [-e^{-0.006x}]_0^{50} = (-e^{-0.006 \cdot 50}) - (-e^{0.006 \cdot 0})$$

$$= -e^{-0.3} + 1 = 1 - e^{-0.3}$$

$$= 1 - 0.740818 \approx 0.2592$$

EXERCISE SET 14.5

1. ▦ Given the lap speeds:

90.791, 89.237, 89.108, 87.926, 86.401, 85.858, 83.271, and 79.669 mph.

The mean is 86.533 mph (Exercise 1, Set 14.2) and the standard deviation is 3.396 mph (see Exercise 1, Set 14.3).

a) What value of the standardized random variable corresponds to 87.533 mph? to 85.533 mph?

b) What speed corresponds to $z = 0.5$? to $z = -0.5$?

c) What percent of the cars had lap speeds within 0.5 standard deviation of the mean?

2. ▦ Given the lap speeds:

91.101, 90.973, 89.257, 86.118, 85.879, 82.438, 81.962, 78.113, and 78.104 mph.

a) What is the mean speed? (See Exercise 2, Set 14.2.)

b) What is the standard deviation? (See Exercise 2, Set 14.3.)

c) What value of the standardized random variable corresponds to 84 mph? to 85 mph?

d) What speed corresponds to $z = 0.5$? to $z = -0.5$?

e) What percent of the cars had lap speeds within 0.5 standard deviation of the mean?

Verify property 3 of the definition of a probability density function over the given interval.

3. $f(x) = 2x$, $[0, 1]$ **4.** $f(x) = \frac{1}{4}x$, $[1, 3]$ **5.** $f(x) = \frac{1}{3}$, $[4, 7]$

6. $f(x) = \frac{1}{4}$, $[9, 13]$ **7.** $f(x) = \frac{3}{26}x^2$, $[1, 3]$ **8.** $f(x) = \frac{3}{64}x^2$, $[0, 4]$

9. $f(x) = \dfrac{1}{x}$, $[1, e]$ **10.** $f(x) = \dfrac{1}{e - 1} e^x$, $[0, 1]$ **11.** $f(x) = \frac{3}{2}x^2$, $[-1, 1]$

12. $f(x) = \frac{1}{3}x^2$, $[-2, 1]$ **13.** $f(x) = 3e^{-3x}$, $[0, \infty]$ **14.** $f(x) = 4e^{-4x}$, $[0, \infty]$

Find k such that each function is a probability density function over the given integral.

15. $f(x) = kx$, $[1, 3]$ **16.** $f(x) = kx$, $[1, 4]$ **17.** $f(x) = kx^2$, $[-1, 1]$

18. $f(x) = kx^2$, $[-2, 2]$ **19.** $f(x) = k$, $[2, 7]$ **20.** $f(x) = k$, $[3, 9]$

21. $f(x) = k(2 - x)$, $[0, 2]$ **22.** $f(x) = k(4 - x)$, $[0, 4]$ **23.** $f(x) = \dfrac{k}{x}$, $[1, 3]$

24. $f(x) = \dfrac{k}{x}$, $[1, 2]$ **25.** $f(x) = ke^x$, $[0, 3]$ **26.** $f(x) = ke^x$, $[0, 2]$

27. A dart is thrown at a number line in such a way that it always lands in the interval $[0, 10]$. Let $x = $ the number the dart hits. Suppose the probability density function for x is given by

$$f(x) = \tfrac{1}{50}x, \quad \text{for} \quad 0 \le x \le 10.$$

Find $P(2 \le x \le 6)$, the probability that it lands in $[2, 6]$.

28. Suppose the situation of Exercise 25, but that the dart always lands in the interval $[0, 5]$, and that the probability density function for x is given by

$$f(x) = \tfrac{3}{125}x^2, \quad \text{for} \quad 0 \le x \le 5.$$

Find $P(1 \le x \le 4)$, the probability that it lands in $[1, 4]$.

29. A number x is selected at random from the interval [4, 20]. The probability density function for x is given by

$$f(x) = \tfrac{1}{16},$$

for

$$4 \le x \le 20.$$

Find the probability that a number selected is in the subinterval [9, 17].

31. A transportation planner determines that the average distance between cars on a certain highway is 100 ft. What is the probability that the distance between cars is 40 ft or less?

33. A telephone company determines the duration t of a phone call is an exponentially distributed random variable with probability density function

$$f(t) = 2e^{-2t},$$
$$0 \le t < \infty.$$

Find the probability that a phone call will last no more than 5 minutes.

35. In a psychology experiment, the time t, in seconds, that it takes a rat to learn its way through a maze is an exponentially distributed random variable with probability density function

$$f(t) = 0.02e^{-0.02t},$$
$$0 \le t < \infty.$$

Find the probability that a rat will learn its way through a maze in 150 seconds, or less.

37. The *time to failure* t, in hours, of a certain machine can often be assumed to be exponentially distributed with probability density function

$$f(t) = ke^{-kt},$$
$$0 \le t < \infty$$

where $k = 1/a$, and a = average time that will pass before a failure occurs. Suppose the average time that will pass before a failure occurs is 100 hours. What is the probability that a failure will occur in 50 hours or less?

---

39. The function $f(x) = x^3$ is a probability density on $[0, b]$. What is b?

30. A number x is selected at random from the interval [5, 29]. The probability density function for x is given by

$$f(x) = \tfrac{1}{24},$$

for

$$5 \le x \le 29.$$

Find the probability that a number selected is in the subinterval [13, 29].

32. A transportation planner determines that the average distance between cars on a certain highway is 200 ft. What is the probability that the distance between cars is 10 ft or less?

34. Referring to the data in Exercise 31, find the probability that a phone call will last no more than 2 minutes.

36. Assume the situation and equation in Exercise 33, but find the probability that a rat will learn its way through a maze in 50 seconds or less.

38. The *reliability* of the machine (probability that it will work) in Exercise 35 is defined as

$$R(T) = 1 - \int_0^T 0.01e^{-0.01t}\, dt,$$

where $R(T)$ is the reliability at time T. Find $R(T)$.

40. The function $f(x) = 12x^2$ is a probability density on $[-a, a]$. What is a?

14.6 CONTINUOUS RANDOM VARIABLES: EXPECTED VALUE— STANDARD DEVIATION—NORMAL DISTRIBUTION

Expected Value

Let us again consider throwing a dart at a number line in such a way that it always lands in the interval [1, 3].

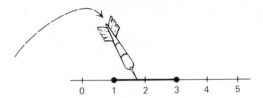

Suppose we throw the dart at the line 100 times and keep track of the numbers it hits. Then suppose we calculate the arithmetic mean (or average) $\bar{x}$ of all these numbers.

$$\bar{x} = \frac{x_1 + x_2 + x_3 + \cdots + x_{100}}{100} = \frac{\sum_{i=1}^{100} x_i}{100} = \sum_{i=1}^{100} x_i \cdot \frac{1}{100}.$$

The expression

$$\sum_{i=1}^{n} x_i \cdot \frac{1}{n}$$

is analogous to the integral

$$\int_{1}^{3} x \cdot f(x)\, dx,$$

where f is the probability density function for x. That is, $1/n$ gives a weight to x_i, and similarly $f(x)$ gives a weight to x. We add all the $x_i \cdot (1/n)$ values when we find $\sum_{i=1}^{n} x_i \cdot (1/n)$; and similarly we add all the $x \cdot f(x)$ values when we find $\int_{1}^{3} x \cdot f(x)\, dx$. Suppose $f(x) = \frac{1}{4}x$. Then

$$\int_{1}^{3} x \cdot f(x)\, dx = \int_{1}^{3} x \cdot \frac{1}{4}x\, dx = \left[\frac{1}{4} \cdot \frac{x^3}{3}\right]_{1}^{3} = \left[\frac{x^3}{12}\right]_{1}^{3}$$

$$= \frac{1}{12}(3^3 - 1^3) = \frac{26}{12} \approx 2.17.$$

Suppose that we keep on throwing the dart and computing averages. The more times we throw the dart, the closer we expect the averages will come to 2.17.

Let x be a continuous random variable over the interval $[a, b]$ with probability density function f.

The *expected value* of x is defined by

$$E(x) = \int_a^b x \cdot f(x)\, dx.$$

The notion of expected value generalizes to other functions of x.

The *expected value* of g(x) is defined by

$$E(g(x)) = \int_a^b g(x) \cdot f(x)\, dx.$$

For example,

$$E(x) = \int_a^b xf(x)\, dx, \quad E(x^2) = \int_a^b x^2 f(x)\, dx, \quad E(e^x) = \int_a^b e^x f(x)\, dx,$$

and

$$E(2x + 3) = \int_a^b (2x + 3)f(x)\, dx.$$

Example 1 Given the probability density function

$$f(x) = \tfrac{1}{2}x, \quad \text{over } [0, 2],$$

find $E(x)$ and $E(x^2)$.

Solution

$$E(x) = \int_0^2 x \cdot \frac{1}{2} x\, dx = \int_0^2 \frac{1}{2} x^2\, dx = \frac{1}{2}\left[\frac{x^3}{3}\right]_0^2$$

$$= \frac{1}{2}\left(\frac{2^3}{3} - \frac{0^3}{3}\right) = \frac{1}{2} \cdot \frac{8}{3} = \frac{4}{3}$$

$$E(x^2) = \int_0^2 x^2 \cdot \frac{1}{2} x\, dx = \int_0^2 \frac{1}{2} x^3\, dx = \frac{1}{2}\left[\frac{x^4}{4}\right]_0^2$$

$$= \frac{1}{2}\left(\frac{2^4}{4} - \frac{0^4}{4}\right) = \frac{1}{2} \cdot \frac{16}{4} = 2.$$

The *mean* μ of a continuous random variable is defined to be E(x). That is,

$$\mu = E(x) = \int_a^b xf(x)\, dx.$$

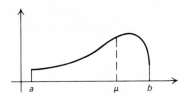 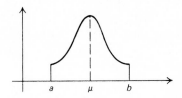

If we could imagine cutting out the region under the curve, the mean is the balance point. Note that the mean can be thought of as an average on the x-axis in contrast to the "average value of a function" that lies on the y-axis.

Standard Deviation

The *variance* σ^2 of a continuous random variable is defined

$$\sigma^2 = E(x^2) - \mu^2 = E(x^2) - [E(x)]^2$$

$$= \int_a^b x^2 f(x)\, dx - \left[\int_a^b x f(x)\, dx \right]^2.$$

The *standard deviation* σ of a continuous random variable is defined

$$\sigma = \sqrt{\text{variance}} = \sqrt{\sigma^2},$$

as before.

Example 2 Given the probability density function

$$f(x) = \tfrac{1}{2}x, \qquad \text{over } [0, 2],$$

find the mean, variance, and standard deviation.

Solution From Example 1.

$$E(x) = \tfrac{4}{3} \quad \text{and} \quad E(x^2) = 2.$$

Then

$$\text{The mean} = \mu = E(x) = \tfrac{4}{3};$$

$$\text{The variance} = \sigma^2 = E(x^2) - [E(x)]^2$$

$$= 2 - \left(\tfrac{4}{3}\right)^2$$

$$= 2 - \tfrac{16}{9}$$

$$= \tfrac{18}{9} - \tfrac{16}{9}$$

$$= \tfrac{2}{9};$$

$$\text{The standard deviation} = \sigma = \sqrt{\tfrac{2}{9}} = \tfrac{1}{3}\sqrt{2} \approx 0.47.$$

Loosely speaking, the standard deviation is a measure of how close the graph of f is to the mean. Note the following examples.

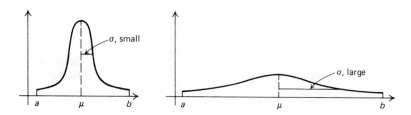

The Normal Distribution

Suppose the average on a test is 70. Usually there are about as many scores above the average as there are below; and the further away from the average, the fewer people there are who get a given score. For example, more people would score in the 80s than in the 90s; and more people would score in the 60s than in the 50s. Test scores, heights of human beings, and weights of human beings are all examples of random variables that may be *normally* distributed.

Consider the function

$$g(x) = e^{-x^2/2}, \quad \text{over the interval } (-\infty, \infty).$$

This function has the entire set of real numbers as domain. Its graph is the bell-shaped curve which follows. Function values are found by using a calculator or Table 4.

$$y = e^{-x^2/2}$$

x	0	1	2	3	-1	-2	-3
y	1	0.6	0.1	0.01	0.6	0.1	0.01

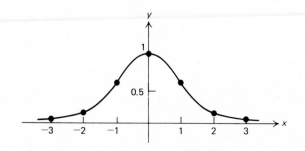

This function has an antiderivative, but that antiderivative has no elementary formula. Nevertheless, it has been shown that its improper integral converges over the interval $(-\infty, \infty)$, and

$$\int_{-\infty}^{\infty} e^{-x^2/2} \, dx = \sqrt{2\pi}.$$

That is, while an expression for the antiderivative cannot be found, there is a numerical value for the improper integral evaluated over the set of real numbers. Note that since the area is not 1, the function g is not a probability density function; but the following is:

$$\frac{1}{\sqrt{2\pi}} e^{-x^2/2}.$$

> **A continuous random variable x has a *standard normal distribution* if its probability density function is**
>
> $$f(x) = \frac{1}{\sqrt{2\pi}} e^{-x^2/2}, \qquad \textbf{over } (-\infty, \infty).$$

This distribution has a mean of 0 and standard deviation 1.
The general case is defined as follows.

> **A continuous random variable x is *normally distributed* with mean μ and standard deviation σ if its probability density function is given by**
>
> $$f(x) = \frac{1}{\sigma\sqrt{2\pi}} \cdot e^{-(1/2)[(x-\mu)/\sigma]^2}, \qquad \textbf{over } (-\infty, \infty).$$

Some examples are

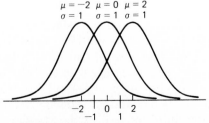

Normal distributions with same standard deviations but different means.

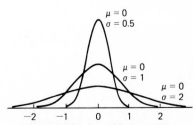

Normal distributions with same means but different standard deviations.

Recall that the standardized random variable z is given by

$$z = \frac{x - \mu}{\sigma}.$$

In terms of z the normal probability distribution can be written

$$f(z) = \frac{1}{\sigma\sqrt{2\pi}} \cdot e^{-z^2/2}, \quad \text{over } (-\infty, \infty).$$

This is the bell-shaped curve shown below.

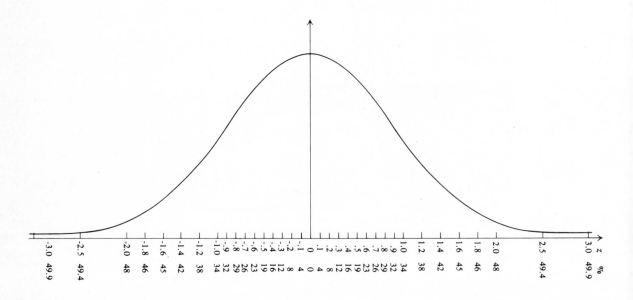

From the figure, we see that there is as much of the curve above the center (z = 0, the standardized mean) as below the center. The curve is symmetrical about z = 0. Between the center and one standard deviation *above* the center (between z = 0 and z = 1), 34% of the data (test scores) should lie. Similarly, between the center and one standard deviation *below* the center (between z = −1 and z = 0), another 34% of the data should lie. Thus, within one standard deviation of the mean (that is between z = −1 and z = 1) should lie 34% + 34%, or 68% of the data.

The normal distribution is extremely important in statistics; it underlies much of the research in the behavioral and social sciences. Because of this, tables of values of the definite integral of the standard density functions have been prepared. Table 6, at the back of the book, is such a table. It contains values of

$$P(0 \leq x \leq t) = \int_0^t \frac{1}{\sqrt{2\pi}} e^{-x^2/2} \, dx.$$

The symmetry of the graph about the mean allows many types of probabilities to be computed from the table.

Example 3 Let x be a continuous random variable with standard normal density. Using Table 6, find:

a) $P(0 \leq x \leq 1.68)$,

b) $P(-0.97 \leq x \leq 0)$,

c) $P(-2.43 \leq x \leq 1.01)$,

d) $P(1.90 \leq x \leq 2.74)$,

e) $P(-2.98 \leq x \leq -0.42)$,

f) $P(x \geq 0.61)$.

Solution a) $P(0 \leq x \leq 1.68)$ is the area bounded by the standard normal curve and the lines x = 0 and x = 1.68. We look this up in Table 6 by going down the left column to 1.6, then moving to the right to the column headed 0.08. There we read 0.4535. Thus

$$P(0 \leq x \leq 1.68) = 0.4535.$$

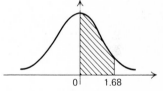

b) Due to the symmetry of the graph,
$P(-0.97 \leq x \leq 0)$
$= P(0 \leq x \leq 0.97) = 0.3340.$

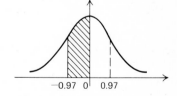

c) $P(-2.43 \leq x \leq 1.01)$
$= P(-2.43 \leq x \leq 0) + P(0 \leq x \leq 1.01)$
$= P(0 \leq x \leq 2.43) + P(0 \leq x \leq 1.01)$
$= 0.4925 + 0.3438$
$= 0.8363$

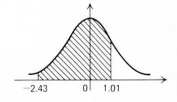

d) $P(1.90 \leqslant x \leqslant 2.74)$
   $= P(0 \leqslant x \leqslant 2.74) - P(0 \leqslant x \leqslant 1.90)$
   $= 0.4969 - 0.4713$
   $= 0.0256$

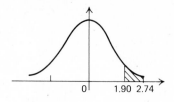

e) $P(-2.98 \leqslant x \leqslant -0.42)$
   $= P(0.42 \leqslant x \leqslant 2.98)$
   $= P(0 \leqslant x \leqslant 2.98) - P(0 \leqslant x \leqslant 0.42)$
   $= 0.4986 - 0.1628$
   $= 0.3358$

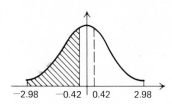

f) $P(x \geqslant 0.61)$
   $= P(x \geqslant 0) - P(0 \leqslant x \leqslant 0.61)$
   $= 0.5000 - 0.2291$

   (Because of the symmetry about the
   line $x = 0$, half the area is on each
   side of the line, and since the entire
   area is 1, $P(x \geqslant 0) = 0.5000$).

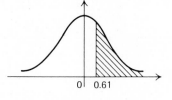

   $= 0.2709$

In many applications, a normal distribution is not standard. It would be a hopeless task to make tables for all values of the mean, μ, and the standard deviation, σ. As before, the transformation

$$z = \frac{x - \mu}{\sigma}$$

standardizes the distribution, permitting the use of Table 6 at the back of the book. That is,

$$P(a \leqslant x \leqslant b) = P\left(\frac{a - \mu}{\sigma} \leqslant z \leqslant \frac{b - \mu}{\sigma}\right),$$

and the probability on the right can be found using Table 6. To see this, consider

$$P(a \leqslant x \leqslant b) = \int_a^b \frac{1}{\sigma\sqrt{2\pi}} e^{-(1/2)[(x-\mu)/\sigma]^2} \, dx,$$

and make the substitution

$$z = \frac{x - \mu}{\sigma} = \frac{x}{\sigma} - \frac{\mu}{\sigma}.$$

Then

$$dz = \frac{1}{\sigma} \, dx.$$

When $x = a$, $z = (a - \mu)/\sigma$; and when $x = b$, $z = (b - \mu)/\sigma$. Then

$$P(a \leqslant x \leqslant b) = \int_a^b \frac{1}{\sigma\sqrt{2\pi}} \, e^{-(1/2)[(x-\mu)/\sigma]^2} \, dx$$

$$= \int_{(a-\mu)/\sigma}^{(b-\mu)/\sigma} \frac{1}{\sqrt{2\pi}} \, e^{-(1/2)z^2} \, dz \qquad \text{(The integrand is now in the form of the standard density.)}$$

$$= P\left(\frac{a - \mu}{\sigma} \leqslant z \leqslant \frac{b - \mu}{\sigma} \right). \qquad \text{(We can look this up in Table 6.)}$$

Example 4 The weights w of the students in a calculus class are normally distributed with mean 150 lb and standard deviation 25 lb. Find the probability that a student's weight is from 160 lb to 180 lb.

Solution We first standardize the weights:

$$180 \text{ is standardized to } \frac{b - \mu}{\sigma} = \frac{180 - 150}{25} = 1.2.$$

$$160 \text{ is standardized to } \frac{a - \mu}{\sigma} = \frac{160 - 150}{25} = 0.4.$$

Then

$$P(160 \leqslant w \leqslant 180) = P(0.4 \leqslant z \leqslant 1.2) \qquad \text{(Now we can use Table 6.)}$$

$$= P(0 \leqslant z \leqslant 1.2) - P(0 \leqslant z \leqslant 0.4)$$

$$= 0.3849 - 0.1554$$

$$= 0.2295.$$

Thus the probability that a student's weight is from 160 lb to 180 lb is 0.2295. That is, about 23% of the students have weights from 160 to 180 lb.

EXERCISE SET 14.6

For each probability density function, over the given interval, find $E(x)$, $E(x^2)$, the mean, variance, and standard deviation.

1. $f(x) = \frac{1}{3}$, $[2, 5]$ **2.** $f(x) = \frac{1}{4}$, $[3, 7]$ **3.** $f(x) = \frac{2}{9}x$, $[0, 3]$ **4.** $f(x) = \frac{1}{8}x$, $[0, 4]$

5. $f(x) = \frac{2}{3}x$, [1, 2]   **6.** $f(x) = \frac{1}{4}x$, [1, 3]   **7.** $f(x) = \frac{1}{3}x^2$, [−2, 1]   **8.** $f(x) = \frac{3}{2}x^2$, [−1, 1]

9. $f(x) = \dfrac{1}{\ln 3} \cdot \dfrac{1}{x}$, [1, 3]   **10.** $f(x) = \dfrac{1}{\ln 2} \cdot \dfrac{1}{x}$, [1, 2]

Let x be a continuous random variable with standard normal density. Using Table 6, find:

11. $P(0 \leqslant x \leqslant 2.69)$ **12.** $P(0 \leqslant x \leqslant 0.04)$

13. $P(-1.11 \leqslant x \leqslant 0)$ **14.** $P(-2.61 \leqslant x \leqslant 0)$

15. $P(-1.89 \leqslant x \leqslant 0.45)$ **16.** $P(-2.94 \leqslant x \leqslant 2.00)$

17. $P(1.76 \leqslant x \leqslant 1.86)$ **18.** $P(0.76 \leqslant x \leqslant 1.45)$

19. $P(-1.45 \leqslant x \leqslant -0.69)$ **20.** $P(-2.45 \leqslant x \leqslant -1.69)$

21. $P(x \geqslant 3.01)$ **22.** $P(x \geqslant 1.01)$

23. a) $P(-1 \leqslant x \leqslant 1)$ **24.** a) $P(-2 \leqslant x \leqslant 2)$

b) What percentage of the area is from −1 to 1?   b) What percentage of the area is from −2 to 2?

Let x be a continuous random variable which is normally distributed with mean $\mu = 22$ and standard deviation $\sigma = 5$. Using Table 6, find:

25. $P(24 \leqslant x \leqslant 30)$ **26.** $P(22 \leqslant x \leqslant 27)$ **27.** $P(19 \leqslant x \leqslant 25)$ **28.** $P(18 \leqslant x \leqslant 26)$

29. The heights h of the students in a calculus class are normally distributed with mean 65 in. and standard deviation 10 in.

a) Find the probability that a student's height is from 67 to 72 in.

b) Find the probability that a student's height is from 60 to 70 in.

c) Find the probability that a student's height is more than 6 ft (72 in.).

30. The daily production N of stereos by a recording company is normally distributed with mean 1000 and standard deviation 50. The company promises to pay bonuses to its employees on those days when the production of stereos is 1100 or more. What percentage of the days will the company have to pay a bonus?

31. The number of daily orders N received by a mail order firm is normally distributed with mean 250 and standard deviation 20. The company has to hire extra help or pay overtime on those days when the number of orders received is 300 or higher. What percentage of the days will the company find it necessary to hire extra help or pay overtime?

32. The scores S on a psychology test are normally distributed with mean 65 and standard deviation 20. A score of 80 to 89 is a B. What is the probability of getting a B?

33. If lightbulbs have a mean life of 270 days with a standard deviation of 30 days, what percent would be expected to last 360 days? If one started with 1000 lightbulbs, how many of them would be expected to last more than 360 days?

34. If transistors have a mean life of 525 days with a standard deviation of 90 days, what percent would be expected to last less than 360 days? If one started with 2000 transistors, how many of them would be expected to last less than 360 days?

35. A lecture series has a mean attendance of 670 and a standard deviation of 110.

   a) If an attendance of at least 500 is necessary to pay expenses, what percent of the time would you expect them not to cover expenses?

   b) If the hall can seat 825, what percent of the time would you expect not to be able to seat all those who come?

37. A farmer's mean crop of soybeans is 1150 bushels with a standard deviation of 240 bushels.

   a) What percent of the time should the farmer expect a crop of less than 1000 bushels?

   b) What percent of the time should the farmer expect a crop of more than 1250 bushels?

36. A movie theater that can seat 720 has a mean attendance of 490 and a standard deviation of 170.

   a) If an attendance of 300 is required to cover expenses, what percent of the time should they expect to cover expenses?

   b) What percent of the time should they expect more to come than they can seat?

14.7 MARKOV CHAINS

A *Markov chain* is a sequence of experiments with certain features which we shall illustrate before presenting a formal definition.

Example 1   *Business, Marketing Surveys.* A child, looking back over the many ice cream cones he has eaten through the years, recalls that:

   a) After he had eaten a vanilla cone, the probability was:

     i) 0 that he would pick vanilla next time,

     ii) $\frac{1}{2}$ that he would pick chocolate next time,

     iii) $\frac{1}{2}$ that he would pick strawberry next time;

   b) After he had eaten a chocolate cone, the probability was:

     i) $\frac{1}{5}$ that he would pick vanilla next time,

     ii) $\frac{2}{5}$ that he would pick chocolate next time,

     iii) $\frac{2}{5}$ that he would pick strawberry next time;

   c) After he had eaten a strawberry cone, the probability was:

     i) $\frac{1}{3}$ that he would pick vanilla next time,

     ii) 0 that he would pick chocolate next time,

     iii) $\frac{2}{3}$ that he would pick strawberry next time.

Assuming that the child's first ice cream cone is vanilla, draw the tree describing possible outcomes through his third ice cream cone.

Solution   The tree can be drawn in a straightforward manner.

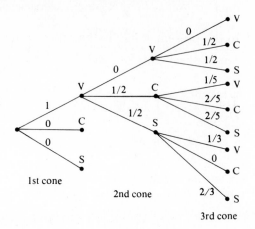

In view of the *repetitive* nature of the example, continuing the tree through further cycles (that is, the fourth and following ice cream cones) becomes increasingly awkward. Hence, it is useful to adopt an alternate way of representing these trials—that is, by means of a *transition diagram*.

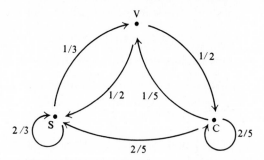

Here the directed line represents a *transition* from one *state* to another (here the state corresponds to a flavor). The number along the line corresponds to the probability that, if one starts in one state, next time he will be in the other state; that is, the probability of transition from one state to the other. The "transition" from one state at one stage to the *same* state at the next stage is represented by a "self" loop. The line is omitted where the transition probability is zero.

This transition diagram illustrates the general features of a *Markov chain*:

    1. The outcome of each experiment (or process, or choice) is one of a *set of discrete states* (a state is another name for an outcome).

2. **The probability for transition from one state to another depends only on the present state (that is, the state one is in and is leaving).**

In the present example the states correspond to flavors. And since the next choice of flavor depends only on the previous choice, the whole process is a Markov chain.

Transition *diagrams* provide a *graphical* way of representing Markov chains. However, for computational purposes, *transition matrices* are more convenient.

We can define a transition matrix T by

$$T = [t_{ij}]_{n \times n},$$

a square matrix, where there are n states and t_{ij} represents the transition probability from state i to state j, so that $0 \leqslant t_{ij} \leqslant 1$. Note that the order of the indices *is* important. Since the object in question must be in one of the n states,

$$\sum_{i=1}^{n} t_{ij} = 1 \qquad \text{for all } i = 1, \ldots, n;$$

that is, the sum of the *row* entries must be 1. There is no corresponding restriction for *column* entries.

Example 2   What is the transition matrix for the problem of Example 1?

Solution   Let vanilla be state 1, chocolate be state 2, and strawberry be state 3. Then

$$T = \begin{array}{c} \\ \begin{array}{ccc} V & C & S \end{array} \\ \begin{bmatrix} 0 & \frac{1}{2} & \frac{1}{2} \\ \frac{1}{5} & \frac{2}{5} & \frac{2}{5} \\ \frac{1}{3} & 0 & \frac{2}{3} \end{bmatrix} \begin{array}{c} V \\ C \\ S \end{array} \end{array}$$

Note that the *row* elements do sum to 1.

Example 3   Given the following matrix, determine whether it qualifies as a transition matrix. If it does, draw the corresponding transition diagram.

$$T = \begin{array}{c} \\ \begin{array}{cccc} 1 & 2 & 3 & 4 \end{array} \\ \begin{bmatrix} \frac{1}{2} & \frac{1}{2} & 0 & 0 \\ \frac{1}{2} & 0 & \frac{1}{2} & 0 \\ 0 & \frac{1}{3} & \frac{1}{3} & \frac{1}{3} \\ \frac{1}{2} & 0 & 0 & \frac{1}{2} \end{bmatrix} \begin{array}{c} 1 \\ 2 \\ 3 \\ 4 \end{array} \end{array}$$

Solution   i) Since the elements are all nonnegative and the row elements all sum to one, we have a transition matrix and can proceed.

ii) Labeling the states 1, 2, 3, and 4, we have:

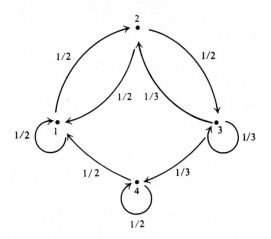

Note that the various states can be located where convenient or advantageous, so that pictorially the transition diagram may not be unique.

Transition matrices are useful in determining the probability of being in various states at later stages.

Example 4   For Example 1, determine the probability that the child will choose each of the different flavors for the second cone; for the third cone.

Solution   Let us solve this problem first by using the tree diagram, then using the transition matrix.

Method 1   It is convenient to describe the initial state of the system by a probability *vector* (here a row matrix),

$$P_0 = [p_1 \quad p_2 \cdots p_n],$$

where p_i $(i = 1, \ldots, n)$ is the probability of being in state i at that stage. Thus, $0 \leq p_i \leq 1$, because p_i is a probability and $\Sigma_{i-1}^n \, p_i = 1$, since the n states exhaust the possibilities. In the present case, the initial probability vector is

$$P_0 = [1 \quad 0 \quad 0],$$

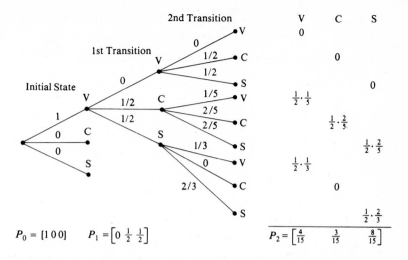

$$P_0 = [1\,0\,0] \qquad P_1 = \left[0\ \tfrac{1}{2}\ \tfrac{1}{2}\right] \qquad\qquad P_2 = \left[\tfrac{4}{15}\quad \tfrac{3}{15}\quad \tfrac{8}{15}\right]$$

since the child's first ice cream cone was vanilla (the first state) and there were three flavors. If the child were equally likely to have picked any flavor, then the initial probability vector would have been

$$P_0 = [\tfrac{1}{3}\ \ \tfrac{1}{3}\ \ \tfrac{1}{3}].$$

Multiplying along branches of the tree and adding among the branches, we obtain the results of the *first* choice as the probability vector

$$P_1 = [0\ \ \tfrac{1}{2}\ \ \tfrac{1}{2}]. \qquad \text{(See figure above.)}$$

The components represent the probability that vanilla, chocolate, or straw-berry will be chosen for the *second* cone, given that the *first* cone was vanilla.

Continuing along the branches of the tree for the *second* choice (that is, the third cone), we obtain

$$P_2 = [\tfrac{4}{15}\ \ \tfrac{3}{15}\ \ \tfrac{8}{15}].$$

The components represent the probability that vanilla, chocolate, or straw-berry will be chosen for the *third* cone, given that the *first* cone was vanilla.

Method 2 As can be seen from the transition *diagram*, the same results can be obtained from the transition *matrix* in the following manner:

$$P_1 = P_0 T,$$

$$P_2 = P_1 T,$$

$$\vdots \qquad \vdots$$

Here,

$$P_1 = [1 \quad 0 \quad 0] \cdot \begin{bmatrix} 0 & \frac{1}{2} & \frac{1}{2} \\ \frac{1}{5} & \frac{2}{5} & \frac{2}{5} \\ \frac{1}{3} & 0 & \frac{2}{3} \end{bmatrix} = [0 \quad \frac{1}{2} \quad \frac{1}{2}],$$

$$P_2 = [0 \quad \frac{1}{2} \quad \frac{1}{2}] \cdot \begin{bmatrix} 0 & \frac{1}{2} & \frac{1}{2} \\ \frac{1}{5} & \frac{2}{5} & \frac{2}{5} \\ \frac{1}{3} & 0 & \frac{2}{3} \end{bmatrix} = [\frac{4}{15} \quad \frac{3}{15} \quad \frac{8}{15}],$$

$$\vdots$$

The numerical computation is the same in both cases, but the transition matrix facilitates the computation.

Alternately, we could substitute the expression for P_1 into the expression for P_2, obtaining:

$$P_2 = (P_0 T)T = P_0 T^2.$$

Thus, here we have

$$P_2 = [1 \quad 0 \quad 0] \cdot \begin{bmatrix} 0 & \frac{1}{2} & \frac{1}{2} \\ \frac{1}{5} & \frac{2}{5} & \frac{2}{5} \\ \frac{1}{3} & 0 & \frac{2}{3} \end{bmatrix}^2 = [1 \quad 0 \quad 0] \cdot \begin{bmatrix} \frac{4}{15} & \frac{3}{15} & \frac{8}{15} \\ \frac{32}{150} & \frac{39}{150} & \frac{79}{150} \\ \frac{4}{18} & \frac{3}{18} & \frac{11}{18} \end{bmatrix}$$

or

$$P_2 = [\frac{4}{15} \quad \frac{3}{15} \quad \frac{8}{15}], \qquad \text{as before.}$$

In general, we can obtain each probability vector from its predecessor,

$$P_n = P_{n-1}T;$$

or directly from the initial probability vector,

$$P_n = P_0 T^n.$$

We now consider what happens in the "long run"; that is, when the number of transitions, n, becomes increasingly large.

Example 5 What fraction of the time will the child of Example 1 pick each flavor ice cream in the "long run"?

Solution The transition matrix for Example 1 was obtained in Example 2 and is

$$T = \begin{bmatrix} 0 & \frac{1}{2} & \frac{1}{2} \\ \frac{1}{5} & \frac{2}{5} & \frac{2}{5} \\ \frac{1}{3} & 0 & \frac{2}{3} \end{bmatrix}.$$

In Example 3, we found that if we started with a probability vector

$$P_0 = [1 \quad 0 \quad 0],$$

then

$$P_1 = [0 \quad \tfrac{1}{2} \quad \tfrac{1}{2}]$$

and

$$P_2 = [\tfrac{4}{15} \quad \tfrac{3}{15} \quad \tfrac{8}{15}].$$

Continuing, we obtain

$$P_3 = P_2 T = [\tfrac{49}{225} \quad \tfrac{48}{225} \quad \tfrac{128}{225}]$$

and so forth

$$\vdots$$

$$P_n = P_{n-1} T.$$

Here we are interested in what happens to P_n as n becomes increasingly large. While it may not be apparent, this sequence of probability vectors is approaching some limit vector, although it does so rather slowly.

Furthermore, we could have started with the initial probability vector

$$P_0 = [0 \quad 1 \quad 0]$$

or

$$P_0 = [0 \quad 0 \quad 1]$$

and find that for increasingly large values of n, they all* approach the *same* limit vector.†

> If these sequences tend to approach some limit vector, then after a while there should be little change from one transition to the next. This leads us to ask what some probability vector $\overline{P}$ must be such that it is the same after a transition as before. That is, we want to find $\overline{P}$ such that
>
> $$\overline{P} = \overline{P}T.$$

Such a probability vector is called a *fixed probability vector*, or *fixed point*.

---

* Or any convex combination of these three initial probability vectors.

† This is true for any *regular* Markov chain, which is the only kind considered here. Further discussion of regular and irregular Markov chains will be found in "Finite Mathematics—A Modeling Approach," Second Edition, by Crown and Bittinger, Addison-Wesley Publishing Co., 1981.

The equation $\overline{P} = \overline{P}T$ can be written $O = \overline{P}T - \overline{P}$, or, since matrix multiplication is distributive,

$$\overline{P}(T - I) = O$$

where I is the identity matrix of appropriate order.

This system of equations, $\overline{P}(T - I) = O$, is homogeneous (which we cannot pursue here in detail, but see Section 3.2) and hence does not have a unique (nontrivial) solution. The solution can be made unique, however, since the probability vector

$$\overline{P} = [\overline{p}_1 \quad \overline{p}_2 \cdots \overline{p}_n]$$

must have components which sum to 1; that is,

$$\sum_{i=1}^{n} \overline{p}_i = 1.$$

The system can now be solved using the echelon method of Chapter 3. For this Example, we have

$$\sum_{i=1}^{3} \overline{p}_i = \overline{p}_1 + \overline{p}_2 + \overline{p}_3 = 1,$$

and

$$\overline{P}(T - I) = O$$

or

$$[\overline{p}_1 \quad \overline{p}_2 \quad \overline{p}_3]\left(\begin{bmatrix} 0 & \frac{1}{2} & \frac{1}{2} \\ \frac{1}{5} & \frac{2}{5} & \frac{2}{5} \\ \frac{1}{3} & 0 & \frac{2}{3} \end{bmatrix} - \begin{bmatrix} 1 & 0 & 0 \\ 0 & 1 & 0 \\ 0 & 0 & 1 \end{bmatrix}\right) = [0 \quad 0 \quad 0],$$

so that

$$[\overline{p}_1 \quad \overline{p}_2 \quad \overline{p}_3]\begin{bmatrix} -1 & \frac{1}{5} & \frac{1}{3} \\ \frac{1}{2} & -\frac{3}{5} & 0 \\ \frac{1}{2} & \frac{2}{5} & -\frac{1}{3} \end{bmatrix} = [0 \quad 0 \quad 0].$$

Thus, the initial echelon tableau is

$\overline{p}_1$	$\overline{p}_2$	$\overline{p}_3$	1
1	1	1	1
-1	$\frac{1}{5}$	$\frac{1}{3}$	0
$\frac{1}{2}$	$-\frac{3}{5}$	0	0
$\frac{1}{2}$	$\frac{2}{5}$	$-\frac{1}{3}$	0

Note that the *columns* of $(T - I)$ become the *rows* of the echelon tableau. Solving, we obtain the final tableau.

$\bar{p}_1$	$\bar{p}_2$	$\bar{p}_3$	1
1	0	0	$\frac{6}{26}$
0	1	0	$\frac{5}{26}$
0	0	1	$\frac{15}{26}$
0	0	0	0

The last row of zeros is evidence of the linear dependence of the system $\bar{P}(T - I) = O$. The fixed probability vector is:

$$\bar{P} = [\begin{smallmatrix} \frac{6}{26} & \frac{5}{26} & \frac{15}{26} \end{smallmatrix}],$$

which does satisfy the fixed-point equation.

We can interpret the significance of the fixed-point vector this way. If the given child in Example 1 is typical of all children, or if the data given is obtained from a survey of many children, then the fixed-point probability vector tells the ice cream manufacturer how much of each flavor ice cream must be made to satisfy the expected demand.

EXERCISE SET 14.7

1. *Business.* A taxi company in a certain town has set up three zones. Taxis picking up a passenger in the first zone have 50% probability of delivering the passenger to that zone and are twice as likely to deliver a passenger to the second zone as to the third zone. A passenger picked up in the second zone will be let off there with a probability equal to that for being delivered to either other zone. A passenger picked up in the third zone is twice as likely to go to the first zone as either to go to the second zone or to stay in the third zone. Draw the transition diagram and find the transition matrix.

2. *Business, Marketing Surveys.* Of car owners surveyed, 60% of the VW owners would buy a VW for their next car while 20% each would buy a Ford or Chevy. Of the Ford owners, 30% would buy a Ford next time, 30% would buy VW, and 40% a Chevy. Of the Chevy owners, 40% would buy a Chevy, 40% a VW, and 20% a Ford. Draw the transition diagram and find the transition matrix.

For each matrix of Exercises 3 through 14, determine whether it qualifies as a transition matrix. If not, state why. If so, draw the transition diagram.

3. $\begin{bmatrix} \frac{1}{2} & -\frac{1}{8} & \frac{5}{8} \\ \frac{1}{3} & \frac{1}{3} & \frac{1}{3} \\ \frac{1}{5} & \frac{2}{5} & \frac{2}{5} \end{bmatrix}$

4. $\begin{bmatrix} \frac{2}{5} & \frac{2}{5} & \frac{1}{5} \\ 0 & 1 & 0 \\ 1 & 0 & 0 \end{bmatrix}$

5. $\begin{bmatrix} \frac{1}{2} & \frac{1}{2} & 0 & 0 \\ \frac{1}{2} & \frac{1}{2} & 0 & 0 \\ 0 & 0 & \frac{2}{3} & \frac{1}{3} \\ 0 & 0 & \frac{1}{3} & \frac{2}{3} \end{bmatrix}$

6. $\begin{bmatrix} \frac{1}{3} & \frac{2}{3} & 0 \\ \frac{1}{2} & \frac{3}{8} & \frac{3}{8} \\ 0 & \frac{2}{3} & \frac{1}{3} \end{bmatrix}$

7. $\begin{bmatrix} 1 & 0 \\ 0 & 1 \end{bmatrix}$
  8. $\begin{bmatrix} 0 & 1 \\ 1 & 0 \end{bmatrix}$
  9. $\begin{bmatrix} 1 & 0 & 0 \\ 0 & 1 & 0 \\ \frac{1}{2} & \frac{1}{2} & 0 \end{bmatrix}$
  10. $\begin{bmatrix} 0 & 1 & 0 \\ 0 & 0 & 1 \\ 1 & 0 & 0 \end{bmatrix}$

11. $\begin{bmatrix} 0 & 1 & 0 \\ 0 & 0 & 1 \\ 0 & 0 & 1 \end{bmatrix}$
  12. $\begin{bmatrix} \frac{1}{2} & \frac{1}{2} & 0 & 0 \\ 0 & \frac{1}{2} & \frac{1}{2} & 0 \\ 0 & 0 & \frac{1}{2} & \frac{1}{2} \\ 0 & 0 & \frac{1}{2} & \frac{1}{2} \end{bmatrix}$
  13. $\begin{bmatrix} \frac{1}{2} & \frac{1}{2} & 0 & 0 \\ 0 & 1 & 0 & 0 \\ 0 & \frac{1}{3} & \frac{1}{3} & \frac{1}{3} \\ 0 & 0 & 0 & 1 \end{bmatrix}$
  14. $\begin{bmatrix} 0 & 1 & 0 & 0 \\ \frac{1}{3} & \frac{1}{3} & \frac{1}{3} & 0 \\ 0 & \frac{1}{3} & \frac{1}{3} & \frac{1}{3} \\ 0 & 0 & 1 & 0 \end{bmatrix}$

15. *Business.* As in Exercise 1, a taxi starts in the second zone. Using a tree, determine its probable location after discharging its second passenger. What is the initial probability vector? Determine the probability vector after the second passenger, two ways.

16. *Business, Marketing Surveys.* As in Exercise 2, assume that initially car ownership is equally divided among VW, Ford, and Chevy. Using a tree, determine the probable ownership distribution for the second car; for the third car. What is the initial probability vector? Determine the probability vector for the second car, and for the third car, two ways.

17. As in Exercise 15, but the taxi starts in the *third* zone. Which method is less work?

18. As in Exercise 16, but the initial distribution is all VW's; is all Fords; is all Chevies.

In each of Exercises 19 through 35, given P_0 and T, determine P_n.

19. $P_0 = [1 \quad 0 \quad 0]$, T from Exercise 4, $P_2 = ?$
  20. $P_0 = [1 \quad 0 \quad 0]$, T from Exercise 4, $P_3 = ?$

21. $P_0 = [\frac{1}{4} \quad \frac{1}{4} \quad \frac{1}{4} \quad \frac{1}{4}]$, T from Exercise 5, $P_2 = ?$
  22. $P_0 = [\frac{1}{5} \quad \frac{4}{5}]$, T from Exercise 7, $P_5 = ?$

23. $P_0 = [\frac{1}{2} \quad \frac{1}{2}]$, T from Exercise 8, $P_1 = ?$
  24. $P_0 = [1 \quad 0]$, T from Exercise 8, $P_1 = ?$

25. $P_0 = [1 \quad 0]$, T from Exercise 8, $P_2 = ?$
  26. $P_0 = [0 \quad 0 \quad 1]$, T from Exercise 9, $P_1 = ?$

27. $P_0 = [0 \quad 0 \quad 1]$, T from Exercise 9, $P_2 = ?$
  28. $P_0 = [\frac{1}{3} \quad \frac{1}{3} \quad \frac{1}{3}]$, T from Exercise 11, $P_2 = ?$

29. $P_0 = [\frac{1}{3} \quad \frac{1}{3} \quad \frac{1}{3}]$, T from Exercise 11, $P_3 = ?$
  30. $P_0 = [\frac{1}{4} \quad \frac{1}{4} \quad \frac{1}{4} \quad \frac{1}{4}]$, T from Exercise 12, $P_1 = ?$

31. $P_0 = [\frac{1}{4} \quad \frac{1}{4} \quad \frac{1}{4} \quad \frac{1}{4}]$, T from Exercise 12, $P_2 = ?$
  32. $P_0 = [\frac{1}{4} \quad \frac{1}{4} \quad \frac{1}{4} \quad \frac{1}{4}]$, T from Exercise 13, $P_1 = ?$

33. $P_0 = [\frac{1}{4} \quad \frac{1}{4} \quad \frac{1}{4} \quad \frac{1}{4}]$, T from Exercise 13, $P_2 = ?$
  34. $P_0 = [\frac{1}{4} \quad \frac{1}{4} \quad \frac{1}{4} \quad \frac{1}{4}]$, T from Exercise 14, $P_1 = ?$

Determine the fixed probability vector for each transition matrix of Exercises 35 through 44.

35. $T = \begin{bmatrix} 0 & 1 \\ \frac{1}{2} & \frac{1}{2} \end{bmatrix}$
  36. $T = \begin{bmatrix} 0 & 1 & 0 \\ \frac{2}{3} & 0 & \frac{1}{3} \\ \frac{1}{3} & \frac{2}{3} & 0 \end{bmatrix}$
  37. $T = \begin{bmatrix} 0 & 1 & 0 \\ 0 & 0 & 1 \\ \frac{2}{5} & \frac{3}{5} & 0 \end{bmatrix}$
  38. $T = \begin{bmatrix} 0 & 1 & 0 \\ 0 & \frac{2}{3} & \frac{3}{5} \\ 1 & 0 & 0 \end{bmatrix}$

39. $T = \begin{bmatrix} 0 & 0 & 1 \\ 0 & 0 & 1 \\ \frac{2}{5} & \frac{3}{5} & 0 \end{bmatrix}$
  40. $T = \begin{bmatrix} \frac{1}{5} & \frac{2}{5} & \frac{2}{5} \\ \frac{1}{2} & 0 & \frac{1}{2} \\ \frac{1}{4} & \frac{1}{4} & \frac{1}{2} \end{bmatrix}$
  41. $T = \begin{bmatrix} 0 & \frac{2}{5} & 0 & \frac{3}{5} \\ 0 & 0 & 0 & 1 \\ 1 & 0 & 0 & 0 \\ 0 & 0 & 1 & 0 \end{bmatrix}$
  42. $T = \begin{bmatrix} 0 & \frac{1}{3} & \frac{2}{3} & 0 \\ 0 & 0 & 1 & 0 \\ 0 & 0 & 0 & 1 \\ \frac{2}{3} & \frac{1}{3} & 0 & 0 \end{bmatrix}$

43. $T = \begin{bmatrix} 0 & 0 & 0 & 1 \\ \frac{1}{2} & 0 & \frac{1}{2} & 0 \\ 0 & \frac{1}{2} & 0 & \frac{1}{2} \\ 0 & 0 & 1 & 0 \end{bmatrix}$

44. $T = \begin{bmatrix} 0 & 0 & \frac{3}{4} & \frac{1}{4} \\ \frac{1}{2} & 0 & 0 & \frac{1}{2} \\ \frac{1}{4} & \frac{3}{4} & 0 & 0 \\ 0 & \frac{1}{2} & \frac{1}{2} & 0 \end{bmatrix}$

45. Using the data from Exercise 35, determine the "long-run" distribution (fixed-point probability vector) of taxi location. By successive squaring, show that each row of T^m is approaching the fixed point.

46. Using the data from Exercise 36, determine the "long-run" distribution of car ownership. By successive squaring, show that each row of T^m is approaching the fixed point.

CHAPTER 14 REVIEW

1. Two fair dice are rolled and the *difference* (in magnitude) between the numbers showing is noted. What is the probability function?

2. For Exercise 1, what is the expected value of this difference?

3. A sea chest contains 10 silver bars and 5 gold ones. Three are drawn at random and the number of gold bars is noted. What is the probability function?

4. For Exercise 3, what is the expected number of gold bars to be drawn?

5. For Exercise 3, what is the variance of the number of gold bars drawn?

6. For Exercise 3, what is the standard deviation of the number of gold bars drawn?

7. A raffle is being held to raise money for a charity. There are 1000 tickets to be sold for $10 each, with a first prize of a three-week vacation in Europe worth $1500, a second prize of one week in lovely downtown Burbank worth $250, and 5 third prizes of $2 tickets to a movie travelogue. What is the expected value of a ticket? How much of the cost of each ticket goes to charity if the printing expenses are $40 and all other labor is volunteer?

8. What is the probability for tails to show twice in 6 flips of a fair coin? List the configurations.

9. Treatment for a certain disease is effective 80% of the time. If six treated patients are surveyed, what is the probability that four of them will be cured?

10. What is the probability function for the problem of Exercise 9?

11. Determine the expected value for the problem of Exercise 9.

12. ▦ Determine the variance and standard deviation for the problem of Exercise 9.

13. An old sea chest contains 10 bars of silver and 5 bars of gold. Three are drawn out at random, the number of gold bars is noted, and the bars are replaced. This is repeated four times. What is the probability for drawing two gold bars three times? *Caution.* Interpret subscripts carefully.

14. Assuming that the heights of female college students have a normal probability distribution with a mean of 5′3″ and a standard deviation of 2.5″, how many students out of a freshman class of 2000 (female) students can be expected to be under 5′ tall?

15. *Political Science.* Of voters sampled, 60% of the Democrats (that is, who voted Democrat in the last election) will vote Democrat in the next election, 20% will vote Republican, and 20% will vote Independent.

Of the Republicans, 40% will vote Democrat and 60% will vote Republican. Of the Independents, 40% will vote Democrat, 20% will vote Republican, and 40% will vote Independent.

a) Assuming that voters are split evenly among the three parties, draw a tree indicating voting patterns through one election.

b) Draw the transition diagram.

16. What is the transition matrix for the problem of Exercise 15?

17. For each matrix, determine whether it qualifies as a transition matrix. If it does, draw the corresponding transition diagram.

a) $T = \begin{bmatrix} \frac{1}{3} & \frac{1}{3} & \frac{1}{3} & 0 \\ \frac{1}{2} & \frac{1}{2} & 0 & 0 \\ \frac{1}{3} & 0 & \frac{1}{3} & \frac{1}{3} \\ 0 & 0 & \frac{1}{2} & \frac{1}{2} \end{bmatrix}$

b) $T = \begin{bmatrix} \frac{1}{8} & \frac{2}{8} & 0 & \frac{5}{8} \\ \frac{1}{9} & \frac{2}{9} & 0 & \frac{5}{9} \\ \frac{1}{2} & 0 & 0 & \frac{1}{2} \\ \frac{1}{4} & \frac{3}{4} & 0 & 0 \end{bmatrix}$

18. For Exercise 15, determine the probability vector for the first election using both a tree diagram and the transition matrix. Assuming the transition matrix does not change for the subsequent election, determine the probability vector for the second election from the transition matrix.

19. Determine the fixed probability vector and long-range properties of the transition matrix:

$$T = \begin{bmatrix} 0 & 1 & 0 \\ \frac{1}{3} & \frac{1}{3} & \frac{1}{3} \\ 0 & 1 & 0 \end{bmatrix}.$$

20. A multiple-choice test consists of 5 questions, each with a choice of 4 answers. If a student guesses answers at random, what is the probability function for the number of correct answers?

21. A multiple-choice test consists of 5 questions each with a choice of 4 answers. If the probability is $\frac{3}{4}$ that a student knows an answer to a question, what is the probability that he gets at least 4 correct?

22. In Exercise 21, what is the number of questions the student should expect to get correct?

23. Given the following probability function, find the expected value.

x	0	1	2	3	4
p	$\frac{1}{9}$	$\frac{2}{9}$	$\frac{3}{9}$	$\frac{2}{9}$	$\frac{1}{9}$

24. Using the data of Exercise 23, find the variance.

25. Using the data of Exercise 24, find the standard deviation.

26. Using the data of Exercise 23, what is the standardized random variable corresponding to $x = 1$?

27. Find k such that $f(x) = kx^3$ is a probability density function over the interval $[0, 2]$.

28. A telephone company determines that the length of time t of a phone call is an exponentially distributed random variable with probability density function

$$f(t) = 2e^{-2t}, \quad 0 \leq t \leq \infty.$$

Find the probability that a phone call will last no more than 1 minute.

Given the probability density function $f(x) = 3x^2$, over $[0, 1]$, find:

29. $E(x)$ **30.** $E(x^2)$ **31.** the variance.   **32.** the standard deviation.

Let x be a continuous random variable with standard normal density. Using Table 6, find:

33. $P(0 \leq x \leq 1.5)$ **34.** $P(0.12 \leq x \leq 2.32)$ **35.** $P(-1.61 \leq x \leq 1.76)$

36. The price per pound p of T-bone steak at various stores in a certain city is normally distributed with mean \$3.75 and standard deviation \$25. What is the probability that the price per pound is \$3.80 or more?

37. In a certain city a review of electoral records indicated that in an election in which the incumbent was:

a) Democratic, the probability was:
   i) 0.4 that the next mayor would be Democratic,
   ii) 0.3 that the next mayor would be Republican,
   iii) 0.3 that the next mayor would be Independent;

b) Republican, the probability was:
   i) 0.4 that the next mayor would be Democratic,
   ii) 0.6 that the next mayor would be Republican,
   iii) 0 that the next mayor would be Independent;

c) Independent, the probability was:
   i) 0.3 that the next mayor would be Democratic,
   ii) 0 that the next mayor would be Republican,
   iii) 0.7 that the next mayor would be Independent.

Assuming that the mayor is originally a Republican, draw the tree describing the possible outcomes. Draw the transition diagram and set up the transition matrix.

38. Given

$$P_0 = [1 \quad 0 \quad 0] \text{ and } T = \begin{bmatrix} \frac{1}{2} & \frac{1}{2} & 0 \\ 0 & \frac{2}{3} & \frac{1}{3} \\ \frac{1}{4} & 0 & \frac{3}{4} \end{bmatrix},$$

find P_2 and the fixed probability vector.

FUNCTIONS OF SEVERAL VARIABLES

15.1 PARTIAL DERIVATIVES

Functions of Several Variables

Suppose a one-product firm produces x items of its product at a profit of $4 per item. Then its total profit $P(x)$ is given by

$$P(x) = 4x.$$

This is a function of *one* variable.

Suppose a two-product firm produces x items of one product at a profit of $4 per item, and y items of a second at a profit of $6 per item. Then its total profit P is a function of the *two* variables, x and y, and is given by

$$P(x, y) = 4x + 6y.$$

This function assigns to the input pair (x, y) a unique output number $4x + 6y$.

Example 1   For $P(x, y) = 4x + 6y$, find $P(25, 10)$.

Solution $P(25, 10)$ is defined to be the value of the function found by substituting 25 for x and 10 for y:

$$P(25, 10) = 4 \cdot 25 + 6 \cdot 10 = 100 + 60 = 160.$$

This means that the two-product firm, by selling 25 items of the first product and 10 of the second, will make a profit of $160.

The following are further examples of functions of several variables, that is, functions of two or more variables.

Example 2 *Price-Earnings Ratio.* The *price-earnings ratio* of a stock is given by the function

$$R(P, E) = \frac{P}{E},$$

where P is the price per share of the stock and E is the earnings per share. Recently, the price per share of Standard Oil of California was $96\frac{7}{8}$ and the earnings per share were $13.50. Find the price-earnings ratio.

Solution
$$R(\$96\tfrac{7}{8}, \$13.50) = \frac{\$96\tfrac{7}{8}}{\$13.50} = \frac{96.875}{13.50} \approx 7.2$$

Example 3 The volume of a rectangular solid is given by

$$V(x, y, z) = xyz,$$

where x is the length, y the width, and z the height. This is a function of three variables.

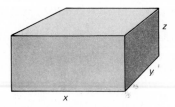

Example 4 The production of a company is given by

$$f(x, y, z, w) = 4x^2 + 5y + z - w,$$

where x dollars are spent for labor, y dollars are spent for raw materials, z dollars are spent for advertising, and w dollars are spent for machinery. This is a function of four variables.

Find $f(3, 2, 0, 10)$.

Solution We substitute 3 for x, 2 for y, 0 for z, and 10 for w.

$$f(3, 2, 0, 10) = 4 \cdot 3^2 + 5 \cdot 2 + 0 - 10$$

$$= 4 \cdot 9 + 10 + 0 - 10 = 36$$

Example 5 Suppose an amount P_0 is invested in a savings account, where interest is compounded continuously at interest rate k. The balance after t years is given by

$$P(P_0, k, t) = P_0 e^{kt}.$$

Find $P(\$100, 0.19, 1)$.

Solution $P(\$100, 0.19, 1) = 100 e^{0.19(1)} = 100(1.209250) \quad (\blacksquare \text{ or Table 4})$

$$\approx \$120.93$$

Example 6 *The gravity model.* The number of telephone calls between two cities is given by

$$N(d, P_1, P_2) = \frac{2.8 P_1 P_2}{d^{2.4}},$$

where d is the distance between the cities, and P_1 and P_2 are their populations.

A constant can also be thought of as a function of several variables.

Example 7 The constant function f is given by

$$f(x, y) = -3, \quad \text{for all inputs x and y.}$$

Find $f(5, 7)$ and $f(-2, 0)$.

Solution Since this is a constant function, it has the value -3 for any x and y. Therefore,

$$f(5, 7) = -3$$

and

$$f(-2, 0) = -3.$$

Partial Derivatives

Consider the function f given by

$$z = f(x, y) = x^2y^3 + xy + 4y^2.$$

Suppose for the moment that we fix y at 3. Then

$$f(x, 3) = x^2 3^3 + x3 + 4 \cdot 3^2 = 27x^2 + 3x + 36.$$

Note that we now have a function of only one variable. Taking the first derivative with respect to x, we have

$$54x + 3.$$

Now, without replacing y by a specific number, let us consider y fixed. Then f becomes a function of x alone and we can calculate its derivative with respect to x. This derivative is called the *partial derivative of f with respect to x*. Notation for this partial derivative is

$$\frac{\partial f}{\partial x} \quad \text{or} \quad \frac{\partial z}{\partial x}.$$

Thus fixing y (treating it as a constant) and calculating the derivative with respect to x, we have

$$\frac{\partial f}{\partial x} = \frac{\partial z}{\partial x} = 2xy^3 + y.$$

Similarly, we find $\partial f/\partial y$ or $\partial z/\partial y$ by fixing x (treating it as a constant) and calculating the derivative with respect to y. We have

$$\frac{\partial f}{\partial y} = \frac{\partial z}{\partial y} = 3x^2y^2 + x + 8y.$$

Partial differentiation can be done for any number of variables.

Example 8 For $w = x^2 - xy + y^2 + 2yz + 2z^2 + z$, find

$$\frac{\partial w}{\partial x}, \frac{\partial w}{\partial y}, \quad \text{and} \quad \frac{\partial w}{\partial z}.$$

Solution

$$\frac{\partial w}{\partial x} = 2x - y$$

$$\frac{\partial w}{\partial y} = -x + 2y + 2z$$

$$\frac{\partial w}{\partial z} = 2y + 4z + 1$$

We will often make use of a simpler notation f_x for the partial derivative of f with respect to x, and f_y for the partial derivative of f with respect to y.

Example 9   For $f(x, y) = 3x^2y + xy$, find f_x and f_y.

Solution
$$f_x = 6xy + y, \quad f_y = 3x^2 + x$$

For the function in the preceding example, let us evaluate f_x at $(2, -3)$.

$$f_x(2, -3) = 6 \cdot 2 \cdot (-3) + (-3) = -39$$

Using the notation $\partial z/\partial x = 6xy + y$, where $z = 3x^2y + xy$, the value of the partial derivative at $(2, -3)$ is given by

$$\left. \frac{\partial z}{\partial x} \right|_{(2, -3)} = 6 \cdot 2 \cdot (-3) + (-3) = -39,$$

but this notation is not as convenient as $f_x(2, -3)$.

Example 10   For $f(x, y) = e^{xy} + y \ln x$, find f_x and f_y.

Solution
$$f_x = y \cdot e^{xy} + y \cdot \frac{1}{x} = ye^{xy} + \frac{y}{x},$$

$$f_y = x \cdot e^{xy} + 1 \cdot \ln x = xe^{xy} + \ln x$$

Economic Interpretations

Recall the functions considered at the beginning of this section:

$$P(x) = \$4x \quad \text{and} \quad P(x, y) = \$4x + \$6y.$$

For $P(x)$, we have

$$\frac{dP}{dx} = \$4,$$

which also happens to be the coefficient in the original function. In such a context, dP/dx is called an *influence coefficient*. It directly influences, in fact it is, the rate of change of P with respect to the number of items x. Similarly, for $P(x, y)$ we have

$$\frac{\partial P}{\partial x} = \$4 \quad \text{and} \quad \frac{\partial P}{\partial y} = \$6.$$

These are also called *influence coefficients*, since they show how the function changes—in one case with respect to x, and in the other case with respect to y.

Geometric Interpretations

Consider a function of two variables

$$z = f(x, y).$$

As a mapping, a function of two variables can be thought of as mapping a point (x_1, y_1) in an xy-plane onto a point z_1 on a number line:

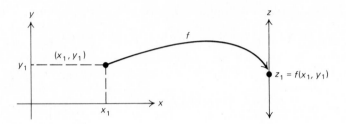

To graph a function of two variables, we need a three-dimensional coordinate system. The axes are usually placed as follows. The line z, called the z-axis, is placed perpendicular to the xy-plane at the origin.

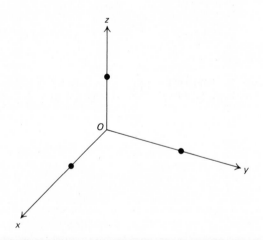

To help visualize this, think of looking into the corner of a room, where the floor is the xy-plane and the z-axis is the intersection of two walls. To plot a point (x_1, y_1, z_1) we locate the point (x_1, y_1) in the xy-plane, and move up or down in space according to the value of z_1.

Example 11   Plot these points: $P_1(2, 3, 5)$, $P_2(2, -2, -4)$, and $P_3(0, 5, 2)$.

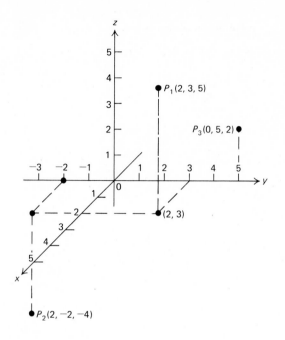

Solution The *graph* of a function of two variables

$$z = f(x, y)$$

consists of ordered triples (x_1, y_1, z_1), where $z_1 = f(x_1, y_1)$. The domain of f is a region D in the xy-plane, and the graph of f is a surface S, as shown below.

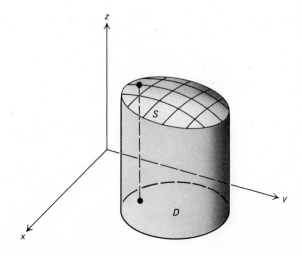

Here are some equations and their graphs.

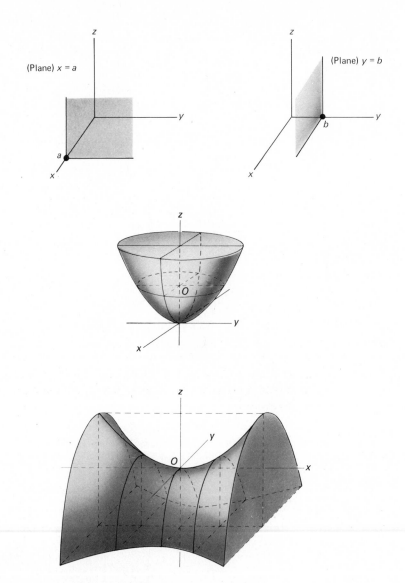

Now suppose we hold x fixed, say at the value a. The set of all points for which $x = a$ is a plane parallel to the yz-plane, so when x is fixed at a, y and z vary along the plane as shown in the following figure.

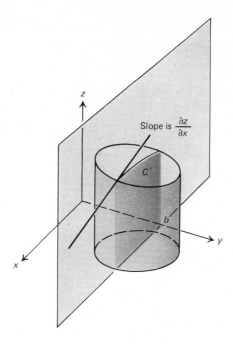

The plane shown cuts the surface S in some curve C as shown. The partial derivative f_y gives the slopes of tangent lines to this curve. Similarly, if we hold y fixed, say at the value b, we obtain a curve C' as shown in the following figure. The partial derivative f_x gives the slopes of tangent lines to this curve.

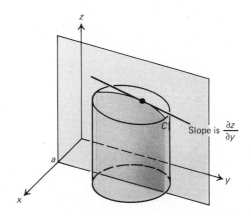

Economic Application—The Cobb-Douglas Production Function

One model of production that is frequently considered in business and economics is the *Cobb-Douglas Production function*:

$$p(x, y) = Ax^a y^{1-a}, \quad A > 0 \quad \text{and} \quad 0 < a < 1,$$

where p is the number of units produced with x units of labor and y units of capital. Capital is the cost of machinery, buildings, tools, and other supplies. The partial derivatives

$$\frac{\partial p}{\partial x} \quad \text{and} \quad \frac{\partial p}{\partial y}$$

are called, respectively, the *marginal productivity of labor* and the *marginal productivity of capital*.

Example 12 A company has the following production function for a certain product:

$$p(x, y) = 50x^{2/3}y^{1/3}.$$

a) Find the production from 125 units of labor and 64 units of capital.

b) Find the marginal productivities.

c) Evaluate the marginal productivities at $x = 125$ and $y = 64$.

Solution

a) $p(125, 64) = 50(125)^{2/3}(64)^{1/3} = 50(25)(4) = 5000$ units

b) $\dfrac{\partial p}{\partial x} = 50\left(\dfrac{2}{3}\right)x^{-1/3}y^{1/3} = \dfrac{100y^{1/3}}{3x^{1/3}}, \quad$ or $\quad \dfrac{100}{3}\left(\dfrac{y}{x}\right)^{1/3},$

$\dfrac{\partial p}{\partial y} = 50\left(\dfrac{1}{3}\right)x^{2/3}y^{-2/3} = \dfrac{50x^{2/3}}{3y^{2/3}}, \quad$ or $\quad \dfrac{50}{3}\left(\dfrac{x}{y}\right)^{1/3}$

c) $\left.\dfrac{\partial p}{\partial x}\right|_{(125,\,64)} = \dfrac{100(64)^{1/3}}{3(125)^{1/3}} = \dfrac{100(4)}{3(15)} = 8\dfrac{8}{9},$

$\left.\dfrac{\partial p}{\partial y}\right|_{(125,\,64)} = \dfrac{50(125)^{2/3}}{3(64)^{2/3}} = \dfrac{50(25)}{3(16)} = 26\dfrac{1}{24}$

How can we interpret marginal productivities? Suppose the amount spent on capital is fixed at, say, $y = 64$. Then if the amount of labor changes by a small amount, production will change by about 9 units. Suppose the amount of labor is held fixed at, say, $x = 125$. Then if the amount of capital spent changes slightly, this will produce a change of about 26 units of production.

A Cobb-Douglas Production function is consistent with the law of diminishing returns. That is, if one input (of either labor or capital) is held fixed while the other increases infinitely, then production will eventually increase at a decreasing rate. With such functions it also turns out that if a certain maximum production is possible, then the expense of more labor, for example, will not prevent that maximum output from still being attainable.

EXERCISE SET 15.1

1. For $f(x, y) = x^2 - 2xy$, find $f(0, -2)$, $f(2, 3)$, and $f(10, -5)$.

2. For $f(x, y) = y^2 + 3xy$, find $f(-2, 0)$, $f(3, 2)$, and $f(-5, 10)$.

3. For $f(x, y) = 3^x + 7xy$, find $f(0, -2)$, $f(-2, 1)$, and $f(2, 1)$.

4. For $f(x, y) = \log_{10}x - 5y^2$, find $f(10, 2)$, $f(1, -3)$, and $f(100, 4)$.

5. For $f(x, y) = \ln x + y^3$, find $f(e, 2)$, $f(e^2, 4)$, and $f(e^3, 5)$.

6. For $f(x, y) = 2^x - 3^y$, find $f(0, 0)$, $f(1, 1)$, and $f(2, 2)$.

7. For $f(x, y, z) = x^2 - y^2 + z^2$, find $f(-1, 2, 3)$ and $f(2, -1, 3)$.

8. For $f(x, y, z) = 2^x + 5zy - x$, find $f(0, 1, -3)$ and $f(1, 0, -3)$.

9. *Price-earnings ratio.* The *price-earnings ratio* of a stock is given by

$$R(P, E) = \frac{P}{E},$$

where P is the price per share of the stock and E is the earnings per share. Recently, the price per share of IBM stock was $287\frac{3}{8}$ and the earnings per share were $23.30. Find the price-earnings ratio. Give decimal notation to the nearest tenth.

10. *Yield of a stock.* The *yield* of a stock is given by

$$Y(D, P) = \frac{D}{P},$$

where D is the dividends per share of a stock and P is the price per share. Recently, the price per share of Goodyear stock was $16\frac{7}{8}$ and the dividends per share were $1.30. Find the yield. Give percent notation to the nearest tenth of a percent.

11. ▧ *Present value.* The present value P of an amount A at interest rate i, compounded n times a year for t years is given by

$$P(A, i, n, t) = A\left(1 + \frac{i}{n}\right)^{-nt}.$$

Find $P(\$10,000, 0.19, 12, 10)$.

12. ▧ *The amount of an annuity.* The amount of an annuity V, where P dollars are invested at the end of each of N years at interest rate i, compounded annually, is given by

$$V(P, i, N) = \frac{P[(1 + i)^N - 1]}{i}.$$

Find $V(\$1000, 0.1875, 20)$.

Find $\dfrac{\partial z}{\partial x}, \dfrac{\partial z}{\partial y}, \dfrac{\partial z}{\partial x}\bigg|_{(-2, -3)}$, and $\dfrac{\partial z}{\partial y}\bigg|_{(0, -5)}$

13. $z = 2x - 3xy$

14. $z = 5y + 2xy$

15. $z = 3x^2 - 2xy + y$

16. $z = 2x^3 + 3xy - x$

Find f_x, f_y, $f_x(-2, 4)$, and $f_y(4, -3)$.

17. $f(x, y) = 2x - 3y$ **18.** $f(x, y) = 5x + 7y$

Find f_x, f_y, $f_x(-2, 1)$, and $f_y(-3, -2)$.

19. $f(x, y) = \sqrt{x^2 + y^2}$ **20.** $f(x, y) = \sqrt{x^2 - y^2}$

Find f_x and f_y.

21. $f(x, y) = e^{2x+3y}$ **22.** $f(x, y) = e^{3x-2y}$ **23.** $f(x, y) = e^{xy}$

24. $f(x, y) = e^{2xy}$ **25.** $f(x, y) = y \ln(x + y)$ **26.** $f(x, y) = x \ln(x + y)$

27. $f(x, y) = x \ln(xy)$ **28.** $f(x, y) = y \ln(xy)$ **29.** $f(x, y) = \dfrac{x}{y} - \dfrac{y}{x}$

30. $f(x, y) = \dfrac{x}{y} + \dfrac{y}{x}$ **31.** $f(x, y) = 3(2x + y - 5)^2$ **32.** $f(x, y) = 4(3x + y - 8)^2$

Find $\dfrac{\partial f}{\partial b}$ and $\dfrac{\partial f}{\partial m}$.

33. $f(b, m) = (m + b - 4)^2 + (2m + b - 5)^2 + (3m + b - 6)^2$

34. $f(b, m) = (m + b - 6)^2 + (2m + b - 8)^2 + (3m + b - 9)^2$

Find f_x, f_y, and f_λ.

35. $f(x, y, \lambda) = 3xy - \lambda(2x + y - 8)$ **36.** $f(x, y, \lambda) = 4xy - \lambda(3x - y + 7)$

37. $f(x, y, \lambda) = x^2 + y^2 - \lambda(10x + 2y - 4)$ **38.** $f(x, y, \lambda) = x^2 - y^2 - \lambda(4x - 7y - 10)$

39. A company has the following production function for a certain product:

$$p(x, y) = 1800x^{0.621}y^{0.379},$$

where p is the number of units produced with x units of labor and y units of capital.

   a) ■ Find the production from 2500 units of labor and 1700 units of capital.

   b) Find the marginal productivities.

   c) ■ Evaluate the marginal productivities at $x = 2500$ and $y = 1700$.

40. A company has the following production function for a certain product:

$$p(x, y) = 2400x^{2/5}y^{3/5},$$

where p is the number of units produced with x units of labor and y units of capital.

   a) Find the production from 32 units of labor and 1024 units of capital.

   b) Find the marginal productivities.

   c) Evaluate the marginal productivities at $x = 32$ and $y = 1024$.

15.2 HIGHER-ORDER PARTIAL DERIVATIVES

Consider

$$z = f(x, y) = 3xy^2 + 2xy + x^2. \tag{1}$$

Then

$$\frac{\partial z}{\partial x} = \frac{\partial f}{\partial x} = 3x^2 + 2y + 2x. \tag{2}$$

Suppose we find the first partial derivative of function (2) with respect to y. This will be a *second-order partial derivative*. Notation for it is as follows.

$$\frac{\partial}{\partial y}\left(\frac{\partial z}{\partial x}\right) = \frac{\partial}{\partial y}\left(\frac{\partial f}{\partial x}\right) = \frac{\partial^2 z}{\partial y\,\partial x} = \frac{\partial^2 f}{\partial y\,\partial x} = 6y + 2.$$

We could also denote the preceding partial derivative using the notation f_{xy}. Then

$$f_{xy} = 6y + 2.$$

Note that in the notation f_{xy}, x and y are in the order (left to right) in which the differentiation is done. In the other symbolisms that order is reversed, but the meaning is not.

Notation for the four second-order partial derivatives is as follows:

$$\frac{\partial^2 z}{\partial x\,\partial x} = \frac{\partial^2 f}{\partial x\,\partial x} = \frac{\partial^2 z}{\partial x^2} = \frac{\partial^2 f}{\partial x^2} = f_{xx}$$ (Take the partial with respect to x, and then with respect to x again.)

$$\frac{\partial^2 z}{\partial y\,\partial x} = \frac{\partial^2 f}{\partial y\,\partial x} = f_{xy}$$ (Take the partial with respect to x, and then with respect to y.)

$$\frac{\partial^2 z}{\partial x\,\partial y} = \frac{\partial^2 f}{\partial x\,\partial y} = f_{yx}$$ (Take the partial with respect to y, and then with respect to x.)

$$\frac{\partial^2 z}{\partial y\,\partial y} = \frac{\partial^2 f}{\partial y\,\partial y} = \frac{\partial^2 z}{\partial y^2} = \frac{\partial^2 f}{\partial y^2} = f_{yy}$$ (Take the partial with respect to y, and then with respect to y again.)

Example 1   For

$$z = f(x, y) = x^2 y^3 + x^4 y + xe^y$$

find the four second-order partial derivatives.

Solution   a) $\dfrac{\partial^2 f}{\partial x^2} = \dfrac{\partial}{\partial x}(2xy^3 + 4x^3 y + e^y)$ (Differentiate twice with respect to x.)

$$= 2y^3 + 12x^2 y$$

b) $\dfrac{\partial^2 f}{\partial y\,\partial x} = \dfrac{\partial}{\partial y}(2xy^3 + 4x^3 y + e^y)$ (Differentiate with respect to x, then with respect to y.)

$$= 6xy^2 + 4x^3 + e^y$$

c) $\dfrac{\partial^2 f}{\partial x\,\partial y} = \dfrac{\partial}{\partial x}(3x^2 y^2 + x^4 + xe^y)$ (Differentiate with respect to y, then with respect to x.)

$$= 6xy^2 + 4x^3 + e^y$$

d) $\dfrac{\partial^2 f}{\partial y^2} = \dfrac{\partial}{\partial y}(3x^2y^2 + x^4 + xe^y)$

(Differentiate twice with respect to y.)

$\qquad = 6x^2y + xe^y$

Note by comparing (b) and (c) above that

$$\frac{\partial^2 f}{\partial y\,\partial x} = \frac{\partial^2 f}{\partial x\,\partial y} \qquad \text{(And similarly, } f_{xy} = f_{yx}.\text{)}$$

This will be true for all functions that we consider in this text, but is *not* true for all functions.

EXERCISE SET 15.2

Find the four second-order partial derivatives.

1. $f(x, y) = 3x^2 - xy + y$ 　　**2.** $f(x, y) = 5x^2 + xy - x$ 　　**3.** $f(x, y) = 3xy$

4. $f(x, y) = 4xy$ 　　**5.** $f(x, y) = x^5y^4 + x^3y^2$ 　　**6.** $f(x, y) = x^4y^3 - x^2y^3$

Find f_{xx}, f_{yx}, f_{xy}, and f_{yy}. (Remember, f_{yx} means differentiate with respect to y, then x.)

7. $f(x, y) = 2x - 3y$ 　　**8.** $f(x, y) = 3x + 5y$ 　　**9.** $f(x, y) = e^{2xy}$

10. $f(x, y) = e^{xy}$ 　　**11.** $f(x, y) = x + e^y$ 　　**12.** $f(x, y) = y - e^x$

13. $f(x, y) = y \ln x$ 　　**14.** $f(x, y) = x \ln y$

Consider the production function

$$p(x, y) = 60x^{2/3}y^{1/3},$$

where p is the number of units produced with x units of labor and y units of capital.

15. Prove that $\dfrac{\partial^2 p}{\partial x^2} < 0$. Interpret this result. 　　**16.** Prove that $\dfrac{\partial^2 p}{\partial y^2} < 0$. Interpret this result.

■

Find f_{xx}, f_{yz}, f_{xy}, and f_{yy}:

17. $f(x, y) = \dfrac{x}{y^2} - \dfrac{y}{x^2}$ 　　　　　　　**18.** $f(x, y) = \dfrac{xy}{x - y}$

15.3   MAXIMUM–MINIMUM PROBLEMS

In this section we shall find maximum and minimum values of functions of two variables.

DEFINITION

A function f of two variables

i) has a relative maximum at (a, b) if

$$f(x, y) \leq f(a, b)$$

for all points in a circular region containing (a, b).

ii) has a relative minimum at (a, b) if

$$f(x, y) \geq f(a, b)$$

for all points in a circular region containing (a, b).

This definition is illustrated in Fig. 1.

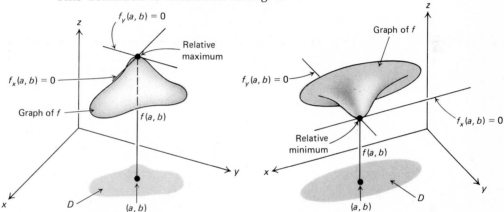

Figure 1

A relative maximum (minimum) may not be an "absolute" maximum (minimum) as illustrated in Fig. 2.

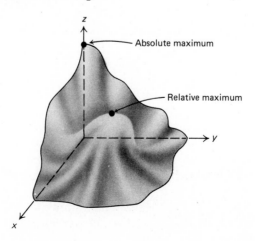

Figure 2

Determining Maximum and Minimum Values

Suppose a function f assumes a relative maximum (or minimum) value at some point (a, b) inside its domain. If we hold y constant at the value b, then $f(x, b)$ is a function of one variable x having its relative maximum value at $x = a$, so its derivative must be 0 there. That is, $f_x = 0$ at the point (a, b). Similarly, $f_y = 0$ at (a, b). The equations

$$f_x = 0, \qquad f_y = 0$$

are thus satisfied by the point (a, b) at which the relative maximum occurs. We call a point (a, b) where both partial derivatives are 0 a *critical point*. This is comparable to the earlier definition for functions of one variable. Thus one strategy for finding relative maximum or minimum values is to solve the above system of equations to find critical points. Just as for functions of one variable, this strategy does *not* guarantee that we will have a relative maximum or minimum value. We have argued only that *if* f has a maximum or minimum value at (a, b), *then* both its partial derivatives must be 0 at that point. Look at Fig. 1. That this does not hold in all cases is shown in Fig. 3.

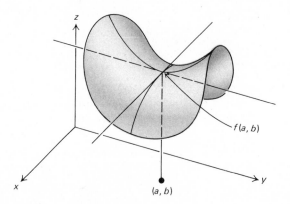

Figure 3

Now suppose we fix y at a point b. Then $f(x, b)$, considered as a function of one variable, has a maximum at a, but f does not. Similarly, if we fix x at a, then $f(a, y)$, considered as a function of one variable, has a minimum at b, but f does not. The point $f(a, b)$ is called a *saddle point*. In other words, $f_x(a, b) = 0$ and $f_y(a, b) = 0$ [the point (a, b) is a critical point], but f does not attain a relative maximum or minimum at (a, b).

A test for finding relative maximum and minimum values that involves the use of first- and second-order partial derivatives is stated below. We shall not prove this theorem.

THEOREM

The D-test. **To find the relative maximum and minimum values of *f*,**

1. **Find f_x, f_y, f_{xx}, f_{yy}, and f_{xy}.**
2. **Solve the system of equations $f_x = 0$, $f_y = 0$.**
   Let (a, b) represent a solution.
3. **Evaluate D where $D = f_{xx}(a, b) \cdot f_{yy}(a, b) - [f_{xy}(a, b)]^2$.**
4. **Then**

   i) **f has a maximum at (a, b) if $D > 0$ and $f_{xx}(a, b) < 0$.**

   ii) **f has a minimum at (a, b) if $D > 0$ and $f_{xx}(a, b) > 0$.**

   iii) **f has neither a maximum nor a minimum at (a, b) if $D < 0$. The**
   function has a *saddle point* at (a, b). See Fig. 3.

   iv) **This test is not applicable if $D = 0$.**

A relative maximum or minimum *may not be an absolute maximum or minimum*. Tests for absolute maximum or minimum are rather complicated. We shall restrict our attention to finding *relative* maximum or minimum values. Fortunately, in most applications relative maximum and minimum values turn out to be absolute maximum and minimum values.

Example 1   Find the relative maximum and minimum values of

$$f(x, y) = x^2 + xy + y^2 - 3x.$$

Solution   **1.** Find f_x, f_y, f_{xx}, f_{yy}, and f_{xy}.

$$f_x = 2x + y - 3, \qquad f_y = x + 2y,$$

$$f_{xx} = 2, \qquad f_{yy} = 2,$$

$$f_{xy} = 1.$$

2. Solve the system of equations $f_x = 0$, $f_y = 0$:

$$2x + y - 3 = 0 \tag{1}$$

$$x + 2y = 0. \tag{2}$$

Solving Eq. (2) for x we get $x = -2y$. Substituting $-2y$ for x in Eq. (1) and solving we get

$$2(-2y) + y - 3 = 0$$

$$-4y + y - 3 = 0$$

$$-3y - 3 = 0$$

$$y = -1.$$

To find x when $y = -1$, we substitute -1 for y in either Eq. (1) or Eq. (2). We use Eq. (2):

$$x + 2(-1) = 0$$

$$x = 2.$$

Thus $(2, -1)$ is our candidate for a maximum or minimum.

3. We have to check to see if $f(2, -1)$ is a maximum or minimum.

$$D = f_{xx}(2, -1) \cdot f_{yy}(2, -1) - [f_{xy}(2, -1)]^2$$

$$= 2 \cdot 2 - [1]^2 = 3.$$

4. Thus $D = 3$ and $f_{xx}(2, -1) = 2$. Since $D > 0$ and $f_{xx}(2, -1) > 0$, it follows that f has a relative minimum at $(2, -1)$ and that the minimum is found as follows:

$$f(2, -1) = 2^2 + 2(-1) + (-1)^2 - 3 \cdot 2$$

$$= 4 - 2 + 1 - 6 = -3.$$

Example 2   Find the relative maximum and minimum values of

$$f(x, y) = xy - x^3 - y^2.$$

Solution   1. Find f_x, f_y, f_{xx}, f_{yy}, and f_{xy}:

$$f_x = y - 3x^2, \qquad f_y = x - 2y,$$

$$f_{xx} = -6x, \qquad f_{yy} = -2,$$

$$f_{xy} = 1.$$

2. Solve the system of equations $f_x = 0$, $f_y = 0$:

$$y - 3x^2 = 0 \tag{1}$$

$$x - 2y = 0. \tag{2}$$

Solving Eq. (1) for y, we get $y = 3x^2$. Substituting $3x^2$ for y in Eq. (2) and solving, we get

$$x - 2(3x^2) = 0$$

$$x - 6x^2 = 0$$

$$x(1 - 6x) = 0. \qquad \text{(Factoring)}$$

Setting each factor equal to 0 and solving, we have

$$x = 0 \quad \text{or} \quad 1 - 6x = 0$$

$$x = 0 \quad \text{or} \quad x = \tfrac{1}{6}.$$

To find y when $x = 0$ we substitute 0 for x in either Eq. (1) or Eq. (2). We use Eq. (2).

$$0 - 2y = 0$$

$$-2y = 0$$

$$y = 0.$$

Thus $(0, 0)$ is one critical value (candidate for a maximum or minimum). To find the other critical value we substitute $\frac{1}{6}$ for x in either Eq. (1) or (2). We use Eq. (2).

$$\tfrac{1}{6} - 2y = 0$$

$$-2y = -\tfrac{1}{6}$$

$$y = \tfrac{1}{12}.$$

Thus $(\frac{1}{6}, \frac{1}{12})$ is another critical point.

3. We have to check both $(0, 0)$ and $(\frac{1}{6}, \frac{1}{12})$ as to whether they yield maximum or minimum values.

$$\text{For } (0, 0): \quad D = f_{xx}(0, 0) \cdot f_{yy}(0, 0) - [f_{xy}(0, 0)]^2$$

$$= [-6 \cdot 0] \cdot [-2] - [1]^2$$

$$= -1$$

Since $D < 0$, it follows that $f(0, 0)$ is neither a maximum nor a minimum, but a saddle point.

$$\text{For } (\tfrac{1}{6}, \tfrac{1}{12}): \quad D = f_{xx}(\tfrac{1}{6}, \tfrac{1}{12}) f_{yy}(\tfrac{1}{6}, \tfrac{1}{12}) - [f_{xy}(\tfrac{1}{6}, \tfrac{1}{12})]^2$$

$$= [-6 \cdot \tfrac{1}{6}] \cdot [-2] - [1]^2$$

$$= -1(-2) - 1$$

$$= 1$$

4. Thus $D = 1$ and $f_{xx}(\frac{1}{6}, \frac{1}{12}) = -1$. Since $D > 0$ and $f_{xx}(\frac{1}{6}, \frac{1}{12}) < 0$, it follows that f has a relative maximum at $(\frac{1}{6}, \frac{1}{12})$ and that maximum is found as follows:

$$f(\tfrac{1}{6}, \tfrac{1}{12}) = \tfrac{1}{6} \cdot \tfrac{1}{12} - (\tfrac{1}{6})^3 - (\tfrac{1}{12})^2$$

$$= \tfrac{1}{72} - \tfrac{1}{216} - \tfrac{1}{144} = \tfrac{1}{432}.$$

Example 3   *Maximizing profit.* A firm produces two kinds of golf balls, one that sells for \$3 each and the other for \$2 each. The total revenue from the sale of x thousand balls at \$3 each and y thousand at \$2 each is given by

$$R(x, y) = 3x + 2y.$$

The company determines that the total cost, in thousands of dollars, of producing x thousand of the $3 ball and y thousand of the $2 ball is given by

$$C(x, y) = 2x^2 - 2xy + y^2 - 9x + 6y + 7.$$

Find the amount of each type of ball that must be produced and sold to maximize profit.

Solution   Total profit, $P(x, y)$ is given by

$$P(x, y) = R(x, y) - C(x, y)$$
$$= 3x + 2y - (2x^2 - 2xy + y^2 - 9x + 6y + 7)$$
$$P(x, y) = -2x^2 + 2xy - y^2 + 12x - 4y - 7.$$

1. Find P_x, P_y, P_{xx}, P_{yy}, and P_{xy}.

$$P_x = -4x + 2y + 12, \qquad P_y = 2x - 2y - 4,$$
$$P_{xx} = -4, \qquad\qquad P_{yy} = -2,$$
$$P_{xy} = 2.$$

2. Solve the system of equations $P_x = 0$, $P_y = 0$:

$$-4x + 2y + 12 = 0 \tag{1}$$
$$2x - 2y - 4 = 0. \tag{2}$$

Adding these equations, we get

$$-2x + 8 = 0.$$

Then

$$-2x = -8$$
$$x = 4.$$

To find y when x = 4, we substitute 4 for x in either Eq. (1) or Eq. (2). We use Eq. (2):

$$2 \cdot 4 - 2y - 4 = 0$$
$$-2y + 4 = 0$$
$$-2y = -4$$
$$y = 2.$$

Thus, (4, 2) is our candidate for a maximum or minimum.

3. We have to check to see if $P(4, 2)$ is a maximum or minimum.

$$D = P_{xx}(4, 2)P_{yy}(4, 2) - [P_{xy}(4, 2)]^2$$

$$= (-4)(-2) - 2^2$$

$$= 4$$

4. Thus $D = 4$ and $P_{xx} = -4$. Since $D > 0$ and $P_{xx}(4, 2) < 0$, it follows that P has a relative maximum at $(4, 2)$. Thus to maximize profit, the company must produce and sell 4 thousand of the $3 golf balls and 2 thousand of the $2 golf balls.

EXERCISE SET 15.3

Find the relative maximum and minimum values.

1. $f(x, y) = x^2 + xy + y^2 - y$

2. $f(x, y) = x^2 + xy + y^2 - 5y$

3. $f(x, y) = 2xy - x^3 - y^2$

4. $f(x, y) = 4xy - x^3 - y^2$

5. $f(x, y) = x^3 + y^3 - 3xy$

6. $f(x, y) = x^3 + y^3 - 6xy$

7. $f(x, y) = x^2 + y^2 - 2x + 4y - 2$

8. $f(x, y) = x^2 + 2xy + 2y^2 - 6y + 2$

9. $f(x, y) = x^2 + y^2 + 2x - 4y$

10. $f(x, y) = 4y + 6x - x^2 - y^2$

11. $f(x, y) = 4x^2 - y^2$

12. $f(x, y) = x^2 - y^2$

In these problems assume that relative maximum and minimum values are absolute maximum and minimum values.

13. *Maximizing profit.* A firm produces two kinds of radios, one that sells for $17 each and the other for $21 each. The total revenue from the sale of x thousand radios at $17 each and y thousand at $21 each is given by

$$R(x, y) = 17x + 21y.$$

The company determines that the total cost, in thousands of dollars, of producing x thousand of the $17 radio and y thousand of the $19 radio is given by

$$C(x, y) = 4x^2 - 4xy + 2y^2 - 11x + 25y - 3.$$

Find the amount of each type of radio that must be produced and sold to maximize profit.

14. *Maximizing profit.* A firm produces two kinds of baseball gloves, one that sells for $18 each and the other for $25 each. The total revenue from the sale of x thousand gloves at $18 each and y thousand at $25 each is given by

$$R(x, y) = 18x + 25y.$$

The company determines that the total cost, in thousands of dollars, of producing x thousand of the $18 glove and y thousand of the $25 glove is given by

$$C(x, y) = 4x^2 - 6xy + 3y^2 + 20x + 19y - 12.$$

Find the amount of each type of radio that must be produced and sold to maximize profit.

15. A one-product company found that its profit in millions of dollars is a function P given by

$$P(a, p) = 2ap + 80p - 15p^2 - \tfrac{1}{10}a^2p - 100,$$

where a = amount spent on advertising, in millions of dollars, and p = price charged per item of the product, in dollars. Find the maximum value of P and the values of a and p at which it is attained.

16. A one-product company finds that its profit in millions of dollars is a function P given by

$$P(a, n) = -5a^2 - 3n^2 + 48a - 4n + 2an + 300,$$

where a = amount spent on advertising, in millions of dollars, and n = number of items sold. Find the maximum value of P and the values of a and n at which it is attained.

■ ─────────────────────────────────

17. *Two-variable revenue maximization.* Boxowitz, Inc., a computer firm, markets two kinds of electronic calculators that compete with one another. Their demand functions are expressed by the following relationships

$$q_1 = 78 - 6p_1 - 3p_2, \qquad (1)$$
$$q_2 = 66 - 3p_1 - 6p_2, \qquad (2)$$

where

p_1, p_2 = the price of each calculator in multiples of \$10,
q_1, q_2 = quantity of each calculator demanded in hundreds of units.

  a) Find a formula for the total revenue function R in terms of the variables p_1 and p_2. [*Hint:* $R = [p_1q_1 + p_2q_2$, then substitute expressions from Eqs. (1) and (2) to find $R(p_1, p_2)$.]

  b) What prices p_1 and p_2 should be charged for each product in order to maximize total revenue?

  c) How many units will be demanded?

  d) What is the maximum total revenue?

Find the relative maximum and minimum values.

18. Repeat Exercise 17, where

$$q_1 = 64 - 4p_1 - 2p_2, \quad \text{and}$$
$$q_2 = 56 - 2p_1 - 4p_2.$$

19. $f(x, y) = e^x + e^y - e^{x+y}$

20. $f(x, y) = xy + \dfrac{2}{x} + \dfrac{4}{y}$

21. $S(b, m) = (m + b - 72)^2 + (2m + b - 73)^2 + (3m + b - 75)^2$

22. An open-top rectangular box is to be made with a 20-meter^2 surface area. Find the dimensions that will yield the maximum volume.

15.4 CONSTRAINED MAXIMUM AND MINIMUM VALUES—LAGRANGE MULTIPLIERS

Before we get into detail let us look at a problem we considered earlier.

Example 1 A hobby store has 20 ft of fencing to fence off a rectangular electric-train area in one corner of its display room. What dimensions of the rectangle will maximize the area?

We maximize the function

$$A = xy$$

subject to the condition or *constraint* $x + y = 20$. Note that A is a function of two variables:

$$A(x, y) = xy.$$

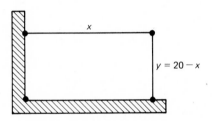

When we solved this earlier, we first solved the constraint for y:

$$y = 20 - x.$$

We then substituted $20 - x$ for y to obtain

$$A(x, 20 - x) = x(20 - x)$$
$$= 20x - x^2,$$

which is a function of one variable. We then found a maximum value using Maximum–Minimum Principle 1. By itself, the function of two variables

$$A(x, y) = xy$$

has no maximum value. This can be checked using the D-test. But, with the constraint $x + y = 20$, the function does have a maximum. We see this pictorially in the figure on the next page.

It may be quite difficult to solve a constraint for one variable. The procedure outlined below allows us to proceed without solving a constraint for one variable.

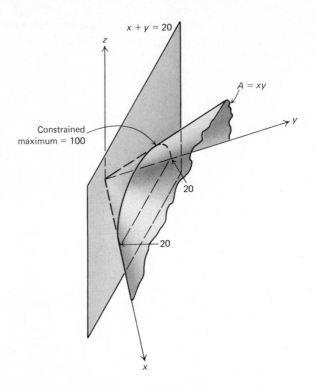

METHOD OF LAGRANGE MULTIPLIERS.   To find a maximum or minimum value of a function $f(x, y)$ subject to the constraint $g(x, y) = 0$,

    1. Form a new function:

$$F(x, y, \lambda) = f(x, y) - \lambda g(x, y).$$

    2. Find the partial derivatives F_x, F_y, and F_λ.

    3. Solve the system

$$F_x = 0, \quad F_y = 0, \quad \text{and} \quad F_\lambda = 0.$$

Let (a, b) represent a solution. We still must determine whether (a, b) yields a maximum or minimum, but we will assume one or the other in the problems considered here.

The variable λ (lambda) is called a *LaGrange Multiplier*. We first illustrate the Method of LaGrange Multipliers in Example 1.

Example 2   Find the maximum value of

$$A(x, y) = xy$$

subject to the constraint $x + y = 20$.

Solution   **1.** We form the new function F given by

$$F(x, y, \lambda) = xy - \lambda \cdot (x + y - 20).$$

Note that we first had to express $x + y = 20$ as $x + y - 20 = 0$.

2. We find the first partial derivatives.

$$F_x = y - \lambda,$$

$$F_y = x - \lambda,$$

$$F_\lambda = -(x + y - 20)$$

3. We set these derivatives equal to 0 and solve the resulting system.

$$y - \lambda = 0 \tag{1}$$

$$x - \lambda = 0 \tag{2}$$

$$x + y - 20 = 0 \tag{3}$$

[If $-(x + y - 20) = 0$, then $x + y - 20 = 0$.]
From Eqs. (1) and (2) it follows that

$$x = y = \lambda.$$

Substituting λ for x and y in Eq. (3) we get

$$\lambda + \lambda - 20 = 0,$$

$$2\lambda = 20,$$

$$\lambda = 10.$$

Thus $x = \lambda = 10$, and $y = \lambda = 10$. The maximum occurs at $(10, 10)$ and is

$$A(10, 10) = 10 \cdot 10$$

$$= 100.$$

Example 3   Find the maximum value of

$$f(x, y) = 3xy$$

subject to the constraint

$$2x + y = 8.$$

[*Note:* f could be interpreted as a production function with budget constraint $2x + y = 8$.]

Solution   **1.** We form the new function F given by

$$F(x, y, \lambda) = 3xy - \lambda(2x + y - 8).$$

Note that we had to express $2x + y = 8$ as $2x + y - 8 = 0$.

2. We find the first partial derivatives.

$$F_x = 3y - 2\lambda$$

$$F_y = 3x - \lambda$$

$$F_\lambda = -(2x + y - 8)$$

3. We set these derivatives equal to 0 and solve the resulting system

$$3y - 2\lambda = 0 \tag{1}$$

$$3x - \lambda = 0 \tag{2}$$

$$-(2x + y - 8) = 0, \quad \text{or} \quad 2x + y - 8 = 0 \tag{3}$$

Solving Eq. (1) for y, we get

$$y = \frac{2}{3}\lambda.$$

Solving Eq. (2) for x, we get

$$x = \frac{\lambda}{3}.$$

Substituting $(2/3)\lambda$ for y and $(\lambda/3)$ for x in Eq. (3), we get

$$2\left(\frac{\lambda}{3}\right) + \left(\frac{2}{3}\lambda\right) - 8 = 0$$

$$\tfrac{4}{3}\lambda = 8$$

$$\lambda = \tfrac{3}{4} \cdot 8 = 6.$$

Then

$$x = \frac{\lambda}{3} = \frac{6}{3} = 2 \quad \text{and} \quad y = \frac{2}{3}\lambda = \frac{2}{3} \cdot 6 = 4.$$

The maximum of f subject to the constraint occurs at $(2, 4)$ and is

$$f(2, 4) = 3 \cdot 2 \cdot 4 = 24.$$

Example 4   *The beverage can problem.* A beverage can firm produces cans which have a volume of 12 oz, or 26 in³. What dimensions yield the minimum surface area? Find the minimum surface area.

Solution   We want to minimize the function s given by

$$s(h, r) = 2\pi rh + 2\pi r^2$$

subject to the volume constraint

$$\pi r^2 h = 26, \quad \text{or} \quad \pi r^2 h - 26 = 0.$$

Note that s does not have a minimum without the constraint.

1. We form the new function S given by

$$S(h, r, \lambda) = 2\pi rh + 2\pi r^2 - \lambda(\pi r^2 h - 26).$$

2. We find the first partial derivatives.

$$\frac{\partial S}{\partial h} = 2\pi r - \lambda \pi r^2 \qquad \frac{\partial S}{\partial r} = 2\pi h + 4\pi r - 2\lambda \pi rh$$

$$\frac{\partial S}{\partial \lambda} = -(\pi r^2 h - 26)$$

3. We set these derivatives equal to 0 and solve the resulting system.

$$2\pi r - \lambda \pi r^2 = 0 \tag{1}$$

$$2\pi h + 4\pi r - 2\lambda \pi rh = 0 \tag{2}$$

$$-(\pi r^2 h - 26) = 0, \quad \text{or} \quad \pi r^2 h - 26 = 0 \tag{3}$$

Note that Eq. (1) can be solved for r:

$$\pi r(2 - \lambda r) = 0$$

$$\pi r = 0 \quad \text{or} \quad 2 - \lambda r = 0$$

$$r = 0 \quad \text{or} \quad r = \frac{2}{\lambda}.$$

Now r = 0 cannot be a solution to the original problem, so we continue by substituting 2/λ for r in Eq. (2):

$$2\pi h + 4\pi \cdot \frac{2}{\lambda} - 2\lambda\pi \cdot \frac{2}{\lambda} \cdot h = 0$$

$$2\pi h + \frac{8\pi}{\lambda} - 4\pi h = 0$$

$$\frac{8\pi}{\lambda} - 2\pi h = 0$$

$$-2\pi h = -\frac{8\pi}{\lambda}, \quad \text{so} \quad h = \frac{4}{\lambda}.$$

Since h = 4/λ and r = 2/λ, it follows that h = 2r. Substituting 2r for h in Eq. (3) yields

$$\pi r^2 (2r) - 26 = 0$$

$$2\pi r^3 - 26 = 0$$

$$2\pi r^3 = 26$$

$$\pi r^3 = 13$$

$$r^3 = \frac{13}{\pi}$$

$$r = \sqrt[3]{\frac{13}{\pi}} \approx 1.6 \text{ in.} \quad (\blacksquare \text{ or Table 1})$$

So when r = 1.6 in., h = 3.2 in., the surface area is a minimum and is about $2\pi(1.6)(3.2) + 2\pi(1.6)^2$, or 48.3 in².

EXERCISE SET 15.4

Find the maximum value of f subject to the given constraint.

1. $f(x, y) = xy; \quad 2x + y = 8$

2. $f(x, y) = 2xy; \quad 4x + y = 16$

3. $f(x, y) = 4 - x^2 - y^2; \quad x + 2y = 10$

4. $f(x, y) = 3 - x^2 - y^2; \quad x + 6y = 37$

Find the minimum value of f subject to the given constraint.

5. $f(x, y) = x^2 + y^2; \quad 2x + y = 10$

6. $f(x, y) = x^2 + y^2; \quad x + 4y = 17$

7. $f(x, y) = 2y^2 - 6x^2; \quad 2x + y = 4$

8. $f(x, y) = 2x^2 + y^2 - xy; \quad x + y = 8$

9. $f(x, y, z) = x^2 + y^2 + z^2; \quad y + 2x - z = 3$

10. $f(x, y, z) = x^2 + y^2 + z^2; \quad x + y + z = 1$

Use the *Method of LaGrange Multipliers* to solve these problems.

11. Of all numbers whose sum is 70, find the two that have the maximum product.

12. Of all the numbers whose sum is 50, find the two that have the maximum product.

13. Of all numbers whose difference is 6, find the two that have the minimum product.

14. Of all numbers whose difference is 4, find the two that have the minimum product.

15. A standard piece of typing paper has a perimeter of 39 in. Find the dimensions of the paper that will give the most typing area, subject to the perimeter constraint of 39 in. What is its area? Does the standard $8\frac{1}{2} \times 11$ paper have maximum area?

16. A carpenter is building a room with a fixed perimeter of 80 ft. What are the dimensions of the largest room that can be built? What is its area?

17. An oil drum of standard size has a volume of 200 gal or 27 ft³. What dimensions yield the minimum surface area? Find the minimum surface area.

18. A juice can of standard size has a volume of 99 in³. What dimensions yield the minimum surface area? Find the minimum surface area.

19. The total sales S of a one-product firm is given by

$$S(L, M) = ML - L^2,$$

where M = cost of materials, and L = cost of labor. Find the maximum value of this function subject to the budget constraint

$$M + L = 80.$$

20. The total sales S of a one-product firm is given by

$$S(L, M) = 2ML - L^2,$$

where M = cost of materials, and L = cost of labor. Find the maximum value of this function subject to the budget constraint

$$M + L = 60.$$

21. A company is planning to construct a warehouse whose cubic footage is to be 252,000 ft³. Construction costs are estimated to be

walls: $3.00 per ft²
floor: $4.00 per ft²
ceiling: $3.00 per ft²

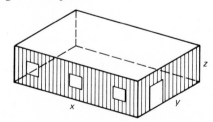

a) The total cost of the building is a function $C(x, y, z)$, where x is the length, y is the width, and z is the height. Find a formula for $C(x, y, z)$.

b) What building dimensions will minimize total cost? What is the minimum cost?

22. A container company is going to construct a shipping container of volume 12 cubic feet with a square bottom and top. The cost of the top and sides is $2 per square foot, and $3 per square foot for the bottom. What dimensions will minimize the cost of the container?

23. A product can be made entirely on Machine A or Machine B, or it can be made on both. The nature of the machines make their cost functions differ:

Machine A: $C(x) = 10 + \dfrac{x^2}{6}$

Machine B: $C(y) = 200 + \dfrac{y^3}{9}$

Total cost is given by $C(x, y) = C(x) + C(y)$. How many units should be made on each machine to minimize total costs if $x + y = 10,100$ units are required?

A company has the following production function for a certain product:

$$p(x, y) = 2400x^{2/5}y^{3/5},$$

where p is the number of units produced with x units of labor and y units of capital. It also determines that each unit of labor costs \$200 and each unit of capital costs \$300. Then total cost of production, or budget, is given by

$$C(x, y) = 200x + 300y.$$

Use the preceding for Exercises 24 and 25.

24. Suppose the budget for production is fixed at \$60,000. What amounts of labor and capital will maximize production?

25. Suppose the number of units produced must be fixed at 360,000. What amounts of labor and capital will minimize total cost?

■ ─────────────────────────────────

Find the indicated maximum or minimum value of f, subject to the given constraint.

26. Minimum: $f(x, y) = xy; x^2 + y^2 = 4$

27. Minimum: $f(x, y) = 2x^2 + y^2 + 2xy + 3x + 2y;$
$y^2 = x + 1$

28. Maximum: $f(x, y, z) = x + y + z;$
$x^2 + y^2 + z^2 = 1$

29. Maximum: $f(x, y, z) = x^2y^2z^2;$
$x^2 + y^2 + z^2 = 1$

30. Maximum: $f(x, y, z) = x + 2y - 2z;$
$x^2 + y^2 + z^2 = 4$

31. Maximum: $f(x, y, z, t) = x + y + z + t;$
$x^2 + y^2 + z^2 + t^2 = 1$

32. Suppose $p(x, y)$ represents the production of a two product firm. We give no formula for p. The company produces x items of the first product at a cost c_1 of each, and y items of the second product at a cost c_2 of each. The budget constraint B is given by

$$B = c_1x + c_2y.$$

Find the value of λ in the LaGrange Multiplier method in terms of p_x, p_y, c_1, and c_2. The resulting equation is called the *Law of Equimarginal Productivity*.

33. A sales manager is trying to maximize effectiveness of the company's sales force, which divides its time between servicing existing accounts and soliciting new accounts. The selling effort can be divided between the two activities as the manager wishes. The 100-person salesforce has 10,000 total hours to employ each month in the field. The sales manager wants to maximize sales volume. Total sales is given by

$$S = \frac{500s}{5 + s} + \frac{250n}{10 + n},$$

where s = service hours and n = new account solicitation hours. How should the total number of selling hours be allocated between the two selling functions?

15.5   APPLICATION: THE LEAST SQUARES TECHNIQUE

The problem of fitting an equation to a set of data occurs frequently. We considered one procedure for doing this in Section 1.6. Such an equation provides a model of the phenomena from which predictions can be made.

For example, in business one might want to predict future sales based on past data. In ecology, one might want to predict future demands for natural gas based on past need. Suppose we are trying to determine a linear equation

$$y = mx + b$$

to fit the data. To determine this equation is to determine the values of m and b. But how? Let us consider some factual data.

The graph shown in Fig. 4 appeared in a newspaper advertisement of the *Indianapolis Life Insurance Company*. It pertains to the total life insurance in force in various years. The same data are compiled in the following table.

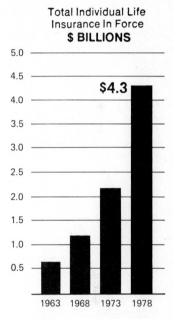

Figure 4

Year, x	1. 1963	2. 1968	3. 1973	4. 1978	5. 1983
Total Individual Life Insurance in Force, in billions, y	$0.6	$1.2	$2.2	$4.3	?

Suppose we plot these points and try to draw a line that fits. Note that there are several ways this might be done (see Fig. 5 and Fig. 6). Each would give a different estimate of the total insurance in force in 1983.

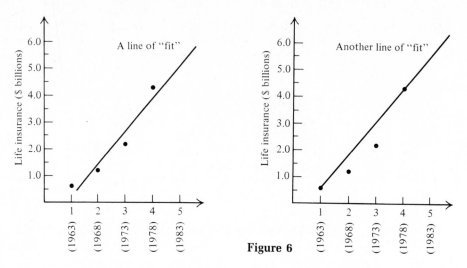

Figure 5   **Figure 6**

Note that time is incremented in fives of years, making computations easier. Consider the data points $(1, 0.6)$, $(2, 1.2)$, $(3, 2.2)$, and $(4, 4.3)$ as plotted in Fig. 7.

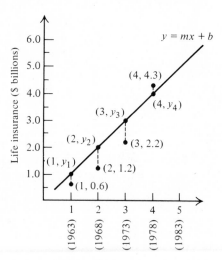

Figure 7

We will try to fit this data with a line

$$y = mx + b$$

by determining the values of m and b. Note the y-errors, or y-deviations, $y_1 - 0.6$, $y_2 - 1.2$, $y_3 - 2.2$, and $y_4 - 4.3$ between the observed points $(1, 0.6)$, $(2, 1.2)$, $(3, 2.2)$, and $(4, 4.3)$ and the points $(1, y_1)$, $(2, y_2)$, $(3, y_3)$, and $(4, y_4)$ on the line. We would like, somehow, to minimize these deviations in order to have a good fit. One way of minimizing the deviations is based on the so-called *least squares assumption*.

LEAST SQUARES ASSUMPTION. The line of best fit is the line for which the sum of squares of the *y*-deviations is a minimum. This is called the *regression line*.

Using the least squares assumption for the life insurance data, we would minimize

$$(y_1 - 0.6)^2 + (y_2 - 1.2)^2 + (y_3 - 2.2)^2 + (y_4 - 4.3)^2 \qquad (1)$$

and since the points $(1, y_1)$, $(2, y_2)$, $(3, y_3)$, and $(4, y_4)$ must be solutions of $y = mx + b$, it follows that

$$y_1 = m1 + b = m + b$$

$$y_2 = m2 + b = 2m + b$$

$$y_3 = m3 + b = 3m + b$$

$$y_4 = m4 + b = 4m + b.$$

Substituting $m + b$ for y_1, $2m + b$ for y_2, $3m + b$ for y_3, and $4m + b$ for y_4 in (1), we have

$$(m + b - 0.6)^2 + (2m + b - 1.2)^2 + (3m + b - 2.2)^2$$

$$+ (4m + b - 4.3)^2. \qquad (2)$$

Thus, to find the regression line for the given set of data, we must find the values of m and b that minimize the function S given by the sum in (2) above.

To apply the D-test, we first find the partial derivatives $\partial S/\partial b$ and $\partial S/\partial m$:

$$\frac{\partial S}{\partial b} = 2(m + b - 0.6) + 2(2m + b - 1.2) + 2(3m + b - 2.2)$$

$$+ 2(4m + b - 4.3)$$

$$= 20m + 8b - 16.6.$$

$$\frac{\partial S}{\partial m} = 2(m + b - 0.6) + 2(2m + b - 1.2)2 + 2(3m + b - 2.2)3$$

$$+ 2(4m + b - 4.3)4$$

$$= 60m + 20b - 53.6.$$

We set these derivatives equal to 0 and solve the resulting system.

$$20m + 8b - 16.6 = 0 \qquad 5m + 2b = 4.15$$
$$\text{or}$$
$$60m + 12b - 53.6 = 0 \qquad 15m + 3b = 13.4$$

The solution of this system is

$$b = -0.95, \qquad m = 1.21.$$

We leave it to the reader to complete the D-test to verify that $(-0.95, 1.21)$ does, in fact, yield the minimum of S. We need not bother to compute $S(-0.95, 1.21)$.

The values of m and b are all we need to determine $y = mx + b$. The regression line is

$$y = 1.21x - 0.95.$$

We can extrapolate from the data to predict the total life insurance in force in 1983.

$$y = 1.21(5) - 0.95 = 5.1.$$

Thus, total life insurance in force in 1983 will be about \$5.1 billion.

The method of least squares is a statistical process illustrated here with only three data points to ease the explanation. Most statistical researchers would warn that many more than three data points should be used to get a "good" regression line. Furthermore, making predictions too far in the future from any linear model may be suspect. It can be done, but the further into the future the prediction is made, the more dubious one should be about the prediction.

The Regression Line for an Arbitrary Collection of Data Points (c_1, d_1), $(c_2, d_2), \cdots , (c_n, d_n)$ (Optional)

Look again at the regression line

$$y = 1.21x - 0.95$$

for the data points $(1, 0.6)$, $(2, 1.2)$, $(3, 2.2)$ and $(4, 4.3)$. Let us consider the arithmetic averages, or means, of the x-coordinates, denoted $\bar{x}$; and the y-coordinates, denoted $\bar{y}$.

$$\bar{x} = \frac{1 + 2 + 3 + 4}{4} = 2.5, \quad \bar{y} = \frac{0.6 + 1.2 + 2.2 + 4.3}{4} = 2.075$$

It turns out that the point $(\bar{x}, \bar{y})$, or $(2.5, 2.075)$, is on the regression line for

$$2.075 = 1.21(2.5) - 0.95.$$

Thus the regression line is as follows

$$y - \bar{y} = m(x - \bar{x}), \quad \text{or} \quad y - 2.075 = m(x - 2.5).$$

All that remains, in general, is to determine m. Suppose we wanted to find the regression line for an arbitrary number of points $(c_1, d_1), (c_2, d_2), \cdots,$ (c_n, d_n).

To do so, find the values m and b that minimize the function S given by

$$S(b, m) = (y_1 - d_1)^2 + (y_2 - d_2)^2 + \cdots + (y_n - d_n)^2 = \sum_{i=1}^{n} (y_i - d_i)^2,$$

where $y_i = mc_i + b$.

Using a procedure like the one we used earlier to minimize S, we can show that $y = mx + b$ takes the form

$$y - \bar{y} = m(x - \bar{x}),$$

where

$$\bar{x} = \frac{\sum_{i=1}^{n} c_i}{n}, \quad \bar{y} = \frac{\sum_{i=1}^{n} d_i}{n}, \quad \text{and} \quad m = \frac{\sum_{i=1}^{n} (c_i - \bar{x})(d_i - \bar{y})}{\sum_{i=1}^{n} (c_i - \bar{x})^2}.$$

Let us see how this works out for the life expectancy example done previously.

c_i	d_i	$c_i - \bar{x}$	$(c_i - \bar{x})^2$	$(d_i - \bar{y})$	$(c_i - \bar{x})(d_i - \bar{y})$
1	0.6	-1.5	2.25	-1.475	2.2125
2	1.2	-0.5	0.25	-0.875	0.4375
3	2.2	0.5	0.25	0.125	0.0625
4	4.3	1.5	2.25	2.225	3.3375

$$\sum_{i=1}^{4} c_i = 10 \qquad \sum_{i=1}^{4} d_i = 8.3 \qquad \sum_{i=1}^{4} (c_i - \bar{x})^2 = 5 \qquad \sum_{i=1}^{4} (c_i - \bar{x})(d_i - \bar{y}) = 6.05$$

$$\bar{x} = 2.5 \qquad \bar{y} = 2.075 \qquad\qquad m = \frac{6.05}{5} = 1.21$$

Thus the regression line is

$$y - 2.075 = 1.21(x - 2.5)$$

which simplifies to

$$y = 1.21x - 0.95$$

Nonlinear Regression (Optional)

It can happen that data do not seem to fit a linear equation; but when logarithms of either the x-values or the y-values (or both) are taken, a linear relationship will exist. Indeed, on considering the graph in Fig. 4 it is not unreasonable to expect this data to fit an exponential function.

Example 1 Use logarithms and regression to find an equation

$$y = Be^{kx}$$

that fits the data. Then estimate the total life insurance in force in 1983.

Year, x	1. 1963	2. 1968	3. 1973	4. 1978
Total individual life insurance in force, in billions, y	$0.6	$1.2	$2.2	$4.3

Solution If we take the natural logarithm of both sides of

$$y = Be^{kx}$$

we get

$$\ln y = \ln B + kx.$$

Note that $\ln B$ and k are constants. So, if we replace $\ln y$ by a new variable Y, the equation takes the form of a linear function

$$Y = mx + b,$$

where $m = k$ and $b = \ln B$.

We are going to find this regression line, but before starting we need to find the logarithms of the y-values.

x	1	2	3	4
$Y = \ln y$	−0.5108	0.1823	0.7885	1.4586

To find the regression line we use the abbreviated procedure described in the preceding part of this section.

c_i	d_i	$c_i - \bar{x}$	$(c_i - \bar{x})^2$	$d_i - \bar{Y}$	$(c_i - \bar{x})(d_i - \bar{Y})$
1	−0.5108	−1.5	2.25	−0.9905	1.4858
2	0.1823	−0.5	0.25	−0.2974	0.1487
3	0.7885	0.5	0.25	0.3088	0.1544
4	1.4586	1.5	2.25	0.9789	1.4684
$\sum_{i=1}^{4} c_i = 10$ $\bar{x} = \frac{10}{4} = 2.5$	$\sum_{i=1}^{4} d_i$ $= 1.9186$ $\bar{Y} = \dfrac{1.9186}{4}$ $= 0.4797$		$\sum_{i=1}^{4} (c_i - \bar{x})^2$ $= 5$	$m = \dfrac{3.2573}{5}$ $= 0.65146$	$\sum_{i=1}^{4} (c_i - \bar{x})(d_i - \bar{Y})$ $= 3.2573$

Thus the regression line is

$$Y - 0.4797 = 0.65146(x - 2.5),$$

which simplifies to

$$Y = 0.65146x - 1.14895.$$

Recall that we were to find k and B. From this equation we know that

$$m = k = 0.65146$$

and

$$b = \ln B = -1.14895.$$

To find B we use the definition of logarithms (or take the antilog) and get

$$B = e^{-1.14895} = 0.3170.$$

Then the desired equation is

$$y = 0.317e^{0.65146x}.$$

Then, using this equation, the total life insurance in force will be

$$y = 0.317e^{0.65146(5)} = \$8.2 \text{ billion}.$$

In conclusion, there are other kinds of nonlinear regression besides logarithmic. For example, a set of data might fit a quadratic equation

$$y = ax^2 + bx + c.$$

In such a case, one can still use regression to find the numbers a, b, and c that minimize the sums of squares of deviations.

EXERCISE SET 15.5

1. The factual data in the table below shows the total sales of Anacomp, Inc. over several years.

Year, x	Sales of Anacomp, Inc., in millions, y
1. 1975	$3.3
2. 1976	5.9
3. 1977	6.2
4. 1978	10.5
5. 1979	16.2

a) Find the regression line.

b) Use the regression line to predict sales in 1989.

3. A professor wanted to predict students' final examination scores, based on their midterm test scores. An equation was determined based on data (see below) on scores of three students who took the same course with the same instructor the previous semester.

Midterm score (%), x	70	60	85
Final exam score (%), y	75	62	89

a) Find the regression line $y = mx + b$. [*Hint:* The y-deviations are $70m + b - 75$, $60m + b - 62$, and so on.]

b) The midterm score of a student was 81. Use the regression line to predict the student's final exam score.

2. Consider the following factual data on natural gas demand.

Year, x	1. 1950	2. 1960	3. 1970
Demand, y (in quadrillion BTU)	19	21	22

a) Find the regression line $y = mx + b$.

b) Use the regression line to predict gas demand in 1990.

c) Use the regression line to predict gas demand in 2000.

4. Consider the following total sales data of a company during the first 4 years of operation.

Year, x	1	2	3	4
Sales (in millions), y	$22	$34	$44	$60

a) Find the regression line $y = mx + b$.

b) Use the regression line to predict sales in the 5th year.

---

5. ▦

a) Find the regression line $y = mx + b$ that fits the set of data in the table.

b) Use the regression line to predict the world record in the mile in 1984.

c) In July 1979 Sebastian Coe set a new world record of 3:49.0 for the mile. How does this compare with what can be predicted by the regression?

[*Hint:* Convert each time to decimal notation; for example, $4:24.5 = 4\dfrac{24.5}{60} = 4.4083.$]

Year, x	World record in mile, y (min:sec)
1875 (Walter Slade)	4:24.5
1894 (Fred Bacon)	4:18.2
1923 (Paavo Nurmi)	4:10.4
1937 (Sidney Wooderson)	4:06.4
1942 (Gunder Haegg)	4:06.2
1945 (Gunder Haegg)	4:01.4
1954 (Roger Bannister)	3:59.4
1964 (Peter Snell)	3:54.4
1967 (Jim Ryun)	3:51.1
1975 (John Walker)	3:49.4

7. ▦

a) Use logarithms and regression to find an equation

$$y = Be^{kx}$$

that fits the set of data in Exercise 1.

b) Use the regression equation to predict sales in 1989.

Compare your answers with those of Exercise 1.

6. ▦

a) Use logarithms and regression to find an equation

$$y = Be^{kx}$$

that fits this set of data.

Year (from 1976), x	0	1	2	3
Population of U.S. (in millions), y	216	218	219	221

b) Use the regression equation to find the population of the U.S. in 1987.

8. ▦

a) Use regression (but not logarithms) to find an equation

$$y = ax^2 + bx + c$$

that fits this set of data.*

Average number of hours of sleep, x	Death rate in one year (per 100,000 males), y
5	1121
6	805
7	626
8	813
9	967

b) Find the death rate of those who average 4 hours sleep, 10 hours sleep, 7.5 hours sleep.

---

* The set of data in Exercise 8 comes from a study by Dr. Harold J. Morowitz.

15.6 APPLICATION: MINIMIZING TRAVEL TIME IN A BUILDING

In multilevel building design, one consideration is travel time between remotest points in a rectangular building with a square base. Let us suppose each floor has a square grid of hallways as shown below.

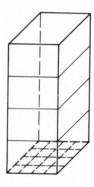

Suppose you are standing at the remotest point P in the top northeast corner of such a building with 12 floors. How long will it take to reach the southwest corner on the first floor? You will be going from point P to point Q in the illustration.

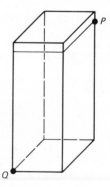

Let us call the time t. We find a formula for t in two steps.

i) You are to go from the twelfth floor to the first floor. This is a move in a *vertical direction*; and

ii) You need to go across the first floor. This is a move in a *horizontal direction*.

The vertical time is h, the height of the top floor from the ground, divided by a, the speed at which you can travel in a vertical direction (elevator speed). So, vertical time is h/a.

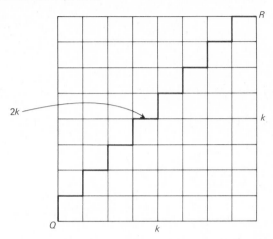

The horizontal time is the time it takes to go across the first level, by way of the square grid of hallways (from R to Q above). If each floor is a square with side of length k, then the distance from R to Q is $2k$. If the walking speed is b, then the horizontal time is $2k/b$. Thus, the time it will take to go from P to Q is a function of two variables, h and k, given by

$$t(h,\ k) = \text{vertical time} + \text{horizontal time} = \frac{h}{a} + \frac{2k}{b}.$$

Now, what happens if we have to choose between two (or more) building plans with the same total floor area, but with different dimensions? Will the travel time be the same? Or will it be different for the two buildings? First of all, what is the total floor area of a given building? Suppose the building has n floors each a square of side k. Then, the total floor area is given by

$$A = nk^2.$$

Note that the area of the roof is not included.

If h is the height of the top floor from the ground and c is the height of each floor, then $n = h/c$. So,

$$A = \frac{h}{c}\, k^2.$$

Let us return to the problem of the two buildings with the same total floor area, but with different dimensions, and find h and k which will minimize $t(h, k)$.

Example 1 *Minimizing travel time.* The objective is to find the dimensions of a rectangular building with a square base that will minimize travel time t between the remotest points in the building. Each floor has a square grid of hallways. The height of the top floor from the ground is h, and the length of a side of each floor is k. The elevator speed is 10 ft/sec and the average speed of a person walking is 4 ft/sec. The total floor area of the building is 40,000 ft². The height of each floor is 8 ft.

Solution We want to find values of h and k that will minimize the function t given by

$$t(h, k) = \frac{h}{10} + \frac{2k}{4} = \frac{1}{10} h + \frac{1}{2} k,$$

subject to the constraint

$$\frac{h}{8} k^2 = 40,000, \quad \text{or} \quad hk^2 = 320,000.$$

We first form the new function T given by

$$T(h, k, \lambda) = \frac{1}{10} h + \frac{1}{2} k - \lambda(hk^2 - 320,000).$$

We take the first partial derivatives and set them equal to 0.

$$T_h = \tfrac{1}{10} - \lambda k^2 = 0 \tag{1}$$

$$T_k = \tfrac{1}{2} - 2\lambda hk = 0 \tag{2}$$

$$T_\lambda = -(hk^2 - 320,000) = 0 \quad \text{or} \quad hk^2 - 320,000 = 0 \tag{3}$$

To clear of fractions, we multiply the first equation by 10 and the second by 2.

$$1 - 10\lambda k^2 = 0 \tag{4}$$

$$1 - 4\lambda hk = 0 \tag{5}$$

$$hk^2 - 320,000 = 0 \tag{6}$$

Solving Eq. (4) for λ, we get

$$\lambda = \frac{1}{10k^2}.$$

Solving Eq. (5) for λ, we get

$$\lambda = \frac{1}{4hk}.$$

EXERCISE SET 15.6

Given the conditions in Exercises 1 through 3, find the values of h and k that minimize travel time

$$t(h, k) = \frac{h}{a} + \frac{2k}{b}$$

subject to the floor-area constraint A given by

$$A = \frac{h}{c} k^2,$$

where

h = height of top floor from the ground (ft)

k = length of side of base (ft)

a = elevator speed (ft/sec)

b = average speed of humans walking in building (ft/sec)

c = height of each floor (ft).

Then find the dimensions of the building.

1. $a = 20$, $b = 5$, $c = 8$, $A = 80{,}000$ ft^2 **2.** $a = 20$, $b = 5$, $c = 10$, $A = 60{,}000$ ft^2

■ ──

3. Find a general solution in terms of a, b, c, and A.

15.7   MULTIPLE INTEGRATION

The following is an example of a *double integral*:

$$\int_3^6 \int_{-1}^2 10xy^2 \, dx \, dy, \quad \text{or} \quad \int_3^6 \left(\int_{-1}^2 10xy^2 \, dx \right) dy.$$

We evaluate a double integral in a manner similar to partial differentiation. We first evaluate the inside x integral, treating y as a constant:

$$\int_{-1}^2 10xy^2 \, dx = [5x^2y^2]_{-1}^2 = 5y^2(2^2 - (-1)^2) = 15y^2.$$

Then we evaluate the outside y integral:

$$\int_3^6 15y^2 \, dy = [5y^3]_3^6 = 5(6^3 - 3^3) = 945.$$

More precisely, the above is called a *double iterated integral*. The word "iterate" means "to do again."

If the dx and dy and the limits of integration are interchanged, as follows,

$$\int_{-1}^{2} \int_{3}^{6} 10xy^2 \, dy \, dx,$$

we would first evaluate the inside y integral, treating x as a constant:

$$\int_{3}^{6} 10xy^2 \, dy = \left[\frac{10}{3} xy^3 \right]_{3}^{6} = \frac{10}{3} x(6^3 - 3^3) = 630x.$$

Then we evaluate the outside x integral.

$$\int_{-1}^{2} 630x \, dx = [315x^2]_{-1}^{2} = 315(2^2 - (1)^2) = 945.$$

Note that we get the same result. This is not always true, but will be for the types of functions we consider.

Sometimes variables occur as limits of integration.

Example 1   Evaluate:

$$\int_{0}^{1} \int_{x^2}^{x} xy^2 \, dy \, dx.$$

Solution   We first evaluate the y integral, treating x as a constant:

$$\int_{x^2}^{x} xy^2 \, dy = \left[\frac{1}{3} xy^3 \right]_{x^2}^{x} = \frac{1}{3} x(x^3 - (x^2)^3) = \frac{1}{3} (x^4 - x^7).$$

Then we evaluate the outside integral:

$$\frac{1}{3} \int_{0}^{1} (x^4 - x^7) dx = \frac{1}{3} \left[\frac{x^5}{5} - \frac{x^8}{8} \right]_{0}^{1} = \frac{1}{3} \left[\left(\frac{1^5}{5} - \frac{1^8}{8} \right) - \left(\frac{0^5}{5} - \frac{0^8}{8} \right) \right] = \frac{1}{40}.$$

Thus,

$$\int_{0}^{1} \int_{x^2}^{x} xy^2 \, dy \, dx = \frac{1}{40}.$$

Geometric Interpretation of Multiple Integrals

Suppose the region G in the xy-plane is bounded by the graphs of continuous functions g and h, and lies between the x-values $x = a$ and $x = b$ in either of the following figures:

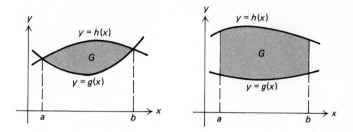

We consider the volume of the solid based on G and capped above by the piece of the surface $z = f(x, y)$ lying over G, where f is a positive (continuous) function of two variables.

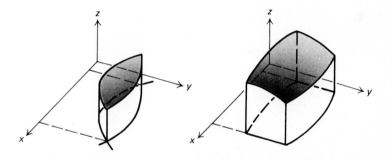

The cross section of this solid in the plane $x = x_0$ is the plane region under the graph of $z = f(x_0, y)$, from $y_1 = g(x_0)$ to $y_2 = h(x_0)$. Its area is:

$$A(x_0) = \int_{y_1}^{y_2} f(x_0, y)\, dy = \int_{g(x_0)}^{h(x_0)} f(x_0, y)\, dy.$$

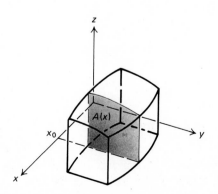

As we vary the slicing plane, the cross section also changes. We can now prove that the volume in question is given by

$$V = \int_a^b A(x)\,dx,$$

or

$$V = \int_a^b \int_{g(x)}^{h(x)} f(x, y)\,dy\,dx.$$

In Example 1, the region of integration G is the plane region between the graphs of $y = x^2$ and $y = x$, as shown on the left below:

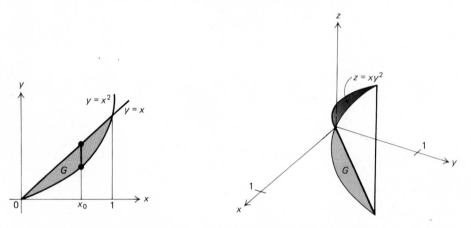

When we evaluated the double integral in Example 1, we found the volume of the solid based on G and capped by the surface $z = xy^2$, as shown on the right above.

Application to Probability

Suppose we throw a dart at a region R in a plane. It lands on a point (x, y). We can think of (x, y) as a continuous random variable that assumes all values in some region R. A function f is said to be a *joint probability density* if

$$f(x, y) \geq 0 \quad \text{for all } (x, y) \text{ in } R$$

and

$$\iint_R f(x, y)\,dx\,dy = 1,$$

where $\iint_R$ refers to the double integral evaluated over the region R.

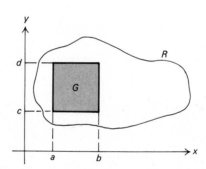

Suppose we want to know the probability that a point (x, y) is in a region G, where G is bounded by the set of points where $a \leq x \leq b$ and $c \leq y \leq d$. This would be given by

$$\int_c^d \int_a^b f(x, y) \, dx \, dy.$$

EXERCISE SET 15.7

Evaluate.

1. $\displaystyle\int_0^1 \int_0^1 2y \, dx \, dy$

2. $\displaystyle\int_0^1 \int_0^1 2x \, dx \, dy$

3. $\displaystyle\int_{-1}^1 \int_x^1 xy \, dy \, dx$

4. $\displaystyle\int_{-1}^1 \int_x^2 (x + y) \, dy \, dx$

5. $\displaystyle\int_0^1 \int_{-1}^3 (x + y) \, dy \, dx$

6. $\displaystyle\int_0^1 \int_{-1}^1 (x + y) \, dy \, dx$

7. $\displaystyle\int_0^1 \int_{x^2}^x (x + y) \, dy \, dx$

8. $\displaystyle\int_0^1 \int_{-1}^x (x^2 + y^2) \, dy \, dx$

9. $\displaystyle\int_0^2 \int_0^x (x + y^2) \, dy \, dx$

10. $\displaystyle\int_1^3 \int_0^x 2e^{x^2} \, dy \, dx$

11. Find the volume of the solid capped by the surface $z = 1 - y - x^2$ over the region bounded above and below by $y = 0$ and $y = 1 - x^2$, and left and right by $x = 0$ and $y = 1$, by evaluating the integral:

$$\int_0^1 \int_0^{1-x^2} (1 - y - x^2) \, dy \, dx.$$

12. Find the volume of the solid capped by the surface $z = x + y$ over the region bounded above and below by $y = 0$ and $y = 1 - x$, and left and right by $x = 0$ and $x = 1$, by evaluating the integral:

$$\int_0^1 \int_0^{1-x} (x + y) \, dy \, dx.$$

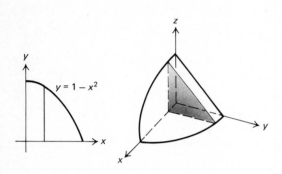

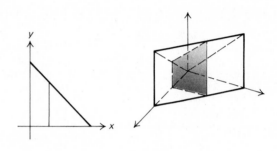

Suppose a continuous random variable has a joint probability density function given by

$$f(x, y) = x^2 + \tfrac{1}{3}xy,$$
$$0 \leq x \leq 1,$$
$$0 \leq y \leq 2.$$

13. Find $\displaystyle\int_0^2 \int_0^1 f(x, y) \, dx \, dy$.

14. Find the probability that a point (x, y) is in the region bounded by $0 \leq x \leq \tfrac{1}{2}$, $1 \leq y \leq 2$, by evaluating the integral:

$$\int_1^2 \int_0^{1/2} f(x, y) \, dx \, dy.$$

■ ———————————————————————————————

A *triple iterated integral* such as

$$\int_r^s \int_c^d \int_a^b f(x, y, z) \, dx \, dy \, dz$$

is evaluated in much the same way as a double iterated integral. We first evaluate the inside x integral, treating y and z as constants. Then we evaluate the middle y integral, treating z as a constant. Finally, we evaluate the outside z integral.

Evaluate these triple integrals.

15. $\displaystyle\int_0^1 \int_1^3 \int_{-1}^2 (2x + 3y - z) \, dx \, dy \, dz$

16. $\displaystyle\int_0^2 \int_1^4 \int_{-1}^2 (8x - 2y + z) \, dx \, dy \, dz$

17. $\displaystyle\int_0^1 \int_0^{1-x} \int_0^{2-x} xyz \, dz \, dy \, dx$

18. $\displaystyle\int_0^2 \int_{2-y}^{6-2y} \int_0^{\sqrt{4-y^2}} z \, dz \, dx \, dy$

CHAPTER 15 REVIEW

Given $f(x, y) = e^x + 2x^3y + y$, find

1. $\dfrac{\partial f}{\partial x}$ **2.** $\dfrac{\partial f}{\partial y}$ **3.** $\dfrac{\partial^2 f}{\partial x^2}$ **4.** $\dfrac{\partial^2 f}{\partial x\, \partial y}$ **5.** $\dfrac{\partial^2 f}{\partial y\, \partial x}$ **6.** $\dfrac{\partial^2 f}{\partial y^2}$

7. Find the relative maximum and minimum values.

$$f(x, y) = x^2 - xy + y^3 - x$$

8. Find the relative maximum and minimum values.

$$f(x, y) = y^2 - x^2$$

9. Consider this data regarding total sales of a company during the first three years of operation.

Year, x	1	2	3
Sales (in millions), y	\$10	\$15	\$19

    a) Find the regression line $y = mx + b$.

    b) Use the regression line to predict sales in the 4th year.

10. Find the maximum value of

$$f(x, y) = 6xy - 4x^2 - 3y^2$$

subject to the constraint $x + 3y = 19$.

11. Evaluate

$$\int_0^2 \int_1^x (x^2 - y)\, dy\, dx$$

12. A company has the following production function for a certain product:

$$p(x, y) = 560x^{1/4}y^{3/4}$$

    a) Find the production from 16 units of labor and 81 units of capital.

    b) Find the marginal productivities.

    c) Evaluate the marginal productivities at $x = 16$ and $y = 81$.

13. *Maximizing profit.* A firm produces two kinds of calculators, one that sells for \$15 each and the other for \$20 each. The total revenue from the sale of x thousand calculators at \$15 each and y thousand at \$20 each is given by

$$R(x, y) = 15x + 20y$$

The company determines that the total cost, in thousands of dollars, of producing x thousand of the \$15 calculator and y thousand of the \$20 calculator is given by

$$C(x, y) = 3x^2 - 3xy + \tfrac{3}{2}y^2 + 6x$$
$$+ 14y - 50.$$

Find the amount of each type of calculator that must be produced and sold to maximize profit.

14. Use natural logarithms and regression to find an equation

$$y = Be^{kx}$$

that fits this set of data.

Year (from 1976), x	0	1	2	3
Population of World (in billions), y	4.0	4.07	4.15	4.23

Find the relative maximum and minimum values.

15. $f(x, y) = x^3 - 6xy + y^2 + 6x + 3y - \frac{1}{2}$

16. $f(x, y) = x^4 + y^4 + 4x - 32y + 50$

17. Minimize

$$f(x, y) = y^2 - 3x^2$$

subject to the constraint $x + y = 1$.

18. Minimize

$$f(x, y, z) = x^2 + y^2 + z^2$$

subject to the constraint

$$x^2 - z^2 = 1.$$

Given $f(x, y) = \dfrac{x - y}{x + y}$, find:

19. f_x **20.** f_y **21.** f_{xx}

22. f_{yy} **23.** f_{xy} **24.** f_{yx}

25. Find the dimensions of a rectangular building with a square base that will minimize travel time t between the remotest points in the building. Each floor has a square grid of hallways. The height of the top floor from the ground is h, and the length of a side of each floor is k. The elevator speed is 10 ft/sec and the average speed of a person walking is 4 ft/sec. The total floor area of the building is 100,000 ft². The height of each floor is 10 ft.

TABLES

Table 1 Powers, Roots, and Reciprocals

n	n^2	n^3	$\sqrt{n}$	$\sqrt[3]{n}$	$\sqrt{10n}$	$\dfrac{1}{n}$
1	1	1	1.000	1.000	3.162	1.0000
2	4	8	1.414	1.260	4.472	.5000
3	9	27	1.732	1.442	5.477	.3333
4	16	64	2.000	1.587	6.325	.2500
5	25	125	2.236	1.710	7.071	.2000
6	36	216	2.449	1.817	7.746	.1667
7	49	343	2.646	1.913	8.367	.1429
8	64	512	2.828	2.000	8.944	.1250
9	81	729	3.000	2.080	9.487	.1111
10	100	1,000	3.162	2.154	10.000	.1000
11	121	1,331	3.317	2.224	10.488	.0909
12	144	1,728	3.464	2.289	10.954	.0833
13	169	2,197	3.606	2.351	11.402	.0769
14	196	2,744	3.742	2.410	11.832	.0714
15	225	3,375	3.873	2.466	12.247	.0667
16	256	4,096	4.000	2.520	12.648	.0625
17	289	4,913	4.123	2.571	13.038	.0588
18	324	5,832	4.243	2.621	13.416	.0556
19	361	6,859	4.359	2.668	13.784	.0526
20	400	8,000	4.472	2.714	14.142	.0500
21	441	9,261	4.583	2.759	14.491	.0476
22	484	10,648	4.690	2.802	14.832	.0455
23	529	12,167	4.796	2.844	15.166	.0435
24	576	13,824	4.899	2.884	15.492	.0417
25	625	15,625	5.000	2.924	15.811	.0400
26	676	17,576	5.099	2.962	16.125	.0385
27	729	19,683	5.196	3.000	16.432	.0370
28	784	21,952	5.292	3.037	16.733	.0357
29	841	24,389	5.385	3.072	17.029	.0345
30	900	27,000	5.477	3.107	17.321	.0333
31	961	29,791	5.568	3.141	17.607	.0323
32	1,024	32,768	5.657	3.175	17.889	.0312
33	1,089	35,937	5.745	3.208	18.166	.0303
34	1,156	39,304	5.831	3.240	18.439	.0294
35	1,225	42,875	5.916	3.271	18.708	.0286
36	1,296	46,656	6.000	3.302	18.974	.0278
37	1,369	50,653	6.083	3.332	19.235	.0270
38	1,444	54,872	6.164	3.362	19.494	.0263
39	1,521	59,319	6.245	3.391	19.748	.0256
40	1,600	64,000	6.325	3.420	20.000	.0250
41	1,681	68,921	6.403	3.448	20.248	.0244
42	1,764	74,088	6.481	3.476	20.494	.0238
43	1,849	79,507	6.557	3.503	20.736	.0233
44	1,936	85,184	6.633	3.530	20.976	.0227
45	2,025	91,125	6.708	3.557	21.213	.0222
46	2,116	97,336	6.782	3.583	21.448	.0217
47	2,209	103,823	6.856	3.609	21.679	.0213
48	2,304	110,592	6.928	3.634	21.909	.0208
49	2,401	117,649	7.000	3.659	22.136	.0204
50	2,500	125,000	7.071	3.684	22.361	.0200

Table 1 (cont.)

n	n^2	n^3	$\sqrt{n}$	$\sqrt[3]{n}$	$\sqrt{10n}$	$\dfrac{1}{n}$
51	2,601	132,651	7.141	3.708	22.583	.0196
52	2,704	140,608	7.211	3.733	22.804	.0192
53	2,809	148,877	7.280	3.756	23.022	.0189
54	2,916	157,464	7.348	3.780	23.238	.0185
55	3,025	166,375	7.416	3.803	23.452	.0182
56	3,136	175,616	7.483	3.826	23.664	.0179
57	3,249	185,193	7.550	3.849	23.875	.0175
58	3,364	195,112	7.616	3.871	24.083	.0172
59	3,481	205,379	7.681	3.893	24.290	.0169
60	3,600	216,000	7.746	3.915	24.495	.0167
61	3,721	226,981	7.810	3.936	24.698	.0164
62	3,844	238,328	7.874	3.958	24.900	.0161
63	3,969	250,047	7.937	3.979	25.100	.0159
64	4,096	262,144	8.000	4.000	25.298	.0156
65	4,225	274,625	8.062	4.021	25.495	.0154
66	4,356	287,496	8.124	4.041	25.690	.0152
67	4,489	300,763	8.185	4.062	25.884	.0149
68	4,624	314,432	8.246	4.082	26.077	.0147
69	4,761	328,509	8.307	4.102	26.268	.0145
70	4,900	343,000	8.367	4.121	26.458	.0143
71	5,041	357,911	8.426	4.141	26.646	.0141
72	5,184	373,248	8.485	4.160	26.833	.0139
73	5,329	389,017	8.544	4.179	27.019	.0137
74	5,476	405,224	8.602	4.198	27.203	.0135
75	5,625	421,875	8.660	4.217	27.386	.0133
76	5,776	438,976	8.718	4.236	27.568	.0132
77	5,929	456,533	8.775	4.254	27.749	.0130
78	6,084	474,552	8.832	4.273	27.928	.0128
79	6,241	493,039	8.888	4.291	28.107	.0127
80	6,400	512,000	8.944	4.309	28.284	.0125
81	6,561	531,441	9.000	4.327	28.460	.0123
82	6,724	551,368	9.055	4.344	28.636	.0122
83	6,889	571,787	9.110	4.362	28.810	.0120
84	7.056	592,704	9.165	4.380	28.983	.0119
85	7,225	614,125	9.220	4.397	28.155	.0118
86	7,396	636,056	9.274	4.414	29.326	.0116
87	7,569	658,503	9.327	4.431	29.496	.0115
88	7,744	681,472	9.381	4.448	29.665	.0114
89	7,921	704,969	9.434	4.465	29.833	.0112
90	8,100	729,000	9.487	4.481	30.000	.0111
91	8,281	753,571	9.539	4.498	30.166	.0110
92	8,464	778,688	9.592	4.514	30.332	.0109
93	8,649	804,357	9.644	4.531	30.496	.0108
94	8,836	830,584	9.695	4.547	30.659	.0106
95	9,025	857,375	9.747	4.563	30.822	.0105
96	9,216	884,736	9.798	4.579	30.984	.0104
97	9,409	912,673	9.849	4.595	31.145	.0103
98	9,604	941,192	9.899	4.610	31.305	.0102
99	9,801	970,299	9.950	4.626	31.464	.0101
100	10,000	1,000,000	10.000	4.642	31.623	.0100

Table 2 Common Logarithms

x	0	1	2	3	4	5	6	7	8	9
1.0	.0000	.0043	.0086	.0128	.0170	.0212	.0253	.0294	.0334	.0374
1.1	.0414	.0453	.0492	.0531	.0569	.0607	.0645	.0682	.0719	.0755
1.2	.0792	.0828	.0864	.0899	.0934	.0969	.1004	.1038	.1072	.1106
1.3	.1139	.1173	.1206	.1239	.1271	.1303	.1335	.1367	.1399	.1430
1.4	.1461	.1492	.1523	.1553	.1584	.1614	.1644	.1673	.1703	.1732
1.5	.1761	.1790	.1818	.1847	.1875	.1903	.1931	.1959	.1987	.2014
1.6	.2041	.2068	.2095	.2122	.2148	.2175	.2201	.2227	.2253	.2279
1.7	.2304	.2330	.2355	.2380	.2405	.2430	.2455	.2480	.2504	.2529
1.8	.2553	.2577	.2601	.2625	.2648	.2672	.2695	.2718	.2742	.2765
1.9	.2788	.2810	.2833	.2856	.2878	.2900	.2923	.2945	.2967	.2989
2.0	.3010	.3032	.3054	.3075	.3096	.3118	.3139	.3160	.3181	.3201
2.1	.3222	.3243	.3263	.3284	.3304	.3324	.3345	.3365	.3385	.3404
2.2	.3424	.3444	.3464	.3483	.3502	.3522	.3541	.3560	.3579	.3598
2.3	.3617	.3636	.3655	.3674	.3692	.3711	.3729	.3747	.3766	.3784
2.4	.3802	.3820	.3838	.3856	.3874	.3892	.3909	.3927	.3945	.3962
2.5	.3979	.3997	.4014	.4031	.4048	.4065	.4082	.4099	.4116	.4133
2.6	.4150	.4166	.4183	.4200	.4216	.4232	.4249	.4265	.4281	.4298
2.7	.4314	.4330	.4346	.4362	.4378	.4393	.4409	.4425	.4440	.4456
2.8	.4472	.4487	.4502	.4518	.4533	.4548	.4564	.4579	.4594	.4609
2.9	.4624	.4639	.4654	.4669	.4683	.4698	.4713	.4728	.4742	.4757
3.0	.4771	.4786	.4800	.4814	.4829	.4843	.4857	.4871	.4886	.4900
3.1	.4914	.4928	.4942	.4955	.4969	.4983	.4997	.5011	.5024	.5038
3.2	.5051	.5065	.5079	.5092	.5105	.5119	.5132	.5145	.5159	.5172
3.3	.5185	.5198	.5211	.5224	.5237	.5250	.5263	.5276	.5289	.5307
3.4	.5315	.5328	.5340	.5353	.5366	.5378	.5391	.5403	.5416	.5428
3.5	.5441	.5453	.5465	.5478	.5490	.5502	.5514	.5527	.5539	.5551
3.6	.5563	.5575	.5587	.5599	.5611	.5623	.5635	.5647	.5658	.5670
3.7	.5682	.5694	.5705	.5717	.5729	.5740	.5752	.5763	.5775	.5786
3.8	.5798	.5809	.5821	.5832	.5843	.5855	.5866	.5877	.5888	.5899
3.9	.5911	.5922	.5933	.5944	.5955	.5966	.5977	.5988	.5999	.6010
4.0	.6021	.6031	.6042	.6053	.6064	.6075	.6085	.6096	.6107	.6117
4.1	.6128	.6138	.6149	.6160	.6170	.6180	.6191	.6201	.6212	.6222
4.2	.6232	.6243	.6253	.6263	.6274	.6284	.6294	.6304	.6314	.6325
4.3	.6335	.6345	.6355	.6365	.6375	.6385	.6395	.6405	.6415	.6425
4.4	.6435	.6444	.6454	.6464	.6474	.6484	.6493	.6503	.6513	.6522
4.5	.6532	.6542	.6551	.6561	.6571	.6580	.6590	.6599	.6609	.6618
4.6	.6628	.6637	.6646	.6656	.6665	.6675	.6684	.6693	.6702	.6712
4.7	.6721	.6730	.6739	.6749	.6758	.6767	.6776	.6785	.6794	.6803
4.8	.6812	.6821	.6830	.6839	.6848	.6857	.6866	.6875	.6884	.6893
4.9	.6902	.6911	.6920	.6928	.6937	.6946	.6955	.6964	.6972	.6981
5.0	.6990	.6998	.7007	.7016	.7024	.7033	.7042	.7050	.7059	.7067
5.1	.7076	.7084	.7093	.7101	.7110	.7118	.7126	.7135	.7143	.7152
5.2	.7160	.7168	.7177	.7185	.7193	.7202	.7210	.7218	.7226	.7235
5.3	.7243	.7251	.7259	.7267	.7275	.7284	.7292	.7300	.7308	.7316
5.4	.7324	.7332	.7340	.7348	.7356	.7364	.7372	.7380	.7388	.7396
x	0	1	2	3	4	5	6	7	8	9

Table 2 (cont.)

x	0	1	2	3	4	5	6	7	8	9
5.5	.7404	.7412	.7419	.7427	.7435	.7443	.7451	.7459	.7466	.7474
5.6	.7482	.7490	.7497	.7505	.7513	.7520	.7528	.7536	.7543	.7551
5.7	.7559	.7566	.7574	.7582	.7589	.7597	.7604	.7612	.7619	.7627
5.8	.7634	.7642	.7649	.7657	.7664	.7672	.7679	.7686	.7694	.7701
5.9	.7709	.7716	.7723	.7731	.7738	.7745	.7752	.7760	.7767	.7774
6.0	.7782	.7789	.7796	.7803	.7810	.7818	.7825	.7832	.7839	.7846
6.1	.7853	.7860	.7868	.7875	.7882	.7889	.7896	.7903	.7910	.7917
6.2	.7924	.7931	.7938	.7945	.7952	.7959	.7966	.7973	.7980	.7987
6.3	.7993	.8000	.8007	.8014	.8021	.8028	.8035	.8041	.8048	.8055
6.4	.8062	.8069	.8075	.8082	.8089	.8096	.8102	.8109	.8116	.8122
6.5	.8129	.8136	.8142	.8149	.8156	.8162	.8169	.8176	.8182	.8189
6.6	.8195	.8202	.8209	.8215	.8222	.8228	.8235	.8241	.8248	.8254
6.7	.8261	.8267	.8274	.8280	.8287	.8293	.8299	.8306	.8312	.8319
6.8	.8325	.8331	.8338	.8344	.8351	.8357	.8363	.8370	.8376	.8382
6.9	.8388	.8395	.8401	.8407	.8414	.8420	.8426	.8432	.8439	.8445
7.0	.8451	.8457	.8463	.8470	.8476	.8482	.8488	.8494	.8500	.8506
7.1	.8513	.8519	.8525	.8531	.8537	.8543	.8549	.8555	.8561	.8567
7.2	.8573	.8579	.8585	.8591	.8597	.8603	.8609	.8615	.8621	.8627
7.3	.8633	.8639	.8645	.8651	.8657	.8663	.8669	.8675	.8681	.8686
7.4	.8692	.8698	.8704	.8710	.8716	.8722	.8727	.8733	.8739	.8745
7.5	.8751	.8756	.8762	.8768	.8774	.8779	.8785	.8791	.8797	.8802
7.6	.8808	.8814	.8820	.8825	.8831	.8837	.8842	.8848	.8854	.8859
7.7	.8865	.8871	.8876	.8882	.8887	.8893	.8899	.8904	.8910	.8915
7.8	.8921	.8927	.8932	.8938	.8943	.8949	.8954	.8960	.8965	.8971
7.9	.8976	.8982	.8987	.8993	.8998	.9004	.9009	.9015	.9020	.9025
8.0	.9031	.9036	.9042	.9047	.9053	.9058	.9063	.9069	.9074	.9079
8.1	.9085	.9090	.9096	.9101	.9106	.9112	.9117	.9122	.9128	.9133
8.2	.9138	.9143	.9149	.9154	.9159	.9165	.9170	.9175	.9180	.9186
8.3	.9191	.9196	.9201	.9206	.9212	.9217	.9222	.9227	.9232	.9238
8.4	.9243	.9248	.9253	.9258	.9263	.9269	.9274	.9279	.9284	.9289
8.5	.9294	.9299	.9304	.9309	.9315	.9320	.9325	.9330	.9335	.9340
8.6	.9345	.9350	.9555	.9360	.9365	.9370	.9375	.9380	.9385	.9390
8.7	.9395	.9400	.9405	.9410	.9415	.9420	.9425	.9430	.9435	.9440
8.8	.9445	.9450	.9455	.9460	.9465	.9469	.9474	.9479	.9484	.9489
8.9	.9494	.9499	.9504	.9509	.9513	.9518	.9523	.9528	.9533	.9538
9.0	.9542	.9547	.9552	.9557	.9562	.9566	.9571	.9576	.9581	.9586
9.1	.9590	.9595	.9600	.9605	.9609	.9614	.9619	.9624	.9628	.9633
9.2	.9638	.9643	.9647	.9652	.9657	.9661	.9666	.9671	.9675	.9680
9.3	.9685	.9689	.9694	.9699	.9703	.9708	.9713	.9717	.9722	.9727
9.4	.9731	.9736	.9741	.9745	.9750	.9754	.9759	.9763	.9768	.9773
9.5	.9777	.9782	.9786	.9791	.9795	.9800	.9805	.9809	.9814	.9818
9.6	.9823	.9827	.9832	.9836	.9841	.9845	.9850	.9854	.9859	.9863
9.7	.9868	.9872	.9877	.9881	.9886	.9890	.9894	.9899	.9903	.9908
9.8	.9912	.9917	.9921	.9926	.9930	.9934	.9939	.9943	.9948	.9952
9.9	.9956	.9961	.9965	.9969	.9974	.9978	.9983	.9987	.9991	.9996
x	0	1	2	3	4	5	6	7	8	9

Table 3 Natural Logarithms (ln x)

x	0.00	0.01	0.02	0.03	0.04	0.05	0.06	0.07	0.08	0.09
1.0	0.0000	0.0100	0.0198	0.0296	0.0392	0.0488	0.0583	0.0677	0.0770	0.0862
1.1	0.0953	0.1044	0.1133	0.1222	0.1310	0.1398	0.1484	0.1570	0.1655	0.1740
1.2	0.1823	0.1906	0.1989	0.2070	0.2151	0.2231	0.2311	0.2390	0.2469	0.2546
1.3	0.2624	0.2700	0.2776	0.2852	0.2927	0.3001	0.3075	0.3148	0.3221	0.3293
1.4	0.3365	0.3436	0.3507	0.3577	0.3646	0.3716	0.3784	0.3853	0.3920	0.3988
1.5	0.4055	0.4121	0.4187	0.4253	0.4318	0.4383	0.4447	0.4511	0.4574	0.4637
1.6	0.4700	0.4762	0.4824	0.4886	0.4947	0.5008	0.5068	0.5128	0.5188	0.5247
1.7	0.5306	0.5365	0.5423	0.5481	0.5539	0.5596	0.5653	0.5710	0.5766	0.5822
1.8	0.5878	0.5933	0.5988	0.6043	0.6098	0.6152	0.6206	0.6259	0.6313	0.6366
1.9	0.6419	0.6471	0.6523	0.6575	0.6627	0.6678	0.6729	0.6780	0.6831	0.6881
2.0	0.6931	0.6981	0.7031	0.7080	0.7130	0.7178	0.7227	0.7275	0.7324	0.7372
2.1	0.7419	0.7467	0.7514	0.7561	0.7608	0.7655	0.7701	0.7747	0.7793	0.7839
2.2	0.7885	0.7930	0.7975	0.8020	0.8065	0.8109	0.8154	0.8198	0.8242	0.8286
2.3	0.8329	0.8372	0.8416	0.8459	0.8502	0.8544	0.8587	0.8629	0.8671	0.8713
2.4	0.8755	0.8796	0.8838	0.8879	0.8920	0.8961	0.9002	0.9042	0.9083	0.9123
2.5	0.9163	0.9203	0.9243	0.9282	0.9322	0.9361	0.9400	0.9439	0.9478	0.9517
2.6	0.9555	0.9594	0.9632	0.9670	0.9708	0.9746	0.9783	0.9821	0.9858	0.9895
2.7	0.9933	0.9969	1.0006	1.0043	1.0080	1.0116	1.0152	0.0188	1.0225	1.0260
2.8	1.0296	1.0332	1.0367	1.0403	1.0438	1.0473	1.0508	1.0543	1.0578	1.0613
2.9	1.0647	1.0682	1.0716	1.0750	1.0784	1.0818	1.0852	1.0886	1.0919	1.0953
3.0	1.0986	1.1019	1.1053	1.1086	1.1119	1.1151	1.1184	1.1217	1.1249	1.1282
3.1	1.1314	1.1346	1.1378	1.1410	1.1442	1.1474	1.1506	1.1537	1.1569	1.1600
3.2	1.1632	1.1663	1.1694	1.1725	1.1756	1.1787	1.1817	1.1848	1.1878	1.1909
3.3	1.1939	1.1970	1.2000	1.2030	1.2060	1.2090	1.2119	1.2149	1.2179	1.2208
3.4	1.2238	1.2267	1.2296	1.2326	1.2355	1.2384	1.2413	1.2442	1.2470	1.2499
3.5	1.2528	1.2556	1.2585	1.2613	1.2641	1.2669	1.2698	1.2726	1.2754	1.2782
3.6	1.2809	1.2837	1.2865	1.2892	1.2920	1.2947	1.2975	1.3002	1.3029	1.3056
3.7	1.3083	1.3110	1.3137	1.3164	1.3191	1.3218	1.3244	1.3271	1.3297	1.3324
3.8	1.3350	1.3376	1.3403	1.3429	1.3455	1.3481	1.3507	1.3533	1.3558	1.3584
3.9	1.3610	1.3635	1.3661	1.3686	1.3712	1.3737	1.3762	1.3788	1.3813	1.3838
4.0	1.3863	1.3888	1.3913	1.3938	1.3962	1.3987	1.4012	1.4036	1.4061	1.4085
4.1	1.4110	1.4134	1.4159	1.4183	1.4207	1.4231	1.4255	1.4279	1.4303	1.4327
4.2	1.4351	1.4375	1.4398	1.4422	1.4446	1.4469	1.4493	1.4516	1.4540	1.4563
4.3	1.4586	1.4609	1.4633	1.4656	1.4679	1.4702	1.4725	1.4748	1.4770	1.4793
4.4	1.4816	1.4839	1.4861	1.4884	1.4907	1.4929	1.4952	1.4974	1.4996	1.5019
4.5	1.5041	1.5063	1.5085	1.5107	1.5129	1.5151	1.5173	1.5195	1.5217	1.5239
4.6	1.5261	1.5282	1.5304	1.5326	1.5347	1.5369	1.5390	1.5412	1.5433	1.5454
4.7	1.5476	1.5497	1.5518	1.5539	1.5560	1.5581	1.5602	1.5623	1.5644	1.5665
4.8	1.5686	1.5707	1.5728	1.5748	1.5769	1.5790	1.5810	1.5831	1.5851	1.5872
4.9	1.5892	1.5913	1.5933	1.5953	1.5974	1.5994	1.6014	1.6034	1.6054	1.6074
5.0	1.6094	1.6114	1.6134	1.6154	1.6174	1.6194	1.6214	1.6233	1.6253	1.6273
5.1	1.6292	1.6312	1.6332	1.6351	1.6371	1.6390	1.6409	1.6429	1.6448	1.6467
5.2	1.6487	1.6506	1.6525	1.6544	1.6563	1.6582	1.6601	1.6620	1.6639	1.6658
5.3	1.6677	1.6696	1.6715	1.6734	1.6752	1.6771	1.6790	1.6808	1.6827	1.6845
5.4	1.6864	1.6882	1.6901	1.6919	1.6938	1.6956	1.6974	1.6993	1.7011	1.7029
5.5	1.7047	1.7066	1.7084	1.7102	1.7120	1.7138	1.7156	1.7174	1.7192	1.7210
5.6	1.7228	1.7246	1.7263	1.7281	1.7299	1.7317	1.7334	1.7352	1.7370	1.7387
5.7	1.7405	1.7422	1.7440	1.7457	1.7475	1.7492	1.7509	1.7527	1.7544	1.7561
5.8	1.7579	1.7596	1.7613	1.7630	1.7647	1.7664	1.7682	1.7699	1.7716	1.7733
5.9	1.7750	1.7766	1.7783	1.7800	1.7817	1.7834	1.7851	1.7867	1.7884	1.7901

Note: Adapted from *Functional Approach to Precalculus*, 2nd ed., Mustafa A. Munem and James P. Yizze (New York, NY: Worth Publishers, Inc., © 1974), pp. 500–501. Reproduced by permission of the publisher.

Table 3 (cont.)

x	0.00	0.01	0.02	0.03	0.04	0.05	0.06	0.07	0.08	0.09
6.0	1.7918	1.7934	1.7951	1.7967	1.7984	1.8001	1.8017	1.8034	1.8050	1.8066
6.1	1.8083	1.8099	1.8116	1.8132	1.8148	1.8165	1.8181	1.8197	1.8213	1.8229
6.2	1.8245	1.8262	1.8278	1.8294	1.8310	1.8326	1.8342	1.8358	1.8374	1.8390
6.3	1.8406	1.8421	1.8437	1.8453	1.8469	1.8485	1.8500	1.8516	1.8532	1.8547
6.4	1.8563	1.8579	1.8594	1.8610	1.8625	1.8641	1.8656	1.8672	1.8687	1.8703
6.5	1.8718	1.8733	1.8749	1.8764	1.8779	1.8795	1.8810	1.8825	1.8840	1.8856
6.6	1.8871	1.8886	1.8901	1.8916	1.8931	1.8946	1.8961	1.8976	1.8991	1.9006
6.7	1.9021	1.9036	1.9051	1.9066	1.9081	1.9095	1.9110	1.9125	1.9140	1.9155
6.8	1.9169	1.9184	1.9199	1.9213	1.9228	1.9242	1.9257	1.9272	1.9286	1.9301
6.9	1.9315	1.9330	1.9344	1.9359	1.9373	1.9387	1.9402	1.9416	1.9430	1.9445
7.0	1.9459	1.9473	1.9488	1.9502	1.9516	1.9530	1.9544	1.9559	1.9573	1.9587
7.1	1.9601	1.9615	1.9629	1.9643	1.9657	1.9671	1.9685	1.9699	1.9713	1.9727
7.2	1.9741	1.9755	1.9769	1.9782	1.9796	1.9810	1.9824	1.9838	1.9851	1.9865
7.3	1.9879	1.9892	1.9906	1.9920	1.9933	1.9947	1.9961	1.9974	1.9988	2.0001
7.4	2.0015	2.0028	2.0042	2.0055	2.0069	2.0082	2.0096	2.0109	2.0122	2.0136
7.5	2.0149	2.0162	2.0176	2.0189	2.0202	2.0215	2.0229	2.0242	2.0255	2.0268
7.6	2.0282	2.0295	2.0308	2.0321	2.0334	2.0347	2.0360	2.0373	2.0386	2.0399
7.7	2.0412	2.0425	2.0438	2.0451	2.0464	2.0477	2.0490	2.0503	2.0516	2.0528
7.8	2.0541	2.0554	2.0567	2.0580	2.0592	2.0605	2.0618	2.0631	2.0643	2.0665
7.9	2.0669	2.0681	2.0694	2.0707	2.0719	2.0732	2.0744	2.0757	2.0769	2.0782
8.0	2.0794	2.0807	2.0819	2.0832	2.0844	2.0857	2.0869	2.0882	2.0894	2.0906
8.1	2.0919	2.0931	2.0943	2.0956	2.0968	2.0980	2.0992	2.1005	2.1017	2.1029
8.2	2.1041	2.1054	2.1066	2.1078	2.1090	2.1102	2.1114	2.1126	2.1133	2.1150
8.3	2.1163	2.1175	2.1187	2.1199	2.1211	2.1223	2.1235	2.1247	2.1258	2.1270
8.4	2.1282	2.1294	2.1306	2.1318	2.1330	2.1342	2.1353	2.1365	2.1377	2.1389
8.5	2.1401	2.1412	2.1424	2.1436	2.1448	2.1459	2.1471	2.1483	2.1494	2.1506
8.6	2.1518	2.1529	2.1541	2.1552	2.1564	2.1576	2.1587	2.1599	2.1610	2.1622
8.7	2.1633	2.1645	2.1656	2.1668	2.1679	2.1691	2.1702	2.1713	2.1725	2.1736
8.8	2.1748	2.1759	2.1770	2.1782	2.1793	2.1804	2.1815	2.1827	2.1838	2.1849
8.9	2.1861	2.1872	2.1883	2.1894	2.1905	2.1917	2.1928	2.1939	2.1950	2.1961
9.0	2.1972	2.1983	2.1994	2.2006	2.2017	2.2028	2.2039	2.2050	2.2061	2.2072
9.1	2.2083	2.2094	2.2105	2.2116	2.2127	2.2138	2.2148	2.2159	2.2170	2.2181
9.2	2.2192	2.2203	2.2214	2.2225	2.2235	2.2246	2.2257	2.2268	2.2279	2.2289
9.3	2.2300	2.2311	2.2322	2.2332	2.2343	2.2354	2.2364	2.2375	2.2386	2.2396
9.4	2.2407	2.2418	2.2428	2.2439	2.2450	2.2460	2.2471	2.2481	2.2492	2.2502
9.5	2.2513	2.2523	2.2534	2.2544	2.2555	2.2565	2.2576	2.2586	2.2597	2.2607
9.6	2.2618	2.2628	2.2638	2.2649	2.2659	2.2670	2.2680	2.2690	2.2701	2.2711
9.7	2.2721	2.2732	2.2742	2.2752	2.2762	2.2773	2.2783	2.2793	2.2803	2.2814
9.8	2.2824	2.2834	2.2844	2.2854	2.2865	2.2875	2.2885	2.2895	2.2905	2.2915
9.9	2.2925	2.2935	2.2946	2.2956	2.2966	2.2976	2.2986	2.2996	2.3006	2.3016

ln 10	= 2.3026	7 ln 10	= 16.1181
2 ln 10	= 4.6052	8 ln 10	= 18.4207
3 ln 10	= 6.9078	9 ln 10	= 20.7233
4 ln 10	= 9.2103	10 ln 10	= 23.0259
5 ln 10	= 11.5129	11 ln 10	= 25.3284
6 ln 10	= 13.8155	12 ln 10	= 27.6310

Examples.

$$\ln 96{,}700 = \ln 9.67 + 4 \ln 10$$
$$= 2.2690 + 9.2103$$
$$= 11.4793.$$

$$\ln 0.00967 = \ln 9.67 - 3 \ln 10$$
$$= 2.2690 - 6.9078$$
$$= -4.6388.$$

Table 4 Exponential Functions

x	e^x	e^{-x}	x	e^x	e^{-x}	x	e^x	e^{-x}
0.00	1.0000	1.0000	0.55	1.7333	0.5769	3.6	36.598	0.0273
0.01	1.0101	0.9900	0.60	1.8221	0.5488	3.7	40.447	0.0247
0.02	1.0202	0.9802	0.65	1.9155	0.5220	3.8	44.701	0.0224
0.03	1.0305	0.9704	0.70	2.0138	0.4966	3.9	49.402	0.0202
0.04	1.0408	0.9608	0.75	2.1170	0.4724	4.0	54.598	0.0183
0.05	1.0513	0.9512	0.80	2.2255	0.4493	4.1	60.340	0.0166
0.06	1.0618	0.9418	0.85	2.3396	0.4274	4.2	66.686	0.0150
0.07	1.0725	0.9324	0.90	2.4596	0.4066	4.3	73.700	0.0136
0.08	1.0833	0.9231	0.95	2.5857	0.3867	4.4	81.451	0.0123
0.09	1.0942	0.9139	1.0	2.7183	0.3679	4.5	90.017	0.0111
0.10	1.1052	0.9048	1.1	3.0042	0.3329	4.6	99.484	0.0101
0.11	1.1163	0.8958	1.2	3.3201	0.3012	4.7	109.95	0.0091
0.12	1.1275	0.8869	1.3	3.6693	0.2725	4.8	121.51	0.0082
0.13	1.1388	0.8781	1.4	4.0552	0.2466	4.9	134.29	0.0074
0.14	1.1503	0.8694	1.5	4.4817	0.2231	5	148.41	0.0067
0.15	1.1618	0.8607	1.6	4.9530	0.2019	6	403.43	0.0025
0.16	1.1735	0.8521	1.7	5.4739	0.1827	7	1096.6	0.0009
0.17	1.1853	0.8437	1.8	6.0496	0.1653	8	2981.0	0.0003
0.18	1.1972	0.8353	1.9	6.6859	0.1496	9	8103.1	0.0001
0.19	1.2092	0.8270	2.0	7.3891	0.1353	10	22026	0.00005
0.20	1.2214	0.8187	2.1	8.1662	0.1225	11	59874	0.00002
0.21	1.2337	0.8106	2.2	9.0250	0.1108	12	162,754	0.000006
0.22	1.2461	0.8025	2.3	9.9742	0.1003	13	442,413	0.000002
0.23	1.2586	0.7945	2.4	11.023	0.0907	14	1,202,604	0.0000008
0.24	1.2712	0.7866	2.5	12.182	0.0821	15	3,269,017	0.0000003
0.25	1.2840	0.7788	2.6	13.464	0.0743			
0.26	1.2969	0.7711	2.7	14.880	0.0672			
0.27	1.3100	0.7634	2.8	16.445	0.0608			
0.28	1.3231	0.7558	2.9	18.174	0.0550			
0.29	1.3364	0.7483	3.0	20.086	0.0498			
0.30	1.3499	0.7408	3.1	22.198	0.0450			
0.35	1.4191	0.7047	3.2	24.533	0.0408			
0.40	1.4918	0.6703	3.3	27.113	0.0369			
0.45	1.5683	0.6376	3.4	29.964	0.0334			
0.50	1.6487	0.6065	3.5	33.115	0.0302			

Table 5 Integration Formulas

(Whenever ln X is used it is assumed that $X > 0$.)

1. $\int x^n \, dx = \dfrac{x^{n+1}}{n+1} + C, n \neq -1$

2. $\int \dfrac{dx}{x} = \ln x + C$

3. $\int u \, dv = uv - \int v \, du$

4. $\int e^x \, dx = e^x + C$

5. $\int e^{ax} \, dx = \dfrac{1}{a} \cdot e^{ax} + C$

6. $\int xe^{ax} \, dx = \dfrac{1}{a^2} \cdot e^{ax}(ax - 1) + C$

7. $\int x^n e^{ax} \, dx = \dfrac{x^n e^{ax}}{a} - \dfrac{n}{a} \int x^{n-1} e^{ax} \, dx$

8. $\int \ln x \, dx = x \ln x - x + C$

9. $\int (\ln x)^n \, dx = x(\ln x)^n - n \int (\ln x)^{n-1} \, dx, n \neq -1$

10. $\int x^n \ln x \, dx = x^{n+1} \left[\dfrac{\ln x}{n+1} - \dfrac{1}{(n+1)^2} \right] + C, n \neq -1$

11. $\int a^x \, dx = \dfrac{a^x}{\ln a} + C, a > 0, a \neq 1$

12. $\int \dfrac{1}{\sqrt{x^2 + a^2}} \, dx = \ln(x + \sqrt{x^2 + a^2}) + C$

13. $\int \dfrac{1}{\sqrt{x^2 - a^2}} \, dx = \ln(x + \sqrt{x^2 - a^2}) + C$

14. $\int \dfrac{1}{x^2 - a^2} \, dx = \dfrac{1}{2a} \ln \left(\dfrac{x-a}{x+a} \right) + C$

15. $\int \dfrac{1}{a^2 - x^2} \, dx = \dfrac{1}{2a} \ln \left(\dfrac{a+x}{a-x} \right) + C$

16. $\int \dfrac{1}{x\sqrt{a^2 + x^2}} \, dx = -\dfrac{1}{a} \ln \left(\dfrac{a + \sqrt{a^2 + x^2}}{x} \right) + C$

17. $\int \dfrac{1}{x\sqrt{a^2 - x^2}} \, dx = -\dfrac{1}{a} \ln \left(\dfrac{a + \sqrt{a^2 - x^2}}{x} \right) + C, 0 < x < a$

18. $\int \dfrac{x}{ax + b} \, dx = \dfrac{b}{a^2} + \dfrac{x}{a} - \dfrac{b}{a^2} \ln(ax + b) + C$

19. $\int \dfrac{x}{(ax + b)^2} \, dx = \dfrac{b}{a^2(ax + b)} + \dfrac{1}{a^2} \ln(ax + b) + C$

20. $\int \dfrac{1}{x(ax + b)} \, dx = \dfrac{1}{b} \ln \left(\dfrac{x}{ax + b} \right) + C$

21. $\int \dfrac{1}{x(ax + b)^2} \, dx = \dfrac{1}{b(ax + b)} + \dfrac{1}{b^2} \ln \left(\dfrac{x}{ax + b} \right) + C$

22. $\int \sqrt{x^2 \pm a^2} \, dx = \tfrac{1}{2}[x\sqrt{x^2 \pm a^2} \pm a^2 \ln(x + \sqrt{x^2 \pm a^2})] + C$

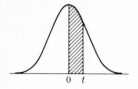

Area = Probability
$$= P(0 \leqslant x \leqslant t)$$
$$= \int_0^t \frac{1}{\sqrt{2\pi}} e^{-x^2/2}\, dx$$

Table 6 Areas for a Standard Normal Distribution

Entries in the table represent area under the curve between $t = 0$ and a positive value of t. Because of the symmetry of the curve, area under the curve between $t = 0$ and a negative value of t would be found in a like manner.

t	0.00	0.01	0.02	0.03	0.04	0.05	0.06	0.07	0.08	0.09
0.0	.0000	.0040	.0080	.0120	.0160	.0199	.0239	.0279	.0319	.0359
0.1	.0398	.0438	.0478	.0517	.0557	.0596	.0636	.0675	.0714	.0753
0.2	.0793	.0832	.0871	.0910	.0948	.0987	.1026	.1064	.1103	.1141
0.3	.1179	.1217	.1255	.1293	.1331	.1368	.1406	.1443	.1480	.1517
0.4	.1554	.1591	.1628	.1664	.1700	.1736	.1772	.1808	.1844	.1879
0.5	.1915	.1950	.1985	.2019	.2054	.2088	.2123	.2157	.2190	.2224
0.6	.2257	.2291	.2324	.2357	.2389	.2422	.2454	.2486	.2517	.2549
0.7	.2580	.2611	.2642	.2673	.2704	.2734	.2764	.2794	.2823	.2852
0.8	.2881	.2910	.2939	.2967	.2995	.3023	.3051	.3078	.3106	.3133
0.9	.3159	.3186	.3212	.3238	.3264	.3289	.3315	.3340	.3365	.3389
1.0	.3413	.3438	.3461	.3485	.3508	.3531	.3554	.3577	.3599	.3621
1.1	.3643	.3665	.3686	.3708	.3729	.3749	.3770	.3790	.3810	.3830
1.2	.3849	.3869	.3888	.3907	.3925	.3944	.3962	.3980	.3997	.4015
1.3	.4032	.4049	.4066	.4082	.4099	.4115	.4131	.4147	.4162	.4177
1.4	.4192	.4207	.4222	.4236	.4251	.4265	.4279	.4292	.4306	.4319
1.5	.4332	.4345	.4357	.4370	.4382	.4394	.4406	.4418	.4429	.4441
1.6	.4452	.4463	.4474	.4484	.4495	.4505	.4515	.4525	.4535	.4545
1.7	.4554	.4564	.4573	.4582	.4591	.4599	.4608	.4616	.4625	.4633
1.8	.4641	.4649	.4656	.4664	.4671	.4678	.4686	.4693	.4699	.4706
1.9	.4713	.4719	.4726	.4732	.4738	.4744	.4750	.4756	.4761	.4767
2.0	.4772	.4778	.4783	.4788	.4793	.4798	.4803	.4808	.4812	.4817
2.1	.4821	.4826	.4830	.4834	.4838	.4842	.4846	.4850	.4854	.4857
2.2	.4861	.4864	.4868	.4871	.4875	.4878	.4881	.4884	.4887	.4890
2.3	.4893	.4896	.4898	.4901	.4904	.4906	.4909	.4911	.4913	.4916
2.4	.4918	.4920	.4922	.4925	.4927	.4929	.4931	.4932	.4934	.4936
2.5	.4938	.4940	.4941	.4943	.4945	.4946	.4948	.4949	.4951	.4952
2.6	.4953	.4955	.4956	.4957	.4959	.4960	.4961	.4962	.4963	.4964
2.7	.4965	.4966	.4967	.4968	.4969	.4970	.4971	.4972	.4973	.4974
2.8	.4974	.4975	.4976	.4977	.4977	.4978	.4979	.4979	.4980	.4981
2.9	.4981	.4982	.4982	.4983	.4984	.4984	.4985	.4985	.4986	.4986
3.0	.4987	.4987	.4987	.4988	.4988	.4989	.4989	.4989	.4990	.4990

ANSWERS TO ODD-NUMBERED EXERCISES

CHAPTER 1

Exercise Set 1.1, p. 9

1. 3, 14   **3.** $\sqrt{3}$, $-\sqrt{7}$, $\sqrt[3]{2}$ **5.** -6, 0, 3, -2, 14   **7.** Rational   **9.** Rational   **11.** Rational
13. Irrational   **15.** Irrational   **17.** Irrational   **19.** Rational   **21.** Irrational   **23.** 12   **25.** 47
27. 7, 7   **29.** -57, -57 **31.** -87 **33.** -16 **35.** -10.3 **37.** $\frac{39}{10}$ **39.** 28   **41.** -49.2
43. 210   **45.** $-\frac{833}{5}$ **47.** 5   **49.** $-\frac{1}{7}$ **51.** $-\frac{3}{49}$ **53.** 25   **55.** -4 **57.** 18   **59.** -11.6 **61.** $-\frac{7}{2}$
63. a) 1.96, 1.9881, 1.999396, 1.999962, 1.999990 b) $\sqrt{2}$ **65.** Identity $(+)$ **67.** Distributive
69. Commutativity $(+)$ **71.** Associativity $(\times)$ **73.** Inverse $(\times)$

Exercise Set 1.2, p. 14

1. $5 \cdot 5 \cdot 5$, or 125   **3.** $(-7)(-7)$, or 49   **5.** 1.0201   **7.** $\frac{1}{16}$ **9.** 1   **11.** t **13.** 1   **15.** $\dfrac{1}{3^2}$, or $\dfrac{1}{9}$

17. 8   **19.** 0.1, or $\dfrac{1}{10}$ **21.** $\dfrac{1}{e^b}$ **23.** $\dfrac{1}{b}$ **25.** x^5 **27.** x^{-6}, or $\dfrac{1}{x^6}$ **29.** $35x^5$ **31.** x^4 **33.** 1

35. x^3 **37.** x^{-3}, or $\dfrac{1}{x^3}$ **39.** 1   **41.** e^{t-4} **43.** t^{14} **45.** t^2 **47.** t^{-6}, or $\dfrac{1}{t^6}$ **49.** e^{4x} **51.** $8x^6y^{12}$

53. $\frac{1}{81}x^8y^{20}z^{-16}$, or $\dfrac{x^8y^{20}}{81z^{16}}$ **55.** $9x^{-16}y^{14}z^4$, or $\dfrac{9y^{14}z^4}{x^{16}}$

Exercise Set 1.3, p. 17

1. 4, 3, 2, 1, 0; 4   **3.** 3, 6, 6, 0; 6   **5.** 5, 6, 2, 1, 0; 6   **7.** $3x^2y - 5xy^2 + 7xy + 2$
9. $-10pq^2 - 5p^2q + 7pq - 4p + 2q + 3$ **11.** $3x + 2y - 2z - 3$ **13.** $5x\sqrt{y} - 4y\sqrt{x} - \frac{2}{5}$
15. $-5x^3 + 7x^2 - 3x + 6$ **17.** $-2x^2 + 6x - 2$ **19.** $6a - 5b - 2c + 4d$
21. $x^4 - 3x^3 - 4x^2 + 9x - 3$ **23.** $9x\sqrt{y} - 3y\sqrt{x} + 9.1$

Exercise Set 1.4, p. 20

1. $6x^3 + 4x^2 + 32x - 64$ **3.** $4a^3b^2 - 10a^2b^2 + 3ab^3 + 4ab^2 - 6b^3 + 4a^2b - 2ab + 3b^2$
5. $a^3 - b^3$ **7.** $4x^2 + 8xy + 3y^2$ **9.** $12x^3 + x^2y - \frac{3}{2}xy - \frac{1}{8}y^2$
11. $2x^3 - 2\sqrt{2}x^2y - \sqrt{2}xy^2 + 2y^3$ **13.** $4x^2 + 12xy + 9y^2$ **15.** $4x^4 - 12x^2y + 9y^2$
17. $4x^6 + 12x^3y^2 + 9y^4$ **19.** $\frac{1}{4}x^4 - \frac{3}{5}x^2y + \frac{9}{25}y^2$ **21.** $0.25x^2 + 0.70xy^2 + 0.49y^4$ **23.** $9x^2 - 4y^2$
25. $x^4 - y^2z^2$ **27.** $9x^4 - 2$ **29.** $4x^2 + 12xy + 9y^2 - 16$ **31.** $x^4 + 6x^2y + 9y^2 - y^4$ **33.** $x^4 - 1$
35. $16x^4 - y^4$ **37.** $a^3 + 3a^2b + 3ab^2 + b^3$ **39.** $x^3 + 3x^2h + 3xh^2 + h^3$
41. $x^3 - 15x^2 + 75x - 125$ **43.** $8x^3 + 36x^2 + 54x + 27$

Exercise Set 1.5, p. 25

1. $3ab(6a - 5b)$ **3.** $(a + c)(b - 2)$ **5.** $(x + 6)(x + 3)$ **7.** $(3x - 5)(3x + 5)$
9. $4x(y^2 - z)(y^2 + z)$ **11.** $(y - 3)^2$ **13.** $(1 - 4x)^2$ **15.** $(2x - \sqrt{5})(2x + \sqrt{5})$ **17.** $(xy - 7)^2$
19. $4a(x + 7)(x - 2)$ **21.** $(a + b + c)(a + b - c)$ **23.** $2x + y - a - b)(x + y + a + b)$
25. $5(y^2 + 4x^2)(y - 2x)(y + 2x)$ **27.** $h(3x^2 + 3xh + h^2)$ **29.** a) 0.81 b) 0.0801 c) 0.008001
31. a) 1.261 b) 0.120601 c) 0.012006001 **33.** a) \$1080 b) \$1081.60 c) \$1082.43 d) \$1083.278
assuming 365 days in a year.

Exercise Set 1.6, p. 32

1. All numbers except 0, 1   **3.** All numbers except 0, 3, -2 **5.** $\dfrac{x - 2}{x + 3}$; All numbers except -3

7. $\dfrac{1}{x - y}$ **9.** $\dfrac{(x + 5)(2x + 3)}{7x}$ **11.** $\dfrac{a + 2}{a - 5}$ **13.** $m + n$ **15.** $\dfrac{3(x - 4)}{2(x + 4)}$ **17.** $(x - y)^2$

19. $\dfrac{x - y - z}{x + y + z}$ **21.** 1 **23.** $\dfrac{y - 2}{y - 1}$ **25.** $\dfrac{x + y}{2x - 3y}$ **27.** $\dfrac{3x - 4}{x^2 - 4}$ **29.** $\dfrac{3y - 10}{(y - 5)(y + 4)}$ **31.** $\dfrac{4x - 8y}{x^2 - y^2}$

33. $\dfrac{3x - 4}{(x - 2)(x - 1)}$ **35.** $\dfrac{5a^2 + 10ab - 4b^2}{(a - b)(a + b)}$ **37.** $\dfrac{11x^2 - 18x + 8}{(x + 2)(x - 2)^2}$ **39.** 0 **41.** $\dfrac{x + y}{x}$ **43.** $\dfrac{a^2 - 1}{a^2 + 1}$

45. $\dfrac{c^3 + 2c^2 + 4c + 8}{c}$ **47.** $\dfrac{xy}{x - y}$ **49.** $x - y$ **51.** $\dfrac{x^2 - y^2}{xy}$ **53.** $\dfrac{1 + a}{1 - a}$ **55.** $\dfrac{b + a}{b - a}$ **57.** $2x + h$
59. $3x^2 + 3xh + h^2$ **61.** x^8

Exercise Set 1.7, p. 40

1. $\{\tfrac{7}{4}\}$ **3.** $\{-8\}$ **5.** $\{120\}$ **7.** $\{0, 3\}$ **9.** $\{0, 2, -\tfrac{1}{3}\}$ **11.** $\{\tfrac{3}{2}, -\tfrac{2}{3}, 1\}$ **13.** $\{\tfrac{1}{2}, 0, -3\}$ **15.** $\{-2\}$
17. $\{6\}$ **19.** $\varnothing$ **21.** $\varnothing$ **23.** $\{8, -5\}$ **25.** $\{\tfrac{5}{3}\}$ **27.** $\{0, 2.1522\}$ **29.** $\{0.94656\}$ **31.** $\{-1, 1, -\tfrac{1}{5}\}$
33. $\{-2, 1, -1\}$ **35.** $\varnothing$

Exercise Set 1.8, p. 44

1. $t = \dfrac{I}{Pr}$ **3.** $P = \dfrac{A}{1 + rt}$ **5.** $a = 3A - b - c$ **7.** $b = \dfrac{at}{a - t}$ **9.** $P = \dfrac{iV}{(1 + i)^N - 1}$ **11.** 19%
13. \$1495   **15.** \$6500   **17.** \$55,000   **19.** \$14,500; \$16,095   **21.** $1\tfrac{34}{71}$ hr   **23.** Mort: 36 hr;
Red: 45 hr   **25.** Attendant should have solved the equation, $x + 4\%x = \$10$, whose solution is
\$9.62. Thus he should have pumped \$9.62 worth of gas instead of \$9.60.

Exercise Set 1.9, p. 49

1. $-\tfrac{4}{5} \leqslant x$ **3.** $x > -\tfrac{1}{12}$ **5.** $x > -\tfrac{4}{7}$ **7.** $x \leqslant -3$ **9.** $x > \tfrac{2}{3}$ **11.** $x < -\tfrac{2}{5}$ **13.** $2 < x < 4$
15. $\tfrac{3}{2} \leqslant x \leqslant \tfrac{11}{2}$ **17.** $-1 \leqslant x \leqslant \tfrac{14}{5}$ **19.** More than 7000 units.   **21.** $60\% \leqslant x < 100\%$ **23.** $(0, 5)$
25. $[-9, -4)$ **27.** $[x, x + h]$ **29.** (p, ∞) **31.** $[-3, 3]$ **33.** $[-14, -11)$ **35.** $(-\infty, -4]$

Chapter 1 Review, p. 50

1. 13, -4, -2, -39, 47, 0   **2.** 13, 47   **3.** All except $\sqrt{3}$ and $\sqrt[3]{7}$ **4.** All   **5.** $\sqrt{3}$, $\sqrt[3]{7}$

6. 13, 47, 0   **7.** -4 **8.** -16 **9.** -8 **10.** 32   **11.** -16 **12.** 162   **13.** -4000 **14.** $\dfrac{29}{24}$

15. $\dfrac{1}{e^k}$ **16.** e^{-13} **17.** $8xy^4 - 9xy^2 + 4x^2 + 2y - 7$ **18.** $x^3 + t^3$

19. $125x^3 + 300x^2b + 240xb^2 + 64b^3$ **20.** $(x^2 - 3)(x + 2)$ **21.** $3a(2a - 3b^2)(2a + 3b^2)$

22. $(x + 12)^2$ **23.** $x(9x - 1)(x + 4)$ **24.** \$920   **25.** $\dfrac{b}{a}$ **26.** 3   **27.** $\dfrac{x - 5}{(x + 3)(x + 5)}$ **28.** $\{6, -3\}$

29. $\{-20\}$ **30.** $\{\frac{27}{7}\}$ **31.** $i = \dfrac{A}{P} - 1$, or $\dfrac{A - P}{P}$ **32.** 60   **33.** $1\frac{1}{2}$ hr   **34.** $[c, d]$ **35.** $x > -4$

CHAPTER 2

Exercise Set 2.1, p. 65

1. a)

Inputs	Outputs
4.1	11.2
4.01	11.02
4.001	11.002
4	11

b) $f(5) = 13$, $f(-1) = 1$, $f(k) = 2k + 3$, $f(1 + t) = 2t + 5$, $f(x + h) = 2x + 2h + 3$

3. $g(-1) = -2$, $g(0) = -3$, $g(1) = -2$, $g(5) = 22$, $g(u) = u^2 - 3$, $g(a + h) = a^2 + 2ah + h^2 - 3$, $g(1 - h) = h^2 - 2h - 2$ **5. a)** $f(4) = 1$, $f(-2) = 25$, $f(0) = 9$, $f(a) = a^2 - 6a + 9$, $f(t + 1) = t^2 - 4t + 4$, $f(t + 3) = t^2$, $f(x + h) = x^2 + 2xh + h^2 - 6x - 6h + 9$
b) Take an input, square it, subtract 6 times the input, add 9.

7.

9.

11.

13.

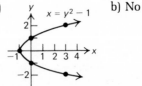

15. Yes   **17.** Yes   **19.** No   **21.** No   **23. a)**   **b)** No

25. $f(x + h) = x^2 + 2xh + h^2 - 3x - 3h$ **27.** $R(10) = \$70$, $R(100) = \$250$ **29.** Increasing
31. Decreasing   **33.** Neither   **35.** Increasing on $[-3, -1]$; decreasing on $[-1, 1]$
37. $-26, 12, 54$ **39.** $0, 22, -50$ **41.** $-5, 25, -25$ **43.** $9, 196, 64$

Exercise Set 2.2, p. 82

1. Horizontal line through $(0, -4)$ **3.** Vertical line through $(4.5, 0)$

5. 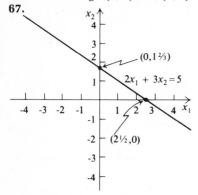   **7.** 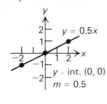   **9.** 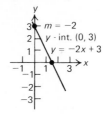   **11.**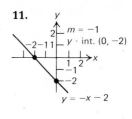

13. $m = -2$, y-int.:$(0, 2)$ **15.** $m = -1$, y-int.:$(0, -\frac{5}{2})$ **17.** $y + 5 = -5(x - 1)$, or $y = -5x$
19. $y - 3 = -2(x - 2)$, or $y = -2x + 7$ **21.** $y = \frac{1}{2}x - 6$ **23.** $y = 3$ **25.** $\frac{3}{2}$ **27.** $\frac{1}{2}$
29. No slope   **31.** 0   **33.** 3   **35.** 2   **37.** $y - 1 = \frac{3}{2}(x + 2)$, or $y + 2 = \frac{3}{2}(x + 4)$, or $y = \frac{3}{2}x + 4$
39. $y + 4 = \frac{1}{2}(x - 2)$, or $y = \frac{1}{2}x - 5$ **41.** $x = 3$ **43.** $y = 3$ **45.** $y = 3x$
47. $y = 2x + 3$ **49.** Neither   **51.** Decreasing   **53.** Increasing
55. a) $C(x) = 40x + 22{,}500$ b) $R(x) = 85x$ c) $P(x) = R(x) - C(x) = 45x - 22{,}500$
d) A profit of \$112,500 e) 500 pairs   **57.** a) $A(x) = 4\%x + 600$, $B(x) = 6\%(x - 10{,}000) + 700$,
for $x > 10{,}000$ b) Solve $B(x) > A(x)$ and get $x > 25{,}000$. That is, Plan B is better when gross sales
exceed \$25,000.   **59.** Line through $(0, 4)$ and $(5, 0)$ **61.** Line through $(0, -4)$ and $(2, 0)$
63. Line through $(0, 4)$ and $(3, 0)$ **65.** Line through $(0, 0)$ and $1, 1)$
67. 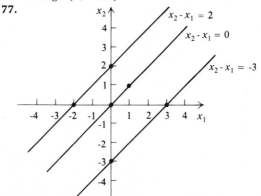   **69.** Horizontal line through $(0, 5)$ **71.** Vertical line through
$(-2, 0)$ **73.** The horizontal x_1-axis   **75.** Horizontal line
through $(0, -3.5)$

77.

Exercise Set 2.3, p. 88

1. No   **3.** Consistent, independent   **5.** Consistent, dependent   **7.** Inconsistent, independent
9. $(2, -1)$ **11.** No solution   **13.** $(-5, 4)$

Exercise Set 2.4, p. 93

1. $(2, -3)$ **3.** $(2, -2)$ **5.** $(6, 2)$ **7.** $(\frac{9}{19}, \frac{51}{38})$ **9.** $(\frac{3}{2}, \frac{5}{2})$ **11.** $(-\frac{1}{3}, -4)$
13. An infinite number of solutions   **15.** No solution   **17.** 13 and 16   **19.** 5 cloth and 15 pigskin
21. 42 L of A, 18 L of B   **23.** \$2000 at 12%, \$2800 at 13%   **25.** $(a, 0)$

Exercise Set 2.5, p. 106

1.

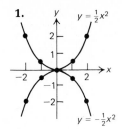

3. See Example 3 for the graph of $y = x^2$. Move it to the right 1 unit to get the graph of $y = (x - 1)^2$.
5. Move the graph of $y = x^2$ 1 unit to the left to get $y = (x + 1)^2$.
7.

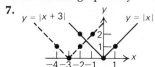

9. See Exercise Set 2.1, Exercise 13, for $y = x^3$. Move it up one unit for $y = x^3 + 1$.

11.

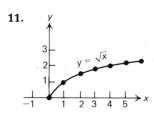

13.

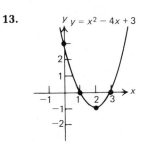

15.

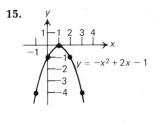

17.

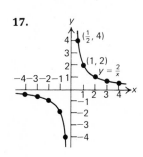

19.

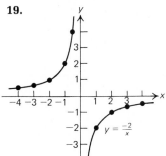

21.

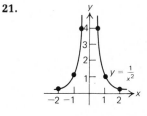

x	-2	-1	$-\frac{1}{2}$	$\frac{1}{2}$	1	2
y	$\frac{1}{4}$	1	4	4	1	$\frac{1}{4}$

23.

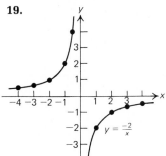

25. $1 \pm \sqrt{3}$ **27.** $-3 \pm \sqrt{10}$ **29.** $\dfrac{1 \pm \sqrt{2}}{2}$ **31.** $\dfrac{-4 \pm \sqrt{10}}{3}$

33. $x^{3/2}$ **35.** $a^{3/5}$ **37.** $t^{1/7}$ **39.** $t^{-4/3}$ **41.** $t^{-1/2}$ **43.** $(x^2 + 7)^{-1/2}$

45. $\sqrt[5]{x}$ **47.** $\sqrt[3]{y^2}$ **49.** $\dfrac{1}{\sqrt[5]{t^2}}$ **51.** $\dfrac{1}{\sqrt[3]{b}}$ **53.** $\dfrac{1}{\sqrt[6]{e^{17}}}$ **55.** $\dfrac{1}{\sqrt{x^2 - 3}}$ **57.** 27   **59.** 16   **61.** 8

63. All real numbers except 5.   **65.** All real numbers except 2, 3.   **67.** $[-\frac{4}{5}, \infty)$ **69.** (2, $4)
71. (1, $4)   **73.** (2, $4)   **75.** 160 thousand   **77.** 12.5%   **79.** 7   **81.** 12

Exercise Set 2.6, p. 110

1. $\frac{5}{3}$ **3.** $\pm\sqrt{2}$ **5.** $\varnothing$ **7.** 4   **9.** $\varnothing$ **11.** -6 **13.** 3, -1 **15.** $\frac{80}{9}$ **17.** $5 \pm 2\sqrt{2}$ **19.** $-\frac{8}{9}$
21. 2   **23.** $\dfrac{-5 + \sqrt{61}}{18}$ **25.** 100, 211

Exercise Set 2.7, p. 113

1. 1, 81   **3.** $\pm\sqrt{5}$ **5.** $-27, 8$ **7.** 16   **9.** 7, 5, $-1, 1$ **11.** 1, 4, $\dfrac{5 \pm \sqrt{37}}{2}$ **13.** $\pm\sqrt{2 + \sqrt{6}}$
15. $-\frac{1}{2}, \frac{1}{3}$ **17.** $-1, 2$ **19.** $-1 \pm \sqrt{3}, \dfrac{9 \pm \sqrt{89}}{2}$ **21.** $\frac{100}{99}$ **23.** $-\frac{6}{7}$ **25.** 2.0486   **27.** 1, 4
29. $\dfrac{2}{51 + 7\sqrt{61}}$, or $\dfrac{7\sqrt{61} - 51}{194}$

Chapter 2 Review, p. 114

1. 6   **2.** $x^2 + 2xh + h^2 + x + h$ **3.** -110 **4.** $m = -3$; y-intercept is (0, 2)   **5.** $y = \frac{1}{4}x - 7$
6. 6   **7.** a) (i) $C(x) = 0.5x + 10,000$ (ii) $R(x) = 1.3x$ (iii) $P(x) = R(x) - C(x) = 0.8x - 10,000$
b) 12,500   **8.** Decreasing   **9.** (3, $16)

10.

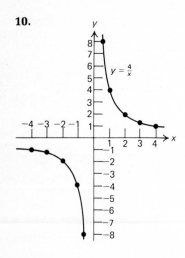

11. t^{-112} **12.** $\dfrac{1}{\sqrt[5]{t^3}}$ **13.** All real numbers except 2, -7

14. $[-2, \infty)$ **15.** $(\frac{3}{2}, \frac{5}{2})$ **16.** An infinite number of solutions

17. 5   **18.** 0, 3   **19.** $\pm\sqrt{\dfrac{3 \pm \sqrt{5}}{2}}$ **20.** 1   **21.** $0_2 \pm \sqrt{3}$

22. $-8, 125$ **23.** 20 hr

CHAPTER 3

Exercise Set 3.1, p. 125

1. $(-3, 2)$ **3.** $(7, 3)$ **5.** $(\frac{5}{2}, -1)$ **7.** $(-3, 5, 7)$ **9.** $(0, 2, 1)$ **11.** $(2, \frac{1}{2}, -2)$ **13.** $(4, 5, 6, 7)$
15. $4100 @ 7%, $4700 @ 8%   **17.** $30,000 @ 5%, $40,000 @ 6%   **19.** 8 white, 22 yellow
21. 150 lb soybean meal; 200 lb corn meal   **23.** $400 @ 7%, $500 @ 8%, $1600 @ 9%

Exercise Set 3.2, p. 134

1. $x_1 = 2 + 3x_2$, $x_2 =$ any number   **3.** No solution   **5.** $x_1 = 1 - x_3$, $x_2 = -x_3$,
$x_3 =$ any number   **7.** $x_1 = \frac{1}{5}x_3$, $x_2 = -\frac{7}{5}x_3$, $x_3 =$ any number   **9.** $x_1 = -\frac{7}{2}x_3$, $x_2 = -\frac{19}{2}x_3$,
$x_3 =$ any number   **11.** $x_1 = 1 + 3x_3$, $x_2 = 4 - 5x_3$, $x_3 =$ any number, $x_4 = -2$ **13.** No solution
15. $x_1 = 19 - 2x_3 - 16x_4$, $x_2 = -6 + 3x_3 + 4x_4$, $x_3 =$ any number, $x_4 =$ any number
17. $x_1 = -1 + 4x_3$, $x_2 = 4 + 2x_3$, $x_3 =$ any number   **19.** $x_1 = 6 - 8x_3 + 3x_4$,
$x_2 = 4 - 4x_3 - 2x_4$, $x_3 =$ any number, $x_4 =$ any number, $x_5 = -5$

Exercise Set 3.3, p. 140

1. 2×2 **3.** 2×3 **5.** $\begin{bmatrix} -1 & 3 \\ 2 & 1 \end{bmatrix}$ **7.** $\begin{bmatrix} -1 & 6 & -7 \\ 4 & 2 & 0 \end{bmatrix}$ **9.** $\begin{bmatrix} 3 & 9 \\ 12 & 6 \end{bmatrix}$

11. $\begin{bmatrix} 5 & 10 & 15 \\ -15 & -10 & -5 \end{bmatrix}$ **13.** $\begin{bmatrix} 3 & 3 \\ 6 & 3 \end{bmatrix}$ **15.** $\begin{bmatrix} -1 & -10 & 1 \\ 2 & 2 & 2 \end{bmatrix}$ **17.** Not possible

19. $\begin{bmatrix} -k & -2k & -3k \\ 3k & 2k & k \end{bmatrix}$ **21.** A **23.** $\begin{bmatrix} 1 & 4 \\ 3 & 2 \end{bmatrix}$ **25.** $\begin{bmatrix} -1 & 3 \\ -2 & 2 \\ -3 & 1 \end{bmatrix}$ **27.** $\begin{bmatrix} -1 & 2 \\ 3 & 1 \end{bmatrix}$

29. $a_{11} = -4$, $a_{12} = 5$, $a_{31} = 1$, $a_{22} = 9$, $a_{32} = 3$, $a_{21} = 0$
31. $X^T = [x_1 \quad x_2 \quad x_3 \quad x_4]$

Exercise Set 3.4, p. 152

1. $AB = [-10]$, or -10; $BA = \begin{bmatrix} -6 & 3 \\ 8 & -4 \end{bmatrix}$ **3.** $AB = [17]$, or 17; $BA = \begin{bmatrix} 18 & 0 & -36 \\ -10 & 0 & 20 \\ \frac{1}{2} & 0 & -1 \end{bmatrix}$

5. $AB = \begin{bmatrix} 7 & -6 & 1 \\ -15 & 12 & 3 \\ -2 & -1 & 8 \end{bmatrix}$, $BA = \begin{bmatrix} 9 & 11 & -10 \\ 3 & 4 & -4 \\ -3 & -1 & 14 \end{bmatrix}$ **7.** $AB = [35 \; -35]$, BA not possible

9. $AB = 0$ **11.** $\begin{bmatrix} 11 & 3 \\ 7 & 2 \end{bmatrix}\begin{bmatrix} x_1 \\ x_2 \end{bmatrix} = \begin{bmatrix} -4 \\ 5 \end{bmatrix}$ **13.** $\begin{bmatrix} 3 & 1 & 0 \\ 1 & -1 & 2 \\ 1 & 1 & 1 \end{bmatrix}\begin{bmatrix} x_1 \\ x_2 \\ x_3 \end{bmatrix} = \begin{bmatrix} 2 \\ -4 \\ 5 \end{bmatrix}$ **15.** $\begin{array}{l} x_1 + 2x_2 = -1 \\ 4x_1 - 3x_2 = 2 \end{array}$

17. $x_1 = -23$, $x_2 = 83$ **19.** $x_1 = \frac{1}{11}$, $x_2 = -\frac{6}{11}$ **21.** $x_1 = -1$, $x_2 = 5$, $x_3 = 1$

23. $(A + B)(A + B) = \begin{bmatrix} 1 & 0 \\ 4 & 4 \end{bmatrix}$, $A^2 + 2AB + B^2 = \begin{bmatrix} -3 & -3 \\ 9 & 8 \end{bmatrix}$ **25.** $\begin{bmatrix} X \\ Y \end{bmatrix}^T = [a \quad b \quad c \quad e \quad f \quad g]$

27. $[A \quad B] = \begin{bmatrix} 2 & -1 & 3 & 0 & 1 & -2 \\ 4 & 1 & 0 & 1 & -3 & 7 \end{bmatrix}$, $[A \quad B]^T = \begin{bmatrix} 2 & 4 \\ -1 & 1 \\ 3 & 0 \\ \hline 0 & 1 \\ 1 & -3 \\ -2 & 7 \end{bmatrix}$ **29.** Yes

Exercise Set 3.5, p. 157

1. -11 **3.** $x^3 - 4x$ **5.** -109 **7.** $-x^4 + x^2 - 5x$ **9.** $\left(-\frac{25}{2}, -\frac{11}{2}\right)$

11. $\left(\dfrac{4\pi - 5\sqrt{3}}{3 + \pi^2}, \dfrac{4\sqrt{3} + 5\pi}{-3 - \pi^2}\right)$ **13.** $\left(\frac{3}{2}, \frac{13}{14}, \frac{33}{14}\right)$ **15.** $\left(\frac{1}{2}, \frac{2}{3}, -\frac{5}{6}\right)$ **17.** $2, -2$

19. $\{x \mid x \leqslant -\sqrt{3} \text{ or } x \geqslant \sqrt{3}\}$ **21.** -34 **23.** 4 **25.** $\begin{vmatrix} L & -W \\ 2 & 2 \end{vmatrix}$ **27.** $\begin{vmatrix} a & b \\ -b & a \end{vmatrix}$ **29.** $\begin{vmatrix} 2\pi r & 2\pi r \\ -h & r \end{vmatrix}$

Exercise Set 3.6, p. 164

1. $a_{11} = 7$, $a_{32} = 2$, $a_{22} = 0$ **3.** $M_{11} = 6$, $M_{32} = -9$, $M_{22} = -29$ **5.** $A_{11} = 6$, $A_{32} = 9$, $A_{22} = -29$ **7.** $|A| = -10$ **9.** $|A| = -10$ **11.** $M_{41} = -14$, $M_{33} = 20$ **13.** $A_{24} = 15$, $A_{43} = 30$ **15.** $|A| = 110$ **17.** -195 **19.** $|A| = -10$, $|B| = 10$; $|A| = -|B|$

21. $|A| = 5$, $|B| = -5$; $|A| = -|B|$ **23.** $\begin{vmatrix} 3 & 7 & 3 \\ 1 & 5 & -3 \\ 4 & 9 & 1 \end{vmatrix}$ **25.** -70 **27.** -4 **29.** 9072

31. -153 **33.** 0 **35.** 0 **37.** -4 **39.** $(x - y)(y - z)(x - z)$ **41.** $xyz(x - y)(y - z)(z - x)$

Exercise Set 3.7, p. 171

1. $A^{-1} = \begin{bmatrix} -3 & 2 \\ 5 & -3 \end{bmatrix}$ **3.** $A^{-1} = \begin{bmatrix} 2 & -3 \\ -7 & 11 \end{bmatrix}$ **5.** $A^{-1} = \begin{bmatrix} \frac{2}{11} & \frac{3}{11} \\ -\frac{1}{11} & \frac{4}{11} \end{bmatrix}$ **7.** $A^{-1} = \begin{bmatrix} \frac{3}{8} & -\frac{1}{4} & \frac{1}{8} \\ -\frac{1}{8} & \frac{3}{4} & -\frac{3}{8} \\ -\frac{1}{4} & \frac{1}{2} & \frac{1}{4} \end{bmatrix}$

9. $A^{-1} = \begin{bmatrix} \frac{1}{3} & 0 & \frac{1}{3} \\ -\frac{2}{5} & \frac{2}{5} & \frac{1}{5} \\ \frac{2}{15} & \frac{1}{5} & -\frac{1}{15} \end{bmatrix}$ **11.** A^{-1} does not exist.   **13.** $A^{-1} = \begin{bmatrix} 1 & -2 & 3 & 8 \\ 0 & 1 & -3 & 1 \\ 0 & 0 & 1 & -2 \\ 0 & 0 & 0 & -1 \end{bmatrix}$

15.–27. See Exercises 1–13   **29.** $\left(-\frac{1}{39}, \frac{55}{39}\right)$ **31.** $(3, -3, -2)$ **33.** A^{-1} exists if and only if $x \neq 0$.

$A^{-1} = \begin{bmatrix} x^{-1} & 0 \\ 0 & 1 \end{bmatrix}$ **35.** A^{-1} exists if and only if $xy \neq 0$. $A^{-1} = \begin{bmatrix} x^{-1} & 0 \\ 0 & y^{-1} \end{bmatrix}$ **37.** A^{-1} exists if and

only if $xyzw \neq 0$. $A^{-1} = \begin{bmatrix} \dfrac{1}{x} & -\dfrac{1}{xy} & -\dfrac{1}{xz} & -\dfrac{1}{xw} \\ 0 & \dfrac{1}{y} & 0 & 0 \\ 0 & 0 & \dfrac{1}{z} & 0 \\ 0 & 0 & 0 & \dfrac{1}{w} \end{bmatrix}$

Exercise Set 3.8, p. 176

1. a) $A = \begin{bmatrix} 0.2 & 0.5 \\ 0.25 & 0.2 \end{bmatrix}$ b) $A_0 = [5 \quad 3]$ c) $(I - A)^{-1} = \frac{10}{53} \begin{bmatrix} 16 & 10 \\ 15 & 16 \end{bmatrix}$ d) $D = [530 \quad 106]^T$

e) $X = [1800 \quad 1820]^T$ f) $x_0 = 14{,}460$ **3.** a) $A = \begin{bmatrix} 0.2 & 0.1 & 0.5 \\ 0 & 0.1 & 0 \\ 0.2 & 0.2 & 0.3 \end{bmatrix}$ b) $A_0 = [0.4 \quad 0.2 \quad 0.3]$

c) $(I - A)^{-1} = \frac{5}{207} \begin{bmatrix} 63 & 17 & 45 \\ 0 & 46 & 0 \\ 18 & 18 & 72 \end{bmatrix}$ d) $D = [230 \quad 207 \quad 69]^T$ e) $X = [510 \quad 230 \quad 310]^T$ f) $x_0 = 154.1$

5. $(I - A)^{-1} = \frac{5}{14} \begin{bmatrix} 5 & 3 \\ 2 & 4 \end{bmatrix}$, $X = [185 \quad 130]^T$, $x_0 = 146.5$

7. $(I - A)^{-1} = \frac{5}{24} \begin{bmatrix} 7 & 1 & 8 \\ 8 & 8 & 64 \\ 7 & 1 & 56 \end{bmatrix}$, $X = [370 \quad 2480 \quad 2050]^T$, $x_0 = 1308$

Chapter 3 Review, p. 177

1. $\begin{bmatrix} 7 & 4 \\ 3 & 1 \end{bmatrix} \begin{bmatrix} x_1 \\ x_2 \end{bmatrix} = \begin{bmatrix} -21 \\ -9 \end{bmatrix}$, $x_1 = -3$, $x_2 = 0$ **2.** $\begin{bmatrix} 3 & -2 & 3 \\ 1 & 1 & -1 \\ 2 & 3 & -5 \end{bmatrix} \begin{bmatrix} x_1 \\ x_2 \\ x_3 \end{bmatrix} = \begin{bmatrix} 24 \\ -7 \\ -32 \end{bmatrix}$, $x_1 = 1$, $x_2 = -3$,

$x_3 = 5$ **3.** $\begin{array}{l} 4x_1 - 8x_2 = -20 \\ 3x_1 - 6x_2 = -15 \end{array}$, $x_1 = -5 + 2x_2$, $x =$ any number **4.** $\begin{array}{l} 8x_1 - 4x_2 = 20 \\ 6x_1 - 3x_2 = 16 \end{array}$, no solution

5. $x_1 = 5 - 6x_3$, $x_2 = 3 + 2x_3$, $x_3 =$ any number, $x_4 = 2$ **6.** No solution **7.** $\begin{bmatrix} -3 & 1 \\ -4 & 1 \end{bmatrix}$

8. $\begin{bmatrix} 2 & 3 \\ 1 & 5 \end{bmatrix}$ **9.** $\begin{bmatrix} -3 & 3 \\ -6 & 1 \end{bmatrix}$ **10.** $\begin{bmatrix} 12 & -8 \\ 20 & -4 \end{bmatrix}$ **11.** $C^T = [2 \quad -3 \quad 4]$ **12.** AB not possible,

$BA = \begin{bmatrix} 5 \\ 7 \end{bmatrix}$ **13.** $x_1 = \frac{1}{2}$, $x_2 = \frac{2}{3}$ **14.** $x_1 = -2$, $x_2 = 3$, $x_3 = 9$ **15.** $\begin{bmatrix} X \\ Y \end{bmatrix}^T = [p \quad q \quad t \quad u]$

16. \$4000 @ 8%, \$5300 @ 10% **17.** $A^{-1} = \begin{bmatrix} 2 & 0 & 1 \\ 3 & 1 & 2 \\ 1 & 0 & 1 \end{bmatrix}$ **18.** -31 **19.** -1 **20.** 0 **21.** 120

22. If a matrix has all 0's below the main diagonal, then its determinant is the product of the elements on the main diagonal. Proof: Expand about the first column.

23. $\begin{vmatrix} 5a & 5b & 5c \\ 3a & 3b & 3c \\ d & e & f \end{vmatrix} = 5(3) \begin{vmatrix} a & b & c \\ a & b & c \\ d & e & f \end{vmatrix} = 0$, since the first two rows are the same.

24. $(b - a)(c - b)(c - a)$ **25.** $X = [146 \quad 156]^T$, $x_0 = 1530$ **26.** No solution

27. $x =$ Any number, $y =$ Any number, $z = 3x - 4y$, $w = 2x + 5y$

CHAPTER 4

Exercise Set 4.1, p. 188

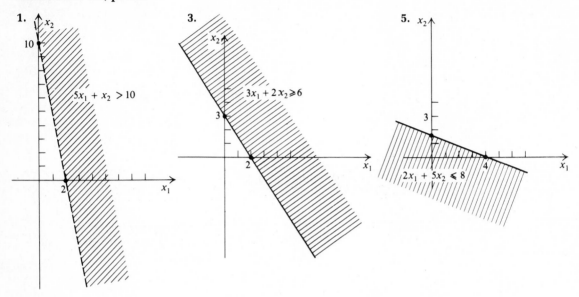

1. $5x_1 + x_2 > 10$

3. $3x_1 + 2x_2 \geqslant 6$

5. $2x_1 + 5x_2 \leqslant 8$

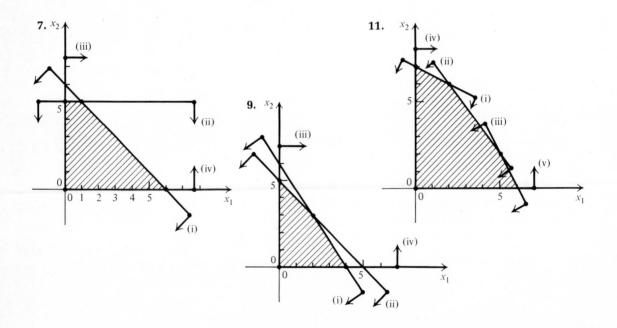

7.

9.

11.

13.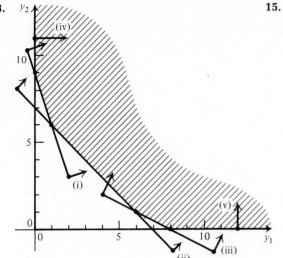

15.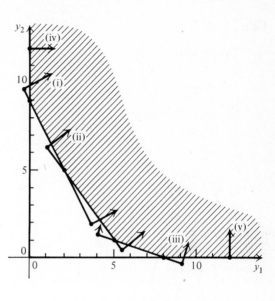

17.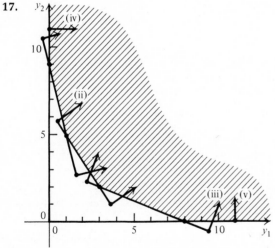

19. a)   i) $x_1 + 2x_2 \leq 6$
      ii) $0 \leq x_1 \leq 5$
      iii) $x_2 \leq -2$
   b)   Nonempty
   c)   Bounded
   d)   No redundancies
   e)   No degeneracies

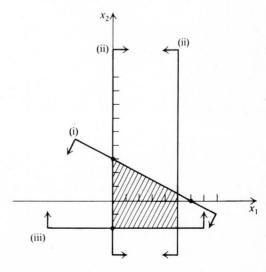

21. a) i) $x_1 \geqslant -3$
ii) $x_1 - 2x_2 \leqslant 4$
iii) $x_2 - 3x_1 \leqslant 9$
iv) $3x_1 + x_2 \leqslant 10$
b) Nonempty
c) Bounded
d) No redundancies
e) No degeneracies

23. a) i) $-3x_1 + 2x_2 \geqslant 6$
ii) $2x_1 + x_2 \leqslant -2$
iii) $x_1 + x_2 \geqslant 4$
iv) $2x_1 + 7x_2 \leqslant 21$
b) Empty
c) Bounded
d) (i) or (ii)
e) No degeneracies

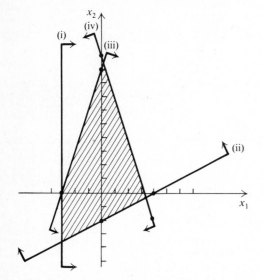

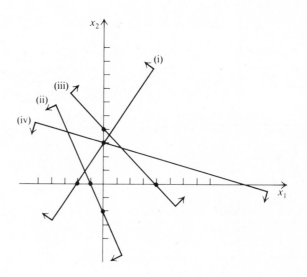

25. a) i) $x_1 \geqslant 0$
ii) $x_2 \geqslant 0$
iii) $x_1 + x_2 \geqslant 2$
iv) $x_1 - x_2 \leqslant 2$
v) $x_2 \leqslant 6$
b) Nonempty
c) Bounded
d) (ii)
e) (2, 0)

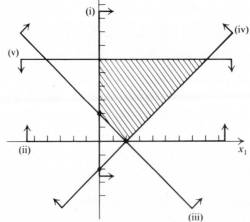

27. a) i) $x_1 + x_2 \leqslant 0$
ii) $2x_1 - 3x_2 \leqslant 15$
iii) $x_2 \leqslant 5$
iv) $x_1 \geqslant 0$
v) $2x_1 + x_2 \geqslant 3$

b) Nonempty ⎰one point,
c) Bounded ⎱$(3, -3)$
d) (iii), (iv)
e) $(3, -3)$

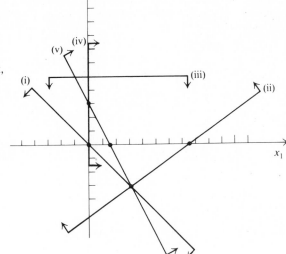

29. a) i) $x_1 \geqslant 0$
ii) $x_2 \geqslant 0$
iii) $5x_2 - 3x_1 \leqslant 15$
iv) $x_1 \leqslant 4x_2$
v) $2x_1 - 5x_2 \leqslant 10$

b) Nonempty
c) Unbounded
d) (ii)
e) $(0, 0)$

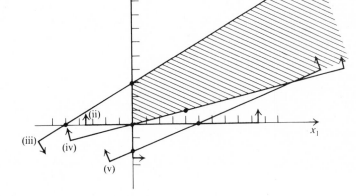

Exercise Set 4.2, p. 194

1. $x_1 = 1$, $x_2 = 5$; $f = 11$ **3.** $x_1 = 2$, $x_2 = 3$; $f = 22$ **5.** $x_1 = 2$, $x_2 = 6$; $f = 30$ **7.** $y_1 = 6$, $y_2 = 1$; $f = 22$ **9.** $y_1 = 5$, $y_2 = 1$; $f = 15$ **11.** $y_1 = 3$, $y_2 = 2$; $f = 19$ **13.** max: $f = 7$ at $(5, -2)$; min: $f = -3$ at $(0, 3)$ **15.** max: $f = \frac{26}{7}$ at $(\frac{24}{7}, -\frac{2}{7})$; min: $f = -\frac{28}{3}$ at $(\frac{1}{6}, \frac{10}{2})$
17. max: $f = \frac{64}{3}$ at $(8, \frac{8}{3})$; min: $f = 0$ for any point on the line segment between $(\frac{24}{11}, \frac{72}{11})$ and $(\frac{5}{4}, \frac{15}{4})$
19. No feasible solution, $\therefore$ no optimum feasible solution, max or min
21. max: unbounded; min: $f = 0$ at $(0, 0)$ **23.** max and min: both have $f = 3$ at $(3, -3)$

Exercise Set 4.3, p. 201

1. Let x_1 = number of suits to be made,
x_2 = number of dresses to be made,
f = income.
Then

$$x_1 + 2x_2 \leq 60,$$
$$4x_1 + 3x_2 \leq 120,$$
$$\max f: f = 120x_1 + 75x_2; \quad x_1, x_2 \geq 0.$$

b) $\begin{bmatrix} 1 & 2 \\ 4 & 3 \end{bmatrix} \begin{bmatrix} x_1 \\ x_2 \end{bmatrix} \leq \begin{bmatrix} 60 \\ 120 \end{bmatrix}$

$\max f: f = \begin{bmatrix} 120 & 75 \end{bmatrix} \begin{bmatrix} x_1 \\ x_2 \end{bmatrix}; \begin{bmatrix} x_1 \\ x_2 \end{bmatrix} \geq \begin{bmatrix} 0 \\ 0 \end{bmatrix}$

c) max income = \$3600 for x_1 = 30 suits
and x_2 = 0 dresses.

3. a) Let x_1 = number of lbs of Mixture I,
x_2 = number of lbs of Mixture II,
f = income
Then

$$0.6x_1 + 0.2x_2 \leq 1800,$$
$$0.3x_1 + 0.5x_2 \leq 1500,$$
$$0.1x_1 + 0.3x_2 \leq 750,$$
$$\max f: f = 0.75x_1 + 2x_2; \quad x_1, x_2 \geq 0.$$

b) $\begin{bmatrix} 0.6 & 0.2 \\ 0.3 & 0.5 \\ 0.1 & 0.3 \end{bmatrix} \begin{bmatrix} x_1 \\ x_2 \end{bmatrix} \leq \begin{bmatrix} 1800 \\ 1500 \\ 750 \end{bmatrix}$

$\max f: f = \begin{bmatrix} 0.75 & 2 \end{bmatrix} \begin{bmatrix} x_1 \\ x_2 \end{bmatrix}; \begin{bmatrix} x_1 \\ x_2 \end{bmatrix} \geq \begin{bmatrix} 0 \\ 0 \end{bmatrix}$

c) max income = \$5,156.25 for x_1 = 1875
lbs and x_2 = 1875 lbs.

5. a) Let x_1 = number of animals of species
A1,
x_2 = number of animals of species A2,
f = total number of animals;
F1: $x_1 + 1.2x_2 \leq 600,$
F2: $2x_1 + 1.8x_2 \leq 960,$
F3: $2x_1 + 0.6x_2 \leq 720.$
$\max f: f = x_1 + x_2; \quad x_1, x_2 \geq 0.$

b) $\begin{bmatrix} 1 & 1.2 \\ 2 & 1.8 \\ 2 & 0.6 \end{bmatrix} \begin{bmatrix} x_1 \\ x_2 \end{bmatrix} \leq \begin{bmatrix} 600 \\ 960 \\ 720 \end{bmatrix}$

$\max f: f = \begin{bmatrix} 1 & 1 \end{bmatrix} \begin{bmatrix} x_1 \\ x_2 \end{bmatrix}; \begin{bmatrix} x_1 \\ x_2 \end{bmatrix} \geq \begin{bmatrix} 0 \\ 0 \end{bmatrix}$

c) max number = 520 for x_1 = 120 and x_2
= 400.

7. a) F1: $x_1 + 1.2x_2 \leq 720,$
F2: $2x_1 + 1.8x_2 \leq 960,$
F3: $2x_1 + 0.6x_2 \leq 600.$
$\max f: f = x_1 + x_2; \quad x_1, x_2 \geq 0.$

c) max number = $\frac{1600}{3}$ (ignore fractions) for
x_1 = 0 and x_2 = $\frac{1600}{3}$. Species A1 would
become extinct (in that area).

Exercise Set 4.4, p. 206

1. a) Let y_1 = number of sacks of soybean
meal,
y_2 = number of sacks of oats,
f = cost
Then

$$50y_1 + 15y_2 \geq 120,$$
$$8y_1 + 5y_2 \geq 24,$$
$$5y_1 + y_2 \geq 10.$$
$$\min f: f = 15y_1 + 5y_2; \quad y_1, y_2 \geq 0.$$

b) $\begin{bmatrix} 50 & 15 \\ 8 & 5 \\ 5 & 1 \end{bmatrix} \begin{bmatrix} y_1 \\ y_2 \end{bmatrix} \geq \begin{bmatrix} 120 \\ 24 \\ 10 \end{bmatrix}$

$\min f: f = \begin{bmatrix} 15 & 5 \end{bmatrix} \begin{bmatrix} y_1 \\ y_2 \end{bmatrix}; \begin{bmatrix} y_1 \\ y_2 \end{bmatrix} \geq \begin{bmatrix} 0 \\ 0 \end{bmatrix}$

c) min cost = \$$\frac{180}{13}$ for y_1 = $\frac{24}{13}$ and y_2 = $\frac{24}{13}$.

3. a) Third constraint $5y_1 + 8y_3 \geq 10$, becomes $5y_1 + 8y_3 \geq 20$. c) min cost $= \$\frac{276}{7}$ for $y_1 = \frac{12}{7}$ and $y_3 = \frac{12}{7}$

5. a) Let $y_1 =$ number of P1 airplanes, $y_2 =$ number of P2 airplanes, $f =$ cost in $ thousands. Then
$$40y_1 + 80y_2 \geq 2000,$$
$$40y_1 + 30y_2 \geq 1500,$$
$$120y_1 + 40y_2 \geq 2400,$$
$$\min f: f = 12y_1 + 10y_2; \quad y_1, y_2 \geq 0.$$

b) $\begin{bmatrix} 40 & 80 \\ 40 & 30 \\ 120 & 40 \end{bmatrix} \begin{bmatrix} y_1 \\ y_2 \end{bmatrix} \geq \begin{bmatrix} 2000 \\ 1500 \\ 240 \end{bmatrix}$,

$\min f: f = \begin{bmatrix} 12 & 10 \end{bmatrix} \begin{bmatrix} y_1 \\ y_2 \end{bmatrix}; \begin{bmatrix} y_1 \\ y_2 \end{bmatrix} \geq \begin{bmatrix} 0 \\ 0 \end{bmatrix}$.

c) min cost $= \$460$ thousand for $y_1 = 30$ and $y_2 = 10$.

7. a)
$$40y_1 + 40y_3 \geq 2000,$$
$$40y_1 + 80y_3 \geq 1500,$$
$$120y_1 + 80y_3 \geq 2400,$$
$$\min f: f = 12y_1 + 15y_3; \quad y_1, y_3 \geq 0.$$

b) $\begin{bmatrix} 40 & 40 \\ 40 & 80 \\ 120 & 80 \end{bmatrix} \begin{bmatrix} y_1 \\ y_2 \end{bmatrix} \geq \begin{bmatrix} 2000 \\ 1500 \\ 2400 \end{bmatrix}$,

$\min f: f = \begin{bmatrix} 12 & 15 \end{bmatrix} \begin{bmatrix} y_1 \\ y_2 \end{bmatrix}; \begin{bmatrix} y_1 \\ y_3 \end{bmatrix} \geq \begin{bmatrix} 0 \\ 0 \end{bmatrix}$.

c) min cost $= \$600$ thousand for $y_1 = 50$ and $y_3 = 0$.

9. Replace $\begin{bmatrix} 2000 \\ 1500 \\ 2400 \end{bmatrix}$ by $\begin{bmatrix} 1600 \\ 2100 \\ 2400 \end{bmatrix}$. a) Set $y_3 = 0$. c) min cost $= \$630$ thousand for $y_1 = 52.5$ and $y_2 = 0$.

11. a) Set $y_2 = 0$.
c) min cost $= \$517.5$ thousand for $y_1 = \frac{55}{2}$ and $y_3 = \frac{25}{2}$.

Exercise Set 4.5, p. 212

1. $90. **3.** 75 lbs
5. $16\frac{2}{3} **7.** $9 per mile
9. 8 **11.** 4000

Chapter 4 Review, p. 213

1,2,3,4,5. (See figure at right.)

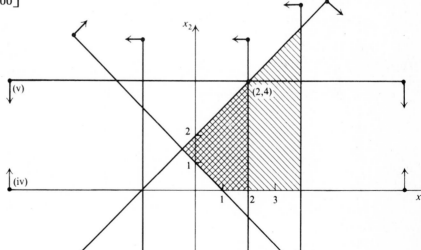
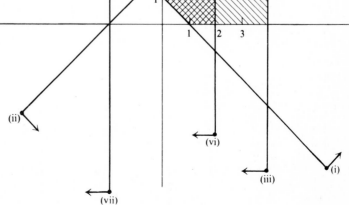

4. a) $(2, 4)$ degenerate; intersection of ii, v, and vi b) Constraints (iii) and (v) redundant

5. Solution set empty **6.** $(\frac{20}{7}, \frac{12}{7})$ **7.** min: $f(-\frac{1}{3}, -\frac{2}{3}) = -\frac{14}{3}$, max: $f(2, 2) = 10$

8. min: $f(-\frac{4}{3}, -\frac{2}{3}) = f(2, 1) = 0$ [any point on the line segment between $(-\frac{4}{3}, -\frac{2}{3})$ and $(2, 1)$], max: $f(0, 2) = 4$.

9.

	Composition		Supply available
	Chairs	Sofas	
Number of units	x_1	x_2	
Wood (feet)	20	100	1900
Foam (lbs)	1	50	500
Material (yds)	2	20	240
Unit price ($)	20	300	Maximize income

$$20x_1 + 100x_2 \leq 1900,$$
$$x_1 + 50x_2 \leq 500,$$
$$2x_1 + 20x_2 \leq 240,$$
$$\max f: f = 20x_1 + 300x_2;$$
$$x_1, x_2 \geq 0.$$

10. $\begin{bmatrix} 20 & 100 \\ 1 & 50 \\ 2 & 50 \end{bmatrix} \begin{bmatrix} x_1 \\ x_2 \end{bmatrix} \leq \begin{bmatrix} 1900 \\ 500 \\ 240 \end{bmatrix}$ $\max f: f = \begin{bmatrix} 20 & 300 \end{bmatrix} \begin{bmatrix} x_1 \\ x_2 \end{bmatrix}$; $\begin{bmatrix} x_1 \\ x_2 \end{bmatrix} \geq \begin{bmatrix} 0 \\ 0 \end{bmatrix}$.

11. $x_1 = 25$, $x_2 = \frac{19}{2}$, $f = 3350$

12. a)

	Composition (tons)		Amount required (tons)
	Ore A	Ore B	
Number of units (tons)	y_1	y_2	
Iron	0.10	0	200
Aluminum	0	0.20	500
Copper	0.02	0.01	100
Cost ($) per ton	10	15	Minimize cost

$$0.1y_1 + 0y_2 \geq 200,$$
$$0y_1 + 0.2y_2 \geq 500,$$
$$0.02y_1 + 0.01y_2 \geq 100,$$
$$\min f: f = 10y_1 + 15y_2; \quad y_1, y_2 \geq 0.$$

13. $f = 75,000$ at $(y_1, y_2) = (3750, 2500)$

b) $\begin{bmatrix} 0.1 & 0 \\ 0 & 0.2 \\ 0.02 & 0.01 \end{bmatrix} \begin{bmatrix} y_1 \\ y_2 \end{bmatrix} \geq \begin{bmatrix} 200 \\ 500 \\ 100 \end{bmatrix}$

$\min f: f = \begin{bmatrix} 10 & 15 \end{bmatrix} \begin{bmatrix} y_1 \\ y_2 \end{bmatrix}$; $\begin{bmatrix} y_1 \\ y_2 \end{bmatrix} \geq \begin{bmatrix} 0 \\ 0 \end{bmatrix}$.

14. Let x_1 = number of lbs of mixture I,
x_2 = number of lbs of mixture II,
f = income.
Then

$$0.8x_1 + 0.6x_2 \leq 100,$$
$$0.01x_1 + 0.03x_2 \leq 10,$$
$$0x_1 + 0.04x_2 \leq 5,$$
$$0.12x_1 + 0.24x_2 \leq 25,$$
$$0.07x_1 + 0.09x_2 \leq 15,$$
$$\max f: f = 0.95x_1 + 1.35x_2; \quad x_1, x_2 \geq 0.$$

$$\begin{bmatrix} 0.8 & 0.6 \\ 0.01 & 0.03 \\ 0 & 0.04 \\ 0.12 & 0.24 \\ 0.07 & 0.09 \end{bmatrix} \begin{bmatrix} x_1 \\ x_2 \end{bmatrix} \leq \begin{bmatrix} 100 \\ 10 \\ 5 \\ 25 \\ 15 \end{bmatrix}, \quad \max f: f = \begin{bmatrix} 0.95 & 1.35 \end{bmatrix} \begin{bmatrix} x_1 \\ x_2 \end{bmatrix}; \quad \begin{bmatrix} x_1 \\ x_2 \end{bmatrix} \geq \begin{bmatrix} 0 \\ 0 \end{bmatrix}.$$

15.

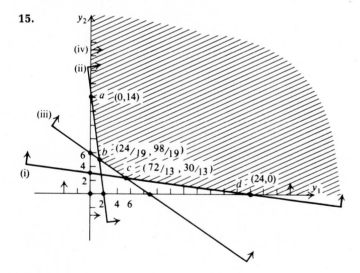

16. Minimum is $6\frac{8}{19}$ when $y_1 = \frac{24}{19}$ and $y_2 = \frac{98}{19}$.   **17.** 6

CHAPTER 5

Exercise Set 5.1, p. 231

1. $x_1 = 1$, $x_2 = 5$, $y_1 = y_2 = 0$; $x_0 = 11$ **3.** $x_1 = 2$, $x_2 = 3$, $y_1 = y_2 = 0$; $x_0 = 22$
5. $x_1 = 2$, $x_2 = 6$, $y_1 = y_2 = 0$, $y_3 = 2$; $x_0 = 30$ **7.** $x_1 = 35$, $x_2 = 0$, $y_1 = 25$, $y_2 = 0$; $x_0 = 4200$
9. $x_1 = 30$, $x_2 = x_3 = y_1 = 0$, $y_2 = 10$, $y_3 = 14$; $x_0 = 90$ **11.** $x_1 = 8$, $x_2 = 3$, $y_1 = 2$, $y_2 = y_3 = 0$;
$x_0 = 19$ **13.** $x_1 = 9$, $x_2 = 4$, $y_1 = 5$, $y_2 = y_3 = 0$; $x_0 = 79$ **15.** $x_1 = \frac{6}{5}$, $x_2 = 0$, $x_3 = \frac{22}{5}$,
$y_1 = y_2 = 0$, $y_3 = \frac{144}{5}$; $x_0 = 22$ **17.** $x_1 = 0$, $x_2 = \frac{9}{4}$, $x_3 = \frac{19}{4}$, $y_1 = \frac{11}{4}$, $y_2 = y_3 = 0$; $x_0 = \frac{75}{4}$
19. No bookcases, 12 desks, 65 tables; max sales = \$6400.

Exercise Set 5.2, p. 243

1. $y_1 = 6$, $y_2 = 1$, $x_1 = 10$, $x_2 = x_3 = 0$; $y_0 = 22$ **3.** $y_1 = 5$, $y_2 = 1$, $x_1 = 2$, $x_2 = x_3 = 0$; $y_0 = 15$ **5.** $y_1 = 3$, $y_2 = 2$, $x_1 = 5$, $x_2 = x_3 = 0$; $y_0 = 19$ **7.** $y_1 = y_2 = \frac{24}{13}$, $x_1 = x_2 = 0$, $x_3 = \frac{14}{13}$; $y_0 = \frac{480}{13}$ **9.** $y_1 = y_3 = \frac{12}{7}$, $x_1 = x_2 = 0$, $x_3 = 4$; $y_0 = \frac{276}{7}$ **11.** $y_1 = 30$, $y_2 = 10$, $x_1 = x_2 = 0$, $x_3 = 1600$; $y_0 = 460$ **13.** $y_1 = 50$, $y_3 = x_1 = 0$, $x_2 = 500$, $x_3 = 3600$; $y_0 = 600$ **15.** $y_1 = 52.5$, $y_2 = 0$, $x_1 = 500$, $x_2 = 0$, $x_3 = 3900$; $y_0 = 630$ **17.** $y_1 = 27.5$, $y_3 = 12.5$, $x_1 = x_2 = 0$, $x_3 = 1900$; $y_0 = 517.5$.   **19.** $y_1 = 4$, $y_2 = 6$, $x_1 = 4$, $x_2 = x_3 = 0$; $y_0 = 76$ (P: $x_1 = 0$, $x_2 = \frac{4}{7}$, $x_3 = \frac{11}{7}$, $y_1 = y_2 = 0$)   **21.** $y_1 = 5$, $y_2 = 7$, $x_1 = x_2 = 0$, $x_3 = 1$; $y_0 = 53$ (P: $x_1 = \frac{9}{7}$, $x_2 = \frac{2}{7}$, $x_3 = y_1 = y_2 = 0$)   **23.** $x_1 = 0$, $x_2 = \frac{7}{4}$, $x_3 = \frac{5}{4}$, $y_1 = \frac{59}{4}$, $y_2 = y_3 = 0$; $x_0 = \frac{19}{4}$ (P: $y_1 = 0$, $y_2 = \frac{1}{8}$, $y_3 = \frac{5}{4}$, $x_1 = \frac{27}{8}$, $x_2 = x_3 = 0$)   **25.** $y_1 = \frac{8}{11}$, $y_2 = \frac{2}{11}$, $y_3 = x_1 = x_2 = 0$, $x_3 = \frac{13}{11}$; $y_0 = \frac{82}{11}$ (P: $x_1 = \frac{29}{11}$, $x_2 = \frac{6}{11}$, $x_3 = y_1 = y_2 = 0$, $y_3 = 4$)   **27.** Cost $0.29 with all soybeans = 288 gms   **29.** Cost $0.91 with 130 gms cheese and 138 gms beef.

Exercise Set 5.3, p. 255

1. Primal degenerate: $x_0 = 12$, $x_1 = 0$, $x_2 = 0$, $x_3 = 4$ Dual nonunique: (1) $y_0 = 12$, $y_1 = 0$, $y_2 = 3$, $y_3 = 0$, (2) $y_0 = 12$, $y_1 = 0$, $y_2 = \frac{9}{4}$, $y_3 = \frac{1}{4}$ **3.** Primal unbounded, dual infeasible.   **5.** Primal degenerate: $x_0 = 12$, $x_1 = 0$, $x_2 = 0$, $x_3 = 3$ Dual nonunique: (1) $y_0 = 12$, $y_1 = 0$, $y_2 = 1$, $y_3 = 1$ (2) $y_0 = 12$, $y_1 = 0$, $y_2 = 0$, $y_3 = 2$.

Exercise Set 5.4, p. 262

Values of basic variables are given; values of nonbasic variables are zero.

1. $x_{11} = 70$, $x_{12} = 80$, $x_{22} = 10$, $x_{23} = 70$; $x_0 = 2230$ **3.** $x_{11} = 70$, $x_{22} = 80$, $x_{31} = x_{32} = 50$; $x_0 = 2850$ **5.** $x_{11} = 15$, $x_{12} = 60$, $x_{14} = 75$, $x_{21} = 30$, $x_{23} = 70$; $x_0 = 2495$ **7.** $x_{11} = 70$, $x_{12} = 10$, $x_{23} = 90$, $x_{31} = 0$, $x_{32} = 110$; $x_0 = 3510$ **9.** $x_{13} = 20$, $x_{14} = 80$, $x_{21} = 25$, $x_{22} = 100$, $x_{31} = 50$, $x_{33} = 100$; $x_0 = 3905$

Exercise Set 5.5, p. 270

Values of basic variables are given; values of nonbasic variables are zero.

1. $x_{12} = x_{25} = x_{31} = x_{44} = x_{53} = 1$; $a_0 = 432$ **3.** $x_{15} = x_{22} = x_{31} = x_{43} = x_{54} = 1$; $a_0 = 439$ **5.** $x_{11} = x_{25} = x_{34} = x_{43} = x_{52} = 1$ or $x_{13} = x_{25} = x_{34} = x_{41} = x_{52} = 1$; $a_0 = 440$ **7.** $x_{12} = x_{25} = x_{33} = x_{41} = x_{56} = x_{64} = 1$; $a_0 = 496$.

Exercise Set 5.6, p. 280

a) See Figure and first arc label.
b) Early start time is first node label.
c) Late start time is third node label.
d) Slack time is difference between the third and first arc labels. Critical path is heavy line.

1.

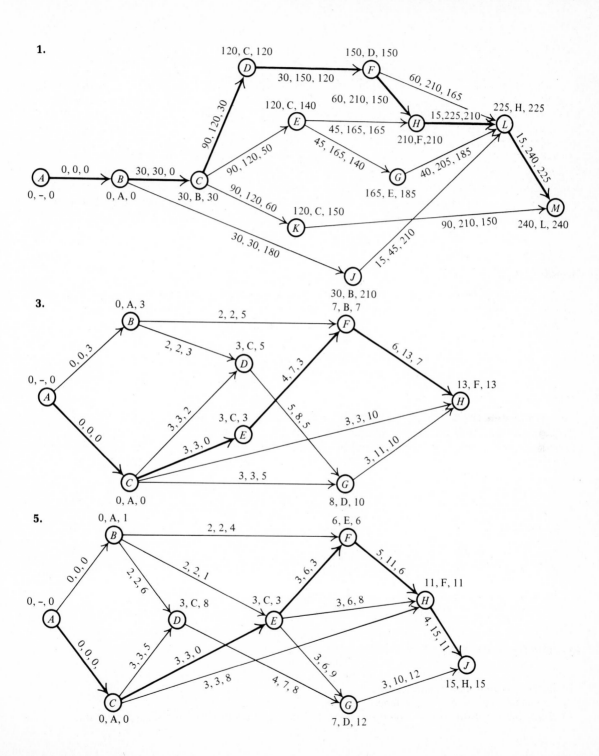

7.

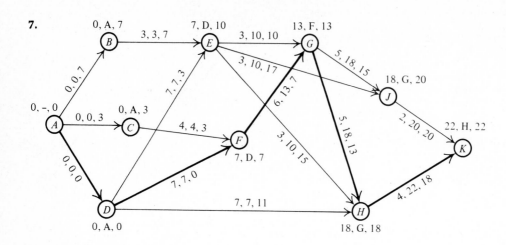

Chapter 5 Review, p. 282

1.
$$20x_1 + 100x_2 + y_1 \qquad\qquad\qquad = 1900$$
$$x_1 + 50x_2 \qquad + y_2 \qquad = 500,$$
$$2x_1 + 20x_2 \qquad\qquad + y_3 = 240,$$

max x_0: $x_0 = 20x_1 + 300x_2 + 0y_1 + 0 \cdot y_2 + 0 \cdot y_3$; $x_i \geq 0$ for all i, $y_i \geq 0$ for all i.

$$\begin{bmatrix} 20 & 100 & 1 & 0 & 0 \\ 1 & 50 & 0 & 1 & 0 \\ 2 & 20 & 0 & 0 & 1 \end{bmatrix} \begin{bmatrix} x_1 \\ x_2 \\ y_1 \\ y_2 \\ y_3 \end{bmatrix} = \begin{bmatrix} 1900 \\ 500 \\ 240 \end{bmatrix}.$$

max x_0: $x_0 = [20 \quad 300 \quad 0 \quad 0 \quad 0][x_1 \quad x_2 \quad y_1 \quad y_2 \quad y_3]^T$, $[x_1 \quad x_2 \quad y_1 \quad y_2 \quad y_3]^T = [0 \quad 0 \quad 0 \quad 0 \quad 0]^T$.

2.

x_1	x_2	y_1	y_2	y_3	1
20	100	1	0	0	1900
1	50	0	1	0	500
2	20	0	0	1	240
−20	−300	0	0	0	0

3. $x_1 = x_2 = 0$; $y_1 = 1900$, $y_2 = 500$, $y_3 = 240$; $x_0 = 0$

4. Second column, second row

5. $x_1 = 25$, $x_2 = \frac{19}{2}$, $y_1 = 450$, $y_2 = y_3 = 0$; $x_0 = 3350$

6.
$$20y_1 + y_2 + 2y_3 \geq 20,$$
$$100y_1 + 50y_2 + 20y_3 \geq 300,$$
$$y_1, \qquad y_2, \qquad y_3 \geq 0,$$

min y_0: $y_0 = 1900y_1 + 500y_2 + 240y_3$

7.
$$0.1x_1 + 0 \cdot x_2 + 0.02x_3 \leq 10,$$
$$0 \cdot x_1 + 0.2x_2 + 0.01x_3 \leq 15,$$
$$x_1, \qquad x_2, \qquad x_3 \geq 0,$$

max x_0: $x_0 = 200x_1 + 500x_2 + 100x_3$

8.

x_1	x_2	y_1	y_2	y_3	1
20	100	1	0	0	1900
1	50	0	1	0	500
2	20	0	0	1	240
-20	-300	0	0	0	0

Initial primal sol.: $x_0 = x_1 = x_2 = 0$, $y_1 = 1900$, $y_2 = 500$, $y_3 = 240$
Initial dual sol.: $y_0 = y_1 = y_2 = y_3 = 0$, $x_1 = -20$, $x_2 = -300$

9.
$$0.1x_1 + 0 \cdot x_2 + 0.02x_3 + \quad y_1 \qquad\qquad = 10,$$
$$0 \cdot x_1 + 0.2x_2 + 0.01x_3 + \qquad\qquad y_2 = 15,$$
$$x_1, \qquad x_2, \qquad x_3, \qquad y_1, \qquad y_2 \quad \geqslant 0,$$
$$\max x_0\colon x_0 = 200x_1 + 500x_2 + \quad 100x_3 + 0 \cdot y_1 + 0 \cdot y_2$$

x_1	x_2	x_3	y_1	y_2	1
0.1	2	0.02	1	0	10
0	0.2	0.01	0	1	15
-200	-500	-100	0	0	0

Initial primal sol.: $x_0 = x_1 = x_2 = x_3 = 0$, $y_1 = 10$, $y_2 = 15$
Initial dual sol.: $y_0 = y_1 = y_2 = 0$, $x_1 = -200$, $x_2 = -500$, $x_3 = -100$

10. Dual (min) solution: $y_1 = 3750$, $y_2 = 2500$, $x_1 = 175$, $x_2 = x_3 = 0$; $y_0 = 75{,}000$
11. Primal (max) solution: $x_1 = 0$, $x_2 = 75$, $x_3 = 500$, $y_1 = y_2 = 0$; $x_0 = 75{,}000$
12. $x_{11} = 40$, $x_{13} = 80$, $x_{21} = 20$, $x_{22} = 50$, $x_{12} = x_{23} = 0$; $x_0 = 1410$
13. $x_{11} = 60$, $x_{13} = 60$, $x_{21} = 50$, $x_{22} = 20$, $x_{12} = x_{23} = 0$; $x_0 = 1370$
14. Same as Example 1 of Section 5.5   **15.** $x_{13} = x_{22} = x_{35} = x_{41} = x_{54} = 1$
16. See Figure and first arc label.   **17.** First node label and first node label of node G.
18. Third node label.   **19.** Difference between third and first node labels.

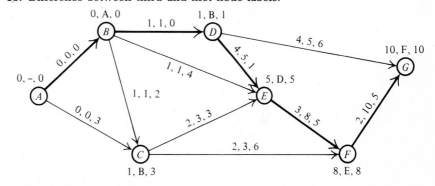

20. $x_1 = 11$, $x_2 = 5$, $y_1 = 5$, $y_2 = y_3 = 0$; $x_0 = 59$.

21. $y_1 = \frac{62}{7}$, $y_2 = \frac{60}{7}$, $x_1 = 0$, $x_2 = \frac{10}{7}$, $x_3 = 0$; $y_0 = \frac{428}{7}$

22. a)
$$
\begin{aligned}
y_1 + \quad y_2 + \quad 5y_3 &\geqslant 4, \\
2y_1 + \quad y_2 + \quad 3y_3 &\geqslant 3, \\
\min y_0: y_0 = 26y_1 + 16y_2 + 70y_3; & \\
y_1, \qquad y_2, \qquad y_3 &\geqslant 0.
\end{aligned}
$$

b) $y_1 = 0$, $y_2 = \frac{3}{2}$, $y_3 = \frac{1}{2}$, $x_1 = x_2 = 0$; $y_0 = 59$

c)
$$
\begin{aligned}
x_1 + 2x_2 + y_1 &= 26, \\
x_1 + \quad x_2 + y_2 &= 16, \\
5x_1 + 3x_2 + y_3 &= 70, \\
x_0 = 4x_1 + 3x_2; & \\
x_1, x_2; y_1, y_2, y_3 &\geqslant 0.
\end{aligned}
$$

d)
$$
\begin{aligned}
y_1 + \quad y_2 + \quad 5y_3 - x_1 &= 4, \\
2y_1 + \quad y_2 + \quad 3y_3 - x_2 &= 3, \\
y_0 = 26y_1 + 16y_2 + 70y_3 &= x_0; \\
y_1, y_2, y_3; x_1, x_2 &\geqslant 0.
\end{aligned}
$$

23.

x_1	x_2	x_3	y_1	y_2	y_3	1
16*	0	−11	1	−5	0	2
−3	1	2	0	1	0	0
5	0	−4	0	−3	1	5
−1	0	3	0	1	0	0

24. a) Primal degenerate: $x_1 = x_2 = x_3 = 0$, $x_4 = 2$, $x_5 = 0$, $x_6 = 5$; $x_0 = 10$. Dual nonunique: $x_1 = 2$, $x_2 = 1$, $x_3 = 1$, $x_4 = x_5 = x_6 = 0$; $x_0 = 10$. b) Primal unbounded; dual infeasible.

25. $x_{12} = 35$, $x_{13} = 10$, $x_{23} = 50$, $x_{31} = 30$, $x_{32} = 35$; $x_0 = 2625$ **26.** $x_{11} = x_{23} = x_{32} = x_{44} = x_{55} = 1$; $a_0 = 35$

27.

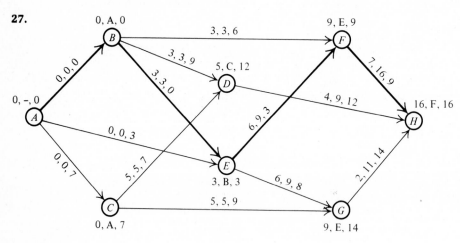

CHAPTER 6

Exercise Set 6.1, p. 290

1. $\frac{1}{2}, \frac{2}{3}, \frac{3}{4}, \frac{4}{5}; \frac{15}{16}$ **3.** $0, \frac{1}{3}, \frac{2}{7}, \frac{3}{13}; \frac{14}{211}$ **5.** 2; 5   **7.** \$1.06; 0.06   **9.** 5; $-\frac{2}{3}$ **11.** 47   **13.** −\$1628.16

15. 45,150   **17.** 690   **19.** $\dfrac{n(n + 1)}{2}$ **21.** \$4.96   **23.** \$18,450

Exercise Set 6.2, p. 296

1. 2   **3.** $-\frac{1}{3}$ **5.** 0.95   **7.** 2187   **9.** $\frac{1}{5^6}$, or $\frac{1}{15,625}$ **11.** $2331.64   **13.** 1016   **15.** $5866.60

17. $2,684,000 approx.   **19.** No   **21.** $12\frac{1}{2}$ **23.** 486   **25.** $12,500   **27.** $32,000,000,000

29. $\approx 3,333,333$; $66\frac{2}{3}\%$ **31.** Assuming 80% of this $7 million is spent again, and so on, the total effect would be $35 million.

Exercise Set 6.3, p. 305

1. a)

Year	Rate of depreciation	Annual depreciation	Book value	Total depreciation
0			$8000	
1	$\frac{1}{4}$ or 25%	$1500	6500	$1500
2	25%	1500	5000	3000
3	25%	1500	3500	4500
4	25%	1500	2000	6000

b) $V_n = \$8000 - (\$1500)n$ c) $-\$1500$

3. a)

Year	Rate of depreciation	Annual depreciation	Book value	Total depreciation
0			$450	
1	$\frac{1}{4}$ or 12.5%	$56.25	393.75	$56.25
2	12.5%	56.25	337.50	112.50
3	12.5%	56.25	281.25	168.75
4	12.5%	56.25	225.00	225.00
5	12.5%	56.25	168.75	281.25
6	12.5%	56.25	112.50	337.50
7	12.5%	56.25	56.25	393.75
8	12.5%	56.25	0	450.00

b) $V_n = \$450 - (\$56.25)n$ c) $-\$56.25$

5. a)

Year	Rate of depreciation	Annual depreciation	Book value	Total depreciation
0			$8000	
1	$\frac{2}{4}$ or 50%	$4000	4000	$4000
2	50%	2000	2000	6000
3		0	2000	6000
4		0	2000	6000

b) $V_n = \$800(0.50)^n$

7. a)

Year	Rate of depreciation	Annual depreciation	Book value	Total depreciation
0			$450	
1	$\frac{2}{8}$ or 25%	$112.50	337.50	$112.50
2	25%	84.38	252.12	196.88
3	25%	63.28	189.84	260.16
4	25%	47.46	142.38	307.62
5	25%	35.60	106.78	343.22
6	25%	26.70	80.08	369.92
7	25%	20.02	60.06	389.94
8	25%	15.02	45.04	404.96

b) $V_n = \$450(0.75)^n$

9. a) $\frac{4}{10}, \frac{3}{10}, \frac{2}{10}, \frac{1}{10}$

b)

Year	Rate of depreciation	Annual depreciation	Book value	Total depreciation
0			$8000	
1	$\frac{4}{10}$	$2400	5600	$2400
2	$\frac{3}{10}$	1800	3800	4200
3	$\frac{2}{10}$	1200	2600	5400
4	$\frac{1}{10}$	600	2000	6000

11. a) $\frac{8}{36}, \frac{7}{36}, \frac{6}{36}, \frac{5}{36}, \frac{4}{36}, \frac{3}{36}, \frac{2}{36}, \frac{1}{36}$

b)

Year	Rate of depreciation	Annual depreciation	Book value	Total depreciation
0			$450	
1	$\frac{8}{36}$	$100	350	$100.00
2	$\frac{7}{36}$	87.50	262.50	187.50
3	$\frac{6}{36}$	75.00	187.50	262.50
4	$\frac{5}{36}$	62.50	125.00	325.00
5	$\frac{4}{36}$	50.00	75.00	375.00
6	$\frac{3}{36}$	37.50	37.50	412.50
7	$\frac{2}{36}$	25.00	12.50	437.50
8	$\frac{1}{36}$	12.50	0	450.00

Exercise Set 6.4, p. 312

1. $2060   **3.** $2560   **5.** a) $2280 b) $2289.80 c) $2295.05 d) $2297.76 e) $2300.52   **7.** $793.83
9. $788.49   **11.** $3450.32   **13.** $1144.90   **15.** $2.41   **17.** 6.25%

Exercise Set 6.5, p. 314

1. 8.16%   **3.** 9.308%   **5.** 8.271%   **7.** 8.328%   **9.** 8.329%   **11.** 13.7%   **13.** 16.8%

Exercise Set 6.6, p. 318

1. $4439.94   **3.** $13,816.45   **5.** $48,594.74   **7.** $1228.29   **9.** $103,399.40   **11.** $3673.84

13. $992.37   **15.** $100.33   **17.** $P = \dfrac{Vi}{[(1 + i)^N - 1]}$

Exercise Set 6.7, p. 323

1. $3387.21   **3.** $7023.58   **5.** $32,702.87   **7.** $760.95   **9.** $139.50   **11.** $548.84

$P = \dfrac{Si}{[1 - (1 + i)^N]}$ **15.** $12,500; you want $1000 of interest each year, so just solve $I = Pit$ for P when $I = 1000, $i = 0.08$, and $t = 1$.

Chapter 6 Review, p. 324

1. 5; 3   **2.** 62   **3.** $31.40   **4.** 1.05   **5.** $155.13   **6.** $1257.79   **7.** Yes, $1086.96

8. a)

Year	Rate of depreciation	Annual depreciation	Book value	Total depreciation
0			$8500	
1	$\frac{1}{4}$ or 25%	$1487.50	7012.50	$1487.50
2	25%	1487.50	5525	2975
3	25%	1487.50	4037.50	4462.50
4	25%	1487.50	2550	5950

b) $V_n = \$8500 - (\$1487.50)n$ c) $-\$1487.50$

9. a)

Year	Rate of depreciation	Annual depreciation	Book value	Total depreciation
0			$8500	
1	$\frac{2}{4}$ or 50%	$4250	4250	$4250
2		1700	2550	5950
3		0	2550	5950
4		0	2550	5950

b) $V_n = \$8500(0.50)^n$

10. a) $\frac{4}{10}, \frac{3}{10}, \frac{2}{10}, \frac{1}{10}$

b)

Year	Rate of depreciation	Annual depreciation	Book value	Total depreciation
0			$8500	
1	$\frac{4}{10}$	$2380	6120	$2380
2	$\frac{3}{10}$	1785	4335	4165
3	$\frac{2}{10}$	1190	3145	5355
4	$\frac{1}{10}$	595	2550	5950

11. a) $1180 b) $1191.02 c) $1194.05 d) $1195.62   **12.** 9.308%   **13.** 18.3%   **14.** $37,089.80
15. $1090.52   **16.** $103,796.58   **17.** $723.77   **18.** $4563.87   **19.** a) $5606.50 b) $5625.59

20. 20,100   **21.** \$13,677.74   **22.** \$723.78   **23.** $S_{\overline{N+M}\rceil k} = \dfrac{(1+k)^{N+M} - 1}{k} =$

$\dfrac{(1+k)^{N+M} - (1+k)^{N} + (1+k)^{N} - 1}{k} = \dfrac{(1+k)^{N+M} - (1+k)^{N}}{k} + \dfrac{(1+k)^{N} - 1}{k} =$

$(1+k)^{N} \cdot \dfrac{(1+k)^{M} - 1}{k} + \dfrac{(1+k)^{N} - 1}{k} = (1+k)^{N} S_{\overline{M}\rceil k} + S_{\overline{N}\rceil k}$ **24.** Similar to Exercise 23.

CHAPTER 7

Exercise Set 7.1, p. 336

1. No   **3.** Yes   **5.** a) Yes b) No   **7.** a) Yes b) Yes   **9.** No, Yes, No, Yes   **11.** Does not exist
13. 41¢   **15.** a) 1, -0.75, -1.56, -1.79, -1.9799, -1.997999; b) Answers may vary; c) -2.
17. -10 **19.** Does not exist.   **21.** $-\frac{3}{2}$ **23.** 12   **25.** $\frac{2}{3}$ **27.** $\frac{1}{2}$ **29.** -0.25 **31.** $2x + 1$
33. a) 0.775, 0.753125, 0.75125, 0.7505, 0.75003125, 0.75000625; b) 0.75 or $\frac{3}{4}$.   **35.** 0   **37.** 5
39. a) \$800, \$736, \$677.12, \$622.95, \$573.11; b) \$5656.12; c) \$10,000.

Exercise Set 7.2, p. 345

1. a) 70, 39, 29, 23 pleasure units/unit of product; b) The more you get, the less pleasure you get
from each additional unit.   **3.** a) $125 \dfrac{\text{million people}}{\text{yr}}$ for each; b) No; c) A: $290 \dfrac{\text{million people}}{\text{yr}}$,

$-40 \dfrac{\text{million people}}{\text{yr}}$, $-50 \dfrac{\text{million people}}{\text{yr}}$, $300 \dfrac{\text{million people}}{\text{yr}}$; B: $125 \dfrac{\text{million people}}{\text{yr}}$ in all intervals;

d) A.   **5.** a) \$93.99, b) \$100, c) $-\$6.01$, d) $-\$6.01$.   **7.** a) 144 ft, b) 256 ft, c) $128 \dfrac{\text{ft}}{\text{sec}}$.
9. \$275,780,000 per day.   **11.** a) $7(2x + h)$; b) 70, 63, 56.7, 56.07.   **13.** a) $-7(2x + h)$; b) -70,
-63, -56.7, -56.07.   **15.** a) $7(3x^2 + 3xh + h^2)$, b) 532, 427, 344.47, 336.8407.   **17.** a) $\dfrac{-5}{x(x+h)}$;
b) -0.2083, -0.25, -0.3049, -0.3117.   **19.** a) -2, b) All -2.   **21.** a) $2x + h - 1$,
b) 9, 8, 7.1, 7.01.   **23.** $2ax + b + ah$ **25.** $\dfrac{\sqrt{x+h} - \sqrt{x}}{h}$

Exercise Set 7.3, p. 356

1. $f'(x) = 10x$, $f'(-2) = -20$, $f'(-1) = -10$, $f'(0) = 0$, $f'(1) = 10$, $f'(2) = 20$.
3. $f'(x) = -10x$, $f'(-2) = 20$, $f'(-1) = 10$, $f'(0) = 0$, $f'(1) = -10$, $f'(2) = -20$.
5. $f'(x) = 15x^2$, $f'(-2) = 60$, $f'(-1) = 15$, $f'(0) = 0$, $f'(1) = 15$, $f'(2) = 60$.
7. $f'(x) = 2$, all 2.   **9.** $f'(x) = -4$, all -4.
11. $f'(x) = 2x + 1$, $f'(-2) = -3$, $f'(-1) = -1$, $f'(0) = 1$, $f'(1) = 3$, $f'(2) = 5$.
13. $f'(x) = \dfrac{-4}{x^2}$; $f'(-2) = -1$; $f'(-1) = -4$; $f'(0)$ does not exist; $f'(1) = -4$; $f'(2) = -1$.
15. $f'(x) = m$, all m **17.** x_0, x_3, x_4, x_6, x_{12} **19.** $x = -3$

Exercise Set 7.4, p. 364

1. $7x^6$ **3.** 0 **5.** $600x^{149}$ **7.** $3x^2 + 6x$ **9.** $\dfrac{4}{\sqrt{x}}$ **11.** $0.07x^{-0.93}$ **13.** $\dfrac{2}{5 \cdot \sqrt[5]{x}}$ **15.** $\dfrac{-3}{x^4}$

17. $6x - 8$ **19.** $\dfrac{1}{4\sqrt[4]{x^3}} + \dfrac{1}{x^2}$ **21.** $1.6x^{1.5}$ **23.** $\dfrac{-5}{x^2} - 1$ **25.** 4 **27.** 4 **29.** x^3

31. $-0.02x - 0.5$ **33.** $-2x^{-5/3} + \frac{3}{4}x^{-1/4} + \frac{6}{5}x^{1/5} - 24x^{-4}$ **35.** $(0, 0)$ **37.** $(0, 0)$ **39.** $(\frac{5}{6}, \frac{23}{12})$
41. $(-25, 76.25)$ **43.** There are none. **45.** Tangent is horizontal at all points on graph.
47. $(\frac{5}{3}, \frac{148}{27})$, $(-1, -4)$ **49.** $(\sqrt{3}, 2 - 2\sqrt{3})$, $(-\sqrt{3}, 2 + 2\sqrt{3})$ **51.** $(\frac{19}{2}, \frac{399}{4})$ **53.** $(60, 150)$
55. $(-2 + \sqrt{3}, \frac{4}{3} - \sqrt{3})$, $(-2 - \sqrt{3}, \frac{4}{3} + \sqrt{3})$ **57.** $(0, -4)$, $(\sqrt{\frac{2}{3}}, -\frac{40}{9})$, $(-\sqrt{\frac{2}{3}}, -\frac{40}{9})$

59. $2x - 1$ **61.** $2x + 1$ **63.** $3x^2 - \dfrac{1}{x^2}$ **65.** $-192x^2$ **67.** $\dfrac{2}{3 \cdot \sqrt[3]{x^2}}$ **69.** $3x^2 + 6x + 3$

Exercise Set 7.5, p. 369

1. a) $P(x) = -0.5x^2 + 46x - 10$ b) $R(20) = \$800$, $C(20) = \$90$, $P(20) = \$710$ c) $R'(x) = 50 - x$,
$C'(x) = 4$, $P'(x) = 46 - x$ d) $R'(20) = \$30$ per unit, $C'(20) = \$4$ per unit, $P'(20) = \$26$ per unit

3. a) $S'(t) = -0.2t + 1.2$ b) $\$100,600$ c) $\$0.8$ thousand/day **5.** $\dfrac{dC}{dr} = 2\pi$ **7.** a) $\dfrac{dV}{ds} = 3s$ b) 30

9. a) $P'(t) = 4000t$ b) $300,000$ c) $40,000$ people/yr

Exercise Set 7.6, p. 374

1. $11x^{10}$ **3.** $\dfrac{1}{x^2}$ **5.** $3x^2$ **7.** $(8x^5 - 3x^2 + 20)\left(32x^3 - \dfrac{3}{2\sqrt{x}}\right) + (40x^4 - 6x)(8x^4 - 3\sqrt{x})$

9. $300 - 2x$ **11.** $\dfrac{300}{(300 - x)^2}$ **13.** $\dfrac{17}{(2x + 5)^2}$ **15.** $\dfrac{-x^4 - 3x^2 - 2x}{(x^3 - 1)^2}$ **17.** $\dfrac{1}{(1 - x)^2}$ **19.** $\dfrac{2}{(x + 1)^2}$

21. $\dfrac{-1}{(x - 3)^2}$ **23.** $\dfrac{-2x^2 + 6x + 2}{(x^2 + 1)^2}$ **25.** $\dfrac{-18x + 35}{x^8}$ **27.** a) $R(x) = x(400 - x) = 400x - x^2$;

b) $R'(x) = 400 - 2x$. **29.** a) $R(x) = 4000 + 3x$; b) $R'(x) = 3$. **31.** $A'(x) = \dfrac{xC'(x) - C(x)}{x^2}$

33. $\dfrac{5x^3 - 30x^2\sqrt{x}}{2\sqrt{x}(\sqrt{x} - 5)^2}$ **35.** $\dfrac{-3(1 + 2v)}{(1 + v + v^2)^2}$ **37.** $\dfrac{2t^3 - t^2 + 1}{(1 - t + t^2 - t^3)^2}$ **39.** $\dfrac{5x^3 + 15x^2 + 2}{2x\sqrt{x}}$

41. $[x(9x^2 + 6 + (3x^3 + 6x - 2)](3x^4 + 7) + 12x^4(3x^3 + 6x - 2)$ **43.** $\dfrac{6t^2(t^5 + 3)}{(t^3 + 1)^2} + \dfrac{5t^4(t^3 - 1)}{t^3 + 1}$

45. $\dfrac{(x^7 - 2x^6 + 9)[(2x^2 + 3)(12x^2 - 7) + 4x(4x^3 - 7x + 2)] - (7x^6 - 12x^5)(2x^2 + 3)(4x^3 - 7x + 2)}{(x^7 - 2x^6 + 9)^2}$

Exercise Set 7.7, p. 380

1. $-55(1 - x)^{54}$ **3.** $\dfrac{4}{\sqrt{1 + 8x}}$ **5.** $\dfrac{3x}{\sqrt{3x^2 - 4}}$ **7.** $-240x(3x^2 - 6)^{-41}$ **9.** $\sqrt{2x + 3} + \dfrac{x}{\sqrt{2x + 3}}$, or $\dfrac{3(x + 1)}{\sqrt{2x + 3}}$ **11.** $2x\sqrt{x - 1} + \dfrac{x^2}{2\sqrt{x - 1}}$, or $\dfrac{5x^2 - 4x}{2\sqrt{x - 1}}$ **13.** $\dfrac{-6}{(3x + 8)^3}$ **15.** $(1 + x^3)^2 \cdot$

$(-3x^2 - 12x^5)$, or $-3x^2(1 + x^3)^2(1 + 4x^3)$ **17.** $4x - 400$ **19.** $2(x + 6)^9(x - 5)^3(7x - 13)$

21. $4(x - 4)^7(3 - x)^3(10 - 3x)$ **23.** $4(2x - 3)^2(3 - 8x)$ **25.** $\left(\dfrac{1 - x}{1 + x}\right)^{-1/2} \cdot \dfrac{-1}{(x + 1)^2}$

27. a) $\dfrac{2x - 3x^2}{(1 + x)^6}$, b) $\dfrac{2x - 3x^2}{(1 + x)^6}$, c) Same. **29.** $C'(x) = \dfrac{1500x^2}{\sqrt{x^3 + 2}}$ **31.** $\$3000(1 + i)^2$

33. $\dfrac{x^2 - 2}{\sqrt[3]{(x^3 - 6x + 1)^2}}$ **35.** $\dfrac{x - 2}{2(x - 1)^{3/2}}$ **37.** $\dfrac{-4(1 + 2v)^3}{v^5}$ **39.** $\dfrac{1}{\sqrt{1 - x^2}(1 - x)}$

41. $3\left(\dfrac{x^2 - x - 1}{x^2 + 1}\right)^2 \cdot \dfrac{x^2 + 4x - 1}{(x^2 + 1)^2}$ **43.** $\dfrac{1}{\sqrt{t}(1 + \sqrt{t})^2}$

Exercise Set 7.8, p. 385

1. $\dfrac{1 - y}{x + 2}$; $-\dfrac{1}{9}$ **33.** $-\dfrac{x}{y}$; $-\dfrac{1}{\sqrt{3}}$ **5.** $\dfrac{6x^2 - 2xy}{x^2 - 3y^2}$; $-\dfrac{36}{23}$ **7.** $-\dfrac{y}{x}$ **9.** $\dfrac{x}{y}$ **11.** $\dfrac{3x^2}{5y^4}$

13. $\dfrac{-3x^2y^4 - 2xy^3}{3x^2y^2 + 4x^3y^3}$ **15.** $\dfrac{dp}{dx} = \dfrac{-2}{2p + 1}$ **17.** $\dfrac{dp}{dx} = -\dfrac{p + 4}{x + 3}$ **19.** \$400 per day, \$80 per day,

\$320 per day. **21.** \$16 per day, \$8 per day, \$8 per day. **23.** 65 mph **25.** a) $\dfrac{dR}{dt} = \$0$ per day

b) $\dfrac{dC}{dt} = \$64$ per day c) $\dfrac{dC}{dt} = -\$64$ per day **27.** $-\dfrac{\sqrt{y}}{\sqrt{x}}$ **29.** $\dfrac{2}{3y^2(x + 1)^2}$ **31.** $-\frac{9}{4}\sqrt[3]{y}\,\sqrt{x}$

Chapter 7 Review, p. 387

1. Yes **2.** No **3.** a) 19, 15.25, 12.61, 12.0601, 12.006001; b) 12. **4.** $3(2x + h)$

5. a) 3.4, 3.9625, 3.985, 3.9997; b) 4. **6.** $(0, 0)$, $(2, -4)$. **7.** $84x^{83}$ **8.** $\dfrac{5}{\sqrt{x}}$ **9.** $\dfrac{10}{x^2}$

10. $\frac{5}{4}x^{1/4}$, or $\frac{5}{4} \cdot \sqrt[4]{x}$. **11.** $-x + 0.61$ **12.** $x^2 - 2x + 2$ **13.** $\dfrac{-6x + 20}{x^5}$ **14.** $\dfrac{5}{(5 - x)^2}$

15. $(x + 3)^3(7 - x)^4(-9x + 13)$ **16.** $-5(x^5 - 4x^3 + x)^{-6}(5x^4 - 12x^2 + 1)$

17. $\sqrt{x^2 + 5} + \dfrac{x^2}{\sqrt{x^2 + 5}}$, or $\dfrac{2x^2 + 5}{\sqrt{x^2 + 5}}$ **18.** a) $P(x) = -0.001x^2 + 48.8x - 60$; b) $R(10) = \$500$,

$C(10) = \$72.10$, $P(10) = \$427.90$; c) $R'(x) = 50$, $C'(x) = 0.002x + 1.2$, $P'(x) = -0.002x + 48.8$;

d) $R'(10) = \$50$ per unit, $C'(10) = \$1.22$ per unit, $P'(10) = \$48.78$. **19.** a) $\dfrac{dM}{dt} = -0.003t^2 + 0.2t$;

b) 9 c) 1.7 words/min. **20.** $-\dfrac{x^2}{y^2}$, $-\frac{1}{4}$. **21.** -0.96 ft/sec. **22.** a) $-2d + 80$ b) 1215 c) 40

23. \$200 per day, \$100 per day, \$100 per day **24.** $15(3x + 2)^4\left(\dfrac{1 + x}{1 - x}\right) + (3x + 2)^5\left[\dfrac{2}{(1 - x)^2}\right]$

25. $\dfrac{-8x^3 - 2x^2 + 8x + 1}{(1 + x^2)^2 \cdot \sqrt{1 + 4x}}$

CHAPTER 8

Exercise Set 8.1, p. 393

1. 0 **3.** $-\dfrac{2}{x^3}$ **5.** $-\frac{3}{16}x^{-7/4}$ **7.** $12x^2 + \dfrac{8}{x^3}$ **9.** $\dfrac{12}{x^5}$ **11.** $n(n-1)x^{n-2}$ **13.** $12x^2 - 2$

15. $-\frac{1}{4}(x-1)^{-3/2}$, or $\dfrac{-1}{4\sqrt{(x-1)^3}}$ **17.** $2a$ **19.** 24 **21.** $720x$

23. $n(n-1)(n-2)(n-3)(n-4)(n-5)x^{n-6}$ **25.** $a(t) = 6t + 2$ **27.** $P''(t) = 200{,}000$

29. $y' = -x^{-2} - 2x^{-3}$, $y'' = 2x^{-3} + 6x^{-4}$, $y''' = -6x^{-4} - 24x^{-5}$ **31.** $y' = \dfrac{1 + 2x^2}{\sqrt{1 + x^2}}$,

$y'' = \dfrac{2x^3 + 3x}{(1 + x^2)^{3/2}}$, $y''' = \dfrac{3}{(1 + x^2)^{5/2}}$ **33.** $y' = \dfrac{11}{(2x + 3)^2}$, $y'' = \dfrac{-44}{(2x + 3)^3}$, $y''' = \dfrac{264}{(2x + 3)^4}$

35. $y' = \dfrac{x - 2}{2(x - 1)^{3/2}}$, $y'' = \dfrac{4 - x}{4(x - 1)^{5/2}}$, $y''' = \dfrac{3(x - 6)}{8(x - 1)^{7/2}}$ **37.** $\dfrac{dy}{dx} = \dfrac{1 + y}{2 - x}$, $\dfrac{d^2y}{dx^2} = \dfrac{2 + 2y}{(2 - x)^2}$

39. $\dfrac{dy}{dx} = \dfrac{x}{y}$, $\dfrac{d^2y}{dx^2} = \dfrac{y^2 - x^2}{y^3}$

Exercise Set 8.2, p. 407

1. a) 41 mph b) 80 mph c) 13.5 mpg d) 16.5 mph e) About 22% **3.** Max. $= 5\frac{1}{4}$ at $x = \frac{1}{2}$; min. $= 3$ at $x = 2$. **5.** Max. $= 4$ at $x = 2$; min. $= 1$ at $x = 1$. **7.** Max. $= \frac{59}{27}$ at $x = -\frac{1}{3}$; min. $= 1$ at $x = -1$. **9.** Max. $= 1$ at $x = 1$; min. $= -5$ at $x = -1$. **11.** None. **13.** Max. $= 1225$ at $x = 35$. **15.** Min. $= 200$ at $x = 10$. **17.** Max. $= \frac{1}{3}$ at $x = \frac{1}{2}$. **19.** Max. $= \frac{289}{4}$ at $x = \frac{17}{2}$ **21.** Max. $= 2\sqrt{3}$ at $x = -\sqrt{3}$; min. $= -2\sqrt{3}$ at $x = \sqrt{3}$. **23.** Max. $= 5700$ at $x = 2400$ **25.** Min. $= -55\frac{1}{3}$ at $x = 1$. **27.** Max. $= 2000$ at $x = 20$; min. $= 0$ at $x = 0$ and $x = 30$. **29.** Min. $= 24$ at $x = 6$. **31.** Min. $= 108$ at $x = 6$. **33.** Max. $= 3$ at $x = -1$; min. $= -\frac{3}{8}$ at $x = \frac{1}{2}$. **35.** Max. $= 2$ at $x = 8$; min. $= 0$ at $x = 0$. **37.** None. **39.** 22506; \$150,000. **41.** 61.25 mph. **43.** Max. $= 3\sqrt{6}$ at $x = 3$; min. $= -2$ at $x = -2$. **45.** Max. $= 1$ at $x = -1$ and $x = 1$; min. $= 0$ at $x = 0$. **47.** None. **49.** Max. $= -\frac{10}{3} + 2\sqrt{3}$ at $x = 2 - \sqrt{3}$; min. $= -\frac{10}{3} - 2\sqrt{3}$ at $x = 2 + \sqrt{3}$. **51.** Min. $= -1$ at $x = -1$ and $x = 1$. **53.** 7

Exercise Set 8.3, p. 418

1. 25 and 25. Max. prod. $= 625$ **3.** No. $Q = x(50 - x)$ has no minimum. **5.** 2 and -2. Min. prod. $= -4$ **7.** $x = \frac{1}{2}$, $y = \sqrt{\frac{1}{2}}$; max. $= \frac{1}{4}$ **9.** $x = 10$, $y = 10$; min. $= 200$ **11.** $x = 2$, $y = \frac{32}{3}$; max. $= \frac{64}{3}$ **13.** $x = 30$ yd, $y = 60$ yd; max area $= 1800$ yd^2 **15.** 13.5 ft by 13.5 ft; 182.25 ft^2 **17.** 46 units; max. profit $= \$1048$ **19.** 70 units; max. profit $= \$19$ **21.** Approx. 1667 units; max. profit $\approx \$5500$ **23.** a) $R(x) = 150x - 0.5x^2$, b) $P(x) = -0.75x^2 + 150x - 4000$, c) 100, d) \$3500, e) \$100 **25.** 20 in. by 20 in. by 5 in.; max. $= 2000$ in^3 **27.** 5 in. by 5 in. by 2.5 in.; min. $= 75$ in^2 **29.** \$5.75, 72,500 (Will the stadium hold that many?) **31.** 25 **33.** 14 in. by 14 in. by 28 in. **35.** $\sqrt[3]{\frac{1}{10}}$ **37.** 4 ft by 4 ft by 20 ft.

39. $x = y = \dfrac{24}{4 + \pi}$ **41.** 9% **43.** a) $C'(x) = 8 + \dfrac{3x^2}{100}$; b) $A(x) - 8 + \dfrac{20}{x} + \dfrac{x^2}{100}$;

c) $A'(x) = \dfrac{x}{50} - \dfrac{20}{x^2}$; d) Min. = 11 at $x_0 = 10$, $C'(10) = 11$; e) $A(10) = 11$, $c'(10) = 11$.

Exercise Set 8.4, p. 425

1. Reorder 5 times per year; lot size = 20.   **3.** Reorder 12 times per year; lot size = 30.

5. Reorder about 13 times per year; lot size = 28.   **7.** $x = \sqrt{\dfrac{2bQ}{a}}$

Exercise Set 8.5, p. 430

1. $\Delta y = 0.0401$; $f'(x)\,\Delta x = 0.04$ **3.** 0.2816, 0.28   **5.** -0.556, -1 **7.** 6, 6
9. $\Delta C = \$2.01$, $C'(70) = \$2$ **11.** $\Delta R = \$2$, $R'(70) = \$2$ **13.** a) $P(x) = -0.01x^2 + 1.4x - 30$;
b) $\Delta P = -\$0.01$, $P'(70) = 0$.   **15.** 4.375   **17.** 10.1   **19.** 2.167

Chapter 8 Review, p. 430

1. $\dfrac{d^3y}{dx^3} = 24x$ **2.** Max. = 9 at $x = 3$.   **3.** Max. = 2 at $x = -1$; min. = -1 at $x = -2$.
4. Max. = 28.49 at $x = 4.3$.   **5.** Max. = 7 at $x = -1$; min. = 3 at $x = 1$.   **6.** None.
7. Min. = $-\frac{13}{12}$ at $x = \frac{1}{6}$.   **8.** Min. = 48 at $x = 4$.   **9.** 4 and -4.   **10.** $x = 5$, $y = -5$;
min. = 50.   **11.** Max. profit = \$24,980; 500 units.   **12.** 40 in. by 40 in. by 10 in.;
max. volume = 16,000 in.³   **13.** 35 times at lot size 35.   **14.** a) $R(x) = x(200 - x) = 200x - x^2$
b) $P(x) = -x^2 + 192x - 5000$ c) 96 d) \$4216 e) \$104 per unit   **15.** $\Delta y = 1.01$, $f'(x)\,\Delta x = 1$

16. 10.2   **17.** a) $A(x) = \dfrac{C(x)}{x} = 100 + \dfrac{100}{\sqrt{x}} + \dfrac{\sqrt{x}}{100}$ b) Min = \$200.01 at $x = 1$

CHAPTER 9

Exercise Set 9.1, p. 441

1.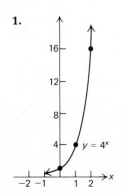

3.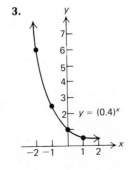

5.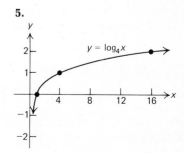

7. $2^3 = 8$ **9.** $8^{1/3} = 2$ **11.** $a^J = K$ **13.** $b^v = T$ **15.** $\log_e b = M$ **17.** $\log_{10} 100 = 2$
19. $\log_{10} 0.1 = -1$ **21.** $\log_M V = p$ **23.** 2.708 **25.** 0.51 **27.** -1.609 **29.** $\frac{3}{2}$ **31.** 2.609
33. 3.218 **35.** 2.9957 **37.** 0.2231 **39.** -1.3863 **41.** 2.3863 **43.** 4 **45.** 2.7726
47. 8.681690 **49.** -4.006334 **51.** 0.6313 **53.** -3.9739 **55.** 6.8091 **57.** -4.5099
59. $t \approx 5$ **61.** $t \approx 4$ **63.** $t \approx 2$ **65.** $t \approx 141$ **67.** $t = \dfrac{\ln P - \ln P_0}{k}$ **69.** ∞

Section 9.2, p. 451

1. $3e^{3x}$ **3.** $-10e^{-2x}$ **5.** e^{-x} **7.** $-7e^x$ **9.** e^{2x} **11.** $x^3 e^x(x + 4)$ **13.** $\dfrac{e^x(x - 4)}{x^5}$

15. $(-2x + 7)e^{-x^2 + 7x}$ **17.** $-xe^{-x^2/2}$ **19.** $\dfrac{e^{\sqrt{x-7}}}{2\sqrt{x - 7}}$ **21.** $\dfrac{e^x}{2\sqrt{e^x - 1}}$ **23.** $(1 - 2x)e^{-2x} - e^{-x} + 3x^2$

25. e^{-x} **27.** ke^{-kx}

29.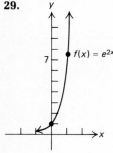

31.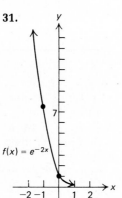

33.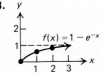

35. 58 days **37.** a) $C'(t) = 50e^{-t}$, b) \$50 million, c) \$.916 million. **39.** a) 18.1%, 69.9%;
b) $P'(t) = 0.2e^{-0.2t}$; c) 11.5. **41.** a) \$58.69, \$78.00; b) \$63.80$e^{-1.1t}$; c) 2.7. **43.** $15(e^{3x} + 1)^4 e^{3x}$

45. $-e^{-t} - 3e^{3t}$ **47.** $\dfrac{e^x(x - 1)^2}{(x^2 + 1)^2}$ **49.** $\dfrac{e^{\sqrt{x}}}{2\sqrt{x}} + \frac{1}{2}\sqrt{e^x}$ **51.** $\frac{1}{2}e^{x/2}\left[\dfrac{x}{\sqrt{x - 1}}\right]$ **53.** $\dfrac{4}{(e^x + e^{-x})^2}$

55. 4, 2.86797, 2.73200, 2.71964, 2.71855

Exercise Set 9.3, p. 456

1. $-\dfrac{6}{x}$ **3.** $x^3(1 + 4\ln x) - x$ **5.** $\dfrac{1 - 4\ln x}{x^5}$ **7.** $\dfrac{1}{x}$ **9.** $\dfrac{10x}{5x^2 - 7}$ **11.** $\dfrac{1}{x \ln 4x}$ **13.** $\dfrac{x^2 + 7}{x(x^2 - 7)}$

15. $e^x\left(\dfrac{1}{x} + \ln x\right)$ **17.** $\dfrac{e^x}{e^x + 1}$ **19.** $\dfrac{2\ln x}{x}$ **21.** a) 1000; b) $N'(a) = \dfrac{200}{a}$, $N'(10) = 20$;
c) Min. = 1000 at $a = 1$. **23.** $\dfrac{-4(\ln x)^{-5}}{x}$ **25.** $\dfrac{15t^2}{t^3 + 1}$ **27.** $\dfrac{4[\ln(x + 5)]^3}{x + 5}$ **29.** $\dfrac{5t^4 - 3t^2 + 6t}{(t^3 + 3)(t^2 - 1)}$

31. $\dfrac{24x + 25}{8x^2 + 5x}$ **33.** $\dfrac{2(1 - \ln t^2)}{t^3}$ **35.** $x^n \ln x$ **37.** $\dfrac{1}{\sqrt{1 + t^2}}$ **39.** e^π

Exercise Set 9.4, p. 461

1. $Q(t) = Q_0 e^{kt}$ **3.** a) $P(t) = P_0 e^{0.09t}$ b) \$1094.17, \$1197.22 c) 7.7 yr **5.** 19.8 yr **7.** 6.9%
9. a) $P(t) = 209 e^{0.01t}$ b) 312 million c) 69.3 yr **11.** a) $P(t) = 216 e^{0.008t}$ b) 225 million
c) 86.6 yr (2062) **13.** a) $N(t) = 50 e^{0.1t}$ b) 369 c) 6.9 yr **15.** 6.9 yr (1983) **17.** a) $k = 0.08$
b) 124 thousand **19.** a) $k = 0.07$, $P(t) = \$90 e^{0.07t}$; b) \$2980 million; c) 9.9 yr (1983).
21. a) $k = 0.06$, $P(t) = \$100 e^{0.06t}$; b) \$332.01; c) 11.6 yr (1978). **23.** 6.18% **25.** 9%
27. $T_3 = \dfrac{\ln 3}{k}$ **29.** Answers depend on particular data. **31.** $\approx$\$66,000,000,000,000 **33.** $\approx$2.2%
35. \$16.64, \$27.71.

Exercise Set 9.5, p. 466

1. \$826.49 **3.** \$22,973.57 **5.** \$4978.71 **7.** a) \$40,000 b) \$5413.41 **9.** a) $k = 0.01$
b) $P(t) = 503,000 e^{-0.01t}$, where t = years since 1960 **11.** 233 million, 173 million

Exercise Set 9.6, p. 471

1. a) $E(x) = \dfrac{400 - x}{x}$, b) $x = 200$. **3.** a) $E(x) = \dfrac{50 - x}{x}$, b) $x = 25$. **5.** a) $E(x) = 1$, for all
$x > 0$; b) Total Revenue $= R(x) = 400$, for all $x > 0$. It has 400 as a maximum for all $x > 0$.
7. a) $E(x) = \dfrac{1000 - 2x}{x}$, b) $x = \dfrac{1000}{3}$. **9.** a) $E(x) = \dfrac{4}{x}$, b) $x = 4$. **11.** a) $E(x) = \dfrac{x + 3}{2x}$,
b) $x = 3$. **13.** a) $E(x) = \dfrac{1}{n}$; b) No, E is the constant $\dfrac{1}{n}$; c) Only when $n = 1$.
15. $E(x) = -\dfrac{1}{x} \cdot \dfrac{1}{L'(x)}$

Chapter 9 Review, p. 471

1. e^x **2.** $\dfrac{1}{x}$ **3.** $-2xe^{-x^2}$ **4.** $\dfrac{1}{x}$ **5.** $e^x - 15x^2$ **6.** $3e^x \left(\dfrac{1}{x} + \ln x \right)$ **7.** $\dfrac{e^x - 3x^2}{e^x - x^3}$
8. $\dfrac{\frac{1}{x} - \ln x}{e^x}$, or $\dfrac{1 - x \ln x}{xe^x}$ **9.** 2.639 **10.** -1.2528 **11.** 2.9459 **12.** $M(t) = M_0 e^{kt}$
13. a) $P(t) = P_0 e^{0.08t}$ b) \$1083.29 c) 8.7 yr **14.** 10 yr **15.** a) $F(t) = 3 e^{0.12t}$, b) 68 billion gal,
c) 5.8 yr **16.** \$24,261.23 **17.** a) $E(x) = \dfrac{5}{x}$, b) $x = 5$. **18.** a) 2000 b) $N'(a) = \dfrac{500}{a}$,
$N'(10) = 50$ c) Min $= 2000$ at $a = 1$ **19.** $\dfrac{-4}{(e^x - e^{-x})^2}$ **20.** $\dfrac{1}{\sqrt{x^2 - 4}}$

CHAPTER 10

Exercise Set 10.1, p. 478

1. $\dfrac{x^7}{7} + C$ **3.** $2x + C$ **5.** $\frac{4}{5}x^{5/4} + C$ **7.** $\dfrac{x^3}{3} + \dfrac{x^2}{2} - x + C$ **9.** $\dfrac{t^3}{3} - t^2 + 3t + C$ **11.** $5e^x + C$

13. $\dfrac{x^4}{4} - \frac{7}{15}x^{15/7} + C$ **15.** $1000 \ln x + C$ **17.** $-x^{-1} + C$ **19.** $f(x) = \dfrac{x^2}{2} - 3x + 13$

21. $f(x) = \dfrac{x^3}{3} - 4x + 7$ **23.** $C(x) = \dfrac{x^4}{4} - x^2 + 100$ **25.** a) $R(x) = \dfrac{x^3}{3} - 3x;$

b) If you sell no products you make no money.   **27.** $s(t) = t^3 + 4$ **29.** $f(t) = \frac{2}{3}t^{3/2} + 2\sqrt{t} - \frac{28}{3}$

31. $f(t) = 400e^{8t}$ **33.** $\dfrac{x^6}{6} - \frac{2}{5}x^5 + \frac{1}{4}x^4 + C$ **35.** $\frac{2}{5}t^{5/2} + 4t^{3/2} + 18\sqrt{t} + C$

37. $\dfrac{t^4}{4} + t^3 + \frac{3}{2}t^2 + t + C$ **39.** $\dfrac{b}{a}e^{ax} + C$ **41.** $\frac{12}{7}x^{7/3} + C$ **43.** $\dfrac{t^3}{3} - t^2 + 4t + C$

Exercise Set 10.2, p. 486

1. 8   **3.** 8   **5.** $41\frac{2}{3}$ **7.** $\frac{1}{4}$ **9.** $10\frac{2}{3}$ **11.** $e^3 - 1 \approx 19.086$ **13.** $\ln 3 \approx 1.0986$ **15.** 51
17. An antiderivative, total cost   **19.** An antiderivative, total sales   **21.** a) $C(x) = 50x - 0.2x^2$
b) $R(x) = 50x + 0.2x^2$ c) $P(x) = 0.4x^2$ d) $P(1000) = \$400,000$ **23.** 155.52   **25.** 16.25   **27.** $3\frac{1}{3}$

Exercise Set 10.3, p. 494

1. $\frac{1}{6}$ **3.** $\frac{4}{15}$ **5.** $e^b - e^a$ **7.** $b^3 - a^3$ **9.** $\dfrac{e^2}{2} + \frac{1}{2}$ **11.** $\frac{2}{3}$ **13.** $\frac{5}{34}$ **15.** 4   **17.** $9\frac{5}{6}$ **19.** 12

21. $e^5 - \dfrac{1}{e}$ **23.** $7\frac{1}{3}$ **25.** $17\frac{1}{3}$ **27.** a) \$2948.26 b) \$2913.90 c) $k = 6.9$, so it will be on the 7th
day.   **29.** \$3600   **31.** $\frac{307}{6}$ **33.** $\frac{15}{4}$ **35.** 8   **37.** 12

Exercise Set 10.4, p. 500

1. $\ln(7 + x^3) + C$ **3.** $\frac{1}{4}e^{4x} + C$ **5.** $2e^{x/2} + C$ **7.** $\frac{1}{4}e^{x^4} + C$ **9.** $-\frac{1}{3}e^{-t^3} + C$

11. $\dfrac{(\ln 4x)^2}{2} + C$ **13.** $\ln(1 + x) + C$ **15.** $-\ln(4 - x) + C$ **17.** $\frac{1}{24}(t^3 - 1)^8 + C$

19. $\frac{1}{8}(x^4 + x^3 + x^2)^8 + C$ **21.** $\ln(4 + e^x) + C$ **23.** $\frac{1}{4}(\ln x^2)^2 + C$, or $(\ln x)^2 + C$

25. $\ln(\ln x) + C$ **27.** $\dfrac{2}{3a}(ax + b)^{3/2} + C$ **29.** $\dfrac{b}{a}e^{ax} + C$ **31.** $e - 1$ **33.** $\frac{21}{4}$

35. $\ln 4 - \ln 2 = \ln \frac{4}{2} = \ln 2$ **37.** $\ln 19$ **39.** $1 - \dfrac{1}{e^b}$ **41.** $1 - \dfrac{1}{e^{mb}}$ **43.** $\frac{208}{3}$

45. a) $P(t) = 2000T^2 - [250,000(e^{-0.1T} - 1)] - 250,000$ b) \$108,025   **47.** $-\frac{5}{12}(1 - 4x^2)^{3/2} + C$

49. $-\frac{1}{3}e^{-x^3} + C$ **51.** $-e^{1/t} + C$ **53.** $-\frac{1}{3}(\ln x)^{-3} + C$ **55.** $\frac{2}{9}(x^3 + 1)^{3/2} + C$ **57.** $\frac{3}{4}(x^2 - 6x)^{2/3} + C$

59. $\frac{1}{8}[\ln(t^4 + 8)]^2 + C$ **61.** $x + \dfrac{1}{x + 3} + C$ **63.** $t - \ln(t - 4) + C$ **65.** $-\ln(1 + e^{-x}) + C$

67. $\dfrac{1}{n + 1}(\ln x)^{n+1} + C$

Exercise Set 10.5, p. 505

1. $xe^{5x} - \frac{1}{5}e^{5x} + C$ **3.** $\frac{1}{2}x^6 + C$ **5.** $\dfrac{x}{2}e^{2x} - \frac{1}{4}e^{2x} + C$ **7.** $-\dfrac{x}{2}e^{-2x} - \frac{1}{4}e^{-2x} + C$

9. $\dfrac{x^3}{3}\ln x - \dfrac{x^3}{9} + C$ **11.** $\dfrac{x^2}{2}\ln x^2 - \dfrac{x^2}{2} + C$ **13.** $(x + 3)\ln(x + 3) - x + C$. Let $u = \ln(x + 3)$,

$dv = dx$, and choose $v = x + 3$ for an antiderivative of v.   **15.** $\left(\dfrac{x^2}{2} + 2x\right)\ln x - \dfrac{x^2}{4} - 2x + C$

17. $\left(\dfrac{x^2}{2} - x\right)\ln x - \dfrac{x^2}{4} + x + C$ **19.** $\frac{2}{3}x(x + 2)^{3/2} - \frac{4}{15}(x + 2)^{5/2} + C$ **21.** $\dfrac{x^4}{4}\ln 2x - \dfrac{x^4}{16} + C$

23. $x^2e^x - 2xe^x + 2e^x + C$ **25.** $\frac{1}{2}x^2e^{2x} + \frac{1}{4}e^{2x} - \frac{1}{2}xe^{2x} + C$ **27.** $\frac{8}{3}\ln 2 - \frac{7}{9}$ **29.** $9\ln 9 - 5\ln 5 - 4$

31. 1 **33.** $\frac{1}{9}e^{-3x}(-3x - 1) + C$ **35.** $\dfrac{5^x}{\ln 5} + C$ **37.** $\frac{1}{8}\ln\left(\dfrac{4 + x}{4 - x}\right) + C$

39. $5 - x - 5\ln(5 - x) + C$ **41.** $\dfrac{1}{5(5 - x)} + \dfrac{1}{25}\ln\left(\dfrac{x}{5 - x}\right) + C$ **43.** $\frac{2}{9}x^{3/2}[3\ln x - 2] + C$

45. $\dfrac{e^t}{t + 1} + C$ **47.** $4\sqrt{x}(\ln \sqrt{x}) - 4\sqrt{x} + C$.   **49.** a) Let $u = x^n$ and $dv = e^x\, dx$.

Then $du = nx^{n-1}\, dx$ and $v = e^x$. Then use integration by parts. b) $x^3e^x - 3\int x^2e^x\, dx =$
$x^3e^x - 3[x^2e^x - 2\int xe^x\, dx] = x^3e^x - 3x^2e^x + 6[xe^x - \int x^0e^x\, dx] = x^3e^x - 3x^2e^x + 6xe^x - 6e^x + C$

Exercise Set 10.6, p. 510

1. a) 1.4914 b) 0.8571   **3.** \$11,250

Chapter 10 Review, p. 511

1. $x + C$ **2.** $200x^5 + C$ **3.** $e^x + \ln x + \frac{8}{11}x^{11/8} + C$ **4.** $\frac{1}{6}$ **5.** $4\ln 3$

6. An antiderivative, total number of words typed in t minutes.   **7.** 12   **8.** $-\dfrac{1}{2}\left(\dfrac{1}{e^2} - 1\right)$

9. $\ln b - \ln a$ **10.** 0   **11.** Negative.   **12.** Positive.   **13.** $\ln(x + 8) + C$ **14.** $-2e^{-0.5x} + C$

15. $\frac{1}{40}(t^4 + 1)^{10} + C$ **16.** $\dfrac{x}{5}e^{5x} - \dfrac{e^{5x}}{25} + C$ **17.** $\dfrac{x^4}{4}\ln x^4 - \dfrac{x^4}{4} + C$ **18.** $\dfrac{2^x}{\ln 2} + C$

19. $\frac{1}{7}\ln\left(\dfrac{x}{7 - x}\right) + C$ **20.** \$49,000   **21.** 95   **22.** $\frac{3}{2}(e^{14} - 1) \approx \$1,803,905$

23. $\dfrac{(\ln x)^4}{4} - \tfrac{4}{3}(\ln x)^3 + 5 \ln x + C$ **24.** $(x + 3) \ln (x + 3) - (x + 5) \ln (x + 5) + C$

25. $(\ln \sqrt{x})^2 + C$ **26.** $\dfrac{x^{100}}{100}\left(\ln x - \dfrac{1}{100}\right) + C$

CHAPTER 11

Exercise Set 11.1, p. 516

1. a) (6, $5), b) $15, c) $9.   **3.** a) (1, $9), b) $3.33, c) $1.67.   **5.** a) (3, $9), b) $36, c) $18.
7. a) (5, $0.61), b) $86.36, c) $2.45.

Exercise Set 11.2, p. 522

1. $131   **3.** $5,610.67   **5.** $340,754.12   **7.** $949.94   **9.** $259.37   **11.** 1,343,724,583 tons
13. By 2001   **15.** 348,811.2 million   **17.** $\displaystyle\int_0^{365} Pe^{0.08 \cdot t/365}\, dt = \dfrac{365P}{0.08}\,(e^{0.08} - 1)$; $379,997.25
19. $33,535.73   **21.** $125,289.70

Exercise Set 11.3, p. 526

1. $17,802   **3.** $511,471.15   **5.** $74.23   **7.** $68.83
9. $\displaystyle\int_0^{365} Pe^{-(0.12/365)t}\, dt = \dfrac{365P}{0.12}\,(1 - e^{-0.12})$; $1719.75

Exercise Set 11.4, p. 530

1. $\tfrac{1}{3}$ **3.** Divergent   **5.** 1   **7.** $\tfrac{1}{2}$ **9.** Divergent   **11.** 5   **13.** Divergent   **15.** Divergent
17. Divergent   **19.** 1   **21.** $30,000   **23.** Divergent   **25.** 2   **27.** $\tfrac{1}{2}$ **29.** $0.93

Exercise Set 11.5, p. 536

1. $y = x^4 + C$; $y = x^4 + 3$, $y = x^4$, $y = x^4 - 796$; answers may vary.
3. $y = \tfrac{1}{2}e^{2x} + \tfrac{1}{2}x^2 + C$; $y = \tfrac{1}{2}e^{2x} + \tfrac{1}{2}x^2 - 5$, $y = \tfrac{1}{2}e^{2x} + \tfrac{1}{2}x^2 + 7$; $y = \tfrac{1}{2}e^{2x} + \tfrac{1}{2}x^2$; answers may vary.
5. $y = 3 \ln x - \tfrac{1}{3}x^3 + \tfrac{1}{6}x^6 + C$; $y = 3 \ln x - \tfrac{1}{3}x^3 + \tfrac{1}{6}x^6 - 15$, $y = 3 \ln x - \tfrac{1}{3}x^3 + \tfrac{1}{6}x^6 - 7$,
$y = 3 \ln x - \tfrac{1}{3}x^3 + \tfrac{1}{6}x^6$; answers may vary.   **7.** $y = \tfrac{1}{3}x^3 + x^2 - 3x + 4$ **9.** $y = \tfrac{3}{5}x^{5/3} - \tfrac{1}{2}x^2 - \tfrac{61}{10}$

11. $y'' = \dfrac{1}{x}$. Then $y'' - \dfrac{1}{x} = 0$

$$\begin{array}{c|c} \dfrac{1}{x} - \dfrac{1}{x} & 0 \\ \hline & 0 \end{array}$$

13. $y' = 4e^x + 3xe^x$, $y'' = 7e^x + 3xe^x$. Then

$$y'' - 2y' + y = 0$$

$$\begin{array}{c|c} (7e^x + 3xe^x) - 2(4e^x + 3xe^x) + (e^x + 3xe^x) & 0 \\ 7e^x + 3xe^x - 8e^x - 6xe^x + e^x + 3xe^x & \\ \hline 0 & \end{array}$$

15. $C(x) = 2.6x - 0.01x^2 + 120$, $A(x) = 2.6 - 0.01x + \dfrac{120}{x}$ **17.** a) $P(C) = \dfrac{400}{(C + 3)^{1/2}} - 40$;

b) $97.   **19.** $y = C_1 e^{x^4}$, where $C_1 = e^C$.   **21.** $y = \sqrt[3]{\frac{5}{2}x^2 + C}$ **23.** $y = \sqrt{2x^2 + C_1}$,
$y = -\sqrt{2x^2 + C_1}$, where $C_1 = 2C$.   **25.** $y = \sqrt{6x + C_1}$, $y = -\sqrt{6x + C_1}$, where $C_1 = 2C$.
27. $y = -3 + C_1 e^{x^2/2}$, where $C_1 = e^C$.   **29.** $y = \sqrt[3]{15x + C_1}$, where $C_1 = 3C$.   **31.** $y = C_1 e^{3x}$,
where $C_1 = e^C$.   **33.** $P = C_1 e^{2t}$, where $C_1 = e^C$.   **35.** a) $P = C_1 e^{kt}$, where $C_1 = e^C$; b) $P = P_0 e^{kt}$.
37. a) $R = k \cdot \ln(S + 1) + C$; b) $R = k \cdot \ln(S + 1)$; c) No units, no pleasure from them.
39. $p = 200 - x$ **41.** $p = \dfrac{C_1}{\sqrt{x}}$

Chapter 11 Review, p. 538

1. $29,192   **2.** $344.66   **3.** 11,098,604 thousand tons   **4.** By 2010   **5.** $30,717.91
6. $15,000   **7.** Convergent, $\frac{1}{4}$ **8.** Divergent   **9.** (3, $16)   **10.** $45   **11.** $22.50
12. $y = \frac{1}{3}x^3 + \frac{3}{2}x^2 - 5x + 7$ **13.** $y = C_1 e^{x^8}$, where $C_1 = e^C$
14. $y = \sqrt{18x + C_1}$, $y = -\sqrt{18x + C_1}$, where $C_1 = 2C$ **15.** $y = C_1 e^{6t}$, where $C_1 = e^C$
16. $y = 5 - C_1 e^{-x^3/3}$, where $C_1 = e^{-C}$ **17.** $y = \pm\sqrt[4]{8t + C_1}$, where $C_1 = 4C$
18. $y = C_1 e^{4x + x^2/2}$, where $C_1 = e^C$ **19.** $p = \dfrac{C_1}{\sqrt[3]{x}}$ **20.** a) $V(t) = 36(1 - e^{-kt})$ b) $k = 0.12$
c) $V(t) = 36(1 - e^{-0.12t})$ d) $V(12) \approx 27.47 e) $t \approx 14.9$ months

CHAPTER 12

Exercise Set 12.1, p. 546

1. $A = \{0, 1, 2, 3, 4, 5, 6, 7, 8, 9, 10\}$, $B = \{1, 2, 3, 4, 5, 6, 7, 8, 9\}$, $C = \{0, 2, 4, 6, 8, 10, 12\}$
3. $A^c = \{11, 12\}$, $B^c = \{0, 10, 11, 12\}$, $C^c = \{1, 3, 5, 7, 9, 11\}$ **5.** True   **7.** False   **9.** True
11. True   **13.** False   **15.** False   **17.** $A^c = \{m, n, r, t, c\}$, $B^c = \{a, e, i, o, u\}$, $C^c = \{i, o, u, m, n, r, t\}$
19. False   **21.** True   **23.** False   **25.** False   **27.** a) 0 b) $\emptyset$ c) 1
29. a) 2 b) $\emptyset$, $\{a\}$, $\{b\}$, $\{a, b\}$ c) 4   **31.** 1, 2, 4, 8, 2^4, 2^n

Exercise Set 12.2, p. 558

1. a) A b) B c) $\{0, 10\}$ d) $\emptyset$ e) A f) $\{2, 4, 8, 10\}$ g) $\{1, 5, 7, 11\}$ h) $\{0, 2, 4, 8, 10, 12\}$ i) $\{10\}$ j) $\{1, 5, 7\}$
3.

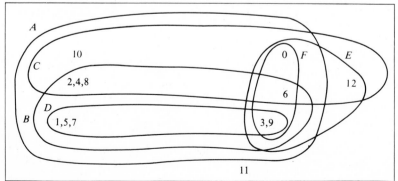

5. a) {e, i, r, t} b) ∅ c) {c, r} d) {i} e) ∅ f) {m, n, r, t} g) ∅ h) {a, e}   **7.** 5   **9.** 4   **11.** 85
13. 47%, 36%, 5%

Exercise Set 12.3, p. 563

1. $E \times F = \{(e, r), (e, t), (i, r), (i, t)\}$ **3.** Yes   **5.** $C \times E = \{(a, e), (a, i), (c, e), (c, i), (e, e), (e, i)\}$
7. 6   **9.** $S = \{I, II, III, \text{none}\}$

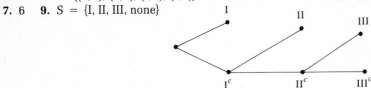

11. $S = \{(AN, CLR), (AN, CLD), (AN, PR),$
       $(N, CLR), (N, CLD), (N, PR),$
       $(BN, CLR), (BN, CLD), (BN, PR)\}$

13. $S = \{(M, S, < 18), (M, S, \geq 18),$
       $(M, M, < 18), (M, M, \geq 18),$
       $(F, S, < 18), (F, S, \geq 18),$
       $(F, M, < 18), (F, M, \geq 18)\}$

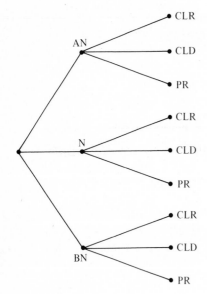

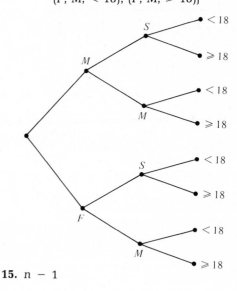

15. $n - 1$

Exercise Set 12.4, p. 571

1. 120   **3.** 1   **5.** 720   **7.** 380   **9.** 2520   **11.** $n(n - 1)(n - 2)$ **13.** $3 \cdot 4 \cdot 2$, or 24
15. $P(4, 4) = 4! = 24$ **17.** $P(4, 2) = 4 \cdot 3 = 12$ **19.** $P(4, 4) = 24$ **21.** $(4 - 1)! = 3! = 6$; no
23. $5 \cdot 5 \cdot 5 \cdot 5 = 625$, $5 \cdot 4 \cdot 3 \cdot 2 = 120$ **25.** a) $5 \cdot 5 \cdot 5 = 125$ b) $5 \cdot 4 \cdot 3 = 60$
27. $7^4 = 2401$, $7 \cdot 6 \cdot 5 \cdot 4 = 840$ **29.** $7^3 = 343$ **31.** 5040, 144, 1440
33. $6! = 720$, $2 \cdot 2 \cdot 2 \cdot 4 \cdot 3! = 192$

Exercise Set 12.5, p. 578

1. 78 **3.** 78 **5.** 7 **7.** $\dfrac{n(n-1)}{2}$ **9.** $\dbinom{6}{4} = 15$ **11.** $\dbinom{10}{7} \cdot \dbinom{8}{5} = 6720$

13. a) $\dbinom{14}{5} = 2002$ b) $\dbinom{6}{2}\dbinom{8}{3} + \dbinom{6}{1}\dbinom{8}{4} + \dbinom{8}{5} = 1316$ c) $\dbinom{6}{1}\dbinom{8}{4} + \dbinom{8}{5} = 476$

d) $\dbinom{6}{4}\dbinom{8}{1} + \dbinom{6}{3}\dbinom{8}{2} + \dbinom{6}{2}\dbinom{8}{3} + \dbinom{6}{1}\dbinom{8}{4} + \dbinom{8}{5} = 1996$ **15.** $\dfrac{11!}{3!\,4!\,2!\,2!} = 69{,}300$

17. $\dfrac{10!}{2!\,3!\,3!\,1!\,1!} = 50{,}400$ **19.** $\dfrac{20!}{2!\,5!\,8!\,3!\,2!} = 20{,}951{,}330{,}400$ **21.** $\dfrac{9!}{3!\,2!\,4!} = 1260$

23. a) $\dbinom{20}{3} = 1140$ b) $\dbinom{20}{3}\dbinom{3}{1} = 3420$ **25.** $5 \cdot 4 \cdot 3 = 60,\ \dfrac{5 \cdot 4 \cdot 3}{3 \cdot 2 \cdot 1} = 10$

27. a) $\dbinom{30}{6} = 593{,}775$ b) $\dbinom{10}{4}\dbinom{20}{2} = 39{,}900$ **29.** $\dbinom{12}{4}\dbinom{8}{4}\dbinom{4}{4} = 34{,}650$

31. $\dfrac{34{,}650}{3!} = 5775$ **33.** 2520, 2520, 1320 **35.** 240

37. a) $\dbinom{8}{0} + \dbinom{8}{1} + \cdots + \dbinom{8}{8} = \displaystyle\sum_{i\,0}^{8}\dbinom{8}{i}$ b) $\displaystyle\sum_{i\,0}^{8}\dbinom{8}{i} = 2^8 = 256$ c) $\displaystyle\sum_{i\,0}^{9}\dbinom{9}{i} = 2^9 = 512$

39. 4 **41.** $13 \cdot 48 = 624$ **43.** $13 \cdot \dbinom{4}{2}\dbinom{12}{3}\dbinom{4}{1}\dbinom{4}{1}\dbinom{4}{1} = 1{,}098{,}240$

45. $\dbinom{13}{5}4 - 36 - 4 = 5108$ **47.** $10 \cdot 4^5 - 36 - 4 = 10{,}200$

49. $P(10, 6) = 10 \cdot 9 \cdot 8 \cdot 7 \cdot 6 \cdot 5 = 151{,}200$ **51.** $C(8, 2) = 28,\ 2C(8, 2) = 56$

53. MATH: $4! = 24$; BUSINESS: $\dfrac{8!}{3!} = 6720$; PHILOSOPHICAL: $\dfrac{13!}{2!2!2!2!2!} = 194{,}594{,}400$

55. $2^7 - 1 = 127$ **57.** $80 \cdot 26 \cdot 9999 = 20{,}797{,}920$ **59.** $C(n, 2) - n = \dfrac{n^2 - 3n}{2}$

61. a) $P(6, 5) = 6 \cdot 5 \cdot 4 \cdot 3 \cdot 2 = 720$ b) $6^5 = 7776$ c) $P(5, 4) = 5 \cdot 4 \cdot 3 \cdot 2 = 120$

d) $P(3, 2) = 3 \cdot 2 = 6$ **63.** $\dbinom{n}{4} = \dfrac{n(n-1)(n-2)(n-3)}{24}$ **65.** 5 **67.** 8 **69.** 6 **71.** 11

Chapter 12 Review, p. 583

1. $A \cup B = \{a, b, c, e, g, f, s\},\ A \cap B = \{b, c, e\}$

2. a) $\{\{1, 2, 3, 4\}, \{5\}\}$ | 1, 2, 3, 4 | 5 |

b) $\{\{1, 2, 3\}, \{4, 5\}\}$ | 1, 2, 3 | 4, 5 |

c) $\{\{1\}, \{2\}, \{3\}, \{4, 5\}\}$ | 1 | 2 | 3 | 4, 5 |

There are other possibilities.

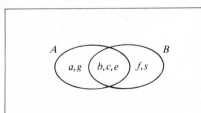

3. $A - B = \{a, g\}$, $B - A = \{f, h\}$, $A^c = \{f, h, i, j, k, \ldots, z\}$, $B^c = \{a, g, i, j, k, l, \ldots, z\}$, $B^c - A^c = \{a, g\}$, shaded as in the accompanying figure.

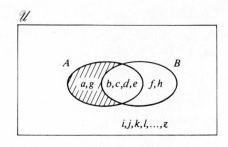

4. 60   **5.** 53   **6.** $S = \{(0, 3), (1, 2), (2, 1), (3, 0)\}$ where each ordered pair = (no. G, no. S)

7.

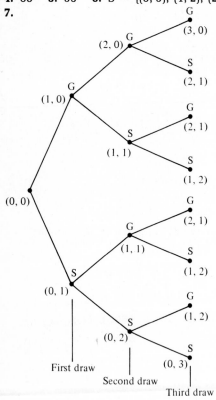

First draw

Second draw

Third draw

8. $A \times B = \{(a, 1), (a, 2), (a, 3), (a, 4), (b, 1),$ $(b, 2), (b, 3), (b, 4), (c, 1), (c, 2), (c, 3), (c, 4)\}$, $\mathcal{N}(A \times B) = 12$ **9.** $5 \cdot 4 \cdot 3 \cdot 2 \cdot 1$, or 120
10. 2^{10}, or 1024   **11.** $5 \cdot 40 \cdot 8$, or 1600
12. $5 \cdot 4 \cdot 3 \cdot 2 \cdot 1$, or 120   **13.** 360
14. a) 5040 b) 2520 c) 840 d) 210
15. $(6 - 1)!$, or 120   **16.** a) $52 \cdot 51$, or 2652
b) $52 \cdot 52$, or 2704   **17.** a) 720 b) 240 c) 144
d) 576   **18.** a) $P(4, 3) = 4 \cdot 3 \cdot 2 = 24$ b) ABC,
ACB, ABD, ADB, ACD, ADC, BAC, BCA, BAD,
BDA, BCD, BDC, CAB, CBA, CAD, CDA, CBD,
CDB, DAB, DBA, DAC, DCA, DBC, DCB

c) $\binom{4}{3} = \dfrac{4 \cdot 3 \cdot 2}{3 \cdot 2 \cdot 1} = 4$ d) $\{A, B, C\}$, $\{A, C, D\}$,
$\{B, C, D\}$, $\{A, B, D\}$ **19.** a) 120 b) 120 c) 126
d) 126

20. $\binom{10}{8} = 45$ **21.** $\binom{7}{4} \cdot \binom{5}{3} = 350$

22. $\binom{3}{1}\binom{4}{1} + \binom{4}{2}$, or 18

23. $\binom{7}{1}\binom{6}{2}\binom{4}{2}\binom{2}{2} = \dfrac{7!}{1!2!2!2!} = 630$

24. 3780   **25.** B   **26.** A   **27.** $\{(a, d), (a, e),$
$(b, d), (b, e), (c, d), (c, e)\}$ **28.** C   **29.** Yes
30. No   **31.** 840   **32.** 35   **33.** 720   **34.** 1

35. $6 \cdot 6 \cdot 6 = 216$ **36.** $\binom{52}{2} = 1326$

37. $5! = 120$

38. $4 \cdot 4 \cdot 4 = 64,\ 4 \cdot 3 \cdot 2 = 24$ **39.** $2 \cdot 4! \cdot 4! = 1152$ **40.** $\dfrac{8!}{1!2!2!1!1!1!} = 10{,}080$

41. $\dbinom{12}{3} + \dbinom{9}{1}\dbinom{12}{2} = 814$ **42.** 35

CHAPTER 13

Exercise Set 13.1, p. 593

1. $\frac{4}{52}$, or $\frac{1}{13}$ **3.** $\frac{13}{52}$, or $\frac{1}{4}$ **5.** $\frac{4}{52}$, or $\frac{1}{13}$ **7.** $\frac{1}{2}$ **9.** $\frac{8}{52}$, or $\frac{2}{13}$ **11.** $\frac{6}{16}$, or $\frac{3}{8}$ **13.** 0   **15.** $\dfrac{\dbinom{7}{2} \cdot \dbinom{8}{2}}{\dbinom{15}{4}} = \dfrac{28}{65}$

17. $\frac{4}{36}$, or $\frac{1}{9}$ **19.** $\frac{1}{36}$ **21.** 0   **23.** $\dfrac{\dbinom{7}{3}\dbinom{8}{2}\dbinom{10}{2}}{\dbinom{25}{7}} = \dfrac{441}{4807}$ **25.** $\dfrac{\dbinom{4}{3} \cdot \dbinom{4}{2}}{\dbinom{52}{5}} = \dfrac{1}{108{,}290}$

27. $\dfrac{\dbinom{4}{4}\dbinom{4}{1}}{\dbinom{52}{5}} = \dfrac{1}{649{,}740}$ **29.** 0   **31.** $\dfrac{\dbinom{10}{2}\dbinom{10}{2}}{\dbinom{20}{4}} = \dfrac{135}{323}$ **33.** a) $\dfrac{\dbinom{5}{1}\dbinom{3}{1}}{\dbinom{8}{2}} = \dfrac{15}{28}$ b) $\dfrac{\dbinom{5}{2}}{\dbinom{8}{2}} = \dfrac{5}{14}$

c) $\dfrac{\dbinom{3}{2}}{\dbinom{8}{2}} = \dfrac{3}{28}$ d) $\frac{5}{14} + \frac{3}{28} = \frac{13}{28}$ **35.** a) $\frac{28}{45}$ b) 17:28 c) 28:17   **37.** a) $\frac{1}{201}$ b) $\frac{3}{250{,}003}$ c) $\frac{3}{500{,}003}$ d) $\frac{2}{201}$

Exercise Set 13.2, p. 601

1. a) 0.77 b) $\frac{9}{14}$ **3.** $\frac{1}{6}$ **5.** a) $\frac{68}{95}$ b) $\frac{27}{95}$ c) $\frac{51}{190}$ d) $\frac{3}{190}$ **7.** a) $\frac{5}{9}$ b) $\frac{4}{9}$ c) $\frac{1}{9}$ **9.** a) $\frac{1}{221}$ b) $\frac{1}{17}$ c) $\frac{4}{17}$ d) $\frac{12}{17}$
11. $\frac{1}{3}$ **13.** $\frac{1}{30}$

Exercise Set 13.3, p. 611

1. $\frac{11}{18}$ **3.** 0.1584   **5.** a) $\frac{1}{4}$ b) $\frac{1}{13}$ c) $\frac{1}{52}$ **7.** a) $\frac{1}{4}$ b) $\frac{13}{51}$ c) $\frac{13}{204}$ **9.** $\frac{1}{3} \cdot \frac{2}{3} \cdot \frac{2}{3} \cdot \frac{1}{3} \cdot \frac{2}{3}$, or $\frac{8}{243}$ **11.** 0.2
13. $(0.90)^6$, or 0.531441; $(0.10)^6$ or 0.000001   **15.** 0.2   **17.** a) $\frac{15}{32}$ b) $\frac{3}{4} \cdot \frac{3}{8} + \frac{1}{4} \cdot \frac{5}{8}$, or $\frac{7}{16}$ c) $\frac{3}{32}$ **19.** $\frac{37}{64}$

21. Left to the student   **23.** $\frac{4}{15}, \frac{23}{45}$ **25.** a) $\dfrac{\dbinom{13}{1}\dbinom{4}{2}\dbinom{12}{3}\dbinom{4}{1}\dbinom{4}{1}\dbinom{4}{1}}{\dbinom{52}{5}} = \dfrac{1760}{4165}$

b) $\dfrac{\binom{13}{1}\binom{4}{3}\binom{12}{2}\binom{4}{1}\binom{4}{1}}{\binom{52}{5}} = \dfrac{88}{4165}$ c) $\dfrac{\binom{13}{2}\binom{4}{2}\binom{4}{2}\binom{44}{1}}{\binom{52}{5}} = \dfrac{198}{4165}$

d) $\dfrac{\binom{13}{1}\binom{4}{2}\binom{12}{1}\binom{4}{3}}{\binom{52}{5}} = \dfrac{6}{4165}$ e) $\dfrac{\binom{13}{1}\binom{4}{4}\binom{48}{1}}{\binom{52}{5}} = \dfrac{1}{4165}$ **27.** $\frac{29}{54}$ **29.** $\frac{20}{27}$

Exercise Set 13.4, p. 620

1. 0.71 **3.** 0.8 **5.** $\frac{11}{15}$ **7.** 0.70018 **9.** 51% $(100\% - 49\%)$ **11.** $(0.4)(0.4) = 0.16$, $(0.6)(0.4) + (0.4)(0.6) = 0.48$ **13.** 5%

Exercise Set 13.5, p. 629

1. 0.5 **3.** $\frac{12}{13}$ **5.** $\frac{1}{13}$ **7.** a) $\frac{3}{7}$ b) $\frac{4}{7}$ **9.** $\frac{3}{4}$; no **11.** 51% should show up, $\therefore$ not independent; O.K. **13.** Yes **15.** $\frac{7}{30}$ **17.** 0.0215 **19.** 14%, 14.5% **21.** $\frac{3}{4}$ **23.** $\frac{2}{3}$ **25.** $\frac{281}{480}, \frac{7}{96}$ **27.** 0.875 **29.** 0.19

Exercise Set 13.6, p. 636

1. $\frac{3}{43}$ **3.** $\frac{4}{7}, \frac{8}{29}$ **5.** $\frac{2}{3}$ **7.** $\frac{49}{89}$ **9.** $\frac{1}{32}$ **11.** 0.16, $\frac{5}{16}$ **13.** $\frac{1}{2}$ **15.** $\frac{17}{30}, \frac{5}{8}$ **17.** $\frac{1}{2}, \frac{297}{400}, \frac{13}{33}$ **19.** $\frac{5}{16}, \frac{1}{2}, \frac{1}{8}$

Chapter 13 Review, p. 638

1. $\frac{1}{17}$ **2.** a) $\frac{5}{36}$ b) $\frac{6}{36}$ c) $\frac{2}{36}$ d) 0 **3.** a) $\frac{23}{34}$ b) 0.37 **4.** a) 1:25 b) 25:1 **5.** 0.63 **6.** 0.76 **7.** $\frac{45}{91}$ **8.** a) $\frac{1}{6}$ b) $\frac{1}{2}$ c) $\frac{1}{12}$ d) Yes **9.** a) $\frac{1}{2}$ b) $\frac{1}{2}$ c) $\frac{1}{4}$ **10.** a) $\frac{1}{6}$ b) 0.132 **11.** $\frac{1}{2} \cdot \frac{1}{2} \cdot \frac{1}{6}$, or $\frac{1}{24}$ **12.** $\frac{1}{6} \cdot \frac{1}{6} \cdot \frac{1}{6}$, or $\frac{1}{216}$ **13.** $(\frac{1}{2})^4$, $\frac{1}{16}$ **14.** a) $\frac{4}{5} \cdot \frac{2}{3}$, or $\frac{8}{15}$ b) $(1 - \frac{4}{5})(1 - \frac{2}{3})$, or $\frac{1}{15}$ c) $\frac{6}{15}$, or $\frac{2}{5}$ **15.** $\frac{5}{32}$ **16.** 0.9 **17.** a) 0.37 b) 0.63 **18.** 0.06 **19.** 0.2 **20.** a) 0.5 b) 0.47 c) 0.56 d) No; $0.47 \neq 0.56$ e) 0.38 **21.** No; $\frac{4}{5} \cdot \frac{2}{3} \neq \frac{3}{5}$ **22.** a) $\frac{200}{450}(0.03) + \frac{150}{450}(0.04) + \frac{100}{450}(0.05)$, or $\frac{17}{450}$ b) $\frac{6}{17}, \frac{6}{17}, \frac{5}{17}$ **23.** a) $p(E^c) = \frac{16}{39}$ b) 23:16 c) 16:23 **24.** 0.9 **25.** $\frac{2}{5}$ **26.** 0.4838 **27.** a) 0.0344 b) No **28.** $\frac{1}{3}$ **29.** a) $\frac{1}{775}$ b) $\frac{60}{775}$ c) $\frac{714}{775}$ **30.** $\frac{3}{5} \cdot \frac{2}{5} \cdot \frac{2}{5} \cdot \frac{2}{5} \cdot \frac{3}{5} = \frac{72}{3125}$ **31.** 0.31 **32.** 0.8; no **33.** a) $\frac{39}{1000}$ b) $\frac{10}{39}, \frac{21}{39}, \frac{8}{39}$

CHAPTER 14

Exercise Set 14.1, p. 646

1.

n	0	1	2	3	4
p	$\frac{14}{323}$	$\frac{80}{323}$	$\frac{135}{323}$	$\frac{80}{323}$	$\frac{14}{323}$

3.

n	0	1	2	3
p	$\frac{1}{14}$	$\frac{6}{14}$	$\frac{6}{14}$	$\frac{1}{14}$

5.

n	0	1	2	3	4	5
p	$\frac{1001}{7752}$	$\frac{3003}{7752}$	$\frac{2730}{7752}$	$\frac{910}{7752}$	$\frac{105}{7752}$	$\frac{3}{7752}$

7.

n	0	1	2	3
p	$\frac{1}{8}$	$\frac{3}{8}$	$\frac{3}{8}$	$\frac{1}{8}$

9.

n_{White}	0	1	2
n_{Red}	3	2	1
p	$\frac{5}{12}$	$\frac{6}{12}$	$\frac{1}{12}$

11.

n	0	1	2	3
p	$\frac{1}{20}$	$\frac{9}{20}$	$\frac{9}{20}$	$\frac{1}{20}$

13.

n	0	1	2	3
p	$\frac{8}{100}$	$\frac{54}{100}$	$\frac{36}{100}$	$\frac{2}{100}$

15.

n	4	5	6	7
p	$\frac{1}{8}$	$\frac{1}{4}$	$\frac{5}{16}$	$\frac{5}{16}$

17.

n	1	2	3	4	5	6	...
p	0	$\frac{1}{2}$	$\frac{1}{4}$	$\frac{1}{8}$	$\frac{1}{16}$	$\frac{1}{32}$	...

Exercise Set 14.2, p. 655

1. 86.533 mph   **3.** \$5.89   **5.** 2 women, 1 man   **7.** 2   **9.** $\frac{3}{5}$ **11.** $\frac{3}{2}$ **13.** $\frac{3}{4}$, 1   **15.** $\frac{3}{2}$ **17.** $\frac{132}{100}$
19. $\frac{93}{16}$ **21.** Betting *with* shooter $E(\overline{X}) = -\frac{7}{495} = -\frac{28}{1980}$ to win. Betting *against* shooter
$E(\overline{X}) = -\frac{3}{220} = -\frac{27}{1980}$ to win. $\therefore$ Better to bet *against* shooter.

Exercise Set 14.3, p. 659

1. 11.530, 3.396 mph   **3.** 1.53, \$1.24   **5.** $\frac{114}{190} = 0.6$, 0.77460   **7.** 0.44, 0.66332

Exercise Set 14.4, p. 665

1.

n	0	1	2	3	4	5
p	$\frac{1}{32}$	$\frac{5}{32}$	$\frac{10}{32}$	$\frac{10}{32}$	$\frac{5}{32}$	$\frac{1}{32}$

; $\frac{5}{2}$, $\frac{5}{4}$, 1.11803

3. 3, 3, $\frac{11}{16}$ **5.** $\frac{3}{16}$, $\frac{5}{2}$, $\frac{5}{4}$, 1.11803   **7.** 0.885735, 0.6, 0.54, 0.73485

9.

n	0	1	2	3	4	5
p	0.00032	0.00640	0.05120	0.20480	0.40960	0.32768

;   4, 0.67232

11.

n	0	1	2	3	4	5
10%p	0.59049	0.32805	0.07290	0.00810	0.00045	0.00001
20%p	0.32768	0.40960	0.20480	0.05120	0.00640	0.00032
30%p	0.16807	0.36015	0.30870	0.13230	0.02835	0.00243

10%, 20%, 30%, 30%

13. $\frac{3}{16}$, $\frac{15}{16}$ **15.** 0.26272, 0.15053

Exercise Set 14.5, p. 675

1. a) $+0.294$, -0.294 b) 88.231 mph, 84.835 mph   c) 37.5%   **3.** $\int_0^1 2x\,dx = [x^2]_0^1 = 1^2 - 0^2 = 1$

5. $\int_4^7 \frac{1}{3}\,dx = \left[\frac{1}{3}x\right]_4^7 = \frac{1}{3}(7-4) = 1$ **7.** $\int_1^3 \frac{3}{26}x^2\,dx = \left[\frac{3}{26}\cdot\frac{x^3}{3}\right]_1^3 = \frac{1}{26}(3^3 - 1^3) = 1$

9. $\int_1^e \frac{1}{x}\,dx = [\ln x]_1^e = \ln e - \ln 1 = 1 - 0 = 1$ **11.** $\int_{-1}^1 \frac{3}{2}x^2\,dx = \left[\frac{3}{2}\cdot\frac{1}{3}x^3\right]_{-1}^1 =$

$\frac{1}{2}(1^3 - (-1)^3) = \frac{1}{2}(1+1) = 1$ **13.** $\int_0^\infty 3e^{-3x}\,dx = \lim_{b\to\infty}\int_0^b 3e^{-3x}\,dx = \lim_{b\to\infty}\left[\frac{3}{-3}e^{-3x}\right]_0^b =$

$\lim_{b\to\infty}[-e^{-3x}]_0^b = \lim_{b\to\infty}[-e^{-3b} - (-e^{-3\cdot 0})] = \lim_{b\to\infty}\left(1 - \frac{1}{3^b}\right) = 1$ **15.** $k = \frac{1}{4}$ **17.** $k = \frac{3}{2}$

19. $k = \frac{1}{5}$ **21.** $k = \frac{1}{2}$ **23.** $k = \frac{1}{\ln 3}$ **25.** $k = \frac{1}{e^3 - 1}$ **27.** $\frac{8}{25}$ **29.** $\frac{1}{2}$ **31.** 0.3297

33. 0.99995 **35.** 0.9502 **37.** 0.3935 **39.** $b = \sqrt[4]{4}$, or $\sqrt{2}$.

Exercise Set 14.6, p. 685

1. $\mu = E(x) = \frac{7}{2}$, $E(x^2) = 13$, $\sigma^2 = \frac{3}{4}$, $\sigma = \frac{1}{2}\sqrt{3}$. **3.** $\mu = E(x) = 2$, $E(x^2) = \frac{9}{2}$, $\sigma^2 = \frac{1}{2}$, $\sigma = \sqrt{\frac{1}{2}}$.
5. $\mu = E(x) = \frac{14}{9}$, $E(x^2) = \frac{5}{2}$, $\sigma^2 = \frac{13}{162}$, $\sigma = \sqrt{\frac{13}{162}}$.
7. $\mu = E(x) = -\frac{5}{4}$, $E(x^2) = \frac{11}{5}$, $\sigma^2 = \frac{51}{80}$, $\sigma = \sqrt{\frac{51}{80}} = \frac{1}{4}\sqrt{\frac{51}{5}}$.
9. $\mu = E(x) = \frac{2}{\ln 3}$, $E(x^2) = \frac{4}{\ln 3}$, $\sigma^2 = \frac{4\ln 3 - 4}{(\ln 3)^2}$, $\sigma = \frac{2}{\ln 3}\sqrt{\ln 3 - 1}$.
11. 0.4964 **13.** 0.3665 **15.** 0.6442 **17.** 0.0078 **19.** 0.1716 **21.** 0.0013 **23.** a) 0.6826
b) 68.26% **25.** 0.2898 **27.** 0.4514 **29.** a) 0.2088 b) 0.3830 c) 0.2420 **31.** 0.62%
33. 0.081, 0.271 **35.** 7 **37.** 10, 9.48683

Exercise Set 14.7, p. 695

1.

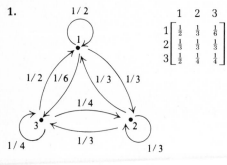

$$\begin{array}{c c}
 & \begin{array}{c c c} 1 & 2 & 3 \end{array} \\
\begin{array}{c} 1 \\ 2 \\ 3 \end{array} & \left[\begin{array}{c c c} \frac{1}{2} & \frac{1}{3} & \frac{1}{6} \\ \frac{1}{3} & \frac{1}{3} & \frac{1}{3} \\ \frac{1}{2} & \frac{1}{4} & \frac{1}{4} \end{array}\right]
\end{array}$$

3. No; negative element in first row.

5.

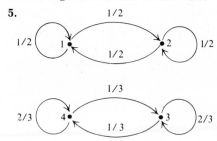

7.

9.

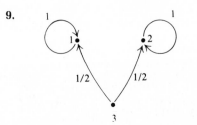

11.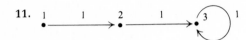

13.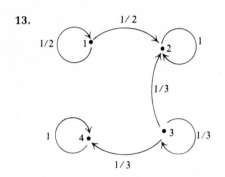

15. First zone: $P_0 = [0 \quad 1 \quad 0]$, $P_1 = [\frac{1}{3} \quad \frac{1}{3} \quad \frac{1}{3}]$, $P_2 = [\frac{16}{36} \quad \frac{11}{36} \quad \frac{9}{36}]$ **17.** $P_0 = [0 \quad 0 \quad 1]$ $P_1 = [\frac{1}{2} \quad \frac{1}{4} \quad \frac{1}{4}]$
$P_2 = [\frac{22}{48} \quad \frac{15}{48} \quad \frac{11}{48}]$ **19.** $P_2 = [\frac{9}{25} \quad \frac{14}{25} \quad \frac{2}{25}]$ **21.** $P_2 = [\frac{1}{4} \quad \frac{1}{4} \quad \frac{1}{4} \quad \frac{1}{4}]$ **23.** $P_1 = [\frac{1}{2} \quad \frac{1}{2}]$
25. $P_2 = [1 \quad 0]$ **27.** $P_2 = [\frac{1}{2} \quad \frac{1}{2} \quad 0]$ **29.** $P_3 = [0 \quad 0 \quad 1]$ **31.** $P_2 = [\frac{1}{16} \quad \frac{3}{16} \quad \frac{7}{16} \quad \frac{5}{16}]$
33. $P_2 = [\frac{9}{144} \quad \frac{79}{144} \quad \frac{4}{144} \quad \frac{52}{144}]$ **35.** $[\frac{1}{3}, \quad \frac{2}{3}]$ **37.** $[\frac{2}{12} \quad \frac{5}{12} \quad \frac{5}{12}]$ **39.** $[\frac{2}{10} \quad \frac{3}{10} \quad \frac{5}{10}]$ **41.** $[\frac{5}{17} \quad \frac{2}{17} \quad \frac{5}{17} \quad \frac{5}{17}]$
43. $[\frac{1}{10} \quad \frac{2}{10} \quad \frac{4}{10} \quad \frac{3}{10}]$ **45.** $[\frac{30}{67} \quad \frac{21}{67} \quad \frac{16}{67}]$

Chapter 14 Review, p. 697

1.

x	0	1	2	3	4	5
p	$\frac{6}{36}$	$\frac{10}{36}$	$\frac{8}{36}$	$\frac{6}{36}$	$\frac{4}{36}$	$\frac{2}{36}$

2. $\frac{70}{30}$ **3.**

x	0	1	2	3
p	$\frac{24}{91}$	$\frac{45}{91}$	$\frac{20}{91}$	$\frac{2}{91}$

4. 1   **5.** $\frac{52}{91}$

6. 0.75593   **7.** $E(\overline{X}) = \$1.76$; to charity $\$8.20$ per ticket

8. $\binom{6}{2} \cdot \frac{1}{2^6} = \frac{15}{64}$

TTHHHH HHTTHH HHHHTT HTHHTH
HTTHHH HHTHTH HHHTTH THHHHT
THTHHH HTHHHT HHHTHT THHHTH
HTHTHH THHTHH HHTHHT

9. $\binom{6}{4}(0.8)^4(0.2)^2 = 0.24576$

10. K is the number cured.

k	p_k
0	0.000064
1	0.001536
2	0.015360
3	0.081920
4	0.245760
5	0.393216
6	0.262144

11. 4.8   **12.** $\sigma^2 = 0.96$, $\sigma = 0.97980$ **13.** $p = \frac{20}{91}$ ($= p_2$ in Exercise 3).

Now $p_3 = \binom{4}{3}\left(\frac{20}{91}\right)^3\left(\frac{71}{91}\right)^1 = 0.033132$ **14.** 240

15. a)

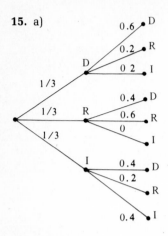

b)

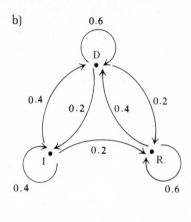

16.

$$\begin{array}{c@{}c} & \begin{array}{ccc} \text{D} & \text{R} & \text{I} \end{array} \\ \begin{array}{c} \text{D} \\ \text{R} \\ \text{I} \end{array} & \left[\begin{array}{ccc} 0.6 & 0.2 & 0.2 \\ 0.4 & 0.6 & 0 \\ 0.4 & 0.2 & 0.4 \end{array}\right] \end{array}$$

17. a) Qualifies

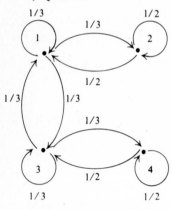

b) Does not qualify. Sum of elements in second row now is less than one.

18. $P_0 = \begin{bmatrix} \frac{1}{3} & \frac{1}{3} & \frac{1}{3} \end{bmatrix}$
$P_1 = \begin{bmatrix} \frac{7}{15} & \frac{5}{15} & \frac{3}{15} \end{bmatrix}$
$P_2 = \begin{bmatrix} \frac{37}{75} & \frac{25}{75} & \frac{13}{75} \end{bmatrix}$

19. $\overline{P} = \begin{bmatrix} \frac{1}{5} & \frac{3}{5} & \frac{1}{5} \end{bmatrix}$

20.

n	0	1	2	3	4	5
p	$\binom{5}{0}\left(\frac{3}{4}\right)^5\left(\frac{1}{4}\right)^0$	$\binom{5}{1}\left(\frac{3}{4}\right)^4\left(\frac{1}{4}\right)^1$	$\binom{5}{2}\left(\frac{3}{4}\right)^3\left(\frac{1}{4}\right)^2$	$\binom{5}{3}\left(\frac{3}{4}\right)^2\left(\frac{1}{4}\right)^3$	$\binom{5}{4}\left(\frac{3}{4}\right)^1\left(\frac{1}{4}\right)^4$	$\binom{5}{5}\left(\frac{3}{4}\right)^0\left(\frac{1}{4}\right)^5$
	$= \dfrac{243}{1024}$	$= \dfrac{405}{1024}$	$= \dfrac{270}{1024}$	$= \dfrac{90}{1024}$	$= \dfrac{15}{1024}$	$= \dfrac{1}{1024}$

21. $\binom{5}{4}\left(\frac{1}{4}\right)^1\left(\frac{3}{4}\right)^4 + \binom{5}{5}\left(\frac{1}{4}\right)^0\left(\frac{3}{4}\right)^5 = \dfrac{648}{1024} = \dfrac{81}{128}$ **22.** $5 \cdot \frac{3}{4} = \frac{15}{4}$ **23.** $\mu = 2$ **24.** $\sigma^2 = \frac{4}{3}$

25. $\sigma = \frac{2}{3}\sqrt{3} \approx 1.155$ **26.** $z = \dfrac{1 - 2}{\sqrt{\frac{4}{3}}} = -\sqrt{\frac{3}{4}}$ **27.** $k = \frac{1}{4}$ **28.** 0.8647 **29.** $E(x) = \frac{3}{4}$

30. $E(x^2) = \frac{3}{5}$ **31.** $\sigma^2 = \frac{3}{80}$ **32.** $\sigma = \frac{1}{4}\sqrt{\frac{3}{5}}$ **33.** 0.4332 **34.** 0.4420 **35.** 0.9071 **36.** 0.4207

37.

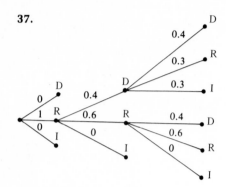 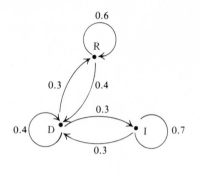

$$\begin{array}{c c c c} & D & R & I \\ D & \begin{bmatrix} 0.4 & 0.3 & 0.3 \\ R & 0.4 & 0.6 & 0 \\ I & 0.3 & 0 & 0.7 \end{bmatrix} \end{array}$$

38. $P_2 = [\tfrac{3}{12} \quad \tfrac{7}{12} \quad \tfrac{2}{12}], \overline{P} = [\tfrac{2}{9} \quad \tfrac{3}{9} \quad \tfrac{4}{9}]$

CHAPTER 15

Exercise Set 15.1, p. 711

1. $f(0, -2) = 0, f(2, 3) = -8, f(10, -5) = 200.$ **3.** $f(0, -2) = 1, f(-2, 1) = -13\tfrac{8}{9}, f(2, 1) = 23.$
5. $f(e, 2) = \ln e + 2^3 = 1 + 8 = 9, f(e^2, 4) = 66, f(e^3, 5) = 128.$
7. $f(-1, 2, 3) = 6, f(2, -1, 3) = 12.$ **9.** 12.3   **11.** \$1518.12

13. $\dfrac{\partial z}{\partial x} = 2 - 3y, \dfrac{\partial z}{\partial y} = -3x, \dfrac{\partial z}{\partial x}\bigg|_{(-2, -3)} = 11, \dfrac{\partial z}{\partial y}\bigg|_{(0, -5)} = 0$

15. $\dfrac{\partial z}{\partial x} = 6x - 2y, \dfrac{\partial z}{\partial y} = -2x + 1, \dfrac{\partial z}{\partial x}\bigg|_{(-2, -3)} = -6, \dfrac{\partial z}{\partial y}\bigg|_{(0, -5)} = 1$

17. $f_x = 2, f_y = -3, f_x(-2, 4) = 2, f_y(4, -3) = -3$

19. $f_x = \dfrac{x}{\sqrt{x^2 + y^2}}, f_y = \dfrac{y}{\sqrt{x^2 + y^2}}, f_x(-2, 1) = \dfrac{-2}{\sqrt{5}}, f_y(-3, -2) = \dfrac{-2}{\sqrt{13}}$

21. $f_x = 2e^{2x + 3y}, f_y = 3e^{2x + 3y}$ **23.** $f_x = ye^{xy}, f_y = xe^{xy}$ **25.** $f_x = \dfrac{y}{x + y}, f_y = \dfrac{y}{x + y} + \ln(x + y)$

27. $f_x = 1 + \ln xy, f_y = \dfrac{x}{y}$ **29.** $f_x = \dfrac{1}{y} + \dfrac{y}{x^2}, f_y = -\dfrac{x}{y^2} - \dfrac{1}{x}$

31. $f_x = 12(2x + y - 5), f_y = 6(2x + y - 5)$ **33.** $\dfrac{\partial f}{\partial b} = 12m + 6b - 30, \dfrac{\partial f}{\partial m} = 28m + 12b - 64$

35. $f_x = 3y - 2\lambda, f_y = 3x - \lambda, f_\lambda = -(2x + y - 8)$
37. $f_x = 2x - 10\lambda, f_y = 2y - 2\lambda, f_\lambda = -(10x + 2y - 4)$ **39.** a) 3,888,064 units

b) $\dfrac{\partial p}{\partial x} = 1117.8\ x^{-0.379}\ y^{0.379} = \dfrac{1117.8\ y^{0.379}}{x^{0.379}} = 1117.8\left(\dfrac{y}{x}\right)^{0.379} \dfrac{\partial p}{\partial y} = 682.2\ x^{0.621}\ y^{-0.621} =$

$\dfrac{682.2\ x^{0.621}}{y^{0.621}} = 682.2\left(\dfrac{x}{y}\right)^{0.621}$ c) 965.8, 866.8

Exercise Set 15.2, p. 714

1. $\dfrac{\partial^2 f}{\partial x^2} = 6$, $\dfrac{\partial^2 f}{\partial y\,\partial x} = \dfrac{\partial^2 f}{\partial x\,\partial y} = -1$, $\dfrac{\partial^2 f}{\partial y^2} = 0$.   3. $\dfrac{\partial^2 f}{\partial x^2} = 0$, $\dfrac{\partial^2 f}{\partial y\,\partial x} = \dfrac{\partial^2 f}{\partial x\,\partial y} = 3$, $\dfrac{\partial^2 f}{\partial y^2} = 0$.

5. $\dfrac{\partial^2 f}{\partial x^2} = 20x^3y^4 + 6xy^2$, $\dfrac{\partial^2 f}{\partial y\,\partial x} = \dfrac{\partial^2 f}{\partial x\,\partial y} = 20x^4y^3 + 6x^2y$, $\dfrac{\partial^2 f}{\partial y^2} = 12x^5y^2 + 2x^3$.

7. $f_{xx} = 0$, $f_{yx} = 0$, $f_{xy} = 0$, $f_{yy} = 0$.   9. $f_{xx} = 4y^2e^{2xy}$, $f_{yx} = f_{xy} = 4xye^{2xy} + 2e^{2xy}$, $f_{yy} = 4x^2e^{2xy}$.

11. $f_{xx} = 0$, $f_{yx} = f_{xy} = 0$, $f_{yy} = e^y$.   13. $f_{xx} = -\dfrac{y}{x^2}$, $f_{yx} = f_{xy} = \dfrac{1}{x}$, $f_{yy} = 0$.

15. $\dfrac{\partial^2 p}{\partial x^2} = -\dfrac{40}{3}x^{-4/3}\,y^{1/3} < 0$, for x and y positive. This says that marginal productivity with respect to labor is decreasing.   17. $f_{xx} = \dfrac{-6y}{x^4}$, $f_{yx} = f_{xy} = \dfrac{2(y^3 - x^3)}{x^3y^3}$, $f_{yy} = \dfrac{6x}{y^4}$.

Exercise Set 15.3, p. 721

1. Min. $= -\tfrac{1}{3}$ at $(-\tfrac{1}{3}, \tfrac{2}{3})$.   3. Max. $= \tfrac{4}{27}$ at $(\tfrac{2}{3}, \tfrac{2}{3})$.   5. Min. $= -1$ at $(1, 1)$.   7. Min. $= -7$ at $(1, -2)$.   9. Min. $= -5$ at $(-1, 2)$.   11. None.   13. 6 (thousand) of the \$17 radio and 5 (thousand) of the \$21 radio.   15. Max. of $P = 35$ (million dollars) when $a = 10$ (million dollars) and $p = \$3$.   17. a) $R(p_1, p_2) = 78p_1 - 6p_1^2 - 6p_1p_2 + 66p_2 - 6p_2^2$; b) $p_1 = 5$ (\$50), $p_2 = 3$ (\$30); c) $q_1 = 78 - 6 \cdot 5 - 3 \cdot 3 = 39$ (hundreds), $q_2 = 33$ (hundreds); d) $R = 50 \cdot 3900 + 30 \cdot 3300 = \$294{,}000$.   19. None.   21. Min. $= \tfrac{1}{6}$ at $(\tfrac{21}{3}, \tfrac{3}{2})$.

Exercise Set 15.4, p. 728

1. Max. $= 8$ at $(2, 4)$.   3. Max. $= -16$ at $(2, 4)$.   5. Min. $= 20$ at $(4, 2)$.   7. Min. $= -96$ at $(8, -12)$.   9. Min. $= \tfrac{3}{2}$ at $(1, \tfrac{1}{2}, -\tfrac{1}{2})$.   11. 35 and 35.   13. 3 and -3.   15. $9\tfrac{3}{4}$ in., $9\tfrac{3}{4}$ in.; $95\tfrac{1}{16}$ in.²; No.   17. $r = \sqrt{\dfrac{27}{2\pi}} \approx 1.6$ ft; $h = 2 \cdot r \approx 3.2$ ft; min. surface area ≈ 48.3 ft².   19. Max. of $S = 800$ at $L = 20$, $M = 60$.   21. a) $C(x, y, z) = 7xy + 6yz + 6xz$; b) $x = 60$ ft, $y = 60$ ft, $z = 70$ ft; \$75,600.   23. 10,000 on A, 100 on B.   25. 150 units of labor and 150 units of capital.

27. Min. $= -\tfrac{155}{128}$ at $(-\tfrac{7}{16}, -\tfrac{3}{4})$.   29. Max. $= \tfrac{1}{27}$ at $\left(\dfrac{1}{\sqrt{3}}, \dfrac{1}{\sqrt{3}}, \dfrac{1}{\sqrt{3}}\right)$ and $\left(-\dfrac{1}{\sqrt{3}}, -\dfrac{1}{\sqrt{3}}, -\dfrac{1}{\sqrt{3}}\right)$.

31. Max. $= 2$ at $(\tfrac{1}{2}, \tfrac{1}{2}, \tfrac{1}{2}, \tfrac{1}{2})$.   33. 4997.5 hr for new account solicitation, 5002.5 hr for service.

Exercise Set 15.5, p. 738

1. a) $y = 3.04x - 0.7$ b) \$44.9 million   3. a) $y = \dfrac{203}{190}x - \dfrac{235}{190}$ b) 85.3

5. a) $y = -0.00582x + 15.3476$ b) 3:48.0 c) Letting $x = 1979\tfrac{7}{12}$, $y = 3:49.6$

7. a) $y = 2.359e^{0.376x}$ b) \$663.1 million

Exercise Set 15.6, p. 743

1. $h = \sqrt[3]{10{,}240{,}000} \approx 217$ ft, $k \approx 54$ ft; dimensions are 54 ft by 54 ft by 225 ft.

3. $h = \sqrt[3]{\dfrac{Aca^2}{b^2}}$, $k = \sqrt[3]{\dfrac{Abc}{a}}$; dimensions are k by k by $h + c$.

Exercise Set 15.7, p. 747

1. 1   **3.** 0   **5.** 6   **7.** $\frac{3}{20}$ **9.** 4   **11.** $\frac{4}{15}$ **13.** 1   **15.** 39   **17.** $\frac{13}{240}$

Chapter 15 Review, p. 749

1. $\dfrac{\partial f}{\partial x} = e^x + 6x^2 y$ **2.** $\dfrac{\partial f}{\partial y} = 2x^3 + 1$ **3.** $\dfrac{\partial^2 f}{\partial x^2} = e^x + 12xy$ **4.** $\dfrac{\partial^2 f}{\partial x\, \partial y} = 6x^2$ **5.** $\dfrac{\partial^2 f}{\partial y\, \partial x} = 6x^2$

6. $\dfrac{\partial^2 f}{\partial y^2} = 0$ **7.** Min. $= -\frac{7}{16}$ at $(\frac{3}{4}, \frac{1}{2})$ **8.** None   **9.** a) $y = \frac{9}{2}x + \frac{17}{3}$, b) \$23.7.

10. Max. $= -19$ at $(4, 5)$ **11.** 5   **12.** a) 30,240 units b) $\dfrac{\partial p}{\partial x} = 140x^{-3/4}\, y^{3/4}$, $\dfrac{\partial p}{\partial y} = 420x^{1/4}\, y^{-1/4}$

c) 472.5, 280   **13.** 5 thousand of \$15 calculator; 7 thousand of \$20 calculator   **14.** $y = 4e^{0.01824x}$
15. Min. $= -\frac{111}{4}$ at $(5, \frac{27}{2})$ **16.** Min. $= -1$ at $(-1, 2)$ **17.** Min. $= \frac{3}{2}$ at $(-\frac{1}{2}, \frac{3}{2})$
18. Min. $= 1$ at $(-1, 0, 0)$ and $(1, 0, 0)$ **19.** $\dfrac{2y}{(x + y)^2}$ **20.** $\dfrac{-2x}{(x + y)^2}$ **21.** $\dfrac{-4y}{(x + y)^3}$ **22.** $\dfrac{4x}{(x + y)^3}$

23. $\dfrac{2(x - y)}{(x + y)^4}$ **24.** $\dfrac{2(x - y)}{(x + y)^4}$ **25.** $h = 184$ ft, $k = 75$ ft; dimensions are 74 ft by 74 ft by 194 ft

INDEX